ISBN 978-1-334-73011-5
PIBN 10620537

This book is a reproduction of an important historical work. Forgotten Books uses
state-of-the-art technology to digitally reconstruct the work, preserving the original format
whilst repairing imperfections present in the aged copy. In rare cases, an imperfection in
the original, such as a blemish or missing page, may be replicated in our edition. We do,
however, repair the vast majority of imperfections successfully; any imperfections that
remain are intentionally left to preserve the state of such historical works.

For support please visit www.forgottenbooks.com

ANNUAL
BURNS CHRONICLE & CLUB DIRECTORY

No. XXIX.
JANUARY, 1920.

PRICE:
Two SHILLINGS.

PUBLISHED BY THE
BURNS FEDERATION.

PRINTED BY
J. MAXWELL & SON,

CONTENTS.

	Page.
Robert Burns as a Volunteer : Some Fresh Facts from the Minute Book of the Corps— *William Will*	5
Proposed Removal of the Highland Mary Memorial : Further Developments	31
Jubilee Anniversary Meeting of the London Robert Burns Club (25th January, 1919)	45
The Manse of Loudoun—*Helen Walters Crawford* ...	68
Burns and Uppermost Clydesdale—*Rev. Wm. M'Millan, M.A., F.S.A.Scot.*	78
Shenstone and Burns—*A. J. Craig*	86
The Heraldry of Burns—*Rev. Wm. M'Millan, M.A., F.S.A.Scot.*	90
Maria Riddell's Letters to Dr James Currie (1796-1805) —*J.C.E.*	110
Francis Grose, Esq., F.R.S., A.S.—*A. J. Craig*	121
Burns Cottage Relics : A Spurious Collection—*J. C. Ewing*	126
Burns's House in Mauchline : The Mackenzie Extension	135
Memorial to Gavin Hamilton at Mauchline	138
Imposing on Burns—*Davidson Cook, F.S.A.Scot.* .	140
Burns and the Duchesses— *Philip Sulley*	147
Club Notes	156
Federation Office-Bearers, &c.	177
Annual Meeting of Federation	181
Club Directory	188

PREFACE.

THE demands upon the space of this issue of the *Chronicle* have necessitated some addition to its bulk, as well as the omission of the " Notes and Queries " : but we hope that the interest of the articles submitted will be deemed sufficient excuse for all faults.

We have to congratulate the Clubs on the resumption of their pre-war activities, and trust their good example will extend year by year to every unit of the Federation.

Our thanks are again due to all who have assisted us in the compilation of the present volume ; and we may add that a comprehensive Index for the whole series is under consideration.

D. M'NAUGHT.

BENRIG, KILMAURS,
      January 1st, 1920.

ROBERT BURNS AS A VOLUNTEER:

SOME FRESH FACTS FROM THE MINUTE BOOK OF THE CORPS.

FEW men of genius have had to run the gauntlet of criticism more searching, more diverse, and more prolonged than Robert Burns. In his own time it was directed chiefly from a rigid ecclesiastical system, and from the general atmosphere of self-righteousness which that creed encouraged. The criticism has been continued in our own day from totally different angles, the insanity-of-genius school regarding Burns less as a conscious sinner, than as the victim of his own genius ; and what may be called the curiosities-of-literature view-point, which finds a fascination in the conflict between his narrow material environment and his spacious spiritual vision. Between all the shafts of criticism Burns has become a sorely battered target, and it would need a vast volume to refute the charges that have been brought against him.

The harsh criticism to which Burns has been subjected is due largely to his biographers—never was man more unfortunate in his biographers—who too readily accepted the sordid stories which probably originated in the minds of the Poet's political opponents, provincial scandal-mongers, and vindictive victims of that wit which " had always the start of his judgment." These stories, handed from inaccurate biographer to unsuspecting biographer, have become part of the voluminous literature that has gathered about the name of the Inspired Ploughman, and that has been drawn upon by those who have directed their shafts at his character.

More than sixty years ago the dull-looking " Excise Register of Censures," discovered at Somerset House, rescued one side of the Poet's character, and now, a hundred

and twenty-two years after Burns's death, an obscure
manuscript volume of the Minutes of the Dumfries Volunteers has come to light to confound the critics still further.
The great value of the new discovery lies in this, that the
Volunteers set up a standard of discipline in some ways
even more rigid than that of the Church, and yet Burns
stands the test and comes off with flying colours.   His
attitude to his military duties shows that his membership
was not, as has been suggested, a mere piece of hypocrisy
meant to deceive or placate his superiors in the Excise,
who told him, when he sought to defend his attitude to
the French Revolution, that his duty was " to act—not to
think."

Burns's work as a Volunteer has hitherto either been
minimised or misinterpreted.   It is true that Allan
Cunningham said that he remembered well " the appearance of that respectable Corps ; .. and I remember the
Poet also—his very swarthy face, his ploughman's stoop,
his large dark eyes, and his indifferent dexterity in the
handling of his arms."*   We know that Colonel de Peyster,
" the honoured Colonel " to whom Burns addressed his
" Ode on Life," declared that Burns faithfully discharged
his soldierly duties, and was the pride of his Corps.   We
have been told further that Burns, when on his deathbed,
is reported to have jocularly pleaded with a friend not to
allow his fellow-Volunteers—" the awkward squad," he
called them—to fire a volley over his grave, and we have
also been told that that volley was fired in the straggling
manner feared by the Poet.   In Ainslie's *Pilgrimage in the
Land of Burns*, printed at Deptford in 1822, is the following :—" Once when the Corps were exercising in firing,
after a few bad discharges, the Captain asked : ' Is this
your erratic genius, Mr Burns, that is spoiling our fire ?'
' No ! it can't be me, Captain,' said Burns, ' for look, I
have forgot my flint.' "   It was Cunningham who said
" It is very true that his accession [to the ranks] was

* " Honest Allan " must always be taken with a pinch of salt.

objected to by some of his neighbours, but these were overruled by the gentlemen who took the lead in the business, and the Poet soon became, as might have been expected, the greatest possible favourite with his brothers-in-arms." This statement will be dealt with later.

This is the gist of practically all that has, up till now, been published regarding Burns's life as a Volunteer.

. Several of his biographers attach so little importance to his enlistment in the Royal Dumfries Volunteers that they do not even mention it. Other writers refer to the Poet's enlistment only as an explanation of the existence of the song, " The Dumfries Volunteers," or as a proof that the Poet was a patriotic Briton, despite his sympathy with the French people. In point of fact, as we shall see, he was not only an enthusiast but a leader of the movement, and that, too, at a period which has frequently been regarded as the least admirable of his short life.

To say, as has been said by more than one essayist, that Burns became a Volunteer " to prove his loyalty to the Government," is an insult to the memory of the Poet. A military life always had an attraction for Burns. Not only did he as a child " strut in raptures up and down after the recruiting drum and bagpipe, and wish myself tall enough to be a soldier," but in 1782, when his flax-dressing venture literally ended in smoke, he consoled himself thus :—

> " O why the deuce should I repine,
>   An' be an ill foreboder ?
> I'm twenty-three, and five-feet-nine,—
>   I'll go and be a sodger !"

Writing to Mrs Dunlop in 1787, and referring to a suggestion made by her, he said : " Would the profits of that [second and third editions of his poems] afford, I would take the hint of a military life as the most congenial to my feelings and situation." Again, a year later, he wrote to Miss Margaret Chalmers : " Your friendship I can count on, though I should date my letter from a marching regiment.

Early in life, and all my life, I reckoned on a recruiting drum as my forlorn hope."

It will thus be seen that Burns needed no great incitement to take up arms when the call came; and there can be no doubt that he became a Volunteer, as so many of his fellow-townsmen and fellow-countrymen did, because he was opposed to the turbulent crowd who would have "set the mob aboon the throne," and wished to do his part in preventing social disorder, and because he believed that his country was in danger of invasion. It was such a crisis as this that would revive the flame kindled in his breast by the story of the Liberator of Scotland, which, as he explained to Dr Moore, the father of General Sir John Moore, "poured a Scottish prejudice into my veins which will boil along there till the floodgates of life shut in eternal rest."

Not only did Burns join the Dumfries Volunteers, but, like Sir Walter Scott in Edinburgh, he assisted in creating the force; he attended a meeting summoned by the Deputy Lord-Lieutenant of that part of the county, Mr David Staig, the Provost of Dumfries (and the father of Jessie Staig, to whom Burns paid several poetical compliments), to discuss how best they could serve their native land in the time of crisis, and when the meeting resolved to form a Volunteer Company, Robert Burns's name was among the signatories to the petition for the necessary permission.

The first entry in the Corps Minute Book referred to, sets out that this meeting, at which the Dumfries Volunteer movement was inaugurated, was held in the Court House, on 31st January, 1795. With the Deputy-Lieutenant were his two bailies and the leading professional and business men of the town, the list and subsequent signatories* including John Syme of Ryedale and James Gray, staunchest of Burns's friends; Dr Maxwell, the friend of the French Revolution; Dr John Harley, John Armstrong, writer, who became secretary to the Corps; Rev. Dr Wm. Burn-

* See Note A, page 20.

side,* chaplain to the Corps, minister of St. Michael's, where Burns occasionally worshipped; Rev. Dr Wm. Babington, Episcopal minister in Dumfries; Thomas White (probably of Dumfries Academy); David Newall, solicitor; Captain John Hamilton, the Poet's landlord; Lieut.-Col. A. S. de Peyster, the "respected Colonel" of the "Ode on Life"; Captain John Finnan, in whose company Burns was later enrolled; James Gracie, banker, the "Gracie, thou art a man of worth"; "Old Q.'s" chamberlain, John M'Murdo, writer, whose praises and those of his daughters, a "bonnie Jean" and "Phyllis the Fair," Burns sang; Francis Shortt, town clerk, a lieutanant in the Corps, and secretary of the Loyal Native Club, which was pilloried by the Poet in the well-known quatrain; Alexander Findlater, his co-worker and superior in the Excise; John Lewars, another Excise Officer, and brother of Jessie, who attended Burns on his deathbed, and who is enshrined in "The Toast" and in several other complimentary verses; and David Williamson, the rendering of whose account for the dying Poet's volunteer uniform drove him into a paroxysm of anger and the humiliating position of having to beg James Thomson and his cousin James Burness for a few pounds.

The meeting on 31st January declared its "sincere attachment to the happy Constitution of Great Britain, and our firm resolution on every occasion to protect the lives and properties of ourselves and fellow-subjects from

---

* At the meeting Mr Staig produced a letter from Dr Burnside in which the reverend gentleman said that although he did not think it perfectly accorded with his professional character and engagements to enrol among the Volunteers, and, if he did, from his rheumatic ailments he could be of very little use in any active service, yet, to show his good wishes towards so useful and laudable a design, he was ready and willing to subscribe for the use of the Corps, to be applied as they might think best, a sum equal to what it would cost him to be completely accoutred and fitted out as one of the line. The Rev. Dr Babington made a similar proposal. Both were accepted, and the thanks of the meeting were voted them for "such a genteel offer."

proffered fee for reparing himself against the day when a foreign foe might ttempt to desecrate the soil of his beloved Caledonia. Th and other conditions of service suggest that the spirit. ihot the person. of Burns was at the draw_ ing up of the rul(and regulations. One rule, for example, gave the rank ad file the power. which they exercised, of selecting the own commissioned officers : another made it nece~say for every man to run the gauntlet of the ballot by thir fellows before enrolment : while, later, fines were impo·d on officers and men who were absent from drill witho good reason. and on those guilty of being the worse for dnk while on parade : while insolent men and overbearin{officers were also subject to the censure of the Committ• and the Corps.

On the 21 of February, 1795. the first election of Captains and leutenants was held in the Court House —Col. de Pvv•r had been elected Major Commandant on the previous av*—and again Robert Burns was present, one of the ~ervty-five men who voted John Hamilton to be first Capta : John Finnan to be second Captain ; and David N(all. Wellwood Maxwell. Francis Shortt, and Thoma~ W te to be Lieutenants. These commissions were gazetted 4th March. 1795.† On the same day as that on which 1e officers were elected, the meeting having adjourned to tl Assembly Rooms, each man was separately balloted for. a majority of votes being necessary for election. It was here. c the 21st of February, 1795, that Robert Burns, as an oginal member, was balloted into the Royal Dumfries Voluteers ; but he did not, as has been so often said, celebratehis enrolment by writing "Does haughty Gaul invasion breat ?" The great national song, which created enthuasm for the national cause from Maidenkirk to John o' Goats, was not written until the month of

* See Note , page 25.

† War Offi·, March 24th [1795]—Dumfriesshire Corps of Volunteers—A. . de Peyster, Esq., to be major commandant ; John Hamilton nd John Finnan, Esq., captains ; David Newall and Wellwood Iaxwell, gentlemen, first lieutenants ; Francis Shortt and Thoas White, second lieutenants.

every attempt of the ambitious, designing, and turbulent who threaten to overturn the laws of our country, and who, by anarchy, sedition, and bloodshed, may endeavour to destroy the sacred bonds of society."

Following this initiatory meeting came another on the 3rd of February, when the offer of service and the rules and regulations* were signed by each of the sixty-three gentlemen who attended. Among the patriotic three score and three again appears the name of the Poet, and it is important, in view of the many statements that have been made as to his want of loyalty, to read in the Minute Book that Burns subscribed his name to the following which, substituting " Fifth " for " Third," is precisely what patriotic Britons were subscribing to in the months immediately succeeding the outbreak of the war in 1914 :—

" We .... hereby declare our sincere attachment to the person and Government of His Majesty King George the Third ; our respect for the happy Constitution of Great Britain... As we are of opinion that the only way we can obtain a speedy and honourable peace is by the Government vigorously carrying on the present war, humbly submit the following proposals to His Majesty for the purpose of forming ourselves into a Volunteer Corps, in order to support the internal peace and good order of the town, as well as to give energy to the measures of the Government."

There was no hesitancy or half-heartedness about the war policy of Robert Burns and his fellow-Volunteers of Dumfries.

One is not surprised to find that Burns enrolled himself in a Corps which undertook " to serve during the present war, without pay, and find our own clothing." The man who—as we hold, notwithstanding Stevenson's unsupported and ungenerous suggestion—out of pure love for the lyric repute of his native country, contributed, without fee or reward of any kind, those priceless songs of his to Thomson's collection, would have spurned any

* See Note B, page 21.

proffered fee for preparing himself against the day when a foreign foe might attempt to desecrate the soil of his beloved Caledonia. This and other conditions of service suggest that the spirit, if not the person, of Burns was at the drawing up of the rules and regulations. One rule, for example, gave the rank and file the power, which they exercised, of selecting their own commissioned officers ; another made it necessary for every man to run the gauntlet of the ballot by their fellows before enrolment ; while, later, fines were imposed on officers and men who were absent from drill without good reason, and on those guilty of being the worse for drink while on parade ; while insolent men and overbearing officers were also subject to the censure of the Committee and the Corps.

On the 21st of February, 1795, the first election of Captains and Lieutenants was held in the Court House —Col. de Peyster had been elected Major Commandant on the previous day*—and again Robert Burns was present, one of the seventy-five men who voted John Hamilton to be first Captain ; John Finnan to be second Captain ; and David Newall, Wellwood Maxwell, Francis Shortt, and Thomas White to be Lieutenants. These commissions were gazetted 24th March, 1795.† On the same day as that on which the officers were elected, the meeting having adjourned to the Assembly Rooms, each man was separately balloted for, a majority of votes being necessary for election. It was here, on the 21st of February, 1795, that Robert Burns, as an original member, was balloted into the Royal Dumfries Volunteers ; but he did not, as has been so often said, celebrate his enrolment by writing " Does haughty Gaul invasion threat ?" The great national song, which created enthusiasm for the national cause from Maidenkirk to John o' Groats, was not written until the month of

* See Note C, page 25.

† War Office, March 24th [1795]—Dumfriesshire Corps of Volunteers—A. S. de Peyster, Esq., to be major commandant; John Hamilton and John Finnan, Esq., captains ; David Newall and Wellwood Maxwell, gentlemen, first lieutenants : Francis Shortt and Thomas White, second lieutenants.

April.* It must not be supposed that those elections and ballots were mere formalities, for there is disagreeable evidence in the Minute Book that in this, as in other matters, the Committee and the Corps took their duties seriously.

The two captains, having been elected, drew the names of the men who were to serve under them ; and to John Finnan, the Captain of No. 2 Company, fell the honour of drawing for his company the name of the most illustrious, and one of the most enthusiastic Volunteers which Great Britain's danger and Napoleon's ambition caused to be enrolled in these islands. With him in the same Company were his great friends Dr Harley, John Syme, James Gracie, and John Lewars.

At the Old Assembly Rooms, on the 28th of March, Burns, with fifty-seven others, took the Oaths of Allegiance and signed the " Rules, Regulations and Bye-Laws for conducting themselves in a military capacity.†

As happens in every well-regulated household or

* There are two versions of the origin of the song, one being that, at a public dinner of the Corps, Burns gave the subtle toast : " Gentlemen, may we never see the French, and may the French never see us." Murmurs of disapprobation greeted the toast— in particular an Army captain took great umbrage at it—for many of the Dumfries people suspected Burns's loyalty because of his sympathy with the Revolution. By some the innocent toast was considered seditious, which shows the inflammable state of their minds. On returning home he threw off the patriotic verses, the appearance of which in the *Dumfries Journal* must have been as gall and wormwood to his enemies and as marrow to the bones of his friends.

" The Poet had been at a public meeting," says Allan Cunningham, in a note to the song, " where he was less joyous than usual ; as something had been expected from him, he made these verses when he went home, and sent them with his compliments to Mr Jackson, editor of the *Dumfries Journal*." His friend, Stephen Clarke, set the words to music, and as has been said, the song was sung from end to end of the country, helped greatly to fill the ranks of the Volunteers, and did more " to stir the mind of the rustic part of the population than all the speeches of Pitt and Dundas, or the chosen Five-and-Forty."

† See Note D, page 26.

society, the Royal Dumfries Volunteers had their little troubles, and in the first one in the history of the Corps we find Robert Burns figuring. A point of good taste was in dispute, and naturally we find Burns's independence asserting itself. We find him, because his spirit of independence was outraged, taking serious and successful action against the Committee, which held several of his great personal friends, among them Col. de Peyster, Captain Hamilton, Captain Finnan, Lieut. White, James Gracie, John Syme, Wm. M'Cracken, and Alexander Findlater. As has been said, the Royal Dumfries Volunteers were, by their own desire, an unpaid Corps ; but as funds were required for necessary outlays in connection with Corps matters, the Committee, at a meeting on 18th May, 1795, appointed several of their number to call on gentlemen and solicit contributions to the Corps funds.

This decision at once met with keen opposition from certain members of the Companies, who sent to the Committee the following letter :—

' Monday Evening.

" Sir,—From what we have learned of the proceedings of our committee to-day, we cannot help expressing our disapproval of the mendicant business of asking a public contribution for defraying the expenses of our Association. That our secretary should have waited on those gentlemen and others of that rank of life who from the first offered pecuniary assistance meets our idea as highly proper, but that the Royal Dumfries Volunteers should go a-begging with the burnt-out cottager and shipwrecked sailor is a measure of which we must disapprove.

" Please, then, Sir, to call a meeting as soon as possible, and be so very good also as to put a stop to the degrading business until the voice of the Corps be heard.

" We have the honour to be "

(Here follow 24 names, including that of Robert Burns.)

There is no external evidence that Burns's hand helped to frame the letter, but the whole spirit of the document and of its phrasing suggests that the Poet, if he did not actually write it, at least had assisted in its composition.

On the 29th May, 1795, a general meeting of the

Corps was held to discuss the matter, and it was conceded that the exertions of the Committee were well meant, and that no reflection could be cast against the members, but it was agreed that no subscriptions should be taken under a guinea ; and the return of all subscriptions below that sum was recommended and the Committee advised to " fall upon some other plan " for providing money taken from volunteering individuals only. No application was to be made " unless to a few independent and wealthy inhabitants who have not come forward with their personal service, and who need not be pointed out, as they are easily known."

Whether or not Burns instigated the opposition to the indiscriminate collection of money for the Corps' upkeep, it is certain that he had been taking a prominent part in the work of the Corps, and had become one of its leading members ; for at the first general meeting after this affair he was chosen one of the eight men appointed by the rest of the Corps to manage its affairs. At the meeting in the Assembly Rooms on 22nd August, 1795, at which Burns was elected to the Committee, sixty members of the Corps were present. Those elected to serve with the Poet were Robert Jardine, Deacon Anderson, John M'Morine, Alexander Brown, Thomas Gordon, Wm. Paton, and Wm. Laidlaw.

This appointment proves that Burns was highly respected and trusted by his fellow-Volunteers, and that he took a keen and active part in the administrative work of the Corps ; and there is ample further evidence in this Minute Book that he was no " slacker." The names of the members present at the meetings are not given regularly, but on the occasions on which the attendance roll is inscribed, Robert Burns's name always appears. But there is more conclusive proof that the Poet was steadfast in his support of the Corps and that he was conscientious in preparing himself for actual work in the field. As has been said, the Corps in its rules authorised a system of fines for non-attendance at drill, unless good and sufficient reasons for absence were given. Non-commissioned officers and privates suffered penalties of 1s for the first offence and 1s 6d for succeeding abstentions from drill ; and officers paid 2s 6d for a first offence and 5s for each succeeding offence. In addition, as has been said, fines were imposed for inebriety when on parade, and for insolence to superior officers. These fines were freely and sternly enforced by the Committee of which Burns was a member, and by the Committees before and after his appointment, lists of names with the amounts of the fines being given in the Minute Book. Privates and officers appear to have been punished without distinction or favour ; and one officer paid repeatedly the penalty for absence from parade. In March, 1796, Charles Smith was sentenced by the Committee to a reprimand at the head of the Corps at the next drill for being absent from guard, and Smith was ordered to pay a fine of 10s ; and at the same meeting George Christie suffered a like punishment for being drunk under arms, and being guilty of unsoldierlike behaviour. Three men who did not turn out were each fined 5s for neglect of duty ; and the Committee, to maintain its own dignity and round off what must have been a strenuous meeting, fined Robert Grainger 5s for making disrespectful remarks regarding the Committee. One of these culprits (Charles Smith) sent a letter of remonstrance to a general meeting of the Corps, but for his pains was found guilty of prevarication and was expelled the Corps, an order being given that the fact should be published in the *Dumfries Journal*. At one meeting—on 24th August, 1795—in the business of which Burns took part, the Committee imposed fines—for non-attendance only—to the extent of £9 6s, those fined including Captain Hamilton, 2s 6d ; Lieut. Francis Shortt, 7s 6d ; and Dr Harley, 1s. The examples quoted prove that no favouritism was shown by the Committee, which makes more important one outstanding fact, namely, that although at the date of the meeting last mentioned the Poet had been a member of the Corps for some seven months—six working months

at least—not once does the name of Robert Burns appear
in a list of those guilty of absenting themselves from drill
or for otherwise offending against the rigidly enforced
rules.

By means of this Minute Book, whose significance
has been overlooked all these years, we are able to trace
Burns to, or almost to, his fatal illness, and incidentally
to nail to the counter one more of the mis-statements of
Currie, the Poet's first editor and perhaps most inaccurate
biographer, who says : " From October, 1795, to the
January following, an accidental complaint confined
him to the house."

We shall see that he was attending to the work of
the Volunteer Corps in November. It has been to all his
biographers a difficult point to decide when actually the
Bard was seized with the long illness which ended fatally.
His own letters are somewhat contradictory ; but however
that may be, Burns attended a Committee Meeting—his
last recorded—on 5th November, 1795, at which he took
part in the preparation for presentation by the Corps of a
Loyal Address to the King. At the Committee Meeting
Colonel de Peyster suggested that an address should be
presented to His Majesty congratulating him on his happy
escape from the late insult upon his sacred person.* A
few members of the Committee had met and made a draft
which he submitted, and which was approved by the
Committee—Burns, as has been said, was a member of
it, and was present at the meeting—for submission to a
General Meeting held at the Court House on the same
day. The address was in the following terms, and was
passed with unanimity :—

" To the King's Most Excellent Majesty, the humble address
of the Royal Dumfries Volunteers.

" Most Gracious Sovereign,—We, your Majesty's most dutiful
and loyal subjects, composing the Corps of the Royal Dumfries Volun-

* The attack on George III. was made in October, 1795, when
the King was on his way to the House of Lords. One result of the
attack was the passing of the Treasonable Attempts Bill.

teers, penetrated by the recent and signal interposition of Divine Providence in the preservation of your most sacred person from the atrocious attempt of a set of lawless ruffians, humbly hope that your Majesty will graciously receive our unfeigned congratulations.

"Permitted by you, Sire, to embody ourselves for the preservation of social tranquility, we are filled with indignation at every attempt made to shake the venerable and, we trust, lasting fabric of British Liberty.

"We have directed our Major Commandant to sign this address in the name of the Corps assembled at Dumfries, 5th November, 1795."

So ended Robert Burns's presence at the Committee meetings; and it is a singular fact, in view of his known anti-Hanoverian opinions, that the Poet's last work as a Committeeman of the Royal Dumfries Volunteers was to take part in the presentation of a loyal address in the warm terms just quoted.

If there be any truth whatever in the statement by Cunningham that Burns's accession to the Royal Dumfries Volunteers was objected to by some of his neighbours on account of political feeling—and we have discovered no substantiation of it—the minutes which have been quoted prove completely that the objections were soon overcome. And if Cunningham be right, the fact that the Poet was so soon at the head of the Corps' affairs was a great personal triumph, and a tribute to his whole-heartedness in the cause which, let it always be remembered to his credit, he was one of the first to espouse.

For the light that it throws on the habits of the Poet at a particularly interesting period of his life, this Minute Book of the Royal Dumfries Volunteers (gifted to the Ewart Library by the inheritrix of Col. de Peyster's estate) is a most valuable and fortunate find. It is important, for it covers part of the time during which, according to his principal detractor, Henley, he was, because of his vicious habits, an outcast from society; and because of those habits was "burnt to a cinder." Here Henley quotes the words reported by an old man as having been uttered by John Syme, Burns's friend, and reads into them—if ever they were spoken, which is doubtful—a meaning that they probably never had.

If Burns's work during the year 1795, his Volunteer year, the year that ended in his fatal illness, which his critics say was the consequence of his drunkenness, be reviewed, we find how impossible the stories are. Is it conceivable that a man, in the condition to which he is said to have descended, could have attended his drills regularly for two hours on two days in every week, attended regularly his Committee meetings—his very presence there is proof that the story of social ostracism was a lie—and assisted in transacting the important and exacting business of a new Volunteer Corps, when arms, accoutrements, and the general paraphernalia of such a body had to be provided and maintained ? Not only is Burns by this Minute Book proved to have been a man of most regular habits, which coincides exactly with his colleague Findlater's and his friend Gray's testimony, and the " Excise Register of Censures," but during those months he was hard at work on his Excise duties, and had contributed to Scottish song some of its most brilliant gems. During his period of strenuous Volunteering, Burns continued his great work for Scottish song by contributing generously to Thomson's work, still refusing to accept payment because he was rendering patriotic work for his native country. Among the numerous songs which he wrote in the busy months of 1795, were the great patriotic song : " Does haughty Gaul invasion threat ?" that trumpet call to Democracy : " A man's a man for a' that " ; one of the finest specimens of his humour, " Last May a braw wooer " ; one of his immortal love songs, " This is no my ain lassie " ; as well as the Heron Ballads. If this strenuous labour—active Volunteering, exacting Excise duties, and the composition of at least three of his greatest songs, all in the compass of some ten months—be the record of a decadent, we should pray that to Scotland might be born to-day another such decadent.

No ; the truth is that though Burns was not a heavy

or a habitual drinker, his craving for convivial company
led him occasionally to drink too much—which in his
verse he glorified and exaggerated—and that he had many
enemies who did not hesitate to enlarge upon his occasional
excesses.   He was a man of great individuality, and consequently he attracted great attention.   The "fierce
light that beats upon a throne" was nothing to the fierce-
ness of the local light that searched every cranny of the
life of the man who died in the humble home in the Mill
Vennel of Dumfries.   The searchlight discovered blemishes.
It could not be otherwise.   Burns was nothing if he was
not open.   There was no hypocrisy in his composition.
He was a seer, far ahead of his fellows, and consequently
misunderstood by many.   He was a political revolutionary,
and therefore looked at askance and suspected by many
of his contemporaries.   He had a vitriolic tongue and
pen which he uséd remorselessly on occasion on those
whom he did not like ; and those victims of his "rough"
tongue, human nature, even in Dumfries, being what it
was, lost no opportunity of retaliating by improving and
spreading tales of his dissipation ; tales, some of them,
which were merely *oral* half a century after the Poet's
death, yet believed, in spite of the *written* evidence of his
contemporaries that he seldom drank to excess, that he
was deeply interested in his family's welfare and education,
that he was a highly respected citizen, and in conversation
a moral purist.   That many doors in Dumfries were
shut to Burns we need not doubt, but the doors that were
closed to him were not closed because of his dissipation,
His political opinions being what they were, his caustic
epigrams and epitaphs on men and women, created a sufficient number of enemies, and consequently the ground was
ready for the seed sown by those who wished to malign
him.   Because they hated his politics, groaned under his
castigations, and were unable to retaliate in kind, they
took the arrows which Burns himself made, put poison
on the tips, and drove them into the reputation of the
greatest genius of his day ; his biographers turned them

in the wound, and the sore is being healed up only now. Is it too much to hope that the facts here presented from the manuscript Minute Book of the Royal Dumfries Volunteers, in the Ewart Library, Dumfries, and the deductions therefrom, will help somewhat towards healing the wound ?

WILLIAM WILL,
President of the London Robert Burns Club.

ADDITIONAL NOTES TAKEN FROM THE MANUSCRIPT MINUTE BOOK.

Note A.

ORIGINAL MEMBERS OF THE ROYAL DUMFRIES VOLUNTEERS.

List of Inhabitants of Dumfries who attended the Inaugural Meeting of the Royal Dumfries Volunteers, on 31st January, 1795.

John Syme.
John Harley.
John Armstrong.
Hugh M'Cornock, junior.
Thomas Gordon.
Thomas White.
Robert Clugston.
Andrew Smith.
Rev. Dr Wm. Babington.
John Kennedy.
George Duncan.
Simon Mackenzie.
John M'Morine.
James Gracie.
James Denniston.
Thomas Glendinning.
William Paton.
David Williamson.
James Mundell.
John Aitken.

Benjamin Bell.
Kinloch Winlaw.
Henry Clint.
James Stott.
David Newall.
Captain John Hamilton.
Lt.-Col. A. S. de Peyster.
Captain John Finnan.
William Laidlaw.
Samuel Clark, junior.
William Hyslop, junior.
William Boyd.
John Hogg.
James Gray.
Deacon Alexander Lookup.
Robert Jackson, junior.
Robert Primrose, junior.
William Hyslop (1).
Alexander Brown.
William Hyslop (2).

William Johnston.

James Grieve.

James Rae.

George Grieve.

John Ferguson.

Riddell M'Naught.

James Graham.

William Richardson.

Hugh Maxwell.

Wellwood Maxwell.

Convener Wm. Hayland.

Deacon Robert Anderson.

William Manderson.

David Blount.

John Brand.

William M'Cracken.

Edward Hyslop.

Robert Grainger.

John M'Cracken.

Thomas Hood.

Alexander Douglas.

Robert Burns.

John Lawson, junior.

William Hamilton, junior.

List of those whose Names were added on 3rd February 1795, to the above, and formed part of the Original Corps.

John M'Murdo.

Francis Shortt.

Thomas Williamson.

David Newall.

Samuel Johnston.

James Spalding.

William Selkirk.

Frazer Richardson.

James M'Clatchie.

A. Findlater.

Alex. Copland.

Andrew Johnstone.

William Wallace.

John Lewars.

John W. Maxwell

Edward Maxwell.

John Weems, junior.

John Coulthard.

John M'Vitie.

John Kerr.

Thomas Boyd.

William Thomson.

Robert Spalding.

Thomas Halliday.

John Caird, junior.

Leonard Smith.

Thomas Grierson.

Note B.

OFFER OF SERVICE AND CONDITIONS.

At the meeting in the Court House, Dumfries, on 3rd February, 1795, at which Mr Staig presided, the Offer of Service and Rules and Regulations, passed unanimously, signed, and sent to the Lord-Lieutenant for the King's acceptance, are in the following terms :—

" Offer of Service by certain Loyal Inhabitants of the

Town of Dumfries, and Rules, Regulations, and Bye-Laws framed for their Government in a Military Capacity—

" We the subscribers, all inhabitants of the burgh and neighbourhood of Dumfries, within the County of Dumfries, do hereby declare our sincere attachment to the person and government of His Majesty King George the Third ; our respect for the happy Constitution of Great Britain ; and our firm resolution on every occasion to protect the lives and properties of ourselves and our fellow-subjects from every attempt of the ambitious and turbulent who threaten to overturn the laws of our country, and who, by anarchy, sedition, and bloodshed may endeavour to destroy the sacred bonds of society ; and, as we are of opinion that the only way we can obtain a speedy and honourable peace is by the Government vigorously carrying on the present war, humbly submit the following proposals to His Majesty for the purpose of forming ourselves into a Volunteer Corps, in order to support the internal peace and good order of the town, as well as to give energy to the measures of Government, to wit :—

" 1. That we shall form ourselves into a Corps, consisting of two companies of infantry, not exceeding fifty men each, including commissioned and non-commissioned officers, to serve under the Lord-Lieutenant for the county of Dumfries, or his deputy for this district, during the present war, without pay, and find our own clothing.

" 2· That each person enrolling himself into the said Corps shall be approved of by the Lord-Lieutenant for the said county or his deputy, and shall take the oath of allegiance.

" 3· That each company shall have a Captain and two Subalterns and the whole commanded by a Major Commandant.

" 4. That the Officers shall have a temporary rank from the King.

" 5, That the Corps shall be allowed to choose their

own officers, who are to be approved by the Lord-Lieutenant or his deputy.

" 6· That the Corps shall not be obliged to march more than five miles from the town of Dumfries.

" 7· That Government shall furnish arms, accoutrements, pipes and drums, and pay one fifer, one drummer. and one drill sergeant for each company, and the Corps shall return their arms and accoutrements when demanded.

" 8· That the members of the said Corps engage to serve as aforesaid only when within the burgh or neighbourhood of Dumfries, and called on in aid of a civil magistrate for the preventing or suppressing of riot, tumult or disorder.

" 9· That the Corps shall choose the Commissioned Officers as aforesaid by ballot ; and the Non-Commissioned Officers shall be chosen in the same manner bv their respective companies.

" 10. That the Corps shall turn out for the purpose of discipline as often as may appear necessary to the Commanding Officer ; and shall, when drawn up under arms, observe the most profound silence, pay all due respect to their officers, and implicitly obey orders without reply.

" 11. That all persons wishing admission into this Corps shall make application to the Secretary, who shall mention such application before the Committees of Management, a majority of whom shall have power to admit ; and upon anv offence or impropriety of conduct committed by any of the members of this Association, and a complaint thereof made by any of the Committee, and a proof of such offence or impropriety brought, the said majority shall have it in their power to pass censure or even to expel from the Corps.

" 12. That the Corps request to be allowed to assume the name of ' The Royal Dumfries Volunteers ' ; and for their uniform to wear a blue coat half-lapelled with red cape and cuffs, and gilt buttons with the letters R.D.V. engraved on them ; a plain white cassimere vest, with small gilt buttons ; white trousers made of Russia tweeling, tied at the ankle ; white stockings ; a black velvet stock ; hair to be worn short, or turned up behind ; a round hat turned up on the left side with a gilt button, a cockade, and a black feather ; their shoes to be tied with black ribbon ; and the only distinction between the officers and privates, in point of dress, is that the Major Commandant and two Captains are to wear two epaulets, and the other Commissioned Officers one."

These proposals were sent to the Duke of Portland, then Home Secretary, who expressed his great pleasure with them, and said it would be more desirable that the gentlemen of the Corps should agree to accept a sum in lieu of arms and accoutrements than that they should be supplied by the Government.   £1 12s 10d would be allowed for each firelock, and 3s 4d for each set of accoutrements.

In this letter, which was read at a meeting in the Court House on 20th February, the Duke of Portland paid a great compliment to the Royal Dumfries Volunteers. " It is not customary," he said, " to allow daily pay in a Volunteer Corps, except to one sergeant per company, but as the Dumfries Volunteers have spiritedly stept forward with an offer of their services and agreed to serve without pay, daily pay will likewise be granted to one drummer and one fifer per company.

The meeting accepted the sum allowed.

" To fix on the shade and kind of blue cloath to be worn by the Volunteers," Colonel de Peyster, Messrs David Williamson, James Rae, Andrew Johnston, and Robert Grainger were appointed a committee ; and directions were given to Messrs Williamson, Rae, and Johnston to purchase " what cloath, white cassimere, and white Russia tweel may be necessary for cloathing the Volunteers, who all promise to purchase their uniforms from one or other of these three gentlemen, and who are also ordered to purchase a sufficient number of hats at about 16s each."

Note C.

COLONEL AND MRS DE PEYSTER.

Colonel Arentz Schuyler de Peyster, who commanded the Royal Dumfries Volunteers during the troublous times of the end of the eighteenth and opening of the nineteenth centuries, was descended from a Huguenot family which had settled in America. He was in the Regular Army, and during the Seven Years' War he commanded at Detroit, Michilimacinac, and in Upper Canada. It was his great tact and decision that enabled Colonel de Peyster to break the Indians from the French service. For some time he commanded the 8th Regiment, and as a Colonel he retired to Dumfries, the native place of Mrs de Peyster, who was a sister of Mr John M'Murdo, one of Burns's great friends and fellow-Volunteers, and Chamberlain to the Marquis of Queensberry. To the Colonel's home, Mavis Grove, Burns was always a welcome visitor, and the fact that the Colonel also courted the Muses formed a further link with the National Poet. The social unrest and the threatened invasion by the French were the causes of the old war-horse again taking up the sword, and although he was over sixty when he took command of the Dumfries Volunteers, he very soon had the Regiment in a state of great efficiency. From the Minute Book of the Corps, which has been so freely quoted from in this work, we take this extract from a Minute of 20th February, 1795: "That Colonel de Peyster shall be Major Commandant of the Corps, who, being present, accepted thereof." At a meeting on the following day called for the selection of officers, the Colonel said he was truly sensible of the honour done him in electing him Major Commandant; and to show her appreciation Mrs de Peyster would provide a stand of colours to be embroidered "with such figures and emblems of loyalty as the Volunteers shall suggest." Mrs de Peyster requested that they would accept the flag as a free gift from her. The meeting considered that a great honour had been conferred on the Corps. The colours were presented with great ceremony on the Square of Dumfries, on the King's Birthday, in 1795. The Rev. Dr Burnside, after prayer, congratulated the Corps on its splendid discipline, for which Colonel de Peyster's persistence in drilling had to be thanked.

Note D.

RULES AND REGULATIONS SIGNED BY VOLUNTEERS ON TAKING THE OATH.

On the 28th March, 1795, in the Old Assembly Rooms, the Deputy Lord-Lieutenant, Mr David Staig, presided over a meeting of fifty-nine members (including Robert Burns) who took the oath of allegiance.

The following "Rules, Regulations, and Bye-laws for conducting themselves in a military capacity, which they fully considered," were adopted and signed by those present :—

"1st.—All resolutions of the Corps, in a body, are to be decided by a majority of votes by ballot.

"2ud.—Every member admitted must take the oaths to His Majesty, previous to having his arms delivered to him. And he is expressly debarred from wearing his side-arms except when called out for the purpose of drilling, or upon other duty ; and no member to appear at the drill in any degree the worse of liquor.

"3rd.—The dress of the Corps shall remain as fixed in the offer of service—at least no alteration shall be made therein without concurrence of four-fifths of the Corps—and as an exact uniformity in this respect is obviously necessary, no deviation from it can be permitted, excepting that white cassimere breeches, buckled at the knee, and half-gaiters conform to a pattern now shown by Colonel de Peyster, shall be substituted in place of white Russia tweel trousers, as formerly agreed on.

"4th.—The Corps shall wear their uniforms on general field days, and may wear them on Sundays or on public occasions, such as the King and Queen's Birthday, assemblies, &c., and on any other occasion they may think proper.

" 5th.—The Corps may provide themselves with short blue jackets, and with red shoulder-straps, capes and cuffs, to be worn in the mornings or on ordinary occasions, with white vests and nankeen trousers buttoned at the ankle ; and the whole to be uniform.

" 6th.—The uniform of the officers, non-commissioned, and private shall be the same, with this distinction, that the officers shall wear swords and epaulets ; and the sergeants, drummers, and fifers, swords only. And when there are no military in town, the drums and fifes to beat the morning and evening duty.

" 7th.—The colours (which have been presented to the Corps by Mrs de Peyster) shall be placed in the custody of the Major Commandant.

" 8th.—Every member of the Corps obliges himself to turn out, for the purpose of drilling, when his attendance is desired by the commanding officer, such musters, however, not to exceed two hours in each day, nor two days in each week ; and the hours most likely not to interfere with business to be appropriated for these purposes ; and the days of meeting to be Friday and Saturday at six in the evening.

" 9th.—The Corps when arrived at such a state of discipline as to think themselves entitled, by a majority of votes, to demand to be reviewed by an officer of such rank as generally presides on such occasions, after being so reviewed, or qualified to meet it, shall not be called above one day in each fortnight or more than two hours in that day, for the purpose of drilling.

" 10th.—The Corps shall appoint a new committee, consisting of the two captains and four lieutenants and of eight non-commissioned officers or privates, to be elected ; the major commandment or senior officer present to preside on all occasions, and to have the casting vote in case of an equality ; and nine to be a quorum. The committee to continue three months.

" 11th.—This committee shall have jurisdiction in all matters of offence committed against the Corps by any of its members, the punishment to extend only to fine, censure, or expulsion from the Corps ; and in certain cases, may extend the punishment to publishing his name and offence in the *Dumfries Weekly Journal.*

" 12th.—This committee shall deliberate on all matters respecting the Corps. In cases of fine and censure its resolutions to pass by a majority of votes and be decisive ; but in questions of expulsion, &c., by the concurrence of three-fourths of the committee, or quorum present—and in this case an appeal to lay to the whole Corps, on the application of the dissenting members.

" 13th.—When the Corps is called out on ordinary field days, for the purpose of drilling, defaulters or absentees on such musters who cannot assign a just and necessary cause of absence to his commanding officer shall be fined in the following sums, viz., non-commissioned officers and privates one shilling for the first offence, and one shilling and sixpence for every offence thereafter ; commissioned officers of every rank, two shillings and sixpence for the first offence, and five shillings for every subsequent offence, but these fines shall not operate against members confined by indisposition, or on journeys of more than seven miles from Dumfries.

" 14th.—That the fines so levied shall be paid to the commanding officer of each Company, and an account of their amount to be kept by the sergeant-major ; such amount to be submitted once a month to the inspection of the committee, who shall direct the expenditure thereof.

" 15th.—The commanding officer to be bound to call a meeting of the committee on the application of any five members in writing.

" 16th.—The Corps, in case of riot, insurrection, accidental fire, public rejoicing, or other necessary occasions to be bound to turn out under arms, on the call of the commanding officer for the time, on an application to him by the civil magistrates of the town or on requisition of the Lord-Lieutenant of the County, or his deputy for this district, in case the service of the Corps is required in the country as stated in their offer of service ; and in cases of fire the beat of the town drum to be the signal for every member to repair under arms to the alarm post, which the commandant will appoint, dressed in their morning jackets.

" 17th.—Any member of the Corps guilty of insolence to his superior officer, whilst on duty, to be subject to fine or censure, or expulsion, if the committee consider the case to merit it.

" 18th.—Any officer guilty of tyrannical behaviour towards any member of the Corps, whilst on duty, to be punished by fine and censure at the discretion of the committee.

" 19th.—Any centinel or private quitting his post when called out upon duty, to be liable to the highest penalty that can be inflicted ; and any officer or private abandoning his post when on duty to be subject to the same.

20th.—Any centinel or private suffering himself to be surprised on duty, or losing his arms, to be subjected in the same manner.

" 21st.—Any member exciting others to neglect their duty, or raising cabals in the Corps, to be subject to the same.

" 22nd.—No discharge shall in future be granted to any member unless he pay twenty guineas towards the incidental expenses of the Corps, except such as from unavoidable causes shall be obliged to remove their residence, in which case they are virtually discharged.

" 23rd.—Any member having occasion to be absent from town for the space of one week or more, and who upon that account cannot attend the muster during that time, shall be bound to give notice thereof to the Commanding Officer of his Company, upon pain of being fined as in the case of unnecessary absence.

" 24th.—In the event of vacancies happening in the commissioned or non-commissioned officers' departments, every member in the Corps subscribing these regulations, and these only, are eligible to the succession, whatever their rank may be.

" 25th.—The Commandant may give occasional necessary oders for the economy and good discipline of the Corps, viz., forming and sizing the companies, care and occasional repair of arms and accoutrements, occasionally altering a drill day or the hour thereof, and such small matters as must necessarily occur, provided they do not in any wise militate against the intent of the foregoing resolution.

" Lastly.—The Corps reserve to themselves liberty to make such new regulations and bye-laws, or to make such alteration on the present, as a majority of them may afterwards think proper. In testimony of all which the Corps have subscribed the foregoing resolution at Dumfries, the twenty-eighth day of March, in the year one thousand and seven hundred and ninety-five, having at the same time taken the oaths to His Majesty."

PROPOSED REMOVAL OF THE HIGHLAND MARY MEMORIAL.

FURTHER DEVELOPMENTS.

IN the *Burns Chronicle* (No. XXVII., 1918) appeared a narrative of the proceedings of Messrs Caird & Co., Shipbuilders, Greenock, to acquire the Old West Parish Church and Graveyard for the purpose of securing greater facilities for the building of the larger vessels necessitated by the demands of modern commerce. With this object in view, they approached the Heritors and Trustees of the Church, but both bodies refused to entertain the proposal ; and so the project was allowed to lapse for a time, and the narrative in the *Chronicle* referred to ended with the announcement of that fact. Early in 1919 the question was taken up by the Corporation of Greenock, which body took steps to procure a Provisional Order for the removal of the church and graveyard on the grounds that they were situated in a slum locality which ought to be swept away as a menace to the public health and an impediment in the way of the improvement of the town. The question came up for discussion at the Annual Meeting of the Federation on 6th September last, a report of which is annexed, together with other information which brings the narrative up to date. Instead of giving a summary of the evidence led before Lord Forteviot by the Federation delegates, we deemed it preferable to lay it before our readers *in extenso*, lest we inadvertently left out any point in which our readers are interested. It will be observed that, by a majority, the Trustees and Kirk-Session of the Church have changed their attitude ; and we may add that certain of the more influential heritors and lairholders have followed their example.

When the question was reached on the agenda paper the President reported on the efforts made by the Executive of the Federation to secure the preservation of the West Kirk and Kirkyard and Highland Mary's grave and monument. In connection therewith he read the following letters :—

Duncan M'Naught, Esq., President of Burns Federation,
Benrig, Kilmaurs, Ayrshire.

North of Scotland Bank Chambers,
31 Cathcart Street,
Greenock, 25th August, 1919.

Dear Sir,

Greenock Improvement Provisional Order, 1919.

As you will have seen from the papers, the Commissioners decided against us in this matter. Leaving all sentiment out of the case and the methods adopted by the shipbuilding firm, it is our view that the necessity for the churchyard for shipbuilding purposes was not proved, and that it is against usual Parliamentary procedure in any case to grant ground for the purpose of a private enterprise. Notwithstanding the result, we think all the objectors are glad that the attempt was made to preserve the old church and churchyard, with their historic associations, and to have shewn that there are still some people left in this utilitarian age with a sense of decency and a reverence for ancient things.

On the adjustment of the clauses referring to Highland Mary's grave, it was arranged as a condition of the settlement that Messrs Caird should give the letter of which we enclose a copy. It was proposed by the promoters that it should rest with the Greenock Burns Club as to the course to be adopted, but we objected to this on the grounds that we considered the negative attitude adopted by the Greenock Burns Club did not warrant any consideration being given to their views. The letter was handed to us on behalf of the Petitioners, with the approval of the Commissioners, and the Petitioners will now be glad to have the Burns Federation views as to which of the three alternatives proposed they would consider should be adopted. We have no doubt our clients will be glad to have carried out any results which the Burns Federation may suggest. We take it there is no immediate hurry to decide the matter, but it is probably advisable that we should be in a position to state as soon as possible what is to be done. We shall therefore be glad if you will put the matter before the Federation at their first meeting.—We are, Yours faithfully,

(Signed) M'NEIL & ROWAN.

Justiciary Buildings,
Glasgow, 12th August, 1919.

Dear Sirs,

Greenock Provisional Order, 1919.

Notwithstanding the terms of the above Order we agree entirely at our expense either (1) to remove the remains of " Highland Mary " and the monument to her memory to such a place of sepulture or site as may be selected by the Executive Committee of the Burns Federation, or (2) to leave the remains interred as at present and to reverse the existing monument to face Laird Street, and to leave sufficient ground around it to be accessible to visitors at all times, or (3) to remove the existing monument and place and maintain a mural tablet in lieu thereof, as shown on the sketch submitted to you, the remains not being disturbed. Failing agreement, the alternative to be adopted shall be decided by the Sheriff-Substitute at Greenock after hearing all parties interested.—Yours faithfully,

For CAIRD & CO., LTD.,

(Signed)   J. W. KEMPSTER,
Managing Director.

To Messrs M'Neil & Rowan,
Solicitors, Greenock.

If they carried their minds back to 1917 they would remember that certain members of the Greenock Burns Club assured the Federation that there was no proposal at that time to remove Highland Mary's grave. They accepted that statement, but as a precaution they appointed a small committee to act along with the Greenock Burns Club should the emergency arise. During the year 1918 the Secretary reported that the committee had never met, that they had had no news from Greenock, and last year they again remitted the whole question to their Executive. In the beginning of 1919 they found that there was a proposal to remove Highland Mary's grave. Application had been made for a Provisional Order to remove the whole of the West Kirk and Kirkyard, this time not by Messrs Harland & Wolff, but by the Corporation of Greenock, who held that it was a slum area. The Executive met twice, and at the second meeting, as things were urgent, they appointed Mr J. C. Ewing and himself to attend the inquiry that was held in the Justiciary Court,

Glasgow, under the chairmanship of Lord Forteviot, and oppose the granting of the Provisional Order so far as it proposed the removal of the grave of Highland Mary. The impression left on his mind by the evidence produced in Court was that it was perfectly clear to him that the Provisional Order was going to be granted. He remembered that Mr Ewing and himself had been sent specially to the inquiry for the purpose of trying to preserve Highland Mary's grave, and therefore he favoured the offer made by Mr Wilson, K.C., counsel for the promoters, that Messrs Harland & Wolff were willing to make a recess in the wall, leaving the monument and the grave exactly as they stood. But it was a necessity that the monument which at present faced into the church should be turned round and made to face the street. This appeared to him to be a very good solution of the difficulty, but of course h · spoke in ignorance of the locality, and he made it clear at the same time that he only spoke for himself, and that he could not bind himself to speak for the Federation. He had given it as his opinion that it would go a great length in placating the Federation if assurances were given and plans drawn and laid before them to show that the grave and the monument would not be further interfered with. The result of the inquiry was that the preamble of the Provisional Order had been proved, and since then he had received several communications from Greenock. The position now, so far as they were concerned, was that they had an offer by the promoters of three alternatives —(1) to remove the remains of Highland Mary and the monument to such a place of sepulture as might be selected by the executive of the Federation ; (2) to leave the remains interred as at present, and to reverse the existing monument so as to face the street ; or (3) to remove the existing monument, and to place and maintain a mural tablet in lieu thereof, the remains not being disturbed. He was not familiar with the locality, and would be glad to hear the views of the Greenock Burns Club. Personally he had quite an open mind on the matter, but he would like to hear an expression of opinion on the alternatives submitted in view of the Order receiving the assent of Parliament.

Ex-Provost Wilson, Pollokshaws, moved that it be left to the Executive of the Federation, in conjunction with representatives of the Greenock Burns Club, with full powers to determine which of the three alternatives they should accept.

Mr Pollock thought they were going a little bit too fast if they imagined that the last word had been said on this subject. Although the preamble of the Order had been proved, he had been informed that if they could create a sufficient amount of national interest in the matter they would make the House of Commons and the House of Lords pause before they gave their final sanction, and certainly they still had two or three months to do a part which some of them had already tried to do. Mr Pollock moved :—

" That this meeting of the Burns Federation, as Burnsians and as Scotsmen, tender their heartiest thanks to Mr R. L. Scott, Mr J. B. Morison, Mr T. B. Rowan, Mr Grierson Macara, and other members of the Greenock Burns Club for their noble and patriotic opposition to the proposal to sell and remove the ancient Greenock West Church and churchyard, and that all present hereby pledge themselves to do all in their power to oppose the passing into law of the Greenock Improvement Provisional Order, 1919, so far as that Order threatens the preservation of this church and churchyard, and so prevent an indelible disgrace being inflicted upon the name and fame of Scotland and Scotsmen. And this meeting further appeals to all Scottish Societies to aid in this opposition, and so maintain the sacredness of all burial grounds in Scotland, and the permanent validity of the title deeds of all lairholders, whether poor or rich."

Proceeding, Mr Pollock urged upon the members of the Federation to write their various Members of Parliament and protest against this proposed desecration. If they did that he was sure they would find their legislators sympathetic and anxious to know all the facts. They did not protest against the Provisional Order in its entirety, but only as it affected the kirkyard, and as a lairholder himself he wanted to know if it was true that the promoters actually assumed that a lairholder had no property in his lair further than the burial rights. He held that the six feet by two of a lairholder was as much his property as if it were a thousand acres.

Mr Grierson Macara, as a lairholder who had opposed the Provisional Order and as a member of the Greenock Burns Club, explained that there were certain circumstances which had prevented the Burns Club from taking any definite action in this matter. These circumstances had been such as to cause suspicion on the part of outsiders as to the intentions of the Greenock Burns Club. The Club, as such, had never been called together to deal with this matter, and therefore those of them who were members of the Club and who felt very strongly about it, had never had a chance of trying to influence the other members to take the action that they would have liked them to take. As they all knew, the preamble of the Order had been proved, but that did not mean that the Order itself had been passed. The Order became a Bill, and the Bill had to go through certain other stages in both Houses of Parliament before it became the law of the realm ; and it was very important that the Burns Federation and all others who had opposed the Order should take no steps to stultify their position before the Bill came up for consideration, because it might be possible to get a blocking motion introduced in Parliament. They were still in the position of opposers of the Order and were still able to take such action as was open to them to oppose it, and there was no reason whatever why they should prejudice that position. It was not at all necessary to take immediate action as regards the letters which the President had read. Neither the Highland Mary statue nor the graveyard itself was going to be interfered with next week. or next month, or even next year. The scheme was a big scheme. It involved the removal of a slum area in the immediate neighbourhood of the graveyard, and nothing could be done to remove that slum area until the people resident there were put into other houses. That could not be done until new houses were built, and they all knew that houses could not be erected before a considerable lapse of time, so that there was really no immediate hurry to accept or take advantage of the options which had been mentioned. He was sure they would all like to do the right thing, and he would suggest to them that as they did not know the surroundings of the place they might take an excursion to Greenock before coming to a decision. He thought they should still adopt a waiting attitude, leaving the matter in the hands of the Executive, and he would suggest that the Executive should co-opt some members of the Greenock Burns Club or some of the petitioners against the Order, and they could call the Federation together if there should be any need to take action quickly. But he was perfectly sure that that emergency would not arise before they had an opportunity of visiting the place and seeing the surroundings and deciding for themselves which of the three options would be the best to adopt. He strongly urged them not to act precipitately or to do anything that would prejudice the rights which the lairholders now possessed.

After some discussion, the amendment was withdrawn, and the whole matter was remitted to the Executive along with representatives of the Greenock Burns Club, with full powers to deal with it in the interests of the Federation.

EVIDENCE AT THE ENQUIRY

Mr DUNCAN M'NAUGHT, *sworn.*

Were you parish schoolmaster at Kilmaurs for fifty-two years ?—Yes.

Are you a justice of the peace for the county of Ayr ?—Yes.

And also registrar for Kilmaurs ?—Yes, at one time, not now.

I think you have been interested in the Burns Federation since its commencement ?—Since 1885.

Were you one of the founders ?—The only one now living.

Have you been a vice-president since the foundation ?—I have held office since the foundation, and been president for nine years.

And editor of the *Burns Chronicle* for twenty-seven years ? —Yes.

The honorary president is Lord Rosebery, and the honorary vice-president Andrew Carnegie ?—Yes. Lord Rosebery takes a very great interest in our Federation.

Tell us what is the Burns Federation ?—It was formed first of all to unify the Burns Clubs throughout the world, so that we could take united action when any question cropped up.

It is the central association with which is linked up every Burns Club throughout the world ?—Yes. Every one is not federated, but they are coming in day by day. Last week we admitted a Burns Club from Sydney and one from Nova Scotia.

How many of those interested in Burns and his works does the Federation represent ?—It is difficult to answer exactly, but the number of Clubs in our Federation is about 262, and, taking the average, I think I represent 15,000 to 20,000 Burnsians. That is exclusive of the Burns Clubs that are not federated. In that sense I represent 40,000 or 50,000.

I think the Burns Federation started the movement for a Chair of Scottish History ?—We were the first to advocate it, eighteen years before it took practical shape.

You contributed £5000 towards the endowment of the chair ? —Yes, out of £20,000. The Corporation of Glasgow took it over, and the £20,000 was raised.

In recent years the Burns Federation has been active, and in some cases successful in national monuments and objects of national interest being preserved ?—Yes.

As an instance of that, you managed to save the Auld Brig of Ayr ?—Yes, it was entirely due to the Federation. We approached Lord Rosebery, and he came to Ayr and addressed a mass meeting, and £10,000 was raised for the saving of the Auld Brig.

I think you also saved the Glenriddel manuscripts ?—Yes. We threatened the directors of the Liverpool Athenæum with a law action, and, through the generosity of Mr Gribbel, we saved these manuscripts. That was due to the Burns Federation.

The alarm as regards this Parish Church and churchyard, and, in particular, Highland Mary's grave, was sounded about May, 1917 ?—Yes, in the *Glasgow Herald*.

When that article appeared, was action taken by the Burns Federation ?—I was receiving letters from all quarters as to what action the Federation was likely to take, and my answer was that the policy would be directed at the September meeting of 1917.

Delegates were present at that meeting from the Greenock Burns Club, and they asked to be heard. We were then told that there was no proposal before Greenock or before the nation to desecrate the tomb of Highland Mary or to remove it. I thought that exceedingly strange, and I suggested a committee to act along with the Greenock representatives. I called a meeting of the committee, to ascertain if there was any danger of the grave being violated. The year 1918 passed, and there was no committee called, no word having reached us from Greenock. It came up again last September, when the secretary reported that the committee had no meeting, and therefore there was no report.

Before anything could be done to the churchyard, legislative sanction had to be obtained ?—I advised the Federation of that in 1917.

Who were the representatives of the Greenock Burns Club ? I think there was a Bailie M'Callum. It was he who assured us there was no proposal before Greenock or before the country. In 1918, when we reached the business, it was suggested that the question be now remitted to the Executive of our standing council, with powers to take whatever steps they thought fit. At that meeting, in September, 1918, there were representatives present from three clubs in Greenock—the Greenock Burns Club, the Cronies' Club, and St. John's Club. I put this motion to the meeting, and there was no counter motion and no dissent. They agreed to the instructions by the Federation that a delegate was to come here and oppose this Order.

So far as the associations affiliated with the Burns Federation are concerned, the proposal to oppose the Order was unanimous ; there was no dissent ?—No ; the feeling was very strong.

I think you and Mr Ewing were appointed to attend the inquiry and oppose the Order ?—That is so.

Is it your desire that the grave and monument of Highland Mary should remain in its present surroundings in the churchyard of the old West Parish Church ?—It is our wish.

I think at one of your meetings it was suggested that the monument was not to be touched ; it was to be left where it was ?— Nothing official reached us, but we heard that there were two proposals by the promoters of this Provisional Order. One was to surround it with a wall. That, so far as I am personally concerned, I would not consider for a moment. The other proposal was to remove it to some other place, to whatever site the Burns Federation should indicate. I paid great attention to the remarks of the learned gentleman who spoke for the promoters, and heard what he said about a wall being built round the statue and the monument turned round the other way. I would like to know what public access to the monument is proposed to be given. I speak only for myself ; I cannot speak for the Federation, but that would appear to me, if this Order is carried, to be the best solution.

The desire of the Federation is that this churchyard and monument and tomb of Highland Mary should remain as they are ? —Most decidedly.

Will you indicate on the map where the tomb and monument are ?—Where the black line crosses the two lines marking the boundary of the churchyard.

And there is, on the opposite wall of the churchyard, a little tablet indicating that immediately inside the wall is the tomb of Highland Mary ?—Yes.

Cross-examined for the Promoters.

By Mr Wilson—Are you here to-day as the result of any re-solution of the Federation authorising you to speak on their behalf ? —I am here to represent them as an accredited delegate.

Who gave you the right ?—The whole question was remitted at the general meeting of September, 1918, and left to the Standing Committee, which has since met. At the last meeting they appointed Mr Ewing and myself to appear here.

It is a delegation from a delegated body ?—No ; from the Standing Committee, which was invested with full powers.

When was the last meeting of the Federation ?—The first Saturday of September, 1918.

Had they before them the alternative proposal which is made on behalf of the promoters, to make a recess and leave the tomb-stone practically where it is, reversed ?—That was not before us.

Did you not know that the Greenock Club, at various meet-ings, have had before them the choice of either adopting that scheme, or, if they preferred it, removing the remains and the re-erection of the monument to some other site ?—That was hearsay to us. The Greenock Burns Club never approached us officially.

Your committee have not been inquiring as to what was going on ?—We were waiting on the Greenock Burns Club, as arranged.

You got no communication ?—No.

And, now that you hear that the promoters are willing, if the Greenock Club prefer it, to reverse the tombstone, make the recess in the wall, and make it accessible from the street outside the ship-building yard altogether, what do you say to that ?—I have given my personal opinion, but, at the same time, I cannot speak for the Federation. That would be the minimum of disturbance.

You have not had a chance ?—A meeting will be held on 6th September ensuing, when the whole question will come up.

Re-examined by Mr Fenton—You have seen the Order that contemplates the removal of all the remains of Highland Mary ?— Yes.

By the Chairman—Would this proposal to reverse the monument in Laird Street remove to some extent your objection ?—I think so. We had a meeting of the Executive on Saturday last, and it appeared to find favour. Our care is Highland Mary's grave, and it is a personal opinion I give that that would be a good solution to the question if the Provisional Order goes through.

As far as Highland Mary's monument is concerned, that would go to some extent to satisfy you ?—Yes.

You are not speaking of the church or the James Watt monument ?—We have nothing whatever to do with that.

By Mr Sturrock—You spoke about the reversing of Highland Mary's monument representing the minimum of disturbance ?— That is precisely how I look at it. The sentiment attaches to the soil in which she is buried, and that would obviate any disturbance of the soil.

Are the Burns Federation perfectly clear that Highland Mary is buried there ?—No doubt whatever.

By Mr Fenton—Is it generally accepted that she was buried there in 1786, that her relative Macpherson brought her there and interred her there in that spot ?—Yes. There is no doubt she was buried there in 1786.

Mr JAMES CAMERON EWING, sworn.

Are you the librarian of the Baillie's Institution, Glasgow ? Yes.

You are a member of the Library Association and the Edinburgh and Glasgow Bibliographical Societies ?—Yes.

You are a vice-president of the Burns Federation ?—Yes.

And a member of the Glasgow Burns Clubs Association ?—Yes.

I think you have been keenly interested in Burns's works for a long time ?—Nearly thirty years.

I think you have collaborated in the production and preparation of editions and have written very extensively on the subject ?—Yes.

Have you been particularly interested in the proposal to remove to another situation the grave of Mary Campbell ?—Yes.

Have you been instructed to come here and oppose this Order by the Executive of the Burns Federation ?—Yes, along with Mr M'Naught.

I think we all know more or less the relations between Burns and Highland Mary ?—Very likely.

Have you any doubt that she was buried in 1786 by a relative called Macpherson ?—None at all. She was buried on or about 12th October, 1786.

The lair had been acquired by Peter Macpherson, and at that

date Highland Mary was buried ?—Yes, or within a day or two afterwards.

I think in 1917 the Burns Federation learned from newspaper articles that it was proposed to acquire the site of her grave for shipbuilding purposes ?—Yes.

How do you regard the presence of such a grave so far as Greenock is concerned ?—I think the presence of that grave is an honour to the town of Greenock, and ought to be respected by all, and particularly by the Corporation and the inhabitants of Greenock.

How do you regard the proposal to remove it ? — A most objectionable proposal, and one that should be opposed.

You think it is a national duty to preserve it ?—I think so.

Do you know that it has been the place to which many people have come ?—Many hundreds of people individually, and also many Burns Clubs have made a point of having an excursion to the West Kirkyard to see the burial-place of Mary Campbell.

It is a Burns shrine ?—Yes, one of the most interesting.

You think that it would be a serious thing if the monument and the dust, or whatever remains there, were removed to another site ?—I do not think that would be desirable at all. I think it would be a desecration. The stone does not matter ; it is the site which is the thing. I think on no consideration at all should the grave be interfered with.

I think in 1842 a monument was erected ?—Yes. Subscriptions were taken in the beginning of 1841, and the foundation stone was laid in January, 1842.

A parchment was placed there recording that the monument was erected by many admirers of Scotia's Bard and Mary Camp bell ?—That is on record.

Are you aware where the contributions for that monument came from ?—They came from all over Scotland, and some from England. The contribution of the people of Greenock was very small.

I think it was the subject of comment at the time ?—Yes, very strong comment.

Tell us what it was.—The honorary treasurer of the movement was a Mr Innes, a member of Her Majesty's Customs in Greenock. Mr Innes put himself to a great deal of trouble in collecting money, and was in communication with Mr John Corbet in Dundee. He wrote to him acknowledging receipt of £20 from Dundee, and in that letter he said, " I cannot brag much of what I have got in Greenock ; they are a pitiful set of devils." That was in 1841.

Mr Wilson told us on the first day in his opening speech that Burns's remains had been removed from one part of the church-yard to another ?—That is the case. Burns was buried in 1796 in St. Michael's Churchyard in Dumfries, and his widow erected, or caused to be erected, a plain slab over his grave. Nineteen years afterwards, in 1815, it was proposed to erect a mausoleum, and an elaborate design was obtained from Mr T. F. Hunt, a famous architect in London at that time. It was proposed to erect it in the southeast part of the churchyard.

That was from one part of the churchyard to another part of the same churchyard ?—Yes.

In an interval of nineteen years ?—Yes. When the grave was opened the coffin was intact, and they were able to put the remains in a new coffin. That, of course, could not be done now with Highland Mary's remains, for the coffin and its contents must long ago have decayed.

You are interested not only in the monument, but mainly in the site where the remains are ?—Particularly in the site.

Is it your desire, as instructed by the Federation, that that monument and grave should remain in their present surroundings ?—Yes.

Cross-examination for the Promoters.

By Mr Watson—Doesn't the inscription on the grave bear that Highland Mary had lain there unnoticed for fifty years ? Unmarked, do you mean'?

Do you not know the inscription by heart ?—It may be so worded, but I cannot carry it in my mind.

The inscription is from Mr Hill's book ; is it correct ?—I think it is a very careless use of the word " unnoticed."

Is that on the inscription ?—It may be.

Is it untrue, or are you in a position to say it is ?—I am in a position to say it is untrue. I would say it is untrue to this extent, that the grave was unmarked as the grave of Highland Mary until 1842.

It does not explain enough ; it was unmarked, and therefore unnoticed ?—There was no stone indicating Highland Mary, but there was Peter Macpherson's stone indicating the grave which he had bought and in which he buried Highland Mary.

In 1842: was that about the time the subscription was asked for ?—It began in 1841.

How much was raised altogether ?—Slightly over £100.

Was that from all over the world ?—I understand so.

Including the pitiful subscription from Greenock ?—Yes.

If this Order was to drop now you run the risk of another pitiful subscription when you next want it ?—I don't know anything about that.

You agree with the views expressed by Mr M'Naught ?—Yes.

Entirely ?—Yes.

Mr Hill also says about the present slab that its artistic merits are not great ; he does not seem to think much of what was put up for £100 ?—Yes.

Re-examined by Mr Fenton—You are not interested in the monument ?—Not much.

Your chief interest is in the site ?—Yes, the site is everything.

By the Chairman—You are representing the Burns Federation. You have got here a great scheme of public improvement for Greenock to sweep away 306 insanitary houses and to develop great shipbuilders, which will be a good thing for Greenock ; do you think that Rabbie Burns would put the interests of this grave above that ?—I should not like to say what Robert Burns might think.

Do you agree if this monument was left in its present situation that that would remove your objection ?—Yes, provided convenient access were given to it.

JUBILEE ANNIVERSARY MEETING OF THE LONDON ROBERT BURNS CLUB.

25TH JANUARY, 1919.

THE brilliant company assembled at this meeting, whose names would extend over several pages of the *Chronicle*, and the notable speeches delivered by eminent men present, have induced us to lay a full report before our readers as a memento of the Great War and contribution to the celebrations which marked the first Year of Peace. The report may also serve the purpose of introducing the sceptical to the mysteries of the January celebrations.

The Right Hon. Robert Munro, K.C. M.P., Secretary for Scotland, in rising to propose " The London Robert Burns Club," was loudly applauded. He said :—

Mr President, my Lord, Ladies, and Gentlemen,—You have heard from the Secretary of the various calamities which have befallen this gathering by reason of the absence of certain guests. I hope you will not regard my presence as a calamity rather than my absence—(laughter)—when I have concluded the few observations which I propose to address to you.

I think that in submitting to you the toast of " The London Robert Burns Club," eloquence and argument are alike superfluous. But a short and simple narrative may be permitted. Your Club is celebrating this year its jubilee. I think you all know what a wealth of well-conceived and well-directed activity is comprised in that short and simple statement of fact. (Hear, hear.) We recall to-night the founder of the Club, Mr Colin Rae Brown. We recall him with appreciation and with gratitude. We recall also the important part which this Club has been privileged to play in the social life of our time. We recall its many activities. We recall its unbounded generosity towards the ailing and the suffering and the poor, and in particular, we recall its war-time activities, which have been as manifold as they have been bountiful. (Applause.)

May I just add this ? The Club stands, as we all know, for the Burns spirit—the spirit of liberty, equality, and fraternity. That spirit is, of course, the negation of the hateful, and, fortunately, discredited doctrines of Prussia with which we have become familiar in recent years. It is, on the other hand, the affirmation of those great principles which have been triumphantly vindicated by the Allies. (Hear, hear.) Surely, then, there never was a time when an institution, breathing and animated by that spirit—a spirit abounding in, and so to speak, aggregated within its borders, and radiating its influence far and wide—I repeat, there never has been a time when such an institution had an opportunity so great and so fruitful as is presented to this Club. Your Club has a great past. In the greater future, whose sun-capped heights are now piercing the mists of the valley, I do not doubt for a moment that your Club will play a worthy and a noble part. In that uncharted future, in that uncharted sea, you have in your President a skilled and experienced captain, and an inspiring leader. It is my privilege to couple his name with the toast. I give you the toast of the " London Robert Burns Club," coupled with the name of Mr William Will.

The toast was received with musical honours.

Mr William Will, the President of the Club, in responding, said :—

My Lord, Ladies, and Gentlemen,—First let me, on behalf of the Club, thank the Secretary for Scotland for the generous words that he has used in submitting this toast, and you for the hand-some manner in which you have received it. We can reciprocate some of the compliments and congratulations which Mr Munro has offered, for we can congratulate him, and we can congratulate his native land upon his reappointment by His Majesty the King as Secretary of State for Scotland. (Cheers.)

· We meet to-night under conditions entirely different from those which last year led to the elevation of a miserable Italian decoction to the position which can only be satisfactorily occupied by His Majesty the Haggis. (Laughter.) Last year the Haggis was under control. Thanks to our invincible Navy and Army, and a determined civil population behind them, the Hun and the Haggis again occupy their proper places—the Hun under control and the Haggis uncon-trolled. (Laughter and applause.) As the Scottish Secretary has said, this evening the London Robert Burns Club celebrates for the fiftieth year the birth of the Poet. Fifty years ago last Hallowe'en, Mr Colin Rae Brown, a Scottish minor poet, with Samuel Lover, the novelist, George Cruickshank, the artist, and others, founded this Club, and in the intervening half a century the members have kept the Burns cult alive in the capital of the Auld Enemy, by means of literary, social, and charitable endeavour. There are differences of opinion as to the origin and functions of Burns Clubs. It is not the case, as cynics, and others with weak digestions, declare, that Burns Clubs exist for the sole and exclusive purpose of giving Scotsmen an excuse for once a year eating Haggis and getting uproariously "fou," for I never yet met a Scotsman who, if he really wanted a glass, or a bottle for that matter, lost any time in searching for an excuse for drinking it. (Laughter.) No ; the Scot is credited with being a highly practical person ; and there were good reasons for the establishment of associations dedicated to the memory of Robert Burns. The Poet was but a short time in his grave when Robert Heron, the brilliant, dissipated, lying, Scottish literary hack, who settled and died in poverty in London, let loose upon his country the first Life of the Poet. Not for the first or last time was local gossip, scandal, and personal animosity converted into biography. Since then there has raged round the Poet's head of gold and feet of clay a fiercer storm than that which roared over Coila on that never-to-be-forgotten 25th of January, 1759. Heron's, and subsequent attacks based on Heron's mis-statements, were so unjust that the antagonism of many men with a sense of decency and fairplay was aroused. They banded themselves together in clubs. They had, besides, the correction of false statements, to promulgate the Poet's message, for Burns, let it be remembered, was the forerunner of Lord Grey and President Wilson with the idea of the League of Nations ; and he was the author of what may well be the hymn of the League of Nations, the "Marseillaise of Humanity." (Applause.) As I have suggested, the work of our Club is not confined to gatherings such as this. We have literary meetings, we have other social functions, and we raise considerable sums of money for charitable purposes. This week, for example, we have handed to the Harry Lauder Fund for Disabled Scottish Sailors and Soldiers over £400. (Applause.) This Club is not a close corporation. Men of many nationalities come together in its membership. The first enrolled member was Samuel Lover, an Irishman ; our first honorary member was Garibaldi, the Italian patriot ; and the Father of our Club is an Englishman, Past President W. Hayward Pitman, a Deputy Alderman of London, a citizen of credit and renown, who with his good lady and family we are delighted to have with us to-night. (Applause.)

The President made further reference to the international character of the Club's membership, and concluded by again thanking the company for their hearty reception of the toast.

The Right Hon. Lord Morris, K.C., LL.D., K.C.M.G., proposed the toast of "The British Imperial Forces." Greeted with applause, Lord Morris said :—

Mr President, Ladies and Gentlemen,—I should like in the first instance to express my thanks to the President and the members of the Burns Club in London, for affording me the opportunity of being present here this evening and taking part in such a distinguished gathering, in celebration of Burns night. In tendering the toast of the " British Imperial Forces " to this gathering, it is almost impossible not to keep before one the fact that in those Imperial Forces the Scottish element has always taken a very important and outstanding place. (Applause.)

To-night we are celebrating the anniversary of the great Poet Burns, the peasant Poet, the farmer Poet, the ploughman Poet of Scotland, and he is typical in his own sphere of what nearly every class of Scotsman is in relation to his sphere. We have just listened to the strains of " Scots Wha Hae," sung in a manner doing credit to the Poet and the sentiment of that great Poet, and we can understand the emotion, the splendid patriotic feeling, that that must inspire in the breasts and hearts and minds of a Scotsman as he marches to battle, preceded by the bagpipes that we have had the advantage of hearing this evening. (Applause.)

The Scottish race is small in number compared with other portions of the Empire, because, after all, there are only something like four millions even to-day in Scotland, but we can appreciate and realise the very important part they have always played in our Empire, especially in relation to the Imperial Forces, who have won and hold that great Empire of which we are the inheritors to-day. And when one comes to analyse the cause and the reason, one cannot but come to the conclusion that the reason is because they are an earnest people. (Applause.) They have always been a very solid, earnest and quiet, but very determined " get there " portion of the Empire. Whether it be their schools, or fighting, or their patriotism, or their religion, they are always in dead earnest. When the British Empire had only six Universities, Scotland had four, and there is no part of the world to which you may go to-day where you will not find Scottish people and Scotsmen on top. Even in London to-day, from the Archbishop of Canterbury right down, you have Scotsmen occupying the most prominent and important positions in the public life of the country, and the same is true in relation to the whole Empire, and the only conclusion is that they are absolutely in earnest in relation to everything. (Applause.)

I heard a most convincing story on that point the other day. A Scottish cabman was driving an American round Edinburgh. He drove him to Holyrood and showed him the historic palace, then took him up Princes Street and showed him the Scott Monument, and then to Arthur's Seat and showed him the glorious scene from there ; but the American was not in any way enthusiastic, and could not see eye to eye with the Scottish cabman, who was telling him all about the beauties of Scotland, and Walter Scott, and "Ivanhoe," and so on. So the cabman took his fare up to the Castle, and told him of its historical associations, but the American still displayed no enthusiasm over it. Coming down the hill, he stopped opposite John Knox's house, and pointing with great pride to it said : "There is John Knox's house." "John Knox," said the American, "Who was John Knox ?" "Damn it, man," said the cabman, "did you never read your Bible ?" (Loud laughter.) That is the faith, the strong faith, that keeps the Scot on top.

The toast I submit to you, ladies and gentlemen, is that of "The British Imperial Forces." I think for the first time in the history of the Empire we can properly and appropriately call it the British Imperial Force, because the war in which we have been engaged and out of which we have come victorious, if it has done nothing else, has united in bonds of undying affection the peoples of the whole Empire. (Loud applause.) It is quite easy to understand that when war was proclaimed between Great Britain and Germany, how the whole of the British Empire and the peoples of all the Dominions, and the far-flung portions of the Empire, responded, without being asked. It is important to remember that the Dominions and the other portions of the Empire did not come to the "rescue" of the Mother Country, as it is improperly stated. They came to co-operate, to take part in the fight for the great principles underlying the war as far as Great Britain was concerned. (Applause.) The Empire itself was built up in the first place by the people of these islands—the Scottish, English, and Irish. When we had not a foot of land outside these islands, men of those races rose up and penetrated to all parts of the world, and by settlement and occupation, and conquest, built up all the great Dominions that we now call the British Empire. The great poet Tennyson, you will remember, said :—

"We sailed wherever ship could sail,
We founded many a mighty State ;
Pray God our greatness may not fail
Through craven fear of being great."

And that is what we have to fear to-day. We have to fear that there may be some who do not fully appreciate the greatness of the inheritance into which we have come, and the wonderful and tremendous responsibilities attaching to the great inheritance. That can be well tested by the fact that four and a half years ago this

Empire and this nation was suddenly called to arms without arms, or protection, and it is only be a miracle that we have got out of the difficulties through which we have passed.   This Empire is greater to-night than ever it was before, and is entirely on a higher plane, and entirely more glorious and more free, because we are not alone free ourselves, but we have saved liberty and civilisation for the whole world.   In saying that, we must not forget that we have purchased it at great price.   The graves in France and Flanders, the thousands of mained and crippled men, the orphans and widows, and the mourners, all tell the story of the price we have paid for the victory, for the great achievement we have won.   It is due entirely to the spirit of self-sacrifice of all the branches of the Imperial Forces. First, the Navy, who made it possible for us to keep the seas open, to feed the people and bring the soldiers from the uttermost parts of the Empire to the home land and to France.   Then the soldiers, the splendid soldiers, who went over and held the line while we were building up a new army of millions of men.   Then all those splendid young fellows who joined our forces, and those equally noble men who manned our submarines and fought down in the depths of the sea, and those who soared and battled up behind the clouds, and then the army of landsmen and landswomen, and the munition workers—all who combined in this great effort in order that the peoples of the world should be free, and in order that civilisation and liberty should continue in the world.   (Applause.)   We remember with gratitude those splendid fellows who have fallen, those who have been maimed for life.

' When shall their glory fade,
O ! the wild charge they made."

But it is only a repetition of what the bull-dog breed amongst us has been doing for centuries.   We did the same in the days when we were fighting Spain, and later, when we were fighting Napoleon.

" Not once, or twice, in this rough island story
The path of duty was the way to glory."

It was so in the days of Wellington, and it was so in the days of the great sailor, Nelson.   In that great victory of which we are proud to boast, Nelson thought only of duty, and whether the sacrifices they were making that day would come up to the expectations of England, and the people at home, who were waiting and expecting and looking for news.   We have no glory, Mr President, great enough for those valiant men, for the members of those services.   We can erect no monument that will fully express the sacrifices they have made.   This land inviolate to-night is their best monument, and with that sentiment I ask you to drink to " The Health of His Majesty's Imperial Forces."   (Loud applause.)

The toast was honoured with great enthusiasm.

Major-General Sir Newton Moore, M.P., K.C.M.G., who responded, was cheered on rising.   He said :—

Mr Lord, Ladies and Gentlemen,—I thank you for the honour you have done me in inviting me here to join with you in honouring the memory of that distinguished Scotsman, Robert Burns.   That honour I greatly appreciate in view of the fact that it was not my privilege, as it is that of most of you here to-night, of having been born in that country represented here by so many distinguished Scotsmen and Scotswomen.   I can only say in extenuation, that not having been privileged to be born in Scotland I desired to associate myself as far as possible with that great country.   The only way I could do it was by marrying a Scots girl.   (Laughter and loud applause.)   I feel that I am voicing your regret when I say that it is our loss that that distinguished sailor, Sir Rosslyn Wemyss, the First Lord of the Admiralty, is not here to-night, but as already explained, he is at present in Paris, connected with the Peace Conference.   (Applause.)

The toast is " The British Imperial Forces," and I have no doubt that it is a result of my connection with the Australian Forces, and as a recognition of the important part they have played in conjunction with the other Imperial Forces of the Crown in this terrible struggle which has recently been brought, we hope, to a successful conclusion, that I am asked to respond.   At the same time, I am not to detain you to-night, because we have later on in the evening an opportunity of listening to a very distinguished Scottish soldier whom we are all delighted to see here to-night, and whom I am pleased to see here, personally, because it was under his auspices that the Australian and New Zealand Forces received their baptism of fire, and made history, as far as Australia was concerned.   (Loud applause.)

Germany made many mistakes in regard to the mentality of other people, but none more than in regard to the Overseas Dominions. (Hear, hear.)   She confidently hoped and thought that they would have refrained from actual intervention.   On the contrary, however, they thought that the great freedom these communities enjoyed carried a correlative duty, and cheerfully undertook to share the burden as well as the benefits of the Empire.   The Overseas Dominions—exclusive of India—supplied no fewer than 1,300,000 men to the fighting forces of the Empire, to which the Germans can at any rate bear first-hand testimony.   So far as I understand, the Australian and New Zealand Forces are not at all favourites with the German army.   (Laughter and applause.)   The valour, courage and determination of the French army and the matchless men of this island—the first hundred thousand—stayed the rush of the enemy on the Marne in September, 1914, and soon convinced the perpetrators of this world war that it was not to be a triumphant march on Paris, but a contest which would test the endurance of the nations concerned.   Now, as I say, Germany made a great mistake.   She did not realise that as far as Britain was concerned colonising is the peculiar penchant of the British race, but that while she (Germany) colonised with an army behind her, we took to peaceful penetration.   We realised that this old country guided our tottering footsteps through the early days of our history ;   and when we arrived at man's estate, and felt we were competent to work out our own destinies without the assistance of the Old Mother of Parliaments, we were granted responsible government, and as a result—while in any case we would spring to the assistance of the Mother country, realising as Lord Morris has said, that it was a matter which ultimately affected ourselves—not only was it the love of the child born of the parent, but it was also the great recognition of the principle that the greater the liberty the greater the loyalty, and this is where the Germans made the mistake.   (Loud applause.)

We all realise to-night the important part the Navy has played. (Applause.)   Lord Morris referred to the fact that it was not only responsible for bringing food to these islands but that it was responsible for the transport of those 1,300,000 men from Overseas, as well as the American contingents which came to join us in the great fight for freedom, and as President Wilson has said, " to make the world safe for democracy." (Applause.)   As far as Australia was concerned, it meant the transporting of 330,000 men over 14,000 miles of water.   We had endeavoured to emulate you to a very small extent by furnishing our own Navy, and it was one of our criusers—the " Sydney "—that laid by the heels the " Emden " at Cocos Island—a feat, I need hardly say, of which Australians are particularly proud.   (Applause.)   Reference has been made to the Air Services and the part they played.   They were a very determining factor indeed in the concluding few weeks of the war, and some three months ago, when I had the privilege of meeting your President in France, we had an opportunity of witnessing the important part that they had played in connection with the concluding period of the war.

As far as the other forces are concerned it is not necessary to speak to an assemblage of Scotsmen.   We know the part that they played, the magnificent example they set, not only to our Overseas Dominions, but to the troops of the Empire ;   and it is very gratifying indeed to me to-night to know that such is the character of your constitution that you are so cosmopolitan as to have entrusted the toast of the Imperial Forces to one who is a distinguished

Statesman in the Dominion of Newfoundland, and also asked me, one who was not of this country, to respond to the toast. (Applause.)

Major the Rev. Charles Gordon (" Ralph Connor "), whose name was also coupled with the response, was given a hearty welcome. He said :—

Mr President, my Lord, Ladies and Gentlemen.—I am not to take more than a minute to express my sense of the very singular and great honour that I have to-night of representing a part of the great army of which we are all so proud—the British Imperial Forces. I happen to be a Canadian, or Scots-Canadian, which is, I might say, an important type of Scotsman, and of Canadian as well. (Laughter.) I feel myself singularly honoured in being called upon to reply for the Canadian Corps. However, it is not my purpose at all to say a word about their deeds. I always think that an army, like a man, that demands a trumpeter for his deeds or his achievements, needs one. I do not think it is necessary for me to elaborate anything the Canadians have done, but in the minute I have I should like to attempt to express on my own behalf, and on behalf of my country, the profound admiration that we all feel for those splendid forces that went out from these islands and held the line and maintained our cause, and the cause of the world's freedom so gallantly, and at such great cost. (Applause.)

Ladies and Gentlemen, I feel quite sure that none of you who has lived here in England or Scotland knows just how the people across the seas regard you, and regard your army. We thought we knew something about Britain's courage, endurance and power of sacrifices ; but I am bound to say we never dreamed of these things so splendidly and gloriously exemplified during these last five years. And what is true of Canada is also true of the other great branch of the Anglo-Saxon race—the Americans. I may say I have had the privilege of being there during the last two years, and I have been through the country from north to south, and east to west, and I say to you Britishers that we ought to get into our hearts and minds that the best of the American people from the first of the war have been heart and soul with us, and that to-day the American heart beats warm and strong and true with the heart of the British nation ; and this is a new thing in the world, and a thing we, ourselves, ought to take, and I hope will take, home to our hearts ; for if we do not get out of this war a greater, and truer, and more united Anglo-Saxon race, then, whatever else we have gained, we have lost so very much, for everyone knows—we know —that when all is said and done, the future of the world, and the future of humanity is in the keeping not of any League of Nations, but mostly and mainly in the keeping of those two great branches of the Anglo-Saxon race. (Loud applause.) May I suggest to you that it should be on our side our utmost endeavour to promote and to make deeper and stronger and truer this Anglo-Saxon unity. (Applause.) I want to say a word about the great British army with which it was our pride and honour to be associated in a very humble way. I suppose you have all read—at least all intelligent people ought to have read—the splendid history of the war by Buchan. In spite of his fine Scottish reserve, I often wish he would show us something of the passion which lies behind those quiet words of his. When I read the story of the British first contingent, the holding of the line at Mons, with that little army of 25,000 against 400,000, with the British backed by 207 guns against 700 guns, and how from Saturday to Sunday, and Monday, and Tuesday, and Wednesday, and Thursday, and for two weeks, they fought every day and marched every night, still holding the line, gentlemen, it made me proud, as never before, to belong to the British nation. (Loud applause.) Whatever has happened in the war since then, whatever glorious deed has been achieved, nothing finer has been done than that done from the Mons to the Marne by the little Army of Immortal Contemptibles. When I was a boy going to High School, I remember we used to read the story of how the gladiators in the arena used to march about before they went to their death, chanting some such song as this, pausing before the Emperor's box : " *Ave Cæsar, moriaturi te salutamus* " (" Hail, Cæsar ! we, who are appointed to death, salute thee.") It seems to me that when that little sacrificial army, the first hundred thousand, left these shores and looked back upon England, with the lights fading in the distance, might well have said " *Ave Britannia, moriaturi te salutamus*," for they were appointed to death. (Loud applause.) They gave themselves freely, gladly, without hesitation, without repining, for their country's good. To that Army it is our honour to drink, to their undying memory, and to their immortal glory, as well as to those who came after them, worthy to stand beside them, and no greater honour can come to a soldier than that they were permitted to stand side by side with that first little army on the Marne. (Loud applause.)

Captain Bruce Bairnsfather, received with loud applause, said :—

Mr President, my Lord, Ladies and Gentlemen —It is very little that I can add to what you have already heard from the distinguished speakers to-night, but I would like to say how honoured

I feel to be here. It is the first time I have every spoken at the Robert Burns Club. I am not a little proud to be asked to reply for the British Army, the Imperial Forces—I am not a little frightened —I may say I would rather go back for another day in the trenches than make a speech ; but still, as I am here on behalf of Old Bill, Bert, and Alf—(laughter)—I would like to thank you very, very much indeed for the toast you have drunk in their honour to-night, and also to tell you that all through those dark days which you have heard about—of Mons, Ypres, and the Somme, and so on, until the light came—there has never been a thought in the lives of those wonderful soldiers, but merely a speculation as to how long it would take. With this one idea they went through the whole darkness, all the time they were there, and—I am sure Old Bill would say the same—they knew that somewhere and sometime there was a better 'ole. (Laughter and applause.) All through those four and a half years of endurance, bloodshed, tribulation and darkness, right through all that period of the war which you have heard of to-night, they have faced everything, until they brought us to a better 'ole ; and all I can say now is, may we never, never leave it. (Loud applause.)

General Sir Ian Hamilton, G.C.B., D.S.O., A.D.C., who, on rising to propose " The Immortal Memory of Robert Burns," had a great ovation, the audience rising and cheering the great soldier enthusiastically. Sir Ian said :—

Were Burns present with us in the spirit to-night at our festival —and for all I know he may be—what would he think of the Committee who have entrusted the precious privilege of discoursing upon his memory to a sodger ? I believe myself his dark eyes would kindle ; I fear his first impulse might be to hurl a few broad Scots expletives about the hall ; for he hated war and all its works worse, much worse, than Auld Hornie, for whom, by the way, he always had a sort of sneaking regard. On the other hand, the sight of the strange khaki kit might soften his heart, and these ribbons, denoting far campaigns. For we know he had a special sympathy with old soldiers who had served in foreign parts. In the " Jolly Beggars " he gives the place of honour to the veteran who sits " neist the fire, in auld red rags," and makes him spout the lines :—

> " I am a son of Mars,
>   Who have been in many wars,
>   And show my cuts and scars
>   Wherever I come ;

This here was for a wench,
And that other in a trench,
When welcoming the French
    At the sound of the drum.

My 'prenticeship I past
Where my leader breathed his last,
When the bloody die was cast
    On the heights of Abram ;
I served out my trade
When the gallant game was play'd,
And the Moro low was laid,
    At the sound of the drum.

I lastly was with Curtis
Among the floating batt'ries,
And there I left for witness
    An arm and a limb :
Yet let my country need me,
With Elliot to lead me,
I'd clatter on my stumps
    At the sound of a drum."

(Applause.)   In another verse he pays the finest tribute to the soldier that ever was paid by anyone in this world, excepting only the compliment paid by our Lord Jesus Christ to the Centurion when He marvelled at this Captain of Legionaries, and declared, " I have not found so great faith, no, not in Israel."   Burns might have gone to the Church for his example, or the Medical Profession, or the Politicians ; but he did not. He took the soldier as his type of the Idealist, and wrote :—

" For gold the merchant ploughs the main,
    The farmer ploughs the manor ;
But glory is the sodger's prize,
    The sodger's wealth is honour."

(Applause.)   Nor can there be any question of Burns's sincerity. He did not know the phrase " Imitation is the sincerest form of flattery," for it was not coined till 1820 ; but he did, in fact, give that voucher for good faith by himself donning the uniform of King George. On the 31st January, 1795, he joined the Royal Dumfries Volunteers ; for although he had written unguarded words about our war with France, he was not going to leave his own country unguarded ; his acts were to speak for themselves. (Loud applause.) There is a remarkable little book now actually in the press ; a book from the pen of one whom many of you here know well, Mr

William Will, to wit ; at the proofs of which I have been privileged to take a peep. The work is based on the recent discovery of a manuscript copy of the Minutes of the Dumfries Volunteers. It would not be fair to expend this treasure trove prematurely, but I am free to say here that the lucky find has knocked some calumnies on the head. The document covers the very period during which Burns has too readily been supposed by some to have been living almost as an outcast in Dumfries ; and it exhibits him instead as sitting on the Committee of the two companies, to which he has duly been elected by popular vote. The Volunteers are a real though tiny force, doing drills for two hours at a stretch, twice a week. Burns seems never to have missed a meeting, but is discovered as a member of Committee, fining absentees from drill. Prevaricators were " fired " from the Corps, but what would our poor Poet have thought had he known that after his death " prevaricators " would take the field and half-persuade Scotland for a period of a hundred and twenty-two years that he had entered the Volunteers as a matter of policy or calculation, and to make a good impression upon the Government ; also, that by 1795, he had " become burnt to a cinder " because of his drunken habits, when actually, as late as the 5th November, 1795, he was neither a cinder in the hearth nor a Cinderella in Society—(laughter)—but rather a live coal, firing enthusiasm and enlivening the slackness of the slackers of Dumfries, by burning their fingers for them. These facts come out incidentally and carry, therefore, twice the weight of facts picked out to prove a particular theory. (Applause.) I doubt whether these statements about Burns and the low estate into which he had fallen would have obtained their exaggerated currency had not his memory got itself too much entangled amongst those amorous and convivial associations which may, indeed, be attributed of a live man, but are not the man's ain sel'. We have concentrated overmuch, some of us, upon the many moving pictures of Jeans, Marys, Nannies, Peggies, Clarindas ; we have allowed ourselves to plunge too deeply after Burns into the entrails of the great chieftain of the puddin' race :—

            " Hey the Haggis o' Dunbar,
                Hey fol de riddle,
            Few were better, mony waur,
                Hey fol de riddle ;
            For to mak' that Haggis fat,
                Hey fol de riddle,
            They put in a stinking cat,
                Hey fol de riddle."

(Loud laughter). That is *not* Burns. All the same, our friend did love haggis and nappy, swats, usquebae, tippeny, whisky toddy, brandy, and rum.   So do we.   Why not ?   *De gustibus non · est disputandum.*

You shouldn't quarrel with a poet for his tastes any more than you should confound his poems with his politics.   (Hear, hear.) Take the man as seriously as he took himself when serious dangers were in the wind.   Picture him in " white kerseymere breeches and waistcoat ;   short blue coat, faced with red, and a round hat surmounted by a bearskin."   Nowadays that sounds like a description of a salmon fly—(laughter)—actually it is a description of the uniform of the Royal Dumfries Volunteers.   Then see him, as Allan Cunningham saw him, " his very swarthy face, his ploughman stoop, his large dark eyes and his indifferent dexterity in the handling, of his arms."

" Burns !" roars the drill sergeant, " haud up yer heid, man ; ye're nae howking tatties the noo !"   Or else, " Can you no keep still ae meenit, Burns ?   Ye'll be neist for dancing the Hielan' Fling wi' Cutty-sark on His Majesty's parade."   (Loud laughter.)   I am sure there was this sort of thing and lots of it.   People with large dark eyes and a stoop who are clumsy in handling their arms have a very lively time of it with the Scottish drill instructor.   The Scots, unlike the Japanese of to-day, or the Normans of the time of the Conquest, have no use for artists in their wars of commerce or of conquest.   A combination of oratory and administrative ability they unwillingly do admit ;   but once a man takes to putting down his thoughts on paper, especially if he drops in a few rhymes among them, the martinets and sergeant-majors of life make up their minds he must be a muddler in affairs.   (Laughter.)

When Oyama captured Port Arthur from the Chinese, he desired his general staff to write a poem on the incident of a little Pekinese dog which was guarding the dead body of its late master. When he wished to decide which of several staff officers had the most quick and sympathetic perceptions, he set them down to write a poem as to whether the blossom of the plum or of the cherry was most beautiful.   By his answer one of them, I may tell you, gave himself away.   He was afraid of displeasing the Field-Marshal, and so he wrote a poem saying both blossoms were equally lovely. He was turned down.   (Laughter.)   At the battle of Hastings, the hero who rode several horse-lengths ahead of everyone at the head of Duke William's cavalry was the minstrel named Taillefer. Tossing his sword in the air and catching it again by the handle, he went straight as a die for King Harold, where he stood grim with his axemen around him.   Bursting through the shield wall as if it had been paper, this artist slew several of the Saxons before he himself was chopped into pieces.   Paderewski to-day is another example of the artist turning to action.   But still, the Scot will have his theory ; the thing cannot be ; revolutions cannot be made with rose-water ; how ridiculous to suppose they can be handled by pianists ! (Laughter.) Burns, struggling earnestly with the manual and platoon, seems so extraordinary a manifestation to several of the citizens of Dumfries (who did not themselves consider the case of the country so dangerous as to call for any personal service from themselves), that they insist on ulterior motives—the Poet must be trying to curry favour with the Excise or to conceal disloyalty under a military cloak ! (Applause.)

Burns was a great Scotsman and a great citizen of the world, as well as a great Poet. His verses have entered into the very vitals of Scotland. The 9th Division, the 15th Division, the 51st Division, and last but not least, the 52nd Division, owe some of their exceeding great valour, believe me, to " Scots Wha Hae !" (Loud applause.) The same with Lovat's Scouts and the Scottish Horse, 4th Highland Mountain Battery, or those two fine Battalions who fought with the incomparable 29th Division at Gallipoli, the 1st K.O.S.B.'s and the 5th Royal Scots. (Applause.)

The girdle of Scottish camaraderie cast about the world by Burns's " Auld Lang Syne " goes round it faster than Shakespeare's " Ariel," faster than Marconi's wireless ; instantaneous, just one huge all-round-the-world handshake between Scotsmen. Burns has said of Scotsmen everything of which the race has reason to be proud, and in return generations of Scotsmen have delighted to do honour to Burns. (Applause.) As to Scotswomen, they know well enough that Burns could never resist a bonnie lassie ; the sex as a whole have appreciated that virile caress. Small wonder, then, that he is among the Immortals. We have it on record that when Burns came to an inn late at night, the servants got out of their beds to sit and listen to his talk ; but when I talk it is the other way about, and everyone wants to get into their beds. (Laughter.) Therefore I will detain you no more, and will propose to you the toast. Speaking for myself, when I drain my own glass I shall be thinking most of Burns, the voluntary soldier. (Applause.) I give you " The Immortal Memory of Robert Burns."

The toast was drunk in solemn silence.

Mr John Murray, C.V.O., D.L., F.S.A., on rising to propose " Scottish Literature," was loudly cheered. He said :—

Mr President, my Lord, Ladies and Gentlemen,—I ask for your sympathy. Sir Ian Hamilton has told you you ought all to be in bed. Well, I have heard of bed-side books, but I doubt if bed-side speeches could be equally acceptable—(laughter)—

and to begin with such a subject as Scottish Literature at this hour of the night is, I can assure you, a great responsibility, and I must ask you to be lenient. I cannot attempt to deal with the whole subject, but with your permission I will take a few stepping stones, and if they are marked to some extent with my own personal experiences, I would beg you to bear with me. For nearly half a century my business has led me to deal with biography. I have been in at the birth, I have conducted them through life, and, too often, I have attended at the obsequies of many biographies. But I maintain that biography is one of the most inexhaustible and unending sources of human interest. I want you to recognise that among biographies there are two which have been pre-eminent, not only in the English tongue, but in the whole of literature. I have spoken to eminent men, statesmen, literary men, and others, and I have asked them to say, " What do you consider the two great biographies of the world ?"—and without exception they have named two, and I think you will guess which they are. Now, why are those great books ? Because the writers of them were in intimate communication and association with their subjects ; because they were men who loved their subjects and had made constant notes of their habits and sayings ; because they were distinguished literary men, and, above all, because they were Scotsmen. Those two biographies are Boswell's *Life of Johnson*, and Lockhart's *Life of Scott*. You must pardon me if I repeat a story that some of you have heard before. My distinguished namesake, the editor of the great English dictionary, told a friend that he had had a remarkable dream. He said, " I dreamt that, Dr Johnson came back to Oxford, and the great men of the place were leading him about and showing him the changes that had taken place since his time. ' Here, Dr Johnson, is this, and here is that. Dr Johnson, do you know that, for the first time, your dictionary has been superseded, and the editor of the new book is a Scotsman ?' Dr Johnson said, ' Sir, in order to be facetious, it is not necessary to be absolutely indecent.' " (Loud laughter.) The idea of a Scotsman editing his book was far too much for him ! Who can read aloud Sir Walter Scott's life from the beginning to the end ? I defy any man or woman who has, as an old Scottish aunt of mine used to say, " bowels of tender mercies, not made of tenpenny nails," to read that last touching volume, when Scott was wearing himself to the death in body and in mind to wipe off debts which, through the indiscretions of a friend, he had been led into. It is one of the most wonderful books of all generations. There is another Scotsman who comes not far off—Thomas Carlyle. He, too, reminds me of the old story of the judge who, addressing a perverse witness, said, " You have a mind so twisted that if a nail could be got into one side of your head, I am convinced it would come out a screw at the other side." (Loud laughter.) Carlyle had that quality, and about him I will also mention a little incident which happened to an old friend of mine. His son came up to London, and he said to him, " I am going to take you to see the two greatest men of the day." He took him to see Herbert Spencer, and he saw an elderly man, looking like a gardener in his Sunday clothes, lying on his sofa, and he said nothing this young man could carry away. Then he took him to Cheyne Walk and introduced him to Carlyle. He told Carlyle the same story—" I have brought my son to see the two greatest men of the day." Carlyle said, " Wha is the ither man ?" When he was told, " Herbert Spencer," Carlyle answered, " Herbert Spencer ! an immeasureable ass !" (Loud laughter.) So much for biography. Mention of Scott leads us to poetry, and here again, I think, we may claim for our brother Scots the highest place. We may call Byron a Scotsman, for was he not brought up in Aberdeen, and was not his mother a Scotswoman ? I have been reminded when thinking of her, of the saying, with which you may have been familiar, of many Americans, when they say that such and such a thing is very good of its kind, " but a damned bad kind." I would say of Byron's mother that she was a very bad instance of a damn good thing, for there are very few Scottish mothers who were as she was. Byron was stung, and he came to his own by the *Edinburgh Review.* It was Scotland that stung him, and it was that that brought out first of all his " English Bards and Scotch Reviewers, in which he made an attack on Scott. My grandfather, when he read it, knowing both men, said : " I will not rest until I have brought those two men together, because I know that when they become acquainted, Byron will never say that again and will repent of it." I still inhabit the house, and the very rooms, where those two men were introduced by my grand-father in 1815, and from that moment they became the firmest of friends. I have also the book, a copy of Byron's own *English Bards and Scotch Reviewers,* annotated in his own handwriting and characteristic style. " This is much too severe " (says the anno-tation) ; " this will never do." " It is only the fact that this book belongs to another man that prevents me from committing this miserable instance of juvenile acrimony to the flames." From that day onwards Byron and Scott never ceased to be the warmest friends. (Loud applause.)

Burns I hardly dare mention, after all that has been said. I should say Burns and Horace stand highest in the world as the writers of lyrics. They invested the everyday things of life with a humanity and reality that can never die, and Burns and Horace will always stand at the head of the great lyrical poets. (Applause.)

I hold in my hand a book that has a very curious history. It is a diary of Burns, and in view of what Sir Ian Hamilton has said, I will venture to read you a few lines, because it is characteristic. Burns was staying at Dumfries with some friends and he wrote in his diary, " Miss—— seems very well pleased with my bardship's distinguishing her, and after some slight qualms which I could easily mark, she sets the titter round at defiance, and kindly allows me to keep my hold ; and when parted by the ceremony of my intro- duction to Mr Somerville, she met me half, to resume my situation. *Nota Bene.*—The Poet within a point and a half of being damnably in love—I am afraid my bosom is still nearly as much tinder as ever." (Laughter.) I ask you, is that not a characteristic touch of Burns ?

Were there time I should like to talk about Stevenson and others, but I must mention two whom this war has brought to light, Mrs Jacob, with her *Songs of Angus,* and Sergeant Lee, who comes from Dundee. (Applause.) He is not only a poet but an artist, and he has illustrated his own book. He began as a private. Then he was taken prisoner, and whether or not he softened the hearts of his captors with the bagpipes, like Orpheus with his lyre, he has now returned, and to a lieutenant's commission. Among the editors of newspapers there are also eminent names. For instance, M'Culloch, editor of the *Scotsman.* Years ago he was asked to speak at the Literary Fund dinner, and he said : " Why am I asked to respond to this toast ? I am not a man of letters. I would never have had anything to do with books if it had not been for three letters of the alphabet, and these are £ s. d."

Alexander Russel, you know, was the eminent editor of the *Scotsman,* and a man of great humour. He was one night walking through the office, and saw a young man writing away hard, and he said, " What are you writing there ?" The young man said : " Oh ! sir, I was just writing an obituary notice of Bailie M." " Is he dead ?" said Russel, " I knew him ; he was a damned fool." The man said, " Yes, sir, he was, and I was just bringing that oot in the paragraph." (Laughter.) Another story, if I am not offending the ladies. Years ago when first the question of women's suffrage was agitated, Russel was asked : " What line will you take in the *Scotsman ?*" and he said : " Ah, well, I would not give the votes to the women, because if you give them a vote they will never rest until they get into the House of Commons, and my ex- perience is that a woman can never have the feelings of a gentleman." (Loud laughter.) Among astronomers, I suppose Sir David Gill took really the first place of his day—kindest of friends, keenest of sportsmen, and most eager about his work. He said : " I was at one time lecturing to the Society of Naval Engineers, and one of the points of my lecture was the marvellous accuracy to which astronomical instruments had been brought. I told them that with an instrument I possessed, I could measure the disc of a three-penny piece a hundred miles off." At the dinner which followed, the chairman, who was a very distinguished man, proposed Sir David's health, and said : " If we had had any doubt as to the nationality of our good friend the lecturer to-day, before his lecture, we clearly can have none now, because I am quite sure that nobody but a Scot would pay the slightest attention to a threepenny piece a hundred miles away !" (Loud laughter.) Another familiar name to you all is James Nasmyth. I was his executor. He was one of the most charming of companions—engineer, inventor, astronomer, horticulturist, artist, and a man full of curious old-fashioned Scottish humour. I remember him saying to me : " Mr Murray, to the best of my knowledge I've never killed anybody in ma life, and I would not like to kill anybody after I am deid. If I was buried in the ground, I feel sure I'll get into somebody's well and poison him, and so you have just got to get me cremated." (Laughter.) And cremated he was. I suppose I am one of the few living now who knew that wonderful man, David Livingstone. He used to come to dinner at my father's house. Pioneer, missionary, naturalist, sportsman, sailor, he will live for all time as one of the greatest writers of travel. (Applause.) Then there was Mrs Somerville, the greatest lady mathematician, who my father and mother saw making point lace without the aid of spectacles at the age of 89 in Naples. I might go on showing you lines of literature in which Scotsmen have been pre-eminent. I dare not venture to speak to you to-night of those distinguished men who have risen in literature during the war. You see them here, and you have heard them, and it would be presumptuous for me to say more, but I would venture to ask you on this occasion to class amongst distin-guished Scottish authors another. We have a general who has commanded armies larger than Napoleon and Wellington together ever commanded, and who has conducted to a successful issue such a war as the world has never known before. He has shown by his recent despatch that if his vocation in life had been to wield the pen and not the sword he would have been prominent in letters. I ask you with me to acclaim Sir Douglas Haig. (Loud applause.) To what is this wonderful pre-eminence of our countrymen due ? I think it is due to two things—independence of mind, and to a curious, strange, originality, in the way of looking at ordinary things. Please drink with me to the toast " Scottish Literature." (Loud applause.)

Lieutenant-Colonel John Buchan, responding to the toast, was heartily cheered on rising. He said :—

Mr President, Ladies and Gentlemen,—I am greatly honoured at being asked to reply to the toast which has been so felicitously and amusingly proposed by my friend, Mr John Murray. At this hour of the evening you will not expect from me any kind of a speech. It is a toast well worthy of drinking, for Scottish literature is one of the many grounds we Scotsmen have for particular pride. We have produced great writers in every branch of literature, and in Burns and Sir Walter Scott we have produced two of the dozen greatest writers in the history of the world. (Applause.) It seems to me rather piquant and paradoxical that this toast should be proposed by one publisher and replied to by another. (Laughter.) For we publishers have been held occasionally to bear rather a bad reputation by men of letters. There was a time when we were a kind of whipping-boy of literature ; now I am led to believe that that position is taken by the politician. We earn our precarious profits by acting as the brokers of genius and, like other brokers, we charge our small fee. It is not an easy task, and I would beg of you not to judge us harshly. You remember that David Balfour told Alan Breck that he intended to become an advocate, and Alan replied : " Man, Davie, that's but a weary trade and a blackguard yin forbye." (Laughter.) I am afraid that the author in his haste is sometimes apt to make that condemnation of the publisher. I think it is too harsh. I believe that the publisher is as honest and amiable a man as other people, and in proof I would recall the fact that as a rule he bears a Scottish name. I would like to be allowed to say one thing before I sit down. A large part of our Scottish literature is written in the vernacular. I cannot call it a dialect. It is far more, it is a great and true language, akin to English but different from it. (Applause.) A language with an extraordinary quality of incisiveness, a language with great structural beauty, of the richest idiom, a language which has been made classic by great writers. Are we to allow that to decay ? Are we to contemplate some time in the future when a large part of the treasure of our literature will be shut to the ordinary reader ? I am afraid that to-day there are very few people, even in Scotland, who know and speak pure Scots. Even in the country districts the old words and idioms are dying on the lips of men, and in the cities the language is becoming a barbarous jargon where there is much more American and Cockney slang than the pure Doric. (Hear, hear.) For that there are many reasons, one of them I am afraid, being a kind of preverse genteelness working among our people. I have known well-to-do men and women in Scotland, whose fathers have run bare-foot, who thought it unbecoming to admit acquaintance with Scottish words. I think it is a national calamity. (Applause.) If we are to remain what we are, a true race, we cannot afford to lose our peculiar speech, and I should like to see good Scots used in every school—and I should like to see every candidate for Parliament heckled in Doric. (Laughter.) I would appeal to those who still know the old tongue to speak it, to use it, and to write it. Happily there are still " just men in Israel." There are to-day Scots writers like Hugh Haliburton, Charles Murray, Violet Jacob, who write idiomatic Scottish verse. I would like to see every " Poet's Corner " in every country paper filled with experiments in the tongue of our forefathers. Do you remember what Sir Walter Scott once said : " If you unscotch us you will make us damned mischievous Englishmen," and the Scottish writer who dares to unscotch himself becomes a damned writer. (Applause.)

I would appeal to this great Club to make it part of their duty to foster the Scottish tongue. (Applause.) I believe there are still people living, Scottish Miltons, at present mute and inglorious, who only want a certain amount of reasonable encouragement. I can give you one example of that second-rate quality.

Some years ago, when I was in South Africa, I had the task of framing a new game statute for the Transvaal, and among other provisions, we made one in regard to the rhinoceros, which was becoming very rare. Under this provision any man found poaching one was fined £80. That was reported in *The Scotsman*, and caught the eye of a gentleman in Lanarkshire, who perhaps, by profession, was a poacher. Anyhow, he wrote the following :—

I've stood wi' baith ma pooches stuffed fou o' pheasants' eggs
And a ten-pund saumon hingin' doon baith ma trouser legs ;
And I've crackit wi' a keeper ; but yon was naethin' serious,
Its a verra different kind o' job to meet a rhinocerious.

I mind when me and Willie killed a Royal in Braemar
And brocht him doon tae Athol by the licht o' mune and star.
I'll no deny the muckle beast contrived tae fash and weary us,
But Royals maun be child's play compared wi' rhinocerious.

I thocht I kenned o' poachin' just as much as ither men,
But noo I see there's twa-three things that still I dinna ken ;
I canna eat, I canna sleep, I'm perfectly deleerious—
I maun awa' tae Africa and poach a rhinocerious.

(Loud laughter.) Ladies and Gentlemen, if there are men living capable of doing as good things as that, for heaven's sake, let us have more of them. (Loud applause.)

Lieutenant-Colonel E. A. Ewart ("Boyd Cable")
who was also well received, said :—

It gives me the greater pleasure to be with you to-night because
I have been trying for three years to get here. For the previous
two years I have had a much more pressing and less pleasing engagement overseas. It is, therefore, an extra pleasure to-night to
meet the members of the Burns Club. I remember the last Burns
Anniversary Dinner I ate was over in France. Somebody discovered
it was Burns night, and I, being the only Scot in the place, was
called upon to make the haggis. We found rice, bully beef, and
Army biscuits, and we made haggis out of it. (Laughter.) That
was all we had, except pepper and salt. However, that is rather
going off the subject of Scottish Literature.

Amongst all I have known of Burns, I think the one thing
that first struck me, and has stuck to me all my life, has been the
songs that we are all familiar with ; and it is extraordinary how those
songs crop up in all corners of the world, and the tremendous appeal
they make, not only to Scots, but to every other English-speaking
person. I have heard a fireman on a tramp steamer making the
fo'csle ring with songs of Burns, and I have heard whole pages of
Burns quoted by a teamster in the back Australian bush. I also
remember hearing a Canadian Highlander in one of the villages
in France trying to teach a French girl " My bonnie dearie."
(Laughter.) I may say he met with an astonishing amount of
success. (Renewed laughter.) I remember a little story of the
first battle of the Somme. It was during a late period of the battle
when, you will remember, we were having a great deal of bad weather
and were living in mud, rain, and misery for weeks on end. One
of the Scottish Regiments was going over the top, to take a certain
objective. Just before the barrage lifted, when there was a great
deal of noise, one of the platoon commanders, a lieutenant, met
his company commander, who was crawling along to see that everything was all ready before they started out. The platoon commander was shouting something at the pitch of his voice, but the
company commander could not hear it, and all he could catch was
something about " not remembering . . . lines." Then the whistle
went to go over, and over they went, and got their first objective.
All the time what was worrying this company commander was
whether the platoon commander had forgotten something very
important. He had heard a question about lines, and he could
only think of the line of his objective, and he thought " If this
young ass has forgotten his line of objective, he is going to throw
the company in the soup." When he got into the first line of shell
holes, he crawled along under a heavy fire to make his way to this
lieutenant's position. Eventually he managed to reach the hole

where the platoon commander was lying, and he tumbled in beside him and asked him · " What was it you had forgotten ?" The lieutenant replied : " I have been trying to think what are the second and third lines of ' Scots Wha Hae !' " (Loud laughter.) That may sound very extraordinary, but these things do happen sometimes. The company commander turned round and said : " You and your ' Scots Wha Hae !' I'll tell you what I'm thinking about. Have you ever heard of the ' Wee, cowerin', tim'rous beastie, O what a panic's in thy breastie ?' " (Loud laughter.)

I was for a certain time in the South African War, where I served in Lovat's Scouts, with the pipes in my ears getting up each morning and lying down each night. We were a mounted regiment, but we had the extraordinary privilege of having the pipes to sound Reveille and Lights Out. The pipes are great hearteners. I remember seeing one of our Scottish Regiments coming out of action. They had had very heavy losses, and were coming out pretty well dead beat, and were just limping along, dragging their feet and looking dead to the world, when they were met by half a dozen pipers. The pipers waited until this handful of men came along, and then they struck up their pipes, and if you had seen those men throw back their heads and brace their shoulders and step out, it would have done you good. (Loud applause.) More than once it has been my privilege to see some of our Highland Regiments go over the top, and the men to lead them out were the pipers every time. It is quite true that " Scots Wha Hae " has done a lot in this war. For all I am indebted to Burns, I am indebted most to his songs, and with all his contributions to Scottish literature, I shall always feel that his songs are the finest we have. (Loud applause.)

This ended the toast list, and the large company formed a great ring round the banqueting hall, and sang " Auld Lang Syne," as it is seldom sung at social gatherings. Past President James Thomson sang the first verse, Miss Mary Mackie took the second verse, and Mr Archie Anderson the third. The company, joining hands, sang the verse beginning, " Then, here's a hand, my trusty fier." When the final hearty cheers had been given the company separated, all agreeing that they had taken part in one of the most successful gatherings ever held in London.

The great bulk of the work fell upon the able and worthy Hon. Secretary (Mr P. N. M'Farlane), whose arrangements were complete, and whose many efforts made the Festival run smoothly from start to finish.

THE MANSE OF LOUDOUN.

I N the year 1763 the Rev. George Laurie succeeded Andrew
Ross in the Parish Church of Loudoun, Ayrshire, and
took up his abode in the Old Manse at Newmilns.   In the
following year the minister brought home a young wife,
and very soon little heads clustered round his board.   The
Old Manse was small and had many inconveniences, and
four years later Mr Laurie, his wife, and children moved
to a more commodious residence only a few hundred yards
from the former house.   The New Manse was built on a
gentle slope beside the road between Galston and Newmilns,
one of the first roads in the country to be made by statute
labour.   The minister planted the space between his house
and the highway with birch and chestnut trees, which in
process of time almost screened the Manse from public view.
The new house had some pretensions to elegance both in
its exterior and interior, although there was a court behind
it, like that of a farmhouse, with byre and stabling forming
two sides of the square.   The country minister long ago,
with his garden and glebe, was usually a bit of a farmer, and
a horse was indispensable for working the glebe and the
minister's use in the visitation of a large parish.   He
almost invariably kept a man to look after the glebe, the
garden, the horse, and the cow, and to do odd jobs about
the house.   Dr Laurie's household included the " minister's
man " as a matter of course.

The new Manse was two storeys in height, with attics.
The ceilings were low, the windows small with many panes,
and the walls thick.   For the period, however, it was a
good house, and a beautiful garden was soon laid out at
the back and side of the building.   Over the front door,
which faced the road, the letters G. L. and M. C. were carved
—the initials of the names of the minister and his wife—

with the date 1768. By-and-bye there was added tho motto, " Jehovah Jireh " (the Lord will provide)—words which may have brought comfort to many both without and within the Manse. The story of this motto is told in this fashion. One day the nurse from the Manse, accompanied by the children, was walking along the road when a stranger stopped to ask whose bonny bairns they were. The nurse replied that they were the minister's children. " That's

LOUDOUN MANSE.

a big family for a minister to provide for " was the reply. When the nurse went home she repeated the story to her mistress, and she, in turn, to her husband. Dr Laurie said little, but on the lintel of the door he caused to be carved the words of trust and confidence mentioned above. The story may be a mere tradition, for Dr Laurie had but three children, while many a contemporary had much less of this world's gear to start their young people in life than the parish minister of Loudoun.

The Rev. George Laurie came of a race of ministers.

His father, the Rev. James Laurie, was minister of Kirk-
michael ; his grandfather, the Rev. John Laurie, had been
minister of Auchinleck ; his great-grandfather, of Newton-
Stewart, in the Stewartry of Kirkcudbright : and his
great-great-grandfather, so it is said, was one of the ministers
who went to Ireland and was present at the founding of the
Presbyterian Church there.   The Rev. George Laurie
was, therefore, the fifth minister in direct descent : nor
did the line end there, for his son succeeded him in Loudoun,
and his grandson became minister of the parish of Monkton.
Mary Campbell, whom young George Laurie married, was
a daughter of Dr Archibald Campbell, Professor of Church
History in the New College of St. Andrews.   In those days
Newmilns was a weaving village, and the weavers worked
in their own houses.   From morning till night the click-
clack of the shuttle might be heard, and both men and
women wrought at the loom.   The low cottages of the
weavers, with their thatched roofs, straggled along the
sides of the river, the church spire and the old tower being
the only outstanding features of the place.   From the
Manse windows the village could be seen to the east, while
to the south there were gently swelling hills in the near
distance, with the river, glancing in the sun, lying between.
In those days salmon were caught in the Irvine, and the
haughty weavers turned up their noses when the royal
fish appeared too often on their tables.   The house already
described is still the parish manse, although considerably
modified from what it was when built almost a century
and a half ago.   Wings have been added with spacious
rooms ; the ceilings of two flats have been heightened
and the attics have disappeared ; new stairs have been
built, windows have been enlarged, and one of the rooms
has been utilised as an entrance hall.   Still it is the old
Manse, with Dr Laurie's initials above the door, the Manse
where he lived and worked, sorrowed and joyed, the resting-
place of many a wayfarer on the highway of life, to one
of whom—footsore at the very threshold of life's journey
—it seemed a perfect haven of peace and joy.

The Manse of Loudoun, called St. Margaret's Hill in Dr Laurie's day, extended its hospitality to some of the best literary society of the times. Dr Laurie himself was no mean scholar. He was well read, an eloquent preacher, had a fine sense of humour, was a racy conversationalist, had great power of discriminating character, and his word had considerable influence in the Church Courts. Apart from the work for his pulpit ministrations, his special study was the early poetry and music of the Celts in Ireland and Scotland, and for true poetry of every kind he had the the most keen appreciation. Among his friends he numbered Principal Robertson, Dr James MacKnight, Dr Blacklock, Dr Hugh Blair, and many others eminent in the world of letters of the day. His wife was a woman of education and of culture. The Manse of Loudoun, therefore, must have formed a little centre of refinement for the whole parish. Newmilns and Darvel were both weaving villages, and the weavers took a keen interest in all political questions. The farmers were absorbed in their own concerns and cared for but little else. Many of them were descendants of Covenanters, and their religious convictions were of a cast-iron kind, rigid and unbending. Of books they knew but little, and their aspirations, as a rule, did not rise above the society of the like-minded whom they met at fairs and markets. Still, in every community there are a few who burst such bonds asunder ; and St. Margaret's Hill, with its occupants of kind heart and large understanding, must have been a breathing-place of wider atmosphere for all aspiring souls in the neighbourhood.

One young farmer knew well its hospitality, and the glimpses of more refined life he saw there made a great impression on him. He was a man, like Saul, head and shoulders above his fellows in mental stature. His name was Robert Burns. Dr Laurie had read his poems, published in Kilmarnock, and had recognised his genius. He invited the Poet to his home again and again. Burns went, and was delighted with the occupants of the Loudoun

Manse. The following well-known lines are from the pen
of Gilbert Burns :—

" The first time Robert heard the spinet played upon was
while on a visit at the house of Dr Laurie, then Minister of the Parish
of Loudoun, a few miles from Mossgiel, and with whom he was on
terms of intimacy. Dr Laurie had several daughters : one of
them played, the father and mother led down the dance, the rest
of the sisters, the brother, the poet, and the other guests mixed
in it. It was a delightful family scene for our Poet, then lately
introduced to the world. His mind was roused to poetic enthusiasm.
and the stanzas were left in the room where he slept."

The stanzas which Gilbert Burns referred to were
as follows :—

O Thou dread Power, who reign'st above.
   I know Thou wilt me hear ·
When for this scene of peace and love
   I make my prayer sincere.

The hoary Sire—the mortal stroke,
   Long, long be pleased to spare,
To bless his little filial flock,
   And shew what good men are.

She, who her lovely Offspring eyes
   With tender hope and fears,
Oh, bless her with a Mother's joys.
   But spare a Mother's tears !

Their hope. their stay, their darling youth.
   In manhood's dawning blush.
Bless him, Thou God of love and truth,
   Up to a Parent's wish !

The beauteous, seraph Sister-band,
   With earnest tears I pray,
Thou knowest the snares on every hand,
   Guide Thou their steps alway.

When soon or late they reach that coast,
   O'er life's rough ocean driven
May they rejoice, no wanderer lost,
   A family in Heaven !"

The " darling youth " mentioned in the verses was
Dr Laurie's son Archibald, who afterwards succeeded his

father. The "hoary sire" was Dr Laurie himself, who had reached the ripe age of fifty-seven ! On the morning after the pleasant evening depicted by Gilbert Burns, Dr Laurie and his family waited in vain for Burns's appearance at the breakfast table. Weary of waiting, Archibald was sent by his father to knock at Burns's door and ask

THE ENTRANCE HALL.

what detained him. The boy went bounding up the stair, but met Burns coming down. "Good morning, Mr Burns, he said. "I hope you slept well last night." "Sleep, my young friend, I scarcely slept at all—I have been praying all night. If you go to my room you will find my prayers upon the table." Young Mr Laurie went to the room and found the verses already quoted. The M.S. is preserved with pride and pleasure in the family of Dr Laurie's descendants until this day. The following letter to Archibald Laurie shews his intimate footing with the poet :—

"Dear Sir,—I have, along with this, sent the two volumes of *Ossian* with the remaining volume of the Songs. *Ossian* I am not in such a hurry about, but I wish the songs, with the volume of the *Scotch Poets*, returned as soon as they can conveniently be despatched. If they are left at Mr Wilson, the bookseller's shop, Kilmarnock, they will easily reach me. My most respectful compliments to Mr and Mrs Laurie, and a poet's warmest wishes for their happiness to the young ladies, particularly the fair musician, whom I think much better qualified than ever David was, or could be, to charm an evil spirit out of a Saul. Indeed, it needs not the feelings of a poet to be interested in the welfare of one of the sweetest scenes of domestic peace and kindred love that ever I saw, as I think the peaceful unity of St. Margaret's Hill can only be excelled by the harmonious concord of the Apocalyptic Zion.—I am, Dear Sir, Yours sincerely, ROBERT BURNS. Mossgiel, 13th November, 1786."

At that time Burns was only twenty-seven years of age, and open to impressions of every kind. He had lived much for such a young man, and the pity is that such a friendship as that of Dr Laurie had not dawned upon him ten years sooner. The whole current of his life might have been changed by such a glimpse of better things, but even as it was, the friendship of Burns with Dr Laurie was the means of altering the Poet's career. The story is almost too well known for repetition, but for the sake of connection we may glance at it here.

Dr Laurie, in his admiration for the work of the young Poet, sent a copy of his poems to his friend Dr Blacklock, and warmly commended Burns to his favour. Weeks passed, and no reply came to his letter. Burns's affairs had reached their acutest stage, and he resolved to set sail for the West Indies, hoping there to redeem his fortune and reputation. Every preparation was made. His trunk was packed and on its way to Greenock, and Burns had even poured out his soul in a farewell song, when a letter came from Dr Blacklock full of encouragement and good cheer, and the poetic temperament which had breathed a farewell but a few days before to friends and

foes, to the bonnie banks of Ayr, to all the charms of Bonnie
Scotland, suddenly bounded to the other extreme, and the
Poet evidently thought he had only to enter the promised
land to possess it.   It was on the way to Mossgiel, after
what he thought was his last visit to Loudoun Manse, that
the poet composed his farewell.   When the tide of Burns's
fortune flowed in upon him Dr Laurie sent him a letter
of friendly counsel.   Burns was in Edinburgh, flattered
and lionized, and Dr Laurie naturally thought the young
man might lose his head in such unwonted circumstances.
In Burns's reply he says that he " had no great temptation
to be intoxicated with the cup of prosperity."   Then he
goes on to say :—

" By far the most agreeable hours I spend in Edinburgh must
be placed to the account of Miss M. Laurie and her pianoforte.   I
cannot help repeating to you and to Mrs Laurie a compliment that
Mr Mackenzie, the celebrated ' Man of Feeling,' paid to Miss Laurie
the other night at a concert.   I had come in at the interlude and
sat down by him, till I saw Miss Laurie in a seat not very far distant,
and went up to pay my respects to her.   On my return to Mr Mackenzie he asked me who she was ?   I told him 'twas the daughter of a
reverend friend of mine in the west country.   He returned there
was something very striking, to his idea, in her appearance.   On
my desiring to know what it was, he was pleased to say : ' She
has a great deal of the elegance of a well-bred lady about her, with
all the sweet simplicity of a country girl.'   My compliments to all
the happy inmates of St. Margaret's Hill."

The young lady referred to was the eldest daughter
of Dr Laurie—Christina, who afterwards became the wife
of Mr Alexander Wilson, bookseller, Glasgow, son of the
Professor of Astronomy in the University of Glasgow.
The correspondence between Dr Laurie and Burns is not
exhausted with the letter quoted, nor was the " Prayer "
the only memento he left in the room which he occupied
in Loudoun Manse.   Burns had a diamond with which he
scratched his sentiments on more than one window, and
on the window of his bedroom in the Manse he wrote :
" Lovely Mrs Laurie, she is all charms."   The writing
on the pane of glass is still in existence—indeed, the sash
enclosing the pane, with several others, was removed to

prevent accidental breakage. Twenty years ago or so it was on exhibition with other Burns relics in Glasgow. " Lovely Mrs Laurie " did not scruple occasionally to rebuke the Poet for what she considered wrong in his ways, and on one occasion she did so, so effectually that the feelings of the Poet were considerably wounded. Enclosed in a book of old poems which he sent to a member of the family shortly afterwards, the following lines were found :—

Rusticity's ungainly form may cloud the highest mind ·
But when the heart is nobly warm, the good excuse will find :
Propriety's cold, cautious rules warm fervour may o'erlook ;
But spare poor Sensibility the ungentle, harsh rebuke."

If Burns sometimes had reason to fear the criticism of " Lovely Mrs Laurie," there was one person in the household who had a like wholesome dread of the Poet. John Brooke, the minister's man, among his miscellaneous duties, was expected to wait at table. Once, during a visit of Burns to the Manse, the invaluable John did not make his appearance. An excuse was given which did not satisfy the mistress of the house. Seeking him out afterwards, Mrs Laurie asked John why he had not been in his usual place. " Deed, Mem," said the worthy, " I was just fleyed to come in, for fear Burns wad mak' a poem on me.

Burns was not the only poet whom Dr Laurie helped to his place in public estimation. James Macpherson was also indebted to him for bringing the poems of O.s'an before discriminating critics, a service which afterwards, when the world had prospered with him. Macpherson either forgot or pretended to forget. What brought out his apparent forgetfulness was the answer which Dr Laurie received when he wrote to Macpherson, as a member of the House of Commons, over some trouble his brother had fallen into as Governor of the Mosquito Shore.

Dr Laurie received his degree from the University of Glasgow in 1791. His son Archibald succeeded him in Lo doun Kirk and Manse. Dr Laurie died in 1837 in his sixty-ninth year, and forty-fourth of his ministry. His wife pre-deceased him fifteen years.   One daughter was married in Glasgow as already stated and his younger daughter became the wife of the minister of Sorn   His son, Archibald, married Anne Adair, sister of Major Adair, the friend of Robert Burns.   The home of the minister's happy boyhood and youth soon resounded with the voices and laughter of his own children—three sons and three daughters grew up to manhood and womanhood within the brown walls of the old Manse.   His eldest son, George James, became the parish minister of Monkton.   He was very happy in his sea-board parish, and is still affectionately remembered in the district.   He was the author of various songs, but none of them ever earned the popularity of the celebrated lyric describing his boyhood in the old Manse of St. Margaret's Hill in Loudoun—

> " Hae ye mind o' Auld Lang Syne.
> When the simmer days were fine,
> When the sun shone brighter far
> Than it's ever done sin syne ?"

which was given in full in a former number of the *Burns Chronicle*.

HELEN WALTERS CRAWFORD.

BURNS AND UPPERMOST CLYDESDALE.

IN the last *Burns Chronicle* there appears an excellent article with a somewhat similar title to the above, from the pen of that well-known writer on Burns topics, Mr Andrew M'Callum. Unfortunately, Mr M'Callum comes no higher up the valley than Lamington, unaware apparently that the National Bard had associations with the parish of Crawford, which forms the uppermost part of the County of Lanark. This parish, it may be noted in passing, is one of the largest in the south of Scotland, and covers an area of over one hundred square miles. It is possible to walk twenty-one miles in a straight line without crossing the parish boundaries. Burns's visits here all took place after he had settled at Ellisland in 1788. His district as an excise officer " marched " with uppermost Clydesdale, and it is not to be wondered at that at times he went over the border. The Rev. W. C. Fraser, in his book on Crawford, relates that Burns visited the parish in his capacity as an Exciseman, and although, as I have said, the parish was outside his district. it is quite probable that he would do so, because part of the parish was—and indeed still is—closely connected with Dumfriesshire. Indeed, the parish of Moffat is partly within the county of Lanark, and the inhabitants of that portion which extends over the boundaries of the northern shire enjoy the blessings of " Lanark Law and Moffat Gospel." Glengeith Toll-house, which sits a little to the south of Elvanfoot Station, on the side of the Clyde, is said to have been a favourite halting-place of the Poet's. In his days it was an inn, and it is said that he wrote some verses on one of its window panes. If so, they have been lost, and all tradition of what they were has perished likewise. We have the consolation of knowing that the verses must have been good ones, for, as Mr

Fraser rather quaintly remarks, " Had they been worthless they certainly would have been preserved."

Leaving now the realm of tradition, we are on firmer ground when we turn to the Poet's own works, and here we find references to at least two visits to an outlying corner of the parish. The villages of Wanlockhead and Leadhills are, as every one knows, the two highest villages in Scotland. They owe their existence

WANLOCKHEAD.

to the lead mines which have been wrought there for centuries, having been discovered in the days when England and Scotland were still separate kingdoms. The villages sit quite close together, the one on the south and the other on the north side of the boundary line between Nithsdale and Clydesdale. In 1791 we find Burns at Leadhills (in the month of August, according to Scott Douglas, December, according to Wallace), probably on some duty connected with the excise. While on this visit he wrote Mrs M'Lehose (Clarinda). She had written him during the summer, without receiving any reply, and it was in answer to a second letter that he penned the epistle which is dated at "Lead hills, Thursday, noon." In the course of the letter Burns states, " I have just a snatch of time." which seems to point to some pressing business in the neighbourhood. The letter contains. however, the " Lament of Mary Queen of Scots," and concludes in rather a pathetic strain. as though the bleak hillsides had made a deep impression on his spirit : " Misfortune seems to take a peculiar pleasure in darting her arrows against ' honest men and bonie lasses.' Of this you are too. too just a proof. but may your future fate be a bright exception to the remark. In the words of Hamlet—

' Adieu. adieu. adieu ! remember me.'

ROBERT BURNS."

This was not, however. the Bard's first visit to the district, for he was here more than a year before. when he wrote, at " Ramage's," the well-known lines addressed to Mr John Taylor—

" With Pegasus upon a day,
Apollo weary flying."

The Poet had ridden up the Mennock Pass, a road, even yet, in spite of improvements. one of the steepest in the south of Scotland. It was frosty weather, and the Poet determined to get his horse's shoes " sharped " before attempting the return journey. The blacksmith at Wanlockhead, being busy at the time. would not at first undertake the job. Luckily Burns's companion. a Mr John Sloan. was intimate with the manager of the mines. Mr John Taylor, who, on being informed of the Poet's wishes, induced the smith to put the horse's " caulkers " in order. The smith's name was Hutchison. and he was wont to boast in later days that he had never been so well paid for his labour as he was by Burns, who " paid him wi' siller. paid him wi' drink. and paid him wi' a sang." Apparently the verses, though addressed to Mr Taylor, had come into the possession of the " son of Vulcan." The lines were first published in Cunningham's edition (1834). The

John Taylor here referred to belonged to Leadhills. where his father's and grandfather's tombstone may still be seen in the cemetery. The inscription may be considered one of the most remarkable in the country. It reads, " Sacred to the memory of Robert Taylor, who was during many years an overseer to the Scotch Mining Company at Leadhills, and died May 6th, 1791, in the 67th year of his age. He is buried by the side of his father. John Taylor,

HIGHEST INHABITED HOUSE IN SCOTLAND.

(Sits near the boundary between Dumfriesshire and Lanarkshire.)

who died in this place at the remarkable age of 137 years. Remarkable indeed ' This old patriarch was of English birth, having first seen the light in Cumberland. He died in May, 1770, and. while there is reason to doubt the accuracy of the statement on the tombstone, there is evidence that he was considerably over the century. He claimed to remember a famous eclipse of the sun which astronomical investigations showed had taken place in 1652. A brother of the John Taylor who assisted Burns was James Taylor, who was associated with Patrick Miller of Dalswinton,

Burns's landlord, in his experiments regarding the application of steam to navigation. Another Leadhills man associated with these experiments was William Symington, to whose memory a handsome monument was erected in the village about thirty years ago. But there is another son of Leadhills whose influence on the Bard is noticeable in his works, and for whose memory Burns had great respect. This is Allan Ramsay, " Honest Allan," who was born at Leadhills in 1686. His father was also an overseer in the mines, but he died at the early age of 24, and his widow, Alice Bower, soon afterwards married a farmer of the name of Crichton, whose farm was in Crawford Moor. Allan attended the old parochial school in Crawford till his departure for Edinburgh in 1701.

Just seven years after the death of Burns this district was visited by two of the best known of English poets, Wordsworth and Coleridge. They journeyed by way of the Mennock, and put up at the " Hopetoun Arms " in Leadhills. They afterwards crossed by a hill road to Crawfordjohn, and there they met with an accident to their gig, which delayed them somewhat. The two poets were accompanied by Miss Wordsworth (Dorothy), and we have a short description of the country as it appeared to her : " Travelled through several reaches of the glen (Glengonnar), which somewhat resembled the valley of the Mennock on the other side of Wanlockhead, but it was not near so beautiful ; the forms of the mountains did not melt so exquisitely into each other, and there was a coldness and, if I may so speak, a want of simplicity in the surface of the earth ; the heather was poor, not covering a whole hillside, not in luxuriant streams and beds interveined with rich verdure, but patchy and stunted, with here and there coarse grass and rushes." It is in every way probable that Burns went through the parish when he visited Edinburgh in 1789. He was then residing at Ellisland, and the direct road was by way of the Dalveen Pass, through Crawford and Abington and on by way of Biggar to the capital. Biggar was regarded by travellers from Mid-

Nithsdale as the half-way house on the way to Edinburgh
—a point used to good purpose bv Joseph Laing Waugh
in one of his delightful sketches of " Robbie Doo." In
the writer's opinion, this was the most likely occasion for
the Bard's visit to the Parish Church of Biggar, though
most writers place it earlier. Dalveen Pass is a
lovely and romantic glen, with its own memories of
the national and Covenanting struggles. It is mentioned

ENTRANCE TO LEADHILLS.

twice by Burns under the title of the " lang glen
and the " lang loan " in his well-known song,
" Last May a braw wooer cam' down the lang glen."
Originally the third line of the fourth stanza ran, " He up
the Gateslack to mv black cousin Bess," but on Thomson
objecting, the Poet changed the words to " He up the lang
loan." " Gateslack," says Burns. " is positively the name
of a particular place, a kind of passage among the Lowther
hills, on the confines of this county " The name is still
given to one of the farms in Durisdeer parish, on
the side of the " lang glen,"

Burns paid his last visit to Edina in November, 1791. He was then resident in Dumfries, and there is no evidence as to what road he took, so he may have traversed Crawford again, but from a remark he makes in a letter to Alex. Cunningham, it seems more likely that he travelled by Moffat and Tweedsmuir. This was the coach road, and the scene of the disaster to the mail coach in the year of the "big snaw," 1827. In the letter referred to he says, " I am sorry I did not know him (Thomson) when I was in Edinburgh, but I will tell you of a plot I have been contriving. You and he shall, in the course of the summer, meet me half way, that is at the ' Bield Inn.' " This meeting, however, never took place. The inn sits close to the highway, opposite the parish church of Tweedsmuir, about two miles south of the better-known Crook Inn. " From Berwick to the Bield," it may be noted, is the Tweedside equivalent of the Scottish " From Maidenkirk to John o' Groats.

The parish which adjoins Crawford is Crawfordjohn, probably one of the most secluded in the south of Scotland so much so, indeed. that " men speak in proverbs," saying, " oot o' the warl' and into Crawfordjohn." Burns's friend, William Johnstone, resided at Clackcleith, on the borders of Sanquhar and Crawfordjohn. This is the " Trusty auld worthy Clackcleith " of the postcript to the " Kirk's Alarm," and as seems likely Burns visited the hospitable home, he would be within a short distance of the boundary of the parish. There is still extant a short letter of Burns in which mention is made of a Crawfordjohn man who, along with " Clackcleith," assisted the Bard in his recovery of old Scots Airs :

" Memorandum for Provost E—— W—— to get from John French his sets of the following Scots airs :—

(1) The auld vowe jumpt owre the tether.

(2) Nine nichts awa, welcome hame my dearie.

(3) A' the nichts o' the year the chapman drinks nae water.

Mr Whigham will either of himself. or through that

worthy veteran of original wit and social iniquity, ' Clackcleith,' procure these. and it will be extremely obliging to
R. B.''

This note must belong to a date after 1793, for it was
in that year that Whigham became Provost of Sanquhar.
John French belonged to a family which was well known
in Crawfordjohn, and is still represented there.   John Black,
who acted with " Clackcleith " as trustee for the creditors
of John Lapraik, the old Scotch bard, was also a Crawfordjohn man.

In conclusion, it may be added that the heroine of
the song, " Yon wild mossy mountains," has been claimed
for Crawford.   To the writer, the scenery described in the
poem seems to fit the district around Elvanfoot better
than that around Covington.   It is difficult to speak of the
" youth of the Clyde " at a point so far down the stream.
Scott Douglas is certainly in error when he refers to the
" Infant Clyde meandering " there.   The river at the base
of Tinto is as large as many a Scottish river is when it enters
the sea.   The " infancy " of the Clyde is in Crawford
parish, whether the source be found in the Little Clyde
or at the head of the Daer, a river, by the way, which gave
a title to the first nobleman with whom the Bard " dinnered."
and whose whole course belongs to uppermost Clydesdale.
The estates which led to the adoption of the title by the
family are now largely in the possession of the Marquis of
Linlithgow.

WM. M'MILLAN,
St. Leonard's, Dunfermline.

SHENSTONE AND BURNS.

TO estimate the influence of Shenstone upon Burns, it will be necessary to recall the position Shenstone had acquired in the literary world, and his standing as a poet, when Burns came under the power of " the bosom-melting throe with Shenstone's art " (*The Vision*), some-where about the year 1778.

Writing about his friend and contemporary, Richard Graves says ·—" Few men have risen with so rapid a pro-gress, and on apparently so slender a foundation, from a state of the utmost obscurity to so great a degree of cele-brity and repute, as Mr Shenstone. Born to a very small paternal estate, which his ancestors cultivated for a sub-sistence, he embellished it for his amusement ; and that in so good a taste as to attract the notice not only of the neighbouring gentry and nobility, but almost of every person in the kingdom who either had, or affected to have, any relish of rural beauties ; so that no one came to see the noble and delightful seat of Lord Lyttelton at Hagley who did not visit with proportionable delight the humbler charms of the Leasowes.

" Mr Shenstone's talents of a different kind have made him as much known and admired for his writings in the elegiac and pastoral styles as he was at first for the elegance of his taste in rural embellishments."

Isaac D'Israeli, in his *Curiosities of Literature*, written 1791-1823, found it necessary to enter upon a vindication to protect the " fine natural genius of Shen-stone " from the fatal injuries inflicted on him by the criti-cism of his contemporaries. Evidently, if Shenstone needed vindication in or about 1800, the period of his highest fame must indeed have been short, but that period during which he enjoyed his highest popularity would be a period immediately preceding Burns's first acquaintance with his Works.

The article in which Shenstone is vindicated contains passages that throw light on the considerable influence Shenstone must have had amongst his contemporaries, and if that influence had been such as to affect the elder D'Israeli, who is credited by his son with being " without a passion or a prejudice," then *a fortiori* they must have had a stronger influence on the susceptible " tinder " heart of the youthful Burns. The passages which illustrate this influence are :—" Why have the *Elegies* of Shenstone, which forty years ago formed for many of us the favourite poems of our youth, ceased to delight us in mature life ? It is perhaps that these *Elegies*, planned with peculiar felicity, have little in their execution. They form a series of poetical truths, devoid of poetical expression ; truths, for notwithstanding the pastoral romance in which the poet has enveloped himself, the subjects are real, and the feelings could not, therefore, be fictitious."

" If Shenstone created little from the imagination, he was at least perpetually under the influence of real emotions. This is the reason why his truths so strongly operate on the juvenile mind, not yet matured ; and thus we have sufficiently ascertained the fact, as the Poet himself has expressed it, ' that he drew his pictures from the spot, and he felt very sensibly the affections he communicates.' "

Consistent with Isaac D'Israeli's estimate, we find the effect of Shenstone very clearly marked in the first Common-place Book of Burns' (1783). Burns had told Dr Moore that when he was at Kirkoswald (1775) " his reading had been enlarged by the very important addition of Shenstone's works." In the Common-place Book the first quotation is from Shenstone—" there are numbers in the world who do not want sense to make a figure, so much as an opinion of their own abilities, to put them upon recording their observations, and allowing them the same importance which they do to those which appear in print " ; and the

second quotation we also find is from Shenstone's first
Elegy—

> " Pleasing when youth is long expir'd to trace
>   The forms our pencil or our pen design'd !
> Such was our youthful air and shape and face ;
>   Such the soft image of our youthful mind."

These quotations shew that Burns's study of Shenstone
was not confined alone to the poems, for the first or prose
quotation is taken from Shenstone's " Egotism XLIV."
in his " Essay on Man and Manners " ; and again the quotation, " stained with guilt and crimsoned o'er with crimes,"
which Burns used in connection with " Blackguards," is
taken from Shenstone's XX. Elegy.

The references to Shenstone in Burns's Common-place
Book can be supplemented by extracts from the letters
of Burns, which almost convince that Shenstone was one
of the " models " whom Burns set up for his self-education
in the realms of poetry, and it is not surprising to find these
influences at work when Burns gives his works to the public.
In the Poet's Preface to the Kilmarnock (1786) Edition of
his Poems, he says, " It is an observation of that celebrated
poet whose divine Elegies do honour to our language, our
nation, and our species, that ' Humility has depressed many
a genius to a hermit, but never raised one to fame.' "

This quotation about " Humility " is taken from
Shenstone's prose works, and is the concluding observation
in the Essay on " Allowing merit in others."   The above
references should be sufficient to shew how large a part,
and how strongly Shenstone worked on Burns's feelings,
and it may not be overstrained when we say that one feels
forced to admit that Shenstone was one of the " models "
of thought and expression that dominated the writing of
the four lines of apology with which Burns introduced the
" commencing poet " to the public :—

> " The simple Bard, unbroke by rules of art,
>   He pours the wild effusions of the heart ·
> And if inspired, 'tis Nature's pow'rs inspired,
>   Her's all the melting thrill, and her's the kindling fire."

Similarities of diction to these four lines are found in Shenstone's Elegy No. 1 :—

> " O lov'd simplicity ! be thine the prize !
>   Assiduous art correct her page in vain !
> His be the palm who, guiltless of disguise,
>   Contemns the pow'r, the dull resource to feign ' "

The first two lines of this verse convey the same sentiments as Burns does.

Again, in Elegy No. 1, is the inspiration :—

> " Write from thy bosom—let not art controul
> The ready pen that makes his edicts known."

And Shenstone emphasises the origin of this simplicity when he says in verse 3 :—

> " Hence ! the faint verse that flows not from the heart."

Again, in verse 6, we find the two lines :—

> " Soft as the line of love-sick Hammond flows,
> 'Twas his fond heart effus'd the melting theme."

Burns's words, " effusions " and " melting," are surely a little more than a coincidence, and it is further noticed that " melting " is the adjective that he, in " The Vision," applies to " Shenstone's art.'

If the writer has not proved his suspicions, amounting to a belief, that Shenstone was the main inspiration for the introductory Apology to the Kilmarnock Edition, he may surely flatter himself that his belief is certainly not groundless.

Other similarities in the works of Shenstone and Burns exist which may form subject-matter for a future paper, but the foregoing notes may serve as an introduction to the influences that Shenstone exercised on the formation of Burns's thoughts.

A. J. CRAIG.

THE HERALDRY OF BURNS.

I CAN imagine that many of the admirers of the Bard
will be somewhat surprised at the title of this paper.
Heraldry seems far removed indeed from the circle in which
Burns moved.   No one could speak with greater power
than he of " a' the tinsel trash o' State," yet it remains a
fact that the Poet who sang " A man's a man for a' that "
also wrote " I am a bit of a herald."   In quite a number
of his letters and poems we have allusions to the " Gentle
Science," and it is to deal with those that this paper is
written.

Burns, like so many of his contemporaries, used a
seal, and it is in connection with his obtaining a new
seal in 1794 that he makes the statement quoted above.
It occurs in a letter to his Edinburgh correspondent, Alexander Cunningham, of date 3rd March, 1794 :   "
There is one commission that I must trouble you with.
I lately lost a valuable seal, a present from a departed
friend, which vexes me much.   I have gotten one of your
Highland pebbles, which I fancy would make a very decent
one ; and I want to cut my armorial bearings on it : will
you be so obliging as to enquire what will be the expense
of such a business ?   I do not know that my name is
matriculated, as the heralds call it, at all, but I have invented arms for myself, so you know I will be chief of the
name ; and by courtesy of Scotland will likewise be entitled
to supporters.   These, however, I do not intend having
on my seal.   I am a bit of a herald, and shall give you,
secundum artem, my arms :—On a field azure a holly-bush
seeded, proper ; in base a shepherd's pipe and crook saltier-
wise, also proper, in chief.   On a wreath of the colours a
woodlark perching on a sprig of bay-tree, proper, for crest.
Two mottoes—round the top of the crest, 'Wood-notes wild ' ;
at the bottom of the shield, in the usual place, ' Better a

wee bush than nae bield.' By the shepherd's pipe and crook I do not mean the nonsense of painters of Arcadia, but a *stock and horn* and a club, such as you see at the head of Allan Ramsay in Allan's quarto edition of the *Gentle Shepherd*" From this it is quite evident that Burns had paid attention to the grammar of heraldry, for no herald could have described the arms more correctly. Heraldic language is sometimes rather mystifying to the ordinary

individual, yet here the Poet shows that he is quite well acquainted with the technical terms used in these matters. The shield is coloured *azure, i.e.,* blue. The holly-bush, pipe and crook are *proper, i.e.,* they are in their natural colours ; while the two latter are placed *saltier-wise in chief,* which means that they are placed in the form of an x in the upper part of the shield. The " wreath " is the twisted fillet of silk which was formerly used to bind the crest to the helmet of the wearer, and the " colours " are those of the arms. With regard to the charges on the shield, Burns was at pains to see that they were engraved properly. His letter to Cunningham indicates that he was afraid that the designer would not fashion the shepherd's pipe correctly. That his anxiety was not without cause is shown by the fact that in a sketch of those arms drawn by one of the leading heraldic painters in Scotland, the very error which the Poet wished to guard against was made and an " Arcadian " pipe introduced.

The *stock and horn* was in some ways a favourite instrument of the Poet's. Writing to Thomson with regard to a plate David Allan (the Scottish Hogarth) was doing for the forthcoming volume of songs, he says · " Tell my friend Allan that I much suspect he has in his plates mistaken the figure of the stock and horn. I have at last gotten one, but it is a very rude instrument. It is composed of three parts—the stock, which is the hinder thigh bone of a sheep, such as you see in a mutton ham ; the horn, which is a common Highland cow's horn, cut off at the smaller end until the aperture be large enough to admit the ' stock.' to be pushed up through the horn until it be held by the thicker end of the thigh bone ; and lastly, an oaten reed. exactly cut and notched like that which you see every shepherd boy have when the corn stems are green and full grown. The reed is not made fast in the bone, but is held by the lips, and plays loose in the smaller end of the stock, while the stock and horn, hanging on its larger end, is held by the hands in playing. The stock has six or seven ventiges on the upper side and one back ventige, like the common flute. This of mine was made by a' man from the braes of Athole. and is exactly what the shepherds were wont to use in that country." In another letter he suggests that in one of the other plates being made for the volume a stock and horn should be placed in the hands of one of the figures, instead of a piece of knitting. Thomson had not the same ideas as his correspondent, for in one of his letters to the Bard he remarks · "I doubt much if it (the stock and horn) was capable of anything but routing and roaring. A friend of mine says he remembers to have heard one in his younger days made of wood instead of your bone, and that the sound was abominable." Apparently Cunningham had had a design prepared for Burns's seal, and had sent it through Thomson to him at Dumfries, for in a letter of May, 1794, to Thomson we have the following : "My seal is all well, except that the holly must be a bush, not a tree, as in the present shield. I also enclose it, and will send the pebble at the first opportunity."

The selection of the shepherd's pipe for the " arms " of a rustic poet is quite easily accounted for. Probably the same feeling suggested the crook, though we might have expected something suggestive of the plough, for the Bard was never a shepherd in the strict sense of the word. It is not so easy to find a reason for the the use of the holly. It is the badge of the clans Mackenzie and Macmillan, but Burns had no connection with either. Apparently, however, he had a special regard for the prickly leaf, for in " The Vision " he pictures " Coila " wearing a wreath of its leaves :—

" Green, slender, leaf-clad holly boughs
  Were twisted, gracefu', round her brows "—

and in the last stanza he pictures her crowning the rustic Bard with her own garland :—

" ' And wear thou this,' she solemn said,
  And bound the holly round my head :
  The polished leaves, and berries red,
        Did rustling play ;
  And, like a passing thought, she fled,
        In light away."

At first sight it seems difficult to understand why he should have associated the holly with the Scottish muse, nor does the plant strike one as furnishing the most appropriate—or the most comfortable—leaves for a head-dress. The Scottish clan badges were generally chosen from evergreen plants. Sir Walter Scott mentions that the downfall of the Stewarts was supposed to be omened by their having chosen the oak, which was not an evergreen, as their distinctive symbol, and this may have influenced the Bard in the choice of the holly for his cognizance. Judging from his poetry, the birch was his favourite tree. There is, however, another reason which may be put forward to account for the Poet's choice. Although a native of Kyle, he was born " upon the Carrick border," and the holly is traditionally associated with the latter district. Culzean, the seat of the Marquis of Ailsa, means *The place of the holly*. The arms of the Irvine family of Drum consist of three bunches of holly leaves, and the tradition regarding them is that when Robert Bruce took up arms in support of his claim to the throne of Scotland, he appointed William de Irvin as his personal attendant, bestowing upon him the arms which he had borne as Earl of Carrick. The supporters of the Drum arms, it may be noted, are two savages *wreathed about head and loins with holly*. The Earldom of Carrick in the Scottish peerage is now held by the eldest son of the King, whose chief Scottish title—after that of Prince of Scotland—is Duke of Rothesay, a fact Burns alludes to in one of his Jacobite songs :—

> " In the rolling tide of swelling Clyde
>   There sits an isle of high degree,
> And a town of fame, whose princely name
>   Should grace the lass of Albanie."

Strictly speaking, armorial bearings are confined to the contents of the shield, and heraldic writers have regarded the appendages, supporters, crest, motto, &c., as being of less importance than the charges ; but although such is the case, these add much to the interest and beauty of the achievement (the complete coat-of-arms).

For crest, Burns chose a " woodlark perching on a sprig of bay-tree," a most appropriate crest, be it said, especially as the lark seems to have been· his favourite among the birds. In early days the crest was actually worn on the helmet, and the Poet's choice was such that it could, without much difficulty, have been transferred to the head-dress. The bay or laurel has been used from time immemorial for the crowns with which heroes were rewarded, and for the garlands with which poet's were crowned. It is probable that this ancient use accounts for its mention here. In the epistle to James Smith, the Bard says of himself :—

> " Then, farewell hopes of laurel-bough
>   To garland my poetic brow,"

and it will be remembered that he wrote " an address to the shade of Thomson on crowning his bust with bays." This he did at the request of the Earl of Buchan, who apparently wished to honour himself as well as the Poet. In a later poem Burns indicates that Thomson had won the " unfading garland " without the aid of any noble's patronage. In the epigram on Elphinstone we have also a reference to " Laurel'd Martial."

The mottoes now claim attention. The first is " Wood-notes wild." The expression was a favourite one with the Bard, and in at least four of his letters he refers to Bonnie Jean's " wood-note wild." The phrase was used by Milton in his " Il Penseroso " (see lines 131-4) :—

> " Then to the well-trod stage anon,
>   If Jonson's learned sock be on,
>   Or sweetest Shakespeare fancy's child
>   Warble his native ' wood-notes wild.' "

It is quite probable that the Scottish Poet, who was an earnest student of Milton, is quoting from his English predecessor, though it is equally possible that the quotation is at second hand. The expression was used by Henry Mackenzie in the review of the Kilmarnock edition published in *The Lounger* for 9th December, 1786. The Bard's first use of the words dates from after his first Edinburgh visit. The motto has a double meaning, indicating the nature of its user's poetry and also the sweetness of the woodlark's melody. A very large number of ancient Scottish mottoes have some allusion to the *crests* of the bearers, and this doubtless influenced the Bard in his choice.

The second motto, " Better a wee bush than nae bield,"

is a proverbial expression still current in the south-west of Scotland. Whether its use here was suggested by the bush in the arms, or whether the bush in the arms was suggested by the motto, is a problem we have no means of solving. In view of the fact, however, that he insisted on a " bush " in his arms, and not a " tree," it appears more probable that the principal charge was suggested by the motto, and not *vice versa*. It will be observed that in the description of his arms Burns says of the second motto that it was to be put " at the bottom of the shield in the usual place " Now, the " usual place " for a motto in Scottish heraldry is above the crest, while, on the other hand, in English heraldry the motto is usually placed below the shield. This is one of the differences between the practices of the two countries. The mistake of placing a Scottish motto according to English use is one that is often made even in quarters where one would expect a better knowledge of these points. Not many years ago one of the Royal Burghs, which had conferred its freedom upon the Bard, invested in a chain of office for its Provost, yet, despite the fact that this Royal Burgh prides itself upon its patriotism, it had its arms marshalled according to the English usage. While the usual rule in Scotland is to place the motto above the crest, it is quite legitimate to put a *second* motto below the shield. Indeed, this is the usual place for a second motto. Sir George Mackenzie, the " Bloody Mackenzie " of Covenanting times, is one of the earliest authorities on Scottish heraldry, and according to him the motto should be placed according to the portion of the arms, shield, crest, or supporters to which it relates. According to this writer, therefore, Burns, even if he had only had the longer motto, would have been quite in order in placing it beneath the shield. Another difference between the practice of Scotland and England may be noted, as it throws some light on another part of the letter relating to the Poet's arms. In the southern country in Burns's day the only persons entitled to " supporters " for their arms were peers of the realm, Knights of the Garter, and a few specially privileged baronets and commoners. In Scotland, on the other hand, the list of such persons is much larger. It includes not only the classes mentioned above, but also representatives of the "minor barons" of Scottish history who sat in Parliament previous to 1587, chiefs of clans, and persons who can prove usage previous to 1672. Burns mentions that, as he has invented the arms for himself, he will be " chief " of the name, and thus " by the courtesy of Scotland will likewise be entitled to supporters.". " These," he adds, " I do not intend having on my seal."

The one thing which strikes every one with a knowledge of the " Gentle science " is the correctness of the Bard's words regarding his arms. In a technical subject such as heraldry it is very easy to make mistakes, but in this case, as has already been stated, there is nothing which could be objected to. When comparison is made with the coats-of-arms taken out under official auspices in the end of the 18th and beginning of the 19th century Burns's design does not in any way suffer by the comparison. All writers are agreed that the average heraldry of the period was anything but good. Indeed, one English writer says that in the years in question " the final degradation of heraldry is to be seen," and the present Lyon King-of-Arms, while not going so far, yet states that then " heraldic art was at rather a low ebb." It cannot be denied, however, that the arms invented for the Poet by himself are quite good, and in accordance with the better practice of earlier days. The arms give us another example of the thoroughness with which the Bard did all that he set his hand to, and afford evidence—if such be required —against the " down grade " theory of his life at Dumfries. The description of the seal was sent to Edinburgh in 1794, but Burns did not receive the completed article until 1796, just two months or so before his death. In April of that year he writes to Thomson that " Mrs Hyslop " (of the Globe Tavern), to whom his letter had been entrusted, " will be a very proper person to bring back the seal you talk of." Apparently a letter from Thomson is amissing. On 4th July, in a postscript, Thomson remarks, " Mrs Hyslop I doubt not delivered the gold seal to you in good condition," and in the next letter from Dumfries we learn that it had arrived safely, the last line being, " many, many thanks for the beautiful seal."

This seal passed to his eldest son, Robert, and from him to the Bard's great-granddaughter, Mrs Thomas, with whom it remained till her death.

There is another seal, however (described in *Burns Chronicle*, No. 4), in the possession of another branch of the family. This is a pencil seal, with the woodlark perching on a branch, and the motto " Wood-notes wild." (It is not mentioned whether the crest is set on a " wreath.") " It is cut in a yellow topaz, set in silver, to screw on the top of pencil case, and bears the appearance of age, as if having been well used. This seal, my father told me, was the Poet's. I feel convinced it is the one the Poet spoke of losing, it is just the size for sealing letters. My father set very great value upon it . as being a genuine relic of my great-grandfather." This extract is from a letter dated " Adelaide, October 10th, 1894," written by Annie Vincent Burns Scott, daughter of Mrs Hutchison, who was, again, the daughter of the Poet's son, James Glencairn. Burns used at least two other seals in his correspondence. The earliest was of no heraldic design, being oval, and showing a figure with harp in hand. It was used as early as 1789. The second is of more interest. It bears a heart transfixed by two arrows. The first letter to which it was affixed is one relating to the birth of the Poet's third son, William Nicol. Scott Douglas draws attention to the seal, " with its symbolic impression, as pregnant with meaning. For, nine days before the date of the birth of William Nicol, the Poet's ' Anna of the gowden locks ' was delivered of a daughter, who was afterwards brought up by Mrs Burns."

It is possible that the seal was designed by the Bard in view of the position he found himself in, but it is hardly likely. The " heart " is a common charge on arms in Scotland, owing, doubtless, to its association with the Douglas family. No fewer than seventy "coats" bearing the heart are recorded in the Public Register of Scottish Arms. One of the coats registered there is very like Burns's seal. Alexander Yeoman has for arms, *argent*, a heart, *gules*, pierced with two darts. Did Burns use a similar design to indicate that he was also a *yeoman* ?

Heraldry in Scotland is regulated by the Lyon Office, at the head of which is Lyon King-of-Arms, commonly, though incorrectly, styled the "Lord Lyon." In that office are kept the heraldic records, genealogies, &c., belonging to the kingdom of Scotland, and on the occasion of his first visit to Edinburgh Burns called there in order to discover, if possible, particulars regarding his family. In the atuobiography which he wrote for Dr Moore the following occurs : " I have not the most distant pretence to what the pye-coated guardians of escutcheons call a gentleman. When at Edinburgh last winter I got acquainted at the Herald's Office, and looking through the granary of honours I there found almost every name in the kingdom. But for me—

  ' My ancient, but ignoble, blood
  Has crept thro' scoundrels since the flood.'

Gules, purpure, argent, &c., quite disowned me." At the time of his visit the Lyon King-of-Arms was John Hooke Campbell of Bangeston ; but it is questionable whether he would take much interest in the office at all, for in the latter end of the 18th century the office of Lyon was treated as a sinecure. Most, if not all, of the work was done by the Lyon-Depute, an office abolished in 1867. The Lyon-Depute of Burns's day was Robert Boswell, a writer to the signet, who also held the office of Lyon-Clerk. In this office he also had a deputy, one Robert Rankin, a solicitor in the city, and the latter probably would be the person who helped the Poet in his researches.

It may not be out of place to say that the foreign-looking words, *gules, purpure, argent, or*, which occur here and in a letter to Mrs Dunlop, are the heraldic terms for red, purple, white (or silver), yellow (or gold). The " pye-coated guardians " were, in addition to the Lyon and his depute, the heralds and pursuivants, all of whom bore titles of some antiquity. The heralds had as titles Albany, Islay, Marchmont, Ross, Rothesay, and Snowdon ; while the pursuivants were Bute, Carrick, Dingwall, Kintyre, Ormond, and Unicorn. There are now only three of each, the other offices having been abolished in 1867. " Pye-coated " refers, of course, to the " tabards " which form the official dress of the heraldic executive, and which bear the Royal Arms in full colour. In pre-Union days the tabards were quartered in accordance with the Scottish form of the Royal Arms, but in Burns's day, as in our own, the English form was used. The Bard, in a letter to Mrs Dunlop, declared that nothing could reconcile him to the common terms, " English Ambassador," " English Court," " the Commons of England," and we can well believe that in this matter also he would not be pleased to see Scottish forms thrust aside for English ones. That Burns knew something of the procedure of the Lyon Office is shown in his works.. The " proclamation " of his early days, " in name of the nine," is as correctly formal as any herald could have made it. Matthew Henderson " held his *patent* for his *honours* immediately from Almighty God," a phrase which gained the admiration of Carlyle In a letter to an unknown correspondent from Ellisland he writes : " When I matriculate in the Herald's Office I intend that my sup-porters shall be two sloths, my crest a slow-worm, and the motto ' Deil tak' the foremost ' " (he was apologising for delay in answering a letter). The only reference to the head of the Lyon Office is in that remarkable letter which Scott Douglas has termed " Literary Billingsgate," where he addresses his correspondent as " Thou Lyon herald to silly etymology."

Of actual coats-of-arms we have been able to discover references to four only, each, however, belonging to a distinguished Scottish family. In the note which Burns added to the copy of " Scots wha hae " presented to Dr Hughes, he relates that well-known incident in Scottish history when Bruce struck down Comyn in the Greyfriars' Church in Dumfries and then rushed out crying, " I doubt I have slain the Comyn." " Do you doubt ? " cried Sir Roger de Kilpatrick, one of his companions, " I'll mak' siccar," whereupon he entered the church and slew the enemy of his king as he lay beside the altar. Burns quotes Kilpatrick's words as " I've sickered him," and adds, " until lately this was the motto of the Closeburn family, but the late Sir Thomas changed it into ' I've made sure.' The crest is still the bloody dagger."

The second reference is to the arms of the house of Douglas, arms which probably figure more prominently in the literature of Scotland than those of any other family. The old ballad depicts the Douglas banner :—

> " The blodye herte in the Douglas arms,
>   His standard stood on hie,
> That every man might full wel knowe,
>   Besyde stood starrés three."

Sir Walter Scott, in " Marmion." writes of the shield carved over the doorway of Tantallon :—

> " Of sculpture rude a stony shield,
>   The bloody heart was in the field
> And in the chief three *mullets stood
>   The cognizance of Douglas blood."

Burns's reference is not so explicit, but it is quite clear :—

> " But cautious Queensberry left the war,
>   The unmanner'd dust might soil his star ;
>   Besides, he hated †*bleeding*."

The last word has a double 'reference—(a) to the bloody heart on the arms, (b) to its wearer's penurious habits. The Douglas arms originally consisted of a shield, *argent*, with a chief, azure, bearing three white stars. After the death of the " Good Sir James " the " bloody heart " was

---

* Mullet is the heraldic term for a star.

† Italics Burns's.

added to commemorate the mission he undertook with a view to carrying the heart of the Bruce to the Holy Land—a mission which, as every one knows, he did not live to fulfil.

William, Duke of Queensberry, succeeded to that title in 1778, and just two years before that, William, the last Earl of Nithsdale, had died. The latter's arms consisted of a double-headed eagle, bearing on its breast a shield with the St. Andrew's Cross thereon. Does this explain the lines ?—

> " Drumlanrig's towers hae tint the powers
>   That kept the lands in awe, man ;
>   The eagle's dead, and in his stead
>   We've gotten a hoody craw, man."

It is true that Burns could not have known the Earl. but as the Earl was a Maxwell, a family which, in the person of its " veteran chief," the Bard admired, it is at least possible that he is alluded to here.

The last reference is rather different. It occurs in the " Election Ballad " :—

> " The Murray, on the auld grey yaud
>   Wi' winged spurs did ride."

Murray of Broughton had eloped with a lady of the name of Johnston, and this is the Poet's pleasant way of alluding to the circumstance. The winged spur was the crest of the family, and there is a tradition in the family that its use was due to the fact that it was a Johnston who warned Bruce (while he was still at the Court of the King of England) of Edward's resentment, by sending him a pair of spurs to which grouse feathers were attached, a hint which was not lost on the hero. At any rate, the flying spur is the crest of the Johnstons to this day, while for their arms they use the saltier and chief of the Bruces with different colours. The home of the Johnstons was Annandale, and probably in no district in all Scotland is the emblem of the leading family to be seen so frequently as the " winged spur " is to be seen there.

One of the ministers mentioned in the Election Ballads

was Muirhead of Urr, who claimed to be chief of the clan Muirhead, and who is said to have been given to boasting of his " lang pedigree." He was not content to sit still under the attacks of the Bard, and in a little brochure published in Edinburgh he gave Burns a stinging reply. It took the form of a quotation from *Martial's Epigrams*, followed by a free translation, and of its smartness there can be no doubt. Burns replied to the minister about a year later in his " Buy Braw Troggin " :—

> " Here's armorial bearings,
> Frae the Manse o' Urr ;
> The crest, an auld crab-apple,
> Rotten at the core."

(The Muirhead arms consisted of three acorns.)

The word "bearings," in an armorial sense, is found in the 1790 Election Ballads, where the Poet summonses to the Whig side " the muffled murtherer of Charles," who—

> " The Magna Charta flag unfurls,
> All deadly gules it's bearing,"

which—as *gules* is the heraldic term for red—gives the " Red Flag " of the revolutionary a greater antiquity than is usually claimed for it.

In the *Edinburgh Journal* the first lines of the " Epitaph on 'Ferguson " are given thus :—

> " No pageant bearings here, nor pompous lay,
> ' No storied urn or animated bust.' "

In the poems of Burns we have quite a number of references to national emblems. Naturally we would expect the thistle to lead the way, but it is interesting. to note that whereas he mentions that emblem four times he mentions the rose forty-three. Indeed, judging from his verses, the rose appears to have been his favourite flower. In its capacity as the floral symbol of England, however. the rose does not appear so very often, the most striking line being that in " The Banks of Devon " ·—

> " And England, triumphant, display her proud rose,"

The white rose was also the badge of the Jacobites, and therefore pleasing to the Poet :—

> " And here's the flower that I lo'e best,
> The rose that's like the snaw."

As the symbol of Scotland the thistle appears three times —

> " The rough burr-thistle spreading wide
> Amang the bearded bear,
> I turn'd the weeder clips aside,
> An' spared the symbol dear."

Again he paints

> " Scotland greetin' owre her thrissle " ;

while, in the third instance, he joins the emblems of the two countries —

> " Our thrissles flourish'd fresh and fair,
> And bonie bloom'd our roses ;
> But Whigs cam' like a frost in June,
> An' wither'd a' our posies."

The only other floral symbol he mentions is the Lily of France, the *Fleur-de-lis* :—

> " Let Bourbon exult in his gay gilded lilies."

In " Caledonia " we meet with quite a number of national emblems, although not all of them are entitled to be called heraldic.   Here we have the Roman eagle, the Norse boar, the Danish raven, as well as the Anglian and Caledonian lions.   The latter are still to be seen in the Royal Arms of Britain.

> " The black-headed eagle, as keen as a beagle,"

the Austrian successor of the eagle of Imperial Rome has also a line in the verses of the Poet.

Every one knows that of late years there has been some dispute as to whether the " Lion Rampant " is a Royal or National flag.   In the summer of 1919 a newspaper correspondence of more than usual interest went on regarding this subject in the columns of the *Glasgow Herald.*   Scottish literature was laid under contribution on both sides, and poets, from Barbour and Blind Harry to Ayton, and from Dunbar and Lindsay to Allan Ramsay and Walter Scott, were freely quoted. But it was rather strange, and perhaps saddening, that not one single quotation was made from the works of the National Bard, although several references to the flag might have been found there. Two references might, if they stood alone, be construed in favour of the " National " position, as when, in " Caledonia," he refers to her as—

" A lambkin in peace, but a lion in war,"

and his first letter to the Earl of Buchan, in which he refers to those places " where Caledonia, rejoicing, saw her bloody lion borne, through broken ranks, to victory and fame." Neither quotation can be called conclusive.

On the other side, we have the lines of the " Address to Edinburgh." When referring to Scotland's kings he writes :—

" Wild beats my heart to trace your steps,
Whose ancestors, in days of yore,
Thro' hostile ranks, and ruin'd gaps,
Old Scotia's bloody lion bore."

And in a letter to Robert Muir from Stirling he delivers his soul thus : " Two hours ago I said a fervent prayer for old Caledonia over the hole in a blue whinstone where Robert de Bruce fixed his Royal Standard on the banks of Bannockburn " These quotations seem to put Burns's view beyond dispute. Nor is that opinion to be wondered at, seeing that he had some acquaintance with the science of heraldry, for all heraldic writers, ancient and modern, Scottish, English, and continental, agree in this, that the lion rampant of red on gold, surrounded by the double tressure flory counter-flory, was the flag of the King of Scots.

It does appear strange, however, that he nowhere mentions specifically the Scottish national flag, the St. Andrew's saltier of white and blue, a fact which is all the more strange when we remember that part of the arms of the royal burgh of Ayr was this very flag. It is possible that the placing of the crook and horn *in saltier* on his arms was suggested by the St. Andrew's cross, but of this there is no evidence. Dr Wallace, in his edition of Chambers's *Life and Works of Robert Burns*, thinks the words in "The Battle of Sherramuir,"

> "And covenant true-blues, man,"

were suggested by the blue banner of the Covenanters. That flag was, of course, simply the National Ensign. Further, the Bard does not appear to have made any mention of the British flag, the first Union Jack, nor, though he mentions many a " burgh toon," and though he was made a freeman of quite a number of them, there is not a single word in his works suggestive of the arms they used. An exception might be made in the case of Dumfries, whose arms show the archangel Michael trampling upon the serpent. In the "Address to the Deil" Michael is introduced, but Burns had not been near Dumfries when that poem was written. Considering that coats-of-arms were honours, and that they usually recalled some heroic deed, we might have expected some reference to those borne by his patrons, the Earl of Glencairn, Lord Daer, and Graham of Fintry, but no such references are to be found. Party colours came in for passing notice :—

> " As Queensberry buff and blue unfurled."

> " Its gude to support Caledonia's cause,
>   And bide by the buff and the blue.'

Burns's attitude towards titles is well known.

> For " marquis, duke, an' a' that "

he had no high regard ; yet he was not a bigot on the matter of titles, for he was prepared to give one to the Scottish patriot :—

> " A title Dempster merits it."

Only one order of knighthood is specifically mentioned, that is the Order of the Garter :—

> " A garter gae to Willie Pitt."

The ribbon of this order is blue, and this probably accounts for the words " Royal Blue " in the Epistle to W. Chalmers :—

" The feeling heart's the royal blue."

All the British orders of Burns's day had as their insignia, star, ribbon, badge and chain, and so the remarks about the " ribbon, star, and a' that " suit any of them. It seems, indeed, likely that Burns deliberately chose to make his remarks on this matter general, for in the first draft of " A man's a man for a' that " one of the lines runs—

" His garters, stars, and a' that."

In the 18th century there were only four British Orders —Thistle, Garter, St. Patrick, and Bath, the ribbons of which were green, blue, sky blue, and red.

Although we have spoken of the " arms " of Burns in this paper, it should be stated that legally Burns had no arms. The King alone can give a grant of arms, and this he does in Scotland through the Court of the Lyon. Indeed, by assuming " arms " as he did, the Bard rendered himself liable to sundry pains and penalties, for as early as 1592 the Scottish Parliament passed an Act declaring that, so far as those who have not the right to do so are concerned, " nane of thame presume or tak' upon hand to bear or use ony armes in tyme coming," under pain of fine or imprisonment, together with the confiscation of all articles upon which the assumed arms have been placed. This is still the law in Scotland, and although its aid is not always invoked, it can be put into use at any time. Quite recently the Treasury, acting on the advice of the Lord Advocate, authorised the prosecution of the magistrates of a Scottish Royal Burgh—well known to all admirers of the Bard—who were using arms which had not been officially recorded. The Lyon King is empowered—and indeed required—to grant arms to all virtuous and well-deserving citizens who may apply for the same. None of Burns's sons took up their father's arms officially, although both Col. William Nicol Burns and Col. James Glencairn

Burns had enlarged gravings of them put on several relics.
The earliest use of them was on the title page of Currie's
edition of Burns, 1800, where, enclosed in an oval border,
they rest upon two branches, one of oak and the other of
laurel. A somewhat similar example occurs in Allan
Cunningham's edition of the Poet's works under the sil-
houette portrait of the Bard.

Fully forty years after Burns's death his arms found
a place on the register in the Lyon Office, when Dr James
Burnes, the eldest son of a cousin of the Poet, a Knight of
the Order of Hanover and a distinguished East India
servant, applied for and received a grant of armorial bearings.
These arms were granted to Dr Burnes and to the " lawful
descendants of his paternal grandfather," and in the base
of the shield was placed what was termed by the Lyon Clerk
" the well-known device of the Poet Burns." The crest
was " Issuant from an eastern crown, an oak shivered
renewing its foliage," and there were two mottoes—
Revirescimus and *Ruinam salutarunt pro rege.* The
first motto, it will be noticed (we are reviving), is an allusion
to the crest. In 1841 Dr Burnes's two brothers, Sir Alexander and Charles, both soldiers (the one a Lieut.-
Colonel and the other a Lieutenant), fell in the disastrous
massacre of the British at Cabul, and ten years later the
Doctor received a new grant of arms, which may be quoted
in full : Arms.—*Ermine,* on a bend azure, an escutcheon,
or, charged with a holly-bush surmounted by a crook and
bugle horn saltier-wise, all proper, being the device of the
Poet Burns ; and on a chief, *gules,* the white horse of Hanover
between two eastern crowns, in allusion to the Guelphic
order conferred on James Burnes, K.H., by King William
IV., and to the distinguished services of him and his brothers
in India. Crests.—On the dexter side, one of augmentation,
in allusion to the devotion to their country of Lieut.-Colonel
Sir Alexander Burnes, C.B., and Lieut. Charles Burnes,
out of a mural crown per pale *vert* and *gules,* the rim inscribed
CABOOL in letters *argent,* a demi-eagle displayed transfixed
by a javelin in bend sinister, *proper.* On the sinister side,

that previously borne, viz., Issuant from an eastern crown, *or*, an oak tree sheered renewing its foliage, proper. Motto —*ob patriam vulnera passi* (suffering for one's native land).

In 1895 Kenneth Glencairn Burns, the great-grandson and direct descendant of Gilbert Burns, the brother of the Poet, matriculated arms. *Ermine,* on a bend *azure,* an escutcheon, *or*, charged in base with a holly-bush in chief, with a shepherd's pipe surmounted by a crook in saltier, all proper. Crest on a wreath *azure,* and *argent* an oak tree shivered renewing its foliage, proper. Mantling, *azure* and *argent.* Motto—*ob patriam vulnera passi.*

It will be observed that in both coats the colour of the Poet's shield has been changed from *azure* to *or* (from blue to gold). In the engraving in Currie's edition the field is correctly represented by horizontal lines as blue.

In conclusion, it may be stated that no person or club is entitled to use the arms of the Bard (except, of course, those who have matriculated arms as above). Any Burns Club inscribing its note-paper, for example, with the Poet's device, is liable to be called in question by the authorities. There is no objection, however, to the various parts—bush, horn, crook, &c.—being used for decorative purposes, or to the whole device being placed on any memorial to the Bard.

Rev. W. M'MILLAN, M.A., F.S.A. (Scot.),
Dunfermline.

MARIA RIDDELL'S LETTERS TO DR JAMES CURRIE, 1796-1805.

PART I.

On Wednesday, 24th July, 1918, there was offered at auction in the galleries of Messrs Sotheby, Wilkinson & Hodge, 34-35 New Bond Street, London, " an interesting collection of autograph letters and documents by, and relating to, Robert Burns." The printed catalogue of the sale did not tell to whom the collection belonged ; but, as most of the documents were addressed to Dr James Currie of Liverpool, probably it came from a descendant of Burns's biographer and editor.

One of the most valuable lots (No. 929) in the collection was " A series of thirty-six autograph letters signed, from Mrs Maria Riddell." That lot was purchased by Mr Charles R. Cowie of Glasgow, and, as none of the letters appears ever to have been printed, he has kindly consented to the publication here of those portions of them which refer to Burns. Unfortunately, however, these letters—a nearly complete sequence—are only one side of the correspondence. Currie's letters to Mrs Riddell are not known now to exist ; not one of them is printed in the *Memoir of James Currie*, edited by his son and published in 1831—indeed, the lady herself appears not to be even mentioned in that work.

The portions of the letters now printed are extracted from the first eleven of the series : No. I. is dated " Halleaths, by Lockerby, 15th October, 1796," and No. XI., " Bloxworth, 28th September, 1797." These eleven letters fill no fewer than 57 quarto pages, in Mrs Riddell's neat script. They are full of interest, for the writer was intimately acquainted with very many prominent persons of her time, and many of these are named in the letters. They exhibit Mrs Riddell as desirous that Currie should write the " Life " of Burns and edit his writings ; and, after Currie had decided to take up the work, as assisting him in several ways.

Attention may be directed to her references to the letters she was receiving from " Clarinda," and to her own " sketch," apparently the tribute to Burns which had been printed in the *Dumfries Journal* shortly after the death of the Poet—to Gilbert Burns, who " reminded me of our Bard in voice and even in the sentiments it conveyed, so much so that his converse was, at the juncture I happened to partake of it, absolutely painful to me " ; and " does he not bear quite an uncomfortable resemblance to our Bard, particularly in his manner of speaking ?—and, finally, to her opinion of Nasmyth's earliest bust-portrait of the Poet as " an excellent resemblance."

J. C. E.

Correspondence between Maria Riddell and
Dr Currie.

No. I.

Halleaths, by Lockerby, N.B.,
15th Oct., 1796.

To have indulged the wish (that has, however, frequently
sprung up on former occasions) of addressing Dr Currie, and pro-
curing myself the pleasure of his acquaintance, might have been
presumptuous ; to neglect the opening his flattering compliment
in desiring Mr Syme to transmit to me the elegant stanzas on the
death of Burns has now afforded me, were surely ingratitude.
Permit me, then, Sir, to return you my warmest acknowledgments
for the honour you have done me by presenting me with a copy of
Mr Roscoe's animated tribute to the memory of our late ever-to-be-
regretted Bard, a favour to which I could have no title, except indeed
that of my long correspondence and intimacy with the object of,
I am well assured, our mutual regret.   You have had the con-
descension to desire my opinion of the poem.   I cannot venture
to give a more particular one than by saying I admire it equally
for the elegant pathos with which it is so frequently replete as for
the indignant energy that glows in the kindred bosom of Burns's
accomplished panegyrist, where he touches on his unfortunate
circumstances in the ill-adapted station he was doomed to fill throughout life, and the scanty tribute paid to his talents by those even
who aspired to the honor of being thought Burns's Patrons and
Protectors.   Farther than this I dare not venture on a critique ;
I can easily perceive some few passages may admit of improvement—
without actually requiring it ; and it would be a daring hand that
offered to superadd one grace where Mr Roscoe has assembled so
many ; if there is to be additional ones, they can only be looked
for from himself.   Dr Currie, unless my friend Syme flattered me,
has in a recent letter to him expressed an intention of giving me
the opportunity of being personally known where I have been so
earnestly desirous of that gratification ever since I had first the
pleasure of an acquaintance with several of Dr Currie's literary
productions.   I propose travelling to the South country in the course
of the ensuing week, and if I can be allowed to entertain a hope of
passing one evening in his society, the trifling circuit of thirty or
forty miles shall be no obstacle to my taking Liverpool in my road
to the Capital.   I have yet time to receive a line from Dr Currie,
should I be so fortunate as to be favoured with one, and if I can

flatter myself with the expectation of meeting with him, it will decide me on bending my steps farther west than I shall otherwise do. I shall hope, too, in that case, that chance or opportunity will indulge me so far as to permit my conveying to Mr Roscoe my sentiments upon his having engaged his Muse in so eloquent yet delicate a monody on a friend I so ardently loved and esteemed. I have promised Syme to bear his commands to you should I have the pleasure of assuring you, in person, how truly—I am, Sir, Yours with respect and gratitude,

MARIA RIDDELL.

No. II.

4 Baker Street, Portman Square,
London, 23rd Nov., 1796.

I fear, my dear Sir, that if you have condescended to think of me at all, it has been to reproach me with inattention in not having availed myself earlier of the pleasure you offered to yield me by a correspondence which, I am well assured, will be productive of so much gratification to me. I did not conclude my travels so soon as I expected ; part of the Saturday and Monday which succeeded those very agreeable days I passed at Liverpool I devoted to the society of Dr Darwin. . . . I can write you nothing of the news of London, as I have not " been in London " yet—that is to say, I have seen none but my own family, and have not once set my foot beyond my threshold. Capt. Riddell is ordered abroad, and my head is yet quite distracted with the investigations requisite for me to make into the labyrinth of affairs I must now again assume the management of during his absence, and I assure you this *quart d'heure* I steal to enquire after you is the first in which I have been able to abstract myself from " the dull realities of life " with which I have been too long occupied. However, I hope soon to be more comfortable, and to hear from you that my friends in Liverpool are all as I wish them, if that is possible. I wrote fully to Syme upon our arrangements—plans, rather—for Burns's publications ; have not yet received an answer, but conclude he has corresponded with you, or you with him, on the interesting subject. I must now conclude. Receive, then, my best wishes and regards, and assure Mrs Currie of them, whose attentions and goodness to me during my *sejour* in Liverpool—and your own—I can never forget. . . . If Mr R. comes soon to London you can return me the MSS. I left with you by him. Farewell, my dear Sir, and continue to believe me, with faithful regard—Your truly obliged, &c.,

· MARIA RIDDELL.

No. III.

London, 9th Dec., 1796.

I am happy to find, my dear Sir, you have recovered your " tranquillity and leisure," since they have procured me the pleasure of hearing from you. . . . Dr Darwin questioned me very much about the late William Smellie, the Author of the *Philosophy of Natural History*, with whom he knew I had been in habits of intimacy and correspondence. He seemed disposed to do justice to Smellie's genius, but expressed himself very indignantly upon that author's attempt at defeating his favourite system of sexualism in the vegetable world. . . . What do you mean by desiring *me* to correct *any* thing of Burns's ? 'Tis asking me " to paint the lily and add a perfume to the violet." I have heard nothing from Syme or Maxwell yet. I doubt you misunderstand each other somehow, or the rest of the Bard's MSS. had been remitted to you ere this time. I had a most inimitable letter from " Clarinda " lately. If you and Mr Roscoe *are* B.'s biographers, I must obtain permission to entrust some of those letters to you. They contain treasures relative to *him*. She wrote to me last by Dr Moyes, who had desired an introduction ; but I find it is not easy for a blind philosopher, his inclination be what it will, to make rendezvous. He called on me, I was absent ; he wrote, or rather his secretary did, and never signified his place of abode. I could not discover it, and I fear he is now gone to Bath as he proposed, and no interview has taken place. . . .—Believe me, much and truly yours,

MARIA RIDDELL.

No. IV.

13 Bridge Street, Westminster,
12th Jan., 1797.

I still think of poor old Smellie with regret ; never did an outside so rough and manners so unpolished cover a warmer and more excellent heart Clarinda is still a faithful correspondent, and her letters full of the most inestimable anecdote for Burns's biographers. I must and will demand permission to communicate to you, when required. Syme has written me a volume of acknowledgments for the effect of my supposed influence with you and your friend. The *dimidium animæ* . . . relative to the undertaking of his publication, &c. By what he writes me I conclude the materials are *chez vous* ere this, and there is great joy in Israel at the prospect of their passing such a crucible. Let me know if you have them yet. . . .

Adieu ! What shall I call you in return for the happy—compound—epithets you have affixed to my designation ? Be what you will, and let me remain your truly obliged and affectionate,

MARIA RIDDELL.

No. V.

Duke Street, St. James's 18,
19th Jan., 1797.

I have just sent to Cadell and Davies to desire an interview and get some of the proposals. How can you—" O you of little faith "—suppose I would " traverse " any arrangement of yours ? Depend, my good friend, on my discretion with regard to Creech. I wish zealously to promote, and never could voluntarily traverse, what you are desirous should be effected, either in the object, the means, agents or measures. Cadell published a little volume of mine a few years ago, but I dare say a trifle so unimportant will scarcely recall me to his memory. Perhaps it is as well we should recommence our acquaintance on a fresh score. I can settle with him what to do with my growing list of subscribers' names. I read the passages relative to her last night to the Duchess of Gordon. She laughed, and was flattered at them ; your eulogium on her benevolence and affability, and your panegyric on her handsome leg and ankle delighted her excessively. She says her leg is as good and well-proportioned, she believes, as when you followed her across the bridge at Edinburgh, and I can answer for the other attributes being equally unimpaired. In addition to hers, the Marquisses of Abercorn and Lorne, Lord Westmorland, Lord Charles Bentinck, Lord John Campbell, Duchesses of Hamilton, Keppel, Craven, the Margraime of Anspach's son, Col. Erskine, Lewis and his father, and a few more names of less note, make up my present list. It is trifling hitherto, but I will spare nothing to increase its magnitude. . . . I wrote yesterday to Clarinda to continue her communications. I conceived it cruel to trespass on her sensibility unless they were likely to be of service to you. I send with this a packet containing her letters. Most of them contain some interesting passages relative to our Poet, those that did not I have destroyed. I declare I think after all, the packet will be scarcely worth its postage, to you even, and there was no such thing as reasonably desiring either peer or commoner to frank so many at a time. This has absolutely been the discreet cause of my withholding them so long from you. I have just number'd them in order for your perusal, and as you asked me once before, have enclosed the copies of some of my letters to Clarinda relative to Burns's death. I send them to you just as she got them copied ; if I had once looked over them I am sure I should have put them into the fire. Clarinda's are, I perceive, too enthusiastic to be perused when one is *de sang froid*, and mine were written under the immediate and powerful impression of circumstances and scenes that affected me extremely, most of them written with great dispatch, much feeling, and little reflection, and at the time of poor B—'s death. Clarinda was, from her talents, misfortunes, and their mutual attachment, a very interesting object to all B—'s friends. Now pray do not display all this nonsensical correspondence, but when you have made what use you can of it, lay it aside to send me back again ; I entrust it to you on that condition only. I have not time to take extracts, so rely on your fidelity in this respect. . . . Adieu ! Believe me, faithfully yours,

MARIA RIDDELL.

[A letter from Mrs Riddell to Dr Currie, written on 6th January, 1797, is missing from the series. It is referred to in No. VI.]

———

No. VI.

Pluvoise, septidi 2 de decade,
London.

. . . . My letter of the 6th ult., which must have passed yours upon the road, will have explained all this business, and I hope I shall now be received into your good grace and favor again, and that the mild beams of your approbation will once more shine upon your faithful and devoted disciple. I answered you fully in all particulars relative to Col. Fullarton, so have nothing new to add on the subject of Burns's affairs. . . .—*Al Dis della Liberta.*

MARIA RIDDELL.

———

No. VII.

London, 17th Feb., 1797.

It was yesterday only that I became apprized of Mr Roscoe's arrival, and the pleasure and gratification I experienced in receiving him were not a little enhanced by his presenting me with your most welcome packet. As I know Syme to be a careless and a very unsuspicious character, I am the less surprized by what you relate to me relative to the unguarded manner in which he suffered the Bard's papers to be transmitted to you. Our friend Syme finds his own occupations press so heavy on him that I dare say he actually had little, if any, time to dedicate to the arrangement of Burns's papers. He has a good head, united to an excellent heart, but I know that in matters of business he wants method ; he is always in a labyrinth of papers and accounts, and, somewhat like the cuttlefish, he obscures himself altogether in a mist of his own creating. I have nothing to offer, farther than what I have dwelt amply upon on former occasions, relative to your assuming the task of bio- graphising Burns. You must, of course, judge for yourself. I can only say I am certain it can be transferred to no better hands than yours, and I trust you will not at all events resign the *Critique* you meditated to any other person. . . . I shall attend to your counsels relative to such of the Bard's MSS. as I am possessed of. As for the lines to Clarinda, unless anecdotes were circulated with them calculated to attach the sentiments to himself, I own I do not see why they can be thought to affix more censurability upon Burns, than the Epistle of Elouise to Abelard did upon Pope. Pray lay those sketches of mine upon the shelf ; something better may be made of them if they contain materials worth working upon, but in the present state you have them with " all their imperfections on their head," some of which are very glaring indeed. What have you done with the copy of B—'s *Poems* I lent you to refer to ? If you know of no private opportunity likely to occur shortly, I shall request you to forward them to me by the ordinary channel ; the two volumes are a necessary *vade mecum* with me. Clarinda's letters, I tell you candidly, I will entrust to no biographer of Burns except yourself, nor do I esteem my yielding the perusal to you justifiable on any other score. I do not know Mr Alison even by name, but Burns's biographer must be a liberal and even an inde- pendant man. These qualifications are not frequent among the Scots Clergy. . . . Believe me, your sincere and faithful

MARIA RIDDELL.

No. VIII.

13 Bridge Street, Westminster,
22nd April, 1797.

Dr Moore has been extremely attentive to me. We talk together of men and books, the living and the dead, very fre- quently of poor Burns, of Roscoe, and, shall I say, not less frequently of Dr Currie ? Why should I say it, for he needs not the assurance of a constant recollection from every one who has once had the satisfaction of knowing him. Moore has just presented me with a copy of his *Edward*, which I never met with before. I do not recognize the author of *Zeluco* in this last production. He raves about Burns, and so does Sheridan. I believe they both sought my acquaintance for no other purpose than to talk of him, and what a society is Sheridan's ! . . . Do you know you appear to us in town to be coquetting in this business of Burns's, and we rail at you a little for it. Roscoe will tell you that. Sheridan and Dr

Moore are both clearly of opinion that this task is calculated for you, and you for it ; that you lose time by all this irresolution ; now the papers are in your possession you cannot retract ; and that your talents do not tally more perfectly with the brilliancy of the undertaking than your character renders the selection completely eligible. Nothing but. enthusiasm prevails now for Burns's writings and memory ; I see little danger of its failing to extend to his biographer, and if it was a service of danger, your heart and head are equally fitted for the support of such an one. No man residing in Scotland should venture on it, that we admit. Moore is just engaged in somewhat of a similar employment with Smollett's writings. I long to hear you are embarked—decidedly and intrepidly embarked. By the way, convey to me, I pray you, the two volumes I left with you of the poor Bard's works ; there remains, too, a MS. or two yet unreturned ; let it be soon, as I leave town next month. . . . Shall I not hear from you soon ?—*Vale—valete.*

MARIA RIDDELL.

This delightful creature has given this small space, my Dear Dr, to tell you that your Graham is well at Portsmouth with his crew at large, with whom he has influence enough to keep clear of this awful mutiny. My compliments to Roscoe and his Rib.—Adieu.

J. MOORE.

No. IX.

[Undated ; but franked " Wimborne,
14th June, 1797. H. Bankes."]

I have had a letter from Syme since I wrote to you last. My earnest solicitations, " my petitionary vehemence," while their success was yet dubious, may satisfy you, more than anything I could now say, of the pleasure your resolution respecting the undertaking of Burns's publication must afford me ; the gratitude and approbation of your fellow citizens, and the spirit of Burns hovering over you, will be a reward, or tribute, worthy such a mind as yours. Pray do not depend too much on Syme's coming to Liverpool ; with all the *bon cœur* and *bonne volonté* in the world, you know him to be " a little mutabilities and variations," as Capt. Fluellen says, and his time is not always his own. I wish you could see G. Burns ; he reminded me of our Bard in voice, and even in the sentiments it conveyed, so much so that his converse was, at the juncture I happened to partake of it, absolutely painful to me. It is very strange, but this said " Song of the Dying " I never even heard of ; I should like to see it. However, I " *will* be quiet, and have patience, and desire my friends to be quiet and

patient and reasonable." Will this satisfy you ? One more such
monition, and 1 " sit like my grandsire cut in alabaster " till you
condescend once more to authorise my being accessible to a little
of that eager avidity for the effusions of Genius or the acquirements
of Science which few are better calculated to encourage and gratify
with me than yourself. . . . Yours very faithfully,

MARIA RIDDELL.

No. X.

Kingston Hall, Wimborne
14th June, 1797.

1 have scrawled out the verses I promised you, my dear Dr,
and I fear, almost illegibly. I have enclosed at the same time a
poem on Burns which was written by a lady in Scotland. You
must return it to me (whether you write by the same opportunity,
and at that time, or not) in two or three days, as it is not my own,
and I promised sacredly to return it to the person who entrusted
me with it, very shortly. It is by stealth I lend it to you. I like
it ; if you think well of it perhaps you will cause it to be copied,
and have it inserted with Roscoe's (if any other tribute will not
appear as superfluous homage after his to departed Genius) at the
beginning of *Burns's Poems*, as these kind of recommendatory poems
often are. This is *ad libitum*, but you will at all rates return it to
me.—*Addio*. Yours (in haste),

MARIA R.

No. XI.

Bloxworth 28th Sept., 1797.

I almost feared, my dear Dr, 1 should never hear from you
again. You can not conceive what a blank your silence creates
in my narrow circle—for it is become so now — of intellectual
pleasures. I have just had a volume likewise from Syme. So
you have had Gilbert Burns with you ! Does he not bear quite an
uncomfortable resemblance to our Bard, particularly in his manner
of speaking ? Did Smyth shew you my last letter to him ? or at
least read you a paragraph that I requested him to communicate
to you relative to some very capital poetry of the Bard's inserted
—not in any edition of his own works—but in Johnson's *Scots Musical
Miscellany* [*Museum*], as well as some in a Selection of Scottish
Songs by Pleyel ? If you have had these pointed out to you it is
very well ; if not, return me a line by the next post and I will copy
and transmit them all to you without loss of time, as Burns marked

all his own in my Copies of those works himself, and there are several without his name prefixed to them at all. Now, be you in ever so indolent a mood, persuade yourself to let me know about this business, as by neglecting this acquisition you not only render your Collection of the Songs incomplete, but lose some that I think may be esteemed among his very best. I conclude you have had the portrait by Nasmyth brought up to Liverpool, which is an excellent resemblance, as it were doing the print injustice to take it from the former engraving. I suppose your artist will be the same who executed the frontispiece of Lorenzo de Medici. For this same subscription I am less a *partée* to be of use, even in the offering of advice, than if I happened to be in the Metropolis. I shall mention to Syme my ideas for the arrangement of the subscription in Scotland ; it must be launched out from Edinburgh in many other channels. I should conceive in all the principal towns, as Glasgow [*sic*], Aberdeen, &c., persons should be appointed to receive subscriptions. The same in England. In London, I should think Moore or any literary person could point out a fashionable and perhaps an honest and liberal bookseller. Cadell or Edwards or some of these people would receive them. I could have spoken to Edwards had I been in town, but Roscoe or Moore must know this part of the business better than myself. Do you propose confining the reception of subscriptions to London ? I should think at Bath, Derby, York, Exeter, and these places, something not inconsiderable might be made. You may depend (at least if I know anything of myself) on my activity and of the full exertion of all my influence as far as it extends or can be extended. In this place—that is a solitary little *ferme ornée* of my youngest Sister's—I can do nothing, and from hence I go in a few days to Christchurch, in Hampshire, a retired sea-bathing quarter, with my Daughter and two of my Nieces, and there I banish myself for five weeks. In fine, I shall live amongst waves and woods till Xmas, after which I go to London, where I will positively lay all and every one of my Vassals under contribution, or in plain English and modester terms, will engage all my friends (who will suffer me to influence them) into setting down their names to this subscription. There is not a soul in London at present, or will be till near the Winter Birthday, so nothing could be effected that way even if I were in town. What then you have to do with regard to setting me in train is to let me know who is appointed to receive Subscriptions in London, and I can get a parcel of proposals to dispose of more readily from thence, or send me a few in separate covers by two or three different day's posts, if you think it necessary. In the meantime I keep this one for myself. My friend the Duchess of Gordon will assist me powerfully, I know, in London, and perhaps we have still some interest even in the North. Do not therefore delay, my good friend, to acquaint me whether the proposals are handed about in Edinburgh yet, and where you arrange that the Subscribers shall set down their names, &c., both there and in London (it cannot be in a private house, of course), and the instant I am *au fait* in these necessary particulars I shall apply to my friends, which I can do by letter, and set down their names for you, even before I go myself to the great city.   I have great hopes that I can be of use to the cause there, and will neglect nothing to benefit it, and partake with Burns's generous benefactors in Liverpool the trouble and the honor of patronising his surviving family. . . .   As to my assisting you in the Biography, I have more zeal, I doubt, than capacity.   You know the nature of " Clarinda's " letters ; I do not know if she could not afford you some assistance.   I will look over her letters to me again.   I left them at Kingston Hall. Yet, after all, they are of so private a nature I am not clear you could make anything of them for your purpose.   I did not mention the little sketch you got from me because I thought it probable you would suffer it to remain in Oblivion, but since you declare so " positively " you will keep it, I must be suffered to interfere as to the use you may chuse to put it to.   I gave it to you in a state of incorrectness for which I feel no toleration (on looking over the duplicate) to my own complaisance in letting you have it, but I shall in future mistrust my faculties of putting a negative on anything you desire.   If you only propose making use of some passages and interweaving them in your own language, you shall have them all to dissect and put together again your own way, but if you mean to put them in *my* terms, you must—mind I swear by all my Gods apprize me of the plan and let me send them to you in a less imperfect form.   I hope to be at least qualified to correct Scotticisms after a twelvemonth's residence south of the Tweed.   Now, remember, I am inflexible on this point. . . .   I was happy to hear from Syme a good account of Mrs C. and your little " Olive branches."   I bid you farewel with regret.—Ever faithfully yours,

MARIA R—

FRANCIS GROSE, Esq., F.R.S., A.S.

THE two portraits of Capt. Grose here reproduced are taken from *The Olio*—a collection of Essays, Anecdotes, Parodies, Bon Mots, Epigrams, Epistles, &c

FRANCIS GROSE. Esq. F.R.S. & A.S.

London, 1796. This Medley by the " Chield amang ye takin' notes " was carefully explored in order to see if it contained any direct reference to Burns. Perusal failed to produce anything nearer the subject sought for than " A dialogue between a traveller from London and a waiter at a Scotch Inn," which took place about 20 miles from Dumfries. The dialogue was intended to bring out the droll specimen of Scotch idiom.

Though success was denied the search for any passages that might have any connection with Burns, *The Olio* is interesting to the Burns student as it brings out in the figure and character of Grose points that had been com mented on by Burns. One of the portraits, page 96, is a caricature by the Author himself, who, we are told by Burns, was " unco slight o' caulk and keel." This sketch represents Burns's " fine, fat, fodgel wight " as a paymaster in the Surry Regiment ; which post did not pay Grose, as his methods of cash-keeping were confined to no books ; and the money transactions, we are told, were conducted by the media of two trousers pockets !—a method of book-keeping that, even with a less generous soul, would have proved unremunerative   To the two portraits we find descriptions, one by Mr Davis, of Wandsworth, and the other by Grose himself. In the former, Grose's picture is thus portrayed :—

> " Grose to my pen a theme supplies,
> With life and laughter in his eyes,
> Oh ! how I can survey with pleasure
> His breast and shoulders' ample measure ;
> His dimpled chin, his rosy cheek,
> His skin from inward lining sleek.
> When to my house he deigns to pass
> Through miry ways to take a glass.
> How gladly ent'ring in I see
> His belly's vast rotundity !
> For though so fat, he beats the leaner
> In ease and bodily demeanour ;
> And in that mass of flesh so droll
> Resides a social, gen'rous soul.
> Humble—and modest to excess,
> Nor conscious of his worthiness,
> He's yet too proud to worship State
> And haunt with Courtly bend the great
> He draws not for an idle word,
> Like modern duellists, his sword,
> But shows upon a gross affront
> The valour of a Bellamont."

The valour of a Bellamont confirms Burns's character as one that " wad rather fa'n than fled." The lines of the picture leave us in no doubt as to Burns's accuracy about the unwieldy proportions of his " kind and funny friend." Grose's own description of himself tells us that the vast rotundity was both fore and aft, when he says (page 97) :—

> " How will the gaping rabble stare,
> At military *pet-en-l'air* !
> Without his joke not one will pass
> My huge rotundity of a—e ;
> What food for each sarcastic snubber
> This load of adventitious blubber !"

The confirmations of rotundity may excuse Burns's reference to Grose in his epigram, when Satan, after viewing Grose a-dying, exclaims :—

> . . . . " By G—d,
> I'll want him ere take such a damnable load."

Though *The Olio* corroborates Burns's jesting remarks about Grose, it does not bear out Grose in the character of Antiquary that Burns paints him in, as a collector of useless articles of vertù, such as " The coins of Satan's coronation " and the " Fouth of auld nick-nackets " described in the late Capt. Grose's *Peregrination Through Sco.land*. From *The Olio* we learn that Grose shewed discretion in his collecting, and one feels forced to the conclusion that most of what Burns said about this adopter of the antiquarian trade was by way of good-natured if exaggerated jests, which would be encouraged by the social Grose.

Amongst the contributions to *The Olio* are three short essays on " The Sketch of a Modern Connoisseur," " Complaint of a wife at her husband's rage for Antiquities," " The Irrational Pursuits of Virtu." The *connoisseur* is held up to ridicule because of the means he adopts to become distinguished as an amateur and capital collector. He purchases at enormous prices, not the best pieces, but the scarcest of each master. The complaints of the wife is that her husband has, by his collections, surrounded her by everything that can remind one of mortality, and that he is an exhibitor to the Society of Antic-Queer-Ones.

The collector of irrational articles of vertu, Mr Jack Cockle, was from his infancy a lover of rarities. At school

E · P I S T L E *

ⱷ THT RIGHT HON. LORD ON——W,

ᴍ.Y LORD,

YOUR friend, in fad condition,
Implores your kind interpofition,
To ward off an impending evil,
The corps is going to the Devil ;

he would give half his week's allowance for a double wall-nut, a white mouse, or a taw of any uncommon size or colour—in short, everything uncommon, whether natural or artificial. As he grew up, his taste dilated. and monstrous births and anatomical preparations were added to the catalogue of his researches, which included a kitten with three eves and a pig with one ear. This singular collector got into trouble by his too strenuously investigating the person of a lady, who, report had it, was one of the remaining descendants of people with tails.

Grose holds each of these three collectors up to ridicule, and as some of their foibles are akin to those that Burns has charged Grose with, one is again forced to the conclusion that Burns's descriptions may have been largely chaff. And also that the incongruities that Grose related in social intercourse may have been taken by Burns as containing a substratum of truth that suited his poetic purpose.

A. J. CRAIG.

BURNS COTTAGE RELICS.

A Spurious Collection.

A T one of the galleries in one of the most famous streets in the world—at Agnew's, Bond Street, London, to be precise—there is now being publicly exhibited " The Burns Cottage Collection, comprising the furniture of the Cottage in which the poet, Robert Burns, was born on January 25, 1759." Thus reads the title-page of the printed catalogue. The wording of the title is not ingenuous, for it gives no indication of the period at which this collection was in the Cottage, though of course the furniture of the Cottage at any time between 1757, when it was built, and 1918 may quite correctly be termed a Burns Cottage collection." But the "foreword" to the catalogue supplies what the title lacks, for it states that certain outstanding articles in the collection " were acquired from the Poet's father, and as such were shown to visitors for many years by John Goudie," tenant of the Cottage, so that the collection claims to include a considerable portion of the furnishing of the Cottage at the time when Robert Burns was born. Believing that the sole interest —and it is very little—attaching to the collection now exhibiting in Bond Street is that of having belonged to one who ran the Cottage as a common public-house, I propose briefly to examine the claim made on its behalf and to show cause why it cannot be accepted. The exhibition, I note with regret, is " under the special patronage " of a Royal personage, who has visited the show, and it has been organised by the London Robert Burns Club, which has failed in its very obvious duty

The world-famous Cottage at Alloway—built by William Burnes himself on land that he had leased, to which in 1757 he brought home his bride, and in which in 1759 his eldest son was born—was the home of the Burnes family from 1757 till 1766. In the latter year William Burnes, with the assistance of his master, Provost William Fergusson of Doonholm, ventured on a small farm at Mount Oliphant, two miles distant from Alloway. But, though he had ceased to inhabit the " auld clay biggin," he remained lessee of the land and proprietor of the house. There is good reason—from documents still existing—to believe that both house and land were let by him to Joseph Norman, seedsman in Ayr, and that afterwards the house, having been put (1779) into " a good and tennable condition," was occupied by David and William Calbreth, wrights in Alloway. In 1781 William Burnes's land and house, being in the market, were purchased by the Incorporation of Shoemakers in Ayr at the price of £160 sterling.

The records of that Incorporation show that the quondam Burnes house was occupied—at a rental of £10 —by Matthew Dick, shoemaker in Ayr, from 1782 till 1801. Dick—the man who turned the Burns Cottage into a public-house—was succeeded in the tenancy by John Maitland, flesher in Ayr, who had " made offer to the trade of £25 10s of yearly rent for a 38 years' tack from Martinmas, 1801, of their houses and land presently possest by Matthew Dick." Maitland appears to have occupied the house for only two years—for what reason is unknown—and in 1803 he sub-let to John Goudie. From Martinmas, 1803, until his death in 1842 " Miller " Goudie, for so he was known, ran the Burns Cottage as a public-house : himself—as John Keats recorded on his visit to the place in 1818—" a mahogany-faced old jackass who knew Burns ; he drinks glasses, five for the quarter, and twelve for the hour." After Goudie's death the business at the Cottage was carried on by his widow until her death in 1843 ; after her death it was continued by their daughter (Mrs Hastings) and her husband until Martinmas, 1845, when the Cottage was let to Davidson Ritchie, who had offered a larger rental than David Hastings.

These are plain statements of fact, mostly from the

" Book pertaining to the Shoemakers' Trade of Ayr,"
which the writer was privileged to examine some years ago,
and they " downa be disputed." It is necessary that
they should be stated before considering the claim made
for the " Burns Cottage Collection."

After the death of Mrs Goudie the " whole household
furniture and other effects situated within Burns' Cottage
and other premises, lately possessed by Mr and Mrs Goudie,"
were sold by public roup on September 30, 1843 ; and two
years later (1845) the effects of the Hastings were disposed
of. Certain of the articles included in the Hastings sale
were purchased by, or for, Mr James Esdaile, of Manchester :
these articles form the " Burns Cottage Collection " which
is the subject of these notes. Some " personal effects and
relics " of the Poet were subsequently acquired by the
gentleman, and these eke out the show in Bond Street.
These " personal effects and relics " as listed in the printed
catalogue, by the way, seem a questionable lot, but they
do not concern us at present.

That Esdaile was none too happy in the possession
of his treasures may be gathered from the fact that they
were exhibited in public on several occasions, but without
finding a purchaser. And so the owner took to offering
them privately ; in 1866 to James M'Kie, the Burns collector and publisher at Kilmarnock, the price being £100 ;
and in 1870 to the Trustees of the Burns Monument at Alloway—" I have fixed on these rare articles the moderate
price of £50," wrote Esdaile. Doubtless other persons
also were offered these " rare articles," but none would
look at them ; and on the death of James Esdaile they
passed to his son, George Esdaile, of Rusholme, Manchester.

Like his father, George Esdaile was a man of easy
faith. He brought himself to believe that he had inherited
a large portion of the furniture that had been in the Cottage
when Robert Burns was born in 1759, and he spent a large
part of his life in attempts to get rid of his Burns inheritance
at a continually increasing price. He advertised freely,
and as freely offered £300 to the agent who would find him

a purchaser for the goods. " I wish the nation would take up the matter," he once wailed, " and restore the Cottage Collection to the Cottage ; what is in the Cottage now is not that which was in the possession of the Goudies since 1792. It is all spurious." He proposed that a company should be formed to acquire his collection. He offered it to any whom he considered a possible purchaser. " If the promoters like, I will construct a facsimile Burns Cottage and put my collection into it in Glasgow for the sum of six thousand pounds, and the relics will sell for much more after," he wrote to the secretary of the Glasgow Burns Centenary (1896) Exhibition. But " nothing was doing."

An offer to sell his gathering to the Corporation of Edinburgh gave Esdaile an unexpected advertisement, though not exactly of the kind he would have desired, and led to the ruin of his hopes. Edinburgh had not had time to forget the scandal of the Burns forgeries (1892) when the offer from Manchester came to it, and was promptly declined. That decision was immediately followed by the irrefutable exposure of Esdaile's claim on behalf of his collection, in the columns of the *Edinburgh Evening Dispatch* (July-October, 1895), by the late Mr Craibe Angus, of Glasgow. Thereafter little was heard of the discredited " Burns Cottage Collection " ; various attempts to exploit it came to nothing, and George Esdaile recently passed to the majority. What the Esdailes—father and son— had failed to do in 73 years the son's executors succeeded in doing in a few months' time. They decided to get rid of the Esdaile " white elephant," and it is betraying no secret to tell now that an offer was made to the Trustees of the Burns Cottage ; of course, it was " turned down." Subsequently—the catalogue tells us—" an acceptable offer was received from a distinguished resident of the United States "—said to be Mr Schwabe—" and it appeared probable that the collection would cross the Atlantic. Fortunately, however, Mr Harry Maconochie, a Scottish gentleman, made a counter-offer to that received from America, and this offer was accepted." As a result these

" fascinating relics and mementoes of the Poet "—again to quote the catalogue—are now exhibited in Bond Street as " kindly lent by Mr Harry Maconochie." The purchase price, it is whispered, was round about £4000.

Writing in 1866 and again in 1870 James Esdaile stated that " this furniture I purchased at the sale of the effects of the then occupant of the auld clay biggin, David Hastings, in 1845." But Esdaile's son time and again repeated that the " Burns relics, comprising virtually the entire contents of the Cottage as the great Poet knew it," were bought at the Goudie sale in 1843. These statements cannot be reconciled. Which is correct ? To that there can be but one answer. Undoubtedly the statement of the father, who purchased the furniture, is correct ; and it is a fair inference that the son desired that the furniture he wished to sell should be associated, not with the little-known David Hastings, who had lived in the Cottage for only two or three years, but with the well-known John Goudie, who had lived in it for 40 years. It is not unlikely, however, that Hastings had acquired some portion of the Goudie furniture sold in 1843. Esdaile consistently refused to produce his " guarantees of authenticity " of the furni-ture, although he persisted that he had them, and that they would be furnished to a buyer at the settlement. Chal-lenged to prove that any one item in his possession had ever belonged to William Burnes, " I assert and can prove," he wrote, " that the Cottage collection was in the Cottage when the Souters of Ayr bought it from the father of the Poet, that such furniture became the property of the miller Goudie in 1792, that it was Goudie's till his death in 1842, that my father bought it, and that I have it now " He asserted—but he never proved his assertion. At another time he offered " a certificate given by the Goudie people. which carries us back to 1792," and which states that the furniture " was the furniture of the Cottage in which Robert Burns was born, and where our father resided for 50 years." But the records of the Incorporation of Shoemakers prove that Goudie resided in the Cottage, not for 50 years, but for

40 years, so that the certificate—even if it were worth anything—" carries us back " only to 1803. What of the 37 years' interval between 1766 and 1803 ? Are we to believe that William Burnes, when he moved from Alloway to Mount Oliphant, left behind him certain important pieces of furniture—" virtually the entire contents of the Cottage "? That Joseph Norman had the use of them, and the two Calbreths ? That the Incorporation of Shoemakers purchased them in 1781, though their records speak only of " houses and land "? That Matthew Dick got them in 1782, handed them on (in 1801) to John Maitland, who in turn passed them on to Goudie in 1803 ? Absurdity could go no further than that.

It is doubtful if Goudie ever stated that any article of furniture in the Cottage of his time had belonged to the Poet's father ; had he done so the fact would almost certainly have been recorded somewhere in print. But no such statement is known. On the contrary, several books published while Goudie was yet alive contain references to the Burns Cottage ; all of them, including the important *New Statistical Account of Scotland*—containing an account of the parish of Ayr, drawn up by one of its ministers in 1837—agree in stating that no part of William Burnes's furniture was then in the Cottage.

Mr Craibe Angus pointed out that the Esdaile furniture is of the character common in country inns of the early nineteenth century, and does not at all resemble the type found in the home of a peasant like William Burnes. And if the Esdaile story were true, why was the furniture left in the Cottage ? Why should William Burnes—the poorest of men in this world's gear—at his first " flitting " leave behind him his eight-day clock, his corner cupboard, his tables and chairs, which he had provided less than nine years before ?

No serious Burnsian believes that any article in the Esdaile collection had the slightest personal association with William Burnes or with any member of his family. " It is all spurious," to quote George Esdaile's own words ;

the relics are Hastings'—may even be Goudie's—furniture, but they are nothing more.

The Esdaile collection has had a past ; but what of its future ?   The " foreword " of the printed catalogue of the exhibition in London announces that " these fascinating relics and mementoes of the Poet will find a home in the county of his birth "   If that means only that they are to be a private possession no one may offer objection, but if it means that they are to be handed over for public exhibition in the county of the Poet's birth—surely that would be adding insult to injury ?   Kyle, Carrick, and Cunningham may be trusted to see to the protest.

J. C. EWING.

TO THE EDITOR, " THE GLASGOW HERALD "

I.

Beurig, Kilmaurs,
7th December, 1918.

SIR.—The thanks of Burnsians everywhere are due to you for granting space in these pressing times for Mr Ewing's opportune article on the above subject, which has now assumed a somewhat serious aspect. For over 35 years this "Esdaile Collection" has been to me what the head of Charles I. was to Uncle Dick. Scarce a year has passed but I have received more than one inquiry as to its genuineness from private individuals, speculators, auctioneers, or public bodies both here and in America, necessitating my setting forth the condemnatory evidence so often that now the mere mention of it induces a sort of mental nausea. Every sort of blandishment has been tried to induce me to assist in its sale, my official position in the Burns Federation conferring, I suppose, a pecuniary value on my name. The most recent inquiries have been from Liverpool and London, among the latter being one from the London Robert Burns Club, to which I lost no time in replying, to put the members on their guard. In face of my communication, I am loath to believe that that Club has deliberately countenanced an exhibition, no article of which, as Mr Ewing conclusively proves, " has the slightest personal association with William Burnes or any of his family." If the London Club and the " royal personage " who visited the show have been " nobbled," it would be interesting to know, apart altogether from the evidence of the recorded facts, how they managed to swallow the transparent absurdity of William Burnes's furniture having been handed down as heirlooms by the successive tenants of the Cottage, from 1766 to 1843, even on the supposition that he (a poor man who required to borrow £100 to stock Mount Oliphant) left his furniture behind him, then only some eight years in use, for behoof of a queue of chance strangers, with or without the usual consideration. True, he had a son named Robert, aged seven years in 1766, of whom the world never heard till twenty years afterwards. Mr Ewing's extracts from the printed catalogue, camouflaged as that document appears to be, leaves the impression that the show is of a nature which can only be characterised in terms which one hesitates to use in a public journal. Should the show come to Ayrshire, the Burns Federation will likely see to it that it gets the reception it merits.—I am, &c.

(Signed)   D. M'NAUGHT,
President, Burns Federation.

II.

7 Stewarton Drive
Cambuslang, 7th December, 1918.

Sir,—I have been much interested in reading the article on above in to-day's *Herald* by Mr J. C. Ewing. It puts very clearly the impossibility of the furniture at present being shown in London as having belonged to the Poet Burns's father. In 1899 I had many communications in connection with an offer from Mr George Esdaile, and latterly from an agent on his behalf, to sell the " furniture and relics," including the first five visitors' books with names from 1829 to 1840 of those visiting the Cottage, to the Mauchline Burns Memorial Museum. The " Collection " was then being shown at Stratford-on-Avon, and comprised " the whole of the original furniture of the Cottage with the exception of the bedstead, which fell to pieces on removal and was thrown out as useless." In an invitation to view the " Cottage Collection," sent to me by Mr Esdaile, besides stating that the " Collection " was sold in 1843, at the " Cottage Birthplace," he also says : " At the sale it was stated that the furniture was that left in the Cottage by the father of the Poet on his selling it in 1766. This statement is corroborated by numerous documents and declarations." Mr Ewing proves the Cottage was not sold till 1871.

With regard to the present exhibition in London, another item in the catalogue seems curious to me—" No. 18, ' Souter Johnnie's ' chair, with the drawers in which he kept his tools." Now, in 1896 I was enabled, through a hint from Mr James Tennant, now of Ayr, and a grandson of Mr John Tennant, " Guid Auld Glen," Burns's friend, to get Souter Johnnie's (John Davidson's) workstool and tools for the Mauchline Burns Memorial Museum. The donors were Messrs John G. Hazel, Dundee, and D. Cowan, Maybole, and they fully authenticated their presentation, which is on show at the Memorial.—I am, &c.

(Signed)   Thos. Killin, *Hon. Treasurer,*

*National Burns Memorial and Cottage Homes
Mauchline.*

BURNS'S HOUSE IN MAUCHLINE.

THE MACKENZIE EXTENSION.

BY the purchase and restoration of the house in which
Robert Burns and Jean Armour began married
life a notable addition to Scottish national shrines was made
nearly five years ago.   That house is at the core of Burns
associations.   Directly opposite stands the scene of the
" Holy Fair "—Mauchline parish kirkyard, where lie four
of the Poet's children and many of his friends and acquain
tances.   Close at hand are Mauchline Castle and Gavin
Hamilton's residence, Nanse Tinnock's, the Cowgate. and
" Poosie-Nansie's," in which the Jolly Beggars

> " Held the splore,
> To drink their orra duddies."

Only a mile away lies Mossgiel, and within easy reach are
Lochlea and Largieside, Tarbolton and Failford, Catrine
and Ballochmyle.   Built of red sandstone and roofed with
thatch, Burns's House faces what for many years was the
" Back Causeway," but now is named " Castle Street."
(By the way, might not the old picturesque name of the street
be restored ?)   From its proprietor and tenant, Archibald
Meikle, tailor in the village, Burns in February or March,
1788, rented one of its upper rooms for Jean Armour, and
here Mrs Burns lived until near the close of that year, when
the new farmhouse on the banks of Nith at Ellisland was
ready for her ; in the interval, her husband records, she
was " regularly and constantly apprentice to my mother
and sisters in their dairy and other rural business " at
Mossgiel.   The house in Back Causeway remained private
property until Whitsunday, 1915, when it was acquired
by the Glasgow and District Burns Association.   After
necessary repairs had been carried out, the Burns room was

opened to visitors, the adjoining apartment was utilised as a museum, and the remaining three rooms were prepared to accommodate deserving old folks. Since it was publicly opened in August, 1915, the house has been visited by large numbers of people, many of them from distant parts of the world ; and exceptional interest has been shown in the Burns room and in the contents of the museum.

The original scheme of the Burns Association was ·limited to the acquisition and utilisation of Burns's House, but the members soon found that an extension of that scheme was desirable, if not inevitable. The former Back Causeway of Mauchline holds other houses that merit special attention from Burnsians. One of these, adjoining the Poet's house, was long known as " the Doctor's Shop," and local tradition has it that Dr John Mackenzie, medical adviser, patron, and friend of the Poet, either resided or had his consulting-room there. That tradition may, or may not, be correct ; but the title deeds show that a bond over the property—which had been purchased in 1778 from James Aird, junior, merchant in Glasgow, by William Nickle or Nicolson, merchant in Mauchline, at the price of £47—was given to Dr Mackenzie in return for the sum of £100, borrowed from him by Nicolson in 1788. Principal and arrears of interest having in 1815 amounted to £130, Nicolson, Mackenzie, and a second bondholder named Robert Paterson entered into a private agreement to sell the property to Mackenzie ; and " Common-Sense," as the author of the " Holy Fair " named him, held the property until Whitsunday of 1831, when he sold it to William Ronald, merchant in Mauchline.

The Book of Robert Burns tells that when Mackenzie entered on professional business at Mauchline he rented a small shop which served as his drug store and consulting-room." It is impossible to prove relation between Charles Rogers's " small shop " and the property in Back Causeway, but it is suggestive that one of the four tenants named in Mackenzie's disposition of 1831 is Dugald Stewart Hamilton (a son of Gavin Hamilton), who had qualified as a physician, and was then in practice at his native place.   Neither is it known that Mackenzie at any time between his marriage in 1791 and his removal to Irvine in 1801 resided in the house on which he held a bond, though it is known that prior to his marriage with Helen Miller—one of the six " belles of Mauchline "—he lodged at the Sun Inn, tenanted by her father, " Auld John Trot " of Burns's " Mauchline Wedding." For 43 years Dr Mackenzie had an interest in the ownership of the property and he may have lived and had his consulting-room in the building ; at that the question must remain for the present.

A fire some years ago had so damaged the quondam Mackenzie building that it was considered unsafe for habitation, and report had it that its owner would not be averse from selling.   The Glasgow Burns Association accordingly entered into negotiations with his agent, and these ended in their acquiring the property as from Whitsunday, 1916. At that time it was decided, on account of conditions arising from the war, to delay restoration of the property.   That work, however, has since been taken in hand, and is now complete : the building has been divided into separate dwelling-houses, and four old people have been placed in possession free of rent and rates.   At the same time the opportunity was taken to extend the accommodation originally provided for a museum in Burns's House.   Many interesting articles have been presented to the Association or purchased by its Museum Committee, and so an additional room has been fitted up and the entire collection re-arranged.   The work of restoration and alteration has been carried out in a most satisfactory manner by Messrs Thomas Findlay & Sons, of Mauchline, to the instructions of Mr Ninian Macwhannell, F.R.I.B.A., who has again freely given his services to the Association, and the entire cost of purchase and restoration has been found by the clubs which compose the Glasgow and District Burns Association, assisted by individual members.

The formal opening of the Mackenzie extension of Burns's House took place on Saturday, 12th April, 1919.

MEMORIAL TO GAVIN HAMILTON AT MAUCHLINE.

HEADSTONE or slab marks the last resting-place in Mauchline parish kirkyard of many of Burns's friends and acquaintances but none points that of the truest of them all. For more than a century Gavin Hamilton, writer and notary in Mauchline, has lain in an unmarked grave, though tradition attributes this regrettable fact to his own desire. Burns and Hamilton appear to have become acquainted in the winter of 1783, when, anticipating trouble with their father's landlord at Lochlea, the brothers Burns (or Burness, rather) took a sub-let of the farm of Mossgiel from Hamilton, who had rented it from the Earl of Loudoun. At that time the elder Burns was not yet even " Coila's Bard " —he was only a farmer, son of the luckless tenant of Lochlea. The two men had much in common, and became fast friends ; and both in his poetry and in his prose the Poet bears testimony to the " generous-hearted, upright " lawyer who patronised and befriended him, particularly at a dark period of his career. It was in return for that patronage and friendship that the Poet dedicated to the lawyer his first volume, the slim paper-covered *Poems chiefly in the Scottish dialect* which issued from the printing press in the summer of 1786. The poetical " Dedication to G—— H——, Esq.," is unique even among poets' dedications, and it fills no fewer than seven pages of print. " 'Twas nae daft vapour," the author tells his patron—

> " But I maturely thought it proper,
> When a' my works I did review,
> To dedicate them, Sir, to you :
> Because (ye need na tak it ill)
> I thought them something like yoursel'."

The record of such a friendship provokes a strong feeling that the burial-place of such a man ought to be at least indicated, even at the disregard of his declared wish (if such was ever made). And so, with the courteous permission of the present representatives of the Hamilton family and of Mauchline Parish kirk-session, a white marble tablet has been affixed to the iron railing which encloses the family burial-place. The tablet is the tribute of Partick (Glasgow) Burns Club, and has been designed and cut by Mr William Vickers, of Glasgow. It carries this brief inscription in leaded letters :—

The burial-place of Gavin Hamilton
(born November, 1751 ; died 5th February, 1805),
the Patron and Friend of Robert Burns.

' The poor man's friend in need,
The gentleman in word and deed."

Erected by the Partick Burns Club, 1919.

The tablet was unveiled by the President of Partick Burns Club on Saturday, 12th April, 1919, and handed over to the Glasgow and District Burns Association, which has agreed to accept custody. This will ensure the future care of a memorial earned by more wise, congenial, and long-sustained friendship than that which commemorates any member of the wide-ranging Burns circle.

IMPOSING ON BURNS.

IN a letter which he wrote to Mrs Dunlop in June, 1793, Burns included his " Epigram on Miss Davies " :—

> " Ask why God made the GEM so small,
>   Any why so huge the Granite ?—
>   Because, God meant mankind should set
>   That higher value on it."

He continues :—

" Though I think this last a pretty enough thought, yet I have been lately outdone by an humble acquaintance of mine, who is reckoned a very clever fellow among his fellow-tanners ; for that is his trade. I do not remember to have heard anything for a good while that has pleased me so much.

EPIGRAM.

> Silence in love shows deeper woe
>   Than words. tho' e'er so witty ;
>   A beggar that is dumb, you know,
>   Deserves the greater pity."

In a Burns Manuscript in the British Museum, entitled " Libel Summons, &c.," a poem too free for general publication, occur the lines :—

> " Hunter, a hearty, willing brother,
>   Weel skill'd in *dead and living leather."

In the edition of *The Merry Muses*, published by the Burns Federation as " A Vindication of Robert Burns," Hunter is twice (pp. 127-8) alluded to as a " shoemaker " ; but in the British Museum Manuscript, Burns has boldly written on the margin opposite the line with the asterisk, " *A Tanner." The poem belongs to the Mauchline period, but it is not impossible that the " tanner " of Burns's asterisk, and the " clever fellow " of the Epigram on Silence, are one and the same. Whether Hunter, or another, the clever tanner was, in his humble way, a literary impostor, for his Epigram is in *The Scots Magazine* for 1740 (volume ii., p. 463), where it is thus printed :—

" ON SILENCE IN LOVE.

(Written by a young lady.)

Silence in love betrays more woe
Than words, tho' ne'er so witty ;
A beggar that is dumb, you know,
Deserves a double pity."

The same lines, headed " On Silence," appear again —nearly half a century later—in the same Magazine (October, 1787, p. 510). It was probably here, or in *The Universal Magazine* for July, 1758, where they bob up again, that the man of leather found the lines which he passed off as his own, deceiving his fellow-nobodies—and Burns.

Such literary impostures are not unheard of even in these days, but in the eighteenth century they were still more common, as witness the following " Acknowledge ments to our Correspondents," taken from *The Universal Magazine* for 1774 :—

" ' The Modern Fine Lady,' though published in a morning paper as a new production, appeared many years ago in Dodsley's *Miscellanies*."

" The paper on ' Jealousy,' by D.D., is filched from Addison's *Spectator*, and would be immediately detected by every reader acquainted with that celebrated English Classic."

" The mathematical question, by Tyro, was inserted and solved in *The Ladies Diary* for the year 1763."

" The ' Ode to Health ' is taken verbatim from Mr Smart's *Poems*."

" The ' Elegy on the late Parliament ' is a servile copy of Dr Arbuthnot's celebrated piece on Colonel Chartres."

" The Verses inclosed by Tyro are below mediocrity, and have already appeared in an evening paper."

All Burnsians are familiar with the song linked with the name of Lapraik, which Burns, in his first Epistle to that " Old Scottish Bard," singled out thus :—

> " There was ae sang, amang the rest,
>   Aboon them a' it pleas'd me best,
>   That some kind husband had addrest
>   To some sweet wife :
>   It thirl'd the heart-strings thro' the breast,
>   A' to the life.
>
> I've scarce heard ought describ'd sae weel,
>   What gen'rous, manly bosoms feel ;
>   Thought I, ' Can this be Pope, or Steele,
>   Or Beattie's wark ?'
>   They tald me 'twas an odd kind chiel
>   About Muirkirk."

The song in question is thus printed in Lapraik's Poems (1788) :—

> " When I upon thy bosom lean,
>   Enraptured I do call thee mine ;
> I glory in those sacred ties
>   That made us one who once were twain ;
> A mutual flame inspires us both—
>   The tender look, the melting kiss ;
> Even years shall ne'er destroy our love,
>   Some sweet sensation new will rise.
>
> Have I a wish ? 'tis all for thee ;
>   I know thy wish is me to please ;
> Our moments pass so smooth away
>   That numbers on us look and gaze.
> Well pleased to see our happy days,
>   They bid us live and still love on ;
> And if some cares shall chance to rise,
>   Thy bosom still shall be my home.
>
> I'll lull me there and take my rest ;
>   And if that aught disturb my fair,
> I'll bid her laugh her cares all out,
>   And beg her not to drop a tear.
> Have I a joy ? 'tis all her own ;
>   Her heart and mine are all the same ;
> They're like the woodbine round the tree,
>   That's twined till death shall us disjoin.

There is not a peculiarly Scots word in these lines, but Burns, in writing it out for *The Scots Musical Museum* (No. 205, vol. iii., 1790), fitted the song with " vernacular kilts " and made various alterations, which we render *kenspeckle* by the use of italics in the version about to follow. The Poet's Manuscript is in the British Museum. On the reverse there is a song beginning, " There's a youth in this city," which is also in Burns's holograph. Turning to the other side of the sheet again, we find that Burns has written at the top, and then deleted, the words " From Lapraik's Poems."

The MS. reads :—

" When I upon thy bosom lean,
　　And fondly clasp thee a' my ain,
I glory in *the* sacred ties
　　That made us ane, wha ance were twain
A mutual flame inspires us baith,
　　The tender look, the melting kiss :
Even years shall ne'er destroy our love,
　　But gie us only change o' bliss.

Hae I a wish ? *it's* a' for thee,
　　I ken thy wish is me to please ;
Our moments pass sae smooth away
　　That numbers on us look and gaze.
Weel pleas'd they see our happy days,
　　Nor Envy's sel' finds aught to blame ;
And ay when ('as' deleted) *weary cares arise,*
　　Thy bosom still shall be my hame.

I'll *lay* me there, and take my rest,
　　And if that aught disturb my *Dear,*
I'll bid her laugh her cares *away,*
　　And beg her not to drap a tear :
Hae I a joy ? it's a' her ain ;
　　United still her heart and mine ;
They're like the woodbine round the tree
　　That's twin'd till Death shall *them* disjom."

In the Preface to his volume, Lapraik says : " In consequence of misfortunes and disappointments he (the author) was, some years ago, torn from his ordinary way of life and shut up in retirement, which he found at first painful and disagreeable. Imagining, however, that he had a turn for rhyming, in order to support his solitude he set himself to compose the following pieces."

Thus, delicately, does he allude to a period he spent in Ayr Jail as a sequence to financial difficulties resulting from the failure of the Douglas and Heron Ayr Bank in June, 1772. The transactions of the bank—which are fully dealt with in *The Scots Magazine* of the time—were not finally closed till August, 1773. It has been stated that Lapraik was a director of the bank, but his name does not figure on the list. I have not been able to put a date to his "retirement," but it must have been some time *subsequent* to June, 1772.

Some disturber of the ghosts of the Muses in old Maga-land discovered a song wonderfully like Lapraik's lyric buried in the pages of an old magazine. It was naturally concluded that Lapraik was an impostor, and had deceived Burns as to the authorship of the song Henley and Henderson, however, in the Centenary Edition (vol. i., p. 380), incline to the opposite view. Their note reads :—

" Lapraik's song . . . . closely resembles one in *Ruddi-man's Weekly Magazine*, 11th October, 1773, ' When on thy bosom I recline,' dated Edinburgh, 11th October, and signed ' Happy Husband.' It has been too rashly inferred that Lapraik plagiarised from this lyric : he may have written it himself."

The Ettrick Shepherd characterised Lapraik as " a very indifferent poet—indeed, no poet at all." But fortunately we are able to deal with his claims to this " ae sang," apart from the consideration of his poetical merits. Of course, as far as the dates given go, he could have written the song, as he states, in prison, and therefore not earlier than the summer of 1772, and published it, as Henley and Henderson suggest, in *The Weekly Magazine or Edinburgh Amusement*, in October, 1773. However, I am in a position to supplement the Centenary Edition's information with data that undoubtedly brands Lapraik as one of the great gang of song-snatchers

I have found the *Magazine* version of the poem in *The Scots Magazine* for April, 1772, p. 207, printed anonymously, and headed " Sonnett by a Husband." Still earlier I get what I take to be the original publication in *The Universal Magazine of Knowledge and Pleasure* for October, 1771, p. ʻ09· Here it is verbatim :—

" SONNET.

By a Husband, but not a modern one.

When on thy bosom I recline,
Enraptur'd still to call thee mine
 To call thee mine for life,
I glory in the sacred ties
(Which modern wits and fools despise)
 Of husband and of wife.

One mutual flame inspires our bliss,
The tender look—the melting kiss
 Ev'n years have not destroy'd ;
Some sweet sensation ever new
Springs up—and proves the maxim true
 That love can ne'er be cloy'd.

Have I a wish, 'tis all for thee ;
Hast thou a wish, 'tis all for me
 So soft our moments move,
That angels look with ardent gaze,
Well pleas'd to see our happy days,
 And bid us live—and love.

If cares arise (and cares will come)
Thy bosom is my softest home,
 I lull me there to rest ;
And is there aught disturbs my fair,
I bid her sigh out all her care,
 And lose it in my breast.

Have I a joy, 'tis all her own,
Or her's and mine are all but one ·
 Our hearts are so intwin'd,
That, like the ivy round the tree,
Bound up in closest amity,
 'Tis death to be disjoin'd   ' CLIO. '

Obviously, all that Lapraik did was to alter—and certainly not for the better—this song of the unknown bard, whose identity is shrouded in the pseudonym " Clio."   Whatever merits Lapraik's effort displays are *here*, down to the very ideas, words, and phrases, *in print*, at least eight months before, like Bunyan, he was " shut up in retirement " and turned to the solace of the quill.

DAVIDSON COOK F S.A. Scot.

BURNS AND THE DUCHESSES.

ANYONE who seeks a knowledge of Burns must study carefully not merely his poems and letters, but the opinions, remarks, and criticisms actually passed on him in his own day. One realises the true character of the man by learning how he appeared to, how he affected, those with whom he came in personal contact. It is by these sidelights that real information can be gained, and the *Chronicle*, and its Editor, have done monumental work in sifting the true from the false, bringing facts into prominence, and exposing baseless fabrications. No stronger light was thrown than the views of those who met him in the height of his fame, when, as a mere ploughman, a peasant by comparison with the refined but affected society of Auld Reekie, he stepped straight into the limelight, and for a brief while became the central figure of the stage, the universally accepted Bard of his native country.

In one fortnight after his arrival in the Capital, he was able to announce that his avowed patrons and patronesses were the Duchess of Gordon, the Countess of Glencairn, with my Lord (Glencairn) and Lady Betty (Cunningham). Son of a gardener turned farmer, brought up in the narrowest circumstances, owing such education as he possessed mainly to his own efforts—how did this man conduct himself in circumstances so alien. so unexpected ? Himself he says : " At Edinburgh I was in a new world. I mingled among many classes of men, but all of them new to me ; and I was all attention to catch the manners as they rise." Keen to observe ; far more keenly observed.

What was the verdict ? Entirely favourable. Possibly the best testimony was that of the Professor of Greek, who, little dreaming that his words would be known and quoted, wrote : " We have got a poet in town whom everybody takes notice of, a ploughman from Ayrshire, who has produced admirable verses, mostly in the Scottish dialect, though some of them are nearly in English. He is a fellow of strong commonsense, and by his own industry has read a good deal of English, both prose and verse." Sir Walter Scott carries greater weight, and his remarks to Lockhart are obviously based on what he had heard, as well as the one brief interview · "A sort of dignified plainness and simplicity. His conversation expressed perfect self-confidence, without the slightest presumption. His address to females was extremely deferential, and always with a turn to the pathetic or humorous. I have heard the Duchess of Gordon remark this." And Mrs Alison Cockburn, poetess and a Queen of society: "The town is agog with the ploughman Poet, who receives adulation with native dignity. The man will be spoiled, if he can spoil; but he keeps his simple manners, and is quite sober."

Princes Burns never met, but next to them there was no one of the time who held a greater position, wielded more influence in Court, politics, and Society than the young Duchess of Gordon, whose approval gave the cachet to Burns as the Lion of the Day in Edinburgh. She was a penniless lass, but of a lang pedigree—a Maxwell of Monreith, noted from childhood for her wild and charming waywardness and high spirit. Her early marriage brought her into high place, where she had full scope. A contemporary remarks that she was a favourite of George III., whose domestic circle she delighted and amused by vivid personifications and delineations of peculiarities and dialects. Mistress of the Doric and Aberdonian, the jargon of Yorkshire, the humour of the Emerald Isle, the King found her a key to museums of natural history, and of national peculiarities. Her influence and popularity proved of great service to natives who appealed to her for preferment. Pitt, carried captive by her wit and importunities, always resolved to give her next appeal a flat refusal; but uninvited she invaded his sanctum, and opening her budget of wit, proceeded to carry her motion. Her husband, Alexander, fourth Duke, who succeeded in 1762, content for a while to follow his gay Duchess in a life of pleasure and excitement, was described as " the greatest subject in Britain, not from his rent roll, but from the number of people whom Providence had put under his government and protection " His rent roll proved unequal to the strain ; troubles arose, and continued. In reality, the Duke, a lang, lang-nebbit northerner, was no fit match for this amazing woman. What he really cared for was sport—a horse, a dog, and a gun. Still he did well for his country by raising four regiments of Fencibles between 1759 and 1799. It was the 1793 battalion in which his Duchess so keenly interested herself, and it was to her recruiting efforts and methods that the name of " Gay Gordons " is attributable. He also planted large areas and beautiful country-sides.

It chanced that Jean Maxwell was not to be the only Duchess to entertain the Poet, nor yet the first. In the course of the Highland tour, 25th August to 16th September, 1787, Burns rode up Tummel River to Blair Castle on Friday, 31st August, to present a letter of introduction to His Grace of Atholl. The Duke was from home, but expected next day, so the Duchess insisted that he should stay overnight.

" Blair—sup with the Duchess—easy and happy from the manners of that family." Josiah Walker, son of the Minister of Dundonald, had made Burns's acquaintance in Edinburgh, and was now resident-tutor to the young Marquis of Tullibardine Like others, the tutor later dilated on his curiosity to see how the Poet would conduct himself in such august company. Of his favourable opinion it is only necessary to quote one sentence : " He tried to exert his abilities, because he knew it was ability alone gave him a title to be there." Remembering Allan Cunningham, and his inventions, one gets to doubt the accuracy of these post-mortem recollections. Anyone who had met Burns in life found keen auditors to his tale, whether fair or foul, and the tale grew in the telling, as did the narrator's self-importance. Later, it was to Walker that Burns sent a letter, enclosing the verses on Bruar Water. The jottings in Burns's diary are quite vivid :—

" Saturday. Visit the scenes round Blair. Ride in company with Sir William Murray and Mr Walker to Loch Tummel. Dine at Blair—Company : General Murray, Orien ; Capt. Murray, an honest tar ; Sir William Murray, an honest, worthy man ; Mrs Graham, *belle et amiable :* Miss Cathcart ; Mrs Murray, a painter ; Duchess and fine family. Dance—sup—Duke ; Mr Graham of Fintry ; Mr M'Laggan ; Mr and Mrs Stewart."

Jean, Duchess of Atholl, eldest of the three beautiful daughters of Lord Cathcart, married in 1774, had at this time seven children—the youngest, six months old, " the smiling little seraph" ; the others " the lovely olive plants." The Duchess, noted for her happy home life, is described by one of her descendants as " a gentle, kindly woman, well read, and with musical and artistic tastes. There are many traces of her books, music, and sketches at Blair. I might specially mention a small book of manuscript music, in which she has drawn a delightful little coloured sketch of her children dancing to the strains of Neil Gow's fiddle." Like her sister, the beautiful Mrs Graham, she died of consumption, in 1790. Neil Gow was at that time violinist at Blair. He had played the day previous for Burns at Dr Stewart's, and Burns describes " his interesting face—his honest, social brow."

John, the fourth Duke, who had succeeded in 1774, is well remembered for his management of his estates and tree planting. The present Duke thus pithily describes him : " The 4th Duke was a particularly go-ahead man for his date, and he did more for agriculture than almost any man in Scotland. He introduced a proper system of farming in Atholl, laid out the farms on lines which are a model at the present day, built good houses (which are still good) and farm buildings, introduced a proper tenancy system which still obtains, did away with all hopeless crofts, and in their place put small profitable farms, and

did so much in the way of forestry that he was known as
John, the Planter.   The woods that he planted have proved
of great value during the war to the country.   His treatise
on larch planting is still a standard work.   He was a great
sportsman, and a man of much energy."   He was also a
strikingly handsome man ;   his portrait appears in the
engraving, " The Death of a Stag in Glentilt."

This two-day visit might well be described by Burns
as one of the happiest events in his life.   Willie Nicol was
there—Walker calls him a robust but clumsy person, and
Burns described him as a loaded blunderbuss at full cock—
but he appears to have kept in the background and caused
no trouble.   Next day, Sunday, they journeyed by
Dalwhinnie, Rothiemurchus, and the Cairngorms, and
paid a visit to Bruar Water, which inspired " The Humble
Petition to the Noble Duke of Athole," a petition promptly
given effect to.   Burns wrote little about children, save
in his farmhouse sketches, so the last verse in praise of
these highly-born he had so lately seen is worth quoting ·—

> " So may, old Scotia's darling hope,
>   Your little angel band,
> Spring like their fathers, up to prop
>   Their honoured native land.
> So may, thro' Albion's farthest ken,
>   To social-flowing glasses,
> The grace be—' Athole's honest men,
>   And Athole's bonnie lasses.' "

It was a week later that Burns and Nicol drove, by way
of Forres and Elgin, from Brodie House to Fochabers.   At
the Gordon Arms the chaise was put up, and Burns proceeded alone to the Castle to pay his respects to the Duchess.
His jotting is :—

" Friday.   Cross Spey to Fochabers—fine palace,
worthy of the generous proprietor.   Dine—company : Duke
and Duchess, Ladies Charlotte and Madeline ;   Colonel
Abercrombie and Lady ;   Mr Gordon and Mr——, a clergyman, a venerable aged figure ; and Mr Hoy, a clergyman
I suppose, a pleasant open manner.   The Duke makes me

happier than ever great man did—noble, princely; yet
mild, condescending and affable, gay, and kind. The
Duchess charming, witty, and sensible—God bless them."

Hoy was not a clergyman, but the librarian. The
clergyman may have been Rev. Dr Couper, parish minister,
who later supplied the details of the unfortunate ending
of the visit. Did Burns actually give his travelling companion the slip? Nicol knew they were come to Gordon

GORDON CASTLE, FOCHABERS.

Castle, the Duchess, the first patron. It looks remarkably
like it. Possibly Nicol, though unobtrusive at Blair, had
not proved suited to such company. Possibly with Brodie
of Brodie, the night before, something had gone wrong to
make that kind host only " truly polite, but not just the
Highland cordiality." Anyway, alone he went, with or
without explanation. Looking at the calls on the road,
it must have been past noon when Fochabers was reached,
and the Poet arrived at the Castle just as the family was
sitting down to the early afternoon dinner. Meal over,
and a glass or two of wine drunk, he could no longer detain

his friend, and rose to leave. The Duke offered to send a servant, and finally dispatched one of his own guests to accompany Burns, with a special invite to Mr William Nicol to favour their Graces with his company for the night. But that obstinate son of Latin prose, having doubtless employed his weary waiting in his usual manner, was beside himself with anger and vexation. The horses were being yoked to the old chaise ; landlord, postboy, everybody being cursed ; the messenger and his message got the same treatment, and Burns either had to part company and be left behind, or go on with the journey instanter. According to local tradition, there was a real collieshangie on the sidewalk.

So on went the ill-matched pair to 'Cullen—to Old Cullen—now blotted out, and there they spent the night. Local tradition records a call on the way, near to Buckie, at a change-house kept by a notable auld wife, but it must have been a waefu' gait. No wonder that next morning, at Banff, " Burns played off some sportive jests at his touchy companion, about some misunderstanding between them at Fochabers." But, seeing who he was, and what he knew he was, the Bard was a most forbearing man through life. It was a sad affair, maybe a serious one. At Blair he met Graham of Fintry—" Fintry, my stay in worldly strife "— who stood his friend in the Excise, and the Gordon influence might have changed his prospects, as the Duchess was at that time so powerful in political circles. She was then in the height of her fame and power, and her husband was then proudly devoted to her. As to the mode of life at the Castle, and the Duchess's management, it is interesting to quote Mrs Rose, of Kilravock, another famous Scotswoman of the time, with whom Burns had stayed part of the day preceding. She was a constant visitor, and, in a letter to a friend, says :—" The manner of living at the Castle was perfectly gay, remote from anything indelicate or foolish. The table was elegant ; no disguised dishes or French cookery—no coquetry—no jealousy—no hard drinking. I could have lived a month in the same style, and looked back on it as a period rationally employed, which is far from being generally the case. The Duchess is a helper of youthful Scots ; has a great gift of homeliness, the Doric, and various dialects." So the gay Duchess was then as good a helpmeet and housewife as her quieter peer of Atholl. Her latter years were as troubled as those of the Poet himself.

Burns sought to make some return by sending the Duke the verses on Castle Gordon, commencing " Streams that glide in orient plains," as poor as anything he ever wrote, possibly reflecting his disappointment. The poem and letter are not at Gordon Castle, nor is the Bruar Water manuscript to be found at Blair.

That Burns very deeply felt the incident is clear from a letter of his, dated Edinburgh, 20th October, 1787, to James Hoy, the old librarian, a quaint, learned Scots character. In it he says : " I shall certainly, among my legacies, leave my latest curse to that unlucky predicament which hurried—tore me away from Gordon Castle. May that obstinate son of Latin prose be curst." The object of the letter was to secure a copy of " Cauld Kail in Aberdeen," written by the Duke, and to enlist his sympathy in Johnson's *Scots Musical Museum*, for which the Poet was working so devotedly. Hoy, in his reply, told him, " If I were not sensible of your fault as well as your loss, in leaving this place so suddenly, I should condemn you to starve one auld kail ; and as for Dick Latine, your travelling companion, I should give him naught but Stra'bogie custocks." The song was sent, along with an order for the *Museum*, and Burns in a letter of 6th November, writes : " The Duke's song charms me. There is I know not what of wild happiness of thought and expression peculiarly beautiful in the old Scottish song style, of which His Grace, old, venerable Skinner, and the late Ross at Lochlee, are the only modern instances that I recollect, since Ramsay, with his contemporaries, and poor Bob Fergusson, went to the world of deathless existence, and truly immortal song." Later Burns copied the verses into his interleaved copy of the *Museum*.

From that date Burns had no further intercourse with his Duchesses. But he was fated to have his name linked with that of the Duchess of Gordon in a fashion that was repugnant and distressing. First the *London Star*, next the *Gazetteer* in March, 1789, fathered on him an offensive lampoon, with the remark that " Mr Burns, the ploughing Poet, who owes much of his good fortune to Her Grace's critical discernment and generous patronage, made this elegant stanza on that occasion " (of a ball in Edinburgh). When Burns learnt of this, he gave a passionate denial, and later it was announced that the true author was the lawyer politician, Henry Dundas, Lord Melville.

After his return to Edinburgh, Burns sat only once at the table of a nobleman, when, at the end of July, 1793, he and Syme visited Lord Selkirk at The Isle, Kirkcudbright.

PHILIP SULLEY.

CLUB NOTES.

[COMMUNICATED.]

THE LONDON ROBERT BURNS CLUB.

REPORT FOR YEAR ENDING 30th APRIL, 1919.

In more than one respect the Club year just closed has been a notable one. In the first place, the members have had the satisfaction of celebrating the Jubilee of the foundation of the Club ; and I think that we who are privileged to be members to-day have a right to feel that we are not disgracing the memory of the Poet or the memories of those who, fifty years ago, by founding the Club, set themselves to the perpetuation of the Poet's message. In every respect our activities are varied and healthy.

In the second place, the year to which we have all bidden good-bye has been notable in that it has seen the end of the great world conflict, and in the only way possible if truth and justice and democracies, and even the common decencies of life are to prevail. Everything that the name of Robert Burns stands for was at stake in this great struggle, and it was unthinkable that they should be trampled upon with impunity by a people, however great. The cost of the travail has been tremendous, and many members of this Club are to-day suffering from wounds that can never be healed on this side of time, caused through the loss of those who have been as dear to them as life itself. Words cannot heal a wounded heart, but it must be some consolation to know that their glorious deaths have not been in vain. The bereaved members of this Club have our sincere sympathy.

The first semi-public event of the Club year was the Welcome Home Luncheon to our friend and fellow-member Mr (now Sir) Harry Lauder, and his good lady, who we most heartily congratulate on the knighthood which has been conferred upon Sir Harry.

Lord Balfour of Burleigh, Lord Glenconner, and the Right Hon. Andrew Fisher, were also among the speakers.

In order to celebrate Hallowe'en, the Club organised a Matinee at the Pavilion, Piccadilly Circus, which was kindly lent by Mr C. B. Cochran. The result of a successful concert, at which many prominent music-hall and concert artistes gave their assistance without fee or reward, was that with members' contributions £414

was handed to the London Committee of the Harry Lauder Fund
for Scottish Sailors and Soldiers. As usual the work of the matinee
fell on the shoulders of Mr M'Farlane, who we thank heartily for
the great success of the gathering.

THE 25th OF JANUARY,

The Birthday Festival, being the Jubilee Festival of the Club
was celebrated at Prince's Restaurant, Piccadilly, under particularly
happy circumstances, and the attendance of members and friends
was most gratifying. (We have been honoured by a full report
of the proceedings in this year's *Chronicle.*)

The year that has passed has had much shadow as well as much
sunshine. The Club has suffered grievous loss by the sudden
death of Past-President Neil Turner, whose memory will not soon
fade in this organisation. Mr Turner, quiet and enthusiastic,
rendered marked service to the Club, and his year of office was one
of great activity and prosperity. We sympathise with Mr Allpress
and Mr Hyde, two members of Committee and active workers, in
the losses they have sustained by domestic bereavement. Mrs
Allpress and Mrs Hyde, whose loss we deplore, were both regular
attenders at our social gatherings, and we feel their deaths to be
personal losses all the more on this account.

In this connection, I must make mention of the serious trials
through which our worthy Vice-president, Mr L. G. Sloan, has passed.
I have on several occasions conveyed to Mrs Sloan the messages
of sympathy from the members. Mr Sloan is obliged to go on a
business tour in the United States and, consequently, for some little
time at any rate, we shall be without his sage advice and assistance.

Financially, and in point of members, the Club is in a flourishing condition. Thanks largely to the Membership Committee,
of which Mr Florence is the Chairman, the roll has been increased
during the year by thirty-four, and as the number of deaths and
resignations is nine, the net increase to our membership is twenty-five.
The Treasurer's report will show a substantial balance to our credit.

Our Pipers have been reinforced by the appointment of Piper
J. C. Archibald, whose assistance at the Festival we appreciated
so greatly. Pipe-Major Reith deserves our thanks for the splendid
services so ungrudgingly given at our various gatherings. Now
that the war is nearly over, we may soon expect the return of Pipe-
Major George Shand, who has been with his regiment, the London
Scottish, since the war began.

We offer to our members Sir George Riddell, Bart., Sir Harry
Lauder, and Mr William Noble, hearty congratulations on honours

conferred.   Sir George Riddell, who is liaison officer between the
British Empire Press and the British representatives at the Peace
Conference, has been presented by the Imperial Pressmen with a
souvenir of his services to them, and the French Government have
honoured him by admitting him to be an officer of the Legion of
Honour.   These tributes to the work and worth of Sir George are
hailed with great pleasure by his many friends in England.

The knighthood to Sir Harry Lauder is an honour which has
been well earned.

To Mr William Noble, who has been appointed to the high
office of Engineer-in-Chief to His Majesty's Post Office, we also
offer our hearty congratulations.   Mr Noble has, from the lowest
rung in his professional ladder, climbed steadily to the very topmost
step.   It was only the other day that we congratulated him on
having had an important Belgian decoration conferred upon him
for services to Belgium during the war.

In bringing my report to an end, I must take this opportunity
of thanking the members of the Committee for their hearty support
during the year ;   and particularly I would like to say how very
greatly the work has been lightened because of the energetic services
of Mr M'Farlane, our Honorary Secretary, who has co-operated
with me on every occasion with great heartiness.   Without Mr
M'Farlane's assistance one dreads to think what the Club would do.

WM. WILL, *President.*

SCOTTISH   BURNS   CLUB.

(In which is Incorporated " Ye Saints Burns Club.")

Progress has been the experience of the Club for the past season.
An average attendance of over eighty was maintained.   Two
Ladies' evenings were held, when Mr MacKerracher provided very
high-class vocal and musical talent.

About 150 were present at the Anniversary.   " The Immortal
Memory " was proposed by Sheriff R. Macaulay Smith, LL.B.
The address was afterwards printed, and is a valuable addition to
Burns literature.

To meet the demand for membership, the Club raised the limit
to 200 ordinary members and 10 honorary members, and the membership is again full.

The Club has sustained a sad loss through the death of Mr W. F.
Frame, the well-known comedian, and one of the Club's most
enthusiastic members.

Undernoted are details of present season's syllabus :—

1919.   SYLLABUS, 1919-1920.
Sept. 22. " Napoleon "—Mr J. K. M'Dowall, J.P.
Oct. 27. Musical Evening (Ladies' Night)—Mr J. G. Mac·
                 · Kerracher.
Nov. 24. " Shakespeare "—Mr George M'Gill.
Dec. 22. " Knox "—Dr James Devon.
1920.
Jan. 19. " Burns "—Mr John Muir.
Jan. 26. " The Immortal Memory "—Alex. Cargill, Esq., Edinburgh.
Feb. 23. " Cromwell "—Mr T. A. Fraser.
Mar. 22. Annual General Meeting at 6.45 p.m.   Musical Evening
                 (Ladies' Night) at 7.30 p.m.

The meetings are held on the fourth Monday of each month,
at 7.30 p.m., from September to March inclusive, in Reid's Rooms,
30 Gordon Street, Glasgow.

J. KEVAN M'DOWALL, *Hon. Secretary.*

GLASGOW BURNS CLUBS ASSOCIATION.

The Association has now completed its twelfth year, and has
42 Clubs affiliated.

All the meetings were largely attended during the year.

The newly-formed Glasgow Masonic Burns Club has been admitted to the membership of the Association.   The payment of
subscriptions has been satisfactory.

The Burns Anniversary was celebrated this year much more
generally than has been possible since the outbreak of war.   A
number of Clubs which had suspended resumed their work, and
the number of celebrations was largely increased.   Several Clubs
took a collection on behalf of the Burns House, Mauchline, including
a collection of £20 from the Bridgeton Club, and £8 from the Tam
o' Shanter.

As usual, the Burns statue was beautifully decorated by the
Scottish Co-operative Wholesale Society, and individual wreaths
were sent by the Rosebery, Sandyford, and Tam o' Shanter Clubs,
and by this Association.

The third Anniversary Sermon was preached on 19th January,
by the Rev. Jas. Barr, of Govan, whose subject was " The Religious
Teaching of Burns."   The Service was the most successful yet held.

There was a crowded congregation; several hundreds of persons being turned away. The collection on behalf of the Mauchline House amounted to £24 11s 2d.

At last Annual Meeting it was agreed to begin a Pension Fund for the beneficiaries of the Mauchline House, and a sum of £15 was voted for that purpose (£5 for each beneficiary), to be paid quarterly.

At a meeting of Committee, held on 12th February, the advisability of the Association securing permanent premises was discussed, and a committee was appointed. So far no suitable site has been found.

The Dr Mackenzie House at Mauchline was formally opened on Saturday, 12th April, and there was a large attendance of members and friends. The weather was excellent. Mrs C. R. Cowie, who presided, was presented with a glove box made from the oak of the old house, and smaller boxes were presented to Mr Ninian M'Whannell, architect, and to the President, Mr M'Kenzie. The various houses and extended Museum were visited, and great satisfaction was expressed on all hands at the arrangements made. Four aged women are now comfortably housed (in addition to those in the Burns House), and pensions are in contemplation.

On the same afternoon Mr Cowie unveiled, on behalf of the Partick Club, a marble tablet on the grave of Gavin Hamilton. The tablet was then entrusted to the care of this Association.

In connection with the removal of the Old West Kirk, Greenock, and the Highland Mary Monument, the Secretary had some correspondence with Mr Rowan, the solicitor who asked the support of the Association in opposing the Greenock Provisional Order. An enquiry in connection with the Order was held in Glasgow in August, at which Mr M'Coll attended to hear the evidence given by Messrs Duncan M'Naught and J. C. Ewing on behalf of the Burns Federation. The opposition proved unavailing, as the Commissioners decided to grant the prayer of the Order, but it was arranged with Greenock Corporation as to the best mode of dealing with the Monument. Since then Mr Alex. Pollock has greatly interested himself in the matter, and the members of this Association have been asked to write their members of Parliament to intervene and oppose the Bill to be promoted by the Greenock Corporation. On Saturday, 25th October, the Special Committee of Burns Federation met in Glasgow and decided that a circular prepared by Mr Alex. Pollock, and approved by a sub-committee of this Association, be sent to every Burns Club in the country. The circular urged Parliamentary action in opposition to the Greenock proposals, and the expense of printing and posting same is to be borne by the Federation.

On 20th September, the Annual Outing to Mauchline took place.   The two houses were visited, and found in excellent order. Several gifts have been added to the Museum since last meeting.

The Annual Meeting of the Association was held in the Bath Hotel on 30th October, and the Secretary and Treasurer reported a flourishing state of affairs.   The following Executive was appointed Hon. Presidents—Alex. Pollock (Rosebery), Hugh M'Coll (Rosebery), Wm. Douglas (Sandyford), Alex. M'Kenzie (National) ;   President— C. R. Cowie (Partick) ;   Vice-Presidents—Wm. Cockburn (Old Kilpatrick), Thos. Killin (Glasgow Mauchline) ;   Secretary and Treasurer—J. Jeffrey Hunter (Tam o' Shanter) ;   Committee— George Armour (Rosebery), Jas. M. Campbell (Bridgeton), Isaac Chalmers (Govan Cronies), R. M. Milholm (Shettleston), A. M'Kay (Barlinnie), Wm. Reid (Bridgeton), A. C. Riddell (Albany), ex-Councillor Sutherland (Primrose), Jas. Tudhope (Carlton), John F. Anderson (Tam o' Shanter), A. R. Young (Primrose), J. M. Brown (Kingston), J. C. Galpine (National), J. S. Ritchie (Clarinda), T. P. Thompson (Tam o' Shanter), Thos. Turnbull (Primrose), J. C. Ewing (Partick), Ninian M'Whannell (Scottish), T. C. F. Brotchie J. D. Sloan (Rosebery), and Wm. Gardiner (Carlton).

J. Jeffrey Hunter, *Secretary.*

TAM O' SHANTER BURNS CLUB.

The Club is now in its sixty-first year.   The session opened with the Annual Meeting, which later resolved itself into a Smoking Concert.   At that meeting the alteration of rules was discussed. It was also agreed that a Roll of Honour of the members of the Club be prepared.   This was done, and presented at the Annual Dinner.

The Annual Dinner took place on 25th January.   Sir John Ure Primrose proposed the " Immortal Memory ."   A collection was taken at the dinner, amounting to £8, and this was given to the Treasurer on behalf of the Mauchline House Fund.

The question of this Club having a School Competition was discussed at a meeting of Committee held on 24th February, and Mr T. P. Thompson was asked to have it in his school in December or January, and this he agreed to do.   A large sum has been promised for prizes.

The Club was represented at the opening of Dr Mackenzie's House, Mauchline, by Messrs J. F. Anderson, Secretary, A. M'Kenzie, and A. Henderson.   On 25th March a Literary and Musical evening, with a Tattie and Herrin' Supper, was held (the first since the war). The Secretary read a paper on " The Theatre in Glasgow," and an excellent musical programme followed.

The Annual Outing took place to Lanark on the first Saturday of June. The members were met by Bailie Lithgow and some members of the Lanark Club, who accompanied the party to the Falls of Clyde. A high tea took place in the Victoria Hotel, and the outing was a great success.

The Club was represented at the Federation meeting and at the M'Lennan Cup Bowling Competition in August.

It was agreed at the last meeting of Committee that the Club should meet every month as was usual before the war, and the lectures are as follows :—

October.   " Internationalism "—Rev. D. Graham.
November.   " A Public Medical Service "—Mr Wm. Jones.
January 24th—" The Immortal Memory " is to be proposed by
    Mr Graham Moffat.
February.   " Oliver Goldsmith "—Mr J. F. Anderson.
March.   " Lord Byron "—Captain Campbell.

The membership stands thus :—Life Members, 44 ; Ordinary Members, 68 ; Honorary Members, 3—total, 115.

The Annual Meeting was held in the Trades House Restaurant on 28th October, when a large company sat down to high tea.   Mr J. F. Anderson presided, and the Rev. David Graham, Redgorton, delivered an excellent lecture on " Internationalism."   Thereafter an Executive was appointed, and a number of new members were admitted.

J. JEFFREY HUNTER, *Secretary.*

GLASGOW LOSSES.

The Glasgow Burns world is the poorer by the deaths during 1919 of a considerable number of prominent men.   We give some particulars of the three most notable, and that in the order of their demise.

Mr JOHN RUSSELL, Timber Merchant, died on 14th July, in his 67th year, after a long illness.   He was a noted chess player, and the chess papers have recorded his exploits in that game.   For a time he was chess editor of the *Glasgow Weekly Citizen.*   The following is an extract from an obituary notice :—

" A most genial man, and a boon companion in a large circle of friends. Mr Russell was highly popular and well liked, having

an excellent fund of humour, and being a ready raconteur and a witty speaker at dinners and suppers. Fond of most intellectual pursuits, his knowledge of literature was extensive, and of Robert Burns he was a fervent admirer, being prominently connected with both the Primrose and Sandyford Burns Clubs, where he had—at least once — proposed ' The Immortal Memory ' most felicitously. He studied and used shorthand writing a lot, and was rather an elegant penman in longhand. In summer he frequently spent a week or two on the Continent travelling with some chosen companion."

The late Mr John Russell.

As a Burns man Mr Russell delivered several lectures which were in great demand at all sorts of societies. The best of these was " Burns and the Deil," which he gave on many occasions. Mr Russell took a great interest in local affairs, and was a member of the old Glasgow Club. His remains were interred in Cathcart Cemetery in presence of a large assembly of mourners.

———

Mr WILLIAM STRAITON, a well-known citizen, was born 13th October, 1863. He for many years occupied an important post in connection with the Glasgow Corporation. Mr Straiton was of a modest and a rather retiring nature, but his outstanding qualities of character and his secretarial abilities were manifest, and were in great demand. As a Burnsian he was for twenty years a member of the Carlton Club, and was its indefatigable and enthusiastic secretary for fifteen years. In this capacity he undertook much valuable work, and in his later years was largely instrumental in carrying out the movement of printing *Burns's Works for the Blind.* For seven years he was also Secretary of the Glasgow and District Burns Clubs Bowling Association, and his arduous work in arranging for the Annual M'Lennan Cup Competitions was performed in his usual thorough manner. Mr Straiton was also a Director of the National Burns Club, and did valuable work as Convener of the Entertainment's Committee. He was also a notable bowler, and

The late Mr Wm. Straiton.

was connected with Hutchesontown Club for twenty years. He was also for several years its secretary, and acted as President in 1917. Mr Straiton was a very robust and active man, but unfortunately fell a victim to a severe internal complaint to which he succumbed on 19th July. He bore his sufferings with unflinching fortitude, and passed away lamented by a wide circle of friends.

The third and best known of the trio is Mr W. F. FRAME, the genial Scotch Comedian, whose name all over the country was a household word. Mr Frame was an artiste of great originality and conspicuous merit, and his fun was always clean and clever. His services were ever at the disposal of those promoting entertainments for any useful charity, and the work he performed in this respect during the war, both in this country and in France, undoubtedly undermined his health. Mr Frame was an enthusiastic Burnsian, and recited many of the Bard's poems with great acceptance. He was frequently an honoured guest at Burns entertainments, and had promised to propose " The Immortal Memory " at the Govan Cronies Club, in January. Mr Frame's services as a temperance reformer and a Freemason have been adequately dealt with elsewhere. The genial Scot was a victim of the Railway Strike, having caught a chill (during the absence of trains) in a long motor journey. His death took place unexpectedly on the morning of 30th October. The funeral service was held in Lansdowne Church, on Saturday, 1st November, and was attended by a large number of Burnsians, who felt the loss as a personal one.

ALBANY BURNS CLUB.

SESSION 1918-1919.

After about 4½ years of the dreadful holocaust in France, Flanders, Egypt, and other Fronts, we have celebrated a glorious and victorious Peace—a Peace which I hope will make war in the future impossible. We look back with horror to the dreadful times we have come through and the anxieties we have had, all through the rapacity, blood-thirstiness, and brutal warfare of a nation wishing for world power. On the other hand we look back with pride on our young lads who so nobly responded to the call of the Motherland, and with sorrow when we think of the many brave lads who laid down their lives on the great Altar of Liberty. May their names never die. It is the intention of the Directors to prepare a

Roll of Honour of Members and Sons of Members who answered their Country's call

No meetings of members of the Club have been held since August, 1914, although the Directors have held a number of meetings in order to keep in touch with matters connected with Burnsiana. The opening meeting of the Club will be held in the Bank Restaurant on Wednesday, 15th October, and the Annual Dinner (the first since January, 1914), will be held on Friday, 22nd January.

The Annual Singing and Reciting Competition from the Works of Burns by the children of Provanside School, under the auspices of this Club was held on Saturday, 1st February. The Gymnasium of the school was filled by a large and appreciative audience. I need scarcely say the competition was a great success, and this result was largely due to the work of Mr Marshall and his assistants in bringing the children to the high degree of efficiency shewn in the rendering of the songs and recitations. Great care seems to have been taken in giving the proper pronunciation of the Doric. The medals were gifted by Past President M'Bride, and the books by Vice-President Craik. The winners of the Club medals were—for Singing, Annie Barron and Thomas Wright ; and for Reciting, Martha M'Neil and David Chalmers. The medals and books were gracefully handed to the winners by Miss Martyn. Past President Headrick occupied the chair.

The Annual Bowling Match of Present and Past Officials of the Club was played in Willowbank Green, on Saturday, 20th September.

The first Summer Outing of the Club since June, 1914, took place on Saturday, 7th June, to Ayr. There was a good attendance, but the weather proving unpropitious, most of the programme had to be dropped.

1919. Syllabus, 1919-1920.

Oct.   15. Opening Remarks—Dr Cullen, President.
Nov.   5. " The Merchants and Guild Crafts of Glasgow "—James Lucas, Esq., M.A., F.E.I.S.
Dec.   3. " Romance of one of Glasgow Public Parks " (Limelight Photos)—John Main, Esq., F.G.S., F.E.I.S.
1920.
Jan.   7. " Bubble and Squeak "—J. Lothian, Esq.
Jan.   22. " Immortal Memory " (Annual Dinner, Grand Hotel, at 6.30)—Rev. A. Gordon Mitchell, D.D., of Killearn.
Feb.   4. " Robert Fergusson "—Past President J. Wilson Bain.
Mar.   3. " Homes and Haunts of Genius in Glasgow " (Lantern Slides)—Rev. Jas. Primrose, D.D.

Robt. Carmichael, *Hon. Secretary.*

NEWBATTLE AND DISTRICT.

Nov.   1. Mr Wm. Kirkwood—Paper.
Dec.   6. Mr D. Jamieson—Paper.
  1920.
Jan. `10· Mr J. Morris—Paper.
Jan.   24. Anniversary Meeting (as arranged).
Feb.   7. Mr J. Carson—Paper.
Feb.   21. Special Meeting. Mr A. Wilkie—Paper.
Mar.   6. Mr J. Callender—Paper.
April   3. Rev. J. N. Macpherson—Paper.

GOVAN FAIRFIELD BURNS CLUB.

REPORT.

We had a successful Motor Run to Mauchline and Tarbolton
on 21st June, when we visited several places of interest to Burnsites.
I take this opportunity of expressing my own regards for the noble
work you are doing on behalf of lovers of Burns all over the world
in compiling the *Chronicle* year after year, and always having something new; and I also am very pleased at the decision come to regarding Highland Mary's grave and memorial.   I believe a satisfactory
settlement will yet be arrived at.   Our Club held a very successful
Theatre Night in the Lyceum, Govan, on 23rd January last, when
our own old friend, Mr W. F. Frame was appearing, and he gave
a " Burns's Night " for our benefit.

Sept.   3. " The Scottish Sabbath "—Mr J. Jeffrey Hunter.
Oct.   1. " The Social Ideal of Burns "—Mr Alex. Pollock.
Nov   5   " The Philosophy of Burns "—Mr J. F. Anderson.
Dec.   3. " Women who Influenced Burns's Life " (Ladies' Night)
               —Mr Jas. Lauder.
  1920.
Jan.   7. " Napoleon "—Mr J. K. M'Dowall, J.P.
Jan.   24. " The Immortal Memory " (Annual Supper)—Mr T.
               M. Walker, M.A.
Feb.   4. Harmony—Members' Night.
Mar.   3. " Burns and Religion "—Mr Ninian M'Whannell, F.R.I.B.A.

JOHN GORDON, *Secretary.*

YE CRONIES BURNS CLUB (GOVAN.)

Annual Report for 1918-1919.

I have to report another successful session in the history of the above Club, and we all trust that in the near future that long-looked-for Peace, which has meant so much to us all, may soon be ours. The massing of events during these last few days has made us wonder if it is really peace, or is it again war. We do find ourselves, however, projecting our minds into the future with that spirit of hopefulness that, when the restrictions with which the cloud of war has enwrapped us are removed, the social intercourse of brotherhood may be resumed on the good old-fashioned lines.

At the beginning of the past session we were again very unfortunate in losing our Secretary, Mr R. Coutts, owing to a very severe trouble in his eyes, which, I am sorry to say, debars him from attending the Club meetings.

In the M'Lennan Cup Bowling Competition last August, one of our rinks (Mr N. M'Kelvie, skip) had the honour of winning second prize after having tied for the premier position. We have added to the walls of our Club-room another picture, namely, " Burns's House in Mauchline," kindly presented to the Club by Past President Isaac Chalmers.

With reference to the Club Roll of Honour, there are at present on the scroll 8 Members, 21 Members' sons, and 13 Members' brothers. Unfortunately this year we have to report one fatal casualty on the Roll of Honour—Sapper Charles B. Moodie, killed in France, his parents receiving the sad news the very day the Armistice was signed. I have also to report the death of one of our old and esteemed members, namely, Mr William Gibson, one who was beloved by all. A deputation of the members attended the funeral, and a beautiful floral wreath was sent from the members.

The membership having been opened out during the year, eleven new members were enrolled. In November we held a Picture Night, which was a great success, and enabled us to send on postal orders to our brave lads on active service on Club Roll of Honour, and we received very nice replies from the recipients thanking the members of the Club for their kindness.

Owing to the food and liquor restrictions it was decided not to hold our Anniversary Supper on the same scale as in former years, but an Extraordinary Meeting of the Club was held in the Club-room on the 25th January—President James Rellie in the chair, and a large turnout of members. Past President Mr Chalmers proposed the " Immortal Memory " in a very impressive manner, and a very pleasant evening was the result.

Owing to the depletion of membership of some of the Burns
Clubs, Club visitations were not so much in evidence this year as
formerly.   On the 15th March we had a deputation from the
Whiteinch Cronies, which proved a very social function.   A deputation of " Ye Cronies " visited Uddingston Masonic Burns Club,
and spent a very enjoyable evening.   Our Club also subscribed
£7 to the Elder Cottage Hospital, and £3 to Merryflatts Military
Hospital.   We have had a very successful year again, all things
considered, and our best thanks are due to our President, Mr James
Rellie, also to the Office-bearers and Committee, who have worked
entirely for the welfare of " Ye Cronies."

WILLIAM STIRRAT, Secretary.

DUNEDIN   BURNS   CLUB.

28th ANNUAL REPORT.

In presenting the Annual Report we cannot let this opportunity
pass without expressing our thankfulness to Almighty God that
the world's greatest war is now nominally closed, and that the British
Empire and her Allies have once more proved victorious.   We
trust that the long-looked-for Peace will soon be recorded, and
that war and rumours of war shall cease for ever.   We also trust
that the present unsettled state of humanity will soon be over, that
all wrongs will be righted, and the world become a better place,
" when man to man the warld o'er shall brithers be an' a' that."

We are glad to be able to report a little headway made during
the period under review.   The membership shows a decided increase on last year, the number on the roll now being 521 (double
328, single 193), as against 429 last year.   Much of this increase
is due to the enthusiasm of our past Secretary, Mr J. Syme.

Financially there is a credit balance for the year of £24 19s 6d,
the receipts being £290 2s 3d, and expenses £265 2s 9d.   We tender
our sincere thanks to Mr James Brown for his continued services
as Honorary Auditor to the Club.

It may be said that the aims of the founders of the Club are
being fulfilled.   A large proportion of the Office-bearers and
members are New Zealanders, and they will be all the better New
Zealanders, and none the less loyal Britons, while they cherish
a liking for the music, songs, and history of the Old Land of their
fathers and mothers.

MONTHLY CONCERTS.

The monthly meetings have been well attended by enthusiastic
audiences, and the standard of the concerts well maintained.

ADDRESSES.

Five addresses were given at the monthly meetings. Our Vice-president, Mr W. B. M'Ewan, gave a limelight lecture at the June meeting, on "The Haunts and Homes of Burns." The views were much appreciated, and the lecture was most interesting and illuminating.

HALLOWE'EN.

The ancient festival of Hallowe'en was again celebrated. His Majesty's Theatre was well filled by an enthusiastic audience, and the whole concert was most successful.

ANNIVERSARY GATHERING.

The Anniversary of the Poet's birth was observed in the Burns Hall, when one of the best Scottish concerts ever held in Dunedin was given to a well-satisfied audience, which taxed the seating accommodation of the Hall to its utmost. Mr James Craigie, M.P., delivered an appropriate address on "Scotland's Treatment of Burns," which was worthy of the occasion.

ROLL OF HONOUR.

Two hundred and five names are now on the Roll, and it may not be complete. The Roll includes members, sons and brothers of members, and if any names are omitted it is desirable that they should be handed to the President or Secretary. We extend our deepest sympathy to the parents and friends who have had the misfortune to lose their sons and relatives during this great conflict.

COMMITTEE.

The meetings of Committee have been well attended. The President desires to place on record his warm appreciation of the splendid help given to him during his term of office by the Vice-presidents and the other Office-bearers, and to all the members and friends who have done yeoman service in helping to carry on the Club's good work. He extends his thanks to the Dunedin Highland Band for their able services, freely given when requested.

WILLIAM BROWN, *President.*

MOSSGIEL BURNS CLUB (GLASGOW).

The Club continues to show a gratifying increase in membership—the number on the roll now being over 100. The Annual Celebration took the form of a Whist Drive and Dance in the Marlborough Rooms, when an attendance of members and friends to the number of 300 was recorded. The proceedings, ably supervised by President M'Nish, were kept going till a late hour in the evening, when a most pleasing function, deemed by all the most successful ever held in the history of the Club, was brought to a close.

The cessation of the war has enabled the Club to arrange a Winter Syllabus for 1919-1920, the opening address, entitled " A Nicht wi' the Jacobites " being given by President M'Nish to a crowded meeting in the Lounge Room of the Y.M.C.A., Eglinton Toll. The papers constituting the rest of the syllabus are of an interesting type, and should prove equally attractive.

1919.   Syllabus, 1919-1920.

Oct. 16. " A Nicht wi' the Jacobites "—President T. W. M'Nish.
Nov 20 " An Hour in Burns's Library "—John Muir, Esq., F.S.A.
Dec. 18. " Jean Armour "—Ernest G. Gray, Esq.
.1920.
Jan. 15. " The Poetry of Burns "—William Robertson, Esq.
Feb. 19. Selected—Rev. T. Stobo Glen, M.A.
Mar. 18. Singing and Reciting Competition of Burns's Songs and
        · Poetry—Children of Abbotsford Public School.

HAMILTON JUNIOR BURNS CLUB.

Report for Session 1918-1919.

The past session of the Hamilton Junior Club was a very active, profitable, and pleasant one. The Annual Meeting was held on the evening of 25th September, when there was a large attendance of the members. In the regretted absence through illness of the President (Mr Wm. Ferguson), Mr D. Cross, Vice-president, occupied the chair. The reports submitted by the Secretary and Treasurer were of a gratifying nature, and showed the fellowship to be in a good financial position.

During the summer months many pleasant Rambles were organised and carried through. The principal of these was the annual visit to Cadzow Forest. The proceeds of the concerts held during the year were allocated as follows :—Royal Infirmary, £11 ; Western Infirmary, £11 ; Victoria Infirmary, £7 ; Dunoon Seaside Homes, £1.

By the death of Mr Arch. Thomson, Minute Secretary, the Club has lost one of its original members. He was a regular attender at our meetings, and always active and interested. His passing is a loss to the Club, and his presence will be missed. The sympathy of the members is also extended to Mr Ferguson, our President, in his protracted illness. He has been a source of much strength to the Club during his fourteen years' membership, and particularly during the years he has occupied the presidential chair. In the month of April, on the occasion of Mr and Mrs Ferguson's golden wedding, the members of the Club presented him with a steel etching of Burns as a token of esteem, and a handsome gold brooch to Mrs Ferguson. The hope is expressed that he may soon be able to rejoin us. Acting on the suggestion made at the Annual Meeting of the Burns Federation, the Club, during the year, endeavoured to inaugurate a competition in connection with the various schools in the burgh, with the object of popularising Burns's songs amongst the younger generation. The Headmasters were approached, and while the proposal was sympathetically received, it was felt that, with the dislocation in the various staffs by the war, the present was not altogether an opportune time to take the matter up. We are not without hope, however, that at some time in the near future, a competition of this kind will be inaugurated. For the past three years the Brotherhood, owing to war restrictions, were deprived of their regular meeting-place in Union Street, where the Club was formed in 1886. Now that these restrictions have been removed, we are able to resume in our old Club-room. The Club meetings are held on the first Monday of each month, at 7.30 p.m., at 1 Union Street, Hamilton, when a warm welcome will be accorded to any member of a Federated Club.

W. WILSON, Secretary.

SHETTLESTON BURNS CLUB.

SECRETARY'S REPORT, 1918-1919.

" Victory " Year has proved a record session in the history of the Shettleston Burns Club, our membership and financial position being ahead of any previous year. This is most encouraging to the Office-bearers and Committee, as it shows keen spirit and enthusiasm amongst our members. On our Ladies' Night a new feature was introduced ; a lecture on " Bird Life," accompanied with limelight illustrations, being given by James D. Sloan, Esq., President of Rosebery Burns Club, to whom we were greatly indebted for a most interesting night's entertainment. Mr Sloan was quite at home on the subject of his lecture, and showed a thorough knowledge of bird life, giving quotations from Burns and other poets, thus adding greatly to the interest of his lecture.

For the M'Lennan Cup Competition six rinks entered. One of our rinks, skipped by Mr James Myles, succeeded in gaining second prize.

During the session our Club sustained a sad blow in the death of our esteemed Treasurer, Mr Thomas Barrie, one of our oldest members, and for many years a most capable, untiring director of our finances.   His genial presence has been greatly missed at our Committee meetings, and future Social Gatherings will be the poorer by the absence of a most earnest and enthusiastic member of our Club.   His good work is being continued by the Secretary until next Annual Meeting.   As proving the good work done by our late Treasurer, Mr Barrie, the 1918-19 financial statement showed an increase in our funds greatly in excess of any previous year.

Children's Competition—singing and reciting works of Burns—is expected to take place during the coming session.   A fund has been inaugurated, showing £2 9s in hand, towards prizes for this event.

I desire to tender my heartfelt thanks to Officials and Members of our Club for the great assistance given me during my year of Secretaryship, and can testify to the good work accomplished by your Committee.

1919.   SYLLABUS, 1919-1920.

Nov. 1. Lectuer : " Philosphy of Robert Burns "
                                —W. M. Douglas, Esq.
Dec. 19. Lecture : " Charles Murray's Poems "
                                —Chas. MacDonald, Esq.
1920.
Jan. 24. Annual Dinner.
March.   Ladies' Night.

                    ROBERT M. MILHOLM, *Hon. Secretary.*

GATESHEAD BURNS CLUB.

RÉPORT.

Since March, 1914, the Gateshead Club has been in abeyance. Twice during the war I tried to get the members together but failed. Now I am trying again, and hope to succeed.   Some of the members were at the Front, many had sons there, and all had friends and relations on active service.   Our Piper, a native of Ayrshire, with his only son John, was out there, although he is now on the wintry side of fifty.   Another member, also an Ayrshire man, Charlie Bond, was engaged at the Front, with, I think, three sons.   Another member, Donald Morrison, had a son, Captain Morrison, killed at Gallipoli, and another badly wounded in France.   Tom Hethering-ton had a son killed in France and another wounded.   But I daresay if I was going over the list of members it would be a similar tale to tell.

I hope our efforts to get the old Club going again will meet with success.

WM. BAIN, *Secretary.*

SUNDERLAND BURNS CLUB.

We have pleasure in submitting the Annual Report of our past year's work and the twenty-second of our Sunderland Burns Club. On all hands we may congratulate ourselves that we have been able to " keep the home fires burning."

ANNIVERSARY CELEBRATION.

At the Anniversary gathering a large company of gentlemen assembled in the North of England Café on Saturday, 25th January, 1919, to celebrate the one hundred and sixtieth Anniversary of our Poet's birth.

The President of the Club, Neil Cameron, Esq., occupied the chair, supported by Lieut.-Col. C. Duncan Johnstone, who submitted the toast of the " Immortal Memory " in fine style, dealing with the outstanding features in the Poet's life. The musical part of the programme was well sustained ; and the Pipe Band, under Pipe-Major Graham, rendered selections, in addition to ushering in the " Haggis."

" CHRONICLE."

We are pleased to report a continued increase of subscribers in our Club to this most excellent publication. We are not by any means satisfied, and hope we shall not be until every member becomes a subscriber. The veteran Editor spares neither time nor energy to make it worthy of the very best in the Burns world. We are assured that a complete set of the *Chronicle* cannot now be purchased for less than £7.

THE PIPE BAND.

The Pipe Band appeared at the Royal Infirmary Fète on Wednesday evening, 19th June, 1918, and rendered an excellent programme in the grounds. An exhibition of Highland Dancing was given by the M'Cue family. Perhaps the most outstanding feature was the parades arranged on behalf of the D.L.I. Prisoners of War Fund on September 16th, 19th, and 23rd, 1918. As a result of this effort the handsome sum of £94 8s 5d was handed over to the Fund.

In Memoriam.

We have to record our loss during the year of John Mather Phillips, 2nd Tyneside Scottish, who fell in action on 2nd September, 1918. A member of our Pipe Band, he joined up shortly after the outbreak of war and crossed over with the Tyneside Brigade early in 1915. He had seen much strenuous work, until he fell as indicated above. The sympathy of the Club was conveyed to the sorrowing widow and family.

We have also sustained another loss by death of an Hon. Vice-president of the Club. The late Mr George Tawse, whose death took place on 26th December, 1918, had been associated with the Club since its inception, and had always taken a keen interest in all its work—always ready and willing to do whatever lay in his power to promote its best interests. By his passing we have lost a valued member and the town a good citizen. The sympathy of the Club was conveyed to his sorrowing widow and daughters.

Roll of Honour.

Pte. Stan. Murray, West Yorkshire Regiment, son of Mr George Murray (late Club Piper).

Pte. W. H. Calvert, Royal Canadian Rifles, son of Mr A. R. Calvert (Vice-president).

Pte. J. M. Phillips, 2nd Tyneside Scottish.

Membership.

We commenced the year with sixty-seven active members. During the year we have lost two by death, resignations and removals from the district account for five, while the new members joining number eleven, leaving us with seventy-one members—a gain of four on the year.

A large company assembled on 18th March to do honour to Colonel C. Duncan Johnstone, who for the evening had laid aside His Majesty's uniform and appeared in Highland Costume. The toast of the evening, " Our Guest," was given by A. W. Semple, Esq., who spoke of the many outstanding features of Colonel Johnstone since he became associated with us, and also on behalf of the Club expressed regret at his departure, but hoped on some future occasion he would be able to pay a visit to the Club, when he would be assured of a most hearty welcome. Colonel Johnstone, on rising to reply had a rousing reception. He thanked the Club for the many pleasant evenings he had spent in Sunderland, and hoped we would continue to prosper and keep the " Lion Flag flying " for the sake of Auld Scotland.

SYLLABUS.

1918.
Oct.   9. " Sir Collin Campbell "—Neil Cameron (President).
Nov.   13. " Gems of Scottish Song "—Mr G. Mackay.
Dec.   11. " Robert Burns the Farmer "—Mr W. M. Donaldson.
1919.
Jan.   8. Scottish Songs of Quaint Humour—Mr W. H. Turner
Jan.   25. " The Immortal Memory "—Lieut.-Col. C. D. Johnstone.
Feb.   12. " On and off the Stage "—Mr Tom Fisher.
Mar.   18. Farewell to Lieut.-Col. C. Duncan Johnstone.
April   9. " Abraham Lincoln "—Mr M. A. R. Calvert.
May   14. Annual Meeting.—Election of Officers.

Let us not forget our Sailors and Soldiers, and our countrymen in particular, through whose bravery and perseverance, enduring untold misery and hardship, we have emerged from the great struggle victorious.

Let us remember, however, the price paid for this freedom and liberty—a price which has taken from us the flower of our manhood.

We humbly and reverently salute our glorious dead, and we hope that we may live worthily of their great sacrifice.   Out of this struggle we see will arise a " League of Nations " which we hope shall prevent any further wars and bring nearer the time—

" When man to man the world o'er
Shall brithers be for a' that."

M. NEILSON, *Hon. Secretary.*

ROSEBERY BURNS CLUB.

SESSION 1918-1919.

A very successful session was carried through under the able Presidentship of Mr Jas. D. Sloan.

The attendances were from 80 to over 100 at the various meetings.

The literary side was prominent, with subjects on art and poetry and all were of a high standard

The Annual Dinner, and Anniversary of our Poet, was revived after several years' omission owing to the war   It was a pleasant function.

We were fortunate in having an outstandingly good Children's Competition, under the superintendence of Mr Jas. Lucas, M.A., at Bluevale School.   There was an attendance of over 800, only limited by the capacity of the hall. The performance of the children was most creditable, and the competition will be repeated in January, 1920.

GLASGOW MASONIC BURNS CLUB.

SESSION 1919-1920

List of Lectures in Masonic Halls, 100 West Regent Street, at 7.30 p.m. prompt.

1919.

Oct. 17. " Burns at Mossgiel : A Literary Fantasy "—George Henderson.

Nov. 21. " The Attraction of Burns " — James Lucas, M.A.

Dec. 30. " Scotland's Debt to Burns " J. S. Jamieson.

1920.

Jan. 23. Scotch Concert. The " Immortal Memory " will be proposed by the Rev. David Graham, B.D., Redgorton, Perth.

Feb. 26. " The Historical Position of Burns " —A. M. Williams, M.A.

Mar. 11. Dance in Burlington House.

Mar. 30. " Jean Armour "—J. Jeffrey Hunter.

April 30. " Holy Willie's Prayer "—Thos. G. Forbes.

The Burns Federation.

INSTITUTED 1885.

Hon President—The Right Hon. The EARL OF ROSEBERY, K.G., K.T.

Hon. Vice-Presidents—WM. WALLACE, LL.D., University Avenue, Glasgow.

Professor LAWSON, D.D., The University, St. Andrews.

Brigadier-General Sir ALEX. GIBB, K.B.E.. R.E., Rosyth.

OFFICE-BEARERS.

President—DUNCAN M'NAUGHT, J.P., Benrig, Kilmaurs.

Vice-Presidents—J. JEFFREY HUNTER, 89 Bath Street, Glasgow.

A. M'CALLUM, *News* Office, Pollokshaws.

JOSEPH MARTIN, J.P., 163 West George Street, Glasgow.

ALEX. POLLOCK, 52 West Nile Street, Glasgow.

W. H. TURNER, 9 The Oaks, Sunderland.

JOHN CARMICHAEL, 49 Park Road, Glasgow.

P. PATERSON, 23 Bruce Street, Dunfermline.

Ex-Bailie MUNRO, J.P., Howard Park Drive, Kilmarnock.

Ex-Provost M. SMITH, J.P., Glencairn Square, Kilmarnock.

Ex-Provost WILSON, 149 Howard Street, Glasgow.

PHILIP SULLEY, F.S.A., Elgin.

HUGH M'COLL, 278 St. Vincent Street, Glasgow.

DAVID MAIN, Lowther Street, Carlisle.

HENRY S. MURRAY, J.P., Glenmayne, Galashiels.

CHARLES R. COWIE, Blythswood Square, Glasgow.

J. C. EWING, Bailie's Institution, West Regent Street, Glasgow.

ALEX. M'KENZIE, 210 Battlefield Road, Langside, Glasgow.

JAMES THOMSON, F.S.A.Scot., 85 Fleet Street, London, E.C.

WILLIAM DOUGLAS, 509 Sauchiehall Street, Glasgow.

THOS. KILLIN, 2 Stewarton Drive, Cambuslang.

Hon. Secretary—THOS. AMOS, M.A., 19 Glebe Road, Kilmarnock.

Hon. Treasurer—Major G. A. INNES, M.B.E., Landsborough Drive, Kilmarnock.

Editor " *Burns Chronicle* "—D. M'NAUGHT, J.P., Benrig, Kilmaurs.

Auditors—Major D. YUILLE, Burns Avenue, Kilmarnock, and Capt. ADAM MACKAY, The Crescent, Prestwick.

Local Representatives—

London—P. N. M'FARLANE, Tallis House, Tallis Street, London. E.C.

North of England—W. H. TURNER, Sunderland.

Glasgow and District—J. JEFFREY HUNTER, 89 Bath Street, Glasgow.

Hon. Secretary of Children's Competitions—ALEX. POLLOCK, 52 West Nile Street, Glasgow (to whom all communications should be addressed).

CONSTITUTION.

1. The Federation shall consist of Hon. Presidents, Hon. Vice-Presidents, Executive Council, and members of each affiliated Club.

2. The Executive Council shall consist of a President, Vice-Presidents, Hon. Secretary, Hon. Treasurer, Editor of the *Burns Chronicle*, and two Auditors—all of whom shall be elected annually, and be eligible for re-election ; also 'of the President, Vice-President, and Secretary, or any other three members of, and nominated by, each affiliated Club, and other gentlemen of eminence as Burnsians nominated by the Executive Council.

3. All Past Presidents of the Federation shall *ex officio* be members of the Executive Council.

4. The Executive Committee shall consist of the Office-bearers of the Federation, who shall meet quarterly, or when called by the Hon. Secretary, for the transaction of the business of the Federation.

5. Federated Clubs outwith the United Kingdom may be represented by proxy at the meetings of the Federation.

OBJECTS OF THE FEDERATION.

1. To strengthen and consolidate by universal affiliation the bond of fellowship existing amongst the members of Burns Clubs and kindred Societies.

2. To superintend the publication of Works relating to Burns.

3. To acquire a fund for the purchase and preservation of Holograph Manuscripts and other Relics connected with the life of the Poet, and for other purposes of a like nature, as the Executive Council may determine.

4. To repair, renew, and where advisable mark with suitable inscriptions any buildings, tombstones, etc., interesting from their association with Burns.

5. To encourage and arrange School Competitions in order to stimulate the teaching of Scottish History and Literature.

RULES.

1. The Headquarters of the Federation shall be in Kilmarnock, the town in which the Federation was inaugurated and carried to a practical issue, and which contains the only properly organised Burns Library and Museum in the United Kingdom.

2. Properly organised Burns Clubs, St. Andrew's Societies, and kindred Associations may be admitted to the Federation by application in writing to the Hon. Secretary, enclosing a copy of Constitution, Rules, and list of members, which shall be submitted to the Executive Committee at their first meeting, and the Clubs shall be enrolled if there are not more than two dissentients.

3. The Registration Fee is 21s, on receipt of which the Diploma of the Federation shall be issued, after being numbered and signed by the President and Hon. Secretary.

4. Members of every Burns Club or kindred Association registered by the Federation shall be entitled to receive a pocket Diploma on payment of 1s. These payments are final—not annual.

5. The funds of the Federation shall be vested in the Executive Committee for the purposes before mentioned.

6. A meeting of the Executive Council shall be held annually on the first Saturday of September, at such place as may be agreed upon, when reports on the year's transactions shall be submitted by the Hon. Secretary and Hon. Treasurer, and Office-Bearers elected for the ensuing year.

7. A meeting of the Executive Committee shall take place some time before the Annual Meeting of the Executive Council, to make the necessary arrangements for the same.

8. All nominations for the office of Vice-President must be lodged with the Hon. Secretar two months before the Annual Meeting.

9. Each Federated Club shall subscribe 10s 6d per annum towards the fund for the publication of the *Burns Chronicle*. Clubs failing to pay this subscription for two consecutive years may be struck off the Roll of the Federation. Any surplus profits resulting from the sale of the *Chronicle* shall be added to the general funds.

10. Notice of any amendment or alteration of the Constitution or Rules of the Federation to be considered at the Annual Meeting must be lodged in writing with the Hon. Secretary not later than 30th June.

BENEFITS.

1. Registered Clubs are supplied free with copies of newspapers containing accounts of meetings, demonstrations, etc., organised, conducted, or attended by the Executive Council of the Federation, and of the Annual Meeting of the Kilmarnock Burns Club.

2. Exchange of fraternal greetings on the anniversary of the Poet's natal day.

3. Members of Registered Clubs who have provided themselves with pocket diplomas are entitled to attend meetings of all Clubs on the Roll of the Federation, they being subject to the rules of the Club visited, but having no voice in its management unless admitted a member according to local form.

4. Members are entitled to be supplied, through the Secretaries of their respective Clubs, with copies of all Works published by the Federation at a discount of 25 per cent.

5. A list of Lecturers, Essayists, and Judges for Children's Competitions will be supplied to Clubs on application.

BOOKS PUBLISHED BY THE FEDERATION.

Burns Holograph Manuscripts in the Kilmarnock Monument Museum, with Notes	1889	1s 6d
Burns Chronicle and Club Directory...	1892	1s 0d
,, ,,	1893	1s 6d
	1894	1s 6d
	1895	1s 6d
	1896	1s 6d
	1897	1s 6d
	1898	1s 6d
,,	1899	1s 6d
,,	1900	1s 6d
,, (out of print)	1901	1s 6d
,,	1902	1s 6d
	1903	1s 6d
	1904	1s 6d
	1905	1s 6d
	1906 ...	1s 6d
	1907	1s 6d
	1908 ..	1s 6d
	1909 .	1s 6d
	1910	1s 6d
	1911	1s 6d
	1912	1s 6d
,, ...	1913	1s 6d
,, ...	1914	1s 6d
,, ...	1915	1s 6d
,, ...	1916	1s 6d
	1917	2s 0d
	1918	2s 0d
,, ...	1919	2s 0d
,, ,,	1920	2s 0d

Copies of the last nine vols. may still be had on application to the Hon. Treasurer.

MINUTES OF THE ANNUAL MEETING

OF THE

BURNS FEDERATION.

CENTRAL HALL, BATH STREET,
GLASGOW, 6th September, 1919.

THE Annual Conference of the Burns Federation was held here to-day. Mr D. M'Naught, J.P., presided, and along with him on the platform were : Messrs H. M'Coll, J. Jeffrey Hunter, Andrew M'Callum, Alex. Pollock, Thos. Killin, ex-Provost Wilson, Alex. M'Kenzie, Joseph Martin, J.P., Captain Douglas, J. Carmichael, and C. R. Cowie, Glasgow ; ex-Bailie Munro, J.P., Major Yuille, Major Innes, M.B.E., and T. Amos, Kilmarnock ; P. N. M'Farlane, London ; W. H. Turner, Sunderland ; and P. Paterson, Dunfermline. The following Delegates were also present :

No. 3, Glasgow Tam o' Shanter—J. F. Anderson, W. Renfrew. J. M. Gillies. No. 9, Glasgow Royalty—G. F. Howarth. No. 14, Dundee—Geo. S. Middleton, Jas. Ogilvie. No. 21, Greenock—J. B. Morrison, A. M'Phail, Grierson Macara. No. 22, Edinburgh— George Williamson, J.P. No. 36, Glasgow Rosebery—J. D. Sloan, T. C. F. Brotchie, A. G. Andrew, W. Craig. No. 50, Stirling— Ridley Sandeman. No. 53, Govan Fairfield—T. Fullarton, Jas. Watson, J. M'Lachlan. No. 57, Thornliebank—T. Haddow, H. Halliday, T. Arbuckle. No. 63, Glasgow Mossgiel—W. Murray, J. M. Blair, Robt. Parker. No. 67, Glasgow Carlton—W. Gardiner. No. 85, Dunfermline United—Robt. Dunlop, Wm. Black. No. 91, Shettleston—Jas. S. Wilson, Robt. Milholm. No. 92, Kilbowie Jolly Beggars—D. Clark, John Deans, W. Crum. No. 97, Kilmar-nock Bellfield—Wm. Flannagan. No. 118 Glasgow Albany—R. D. Donaldson, Robt. Carmichael. No. 121, Hamilton Junior—John M'Millan, Robt. Brown, Wm. Wilson. No. 128, Cowdenbeath Glencairn—T. Harrower, T. Wilson, W. Archibald. No. 133, Newart-hill—T. Law, G. Horn. No. 135, Partick Western—Allan Stark. No. 139, Glasgow National—John G. Calpine. No. 148, Greenock Cronies—G. Cameron, A. M'Gavin. No. 153, Scottish—A. Camp-bell. No. 159, Walker-on-Tyne—John M'Kay. No. 169, Glasgow and District—J. Tudhope. No. 175, Meikle Earnock—Jas. Shepherd, A. Laird, R. Lees. No. 181, Glasgow Primrose—G. J. M'Callum, Jas. Lamb. No. 182, Stane Mossgiel—Jas. Whitefield Alex. Walker. No. 184, Blairadam Shanter—George Burden. No. 189, Clydebank Barns o' Clyde—A. Homewood, Jas. Kean, J. Hutcheon. No. 192, Ayrshire Association—Wm. Lennox. No. 199, Newbattle and District—J. Haldane, D. Richardson, P. Gray. No. 202, Govan Ye Cronies—M. Stirling, J. Hutchison, J. Rollie, I. Chalmers, E. J. Tait, J. M'Kinnon. No. 203, Dennistoun Jolly Beggars—A. Hainey, T. Millar, G. Thomas. No. 207, Cambuslang Wingate—D. Beck, A. Dunn, W. Stewart. No. 218, Bannockburn Empire—G. Forsyth, D. Forsyth. No. 223, Glasgow Auld Clinkum

Jas. Muir. No. 226, Dumfries—John M'Burnie. No. 234,
Glasgow Southern Merchants—W. Patrick. No. 243, Paisley St.
James—J. Stewart, W. Alexander, J. M'Kechnie. No. 244, Dalmuir
—J. Holmes, Wm. Boyle. No. 245, Kinnaird—Jas. Turnbull,
Jas. Wallace, A. Reid. No. 246, Lochore and Rosewell Shanter—
T. Wilson, Alex. Ross. No. 250, Cowdenbeath Tam o' Shanter
—J. Black, J. Duff. No. 251, Glencraig—R. Glencross, T. Ferguson.
No. 258, Buck's Head Armadale—J. Mack, J. Stevenson, W.
M'Alpine. No. 259, Bonnyrigg—Jas. B. Howden, D. Blyth. No.
260, Tarbrax—John M'Kee.

The Secretary read the Minutes of the previous Annual Conference and also his Annual Report, both of which were approved.

The Treasurer submitted his Annual Statement, which showed
a balance at the credit of the Federation of £183 19s 9d.

The Editor reported that he had made arrangements for another
issue of the *Chronicle*. On the motion of Mr M'Coll, the Editor was
thanked for his services, and the sum of £25 for payment of contributions to the *Chronicle* was voted by the meeting.

Mr Alex. Pollock reported a decrease in the number of School
Competitions during the war, but hoped there would be a renewal
of interest in this work during the next year or two.

Mr Chas. R. Cowie gave an interesting account of the inaugura-
tion of Dr Mackenzie's House at Mauchline as homes for deserving
old ladies. He also mentioned that, through the help of Partick
Burns Club, a marble tablet in memory of Gavin Hamilton had been
erected in Mauchline Churchyard.

The President detailed the efforts made by the Executive of the
Federation to secure the preservation of the West Kirk and Kirkyard of Greenock and Highland Mary's Grave and Monument. He
placed before the meeting the three options concerning Highland
Mary's grave, which had been offered by the promoters of the
Provisional Order, at the instruction of Messrs Harland & Wolff:—
1st—To remove the remains of Highland Mary and monument to
such a place of sepulture as might be selected by the Executive of
the Federation ; 2nd—To leave the remains interred as at present,
and to reverse the existing monument so as to face the street ;
3rd—To remove the existing monument, and to place and maintain
a mural tablet in lieu thereof, the remains not being disturbed."

Ex-Provost R. Wilson moved that it be left to the Executive
of the Federation, in conjunction with the representatives of Greenock
Burns Club, with full powers, to determine which of the three options
they should accept.

Mr Alex. Pollock moved the following motion : That this meeting
of the Burns Federation, as Burnsians and as Scotsmen, tender their
heartiest thanks to Mr R. L. Scott, Mr J. B. Morison, Mr T. B. Rowan,
Mr Grierson Macara, and other members of the Greenock Burns
Club for their noble and patriotic opposition to the proposal to sell
and remove the ancient Greenock West Church and churchyard ;
and that all present hereby pledge themselves to do all in their power
to oppose the passing into law of the Greenock Improvement Provisional Order, 1919, so far as that Order threatens the preservation
of this church and churchyard, and so prevent an indelible disgrace

being inflicted upon the name and fame of Scotland and Scotsmen. And this meeting further appeals to all Scottish Societies to aid in this opposition, and so maintain the sacredness of all burial grounds in Scotland, and the permanent validity of the title deeds of all lair-holders. whether poor or rich.

Mr Alexander Williamson, J.P., Edinburgh, seconded the motion.

Mr Pollock urged the Delegates to write to their Members 'of Parliament and protest against the proposed desecration.

Mr Grierson Macara, Greenock, said there was no immediate need to hurry in accepting the options which had been mentioned, and he suggested that, as many of the Executive Committee did not know the surroundings of the grave, they should visit Greenock before coming to a decision. He thought they should leave the matter in the hands of the Executive, with powers to co-opt some members of the Greenock Burns Club or some of the petitioners against the Order.

After some discussion, and the withdrawal of Mr Pollock's motion, it was agreed to remit the whole matter to the Executive. along with representatives from each of the federated Greenock Burns Clubs. The Committee was to be called together should there be need to take immediate action.

On the motion of Mr M'Coll, it was agreed to admit Ayr Burns Club to the Federation, on condition that they take the number vacant when they make their application.

To prevent confusion between the London Robert Burns Club and the London Burns Club (Scots), it was agreed that the latter club would only be admitted to the Federation under the name of the London Scots' Burns Club.

The President reported that Mr John Gribbel was unable to leave America at present, and therefore the presentation of the Gribbel Album would be postponed

On the motion of Mr M'Coll, seconded by Mr W. H. Turner, it was agreed to re-elect the office-bearers.

Mr P. N. M'Farlane, on behalf of London Robert Burns Club. invited the Federation to hold its next Annual Conference in London and the invitation was unanimously accepted.

A vote of thanks to the President terminated the meeting.

THOMAS AMOS, *Hon. Secy.*

184

List of Clubs which have Subscribed to the Publishing Fund.

Club	£	s	d
Airdrie	0	10	6
Alexandria	0	10	6
Alloway	0	10	6
Arbroath	0	10	6
Armadale Star	0	10	6
,, ,, (arrears)	0	10	6
Armadale Buck's Head	0	10	6
Auchinleck Boswell	0	10	6
Baillieston Caledonia	0	10	6
Bannockburn Empire	0	10	6
Birmingham	0	10	6
Birtley	0	10	6
Blairadam Shanter	0	10	6
Bonnyrigg A Man's a Man	0	10	6
,. ,, (arrears)	0	10	6
Brechin	0	10	6
Bristol	0	10	6
Burnbank	0	10	6
Cambuslang Wingate	0	10	6
Chattanooga	0	10	6
Clydebank Barns o' Clyde	0	10	6
Cowdenbeath Glencairn	0	10	6
Cowdenbeath Tam o' Shanter	0	10	6
Cupar	0	10	6
Dalmuir	0	10	6
Derby	0	10	6
Dublin	0	10	6
Dumfries	0	10	6
Dumfries Burns Howff	0	10	6
Dundalk and District	0	10	6
Dunfermline United	0	10	6
Dundee	0	10	6
East Calder	0	10	6
Edinburgh Ninety	0	10	6
,, ,, (arrears)	0	10	6
Elgin	0	10	6
Fauldhouse	0	10	6
Galashiels	0	10	6
Garelochhead	0	10	6
Gateshead and District	0	10	6
Glasgow Tam o' Shanter	0	10	6
Glasgow Primrose	0	10	6
Glasgow Thistle	0	10	6
Glasgow Royalty	0	10	6
Glasgow Carrick	0	10	6
Glasgow Dennistoun Jolly Beggars	0	10	6
Glasgow Mossgiel	0	10	6
Glasgow Carlton	0	10	6
Glasgow Mauchline Society	0	10	6
Glasgow Albany	0	10	6
Glasgow National	1	1	0
Glasgow Kingston	0	10	6
Glasgow Auld Clinkum	0	10	6
Glasgow Southern Merchants	0	10	6
Glasgow and District	0	10	6
Glasgow Rosebery	0	10	6
Glasgow Scottish	0	10	6
Glencraig	0	10	6
Govan Fairfield	0	10	6
Govan Cronies	0	10	6
Greenock	0	10	6
Greenock Cronies	0	10	6
Greenock St. John's	0	10	6
Greenock Victoria	0	10	6
Hamilton	0	10	6
Hamilton Mossgiel	0	10	6
Hamilton Junior	0	10	6
Hawick	0	10	6
Helensburgh	0	10	6
Hull	0	10	6
Jedburgh	0	10	6
Kilbowie Jolly Beggars	0	10	6
Kilmarnock	0	10	6
Kilmarnock Jolly Beggars	0	10	6
Kinnaird Falkirk	0	10	6
Kirn	0	10	6
Lanark	0	10	6
Larkhall Thistle Lodge	0	10	6
London Robert Burns Club	0	10	6
Londonderry	0	10	6
,, (arrears)	1	1	0
Meikle Earnock	0	10	6
Mid-Argyll	0	10	6
Midcalder Tam o' Shanter	0	10	6
Muirkirk Lapraik	0	10	6
Newbattle and District	0	10	6
Newarthill	0	10	6
Newton-on-Ayr	0	10	6
Oregon, U.S.A.	0	10	6
Paisley	0	10	6
Paisley Charleston	0	10	6
Paisley St. James	0	10	6
Paisley St. Mirren	0	10	6
Port-Glasgow	0	10	6
Partick Western	0	10	6
Portobello	0	10	6
Prestonpans	0	10	6
Row	0	10	6
Shettleston	0	10	6
Shiremoor Blue Bell	0	10	6
Stane Mossgiel	0	10	6
Stirling	0	10	6
Stonehouse Jolly Beggars	0	10	6
Sunderland	0	10	6
Sydney Anniversary	0	10	6
Thornliebank	0	10	6
Tollcross	0	10	6
Uddingston Masonic	0	10	6
Uphall	0	10	6
Walker, Newcastle	0	10	6
Wallsend-on-Tyne	0	10	6
Whitehaven	0	10	6

Alphabetical List of Federated Clubs.

No. 40. Aberdeen
84. Abington
23. Adelaide
20. Airdrie
143. Airdrie Gateside
2. Alexandria
6. Alloa
252. Alloway
82. Arbroath
174. Ardrossan Castle
257. Armadale Star
258. Armadale Buck's Head
232. Arniston
224. Ashington
238. Atlanta
123. Auchinleck
19. Auckland
192. Ayrshire Association
157. Baillieston Caledonia
218. Bannockburn Empire
99. Barlinnie
12. Barrow-in-Furness
64. Beith
15. Belfast
167. Birmingham
248. Birtley
30. Blackburn
125. Blackburn-on-Almond
184. Blairadam Shanter
240. Blawarthill
95. Bolton
29. Bolton Juniors
119. Bonhill
142. Bonnybridge
259. Bonnyrigg
76. Brechin
120. Bristol
114. Brodick
106. Broxburn Roseberv
230. Burnbank
185. Burton
228. Calderwaterhead
Callander
110. Cambuslang
207. Cambuslang Wingate
87. Campsie

No. 71. Carlisle
102. Carlisle Border
201. Carlisle Newtown
81. Carstairs Junction
171. Chattanooga, U.S.A.
11. Chesterfield
51. Chicago
138. Cleland
166. Cleveland Scottish
Association
93. Clydebank
189. Clydebank Barns o' Clyde
103. Coalburn Rosebery
233. Coalburn Clachan
208. Colorado Springs
79. Corstorphine
127. Cowdenbeath Haggis
128. Cowdenbeath Glencairn
250. Cowdenbeath Tam o'
Shanter
42. Crieff
241. Crook
66. Crossgates
45. Cumnock
86. Cumnock The Winsome
Willie
62. Cupar
179. Dailly
244. Dalmuir
35. Dalry
158. Darlington
122. Darnconner
55. Derby
37. Dollar
146. Dublin
10. Dumbarton
52. Dumfries Mechanics
104. Dumfries Oak
226. Dumfries
112. Dumfries Howff
204. Dundalk
14. Dundee
69. Dunedin
85. Dunfermline United
80. Dunoon Cowal
188. Duns Working Men

No. 134. Duntocher Heron
    5. Earlston
  229. Eastbourne
  108. East Calder
  155. East Stirlingshire
   22. Edinburgh
  111. Edinburgh South
  124. Edinburgh Ninety
  149. Elgin
  217. Eskdale
  126. Falkirk
  231. Fauldhouse
  262. Fifeshire Association
   44. Forfar
  187. Galashiels
   90. Garelochhead
  163. Gateshead and District
    3. Glasgow—Tam o'Shanter
    7.   ,,   Thistle
    9.   ,,   Royalty
   24.   Bank
   27.   ,,   Springburn
   33.   ,,   Haggis
   34.   ,,   Carrick
   36.   ,,   Rosebery
   38.   ,,   Jolly Beggars
   39.   ,,   St. David's
   41.   ,,   Dennistoun
   43.   ,,   Northern
   47.   ,,   St. Rollox
   49.   ,,   Bridgeton
   61.   ,,   Glencairn
   63.   ,,   Mossgiel
   67.   ,,   Carlton
   68.   ,,   Sandyford
   70.   ,,   St. Rollox
                  JollyBeggars
   74.   ,,   Mauchline Soc.
   78.   ,,   Ardgowan
   83.   ,,   Co-operative
   88.   ,,   Caledonian
  107.   ,,   Hutcheson-
                  town
  109.   ,,   Caledonia
  117.   ,,   Southern
  118.   ,,   Albany
  139.   ,,   National
  145.   ,,   Central
  153.   ,,   The Scottish
  129.   Gorbals
  164.   ,,   Kinning Park
  180.   ,,   Tollcross
  181.   ,,   Primrose
  203.   ,,   Dennistoun
                  Jolly Beggars
  206.   Daisy

No. 213. Glasgow—Kingston
  223.   ,,   Auld Clinkum
  234.   ,,   Southern Mer-
                  chants
  255.   ,,   Cathcart
  263.   ,,   Masonic
  169. Glasgow and District
  251. Glencraig
  198. Gorebridge Jolly Beggars
   59. Gourock Jolly Beggars
   53. Govan Fairfield
  202. Govan Cronies
  116. Greenloaning
   21. Greenock
  148. Greenock Cronies
  209. Greenock St. John's
  152. Hamilton
  100. Hamilton Mossgiel
  121. Hamilton Junior
  136. Hamilton Royal Oak
  235. Hamilton Glencairn
  210. Hardgate Auld Hoose
  239. Hawick
  2?5 Helensburgh
  222. Hull
  137. Ipswich
  173. Irvine
   96. Jedburgh
  154. Johannesburg, S.A.
   92. Kilbowie
    0. Kilmarnock
   97. Kilmarnock Bellfield
  150. Kilmarnock Jolly
                  Beggars
  178. Kilmarnock Begbie's
  186. Kilmarnock Glencairn
  245. Kinnaird
  115. Kippen
   58. Kirkcaldy
   75. Kirn
   98. Lanark
  144. Larbert and Stenhouse-
                  muir
  170. Larkhall
  211. Larkhall Thistle
   73. Lenzie
   18. Liverpool
  247. Lochgelly
  ?46. Lochore
       London
  183. Londonderry
   28. Mauchline Jolly Beggars
  175. Meikle Earnock
  214. Melrose
  249. Mid-Calder Tam o'
                  Shanter

No. 194. Middlebie
242. Montrose
8. Morpeth (dormant)
101. Motherwell
56. Muirkirk Lapraik
65. Musselburgh
199. Newbattle and District
32. Newark
133. Newarthill
156. Newcastle and Tyneside
256. Newton-on-Ayr
131. Nottingham
17. Nottingham (dormant)
151. Old Kilpatrick
172. Oregon, U.S.A.
48. Paisley
77. Paisley Gleniffer
161. Paisley Charleston
243. Paisley St. James
205. Paisley St. Mirren
72. Partick
135. Partick Western
227. Penrith
26. Perth
54. Perth St. Johnstone
162. Plymouth and District
140. Pollokshaws
190. Port-Glasgow
212. Portobello
221. Prestonpans
264. Prestonpans Jolly
Beggars
177. Prestwick
176. Renfrew
191. Renfrew Moorpark

No. 168 Riccarton
132. Riccarton Kirkstyle
130. Row
105. Rutherglen
193. Rutherglen Jolly Beggars
216. Rutherglen Royal Burgh
31. San Francisco
91. Shettleston
195. Shiremoor
13. St. Andrews
220. St. Louis, Mo., U.S.A.
182. Stane Mossgiel
50. Stirling
141. Stonehouse
147 Stonehouse Haggis
200. Stonehouse Jolly Beggars
89. Sunderland
16. Sydney
261. Sydney Anniversary
260. Tarbrax
215. Thorniewood
57. Thornliebank
219. Uddingston
237. Uddingston Masonic
94. Uphall
113. Vale o' Leven Glencairn
159. Walker-on-Tyne
165. Wallsend-on-Tyne
46. Warwickshire
160. Whitburn
236. Whitehaven
197. Winnipeg
25 Winnipeg St. Andrew's
Society
60. Wolverhampton

DIRECTORY

OF

BURNS CLUBS AND SCOTTISH SOCIETIES

ON THE

ROLL OF THE BURNS FEDERATION, 1920.

No. 0—KILMARNOCK Burns Club. Instituted 1808. Federated 1885. Place and date of meeting, George Hotel, 24th January. President, Sheriff Robertson, Crookedholm House, Kilmarnock ; Vice-president, James Lang, Grougar Bank, Kilmarnock ; *Secretary,* Thomas Amos, M.A., 19 Glebe Road, Kilmarnock. Committee—Ex-provost Smith, J.P.; D. M'Naught, J.P.; Major G. A. Innes, M.B.E.; Bailie Wm. M'Menan, B.A. ; Major D. Yuille ; John Cuthbertson, M.B.E. ; Jas. Middleton, J.P.

No. 1 The LONDON Robert Burns Club. Instituted 1868. Federated 1885. Place of meeting, Holborn Restaurant, W.C. President, Wm. Will, Tallis House. Tallis Street, London, E.C.4 ; Vice-president, L. G. Sloan, The Pen Corner, Kingsway, W.C. ; *Secretary,* P. N. M'Farlane, Tallis House, Whitefriars, London, E.C.4 ; Treasurer, C. J. Wilkinson-Pimbury. Special features of Club— Historical and literary research work ; social gatherings ; Scotch dancing classes, &c.

No. 2 ALEXANDRIA Burns Club. Instituted 1884. Federated 1885. Place and date of meeting, Village School, 1st Friday each month. President, Richard Stevenson, Stevenson Place, Alexandria ; Vice-president, Donald M'Dougall, Bridge-End Tavern, Bonhill, Alexandria ; *Secretary,* Duncan Carswell, Linnbrane Terrace, Alexandria; Treasurer, James Merrilees, Charleston House, Alexandria. Committee—Dougal Stevenson, Richard Thomson, John Barton, William M'Gregor, Harry Flowers, and John M'Crae

No. 3—GLASGOW Tam o' Shanter. Instituted 1880. Federated 1885. Place and date of meeting, Trades House Restaurant, 89 Classford Street, Glasgow, last Monday of winter months. President, Wm. Renfrew, 29 Park Road, Glasgow ; Vice-president, T. M. Hamilton, 101 St. Vincent Street, Glasgow ; *Secretary,* J. Jeffrey Hunter, 89 Bath Street, Glasgow. Committee—H. J. Attmann, J. Ballantine, Wm. Black, Jas. Fraser, And. Henderson, J. H. Hurll, Alex. Izat, Hugh M'Coll, Alex. M'Kenzie, Dr J. F. M'Lachlan, J. D. M'Lachlan, Bailie Jno. Smith, T. Smith,

T. P. Thompson, Hugh Lynn, Gerrard Morrison, and J.
F. Anderson. Special features of Club—Literary evenings
and useful movements for the promotion of the Burns cult.

No. 4—CALLANDER Burns Club. Instituted 1877. Federated
1885.

No. 5—ERCILDOUNE Burns Club. Instituted 1885. Federated
26th November, 1835. Secretary, A. M. Black, Market
Place, Earlston.

No. 6—ALLOA Burns Club. Instituted 1873. Federated 1885.

No. 7—GLASGOW Thistle Burns Club. Instituted 1882. Fede-
rated 1885. Place of meeting, 9 Miller Street, Glasgow.
President, Councillor Alex. Allan, 13 Eglinton Street,
Glasgow ; Vice-president, Dr Jas. Macdonald, Hawk-
head ; Secretary, John Vallance, 57 College Street, Glasgow;
Treasurer, John Eadie, 5 Miller Street, Glasgow.

No. 8—MORPETH and District Burns Club.

No. 9—GLASGOW Royalty Burns Club. Instituted January,
1882. Federated January, 1886. Date of meeting,
First Thursday in October. President, James Macfarlane,
49 Bath Street, Glasgow ; Vice-president, David Gunn,
4 Finnieston Street, Glasgow ; Secretary, George F.
Howarth, 14 St. Vincent Place, Glasgow.

No. 10—DUMBARTON Burns Club. Instituted 1859. Federated
1886. Place and date of meeting, Elephant Hotel, 26th
January, 1920. President, David Clague, Strathdene,
Dumbarton ; Vice-president, A. Y. Allan, Aitkenbar
Farm, Dumbarton ; Secretary, J. M. Menzies, 69 High
Street, Dumbarton. Committee—J. M'Pherson, C.
M'Kinnon, H. W. Ballardie, R. M'Murray. J. B. Cameron,
D. Blackstock, and J. M'Clelland. Special feature of Club,
—Celebration of the Poet's Birthday.

No. 11—CHESTERFIELD Burns Society. Federated 1886.

No. 12—BARROW-IN-FURNESS Burns Club. Federated 1888.

No. 13—ST. ANDREWS Burns Club. Instituted 1869. Fede-
rated 1886. Place of meeting, Various. President, Wm.
Macbeth Robertson, Esq., Solicitor, Market Street, St.
Andrews ; Secretary, David Fraser, Lilybank, St. Andrews.

No. 14—DUNDEE Burns Club. Instituted 1860. Federated 5th
March, 1886. Place and date of meeting, Club Rooms,
36 Nethergate, Dundee, nightly. President, John A.
Purves, 339 Clepington Road, Dundee : Vice-president,
David T. Dewar, 36 Nethergate, Dundee ; Secretary,
George S. Middleton, 36 Nethergate, Dundee ; Treasurer,
J. G. Knowles ; Auditors, R. Watson and J. Anderson :
Librarian, W. F. Mitchell. Committee—Messrs J. Ogilvie,

J. Neilson, and D. Brown. Special features of Club Literary and recreation.

No. 15—BELFAST Burns Club. Instituted 1872. Federated 1886.

No. 16—SYDNEY Burns Club, N.S.W. Instituted 1880. Federated 1886. *Secretary,* W. Telfer, School of Art, Pitt Street, Sydney.

No, 17—NOTTINGHAM Scottish Society. Federated 1886.

No. 18—LIVERPOOL Burns Club. Instituted 1866. Federated 1886. *Secretary,* Major R. S. Archer, V.D., 6 Devonshire Road, Princes Park, Liverpool. No meetings since outbreak of war. Hope to resume in January, 1920.

No. 19—AUCKLAND Burns Club. Instituted 1834. Federated 1886.

No. 20—AIRDRIE Burns Club. Instituted 1885. Federated 1886. Place and date of meeting, Royal Hotel, Airdrie, 25th January. President, Lieut.-Colonel J. M. Arthur, C.M.G., D.S.O., Glentore, Airdrie ; Vice-president, Geo. E. Swinhoe, Albert House, Airdrie ; *Secretary,* Major G. B. Motherwell, T.D., Solicitor, 4 East High Street, Airdrie. Committee—Robert Eadie, C. R. Larkman, D. Martyn, J. B. Chapman, and Wm. M'Gregor. Special features of Club—Surplus funds distributed each year among local charitable societies, &c.

No. 21 GREENOCK Burns Club (The Mother Club). Instituted 1802. Federated 1886. Place of meeting, 36 Nicolson Street. President, Hugh M'Lean, Esq., Elmhurst, Newark Street ; Vice-presidents, R. L. Scott, Balclutha, Greenock, and D. M'Callum, 21 Cathcart Street ; *Secretary,* George B. Grieve, 25 Robertson Street, Greenock. Special features of Club—To further the interest and study of Scottish Literature, and promote a fuller knowledge of the Works of Burns and other Scottish writers.

No. 22 EDINBURGH Burns Club. Instituted 1848. Federated 1886. President, George Williamson, J.P., 178 High Street, Edinburgh ; Vice-president, Robert Walker, 6 Royal Terrace, Edinburgh ; *Interim Secretary,* Thomas Liddle, S.S.C., 5 Hill Street, Edinburgh.

No. 23 ADELAIDE South Australian Caledonian Society. Instituted 1881. Federated 1886. *Secretary,* H. Tassie, Gray's Arcade, Adelaide, S.A.

No. 24—GLASGOW Bank Burns Club. Instituted 1884. Federated 1886.

No. 25—WINNIPEG St. Andrew's Society. Federated 1886. *Secretary,* David Philip, Government Buildings, Winnipeg.

No. 26—PERTH Burns Club. Instituted 1873. Federated 1886.

No. 27—SPRINGBURN Burns Club. Instituted 1884. Federated 1886.

No. 28—MAUCHLINE Jolly Beggars Burns Club.

No. 29—BOLTON Juniors Burns Club. Instituted 1881. Federated 1886.

No. 30—BLACKBURN Burns Club. Instituted 1834. Federated 1886. *Secretary*, Robt. Ferguson, 9 Tacketts Street, Blackburn, Lancs.

No. 31—SAN FRANCISCO Scottish Thistle Club. Instituted 1882. Federated 1886. *Secretary*, Geo. W. Paterson, 801 Guerero Street, San Francisco, U.S.A.

No. 32—NEWARK Burns Club, U.S.A. Federated 1886.

No. 33—GLASGOW Haggis Burns Club. Instituted 1872 Federated 1886. Place and date of meeting, Ferguson and Forrester's, 36 Buchanan Street, last Tuesday from October till March. President, Robert Hamilton, Invershin, Newlands, Glasgow; *Secretary*, William S. Baird, 121 West George Street, Glasgow.

No. 34 CARRICK Burns Club. Instituted 1859. Federated 1887. Place and time of meeting, 62 Glassford Street, Glasgow, 7 p.m. President, R. A. Wood, Rosevale, Kilmarnock Road, Giffnock; Vice-president, T. J. Jamieson; *Secretary*, David Sutherland, 123 Frederick Street, Glasgow; Treasurer, Wm. Morrison, 62 Glassford Street, Glasgow. Special feature of Club—To keep the memory of Burns ever green.

No. 35—DALRY Burns Club. Instituted 1825. Federated 1887. Place and date of meeting, Turf Inn, Friday, 23rd January, 1920. *Secretary*, Patrick Comrie, Waterside, Dalry.

No. 36—ROSEBERY Burns Club. Instituted 1885. Federated 1887. Place and date of meeting, Bath Street, 2nd Tuesday of month. *Secretary*, Alexander Pollock, 52 West Nile Street, Glasgow; Treasurer, Ronald Johnstone, 85 Roslea Drive, Glasgow. Special features of Club—A course of monthly lectures on various literary subjects; inter-visitation of sister Burns Clubs to promote brotherly feeling and mutual assistance; encouragement of the young to learn the songs and poetry of Scotland by school competitions and prizes. Jointly with the Carlton Club the Rosebery Club have carried through the publication of Burns's Works in Braille type, whereby the blind are able to read Burns for themselves. An edition of the Poet's works in " Moon " type for blind people who are unable to read Braille has also been issued.

No. 37—DOLLAR Burns Club. Instituted 29th December, 1887. Federated 30th December, 1887. *Secretary*, D. Kilpatrick, Station Road, Dollar.

No. 38—GLASGOW Jolly Beggars Burns Club. Instituted 1877. Federated 1888.

No. 39—GLASGOW St. David's Burns Club. Instituted 1887. Federated 1889.

No. 40—ABERDEEN Burns Club. Instituted 1887. Federated 1889.

No. 41—DENNISTOUN Burns Club. Instituted 1887: Federated 1889.

No. 42—CRIEFF Burns Club. Instituted 1889. Federated 1891.

No. 43—GLASGOW Northern Burns Club. Federated 1891.

No. 44—FORFAR Burns Club. Instituted 1890. Federated 1891.

No. 45—CUMNOCK Burns Club. Instituted 1887. Federated 1891. *Secretary*, John Hume, solicitor, Cumnock.

No. 46—WARWICKSHIRE Burns Club. Instituted 1880. Federated 1891.

No 47—GLASGOW St. Rollox Burns Club. Instituted 1889. Federated 1891.

No. 48—PAISLEY Burns Club. Instituted 1805. Federated 1891. Time of meeting, First Thursday each month, October to May inclusive. President, Colonel James Cook, Laigh Park, Paisley; Vice-president, Dr R. S. Penman, The Grange, Meikleriggs, Paisley; *Secretary*, Julius F. M'Callum, Mayfield, Sunnyside, Paisley. Special feature of Club—Literary and social.

No. 49 BRIDGETON Burns Club. Instituted 1870. Federated 30th November, 1891. Place of meeting, Albert Hall, Main Street, Bridgeton (Jubilee Dinner, Grosvenor, 24th January, 1920). President, David M. Kennedy, Glencoral, South Beach, Troon; Vice-president, James W. Shaw, J.P., 67 Marquis Street, Bridgeton; *Secretary*, John G. S. Sproll, 354 Duke Street, Glasgow; Treasurer, William Reid, 49 West George Street, Glasgow; Past President, David S. Brown, 79 Canning Street, Glasgow. Special feature of Club—School Competitions, &c.

No. 50—STIRLING Burns Club. Instituted 1887. Federated 1891. President, William A. Weir, Forth Crescent, Stirling; Vice-president, Judge M'Culloch, Clarendon Place, Stirling; *Secretary*, Alexander Dun, 37 Murray Place, Stirling; Treasurer, J. P. Crawford. Committee—John Craig, Ridley Sandeman, J. W. Paterson,

Bailie Leslie, John Crawford, W. L. Thomson, David
Dick, Judge Barker, J. S. Henderson, Robert Gray, James
Duncanson, William Law, William Brown, D. M'Dougall,
Peter M'Donald, John Ferguson, Alex. Learmonth, and
A. Macintosh.

No 51—CHICAGO Caledonian Society.   Federated 1892.

No 52—DUMFRIES Mechanics Burns Club.   Federated 1892.

No 53—GOVAN Fairfield Burns Club.   Instituted 25th January,
1886.   Federated 23rd September, 1892.   Place and date
of meeting, Eden Villa, 8 Carmichael Street, Govan,
1st Wednesday, September to March.   President, Arch.
B. Allison, 22 Hayburn Crescent, Partick ; Vice-president,
John Donald, 883 Govan Road, Govan ; Secretary, John
Gordon, 13 Hutton Drive, Govan ; Treasurer, Alex.
George ; Past President, M. G. C. Campbell ; Bard,
Walter Mackay : Steward, George Anderson.   Committee
—J. M. Watson, R. C. Hill, J. Gillespie, J. Hair, and
J. M'Lachlan.   Special features of Club—To foster the
love of Burns, and to promote social intercourse with
other Burns Clubs by having members of their Clubs
addressing us, and by our Club visiting other Clubs.

No. 54—PERTH St. Johnstone Burns Club.   Federated 1892.

No 55—DERBY Burns Club.   Instituted 1892.   Federated 1892.
Place of meeting, Royal Hotel, Derby.   President, T. E.
Campbell, 7 Wilson Street, Derby ; Vice-president,
Dr J. A. Watt, The Walnuts, Littleover, Derby : Secre-
tary, Chas. Carmichael, 180 Porter Road, Derby ; Hon.
Treasurer, R. B. Muir, Derby Road, Belper.   Special
features of Club—To unite Scotchmen, and to foster a
spirit of friendship, social and intellectual intercourse
among the members.   Annual Dinner—Royal Hotel,
Derby, 23rd January, 1920 ; Annual Dance—Royal
Hotel, Derby, 31st December, 1919 ; also lectures and
social evenings during the year.

No. 56—LAPRAIK (Muirkirk) Burns Club.   Instituted 1893.
Federated 1893.   President, C. P. Bell, Main Street,
Muirkirk ; Vice-president, Peter Mackie, c/o Mrs Fer-
guson, Main Street, Muirkirk ; Secretary, Hugh Bell,
Roslyn, Wellwood Street, Muirkirk : Treasurer, And.
Pringle, Ironworks Cottages, Muirkirk.   Committee—
Thos. Weir, Jno. Taylor, Edgar Anderson. Jas. Hazel,
Wm. Patrick, Wm. Brown, Arch. Fairbairn, Thos. Hazel,
Special features of Club—Annual Celebration and edu-
cational.

No. 57—THORNLIEBANK Burns Club.   Instituted 1891.   Federated 1893.   Place and time of meeting—Village Institute,
8 p.m.   President, Thomas P. Winter, Elswick, Thornliebank ; Vice-president, James H. M'Millan, Woodlands
Shawlands, Glasgow ; Secretary, Thomas Haddow, Hill-

side Terrace, Thornliebank ; Treasurer, Hugh Halliday,
27 Kennishead Road, Thornliebank ; and 15 members
of Committee. Special features of Club—School children's
competitions, Scotch concert, annual outing, Hallowe'en
festival, Anniversary dinner, and Club monthly meetings.

No. 58—KIRKCALDY Burns Club. Federated 1892.

No. 59—GOUROCK Jolly Beggars Burns Club. Instituted 1893.
Federated 1893. Secretary, Robt. M'Gechan. 2 Torridon
Terrace, 19 Cardwell Road, Gourock.

No. 60—WOLVERHAMPTON Burns Club. Federated 1893.

No. 61—GLASGOW Glencairn Burns Club. Federated 1893.

No. 62—CUPAR Burns Club. Instituted 1892. Federated
1893. President, Col. Sir Alexander Sprot, M.P., Stravithie, Fife ; Vice-president, Provost James Stark, Mill-
bank, Cupar ; Secretary, David F. Esplin, Dundee Courier
Office, Cupar ; Treasurer, Bailie Geo. White ; Chairman
of Committee—Geo. Innes.

No. 63—MOSSGIEL Burns Club. Instituted 1893. Federated
1893. Place of meeting, Y.M.C.A. Rooms, Eglinton Toll.
President, Thos. W. M'Nish, 82 Cumberland Street, S.S. ;
Vice-president, Wm. Murray, 92 Albert Drive, Crosshill ·
Secretary, Joseph M'Gregor, 45 Abbotsford Place, Glasgow ;
Treasurer, R. Parker. Committee—J. M. Blair, W.
Morrison, J. Sanders, J. Coulter, W. Brownlee, Wm.
M'Neil, R. Johnston, and C. Sharpe. Special features
of Club—Annual celebration on 25th January ; reunions
for the cultivation of social and intellectual intercourse
amongst members ; encouragement of Scottish literature;
summer trip to some poetic spot rendered famous by the
Poet ; and school children's competitions.

No. 64—BEITH Burns Club. Instituted 1892. Federated 12th
December, 1893.

No 65—MUSSELBURGH Federated Burns Club. Instituted
1886. Federated 3rd January, 1894. Secretary, Herbert Millar, solicitor, High Street, Musselburgh.

No. 66—CROSSGATES Burns Club. Federated 1894.

No. 67—CARLTON Burns Club. Instituted 1894. Federated
1894. Place and date of meeting, Arcade Cafe, Glasgow.
2nd Tuesday each month. President, Wm. Gardiner,
26 Holyrood Quadrant, Glasgow ; Vice-president, Wm.
Henderson, 912 Sauchiehall Street, Glasgow ; Secretary,
John C. Brown, 5 Brownlie Gardens, Tollcross, Glasgow ;
Treasurer, James Tudhope, 16 Whitehill Street, Dennis-
toun. Directors—Duncan Cameron, John Gray, Matt.
M. Duff, John C. Galpine, Jas. M'Blane, Geo. Edward,
R. Westwater, Hugh Dickie, and J. Clark, with the Past

Presidents *ex officio.* Special features of Club—The perpetuation of the memory of Robert Burns, and the intellectual and social intercourse of its members by such means as may from time to time be arranged.

No. 68—SANDYFORD Burns Club. Instituted 13th December, 1893. Federated 1894. Place and time of meeting, Grand Hotel, 7.30 p.m. Hon. President, A. P. Hamilton, 100 West Regent Street, Glasgow ; President, ex-Bailie Jas. Gardiner, " Overwood," Fleurs Avenue, Dumbreck, Glasgow ; Vice-president, Wm. Thomson, 493 St. Vincent Street, Glasgow : *Secretary,* W. Smith Tait, C.A., 79 West Regent Street, Glasgow. Committee—Jas. Wells, A. Wood Smith, J. M'Naught Campbell, Captain W. M. Douglas, James Michie, David Dalrymple, Wm. Turner, Jas. Miller, Duncan Taylor, Alex. Duthie, Jas. Allan, and Harry Guest.

No. 69—DUNEDIN Burns Club. Federated 1894.

No 70—GLASGOW St. Rollox Jolly Beggars Burns Club. Federated 1891.

No. 71—CARLISLE Burns Club. Instituted 1889. Federated 1895. *Secretary,* Thomas George Beattie, 200 Warwick Road, Carlisle.

No. 72—PARTICK Burns Club. Instituted 1885. Federated 1895. President, Charles R. Cowie, Woodend House, Partickhill, Glasgow ; Vice-president, ex-Bailie Geo Douglas, Manhauset, Bishop's Road, Jordanhill, Glasgow ; *Secretary and Treasurer,* David Crawford, solicitor, 213 West George Street, Glasgow.

No. 73—LENZIE Burns Club. Federated 1896.

No. 74—GLASGOW Mauchline Society. Instituted 1888. Federated 1895. President, J. Leiper Gemmill, 162 St. Vincent Street, Glasgow ; Vice-president, John Hyslop, Ashton, Douglas Gardens, Uddingston ; *Secretary,* William Campbell, 166 Buchanan Street, Glasgow ; Treasurer, Thos. Killin, 7 Stewarton Drive, Cambuslang. Special features of Club—To promote sociability among natives of Mauchline and friends, and manage the National Burns Memorial and Cottage Homes, Mauchline.

No. 75—KIRN Burns Club. Instituted 25th January, 1892. Federated 10th February, 1896. Place and date of meeting, Queen's Hotel, Kirn, 25th January. President, ex-Provost Dobie, Clydesdale Bank Buildings, Dunoon : Vice-president, Peter F. More, British Linen Bank Buildings, Dunoon ; *Secretary,* John Macnair, house factor, Kirn ; Treasurer, Provost Lees, Fernycrag, Kirn : Committee—Col. Maconachie, G. A. Fraser, H. Hamilton, A. M'Gregor, A. Kates, and G. Johnston. Secretary and Treasurer of Debating Branch, J. J. Boyd, Norwood

Cottage, Kirn. Special features of Club—Singing and reciting competitions for children ; annual excursion ; debating and recreation branch ; carpet bowling, &c., in Kirn Hall three times every week.

No. 76—BRECHIN Burns Club. Instituted January, 1894. Federated 7th March, 1896. President, William Anderson, 2 Airlie Street, Brechin ; Vice-president, Charles Thomson, Eastbank, Brechin ; Secretary, F. C. Anderson, 10 St. Mary Street, Brechin. Committee—J. A. Hutcheon, J. Scott Lindsay, J. S. Melrose, J. S. Lammond, Robert Anderson, Alex. Norrie, and David K. Laing.

No. 77—PAISLEY Tannahill Burns Club. Instituted 1892. Federated 1896.

No. 78—GLASGOW Ardgowan Burns Club. Instituted 1893. Federated 1896.

No 79—CORSTORPHINE Burns Club. Instituted 1887. Federated 1896. Secretary, W. M. Wilson, 7 Belgrave Place, Corstorphine.

No. 80—DUNOON Cowall Burns Club. Instituted 1896. Federated 1896.

No. 81—CARSTAIRS Junction Burns Club. Instituted 1896. Federated 1896.

No. 82—ARBROATH Burns Club. Instituted 1888. Federated 1896. President, Dr J. D. Gilruth, Hyde Park House, Arbroath ; Vice-president, John R. W. Clark, solicitor, Arbroath ; Secretary, Ernest F. Cobb, Town Chamberlain Arbroath ; Treasurer, F. W. Moon, solicitor. Arbroath.

No. 83—GLASGOW Co-operative Burns Club. Instituted 1896. Federated 1896.

No. 84—ABINGTON Burns Club. Federated 1896.

No. 85—DUNFERMLINE United Burns Club. Instituted 1812. Federated 12th November, 1896. Date of meeting, 23rd January, 1920. Hon. Presidents, The Right Hon. The Earl of Elgin, Broomhall, Dunfermline ; Sir Alex. Gibb, K.B.E., C.B., Gruimard House, Aultbea, Ross-shire ; Sir Richard Mackie, Leith ; and ex-Bailie Stewart Dunfermline ; Hon. Vice-presidents, W. D. Imrie, Wm Black, P. Donald, Thos. Dow, and R. Taylor ; President, A. P. Machain, solicitor, Kinchello, Venturefair Avenue Dunfermline ; Vice-president, Robt. Hutchison, Dunfermline ; Secretary, P. Paterson, Kimmis House, Kimmis Place, Dunfermline. Committee — John Brown, R. Dunlop, P. Donald, Wm. Black, R. Taylor, Thos. Lessells, Fred W. Yates.

No. 86 CUMNOCK Winsome Willie Burns Club. Instituted 1856. Federated 1896.

No. 87—CAMPSIE Burns Club. Instituted 1890. Federated 1896.

No. 88—GLASGOW Caledonian Burns Club. Instituted 1896. Federated 1897.

No. 89—SUNDERLAND Burns Club. Instituted January, 1897. Federated April, 1897. Place and date of meeting, Palatine Hotel, 2nd and 4th Wednesdays October to March; 2nd Wednesday April, May, and September, at 7.30 p.m. President, Dr A. Stevenson, 147 Chester Road, Sunderland; Vice-president, A. R. Calvert, 11 Side Cliffe Road, Roker, Sunderland; Secretary, M. Neilson, 14 East Whickham Street, Sunderland; Treasurer, A. W. Semple; Librarian, G. Mackay; Auditor, W. S. Gibson; Trustees, W. H. Turner and G. Mackay; Hon. Pipe-Major, W. Graham. Committee—Messrs Condie, Donaldson, Fisher, Shaw, and M'Lagan. Special features of Club—Anniversary celebration, ladies' night, reading of papers, and pipe band. Visitors cordially welcomed.

No. 90—GARELOCHHEAD Burns Club. Instituted 18th November, 1895. Federated 25th March, 1897. Place and time of meeting, Garelochhead Hotel, 8 p.m. President, David Stark, Argyle House, Garelochhead; Vice-president, Duncan M'Keichan, Mambeg, Garelochhead · Secretary, John Burnett, 1 Glencairn Terrace, Garelochhead. Committee—Major D. B. Anderson, P. M'Farlane, I. Martin, W. Grieve, John Douglas, J. Gray, W. Espie, J. Miller. Special feature of Club—Whereas we as Scotchmen could meet to honour Scotland's National Bard.

No. 91 SHETTLESTON Burns Club. Instituted 1897. Federated 1897. Place of meeting, "Sloan's Arcade Cafe. Hon. Presidents, William Reid, F.E.I.S., John Cresswell, John Ramsay, Robert, M. Milholm, and James S. Wilson; President, James Lucas, M.A., ' Huntly Terrace, Shettleston; Vice-president, John M'Farlane, 6 Gordon Terrace, Shettleston; Secretary, Robert M. Milholm, 7 Somerville Place, Glasgow, East; Treasurer, Edwin S. Thompson, Ardshiel, Shettleston. Committee—John Brown, A. Cresswell, J. Seton Smith, M.A., Geo. Glendinning, Geo. Farmer, H. Fletcher, Wm. Ross, Jas. Miller. Special features of Club—A literary centre as well as social; lectures on Scottish life and literature by authorities on various subjects and writers. Prizes are provided by the Club for the pupils of the Shettleston school to foster study of the Works of Burns. Visitors are always welcomed at any of the Club's meetings.

No 92—KILBOWIE Jolly Beggars Burns Club. Instituted 1896. Federated 1897. Place and date of meeting, Cross Restaurant, alternate Tuesdays, 7 p.m. President, A. M'Donald, 53 Montrose Street, Clydebank; Vice-president, D. J. Clark, 150 Kilbowie Road, Clydebank; Secretary, William Crum, 34 Granville Street, Clydebank.

Committee—D. M'Williams, J. Walker, Abbott, Bilslaw, Blair, Donnolly, Davidson, Deans, Gill, Morrison, Philip, Scott. Special features of Club—The cultivation of a better knowledge of the Poet and his Works, and the study of Scottish literature by the reading of papers, &c., both original and selected.

No. 93—CLYDEBANK Burns Club. Federated 1897.

No. 94—UPHALL Tam o' Shanter Burns Club. Instituted 1885. Federated 12th September, 1897. Place of meeting, Ross's Hall, Uphall. President, Jas. Spence, Beechwood Cottages, Uphall Station, Uphall; Vice-president, Hugh Kilpatrick, Rennie's Buildings, Uphall; *Secretary*, Jas. Purdie, Hawthorn Place, Uphall; Treasurer, Robt. Denholm, Pumpherston, Mid-Calder.

No. 95—BOLTON Burns Club. Instituted 1881. Federated 1897.

No 96—JEDBURGH Burns Club. Instituted 1869. Federated 13th November, 1897. Place of meeting, Royal Hotel, Jedburgh. President, ex-Provost Boyd, Bongate Cottage; *Secretary*, William Renilson, Maitland House, Jedburgh; Treasurer, Joseph Tweddle, Castlegate, Jedburgh. Committee—Provost W. Oliver, ex-Bailie A. Walker, J. Oliver, Wm. Swanston, Peter Carruthers, John Brown, Jas. Cree.

No. 97—KILMARNOCK Bellfield Burns Club. Instituted 1895. Federated 1898. Vice-president, Daniel Picken, Glebe Avenue, Kilmarnock.

No. 98—LANARK Burns Club. Instituted 1891. Federated 1898. Place and time of meeting, Market Inn, 7.30 p.m. President, A. S. Boyd, 2 Cordelier Terrace, Lanark; Vice-president, S. Wyatt, Village House, New Lanark; *Secretary*, Thomas Veitch, Dalblair, Wheatland Drive, Lanark. Committee —T. Lithgow, W. Brown, H. Beveridge, James Howe, Robert Flemington. Special features of Club—Social and musical evenings held monthly during winter months.

No. 99—BARLINNIE Burns Club. Instituted 1893. Federated 1898. *Secretary*, Alexander Mackay, 10 Officers' Quarters, Barlinnie, Glasgow.

No. 100—HAMILTON Mossgiel Burns Club. Instituted 1892. Federated 4th April, 1898. Place and date of meeting, Masonic Hall, Hamilton, first Tuesday of every month, except June, July, and August, 7.30 p.m. President, ex-Bailie Robt. Anderson, Roberton, Anderson Street, Burnbank, Lanarkshire; Vice-president, James M'Cartney, 99 Quarry Street, Hamilton; *Secretary*, Wm. Sommerville, 5 Jackson Street, Blantyre; Treasurer, Wm. Hamilton, Burnfoot, Bent Road, Hamilton.

No 101—MOTHERWELL Workmen's Burns Club. Federated 1898.

No. 102—CARLISLE Border Burns Club. Instituted 1898. Federated 1898.

No. 103—COALBURN Burns Club. Federated 1898.

No. 104—DUMFRIES Oak Burns Club. Federated 1898.

No. 105—RUTHERGLEN Cronies Burns Club. Instituted 1896. Federated 1898.

No. 106—BROXBURN Rosebery Burns Club. Federated 1898.

No. 107—HUTCHESONTOWN Burns Club. Instituted 1897. Federated 1898. *Secretary*, Robert A. Sinclair, 4 Govanhill Street, Crosshill, Glasgow.

No 108—EAST CALDER and District Jolly Beggars Burns Club. Instituted 25th January, 1897. Federated 17th January, 1899. Place and time of meeting, Grapes Inn, East Calder, 7 p.m. President, James Millar, Burnhouse, East Calder ; Vice-president, Andrew Cunningham, Oakbank, Mid-Calder ; *Secretary*, John Watson, 46 Oakbank, Mid-Calder. Committee—John A. Forbes, James Robertson, David Watt, Alex. Henderson, Wm. Boyd.

No. 109 GLASGOW Caledonia Burns Club. Instituted 1898. Federated 1899.

No. 110—CAMBUSLANG Burns Club. Instituted 1850. Federated 1898.

No. 111—SOUTH EDINBURGH Burns Club. Instituted 1889. Federated 1899.

No. 112—DUMFRIES Burns Howff Club. Instituted 1889. Federated 10th August, 1899. Place and date of meeting, Globe Hotel, monthly. President, John Maxwell, English Street, Dumfries ; Vice-president, John Houston, High Street, Dumfries ; *Secretary*, Thomas Laidlaw, 3 St. Michael's Terrace, Henry Street, Dumfries ; Treasurer, Thos. Robertson. Committee—J. M'Alister, J. L. Armstrong, Jas. Smith, G. Johnstone, Wm. Scott, N. Ramsay, A. Hutchison, J. W. Blackley, and Wm. Geddes.

No. 113 VALE OF LEVEN Glencairn Burns Club. Instituted 1897. Federated 1899. Place and date of meeting, Albert Hotel, Alexandria, last Saturday of month, at 6.30 p.m. President, Hugh M'Vean, Mossgiel, Dalmonach Road, Bonhill ; Vice-president, Alexander Campbell, 82 Bridge Street, Alexandria ; *Secretary*, Daniel Macmillan, Smollett Street, Alexandria ; Treasurer, Peter Burdon, Viewforth, Balloch. Committee — Daniel M'Innes,

William Gibb, John James, James Burdon, and Thomas Nicol. Special features of Club—Celebration of 25th January ; summer outing ; and occasionally short papers by members.

No. 114—BRODICK Burns Club. Instituted 1899. Federated 1900.

No. 115—KIPPEN and District Burns Club. Instituted 1896. Federated 1900. *Secretary*, Samuel Thomson, Pointend, Kippen.

No. 116—GREENLOANING Burns Club. Instituted 1889. Federated 1900. *Secretary*, James Bayne, Kinbuck, Dunblane.

No. 117—GLASGOW Southern Burns Club. Instituted 1899. Federated 1900.

No. 118—GLASGOW Albany Burns Club. Instituted 1900. Federated 1900. Place and time of meeting, The Bank Restaurant, Queen Street, 7 o'clock. President, William Cullen, M.D.. 3 Queen's Crescent, Glasgow, W. ; Vice-presidents, Isaac Craik, Glenara, Cambuslang, and A. C. Riddall, 23 Shamrock Street, Glasgow ; *Secretary*, Robert Carmichael, 89 Elderslie Street, Glasgow ; Joint Treasurers, S. B. Lithgow, 4 Boleyn Road, Pollokshields, and D. Annand. 177 Ingram Street, Glasgow ; Librarian, William Dall, 105 Kenmure Street, Pollokshields ; Director of Harmony, Alexander Gray, 115 Bain Street, Calton. Glasgow. Directors—R. D. Donaldson, Wm. M'Naughton, J. R. Mirrlees, D. C. Kennedy, W. H. Macdonald, and J. N. Murdoch. Past Presidents, J. Wilson Bain, James Taylor, John A. Headrick, James Raeside, and Thomas M'Bride. Special features of Club—Lectures and harmony, and to cultivate a knowledge of the works of Burns among school children, in connection with which a competition is held yearly and medals and volumes given to the successful competitors. Annual subscription, 2s 6d. Life membership, £1 1s. The meetings of members are held in the Bank Restaurant, 41 Queen Street, on the first Wednesday of the months of October and March, at 7 o'clock evening. The Annual Dinner will be held in the Grand Hotel ; the " Immortal Memory " being proposed by the Rev. Gordon Mitchell, D.D., of Killearn.

No. 119—BONHILL Burns Club. Instituted 1900. Federated 1900.

No. 120—BRISTOL Caledonian Society (an incorporation of the Bristol Caledonian Benevolent Society, instituted 1820, and the Bristol Burns Club, instituted 1894). Incorporated 1898. Place and time of meeting, 2 Bristol Bridge, Bristol, 7.30 p.m. *Secretary*, A. K. Simpson, 2 Bristol Bridge, Bristol. Chairman of Committee, John Turnbull, 1 Baldwin Street, Bristol. Special features of Club —Benevolent, social, and literary.

No. 121—HAMILTON Junior Burns Club. Instituted September. 1886. Federated April, 1901. Place and date of meeting, Mrs R. Bell's, Union Street, Hamilton, first Monday each month. President, David Cross, 127 Quarry Street, Hamilton : Vice-president, George Gilmour, 65 Brandon Street, Hamilton ; *Secretary and Treasurer*, William Wilson, 5 Haddow Street, Hamilton ; Minute Secretary, J. M'Millan. Committee—J. Brown, R. Smith, G. Fleming, and J. Thomson. Stewards, T. Muir and W. Mitchell. Special features of Club—Reading of essays on various subjects, concerts, competitions, summer rambles, and social evenings. (40 members.)

No. 122—DARNCONNER Aird's Moss Burns Club. Instituted 4th November, 1901. Federated 4th November, 1901. *Secretary*, William Naismith, Darnconner, *via* Auchinleck.

No. 123—AUCHINLECK Boswell Burns Club. Instituted 25th January, 1900. Federated, 10th December 1901. Place of meeting, Market Inn, Auchinleck. President, Peter Strachan, Dalsalloch, Auchinleck ; Vice-president, John Black, Dalsalloch, Auchinleck ; *Secretary*, William Hall, Dalsalloch Auchinleck : Steward, David Muir, Dalsalloch, Auchinleck

No. 124 EDINBURGH Ninety Burns Club. Instituted 1890. Federated 1902. Place of meeting, Ferguson & Forrester's, Princes Street. President, William H. Riddell, 60 Grange Road, Edinburgh ; Vice-president, J. Augustus Beddie, 11 Merchiston Crescent, Edinburgh ; *Secretary*, W. J. S. Dalling, solicitor, 173 Bruntsfield Place, Edinburgh ; Treasurer, John Wilson, 66 High Street, Edinburgh. Special features of Club — Anniversary dinner, dance, at-home, excursion, and business meetings.

No. 125 BLACKBURN-ON-ALMOND Rabbie Burns Club. Instituted 1900. Federated 1902. *Secretary*, Robt. Carlyle, West-end, Blackburn, Bathgate.

No. 126—FALKIRK Burns Club. Instituted 1866. Federated 1902. President, James M. Wilson, Arnotfield, Falkirk ; *Secretary and Treasurer*, R. S. Aitchison, solicitor, 2 Bank Street, Falkirk.

No. 127—COWDENBEATH Haggis Burns Club. Instituted 1903. Federated 1903.

No. 128—COWDENBEATH Glencairn Burns Club. Instituted 1893. Federated May, 1903. Place and date of meeting, Raith Arms Inn, Cowdenbeath, every alternate Friday, from October to April, monthly April to October. Hon. President, Wm. Breingan ; Hon. Vice-president, D. Bowie ; President, Thos. Harrower, 41 Arthur Street. Cowdenbeath ; Vice-president, John Liddel, 39 Arthur Street, Cowdenbeath ; *Secretary*, E. Hunter, 31 Arthur Place, Cowdenbeath ; Treasurer, Thos. Wilson ; Bard, J. R. Murray ; Master of Ceremonies, Jas. M'Kenzie.

Committee—Councillor John Sheddon, P. Banks, J. Banks, Wm. Archibald, Wm. Foster, and R. Barker. Special features of Club—The mutual improvement of the members, and the celebration of the Poet's birthday.

No. 129 GORBALS Burns Club. Instituted 1902. Federated 1903.

No. 130—ROW Burns Club. Instituted 6th February, 1902. Federated 1903. Place and date of meeting, Colquhoun Arms, January, June, and October, at 8 p.m. President, Major John M'Farlane, 1 West Clyde Street, Helensburgh ; Vice-president, W. Fraser, F.E.I.S., Clarkfield, 29 Campbell Street, Helensburgh ; *Secretary*, Robert Sloan, Hollylea, Row, Dumbartonshire ; Treasurer, George Walker, Luggray Lodge, Row. Special features of Club—Social intercourse among its members.

No. 131—NOTTINGHAM Scottish Association. Instituted 1902. Federated 1903. President, John Crawford, J.P., Springfield, Bulwell, Nottingham ; *Secretary*, John Currie, 24 Arboretum Street, Nottingham.

No. 132—RICCARTON Kirkstyle Burns Club. Instituted 1904. Federated 1904.

No. 133—NEWARTHILL Burns Club. Instituted 26th September, 1903. Federated 28th March, 1904. Place and date of meeting, Mrs H. Watson's, last Saturday every month, at 6.30 p.m. President, John Henshaw, Church Street, Newarthill, Motherwell ; Vice-president, Thomas Law, Allan Place, Newarthill, Motherwell ; *Secretary*, Duncan Crawford, 267 High Street, Newarthill, Motherwell. Committee—Thos. Crombie, Thos. Nimmo, and Thos. M'Alpine.

No. 134—DUNTOCHER Heron Burns Club. · Instituted 1897. Federated 1904.

No. 135—PARTICK Western Burns Club. Instituted 1903. Federated 1904. President, Allan Stark, 58 Queensborough Gardens, Hyndland, Glasgow ; Vice-president, John Lockhart, 7 Elm Street, Whiteinch, Glasgow : *Secretary*, William Roy, 47 Byres Road, Partick, Glasgow.

No. 136—HAMILTON Royal Oak Burns Club. Instituted 1898. Federated 1904.

No. 137—IPSWICH Burns Club. Instituted 1902. Federated 1904.

No. 138—CLELAND Burns Club. Instituted 1904. Federated 1904.

No. 139—GLASGOW National Burns Club, Ltd. Instituted 1904. Federated 30th November, 1904. Place of meeting, The Club Rooms, 21 India Street, Glasgow. President, Thomas M. Hamilton, 101 St. Vincent Street, Glasgow ; Vice-president, John G. Galpine, 9 Yarrow

Gardens, Glasgow, W. ; *Secretary*, Wm. Hamilton, 42 Seymour Street, Crossmyloof, Glasgow. Special features of Club—The promotion of the study of Burns's Works and Scottish literature generally ; the collection of books, prints, and pamphlets connected therewith ; and social intercourse, mutual helpfulness, mental and moral improvement, and rational recreation.

No. 140—POLLOKSHAWS Burns Club. Instituted 1865. Federated 1905. *Secretary*, Jas. Milne, Burgh Halls, Pollokshaws.

No. 141—STONEHOUSE Burns Club. Instituted 1904. Federated 1905.

No. 142—BONNYBRIDGE Burns Club. Instituted 1905. Federated 1905.

No. 143—AIRDRIE Gateside Burns Club. Instituted 1904. Federated 1905.

No. 144—LARBERT and STENHOUSEMUIR Temperance Burns Club. Instituted 1904. Federated 1905.

No. 145—GLASGOW Central Burns Club. Instituted 1905. Federated 1905.

No. 146—DUBLIN Burns Club. Instituted 1905. Federated 1905. Place of meeting, as arranged. President, George P. Fleming, Drumnagh House, Inchicore, Dublin ; *Secretary*, John Farquhar, 7 Fairview Avenue, Clontarf, Dublin.

No. 147 STONEHOUSE Haggis Burns Club. Federated 1905.

No. 148—GREENOCK Cronies Burns Club. Instituted January, 1899. Federated 9th November, 1905. Place and date of meeting, 15 Charles Street, first Wednesday each month, October till April. President, George Cameron, 7 Mount Pleasant Street, Greenock ; Vice-president, Alex. M'Gavin, 7 Finnart Street, Greenock ; *Secretary*, David Braid, 67 Dempster Street, Greenock ; Treasurer, Joseph Innes, 5 Brachelstone Street, Greenock. Special features of Club—To cherish the name of Robert Burns and foster a love for his writings, and generally to promote good-fellowship.

No. 149 ELGIN Burns Club. Instituted 20th December, 1900. Federated 1905. Place and date of meeting, Elgin, January. Hon. President, Sheriff Dunlop, Mar Lodge, Elgin ; President, Alex. Gillan, Maida, Elgin ; *Secretary*, John Foster, Sheriff-Clerk of Morayshire, Elgin ; Treasurer, J. B. Mair, M.V.O., Chief Constable of Morayshire, Elgin. Committee—T. R. Mackenzie, J. S. Shiach, Philip Sulley, and John Wither.

No 150—KILMARNOCK Jolly Beggars Burns Club, Instituted 1905. Federated 1905. Place and date of meeting, " Wee Thack," last Friday of each month, and every Saturday at 7.30 p.m. President, Geo. Smith Stevenson, Craigneigh, Kilmaurs ; Vice-president, Wm. Willock. 65 King Street, Kilmarnock ; Secretary, Andrew Niven, 17 Fullarton Street, Kilmarnock ; Treasurer, David Mitchell, Fairyhill Road, Kilmarnock. Special features of Club—To foster and maintain an intimate and thorough knowledge of the Life and Works of Burns ; to celebrate the anniversary of his birth in supper, song, and sentiment ; and to propagate and encourage a kind, social, and brotherly feeling one towards another.

No. 151—OLD KILPATRICK Burns Club. Instituted 1900. Federated 20th January, 1906. Place and time of meeting, Gentles Hall, every month, at 7.30 p.m. President, William Cockburn, N.-B. Station House, Bowling ; Vice-president, Robert Newlands, Gavinburn Place, Old Kilpatrick ; Secretary, Robert Smith, Maryville, Old Kilpatrick ; and 8 Committee-men. Special features of Club—Nothing special in the way of social or educational events owing to the serious time : but all helping, as in the past three years, to send a parcel to all brave lads who have left our district and area.

No. 152—HAMILTON Burns Club. Instituted 1877. Federated 1906. Place of meeting, Commercial Hotel, Hamilton. President, Sheriff Hay Shennan, Angus Lodge, Hamilton ; Vice-president, David M. Andrew, Wellhall Road, Hamilton ; Interim Secretary, David N. Cross, Bank of Scotland Chambers, Hamilton ; Treasurer, W. Martin Kay, Chambers, Bank of Scotland, Hamilton. Special features of Club—No meetings have been held during the past year. It is proposed to make a beginning on an early date.

No. 153—SCOTTISH Burns Club (in which is incorporated " Ye Saints Burns Club.") Instituted 1904. Federated 1906. Place and date of meeting, Reid's Rooms, 30 Gordon Street, Glasgow, fourth Mondays, at 7.30 p.m. President, S. B. Langlands, Corrymeela, 1413 Pollokshaws Road, Shawlands ; Vice-presidents, ex-Bailie Arch. Campbell, Park Lodge, 62 Albert Drive, Pollokshields, and D. S. MacGregor, 185 West Regent Street, Glasgow ; Secretary, J. Kevan M'Dowall, 180 Hope Street, Glasgow ; Treasurer, R. W. Reddoch, 35 Bellwood Street, Langside ; Financial Secretary, J. D. Bauchop, LL.B., 9 Blythswood Square, Glasgow ; Auditors, Jas. B. M'Pherson and D. M. MacIntyre, M.B.E., F.C.I.S. ; Bard, Thos. Cree. Committee—J. K. M'Dowall, J.P., J. S. Downie, M.A., N. MacWhannell, F.R.I.B.A., I.A., J. S. Gregson, Jas. Macfarlane, Geo. M'Gill, and J. G. MacKerracher, with President, Vice-presidents, Secretaries and Treasurer ex officio. Special features of Club —Burnsiana and literature ; Motto—" The Heart aye's the part aye." The Club is conducted on temperance principles.

No. 154—JOHANNESBURG Burns Club: Instituted 1900. Federated 1906. *Secretary*, Richard Rusk, solicitor. Natal Bank Buildings, Market Square, Johannesburg.

No. 155—EAST STIRLINGSHIRE Burns Club. Instituted 25th January, 1905. Federated 1st September, 1906. Place and date of meeting, Cross Roads Inn, Gainsford, quarterly. President, Alex. Cruickshanks, Union Buildings, Carron Road, Falkirk; Vice-president, William Galbraith, M'Callum Terrace, Carron Road, Falkirk; *Secretary*, Alex. Glen, 21 Gordon Terrace, Carron Road, Falkirk; Treasurer, Jas. M'Williams. Committee—John Dow, Jas. Cook, Jas. Morison. Special features of Club— To foster and maintain an intimate and thorough knowledge of the life and works of Burns; to celebrate the anniversary of his birth in supper, song, and sentiment.

No. 156—NEWCASTLE and TYNESIDE Burns Club. Instituted 1864. Federated 4th October, 1906. Place and date of meeting, Central Exchange Hotel, Fridays, 7 o'clock. President, William Maxwell, 88 Osborne Road, Newcastle-on-Tyne; Vice-president, R. M. Graham, c/o Bainbridge & Co., Market Street, Newcastle-on-Tyne; *Secretary*, James H. M'Kenzie, 15 Otterburn Avenue, Gosforth, Newcastle-on-Tyne; Treasurer, John Dempster, 51 Northumberland Street, Newcastle-on-Tyne. Special features of Club—To associate Scotsmen and all admirers of Burns; to cultivate literary pursuits; to preserve an interest in Scottish manners, customs, and affairs, and for purposes of a kindred character.

No. 157—BAILLIESTON Caledonian Burns Club. Instituted 25th January, 1901. Federated 5th October, 1906. Place and time of meeting, Free Gardeners' Hall, at 8 o'clock. President, Charles Paterson, 55 Muirside Road, Baillieston; Vice-president, James Adams, 152 Main Street, Baillieston; *Secretary*, Robert Watson, 55 Muirside Road, Baillieston. Committee—Wm. Lockhart, D. Johnstone, W. Scott, R. Lyle, D. M'Farlane, A. Hannah, and Z. Ross. Special features of Club—To cherish the name of Robert Burns and to foster a love for his writings, and generally to encourage a taste for Scottish literature and history; and to celebrate the memory of our National Bard by an annual social meeting, to be held on 25th January, or as near thereto as possible.

No. 158—DARLINGTON Burns Association. Instituted 8th March, 1906. Federated 18th October, 1906. *Secretary*, Robt. M. Liddell, 37 Langholm Crescent, Darlington.

No. 159—WALKER Burns Club. Instituted 1892. Federated 11th November, 1906. Place of meeting, Royal Hotel, Walker. President, Jno. Keith, 633 Welbeck Road, Walker; Vice-presidents, Dr W. Hutchinson and H. F. Caldwell, Welbeck Road, Walker; *Secretary*, Andrew D. Bell, 717 Welbeck Road, Walker, Newcastle; Treasurer,

Robt. M'Rory, 26 Eastbourne Gardens, Walker. Special features of Club—To promote the cultivation of a better knowledge of the Poet and his works ; to bring together Scotsmen and other admirers of Burns ; also promoting Scottish concerts.

No. 160—WHITBURN Burns Club. Instituted 1906. Federated 1906.

No. 161—CHARLESTON Burns Club, Paisley. Instituted 25th January, 1905. Federated 20th December, 1906. Place and date of meeting, 17 Stevenson Street, quarterly. President, Hector Craig, Morag, Hawkhead Road ; Vice - presidents, Peter Shannon, 14 Greenlaw Avenue, and Thos. Peacock, 17 New Stock Street ; *Secretary*, Andrew Walker, 16 Stevenson Street ; Auditors, Hugh Black and Alex. Glasgow. Special features of Club—The propagation of the knowledge of the writings of Burns in the district ; the promotion of a friendly feeling among the members and kindred clubs ; and the celebration of the Poet's birth.

No 162—PLYMOUTH and District Caledonian Society. Instituted 8th February, 1898. Federated 8th March, 1907. *Secretary*, P. Robertson, 89 Alcester Street, Devonport.

No. 163—GATESHEAD and District Burns Club. Instituted 1887. Federated 1907. Place and date of meeting, Royal Hotel, first Thursday of each month, September to April. President, E. Johnston, 140 Westminster Street, Gateshead-on-Tyne ; Vice-president, Thomas Hetherington, 3 St. Edmund's Place, Gateshead-on-Tyne ; *Secretary*, Wm. Bain, 142 Westminster Street, Gateshead-on-Tyne ; Treasurer, George J. Porter, Painter and Decorator, Durham Road, Gateshead-on-Tyne ; Piper, Pipe-Major Strachan, The Tyneside Scottish, 20 Diamond Street, Wallsend-on-Tyne. Special features of Club— To associate Scotsmen and admirers of Burns ; to keep up Scotch customs and study works of Burns.

No. 164—KINNING PARK Burns Club. Instituted 1881. Federated 1907. *Secretary*, John Downie, 29 Melville Street, Pollokshields, Glasgow.

No. 165—WALLSEND Burns Club. Instituted 1898. Federated 18th April, 1917. Place of meeting, Assembly Rooms, Wallsend-on-Tyne. President, D. Walters, 35 North Road, Wallsend-on-Tyne ; Vice-president, James Heron, 15 Curzeon Road, Wallsend-on-Tyne ; *Secretary*, Andrew Gray, 3 Burn Avenue, Wallsend-on-Tyne. Committee —Messrs Liddle, Cox, Polson, Johnston, Carter, Glass, Gillespie, and M'Farlane. Special features of Club—To associate Scotsmen and admirers of Burns ; to cultivate literary pursuits and love of Scottish song and story by promoting Scotch concerts ; also to preserve an interest in Scottish manners, customs, and affairs.

No. 166—CLEVELAND Scottish Association. Instituted 1907. Federated 1907. *Secretary*, A. Wallace, 6 Royal Exchange, Middlesborough.

No. 167—BIRMINGHAM Burns Club. Instituted June, 1906. Federated 13th November, 1907. Place and time of meeting, Grand Hotel, Birmingham, 7.30 p.m. President, John Calder, Ashmount, Tanworth Lane, Shirley, Worcestershire ; Vice-presidents, Wright Murray, 130 Oakwood Road, Sparkhill, Birmingham, and Jas. Ramsay, 101 Sandford Road, Moseley, Birmingham ; *Secretary*, Chas. MacGregor, 161 Great Charles Street, Birmingham ; Treasurer, Robert M'Kenzie, 50 Stirling Road, Edgbaston, Birmingham. Special features of Club—(1) To cherish the name of Robert Burns, to foster a love for his writings, to celebrate the anniversary of his birthday ; (2) to promote social and friendly intercourse amongst Scotsmen and Scotswomen resident in Birmingham and district.

No. 168 RICCARTON Burns Club. Instituted 7th February, 1877. Federated 14th January, 1908. *Secretary*, Jas. P. Moir, Craigallan, 39 Campbell Street, Riccarton.

No. 169—GLASGOW and DISTRICT Association of Burns Clubs and Kindred Societies. Instituted 1907. Federated 1908. Place of meeting, Royal Hotel, Sauchiehall Street Glasgow. President, C. R. Cowie, 20 Blythswood Square, Glasgow ; Vice-presidents, Wm. Cockburn, N.B. Station, Bowling, and Thos. Killin, Stewarton Drive, Cambuslang ; *Secretary*, J. Jeffrey Hunter, Solicitor, 89 Bath Street, Glasgow. Committee—A. Pollock, Hugh M'Coll, Wm. Douglas, Alex. M'Kenzie, G. Armour, Jas. M. Campbell, Isaac Chalmers, R. M. Milholm, A. M. Kay, Wm. Reid, A. C. Riddell, ex-Councillor Sutherland, Jas. Tudhope, J. F. Anderson, A. R. Young, J. M. Brown, J. C. Galpine, J. R. Ritchie, T. P. Thompson, Thos. Turner, J. C. Ewing, Ninian M'Whannell, T. C. W. Brotchie, J. D. Sloan, Wm. Gardiner. Special features of Club—To further the interests of the Burns cult by promoting closer union between the clubs in the district and bringing the members of these clubs into more harmonious relationship, and to take the initiative in instituting and recommending movements likely to be beneficial to the cult.

No. 170 LARKHALL Thistle Burns Club. Instituted November, 1906. Federated 18th April, 1908. President, John Crozier Hislop, 17 Percy Street, Larkhall ; *Secretary*, William Nicol, Machan, Larkhall.

No 171—CHATTANOOGA Burns Society, Tenn., U.S.A. Instituted 25th January, 1908. Federated, 2nd June, 1908. Time of meeting, Annual Dinner, 25th January. President, James Francis Johnston, 505 Walnut Street, Chattanooga, Tenn. ; Vice-president, Col. Milton B. Ochs, *Times* Building, Chattanooga, Tenn. ; *Secretary*, Col. R. B. Cooke, National Soldiers' Home, Tenn. Committee—N. Thayer Montague, Frank Spurlock, Garnett

Andrews. Special features of Club—Annual dinner, papers, lectures, collection of library.

No. 172—OREGON Burns Club, Portland, Oregon, U.S.A. Instituted 25th January, 1908. Federated December, 1908. Place of meeting, Chamber of Commerce Building. President, William Bristol, Attorney, Wilcox Building, Portland, Oregon ; Vice-president, Judge George J. Cameron, Chamber of Commerce Building, Portland, Oregon ; Secretary, Alexander T. Smith, 143 Hamilton Avenue, Portland, Oregon. Committee—Dr W. T. Williamson, James Hislop, Alex. G. Brown, Alex. Muirhead. Special features of Club—Meet once a year on January 25th to celebrate the anniversary of the birth of the greatest poet of humanity, the immortal Robert Burns.

No. 173—IRVINE Burns Club. Instituted 1826.. Federated, 18th November, 1908. Place and date of meeting, King's Arms Hotel, 25th January. President, John Irving Moffat, Eastwood, Irvine ; Vice-president, A. M. Watson, Dyrochburn, Irvine ; Secretary, R. M. Hogg, Stratford, Irvine · Treasurer, Robert F. Longmuir, Roseville, Irvine.

No 174—ARDROSSAN Castle Burns Club. Federated 1908. Secretary, Wm. Gibson, Hill Cottage, 90 Glasgow Street, Ardrossan.

No 175—MEIKLE EARNOCK Original Burns Club. Instituted 16th March, 1906. Federated 21st December, 1908. Place of meeting, John Crowe, Cadzow Vaults, Hamilton. President, James Shepherd, 2 Moore Street, Cadzow, Hamilton ; Vice-president, Alex. Laird, 50 Eddlewood Buildings, Hamilton ; Secretary, John Hepburn, 36 Eddlewood Buildings, Hamilton. Committee—Andrew Hamilton, William Pollock, Robert Lees, William Ross. Special features of Club—To keep ever green the memory of Scotia's greatest son, and disseminate the principles he strove to inculcate.

No. 176—RENFREW Burns Club. Federated 6th December, 1898. Secretary, Wm. S. Cochran, 20 Renfield Street, Renfrew.

No. 177—PRESTWICK Burns Club. Instituted 1902. Federated 1908.

No. 178—KILMARNOCK Begbie's Burns Club. Instituted 1908. Federated 1909. Place and date of meeting, Angel Hotel, third Wednesday of each month. President, John Stewart, 12 Hill Street, Kilmarnock ; Vice-president, Andrew Sinclair, 65 M'Lelland Drive, Kilmarnock ; Secretary, William Lennox, 11 Nursery Avenue, Kilmarnock. Committee—John Brown, A. M'D. Anderson, David Lang, John Douglas, and Wm. Muir. Special features of Club— Reading of papers relative to the works of Burns and kindred subjects ; celebrating the birthday of the Poet.

No 179—DAILLY Jolly Beggars Burns Club. Instituted 22nd January, 1902. Federated 22nd January, 1902.

No. 180—TOLLCROSS Burns Club. Instituted 1908. Federated 1908. Place, date, and time of meeting, Fullarton Hall, Tollcross, first Friday of month, 7.30 p.m. President, John Caldwell Brown, 5 Brownlee Gardens, Tollcross, Glasgow ; Vice-president, Charles Boyd, 399 Wellshot Road, Tollcross, Glasgow ; Secretary, James L. Cowan, Clydeside Terrace, Tollcross, Glasgow : Treasurer, W. Clarke ; Past President, A. M. Shaw. Directors—Messrs John Kerr, John Jack, D. Beveridge, R. Ritchie, A. Marshall, and A. Wilson. Special features of Club—To cherish the name of Robert Burns and foster a love for his writin.s, and generally to encourage a taste for Scottish literature.

No. 181—GLASGOW Primrose Burns Club. Instituted 1901. Federated 1909. Place and time of meeting, Grand Hotel, 7.30 p.m. President, Thos. S. Turnbull, 310 Golfhill Drive, Dennistoun, Glasgow ; Vice-president, Geo. J. M'Callum, 44 West George Street, Glasgow ; Joint Secretaries, Geo. R. Hunter, 55 Seamore Street, Glasgow, and Robt. L. Swann, 104 Hanover Street, Glasgow ; Treasurer, Mr John Wall, 263 Hope Street, Glasgow. Special features of Club—To foster an intimate acquaintance with the works of our National Bard, Robert Burns, by school essay competitions, monthly lectures and musical evenings, and anniversary dinner.

No. 182 STANE (Shotts) Mossgiel Burns Club. Instituted 3rd February, 1908. Federated 24th February, 1909. Place and date of meeting, Stane Hotel, first Friday of each month, except June and July. President, Ja. Cairns, 121 Torbothie Road, Stane, Shotts ; Vice-president, William Rodger, 104 Main Street, Stane, Shotts ; Secretary, Alexander Walker, 9 Torbothie Road, Stane, Shotts ; Treasurer, Jas. White, 1 Stane Place, Stane, Shotts. Special features of Club—Papers read on the Poet's works and Scottish literature, school competitions, celebration of anniversary.

No. 183 LONDONDERRY Burns Club and Caledonian Society. Instituted October, 1905. Federated 15th June, 1909. Place of meeting, Presbyterian Working Men's Institute, Diamond, Londonderry. President, Alexander Maclean J.P., Victoria Park, Londonderry ; Vice-presidents, Geo. P. Findlay, Thomas Wallace, Jas. MacLehose, W. G. S. Ballantyne, A. Wightman, and G. Burns ; Joint Secretaries, Wm. Baxter, 12 Harding Street, and Jas. MacLehose, Abercorn Place ; Treasurer, Jas. F. Wands, Ebrington Gardens ; Chairman of Committee, Thos. Wallace. Special features of Club—The objects of the society shall be to cherish the memory of Burns ; to study his works ; to discuss poets and poetry in general ; to endeavour by these means, or in such other manner as may be approved, to cultivate a closer social union amongst all classes of

Scotsmen and other sympathisers with the objects of the
club in Londonderry and neighbourhood ; to provide a
fund, by annual subscription, whereby Scotsmen in poor
and necessitous circumstances may be relieved ; and to
defray working expenses. Applications to be made to
the Hon. Secretary.

No. 184—BLAIRADAM Shanter Burns Club. Instituted 21st
August, 1907. Federated 29th August, 1909. Place,
date, and time of meeting, Blairadam Tavern, alternate
Saturdays, at 4 p.m. President, James Wilkie, Hutton's
Buildings, Black Road, Kelty ; Vice-presidents, Adam
Lees, Adam's Terrace, Kelty, and Arthur Bennett, Stewart's
Buildings, Main Street, Kelty ; Secretary, Thos. C. Ander-
son, Blairforge, Blairadam ; Treasurer, Geo. Burden.
Committee—Wm. Clark, Robt. Beveridge, Wm. Brown,
Wm. Fyfe. Special features of Club—Recitations, songs,
and readings.

No. 185—BURTON Burns Club. Instituted 1908. Federated
1909.

No. 186—KILMARNOCK Glencairn Burns Club. Instituted 1909.
Federated 1910. Secretary, John Thorburn, 12 Fairyhill
Road, Kilmarnock.

No. 187—GALASHIELS Burns Club. Instituted 10th December,
1908. Federated 9th December, 1909. Place of
meeting—Burgh Buildings. Hon. president, Right
Hon. Robert Munro, K.C., M.P. ; President,
Councillor George Hope Tait ; Vice-presidents, Provost
Dalgleish, H. S. Murray, A. L. Brown ; Secretary, George
Grieve ; Treasurer, John Hodge, jun. Committee—
W. Addison (chairman of committee), H. M. Tait, David
Hislop, W. Young, L. Lennox, Chief Constable Noble,
Jas. Walker, Councillor Thos. Brown, Thos. Lamb, ex-
Provost Riddle, P. Whyte, Councillor Kemp, Councillor
G. T. Sanderson, and ex-Provost Sutherland.

No 188—DUNS Working Men's Burns Club. Instituted 1902.
Federated 1910. Secretary, Robt. Cameron, British Linen
Bank, Duns.

No. 189—CLYDEBANK Barns o' Clyde Burns Club. Instituted
1908. Federated 9th December, 1909. Place and time
of meeting, Whitecrook Hall, 7.30 p.m. President,
George Latto, 23 Cochno Street, Whitecrook, Clydebank ;
Vice-president, James Fowler, 6 Viewfield Terrace,
Clydebank ; Secretary, John Abercrombie, 84 Glasgow
Road, Clydebank ; Treasurer, Alf. Homewood. Special
features of the Club—To extend the good work of the
Poet, and to keep for ever green the memory of
the Immortal Bard, Robert Burns, the Patriot and the
Prince of Song.

No 190—PORT-GLASGOW Burns Club. Instituted 13th January,
1910. Federated 5th April, 1910. Place and date of

meeting, Temperance Institute, third Thursday in month.
President, Wm. R. Niven, Firth View, Port-Glasgow;
Vice-president, John A. Borland, Balfour Place, Port-
Glasgow; *Secretary*, James Hicks, 20 John Wood Street,
Port-Glasgow; Treasurer, Wm. M'Dougall, Glenhuntly
Terrace, Port-Glasgow; Stewards, C. Young (chief), G.
Anderson, D. Crombie; Auditors, A. Ogilvie and J.
Louden. Committee—C. Young, W. Welsh, M. Phillips.

No. 191 MOORPARK Burns Club. Instituted 1908. Federated
1910. *Secretary*, Ebenezer Inglis, Glasdale, Fauldshead
Road, Renfrew.

No. 192—AYRSHIRE ASSOCIATION of Federated Burns Clubs.
Instituted 1908. Federated 1910. Place and date of
meeting, Quarterly, at various places and times in the
county. President, Andrew Sinclair, 65 M'Lelland
Drive, Kilmarnock; *Secretary*, William Lennox, 11
Nursery Avenue, Kilmarnock. Committee—Archibald
Laird, James Moir, Hugh Campbell, Wm. Hall, John
M'Gregor, and James Queay. Special features of Club
—To further the interests of the Burns cult by promoting
closer union between the Clubs in the county, and to render
all possible assistance to the work of the Federation.

No. 193—RUTHERGLEN Jolly Beggars Burns Club. Instituted
1910. Federated 1910.

No. 194—MIDDLEBIE Burns Club. Instituted 1909. Federated
1910. *Secretary*, Walter A. Mather. Donkins House,
Kirtlebridge, Ecclefechan.

No. 195—SHIREMOOR Blue Bell Burns Club. Instituted November, 1906. Federated November, 1910. Place and date
of meeting, Blue Bell Inn, every second Saturday in the
month. President, John Wilson, 11 Duke Street, Shiremoor, Northumberland; Vice-president, Robert Fyfe,
19 Percy Street, Shiremoor, Northumberland; *Secretary*,
James Fyfe Wilson, 11 Duke Street, Shiremoor, Northumberland. Committee—J. Peacock, E. Peacock, J.
Young, T. Bryan, F. Wilson, and Jas. Sneddon.

No 196—MID-ARGYLL Burns Club. Instituted 11th January,
1909. Federated 27th December, 1910. Place of
meeting, Royal Hotel, Ardrishaig. President, John
Campbell, Glenfyne House, Ardrishaig; Vice-president,
Robert Finlay, Royal Hotel, Ardrishaig; *Secretary*,
Andrew Y. Roy, Tigh-an-Eas, Ardrishaig. Committee—
Wm. C. Harvey, J. M. Montgomerie, Alexander Blue,
Archibald Campbell, John M'Alister, Archibald MacBain,
and John M'Arthur. Special features of Club—Celebration of the Poet's birthday and to encourage the
study of his works.

No. 197 WINNIPEG Burns Club. Instituted 1905. Federated
1911. *Secretary*, A. G. Kemp, Box 2886, Winnipeg.

No. 198—GOREBRIDGE Twenty-five Jolly Beggars Burns Club. Federated 28th November, 1913. *Secretary*, John Duncan, 5 Slate Row, Arniston, Gorebridge.

No. 199—NEWBATTLE and DISTRICT Burns Club. Instituted October, 1910. Federated November, 1910. Place and date of meeting, Bowling Green Pavilion, Newtongrange, first Saturday in each month from November to April. President, George Humphrey, Saughs, Newtongrange; Vice-president, Wm. Carson, Saughs, Newtongrange; *Secretary*, James Kennedy, 14 Lingerwood Road, Newtongrange, Mid-Lothian. Committee—P. Gray, P. Dickson, J. Samuel, D. Richardson, D. Pryde, J. Brown, J. Gilmour, J. Currie, G. M'Intosh, T. Dalgleish, J. Haldane, J. Millar. Special features of Club—The encouragement of social intercourse amongst the members and kindred Clubs; the celebration of the Poet's birth; an annual trip; meetings for the reading of literary papers relative to the life of Burns and kindred subjects; to encourage the taste for the works of Burns, and encouragement of the young to learn the songs and poetry of our National Poet by school competitions; promoting concerts during the winter months (as a result of these concerts we were successful in raising over £250 in the last four years for local charities).

No. 200—STONEHOUSE Jolly Beggars Burns Club. Instituted 1911. Federated 21st March, 1911. Place and date of meeting, Buckshead Inn, every alternate Friday. President, Samuel Kennedy, Queen Street, Stonehouse; Vice-president, Daniel Todd, Angle Street, Stonehouse; *Secretary*, Matthew Steel, Camnethan Street, Stonehouse; Treasurer, Robt. Anderson, Buckshead Inn, Stonehouse. Special features of Club—To promote social intercourse among people in the village.

No. 201—CARLISLE Newtown Burns Club. Instituted November, 1910. Federated 27th April, 1911.

No. 202—GOVAN Ye Cronies Burns Club. Instituted 1895. Federated 1911. Place and date of meeting, Red Lamp, Govan, second Saturday, June till March, at 5 p.m. President, Matthew Stirling, 13 Hutton Drive, Govan; Vice-president, James Hutchison, 10 Earle Street, Scotstoun · *Secretary*, James Rellie, 18 Elder Street, Govan; Treasurer, Lachlan M'Laine; Past Presidents, A. Nicol, J. Chalmers, and E. J. Tait. Committee—A. M'Dowall, W. Parker, D. Thomson, M. Wardrop, and T. R. Graham. Special features of Club—That the members of the Club shall consist of men who honour and revere the memory of Burns; that the membership shall not exceed 100 in number, and each candidate for membership must be a Freemason; to promote social and friendly intercourse amongst its members.

No. 203—DENNISTOUN Jolly Beggars Burns Club. Instituted 25th January, 1911. Federated 6th June, 1911. Place and date of meeting, Chalmers Street Halls, last Thursday of month. President, A. Hainey, 39 Brandon Street, Dennistoun, Glasgow; Vice-president, Wm. M'Kay, 7 Forrest Street, Mile End, Glasgow; *Secretary*, Wm. Fulton, 4 Parkhouse Lane, Dennistoun, Glasgow. Federation delegates—G. F. Thomas, 85 Eveline Street; G. Newman, 24 Brownpark Drive. Special features of Club —The celebration of the birth of Robert Burns; occasioual re-union for the cultivation of social and intellectual intercourse amongst members and friends; and the encouragement of Scottish literature.

No. 204—DUNDALK and DISTRICT Burns Club. Instituted January, 1909. Federated July, 1911. President, W. G. Minchin, Castle Road, Dundalk; Vice-president, W. B. Cree, Jocelyn Street, Dundalk; *Secretary*, Geo. Williamson, 53 Castle Road, Dundalk.

No. 205—PAISLEY ST. MIRREN Burns Club. Instituted September, 1911. Federated September, 1911. Place of meeting, 44 Old Sneddon Street. President, John Brown, Rutherglen; Vice-president, Aaron Jones; *Secretary*, Robert Crawford, 44 Old Sneddon Street, Paisley. Special feature of Club — To maintain the interest of Burns.

No. 206 GLASGOW Daisy Burns Club. Instituted 1911. Federated 1911.

No. 207—CAMBUSLANG Wingate Burns Club. Instituted 1908. Federated 1912. Place and date of meeting, Masonic Hall, first Saturday each month. President, James Young, 44 Glasgow Road, Cambuslang; Vice-president, James M. Smith, 623 Main Street, Tollcross; *Secretary*, Robert Forrester, 156 Hamilton Road, Cambuslang; Assistant Secretary, Robt. Tait; Treasurer, John M'Cracken; Assistant Treasurer, Wm. Stewart; Stewards, John Williamson and Thos. M'Gilvray; Hon. Members— Wm. M'Lean, Duncan M'Gilvray, A. Young, Wm. Young, R. Tait, John Smith, Dan Smith, Joseph Laird, John M'Ginn. Committee—Alex. Nelson, John M'Dermid, John Ferguson, Dugal Wright, Jas. Waddell, Thos. Dick. Special features of Club—Furtherance of Scottish song and sentiment.

No. 208 COLORADO SPRINGS and DISTRICT Caledonian Society. Instituted 1897. Federated 1912. Chief, W. W. Campbell, Golf Club, Colorado Springs, Colorado, U.S.A.; First Chieftain, John Grant, 162 South Nevada, Colorado Springs; Second Chieftain, D. W. Smith; Third Chieftain, P. D. Campbell; *Secretary*, William B. Dunlop, 219 North Cascade Avenue, Colorado Springs; Treasurer, Thos. MacLaren.

No. 209 GREENOCK St. John's Burns Club. Instituted 13th August, 1903. Federated 17th August, 1912. Place of meeting, Masonic Temple. President, Robert Brown,

14

69 Dempster Street, Greenock ; Vice-president, George
Blake, 45 Regent Street, Greenock ; *Secretary*, J. A. Hamilton, 6 Corwood Street, Greenock ; Treasurer, J. P. Millar,
28 Bruce Street, Greenock.

No. 210—HARDGATE Auld Hoose Burns Club. Instituted 28th
September, 1912. Federated 30th September, 1912.

No. 211—LARKHALL Thistle Lodge Free Gardeners, No. 15.
Instituted May, 1912. Federated 12th October, 1912.
Secretary, Alex. Henderson, 65 London Street, Larkhall,
Lanarkshire. Special features of Club—To foster the
knowledge of the works of Burns, and to elevate the minds
of our members.

No. 212—PORTOBELLO Burns Club. Instituted 25th January,
1892. Federated October, 1913. President, Very Rev.
H. S. Reid, M.A., Dean of Edinburgh, 19 Abercromby
Place, Edinburgh ; Vice-president, James Hastie, J.P.,
3 Queen's Bay Crescent, Portobello ; *Secretary*, William
Baird, J.P., F.S.A.Scot., Clydesdale Bank House, Portobello ; Treasurer, J. L. Jenkins, 2 Windsor Place, Portobello. Special features of Club—Cultivating a friendly
feeling among the members ; giving lectures ; encouraging
the young of Portobello in the study of Scottish literature,
and particularly the poetry of Robert Burns ; giving book
prizes to the schools. - Our annual festival was resumed
last January (after a suspension of four years during the
war) and was a brilliant success, the toast of the evening
by Rev. L. Maclean Watt and the musical programme
being of a first-class order.

No. 213—GLASGOW Kingston Burns Club. Instituted November,
1912. Federated 11th January, 1913. Place and date
of meeting, Wheat Sheaf Tea Rooms, 263 Paisley Road,
second Thursdays, October to March (inclusive). President, John M'Laren, 318 Paisley Road, Glasgow ; Vice-
president, Ernest G. Gray, 2 Herriet Street, Pollokshields ;
Secretary and Treasurer, Hugh A. Begg, 104 Weir Street,
Glasgow, S.S. Directors—John M. Brown, John Baird,
William Robertson, Alex. C. Baird, John Logan, J.P.,
Robert M'Lachlan, and James M'Millan. Special features
of Club—To commemorate the genius of Robert Burns
and foster a love for his writings, and to encourage the
taste for Scottish literature and music generally ; to celebrate his birthday on the 25th January, or as near thereto
as possible. Ladies are invited to all meetings this session.

No. 214—MELROSE Burns Club. Federated 22nd February,
1913. President, Dr Henry Speirs, St. Dunstan's, Melrose ; Vice-president, Geo. Sanderson, Westhill, Melrose ·
Secretary, Geo. Mackenzie, High Street, Melrose.

No. 215—THORNIEWOOD Burns Club. Instituted 26th February, 1911. Federated 24th February, 1913. *Secretary*,
W. Kerr, 54 Thorniewood, Uddingston.

No. 216—RUTHERGLEN Royal Burgh Burns Club. Instituted March, 1913. Federated May, 1913. *Secretary*, James E. Murray, 94 Mill Street, Rutherglen.

No 217—ESKDALE Burns Club. Federated 29th April, 1913. President, Clement Armstrong, F.S.A.Scot., Eskholm ; Vice-president, Thomas Bell, Townfoot ; *Secretary*, Wm. Pendreigh, Brewery House, Langholm. Committee— James Barr, Wm. Murray, David Calvert, and Robt. Irving.

No. 218—BANNOCKBURN Empire Burns Club. Instituted 25th January, 1913. Federated 13th June, 1913. Place and time of meeting, Commercial Hotel, Bannockburn, 7 p.m. President, William R. Lennie, Newlands, Bannockburn ; Vice-president, Thomas Rattray, West Murrayfield, Bannockburn ; *Secretary*, William Wark, Helenslea, Bannockburn ; Treasurer, James Kirkwood, Cauldhame, Bannockburn. Committee—Messrs Fulton, Smith. Neil, Palmer, Still, Wilson, Forsyth, and M'Gilchrist. Special features of Club—Monthly meetings during the year (our meetings consist of recitations and songs, and tend to create good-fellowship amongst our members) ; and to render all possible assistance to the work of the Federation.

No. 219—UDDINGSTON Burns Club. Instituted 1st April, 1913. Federated 21st June, 1913. Place and date of meeting, Magdala Hall, second Tuesday, 6.30 p.m. President, Thomas Hamilton, 12 Alpine Terrace, Uddingston ; Vice-president, John Hosie, 29 Greenrigg Street, Uddingston ; *Secretary*, John Meikle, 84 Avondale Terrace, Main Street, Uddingston ; Treasurer, John Hunter, jun., Committee—N. M'Donald, J. Leitch, T. Simpson, J. Ferguson, Wm. Fulton. Special features of Club—The moral and intellectual improvement of its members by the reading of essays and conversation on Burns's works, or any subject that may be for the well-being of the Club.

No. 220 ST. LOUIS Burns Club, Mo., U.S.A. Instituted 1904. Federated 1913. Date of meeting, 25th January. President, W. K. Bixby, Century Building, St. Louis, Mo. ; Vice-president, David R. Francis, St. Louis, Mo. ; *Secretary*, Walter B. Stevens, Jefferson Memorial, St. Louis Mo. ; Treasurer, Hanford Crawford, 722 Chestnut Street, St. Louis, Mo. Special features of Club—Annual meetings ; issuing printed reports from time to time.

No. 221—PRESTONPANS Burns Club. Instituted 25th January, 1913. Federated 16th August, 1913. *Secretary*, T. W. Watson, Moat House, Prestonpans.

No. 222—HULL Burns Club. Instituted 1869. Federated 1913. Place and date of meeting, Hammond's Cafe, Hull, third Friday of month, 7.45 p.m. President, Councillor Dr G. W. Lilley, J.P., 22 Williamson Street, Hull ; Past

President, Councillor W. Hakes, F.R.G.S., 61 Louis Street, Hull; *Joint Secretaries*, Robert A. Spiers, 22 Telford Street, Hull, and Albert Hockney, 51 Clumber Street, Hull; Hon. Treasurer, John R. Robinson, 20 Spring Street, Hull. Special features of Club—Social and literary. Membership, 240.

No. 223 GLASGOW Auld Clinkum Burns Club. Instituted 3rd April, 1913. Federated 6th October, 1913. Place and date of meeting, Masonic Halls, Overnewton, first Saturday each month. President, Charles M'Kinna, 4 Morrin Square, Glasgow; Vice-president, Jas. Wilson, 1314 Argyle Street, Glasgow; *Secretary*, Thos. Balcomb, 84 Henderson Street, Glasgow, N.W.; Treasurer, P. Moir, 16 Blackie Street, Overnewton, Glasgow. Delegates—J. Muir and J. Wilson, sen. Special features of Club—Annual trip; celebration of the Poet's birthday; literary and musical evenings; occasional short papers by members, and otherwise to encourage interest in the work and teaching of Scotia's National Bard.

No. 224 ASHINGTON Burns Club. Instituted 1891. Federated 1913. Place of meeting, Portland Hotel. President, Dr F. Beaton; Vice-president, Dr J. M'Lean; *Secretary*, D. Robertson, 20 Sixth Row, Ashington; Treasurer, S. W. Strong. Special feature of Club—Celebration of Burns anniversary.

No. 225—HELENSBURGH Burns Club. Instituted 2nd February, 1911. Federated 14th November, 1913. Place of meeting, as advertised. President, John Brown, Cairndhu Lodge, Helensburgh; Vice-presidents, Silas Maclean, 52 John Street, Helensburgh, and John Somerville, Woodland Place, Helensburgh; *Secretary*, Robert Thorburn, Albion Cottage, Helensburgh.

No. 226 DUMFRIES Burns Club. Instituted 18th January, 1820. Federated 1913. Place and date of meeting, Annual Meeting, Sheriff Court-house, Dumfries, first week in November. President, R. A. Grierson, Solicitor and Town Clerk, Dumfries; *Secretary*, John M'Burnie, Sheriff Court-house, Dumfries. Committee—G. B. Carruthers, David Fergusson, David H. Hastie, W. A. Hiddleston, Dr Joseph Hunter, and A. C. Penman. Special features of Club are—(a) To maintain the Burns Mausoleum in good repair, and provide for its proper supervision; (b) To discharge the obligations laid upon the Club by the testamentary disposition of Colonel William Nichol Burns, with respect to Burns's House and the Mausoleum; (c) To celebrate in suitable manner the anniversary of the Poet's birth, and to honour his memory in such other ways as may be from time to time determined; (d) To foster a knowledge of the life and works of Burns by means of an annual competition amongst local school children, prizes being awarded to the successful competitors.

No. 227—PENRITH Burns Club. Instituted 27th January, 1911. Federated 1913. Place of meeting, Station Hotel. President, D. S. M'Ghie, Kirkby Thore, near Penrith ; Vicepresident, Thomas Heskett, Plumpton Hall, Plumpton, Penrith ; *Secretary*, J. S. M'Grogan, 94 Lowther Street, Penrith, Cumberland ; Treasurer, R. Gardiner, 8 Brunswick Square, Penrith. Special feature of Club—Honour to memory of Burns.

No 228—CALDERWATERHEAD Burns Club. Federated 23rd May, 1914. *Secretary*, Wm. R. Moir, Mossbank, Hall Road, Shotts.

No. 229—EASTBOURNE and DISTRICT Scottish Association. Federated 23rd May, 1914. President, Sir John Nisbet Maitland, 69 Silverdale Road, Eastbourne ; Vice-president, Alex. Campbell, 14 Blackwater Road, Eastbourne ; *Secretary*, R. Prentice, 110 Terminus Road, Eastbourne.

No. 230—BURNBANK Burns Club. Instituted November, 1913. Federated 23rd May, 1914. *Secretary*, William Jamieson, 140 Glasgow Road, Burnbank, Hamilton.

No. 231—FAULDHOUSE and EAST BENHAR Burns Club. Instituted 1898. Federated 23rd May, 1914. Place of meeting, Caledonian Hotel, Fauldhouse. President, John Salmond, Co-operative Buildings, West End, Fauldhouse ; Vice-president, T. Forsyth, Caledonian Hotel, Fauldhouse ; *Secretary*, John Kinniburgh, Co-operative Buildings, West End, Fauldhouse ; Treasurer, R. Clark. Committee—Thos. Glencorse, Wm. Forsyth, R. Mutter, and George Hardie. Special features of Club—Receiving invitations and visiting other Clubs' meetings ; on the last Saturday of every month, at 6 o'clock, for songs and sentiments from Burns's works.

No. 232 ARNISTON Tam o' Shanter Burns Club. Federated 23rd May, 1914. *Secretary*, George Russell, 1 Victoria Street, Arniston, Gorebridge.

No. 233—The CLACHAN Burns Club. Instituted February, 1914. Federated 23rd May, 1914. *Secretary*, Donald M'Leod, Ivy Cottage, Braehead, Coalburn.

No 234—GLASGOW Southern Merchants' Burns Club. Instituted 1914. Federated 1914. President, Bailie Campbell, Govan Road, Glasgow ; Vice-president, W. L. Hutchison, 1 and 3 Cathcart Road, Glasgow ; *Secretary*, A. J. Ruglen. 36 Dundas Street, Glasgow (City).

No. 235—HAMILTON Glencairn Burns Club. Instituted 1894. Federated 8th August, 1914.

No. 236—WHITEHAVEN Burns Club. Instituted 24th January, 1914. Federated August, 1914. Place and date of meeting, Masonic Hall, Duke Street, Whitehaven, in January, March, and November. President, Dr J. F. Muir, Scotch Street, Whitehaven ; Vice-president, Dr Dickson, Queen Street, Whitehaven ; *Secretary*, John Davidson, 9 Edge Hill Terrace, Whitehaven. Committee—A. Anderson, R. T. Bell, J. R. Clark, A. Dickson, Wm. Glenn, Geo. Hill, A. Lockhart, H. M'Intosh, J. Murray

W. H. Miers, T. Preston, Jas. Shields, P. Turner, J. D. Wood, and J. Young. Special features of Club—To foster a knowledge of the life and works of Robert Burns, and to perpetuate his memory by an annual festival on the 25th January.

No. 237—UDDINGSTON Masonic Burns Club. Instituted July, 1914. Federated 8th August, 1914. Place of meeting, Rowan Tree Inn Hall, Uddingston. President, James Donald, Bothwell Castle, Bothwell; Vice-president, Thomas Cameron, Gas Works Cottage, Uddingston; *Secretary*, Owen Williams, 103 Walter Street, Alexandra Park, Glasgow; Treasurer, Thomas Barr, 4 Croftbank Place, Uddingston. Committee—David N. Miller, Alfred Russell, William Lumsden. Special features of Club— To celebrate in suitable manner the anniversary of the Poet's birth, and to honour his memory in such a way as may be from time to time determined.

No. 238 ATLANTA, Ga., Burns Club, U.S.A. Instituted 1896. Federated August, 1914. Place and date of meeting, Burns Cottage, Atlanta, Ga., first Wednesday each month. President, Dr Jno. Osman, 584 So. Boulevard, Atlanta, Ga., U.S.A.; Vice-presidents, A. A. Craig, Box 582, Atlanta, Ga., and H. H. Cabaniss, Atlanta, Ga.; *Secretary*, A. A. Craig, P.O., Box 582, Atlanta, Ga., U.S.A.; Treasurer, E. F. King; Superintendent of Grounds, W. L. Smith; Historian, R. M. M'Whirter. Special feature of Club—The only permanent replica of the Burns Cottage extant.

No. 239 HAWICK Burns Club. Instituted 1878. Federated 17th August, 1914. Place and date of meeting, 12 Teviot Crescent, open daily (except Sundays) from 10 a.m. to 10 p.m. President, John Hume, 5 Wellington Road; Vice-president, Wm. Fairholm, 12 Dickson Street; *Secretary*, Alex. Pringle, 24 Garfield Street. Committee —Peter Walker, Thos. Laidlaw, John Halliday, Robert Butler, George Brooks, James Murray, Special features of Club—To honour the name of Robert Burns; to celebrate the anniversary of his birth, and otherwise help to perpetuate his memory; to afford the members the means of social intercourse, mutual helpfulness, intellectual improvement, and social recreation.

No. 240 BLAWARTHILL Burns Club. Federated 6th December, 1914. President, Wm. Blair; Vice-president, J. Paterson; *Secretary*, T. G. King, 917 Yoker Road, Yoker; Treasurer, D. J. Lindsay.

No. 241—CROOK Burns Club. Instituted 1906. Federated 4th January, 1915. *Secretary*, A. B. Rutherford, Church Street, Crook, Co. Durham.

No. 242—MONTROSE Burns Club. Instituted 1908. Federated 1915. *Secretary*, Jas. Cumming, Town Clerk's Office, Montrose.

No. 243—PAISLEY St. James Burns Club. Instituted 1912. Federated 1915. Place of meeting, 7 Love Street, Paisley. President, John P. Stewart, 6 Blythswood Drive, Paisley;

Vice-president, Wm. Alexander, 28 Glen Street, Paisley ; *Secretary*, John M'Kechnie, 2 Douglas Terrace, Abbotsinch, Paisley ; Treasurer, James Fleming, 33 Glen Street. Paisley. Special features of Club—The encouragement of social intercourse amongst the members and kindred Clubs ; the celebration of the Poet's birth ; meetings for the reading of literary papers relative to the life and works of Burns, and kindred subjects.

No. 244—DALMUIR Burns Club. Instituted 1914. Federated 1916. Place and date of meeting, Trades Hall, third Thursday of each quarter, also Hallowe'en and annual festival. President, Bailie Jno. Young, The Crescent, Dalmuir ; Vice-president, R. Ferguson, Learig Place, Dalmuir ; *Secretary*, Alex. Dillon, 21 Trafalgar Street, Dalmuir ; Literary Secretary and Bard, Jno. Rae. Special features of Club—The perpetuation of the memory of our National Bard and the cultivation of Scottish literature and poetry.

No. 245—KINNAIRD Victoria Burns Club. Instituted October, 1910. Federated 3rd January, 1917. Place and date of meeting, Victoria Inn, Carronshore, second Saturday each month at 6 p.m. President, James Turnbull, Bothy Row, Carronshore, by Carron ; Vice-president, Alexander Reid, North Main Street, East End, Stenhousemuir : *Secretary*, George Jenkins, Kinnaird, by Falkirk. Committee—George Cowan, John Waugh, James Binnie, Joseph Wallace, Samuel Marshall. Special features of Club—To meet in a social capacity ; to uphold the name of Burns and his works ; to create a friendly spirit amongst the members ; and to assist the Burns Federation.

No. 246 LOCHORE and ROSEWELL Shanter Burns Club. Instituted 29th September, 1916. Federated 15th January, 1917. Place and date of meeting, Rosewell Bar, every second Saturday. President, Wm. Morton, 138 Waverley Street, Lochore ; Vice-president, Thos. Wilson, Dumbiedykes, Lochore ; *Secretary*, Robert Davidson, Ballingry Road, Lochore. Committee—Jas. Dunn, A. Rankine, A. Arnot, Thos. Hunter, John Young, Henry Davidson. Special features of Club—The encouragement of sound intercourse among admirers of the Poet by means of literary and social meetings (as the committee may adopt).

No. 247 LOCHGELLY Thirteen Jolly Beggars Burns Club. Instituted 12th March, 1916. Federated 1st September, 1917.

No. 248—BIRTLEY Burns Club. Instituted 10th December, 1915. Federated 18th October, 1917. Place and date of meeting, Railway Hotel, Birtley, alternate Thursdays, 7.30 p.m. President, T. Fenwick, Harras Bank, Birtley, Co. Durham ; Vice-president, John Young, Durham Road, Birtley, Co. Durham ; *Secretary*, James Mann, Wellington House, Station Road, Birtley, Co. Durham ; Assistant Secretary, J. W. Stirling ; Treasurer, Dr J. Johnston, Brookside Birtley, Co. Durham ; Organist, R. H. Richardson. Committee—R. Wade, R. G. Wilson, A. Stewart, R. H. Robson, T. Foster, G. Jackson. Special features of Club—To

celebrate in a suitable manner the Poet's birth, and to
honour his memory in such other way as may from time
to time be determined ; social well-being of the members ;
to institute competitions in local schools in Scottish songs
and literature.

No. 249—MID-CALDER Tam o' Shanter Burns Club. Instituted
29th September, 1916. Federated 23rd November, 1917.
Place and date of meeting, Market Inn, Mid-Calder, first
Saturday each month. President, Jas. Denholm, Pum-
pherston, Mid-Calder ; Vice-president, Thos. Dalziel,
Oakbank, Mid-Calder ; Secretary, D. M'Kerracher, North
Gate, Livingston, Mid-Calder.

No. 250 COWDENBEATH Tam o' Shanter Burns Club. Instituted 19th October, 1917. Federated 28th November,
1917. Place and date of meeting, Crown Hotel, monthly
(Saturdays) at 5.30. President, John Black, 25 Natal
Place, Cowdenbeath ; Vice-president, Robert Macgregor,
10 Sligo Street, Lumphinnans ; Secretary, George Marshall,
38 Natal Place, Cowdenbeath ; Treasurer, John Duff.
Committee—R. Brownlie, W. Jack (Bard), A. Bradford
(Croupier). Special features of Club—To promote
friendly intercourse amongst its members ; celebrating
the Poet's anniversary.

No. 251 GLENCRAIG Burns Club. Instituted February 9th,
1918. Federated November 23rd, 1918. Place and
date of meeting, Hunter's Bar, third Saturday of month
from September till April. President, Robert Glencross,
Lofty View, Glencraig ; Vice-president, Thomas Ferguson,
125 South Glencraig ; Secretary, John Duncan, 4 Flockhouse, Lochore, Glencraig. Committee—Jas. Salmond,
Alex. Murdoch, Robt. Hutchison, John Dodds, John
M'Callum, Robt. Moffat.

No. 252—ALLOWAY Burns Club. Instituted 1908. Federated
1918. Place of meeting, Alloway. President, John B.
Fergusson, of Balgarth, Alloway, Ayr ; Vice-president,
James Turnbull, The Schoolhouse, Alloway, Ayr ; Secretary, Andrew J. Gray, 29 Northpark Avenue, Ayr. Committee—Rev. J. M. Hamilton, T. Auld, J. R. Dickson
A. Cunningham, J. Grant, and A. Harvey.

No. 253—GALSTON Jolly Beggars Burns Club. Instituted 1916.
Federated 1918. Place and date of meeting, Burns
Tavern, Galston, Monday, at 6.30 p.m. President,
Alex. Hunter, Barr Street, Galston ; Vice-president,
John Luke, Orchard Street, Galston ; Secretary, John
Morton, 26 Garden Street, Galston. Committee—
Adam Aitken and Jas. M'Caw. Special features of Club
—Social and literary.

No 254—GREENOCK Victoria Burns Club. Instituted 2nd
October, 1914. Federated 1918. Place and date of meeting, Co-operative Hall, monthly. President, Dr Milne,
Hillend House, East Crawford Street, Greenock ; Vice-
president, D. Clark, 2 Octavia Street, Port-Glasgow ;
Secretary, Matthew W. Linn, 19 Belville Street, Greenock.
Special features of Club—Monthly lectures ; draughts,
dominoes, darts, cards, and bagatelle competitions ; to
cherish the name of Robert Burns, to foster a love for his
writings, and generally to promote good-fellowship.

No 255—CATHCART Burns Club. Instituted January 22nd, 1916. Federated January 15th, 1919. Place of meeting, Unionist Rooms, Clarkston Road, Cathcart. President, William Glen, 9 Holmhead Street, Cathcart ; Vice-president, Robert Laurie, 1132 Cathcart Road, Mount Florida, Glasgow : Secretary, David B. Wilson, 9 Craig Road, Cathcart. Special feature of Club—Monthly meetings at which papers are read, followed by discussion.

No. 256 NEWTON-ON-AYR Burns Club. Instituted August, 1904. Federated 1919. Place and date of meeting, Robert Burns Tavern, Ayr, Thursdays. Hon. President, Sir George Younger, Bart, M.P. ; President, John S. Jackson, 23 Bellesleyhill Avenue, Ayr : Vice-president. H. M. Giles, Southcote, Prestwick ; Secretary, James Dobbie, 1 Falkland Park, Ayr ; Treasurer, Thos. Sands. Committee—W. M'Dowall, Thos. M'Creadie, R. Morris, D. Mullen, Thos. Reid. Auditors, D. Mullen and Jas. Templeton. Special features of Club—To promote among the members the knowledge of Scottish history, literature, and music, and especially of the life and works of Burns.

No. 257 ARMADALE Star Burns Club. Instituted 2nd February, 1918. Federated 17th May, 1919. Place and date of meeting, Star Inn, first Saturday, monthly, 6 p.m. President, Thomas Milne, Star Inn, Armadale ; Vice-president, James M'Hattie, Heather Field, Armadale ; Secretary, Benjamin Reid, 32 East Main Street, Armadale · Treasurer, Alexander Samuels. Committee—R. Currie G. Menzies, R. Cunningham, H. Nisbet, H. Imrie.

No. 258—ARMADALE Buck's Head Burns Club. Instituted, 12th October, 1918. Federated 17th May, 1919. Place and date of meeting, Masonic Hall, Armadale, third Saturday of each month, 6 p.m. President, John Mack, Polkemmet Cottage, Armadale, West Lothian ; Vice-president, William M'Alpine, Unity Terrace, Armadale, West Lothian ; Secretary, John Stevenson, 24 Hardhill Terrace, Armadale, West Lothian ; Treasurer, John Henderson, 36 Hardhill Terrace. Committee—Meikle M'Lay, Wm. Ferguson, James Hasten, James Dunn, John Peden. Special features of the Club—To consider and discuss subjects, questions, and reading of papers directly concerning Burns and his works ; to promote the efficiency, knowledge, and attainments of the members on the works and life of Rabbie Burns ; visitation to places of interest and kindred Clubs ; anniversary dinner celebration ; holding of Hallowe'en special night ; annual public schools competition ; visitors cordially invited.

No. 259- BONNYRIGG A Man's a Man for a' That Burns Club. Instituted 5th April, 1919. Federated 6th June, 1919. Place and date of meeting, Calderwood Arms, Bonnyrigg, last Saturday of every month. President, David Blyth, Hoggan's Buildings, Polton Road, Bonnyrigg ; Vice-president, John Shanks, 43 Polton Street, Bonnyrigg ; Secretary, George Weatherston, 8 Camp View, Bonnyrigg ; Treasurer, John Anderson. Committee—A. Hill, A. Ross, J. M'Lean, J. Crozier, G. Scott, J. B. Howden, N. Peacock.

No 260—TARBRAX Jolly Beggars Burns Club. Instituted 25th January, 1919. Federated 17th May, 1919. Place and date of meeting, Schoolroom, Tarbrax, 26th January, 1920, 8 p.m. President, David Black, Moorview, Tarbrax, Cobbinshaw ; Vice-president, J. R. Roberts, Fineview, Tarbrax, Cobbinshaw ; Secretary, Hugh M'Glone, 239 Tarbrax, Cobbinshaw ; Chairman of Committee, Robert Crichton, New Houses, Tarbrax, Cobbinshaw. Special features of Club—To meet and celebrate at the annual anni. versary ; to keep in touch with the admirers of our National Poet ; to hold competitions on the works of Burns for school children, and thus help to keep the young in touch with his works (we have held three competitions and all have been great successes).

No. 261—SYDNEY ANNIVERSARY Burns Club, N.S.W. Fede. rated September, 1919. Secretary, David R. Rogers, Bannockburn, Marlowe Street, Campsie, Sydney, N.S.W.

No. 262—FIFESHIRE Burns Association. Instituted 17th May, 1919. Federated 6th September, 1919. Place of meet. ing, Affiliated Clubs Meeting Rooms. President, A. T. Macbain, Solicitor, Kincholle, Venturefair Avenue, Dunfermline ; Vice-presidents, Jas. Wilkie, Black Road, Kelty, and R. Glencross, Loftyview Glencraig, ; Secretary and Treasurer, Geo. Marshall, 38 Natal Place, Cowden. beath ; Bardess, Miss M. Moir, Kingskettle, Cowdenbeath. Committee—W. Whisker (Lochgelly Jolly Beggars), T. Anderson (Kelty Shanter), T. Davidson (Lochore), T. Murdoch (Glencraig), E. Hunter (Cowdenbeath Glencairn), T. Paterson (Dunfermline). Special features of Association —To further the interests of the Burns cult by promoting closer union between Clubs and kindred Societies, and bringing them into more harmonious relationship.

No. 263—GLASGOW Masonic Burns Club. Instituted 31st January, 1919. Federated 23rd September, 1919. Place and date of meeting, Royal Restaurant, Glasgow, last Fridays October to April. President, J. S. Jamieson, Glenwood, Newlands ; Vice-president, John Waddell ; Secretary, H. Stuart Girvan, B.L., Solicitor, 252 West George Street, Glasgow ; Treasurer, A. D. Campbell, 182 Trongate ; Directors of Music, J. S. Leslie and Wm. Lochrie. Directors —Hugh M'Quat, Jas. Veitch, Wm. Millar, J. T. Grady, Jas. Thomson, Richard Scott.

No 264 PRESTONPANS Jolly Beggars Burns Club. Instituted 28th June, 1919. Federated 20th September, 1919. Place and date of meeting, Queen's Arms Hotel, first Saturday in month, at 4 p.m. Hon. President, Wm. Brown ; President, William Edmond, Harlaw Hill, Prestonpans ; Vice-president, David Bruce, 90 Mont. gomery Street, Edinburgh ; Secretary, Wm. M'Leod, 15 Crown Square, Prestonpans ; Treasurer, Wm. Cunning. ham ; Bard, Andrew M'Leod ; Croupiers, George and Wm. Doigg ; Editor, Wm. Watt. Special features of Club—Scottish literature ; study and rehearsal of Burns's works ; educating the young into the works of Burns.

J. MAXWELL & SON, Printers and Lithos., High Street, Dumfries.

Burns Chronicle & Club Directory

No. XXX.

January, 1921.

Price

Three Shillings.

Published by the
BURNS FEDERATION.

Printed by
ROBERT DINWIDDIE,

BURNS CHRONICLE & CLUB DIRECTORY

No. XXX.

JANUARY, 1921.

PRICE

THREE SHILLINGS.

PRINTED BY
ROBERT DINWIDDIE.

PUBLISHED BY THE
BURNS FEDERATION.

CONTENTS.

	Page.
Mr Gribbel's Visit to Scotland	5
To Mr John Gribbel—*W. Munro*...	19
The Burnsian Welcome—*T. C. F. Brotchie*	19
Elegy on Stella—*Davidson Cook*	29
Burns and Creech—*Editor*	39
Two Artists of the People—*Albert Douglas*	54
Shenstone and Burns (II.)—*A. J. Craig*	67
Robert Burns, Antiquarian—*Philip Sulley*	81
At Brow and After—*J. T. G.*	86
Removal of the Highland Mary Memorial	87
Highland Mary Memorial at Failford	92
At Mary's Shrine—*Chas. L. Brodie*	94
Maria Riddell's Letters to Dr Currie (II.)—*J. C. E.*	96
Dumfries Burns Club Centenary Celebration	109
The Poet's Insight—*James Brown*	117
Reviews	119
The Poet's Genealogy—*K. G. Burns*	120
Club Notes	125
Notes and Queries	153
Federation Office-bearers, &c.	166
Annual Meeting of Federation	170
Club Directory	181

PREFACE.

THE phenomenal demand for the *Chronicle* last year—
the whole issue was sold out within eight days after publication—occasioned much disappointment amongst the
Clubs whose orders had been inadvertently delayed. The
national shortage of paper restricted the issue to the average
of the war period, but arrangements have now been made
to cope with the ever-increasing demand.

The chronicling of current events has demanded
so much space in the current issue that several articles
of merit have been unavoidably held over.

Owing to the serious illness of Mr Albert Douglas
the compiler of the general Index to the *Chronicle*, its
publication has been delayed, but it is expected that it
will be ready for delivery early in February.

The Editor's thanks are again due to all who have
assisted him in preparing this year's volume.

D. M'NAUGHT.

BENRIG, KILMAURS,
  January 1st, 1921.

VISIT OF MR JOHN GRIBBEL TO SCOTLAND.

THE great debt which Scotland owes to Mr John Gribbel of Philadelphia, who restored the Glenriddel MSS. of Robert Burns to the Nation after they had been unwarrantably disposed of by the Directors of Liverpool Athenæum, can never be adequately discharged ; but the Burns Federation embraced the opportunity of a visit of Mr Gribbel to the " land of the mountain and flood," to mark its heartfelt appreciation of his generous action and his munificent gift. On Tuesday, 27th July of this year, the Federation entertained Mr Gribbel at dinner in the Grand Hotel, Glasgow, and presented him with a splendid album containing an illuminated address and drawings in oils, water colours, and black-and-white by no fewer than 36 famous Scottish artists. Under the guidance of the Office-bearers of the Federation, Mr Gribbel made a tour in the land of Burns, visiting Ayr, Alloway, and Kirkoswald on Thursday, and Kilmarnock, Mauchline, and Tarbolton on Friday. Mr Gribbel has been greatly delighted with his visit to Scotland and with the hearty reception accorded him everywhere by the admirers of the National Poet.

THE DINNER AND PRESENTATION.

The dinner and presentation passed off with the utmost success, the company being large and representative, and the proceedings being characterised by intense enthusiasm. Mr Duncan M'Naught, J.P., Kilmaurs, President of the Federation, occupied the chair, supported on the right by the guest of the evening, Mr Gribbel ; Sir Robert Cranstoun, Edinburgh ; Sir D. M. Stevenson, Glasgow ; Mr Hugh M'Coll, Glasgow ; Ex-Bailie Munro, Kilmarnock ;

Mr Alexander Pollock, Mr T. Maxwell, Mr J. Connell, Glasgow ; and Mr Thomas Amos, M.A., Hon. Secretary of the Federation ; and on the left by ex-Provost Mathew Smith, Kilmarnock ; Mr A. Brownlie Docharty, artist ; ex-Provost Wilson, Govan ; Mr T. C. F. Brotchie, curator of the Art Galleries, Glasgow ; Mr Philip Sulley, Edinburgh ; and Mr George A. Innes, M.B.E., Hon. Treasurer of the Federation. The Croupiers were Mr Charles R. Cowie, Partick ; Mr Tom Hunt, Artist ; Mr Thomas Killin, Glasgow Mauchline Society ; and Mr J. C. Ewing, Baillie's Institution, Glasgow ; and amongst others present were Mr David Yuille, Mr Adam Mackay, and Mr J. P. Dickson, Kilmarnock ; Mr J. Leiper Gemmill, Mr Alexander Mackenzie, Mr John Carmichael, ex-Bailie Douglas, and Captain Douglas, Glasgow ; Mr Peter Paterson, Dunfermline ; Mr James Thomson, London ; Mr W. H. Turner and Mr A. W. Semple, Sunderland, &c. The company numbered about 150. During the service of the dinner, which was admirably purveyed, several Scottish selections were skilfully played on the pianoforte.

The Chairman, in a few opening remarks, said—

He had to congratulate the Executive of the Federation and the Federation itself on the grand turnout that night in order to do honour to Mr Gribbel. It was a very awkward season of the year for a meeting of that kind, and he knew that some of them must have exercised a considerable amount of self-denial in order to be there, but he hoped that they would not consider their time misspent. The next remark he would make was on the unusual brevity of the toast list. The Executive thought that it would be better to have very few formal toasts, and leave the remainder to take care of themselves. If any gentleman felt inspired to say anything afterwards they would be very glad to afford him an opportunity. The last remark he had to make was that the speeches were to be brief. (Laughter.) Of course from that they excepted their honoured guest, Mr Gribbel, who would have *carte blanche* in that respect.

The Chairman then proposed the loyal toasts, which were heartily honoured. He also proposed a toast to the President of America, " that wise, far-seeing man, Mr

Woodrow Wilson." (Applause.) The company responded to the toast by singing " He's a jolly good fellow."

Mr Cowie, in proposing " The Imperial Forces," and
referring to the part that America had taken in the
war, said—.

That the poems and songs of Burns had done more than anything else to cement America and this country together. They
all knew how enthusiastic the Americans were over Burns. His
songs resounded throughout the land, and it was believed that these
would have an ever-increasing influence in binding the two countries
more closely together.

Sir Robert Cranstoun replied to the toast, and after
referring to Mr Gribbel as " our most worthy and most
welcome guest," he spoke of the camaraderie that existed
amongst the fighting forces during the war, their one idea
being " their God, their King, and their country." They
had fought for the love of God, the honour of the King,
and the welfare of the people.

The Chairman, in proposing the toast of the evening
" Our Guest, Mr Gribbel," said—

That a long-looked-for occasion had come at last. He was
not going to inflict upon them the story of the Glenriddel Manu
scripts. The facts were as well known to them as to himself.
Suffice it to say, that whenever the alarm was sounded in this country
every Burnsian sprang to his feet, and they all did what they could
to prevent the manuscripts from going across the Atlantic, but
without success. When the Manuscripts came into the hands of
Mr Gribbel it was not for the purpose of adding to his own collection.
He sent them back to Scotland as a gift to the Nation—(applause)
—not in any ostentatious spirit, because that was contrary to his
nature—not to ingratiate himself with Burnsians over the Empire,
but from a sheer sense of duty. (Applause.) The outstanding
characteristic of Mr Gribbel was an abounding love of Scotland
and everything Scottish. At an early date he (the Chairman) had
suspected that there was a strong strain of Scottish blood in Mr
Gribbel. He had turned up all the authorities he could think of
—all the place-names and surnames in Scotland, but with very
little effect. He was on the wrong trail. The name was not
" Gribb-el " but " Gri-bbel," and Bell was a common name in
Scotland. It was a well-known name in Glasgow. Not long

ago they had Sir James Bell in the civic chair as Lord Provost of the city. In olden times they had the Black Douglases and the Red Douglases, and he was perfectly certain that it would take little research to discover the " Grey-bells " of that ilk. (Laughter.) He was perfectly serious ; for they had only to look at their worthy guest to see that as the years had gone on he had developed in a very high degree the family characteristics. If his forefathers did not go over with the Pilgrim Fathers in 1620 it was doubtless because they were there already. (Laughter.) With regard to Mr Gribbel's character he must speak with bated breath. The most flattering reports had come about his character and worth. From London they had received word that Mr Gribbel was about the best specimen of the American that had ever crossed the Atlantic. (Applause.) Putting that aside, they all knew of his connection with that organ of public opinion, the *Philadelphia Ledger*. Most of them would remember the extracts from the *Ledger* that appeared in the London and Scottish daily papers, showing that the *Ledger* had been strongly pro-Ally, and he could corroborate that from correspondence which he had had with Mr Gribbel. After the first few letters the subject of the Glenriddel Manuscripts dropped out of the correspondence, and the war took its place. He (the Chairman) remembered. telling him about his own sons, and Mr Gribbel replied that even that brought the war nearer to him and to his door, and when the American Nation sprang to arms the sons of their guest were amongst the first to land in France. (Applause.) Some of them had returned home, but one at least had shed his blood in the great cause for which they were all fighting. Proceeding, the Chairman said that he considered it a very high honour to present the album in name of the Burns Federation. At first they had thought of presenting him with a testimonial of some kind or other. but they had some difficulty in coming to a conclusion as to the form it should take, and at last they made up their mind to present him with an illuminated address. This took root and grew, and then they appealed to the Scottish artists, who responded to them in the most generous spirit. (Applause.) He need not say a single word as to the pecuniary value of the album. All he need say was that it was a Glasgow production and executed in the highest style of the art. Their friend, Mr Connell, had made sure of that. (Applause.) Its value would doubtless be enhanced in the future, when the Gribbel Album would be carefully scanned in order to discover the early efforts of the grand old masters of the Glasgow School. (Applause.) It only remained with him now to call upon their worthy Secretary, Mr Amos, to read the text of the illuminated address, and he might tell them that it was not an array of meaningless words, because the matter had been remitted to a special committee, and every word and every phrase had been carefully weighed and considered. When they heard these words from the lips of Mr Amos they were to understand that these honestly but insufficiently conveyed to Mr Gribbel their opinion of him as a man and their sense of gratitude for the great benefit that he had conferred upon the Scottish Nation. (Loud applause.)

Mr Amos read the address, which was in the following terms :—

" To John Gribbel, Esq., of Anstell Hall, Wyncote,
        Pennsylvania, U.S.A.

    " SIR,—The Burns Federation, representing many thousands of the admirers of Robert Burns throughout the world, take the occasion of your visit to Scotland to offer you their heartfelt thanks for your generosity in restoring to Scotland the great collection of the Poet's writings known as the Glenriddel MSS.

    " These precious relics seemed irretrievably lost to Scotland till they came into your hands, when you unhesitatingly showed your appreciation of the most fitting place for their permanent preservation and your wisdom in the arrangements for making them available for inspection and study in Edinburgh and Glasgow.

    " Your generous action has evoked throughout Scotland feelings of the warmest gratitude. We here seek to express that gratitude in a volume containing, besides this address, drawings of scenes associated with the life and writings of the Poet—the works of eminent Scottish artists. We ask you to accept the volume, accompanied by the earnest hope that it will be cherished by yourself and your descendants as a reminder of a nation's gratitude called forth by your munificence.

    " Signed on behalf of the Burns Federation.
        ROSEBERY, Hon. Pres.
        WM. WALLACE, ALEX. LAWSON, JAS. SIVEWRIGHT, Hon.
            V.-P.'s.
        D. M'NAUGHT, Pres.   THOS. AMOS, Hon. Secy.
        GEO. A. INNES, Hon. Treas.
        HUGH M'COLL, J. JEFFREY HUNTER, ALEX. POLLOCK,
            J. C. EWING, J. CONNELL, DANIEL STEVENSON,
            A. INCHES."

The Chairman then called upon the company to pledge the toast of " Mr and Mrs Gribbel and Family " in an overflowing bumper.

The toast was honoured with tremendous enthusiasm, and " He's a jolly good fellow " was sung with great heartiness.

Mr Gribbel, on rising to reply, received quite an ovation, the company springing to their feet and cheering vociferously.

" He would have to be a very insensible man," said Mr Gribbel in his opening sentence, "who could sit in his chair here to-night and hear unmoved the things that Mr M'Naught has said, even if one's own judgment could go so far as his kindness has gone. I confess to you that had I known the embarrassment that might present itself to me standing before you to-night, I think that Scotland would have got the Glenriddel Manuscripts anonymously." (Laughter and applause.) Proceeding, Mr Gribbel said that their kindness had made an impression not to be put into words —it could only be felt ; and as long as consciousness endured, the kindness of Scotland to him for doing a thing for which he deserved no credit—he simply did it because he loved to do it—would be gratefully remembered. When he sent these manuscripts to Scotland he had the impression that they would be received and given a permanent home, which was all he sought for ; but he little thought that Scotsmen, aye, and Scotswomen, the wide world over would express to him the gratitude he had received in hundreds and hundreds of letters. Nearly four years ago, being a little racked in nerves and suffering from sleeplessness, largely due to the war and the attitude of the American Government in holding out of it so long, he made up his mind to get away from civilisation, away from business and correspondence, and after some wandering he found himself in the Arizona desert. There he was told that some distance off he would find a Scotsman named Campbell. This man had been at a trader's post there for forty years. He had gone out dying of tuberculosis, and, like every other Scotsman, he found the very thing he was hunting for. He found an atmosphere that he could breathe and live in, and during all these years he had been out there thriving, and had amassed a competence, but he was a bit short-grained in the temper. (A voice—" Like a Scotsman again," and laughter.) About six o'clock one evening as he and his friend were going over the Divide, they saw a dry lake in front of them, and he said to his friend, " We're coming to Campbell's." They went over the lake—they called it a lake, though there had been no water in it since the Flood—and he saw against the sunset two little bumps, as they seemed to be, in the landscape. He said to his friend, " That is Campbell's "; and as they drew up in front of the store they saw the old man sitting on an up-ended box, leaning over another box on which lay an unopened book, on the top of which was an open book. Campbell had spent forty years in that wilderness, dealing with ranchers, Indians, and cowboys, and the book he was reading was Locke's *On the Human Understanding*.

He tried to get into conversation with him, but did not succeed very well. He walked around him and behind him, and discovered that the unopened book was *Chambers' Encyclopædia.* He continued his efforts to get into conversation with him, and finally the old man ' loosened out," as they said in the States. He " loosened

Mr JOHN GRIBBELL, Philadelphia, U.S.A.

out " to the extent of saying " Whaur are ye frae ?" (Laughter.) He said that he was from Philadelphia. After a little Campbell asked, " What may be your name ?" and he replied that it was Gribbel. Without looking up, Campbell asked, " Are there many of your family there ?" and he answered, "No." Then the old man went on reading for two or three minutes, and afterwards asked, " Did you ever hear of John Gribbel in Philadelphia ?" He (Mr Gribbel) said that that was his name, and the old man continued reading Locke's *On the Human Understanding*. (Laughter.) After a while he said, " Do you do any reading yourself ?" He answered " Yes," and added that he got a great deal out of British poets. "Do you read Burns?" asked Campbell. "Yes," said Mr Gribbel, " Burns is my chief joy." Then the old man unfolded his arms and put out his hand and said, " Are you the man ?" and he replied, " I am." (Laughter and applause.) And yet the Scot was said not to be sympathetic or sentimental ! It was only the ignorant who made such an assertion. Campbell insisted that he (Mr Gribbel) should sleep in his own bed that night, and would not allow him to erect his tent on the sands. In the morning he asked the old man how he came to know about the Glenriddel Manuscripts, seeing that he had not been at Los Angelos or San Francisco or Chicago for forty years " Ah ! man," was the reply, " I have been taking in an Aberdeen journal for forty years." When he (Mr Gribbel) came to leave he had to settle with Campbell for some stores, and the amount was paid even to the changing of half-a-cent—that was a business transaction ; but when he offered to pay 'for the hospitality that had been extended to him the old man would not hear of it, and he (Mr Gribbel) had to apologise for insisting upon it. Lying on the counter there was a copy of the *Saturday Evening Post*, to which he (Mr Gribbel) had given a good deal of attention, and when Campbell turned round to give him his change he looked up to him with a sarcasm not to be put in words, and said, " That's nothing for the like o' you—it is purely commercial." (Laughter.) Proceeding, Mr Gribbel said that he had often remarked in the States that he had not a drop of Scottish blood in his veins. He was very glad that night to have got the assurance—and he would have made the journey to Scotland to have got it—that the Chairman had made ; for he had been hugging the delusion that whilst he was not Scottish by ancestry, perhaps they would have a place for him because he was a Scot in his choice of their love. He was glad to have the Chairman's assurance that somewhere in his line there was a Scottish root, and in order not to disturb it he undertook not to search closer into his ancestry. (Laughter.) While he was not Scottish by ancestry, he rejoiced to say one thing out of a full heart, that he was Scottish by posterity—(laughter)—for all his grandchildren were Douglases and Campbells. Shortly after the Glenriddel Manuscripts were sent to Scotland a great Scottish newspaper had paid him a compliment that he prized very highly. In a leading article it said : " Mr Gribbel says that he has not a drop of Scottish blood in his veins. Be that as it may—let the truth be told, he is fit to be a Scotsman." (Applause.) The measure of gratitude expressed in that article he had never seen equalled. It had been his great privilege as a boy from seven to fourteen years of age to enjoy the company and the companionship of a dear old man who came to live in Philadelphia as his father's near friend. Night after night his youthful imagination had been fired as the old man recounted the *Tales of the Borders* and stirring stories in Scottish history. He quoted from Ferguson and Ramsay, and he taught him Burns. When he (Mr Gribbel) went to school he knew Burns ; aye, he knew more, for that dear old Scotsman had taught him the Ayrshire dialect. (Applause.) He could see and hear him now as he sat crooning—

" O' a' the airts the wind can blaw."

And he generally stood up when he recited—

" Is there, for honest poverty,
That hings his head, and a' that ?
The coward-slave, we pass him by,—
We daur be puir for a' that !"

When he recited " Scots wha hae " he (Mr Gribbel) always got up too. (Applause.) Should he live to be as old as Methuselah he would never forget those early days, and it was one of the joys of his life that now, on his native heath, he could pay this tribute to the character and worth and scholarship of the dear old Scotsman who gave him his bent towards Scottish history and literature— James Macphail of Falkirk. (Applause.) All the world was deeply indebted to Scotland, and his own country was specially indebted to it for one thing—John Knox and the gift of the public schools. In the United States they had the most tremendous experiment in humanity that the sun had ever shone upon, and the thing that was going to solve their problem—thank God—was the public school ; for while the foreigner remained prejudiced to the flag he was raised under, the children went to the public school and came out Americans. A second great gift for which his country was indebted to Scotland was Robert Burns. (Applause.) He was not going to weigh the relative merits of Robert Burns and John Knox, but if he had to choose he would take Burns and trust the future for John Knox. The great debt that English literature owed to Scotland was that it produced the man who turned the whole English speaking and reading world back from the artificialities of Pope and Dryden to nature. Burns wrote :—

" Wee, modest, crimson-tipped flow'r,
Thou's met me in an evil hour ;
For I maun crush amang the stoure
Thy slender stem :
To spare thee now is past my pow'r,
Thou bonie gem."

Had Burns not written that, he (Mr Gribbel) would hazard the opinion that Tennyson, the finest product of the British School, would never have penned—

"Flower in the crannied wall,
I pluck you out of the crannies,
I hold you here, root and all, in my hand,
Little flower—but if I could understand
What you are, root and all, and all in all,
I should know what God and man is."

(Applause.) There was another great debt that his country owed to Scotland. He attended many dinners every winter in the States, and the guests never parted without joining hands and singing "Auld Lang Syne." Oh! the influence of Burns. We were yet too close upon him to get the true perspective of his real worth. Whatever value they might place upon the Glenriddel Manuscripts he felt that his own debt to Scotland was just begun to be discharged. In these days we heard a great deal of talk about the League of Nations. He was not a statesman—just a plain business man; but there was one thing he would say, and it was this, that this war-torn, hungry, aching world was needing more than a League or Nations—it was needing a closer understanding and sympathy between Great Britain and the United States. (Applause.) If they would grant that and see it brought about, both he as an American citizen and they as Britons would trust a League of Nations that grew out of that sympathy. What should he say to them for this outpouring of their generosity in the presentation of this album ? What should he say to those artists of Scotland who did this beautiful work of love to a stranger ? The English language was too limited for him, and even the Ayrshire dialect was not equal to the occasion. (Laughter.) He would enter into a contract with them. He would contract to take this album to the United States, to preserve it among his own most treasured possessions, and to hand it down to his children as one of the dearest things he had to leave them, with the intention that they in turn would hand it down to their children, and remember that their father or grandfather, as the case might be, was a bounden debtor to Scotland. (Loud applause.)

Mr Alex. Pollock proposed " The Artists."

The artists, he said, had given their work as a labour of love, and he imagined that they had done so because they were men of vision. "Where there is no vision the people perish." There was no fear of Scotland perishing as long as she had artists with the spirit and enthusiasm and patriotism that these thirty-six had shown in contributing to the Gribbel Album. (Applause.)

Mr A. Brownlie Docharty, whose name was coupled with the toast, said—

That it was with the greatest diffidence and respect that he rose to thank them for the manner in which the toast had been proposed and received. In the first place, because he was speaking on behalf of his fellow-artists, amongst whom there were those who could have put in language their combined thoughts, on so memorable an occasion as that, much better than he could. In the second place, because what was to be said and what had been done was connected with the name of our National Bard—that perfect artist—(applause)—he who had the clearest perception of the Eternal Verities, and the power to give them to this poor world of ours that all who tasted could understand. He was sure he was speaking on behalf of his fellows when he affirmed that it was with this feeling of reverence that those sketches had been given—(applause)—and also as a mark of brotherly fellowship to one who had so nobly shown himself not only a lover of Burns but a doer as well. " By their works ye shall know them," and that night Mr Gribbel had proved himself to them an artist to his finger-tips. It might seem fitting that in a few words he should testify to the fountain of inspiration the genius of Burns had given to the art they practised—that fountain the purest and best, a river of living waters, clear and certain, an unwavering interpretation of God and Nature's own truth. (Applause.) They found therein every essential of Art in its greatest purity. It therefore seemed to him a very happy thought that those concerned in devising some tangible mark of Mr Gribbel's poetic sense of artistic right should have given his brother-artists and himself an opportunity to do something in this sequence in the history of our Bard. At the proper call the artist was always ready, and an appeal like this was quite to the mind and liking of all who admired what was good and right. Again he thanked them all for their appreciation of what the artists had done. (Applause.)

Mr Thomas Killin, in proposing " The Chairman "—

Referred to Mr M'Naught as a thorough Scot and a true Burnsian. In season and out of season, by letters and articles in the press and through the Federation organ, *The Chronicle*, he had nobly defended Burns against the calumnies and aspersions that had been cast upon his character and career, and he had been amongst the foremost to give the Poet his true character as a man. (Applause.) As Editor of the *Burns Chronicle*, Mr M'Naught was known over the world wherever the English language was spoken as the prophet, priest, and king of the Burns cult, and for anyone to attempt to add to his name and fame as a Burnsian would be attempting to paint the lily or add to the fragrance of the rose.   (Applause.)

The Chairman, in replying, said—

That his Burns work had been from the beginning a labour of love.   He felt that there was a duty upon him to defend the character of Burns.   It was very much needed.   Things that were not facts at all had passed into belief, and it was a hard task; but he had done his best, and as long as he had health and strength he should con. tinue his labour of love.   (Applause.)

The proceedings then terminated with the singing of " Auld Lang Syne."

The proceedings were enlivened at intervals by Scottish songs, tastefully rendered by professional singers specially engaged for the occasion.

The Presentation Album.

Each of the 36 drawings has been mounted, and a leaf of vellum with the autograph signatures of the artists prefixed.   These, with a specially-prepared print of Archibald Skirving's noble drawing of the Poet ;   an " historical note " telling the 130 years' history of the Glenriddel Burns Manuscripts from their inception by Burns or Riddell until their gift to Scotland in 1913 ;   and the Burns Federation's Address of thanks, constitute the offering to Mr Gribbel.   The address, written throughout in black and red heightened by gold, is dated from " Kilmarnock, 17th September, 1914," and is signed by the Earl of Rosebery and the other Honorary Office-bearers of the Federation, by the eight members of the Album Committee, and by the Lord Provosts of Edinburgh and Glasgow at that date —Sir Robert K. Inches and Sir D. M. Stevenson.

Address and drawings have been bound in a levant morocco of dark green, with the " end-papers " of green watered silk ;   and the boards have been decorated in a severely-plain and dignified style, the " arms " of the Poet, as sketched by himself, being introduced. The volume is enclosed in a morocco-covered case, the whole forming a memorial at once sumptuous and impressive, worthy of the Scottish givers, and not unworthy of the American recipient. It should be added that the Address was executed by Mr John Brown, and the binding of the volume by Messrs William Muir & Co., both of Glasgow. The Album Committee of the Burns Federation were greatly indebted to Mr James D. Connell and Mr William Stewart for assistance in the preparation of their tribute to Mr Gribbel; in acknowledgment they, with the artists, were the guests of the Federation at the presentation.

CONTRIBUTORS.

The following artists made contributions to the album :—

Sir DAVID MURRAY, R.A., A.R.S.A., A.R.W.S., R.S.W., 1 Langham Chambers, Portland Place, London, W.

A. K. BROWN, R.S.A., R.S.W., 152 Renfrew Street, Glasgow.

R. B. NISBET, R.S.A., R.S.W., Bardon, Ferntower Road, Crieff.

J. WHITELAW HAMILTON. A.R.S.A., R.S.W., The Grange, Helensburgh

JAMES RIDDEL, R.S.W., Caerketton, Colinton, near Edinburgh.

A. S. BOYD, R.S.W., The Hut, 17 Boundary Road, St. John's Wood, London.

R. W. ALLAN, R.S.W., R.W.S., 62 Buckingham Gate, London, S.W.

ARCHIBALD KAY, R.S.W., Woodend, Callander.

T. C. F. BROTCHIE, F.S.A., Art Galleries, Kelvingrove

A. BROWNLIE DOCHARTY, 3 Jane Street, Glasgow.

WILLIAM WALKER, 35 Redcliffe Square, London, S.W.

JOHNSTONE BAIRD, 48 Thornton Avenue, Streatham Hill, London S.W.

JOHN HENDERSON, 207 West Campbell Street, Glasgow.

TAYLOR BROWN, The Studio, Stewarton.

J. MORRIS HENDERSON, 207 West Campbell Street, Glasgow.

FRED A. FARRELL, 185 Bath Street, Glasgow.

FRANCIS DODD, 51 Blackheath Park, London, S.E.

H. MACBETH RAEBURN, 55a Maida Vale, London, W.

W. A. GIBSON, 7 Great Western Terrace, Glasgow.

TOM MAXWELL, Chimiez, West Kilbride.

JOHN M'GHIE, 351 Renfrew Street, Glasgow.

TOM H. MACKAY, 101 St. Vincent Street, Glasgow.

COLIN G. MITCHELL, 104 West George Street, Glasgow.
J. HAMILTON MACKENZIE, R.S.W., 242 West George Street, Glasgow.
DAVID FULTON, R.S.W., 183 West George Street, Glasgow.
THOMAS HUNT, R.S.W., 88 Bath Street, Glasgow.
HENRY MORLEY, The Gables, St. Ninian's, Stirling.
JAMES PATERSON, R.S.A., R.S.W., R.W.S., 17 India Street, Edinburgh.
T. CORSAN MORTON, 45 Inverleith Row, Edinburgh.
ANDREW F. AFFLECK, 17 Salisbury Road, Edinburgh.
PATRICK DOWNIE, R.S.W., Netherbank, Largs.
WALTER M'ADAM, R.S.W., 259 Sauchiehall Street, Glasgow.
CHARLES R. DOWELL, 101 St. Vincent Street, Glasgow.

We give the following extract from an enthusiastic report of the Gribbel function read to the Sunderland Club by Mr A. W. Semple :—

It was a most appropriate speech, and the fact that Mr Gribbel delivered it without notes was an accomplishment any orator might have envied. Yet he claimed to be just a plain business man, but the company took him at their own valuation, and voted him one of the jolliest good fellows that had ever graced a Burns Federation function. After honouring the Artistes and Chairman, the latter said—as the Kilmarnock contingent had to leave for home shortly after nine o'clock, he would vacate the chair, and he suggested that Mr Cowie should preside and carry on for an hour or so longer. During the interval we were shewn the contents of the album, which is, I believe, unique in the annals of art. The meeting was resumed, and the singing of the three Scottish artistes—Miss Marquis, soprano; Miss Norman, alto; and Mr Macgregor, baritone, was a musical treat of the highest order. Near the close of the function Mr Pollock referred to the fact that a deputation from the Sunderland Club was present, and suggested that Mr Turner should be called on for a few words. The Chairman accepted the suggestion, and Mr Turner delivered an impromptu speech that fairly brought down the house, and confirmed the Sunderland Burns Club's reputation as one of the most loyal Clubs that appeared on the roll of the Federation, and it also added to Mr Turner's well-known reputation as an after-dinner speaker. I am sure the memories of that memorable night will long remain fragrant in the minds of all present as one of the most pleasant chapters in the history of the Burns Federation.

TO MR JOHN GRIBBEL.

Gribbel ! Ye honoured of the Scots.
　　Who, o'er the broad Atlantic sea,
Saved from Liverpudlian plots
　　And set a valued treasure free.
With liberality of thought,
　　Unostentatious to the core,
Full of munificence you sought
　　This gem for Scotland to restore.

Your just interpretation which
　　Should govern the unwritten law—
That worth belongs both to the rich
　　And those who " farther canna fa' " ;
But every noble soul who earns
　　A country's patriotic pride—
His work will charm the world, like Burns,
　　And through eternity abide.

'Twas thoughts like these that weighed with you
　　And no doubt centred in your mind ·
With breadth of vision known to few
　　You taught a lesson to mankind.
If mortal men could bridge the bourne,
　　And touch immortals o'er the way,
Then, Robert Burns, we'd surely learn,
　　Would join in hon'ring you this day.

Kilmarnock.　　　　　　　　　　　　W. MUNRO.

THE BURNSIAN WELCOME.

(To be sung to the old American air, " John Brown's Body.")

We welcome Johnnie Gribbel frae the land across the sea
For it's to noble chiels like him all honour we maun gie ;
He comes from where " Old Glory " waves, the country o' the free,
　　The land o' the Stars and Stripes.

CHORUS—

Welcome, welcome to the land o' heath and glen,
Welcome, welcome to the land o' loch and ben,
Welcome, welcome to the land o' honest men,
　　Welcome to the land o' Burns !

Ye meet us here in Glesca' toon beside the famous Clyde,
And eke the wale o' westland men, M'Naught, shall be your guide,
To wander by the theekit cot where bonnie Doon doth glide
  And our great Scots Poet was born !

CHORUS.

There's no' a chiel among us a' but's Scottish to the core ;
We dearly lo'e an unco' man, and whiles a wee bit splore ;
To leal hearts frae the ither side we never steek the door,
  And their welcome's seldom " dry."

CHORUS.

The time will come when man to man a' brithers kind shall be,
That vision great of Robert Burns shall stretch from sea to sea ;
Let's do our best to give it shape and then we shall be free
  That's the star o' the 25th !

CHORUS

  Welcome, welcome to the land o' heath and glen,
  Welcome, welcome to the land o' loch and ben,
  Welcome, welcome to the land o' honest men,
   Welcome to the land o' Burns.

Glasgow.   T. C. F. BROTCHIE.

MR GRIBBEL IN AYRSHIRE.

IN AYR DISTRICT.

ON Thursday, 5th August, the Officials of the Burns
Federation met Mr Gribbel at Ayr Station, and
proceeded to Turner's Bridge, from which a fine view of
the Auld Brig was obtained.   They then proceeded to
the Auld Brig, where Mr Hyslop, acting as guide, showed
the many points of interest.   Mr Gribbel was much
interested in the story of the successful efforts which had
been made some years ago to strengthen the bridge and
keep it as a monument for all time.   After visiting the
Auld Kirk the party proceeded to the Town Hall, where
Provost Morton, supported by the Magistrates and local
Burnsians, extended Mr Gribbel a hearty welcome.
Amongst those present were Mr George Willock, President
of the Ayr Burns Club ; ex-Provost Hunter, Ayr ; Bailie
Murray, Bailie Terry, ex-Bailie Milne, Treasurer M'Donald,
Dean of Guild Stewart, Councillor D. A. Wallace ; Mr
P. A. Thomson, Town Clerk ; Mr T. L. Robb, Town
Chamberlain ; Mr T. Hart, C.A., Glasgow, Burgh Auditor ·
Mr J. D. Sloan, Glasgow ; Mr James Hyslop, and Mr
Robert Stewart.

After lunch Burns's Cottage and Monument were
visited.   In the Cottage Museum the guest of the day
would fain have lingered long over the many fine manuscripts and other Burns treasures which are housed there.
After tea in the Doon Gardens, the party proceeded to
Kirkoswald, where the Rev. Mr Muir took the party through
Souter Johnnie's house, which is at present being over-
hauled, but is being kept as far as possible in its original
condition.   The visit to the old Church and Burial Ground
was much enhanced by the Rev. Mr Muir's extensive
knowledge of local history and legend, while the condition
of the churchyard, for which he is mainly responsible, was

much admired by Mr Gribbel, who expressed his appreciation in no unstinted way.

In Kilmarnock and District.

Mr Gribbel arrived in Kilmarnock on Friday morning with the ten o'clock train from Glasgow. He was met by the officials of the Burns Federation and by Provost James Smith, ex-Provost Mathew Smith, and Mr John Haggo, Town Chamberlain. The party visited the historic Laigh Kirk, the scene of Burns's poem, " The Ordination," and afterwards proceeded to the Burns Monument in the Kay Park. Mr Gribbel was highly pleased with the external appearance of the structure, and he regards the statue as one of the finest he has seen anywhere. He spent a considerable time in the interior, being very deeply interested in the unique collection of Burns manuscripts and the numerous editions of the Poet's works, and he warmly congratulated the community, through the Provost, on having such a rich store of Burnsian treasures. The party afterwards visited the Dick Institute, which he described as one of the finest buildings he had seen in any provincial town, and he was much interested to learn that it had been utilised as an Auxiliary Red Cross Hospital during the war. After having a passing glimpse at the old building in Waterloo Street where the famous first edition was printed, the party adjourned to the Club, where an excellent luncheon was admirably served. Mr M'Naught occupied the chair, and ex-Provost Smith officiated as croupier. The others present, besides Mr Gribbel, were Provost James Smith, ex-Bailie Finlay, Mr Amos, Mr Innes, Mr D. Yuille, Mr George Clark, Mr John Haggo, and Mr J. P. Dickson.

After luncheon Mr Gribbel and the officials of the Burns Federation proceeded to Tarbolton in two cars, travelling *via* the Ayr Road. The weather was bright and bracing, and the run was thoroughly enjoyed. Ex-Provost Smith and Mr M'Naught pointed out to Mr Gribbel the principal features by the way, and he was particularly interested in the Wallace Monument at Barnweil. On reaching Tarbolton the visitors were received by the Rev. James Higgins, B.D., who entertained them in the Manse and afterwards showed them round his extensive and well-kept garden. He then took them to Mrs Murchie's and the Masonic Hall, where they saw Burns manuscripts and also Masonic jewels which had been worn by the Poet, and in these Mr Gribbel displayed the keenest interest. He sat for a few minutes in the chair in which Burns " presided o'er the sons of light," and held in his hand the mallet which the Poet had used while acting as Master of the Lodge. A visit was afterwards paid to the last of the handloom weavers in Tarbolton. Mr Gribbel had never seen a handloom before, and with the keenest interest he watched the weaver plying his shuttle in the making of a web of silk. Mr Higgins gave an order to weave a silk muffler for Mr Gribbel, who returned thanks and said that he would prize this as one of his most cherished possessions. The tourists then proceeded to Mauchline, stopping for a short time at Failford to look at the site which has been proposed for the erection of a memorial to Highland Mary. The journey was continued to the Burns Memorial Tower and Cottage Home, where the visitors were met by Sir Archibald M'Innes Shaw, Mr J. Leiper Gemmill, and Mr Thomas Killin, representing the Glasgow-Mauchline Society.

Sir Archibald M'Innes Shaw, in name of the Society, welcomed Mr Gribbel, and assured him that they counted it a great honour that he had come to see Mauchline and the good work which was being carried on there by the Society.

The visitors ascended the long narrow flight of stairs and from the top of the Tower had a splendid view of the countryside. Mr Gribbel was perfectly enchanted with the delightful prospect. The fine collection of Burns relics was inspected with much interest. Under the guidance of Mr Leiper Gemmill, Mr Gribbel visited several of the

Cottage Homes and chatted freely with the occupants. " A blessed work " was the phrase in which he described the efforts of the Glasgow-Mauchline Society to perpetuate the name and fame of Burns and at the same time to provide comfortable homes to worthy old people in the evening of their days. Returning to Mauchline Mr Gribbel was shown through the Burns House and Dr M'Kenzie's House, which have been in recent years restored by the Glasgow Burns Clubs Association and are also occupied by aged people. The party then proceeded to Ballochmyle, where they were entertained to tea by Sir Archibald and Lady M'Innes Shaw, where Mr Gribbel remained over the week-end.

During the week-end Mr Gribbel visited various places of interest in and around Mauchline. On Saturday they journeyed to Cumnock and inspected many treasures and relics in Dumfries House, afterwards partaking of tea in the Dumfries Arms Hotel.

LUNCHEON IN GLASGOW.

On Thursday Mr Gribbel was entertained at luncheon in the City Chambers, Glasgow, by Lord Provost Stewart, who is an Ayrshire man, being a native of Muirkirk. The company included Mrs Gribbel, Mrs Stewart, and Miss Stewart ; four ex-Lord Provosts—Sir Samuel Chisholm, Sir D. M. Stevenson, Sir Archibald M'Innes Shaw, and Sir Thomas Dunlop ; Sir John Samuel ; Mr Pitt, the City Librarian ; Mr J. Leiper Gemmill ; Mr D. M'Naught, ex-Provost Smith, and Mr Thomas Amos, M.A., Kilmarnock, representing the Burns Federation, &c. The Lord Provost, in graceful terms, proposed the health of Mr Gribbel, who happily replied, and the only other toast was that of " The Lord Provost," which was given by Sir Samuel Chisholm.

MR GRIBBEL AT DUMFRIES.

MR GRIBBEL visited Dumfries on Wednesday, 11th August, where he was accorded a civic welcome, and later entertained to luncheon by Dumfries Burns Club. Mr Gribbel has spent several weeks in Scotland, and in the course of his journeyings he has visited most of the scenes amid which the life of the Poet was spent, while he has been honoured by various Burns Clubs, and entertained by the Burns Federation and the Corporation of Edinburgh. A man of wide interests, Mr Gribbel has a strong and attractive personality, and is very desirous of seeing the ties between this country and America strengthened, and his keen friendship for Britain has been manifested in many influential ways.

On arrival he was greeted by Mr R. A. Grierson, President of Dumfries Burns Club; Mr John M'Burnie, Secretary; Provost Macaulay; and Dr Hunter, Dumfries, who were joined by Mr Duncan M'Naught, Kilmarnock, President of the Burns Federation; Sir Alexander Walker, and ex-Provost Smith, Kilmarnock.

The party proceeded to the Town Hall, where several precious Burns relics were shown by Mr G. W. Shirley, Librarian, along with a number of documents relating to early periods in the history of the burgh. The Provost afterwards formally welcomed Mr Gribbel, and there were present at this ceremony, in addition to those mentioned, Bailie Connolly, Bailie Kelly, Dean Lockerbie, Judge Smart, Judge Farrow, Mr M. H. M'Kerrow, and Mr John Gibson.

Mr Gribbel was afterwards entertained to luncheon in the Royal Restaurant by Dumfries Burns Club, who also extended an invitation to the Provost and Magistrates to be present.

Mr R. A. Grierson, President of Dumfries Burns Club,

piesided at the principal table, and he was accompanied
on his right by Mr Gribbel, Sir James Crichton-Browne,
Mr Duncan M'Naught, Kilmarnock, President of the Burns

MR GRIBBEL'S VISIT TO THE MAUSOLEUM.

The names (reading from left to right) are as follows :—*Back Row*—Mr Duncan M'Naught
(Kilmarnock), Mr M. H. M'Kerrow, Mr John M'Burnie, Dr Hunter, Ex-Provost Smith
(Kilmarnock), and Mr G. W. Shirley.   *Front Row*—Mr R. A. Grierson, Mr Gribbel,
Provost Macaulay, Sir Alexander Walker (Kilmarnock).

(Reproduced by kind permission of the " Dumfries Courier and Herald.")

Federation ;   and ex-Provost Smith, President of Kilmarnock Burns Club ;   and on his left by Sir Alexander
Walker, Kilmarnock ;   Provost Macaulay, Dumfries ;

and Mr John M'Burnie, Secretary, Dumfries Burns Club. The others present were :—Mr John Maxwell, President, Dumfries Burns Howff Club, and Mr Thomas Laidlaw, Secretary ; Mr Hugh S. Gladstone of Capenoch ; Mr C. Oliverson, Weston Norwich ; Provost Arnott, Maxwelltown ; Dr Hunter, Dumfries ; Mr James Carmont, Castledykes ; Mr John Symons, Writer ; Mr R. D. Maxwell, Editor of the *Courier and Herald ;* Mr Jas. Reid, Editor of the *Standard ;* Mr John Gibson, Mr J. E. Blacklock, Mr G. B. Carruthers, Mr David Fergusson, Mr M. H. M'Kerrow, Mr G. W. Shirley, Treasurer Grieve, Dean Lockerbie, Bailie Kelly, Bailie Connolly, Bailie M'Lachlan, Judge O'Brien, Judge Smart, and Judge Farrow. The croupiers were Mr J. H. Balfour-Browne, K.C., of Goldielea ; and Mr James Geddes, solicitor, Dumfries.

After luncheon a tour of the various places in and around Dumfries associated with the Poet was made. A short stay was made at Dunscore Old Churchyard, where close to the public road but almost unobservable from the highway were buried the remains of Robert Riddell of Glenriddell, to whom the Glenriddel Manuscripts were originally gifted. The grave, which is somewhat overgrown and carries one's thoughts back to the " resurrecting " days of Burke and Hare, was closely examined by Mr Gribbel and the company. In the course of conversation Mr Gribbel remarked that a descendant of Robert Riddell's was at present Chief Justice in the Appeal Court for the Province of Ontario, and that he corresponded with him regularly. In passing, notice was also taken of the grave of Sir Robert Grierson of Lagg, notorious in the days of the Covenanters. Proceeding less than half a mile further, the company visited Ellisland. Here the visitors were met by Mr John Grierson, the farmer, who conducted them down the famous " Shanter walk " close by " the winding Nith," and pointed out all places of literary and historic association with the Poet, both outside and inside the farmhouse. Friars' Carse was next visited, and there the company were met and welcomed by Mr and Mrs Dick-

son.   They were conducted by Mr Dickson over the rooms
in the mansion-house associated with the Poet, and in the
billiard room were shown the manuscripts in the Poet's
handwriting of " The Whistle," " Thou whom chance
may hither lead," and " The wounded Hare," and also a
letter, dated 10th January, 1792, all of which are carefully
preserved and greatly valued.   A tour was also made
of the beautiful grounds of Friars' Carse, and a visit made
to the Hermitage, where Burns frequently sat, and where
he penned many of his sweetest songs.   Returning to Dumfries about six o'clock, the company visited the Mausoleum
and the old Church of St. Michael's.   Burns's House was
next visited, and Mr Gribbel was greatly interested in the
various relics.   Visiting Burns's room in the Globe Hotel,
Mr Gribbel had a seat on the chair of the Poet there.   The
exterior of the house in Bank Street which Burns occupied
when he came to Dumfries from Ellisland was also viewed.

   After tea in the Station Hotel, Mr Gribbel, accompanied
by Sir Alexander Walker, ex-Provost Smith, and Mr
M'Naught, returned to Glasgow highly delighted with the
day's proceedings.

"ELEGY ON STELLA"·

A BURNS MYSTERY SOLVED.

Abridged by the author from two articles in *The Bookman* (April, 1919—August, 1920), by kind permission of the Editor, to whom we are also indebted for the use of the illustrations.

IN nearly every modern edition of Burns's Poems there appears a piece entitled " Elegy on Stella." It was first introduced into the Burns fold in Macmillan's two-volume Golden Treasury edition of 1865, the editor of which, Alexander Smith the poet, ·found the poem in Burns's handwriting, in a Commonplace Book of the Bard's, which had been acquired by the publishers. This relic, known as the Edinburgh Commonplace Book, to distinguish it from an earlier one which was privately printed in 1872, was published *in extenso* in *Macmillan's Magazine*, vols. 39-40 (1879). The manuscript is now in the Alloway Cottage Collection, having been purchased for £365 in 1897.

In transcribing the Elegy, Burns did not claim authorship, but introduced it thus :—

" The following poem is the work of some hapless, unknown son of the Muses who deserved a better fate. There is a great deal of the ' voice of Cona ' in his solitary, mournful notes, and had the sentiments been clothed in Shenstone's language they would have been no discredit even to that elegant poet."

Professor William Jack, who edited the Common-place Book for *Macmillan's Magazine*, in the course of a lengthy annotation of the Elegy says :—

" Alexander Smith is of the opinion that the poem is not by Burns. *Pace tanti vivi*, I think it is ... Burns was perpetually writing Elegy. Nothing is more certain than that all through all his early life he felt himself to be some hapless, unknown son of the Muses, and that the ' voice of Cona,' the music of Ossian, full of the melancholy wail of the western waves, was often in his ears. As for the disclaimer of the authorship, Burns had previously tried that innocent mystification, like thousands of bashful authors before and since his day .. The much-loved Stella of the Poet is no doubt his Highland Mary ; and Jean Armour, the mother of his children, still very dear to a heart for which one love was seldom sufficient, is the Vanessa of the dim background."

Professor Jack further opined that the friend who was in Burns's thoughts " when he wrote the Elegy " was probably Richard Brown (mentioned in the famous letter to Dr Moore), whose sea perils, and the tender tragedy of poor Highland Mary, were probably both reflected in these mournful verses, which, he ventured to think, " no man but Burns then living could have written."

In a letter from Burns to Mrs Dunlop dated 8th July, 1789, an epistle not to be found in any edition of the Poet's Works but included in the *Robert Burns and Mrs Dunlop Correspondence* (Hodder & Stoughton, 1898), he once more transcribed the Elegy, introducing it in this fashion :—

" I some time ago met with the following Elegy in MS., for I suppose it was never printed, and as I think it has many touches of the true tender, I shall make no apology for sending it you : perhaps you have not seen it.

[Here he transcribes the Elegy.]

I have marked the passages that strike me most. I like to do so in every book I read . . ."

The ordinary inedited editions of Burns include the Elegy, transcribed by the Poet without comment, leaving it to be assumed that it is as authentic as " Tam o' Shanter." Editors generally, beginning with its sponsor, have looked upon it as doubtful. Smith says : " Still, the Elegy, so far at least as the editor is aware, exists nowhere else." In Henley and Henderson's Centenary Edition it is classed among the " Improbables," and the editors say there is no earthly reason for attributing the thing to Burns. William Wallace, who edited the Burns-Dunlop Correspondence, speaks of the Poet's description of the origin of the " Elegy on Stella " as " mystifying."

The mystery seemed incapable of solution and, in

spite of editorial doubts, there was the lurking idea that, after all, Burns might have composed the poem, for in a letter to Mrs Dunlop dated 17th December, 1788, after transcribing *his* famous " Auld Lang Syne," he followed with these similarly mystifying words : " Light be the turf on the breast of the Heaven-inspired poet who composed this glorious fragment !"

Assuming, however, that Burns was not repeating the " unknown poet " subterfuge in regard to the Stella Elegy, and that his two explanations, in addition to being consistent, were also correct, the fact that he supposed " it was never printed " was not calculated to encourage research.   And yet, with a faith begotten of some kind of literary second-sight, I started, beginning with Volume I., 1739, searching through a set of *The Scots Magazine*, which I had added to my " tool-books," full of the idea of finding this mysterious Elegy on Stella.   And at last I found it.   Here, on page 156 of Volume XXXI., March, 1769, *printed when Burns was a boy of ten*, was the identical poem.

The poet who wrote it signed the Elegy " Gallovidianus," and fifteen pieces over that pseudonym appeared in *The Scots Magazine*.   They will be found as follows :—

1766—p. 655 ; 1767—pp. 95, 198, 265, 313, 435 ; 1768—pp. 97, 317, 431, 652 ; 1769—pp. 156, 260 ; 1770—pp. 36, 615 ; 1772 —p. 94.

The poems are mostly Elegies, and several of them have as their theme the love-tragedy of the Poet and his Stella.   Though it has been so termed, the poem ascribed to Burns is not, strictly speaking, an " Elegy on *Stella* " at all, for *she* is not " the ever dear inhabitant below " to whom the first fifteen verses are devoted, the Poet's greater grief o'erflowing all with the transition to Stella— " Like thee, cut off in early youth "—in the last five stanzas only.

However, in *The Scots Magazine* for January, 1770, there is an Elegy on Stella—the first of the series graced

156   POETICAL ESSAYS.   Vol. xxxi.

E L E G Y.

Strait is the spot, and green the sod,
  On which my sorrows flow;
And soundly rests the ever-dear
  Inhabitant below.

Pardon my transport, gentle shade!
  While o'er this turf I bow;
Thy earthly house is circumscrib'd,
  And solitary now.

Not one poor stone to tell thy name,
  Or make thy virtues known;
But what avails to me, to thee,
  The sculpture of a stone?

I'll sit me down upon this turf,
  And wipe away this tear;
The chill blast passes swiftly by,
  And flits around thy bier.

Dark is the dwelling of the dead,
  And sad their house of rest;
Low lies thy head, by Death's cold arm
  In awful fold embrac'd.

I saw the grim avenger stand
  Incessant at thy side;
Unseen by thee, his deadly breath
  Thy lingering frame destroy'd.

Pale grew the roses on thy cheek,
  And wither'd was thy bloom;
Till the slow poison brought thy youth,
  Untimely to the tomb.

Thus, wasted from the ranks of men,
  Youth, Health, and Beauty fall;
The ruthless ruin spreads around,
  And overwhelms us all.

Behold where, round thy narrow house,
  The graves unnumber'd lie!
The multitudes that sleep below
  Existed but to die.

Some, with the tott'ring steps of age,
  Trode down the darksome way;
And some, in youth's lamented prime,
  Like thee were torn away.

Yet these, however hard their fate,
  Their native earth receives;
Amidst their weeping friends they died,
  And fill their fathers graves.

From thy lov'd friends, where first thy breath
  Was taught by Heaven to flow,
Far, far remov'd, the ruthless stroke
  Surpris'd, and laid thee low.

At the last limits of our isle,
  Wash'd by the western wave,
Touch'd with thy fate, a thoughtful bard
  Sits lonely on thy grave.

Pensive he eyes, before him spread,
  The deep outstretch'd, and vast;
His mourning notes are borne away,
  Along the rapid blast:

And while, amidst the silent dead,
  Thy hapless fate he mourns,
His own long sorrows freshly bleed,
  And all his grief returns.

Like thee, cut off in early youth,
  And flower of beauty's pride,
His friend, his first and only joy,
  His much-lov'd Stella died.

Him too the stern impulse of fate
  Resistless bears along;
And the same rapid tide shall whelm
  The poet and the song.

The tear of pity which he shed,
  He asks not to receive;
Let but his poor remains be laid
  Obscurely in the grave.

His grief-worn heart, with truest joy
  Shall meet the welcome shock;
His airy harp shall lie unstrung,
  And silent on the rock.

Oh my dear maid! my Stella! when
  Shall this sick period close,
And lead thy solitary bard
  To his belov'd repose?

              GALLOVIDIANUS.

A S O N G.

As Strephon rov'd, a guileless youth,
  Where Nature paints the varied year,
Conscious at once to love and truth,
  He sigh'd—and dropt a silent tear.

The feather'd quire around him sung,
  To soothe the anguish of his breast;
Then, falt'ring accents from his tongue,
  The anguish which they sooth'd express'd.

Ye songsters, of the vocal grove,
  How wing'd with joy your moments fly!
No pangs you feel, and yet you love!
  Thrice happy! happier far than I.

I listen to your warbling throats,
  My heart responding to the strain;
And, as ye pour the melting notes,
  They lull, or seem to lull, my pain.

Those vales, and plains, and groves I rang'd,
  With heart compos'd, as well as you;
Till Strephon's fate Belinda chang'd,
  A throbbing breast he never knew.

Enamouring glances, from her eyes,
  She darted to my inmost soul;
All my unguarded peace her prize!
  Myself a slave, at her controul!

To this I patiently submit,
  Nor e'en in secret sighs repine;
Yet reason whispers, it is fit,
  Her heart should in return be mine.

But, should th' unheeded whisper die,
  And she elsewhere her heart bestow;
In pining sorrow though I die,
  Still may she live secure from wo.

From her, may Heav'n a fate like mine
  Avert; if she refuse to save,
Give bliss to her, ye pow'rs divine!
  To me—'tis all I ask—a grave.

                   THE

with a descriptive title, which is " The Death of Stella "
In the opening stanzas the unhappy poet, who in a previous
piece has described how he killed his beloved's brother
with his " shrinking sword," reproaches himself for being
alive, and mourns his Stella in the words :—

> " Oh ! she is gone for whom the valiant strove !
> For whom the Graces pour'd their choicest store !
> For whom the Muse her fairest garlands wove !
> My friend, my lovely Stella, is no more !''

That Burns did not write the so-called " Elegy on
Stella " is demonstrated beyond dispute, and that being
so it may have seemed of comparatively little consequence
to probe further, but Gallowegians and others wanted to
know who " Gallovidianus " was.   Unfortunately I was
not able to enlighten them, as I could find no clue to the
identity of the poet, in spite of much seeking in the pages
of *The Scots Magazine*.   Ultimately, after following many
a blind trail, Mr John A. Fairley, author of the *Bibliography
of Robert Fergusson*, &c., made me aware of the fact that
" Gallovidianus " had also contributed to the *Dumfries
Weekly Magazine*, and kindly suggested that Mr G. W.
Shirley, the Librarian of Dumfries and Maxwelltown
Ewart Public Library, might be able to furnish details.   I
accordingly wrote to Mr Shirley asking for particulars
of these contributions of " Gallovidianus," at the same
time emphasising the importance of sifting for any possible
clue to the identity of Stella's bard.

As the result of Mr Shirley's researches, he informs
me that the name " Galovidianus " (*sic*) first appears in
the *Dumfries Weekly Magazine* of April 30th, 1773, attached
to a letter to the Editor exposing a piece of plagiarism
of which the latter had been made the victim.   In the
issue of 19th May, 1773, appears an article on " Tale-
bearing," signed " Juvenis Galovidianus," whose habit
was given as the " Banks of Cairn "   The third appearance is on 14th August, 1773, when an Elegy was printed,
beginning " Far from the noisy world apart," and dated

at " P—t Patrick, 14th August," signed " Galovidianus '
(*sic*). Evidently these three efforts were *not* from the
pen of the real " Gallovidianus," for the following indignant
letter from that poet appeared in the issue of 12th October,
1773 :—

" Gentlemen,—You will inform such of your readers as may
think it of any consequence, that the Gentleman who appeared
in one of your late magazines under the signature of ' Gallovidianus '
(*sic*) is not the author who wrote lately under that signature in *The
Scots Magazine*. Intreat that Gentleman that he will have the
humanity to spare other people's signatures and that he will date
his melancholy endeavours from some other place than P—t Patrick.
Beg of him that he will adopt a signature of his own ; and assure
him that if he does this nobody will probably interfere with it.

M."

An editorial footnote ran :—

" We are assured that the *real* ' Gallovidianus ' will favour us
with some of his performances soon."

Sure enough, on 26th October, 1773, appears a poem
" On the Death of George Marshall, late Vintner in Dumfries," signed " Gallovidianus."

Mr Shirley writes :—

" Considering the sarcastic letter above, I came to the conclusion that the real ' Gallovidianus ' had felt himself insulted by
the Elegy, and lived in Portpatrick, and that his name began with
' M.' Chancing to be working with Scott's *Fasti Ecclesiæ Scoticanæ*,
I turned up Portpatrick and found a note on John Mackenzie, and
a book entitled *Ocean, Stella, and other Poems*, 1816. Shortly
afterwards I asked Mr A. E. Hornel, the artist, who bought the
collection my note was taken from, if he had the book, and if the
author was ' Gallovidianus.' He said, curiously enough, he had
handled it that same morning, and the author was the ' Gallovidianus '
of *The Scots Magazine*."

It will thus be seen that, though hinging on my
investigations, the credit of establishing the identity of
" Gallovidianus " belongs to Mr Shirley. His communi-
cation sent me to Scott's *Fasti*, where I found that
John Mackenzie, son of Niven Mackenzie, Clayholes,
Stranraer, had studied theology under Dr Traill, in the

University of Glasgow.   It is stated that while residing
at Logan he was licensed by the Presbytery 4th September,

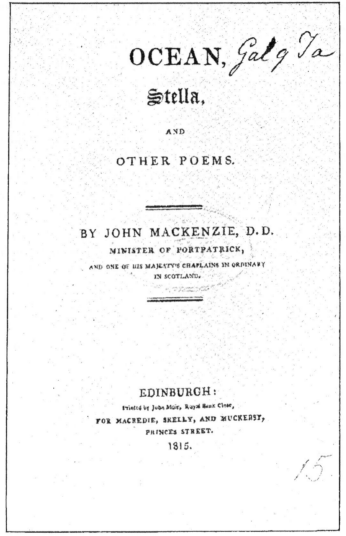

(Photo by Donald Macbeth, London.)

FACSIMILE TITLE PAGE OF JOHN MACKENZIE'S POEMS.
(From the copy in the British Museum.)

1771 (his blank year in *The Scots Magazine*), and ordained
Minister of Portpatrick on 18th March, 1773.   He died
the father of the Synod, on 21st December, 1836, in the

ninety-third year of his age, and the sixty-fourth of his ministry. He published a volume of Sermons in 1800, to which I turned in the hope of finding a portrait of " Gallovidianus," but unfortunately the book has no such embellishment.

Scott's *Fasti* is a year wrong with the date of *Ocean, Stella, and other Poems*, as will be seen by the title page which we reproduce in *facsimile*. This vital volume of 158 pages (British Museum copy, 994, e. 26), though it does not once mention *The Scots Magazine*, nor hint at the name of " Gallovidianus," affords ample evidence that *he* and its author, the *Rev. John Mackenzie*, are one and the same. In addition to the *Dumfries Weekly Magazine* poem (page 101), it contains no fewer than *eight* of the fifteen poems published by and signed " Gallovidianus " in *The Scots Magazine*.

The minister-poet of Portpatrick does not include in " Stella," as published in four parts in his volume of Poems, the—to us all-important—" Elegy on Stella " which won the appreciation of Burns. I was not surprised at the omission, for it must be obvious to all who read the poem analytically that the title favoured in most editions of Burns is a misnomer. Though not included in " Stella," *Mackenzie's* volume of verse does contain (page 93), under the title " Incognita," the very poem transcribed by, and ascribed to, Burns—the identical twenty stanzas published in *The Scots Magazine* of March, 1769, and composed by " Gallovidianus " (a young poet of twenty-five) in the little Wigtownshire coast village of Port-Logan :—

> " At the last limits of our isle,
>   Washed by the western wave,
>   Touched by thy fate a thoughtful bard
>   Sits lonely on thy grave.
>
>   Pensive he eyes, before him spread,
>   The deep, outstretched and vast ;
>   His mourning notes are borne away
>   Along the rapid blast."

The 1815 volume has a few trifling variations, but nothing worth noting till we come to the last verse, which is recast thus :—

> " Transporting thought, my maid, for then
> This sickening scene shall close ;
> And lead thy solitary bard
> To his belov'd repose."

There remains the question as to the personality of Stella, and the reality or otherwise of the Poet's love-tragedy—the killing of her brother, and the death of

KIRKMAIDEN PARISH CHURCHYARD

" At the last limits of our Isle,"
where " Gallovidianus " composed the Elegy ascribed to Burns.

Stella.   Fortunately all speculation on these matters is ended by Doctor Mackenzie's preface (page 7), in which he remarks :—

" In Stella, though he speaks in the first person, he hopes it is unnecessary to say that the author is not the hero.   It was composed at an early period, when the passions are in their strength. The only competent question is, whether he has given a true delineation of the passion he describes, and of the sentiments and feelings which arise out of the situation.   For this, and this only, he considers himself responsible."

So the Stella of " Gallovidianus," as explained by Mackenzie, was a poetic creation, and the poet's *pen* was mightier than his *sword*, even to the slaying of her " haughty brother." Yet we find in one of his " other poems " that tragedy came to the Poet's door in grim reality— he lost a son, Captain John Mackenzie, who in 1809 fell leading a forlorn hope in battle. Many who in these nearer days have drank the same bitter cup, will read with a deep understanding this tender verse of the forgotten poet of the Manse of Grey Galloway :—

> " Shade of my dear departed boy,
>   Say what the cause can be
> That I can sing of others' woes,
> Their hopes, their fears, their griefs disclose,
>   But cannot sing of thee ?
> My wild harp grovelling on the ground,
> From passing winds may catch a sound,
>   But low and sad the melody."

DAVIDSON COOK, F.S.A.

16 Pollitt Street. Barnsley.

BURNS AND CREECH.

FROM all that can be gathered from what is recorded of him, William Creech, Burns's Edinburgh publisher, appears to have been a man possessing many admirable qualities, none of which specially fitted him for the proper conducting of a publishing or any other business. He was dilatory and procrastinating, naturally averse to the routine work of business, which he left entirely in the hands of subordinates, and spent his time in holding levées in his private residence with probable customers of literary predilections, which were usually adjourned to his place of business each day as occasion dictated. All accounts agree that he had a keen eye for his own interests, and could drive a hard bargain when it came to be a question of money—so much so that he was reputed stingy and the reverse of punctual in the payment of his liabilities. That Burns was dissatisfied with the treatment accorded him is evident from the language he uses in several of his letters complaining of the difficulty he experienced in obtaining a final settlement with Creech, who kept him hanging about Edinburgh for months with fair promises which were repeatedly broken, and consequently again and again upset the arrangements he had made to leave the city lest it might be said he had out-stayed his welcome. Moreover, the fact that Burns had no other resource to fall back upon to defray the expense of maintaining himself in Edinburgh, showed a want of consideration on the part of Creech totally indefensible. The money received for the copyright must have been wellnigh exhausted by the end of 1787, and we can guess how the prospect of running into debt through no fault of his own would affect the independent spirit of Burns. That he did not submit to Creech's inconsiderate treatment without protest is made manifest by the letters referred to. He wrote him more than once in sharply pointed terms, he tells us, and received in reply communications which, he leads us to believe, were not uniformly in an apologetic vein. What were the exact terms in which each expressed himself we know not, for they have never been vouchsafed to the public. Dr Currie, who apparently perused the correspondence, remarks that he could find no proof in it of ill-usage of the Poet by Creech ; and it is said he submitted it to Margaret Chalmers, who advised him to destroy it, which was accordingly done. This, as we take it, refers only to the Burns side of the correspondence. The other, we have somewhere seen it stated, is still in the possession of Creech's descendants ; if so, the obvious way of proving the correctness of Dr Currie's verdict is to publish the letters received by Creech, for the purpose of making clear whether Burns's grounds of complaint were justifiable or not. Creech's delay in coming to terms had other and more deplorable results. If Burns had been enabled to adhere to the time-table of engagements he had drawn out in 1787, the " Clarinda " entanglement would never have had a beginning. He had returned from Ayrshire to settle finally with Creech, and intended to leave the city at the beginning of December. On the 4th of that month he was introduced, in Miss Nimmo's house, to Mrs M'Lehose ; the accident to his leg happened a day or two afterwards, and this led to the " Clarinda " correspondence which was carried on during the period of his confinement to his room. To comment at length on this passage in the Poet's life would be out of place here. Suffice it to say that he left Mauchline in 1786, with the certificate of bachelorhood in his pocket granted by Mr Auld, who was kept in ignorance of his irregular marriage with Jean Armour ; and this may have had the effect of unsettling his mind on the validity of said marriage, and leading him to believe that he was still a single man. His letter to Ainslie of 3rd March 1788, however, clearly proves that he was ever haunted with the gravest doubts of its reliability. When the real state of matters was revealed

to Mr Auld, and the private marriage publicly declared in
1788, the Sessional reproof was confined to the irregularity
of the marriage, from which it followed that all Jean's
children were born in lawful wedlock.   Burns's relations
with " Clarinda " have been so often referred to by his
censors to his disadvantage that this fact alone gives
to Creech's dilatory habits a sinister significance which
otherwise would have given them less importance in the
Burns narrative.

Through the courtesy of Mr W. H. Turner, a leading member of the Sunderland Burns Club, we were, many
years ago, put in possession of a correspondence on " Burns
and Creech," which had appeared in the columns of a local
newspaper, and which we have kept *in retentis* ever since
in the hope that further information on the subject might
be discovered during the intervening years ;   but as that
hope has been disappointed, we deem it incumbent on us
to lay the said correspondence before our readers.   Both
disputants state their cases so lucidly and moderately
that nothing need be added to aid the reader in coming
to the right conclusion.   We append a short sketch of
Creech's life as an appropriate preface to the discussion.

William Creech was born at Newbattle, near Edinburgh, on 21st April, 1745.   He was the son of the Rev.
Wm. Creech, parish minister of Newbattle, and Mary
Buler, his wife, an English lady, related to an aristocratic
family in Devonshire.   His father died at the early age
of forty, a few months after the birth of his son, leaving
a widow and two young daughters, both of whom died in
1749.   Mrs Creech retired to Dalkeith, and afterwards
removed to Perth, where the education of her son was
begun.   Returning to Dalkeith, he was put under the
tuition of Dr Robertson, minister of Kilmarnock, the
sons of the Earl of Glencairn being his fellow-pupils,
with whom he contracted a warm and lasting friendship.
After completing his education, he removed with his mother
to Edinburgh, where he was assumed a partner in the firm
of Kincaid and Fell, printers to the King, ultimately

succeeding to the business on the retiral of the seniors. At one time he attended the medical classes of the University of Edinburgh with a view to qualifying for that profession, but that idea was abandoned, and he went to London to gain more experience in the bookselling trade. In 1770, he made the " grand tour " through Holland, France, Switzerland, and Germany with Lord Kilmaurs. eldest son of the Earl of Glencairn, and returned home well fitted to engage in the line of business he had chosen for himself. He became publisher for most of the *literati* of the period, and founded a new era in the literature of Edinburgh by the publication of the periodicals *The Mirror* and *The Lounger*, both of which enjoyed great popularity. He became a magistrate of the city in 1788, and filled the office of Lord Provost from 1811 to 1813. He was highly respected in literary and public life, and still more distinguished in social circles, in which he was universally admired for his never-failing humour and engaging manners We extract the following from an obituary notice which appeared in the *Courant* of 19th January, 1815.

" He was an excellent and an elegant scholar ; and although, from the extent of his business as one of the most eminent booksellers of his day, and his many social engagements, he had little leisure to direct his mind to any deliberate literary work, yet the frequent light pieces and essays which came from his pen evinced the elegance of his taste, his knowledge of character, and his capability of a higher attainment in composition had he chosen to aim at it. Several of these essays were afterwards collected into a volume entitled *Edinburgh Fugitive Pieces.* He will be long remembered by the numerous circles to whom his many pleasing qualities so much endeared him, and who now so sincerely regret that he is lost to them for ever."

Mr Creech was never married. During his term of magistracy, a woman of the town, who called herself Margaret Burns, but whose real name was Mathews, a native of Durham, was charged with keeping a disorderly

house. She was found guilty, and sentenced to be
" banished forth of the city and liberties for ever." She
appealed to the Court of Session, where the case was decided
in her favour, which greatly annoyed Mr Creech. This
" unfortunate " is the " Madamoiselle Burns " referred to
in the Poet's " Cease, ye prudes, your envious railing."
Following on the reversal of the magistrates' finding, several
squibs were circulated at their expense. One of them—
a coarse piece of clownish horse-play—appeared in a London
journal, in which it was announced that " Bailie Creech,
of literary celebrity in Edinburgh, was about to lead the
beautiful and accomplished Miss Burns to the hymeneal
altar." Mr Creech immediately threatened an action for
damages, which produced the following apology from
the offending journal : " In a former number we noticed
the intended marriage between Bailie Creech of Edinburgh
and the beautiful Miss Burns of the same place. We
have now the authority of that gentleman to say that
the proposed marriage is not to take place, matters having
been otherwise arranged to the mutual satisfaction of both
parties and their respective friends." The wonder is
that Mr Creech accepted this evasive and ambiguous withdrawal as satisfactory solatium, the reason probably being
that it was everywhere received as a joke of the clumsiest
and most self-evident character.

In the present issue of the *Chronicle* will be found
two exceedingly frank references to Creech (see " Maria
Riddel's Letters "), expressed in the " rattlepate " style
characteristic of her correspondence with Dr Currie when
the latter was engaged on the Liverpool edition. On
6th December, 1797, she writes :—

" Creech, however, should be avoided like plague or pestilence ;
he is a great rogue as well as an intolerable pedant."

Again, on 7th July, 1798 :—

" If the new plan for the publication of the Works *in toto* answers,
it will be excellent ; but if you can exorcise the *dæmon* of covetousness out of old Creech—the Age of Miracles is indeed not past ! "

We refer the reader to the context for explanation of the circumstances which induced her to express herself in terms so much the reverse of flattering.

EDITOR.

BURNS AND CREECH.

SIR,—In his article in your paper on Newbattle Churchyard, Mr Carrick refers to Creech, the publisher, whose father was minister in Newbattle, as " one of the best of Robert Burns's friends." Are not the facts of the case rather against this statement ? Creech certainly published Burns's poems, but was so remiss and dilatory in settling accounts that the Poet's wrath against him waxed very fierce. In a letter to Dugald Stewart, he projected a poem, which was to be called " Creechiad, or the Poet's Progress," in which, judging from the fragment that survives, the bookseller's character was to be severely handled. No one can read the lines beginning—

> " A little, upright, pert, tart, tripping wight,
> And still his precious self his dear delight,"

and ending—

> " His meddling vanity, a busy fiend,
> Still making work, his selfish craft must mend,"

without duly appreciating the scorn and aversion Burns felt for this best friend of his. Even granting that they were in some measure reconciled in after days, enough is left to make the cautious historian hesitate before committing himself to the sweeping assertion that Creech was one of Burns's best friends. The article otherwise was interesting and enjoyable to yours, &c.,

HISTORY.

SIR,—I am much obliged to your kind and courteous correspondent, " History," for his letter on the above subject. The criticism, which he offers in such a polite and pleasant manner, as to Creech having been Burns's best friend, or, at any rate, one of his best friends, was made some months ago in the *Glasgow Herald* in a review of the little volume entitled *William Creech*, which was published to assist in the raising of the Creech memorials in Newbattle Church and Churchyard. Like " History," the Glasgow reviewer questioned altogether Creech's claim to be considered what I ventured to call him—" Robert Burns's best friend." I still feel justified in describing him in these terms generally.

The sarcastic references of the " Creechiad," and Burns's cutting description of his benefactor quoted by " History," were the expression of a single difference and quarrel with Creech over the financial settlement of the second edition of Burns's songs and poems. It is the only instance on record of any quarrel between them, and in the end Burns declared that Creech's settlement had been quite fair and honourable. In a moment of passion and irritation he wrote of his friend and benefactor in an exceedingly acid way, but when calmer judgments prevailed with him he wrote to his bosom friend, Mrs Dunlop : " Through Mr Creech, who has at last settled amicably and fully as fairly as could have been expected with me, I clear about £440-50." This letter was written on 25th March, 1789, and a few days later, on 1st April, 1789, Mrs Dunlop wrote the Poet advising him to use Creech's influence to procure for him the Chair of Agriculture in Edinburgh—a suggestion which would never have been made unless Burns really was sure of Creech's support and friendly interest. Most friendships have an occasional something to mar them, and this is the only instance recorded of any hitch or bad feeling between the Poet and the publisher-provost, whom, in his letters, he invariably addressed with the greatest courtesy and friendliness. A careful perusal of the lives of Burns by Currie, Allan Cunningham, Robert Chambers, Hamilton Paul, &c., and of the Poet's own letters and works, adds to my conviction, while many additional sidelights on that friendship are cast by the Dunlop correspondence and other contemporary letters and publications.

1. In Dr Lawrie, minister of Loudon, and Dr Blacklock, the blind poet and divine, Burns had his earliest helpers, but it was not until Burns came to Edinburgh with an introduction to Creech that his fame was really made. Creech was then at the very summit of his social and literary position, and the intellect of Scotland gathered in his rooms beside St. Giles' Cathedral for the interchange of ideas. At Creech's " levées," which were the central meeting places of literary, dramatic and artistic people, there were always to be found such lights as these : Lord Kames, Dr Blair, Dr Beattie, Dr Gregory, Mackenzie, Ferguson, Reid, Dugald Stewart, Dr Adam, Howe, Ogilvie, Lords Woodhouselee, Monboddo, &c. Creech gave Burns his introduction to this, the most powerful and influential group in Scotland, and warmly took him by the hand himself.

2. Creech published several literary journals—the most influential literary papers of the day—devised and conducted after the model of Addison's *Spectator*. Creech sounded young Burns's praises in these over and over again, more especially in the *Lounger* (No. 97, Saturday), where an account is given of " Robert Burns, the Ayrshire Ploughman : with extracts from his poems."

3. Burns himself says that as the result of such social and literary encouragement he found himself "suddenly translated from the veriest shades of life into the presence, and, indeed, into the society of the best."

4. "James, Earl of Glencairn—the last to hold the title—by his generous patronage of an Ayrshire peasant, gilded his coronet with imperishable glory, and shed a parting ray of light on the dying honours of his house." These are my words in the preface to *William Creech*. Yes, but who brought Glencairn's powerful influence to bear on Burns—an influence which Burns over and over again gratefully acknowledges? It was William Creech, whose widowed mother had as boarders in her house in Dalkeith the two sons of the then Earl of Glencairn. The friendship struck up between the boy Creech and the two little noblemen-boarders was affectionate, intimate, and life-long. Taking advantage of this close relationship, Creech in after years enlisted the interest of his old schoolfellow, who became Earl of Glencairn, on behalf of the struggling Ayrshire Poet. Had young Glencairn and Creech not been brought up together by Mrs Creech in Dalkeith, and sat together in Dalkeith Academy as "Barclay's scholars," Burns would never have enjoyed Glencairn's powerful help and patronage.

Burns might well dedicate the enlarged edition of his poems—the Edinburgh edition—to the Earl and the Caledonian Hunt; it was a well-deserved compliment. But Burns would never have had that patronage had it not been for the early boyish connection between Creech and the youthful nobleman.

5. Creech published Burns's poems for him, though it was a very considerable risk. Burns declares that his publisher acted in perfect honour and fairness in a business capacity, and as a matter of fact Creech's edition put £500 into the Poet's pocket—a very practical form of friendship.

6. Apart from other complimentary and grateful references, the well-known address of Burns to "Willie Creech" is sufficient proof of the Poet's grateful appreciation of one who from a practical point of view still seems to me to have been altogether his best friend.

Though a delightful humorous vein runs through the whole piece, there is still enough to show the warm gratitude and affection which the Ayrshire Bard felt for the man who put him on his feet, and whom he over and over again addresses as "my honoured friend."

For these reasons I have ventured thus to characterise and speak of Creech, and I feel justified in continuing to do so, until some more "cautious historian" brings contrary facts to light. —I am, &c.

J. C. CARRICK.

Newbattle, 7th June, 1904.

Sir,—I am obliged to Mr Carrick for his lengthy and courteous reply to my note on the above subject ; but he must permit me to say that nothing it contains leads me to alter my opinion or to understand his. He seeks to minimise the historical quarrel between Burns and Creech as " the only instance on record of any quarrel between them." This is rather on the lines of the excuse offered by the man who was accused of inebriety, that " he had been drunk only once for the last twenty years," and which was found to cover the fact that he had never been sober all that time ! If there was only one quarrel between Burns and his publisher it was long enough and bitter enough to cut up into a score of average misunderstandings.

The facts of the case seem to be these. Creech was a cautious man of business, and very naturally looked on the products of Burns's muse from the intelligible standpoint of profit ánd loss. " As to the merit of the book and its interest," he frankly said. " there can be no doubt ; the question of sale is what I have to consider." It is also extremely natural, having undertaken to produce the work, he should speak warmly of it in some of the numerous and short-lived journals he issued. But the praise of a publisher for the wares he has to dispose of need not be interpreted as the sign of a warm and devoted friendship to the man who had originally produced them.

In the after transactions that ensued between author and publisher, one is bound to say that Creech does not appear to very high advantage. It seems impossible to acquit him of remissness and negligence in his dealings with the Poet, though one may not be quite prepared to go so far as some historians and accuse him of craft or worse. The impression that would be left on the minds of most unbiassed readers after a careful study of the subject is that Creech, with some sincere admiration for Burns, looked upon him in a strictly professional light, and was not averse to making out of him as much grist for the mill as he could. All which is quite natural and right enough, but contains not the least warrant for embalming him in history as " one of the best friends Burns ever had."

To show that the above is well within fact let me quote some references that Burns makes to Creech in his correspondence. To save space I omit the names of those who received the letters, but give the dates —

Sept. 28, 1787.—" I am determined not to leave Edinburgh till I wind up my affairs with Mr Creech, which I am afraid will be a tedious business."

Nov. 6, 1787.—" This day will decide my affairs with Creech. Things are, like myself, not what they ought to be ; but better than what they appear to be."

January, 1788.—" I have broke measures with Creech, and last week I wrote him a frosty keen letter.   He replied in terms of chastisement, and promised me, upon his honour, that I shall have the account on Monday ; but this is Tuesday, and yet I have not heard a word from him.   God have mercy upon me, a poor ... incautious, duped, unfortunate fool."

May 25. 1788.—" I am really uneasy about that money which Mr Creech owes me per note in your hand."

January 4, 1789.—" I cannot boast of Mr Creech's ingenuous fair dealing to me.   He kept me hanging about Edinburgh from 7th August, 1787, until the 13th April, 1788, before he would give me a statement of affairs ; nor had I got it even then but for an angry letter I wrote him, which irritated his pride.   I could—not a tale, but a detail, unfold ; but what am I that I should speak against the Lord's anointed Bailie of Edinburgh ?"

And then this, after two years :—

October, 1791.—" I have not been so lucky in my farming. Mr Miller's kindness has been just such another as Creech's was : but this for your private ear :—
    ' His meddling vanity, a busy fiend,
      Still making work, his selfish craft must mend.'

By the way, I have taken a d——d vengeance of Creech.   He wrote me a fine, fair letter telling me that he was to print a third edition ; and as he had a broker's care of my fame, he wished to add every-thing new I have written since, and I should be amply rewarded with—a copy or two to present to my friends ! He has sent me a copy of the last edition to correct, but I have as yet taken no notice of it, and I hear he has published without me.   You know, and all my friends know, that I do not value money ; but I owed the gentleman a debt which I am happy to have it in my power to repay."

Pretty good all this between the best of friends !

Mr Carrick makes much of the fact of Creech having procured for Burns the notice and patronage of the Lord Glencairn.   Again, with the utmost courtesy, is this a fact ?   My friend's words are : " Had young Glencairn and Creech not been brought up together by Mrs Creech in Dalkeith, Burns would never have enjoyed Glen-cairn's powerful help and patronage."   The real facts are these : Provost Ballantyne of Ayr introduced the Poet to Mr Dalrymple of Orangefield, who was a near relative by marriage to Glencairn, to whom he introduced Burns.   It was after this that Lord Glen-cairn showed practically his interest in Burns by bringing him into contact with Creech as a possible publisher.   Burns's own words are, in 1786 : " I have found (in Edinburgh) a worthy warm friend in Mr Dalrymple of Orangefield, who introduced me to Lord Glencairn, a man whose worth and brotherly kindness to me I shall remember when time will be no more." This is surely explicit enough as to the channel of acquaintanceship with Lord Glencairn.

One has no quarrel with Creech. All that a student of the past, who has no theory to support, desires, is to strip him of borrowed, or rather of bestowed plumes. To call Mr Creech " one of the best friends Burns ever had," in the face of the facts may be charity, but to my humble thinking it is far from being

HISTORY.

SIR,—There seems little use in continuing a correspondence in which one side consistently ignores evidence and statements which do not support it. " History " brings up all the references to the quarrel between Burns and Creech, and occupies half a column with the extracts. In my little book on *William Creech* I have given due justice and have quoted the sarcastic lines of Burns as to his publisher friend, but all " History's " quotations are reduced to worthlessness when Burns himself negatived all he had said and written in prose and verse against Creech by declaring that at last Creech gathered in the profits of his poems and had been quite " amicable and fair." The hard-up Poet grumbled through a couple of years as to not getting money, but at last he was quite satisfied.

As to Glencairn's patronage, I am quite aware that it was Glencairn who brought Burns to Creech. The formal introduction of Burns to Glencairn was, I am aware, through Dalrymple ; but this does not invalidate my statement that the early relationship between Creech and Glencairn as boys together made both take a warmer interest in the struggling Poet than they would otherwise have done. Indeed, " History's " reference to Burns's formal introduction to Glencairn is only another proof of Creech's power ; for that nobleman could think of no kinder or more practically helpful turn that he could do to the struggling ploughman than introduce him to his old schoolfellow and friend, Willie Creech. For old friendship's sake Creech interested himself in Burns and changed Glencairn's formal and casual patronage into warm interest and practical helpfulness.

" History " calmly passes over all the proofs which I offered of Creech's friendly interest in Burns, his admitting him into the inner literary circle, his advertisement of the ploughman's genius and power in his magazines, his publishing of his works, and the undoubted fact that Creech practically opened the doors of Edinburgh learning and Society to the Ayrshire peasant. Burns acknowledged all this with gratitude. Cromek's *Reliques of Burns*

has many such references.   Take the Poet's letter to his publisher
of 13th May, 1787 : " My honoured friend, the inclosed I have just
wrote nearly extempore in a solitary inn in Selkirk after a miserable
wet day's riding.   Yesterday I dined with Lady Hariet, sister
to my noble patron, *quem deus conservet* [Glencairn's sister-in-law,
Lady Harriet Dunn].   I could write till I would tire you as much
with dull prose as I daresay by this time you are with wretched
verse.   But I am jaded to death, so with a grateful farewell, I
have the honour to be, good sir, yours sincerely, Robert Burns."
What was the use or purpose of Burns writing " Willie's awa' " unless
he meant the sentiments of gratitude and respect ?

Eliminating the references in Burns's letters and poem to the
unfortunate quarrel between Poet and publisher as to gathering
in the profits, which Burns declared was finally accomplished honour-
ably and fairly, I can see nothing to point to anything but friendship
between the two.   And certainly it would have been strange if the
warm and generous heart of the Ayrshire Poet had not responded
to the help and patronage of one who had so much power and
influence in his hands.   In my preface to *William Creech* I ventured
to say, after enumerating the friendships of Lawrie, Blacklock, Glencairn, and Dugald Stewart, that " probably the most practical and
useful friend Burns ever had was Willie Creech, who in song and
letter is often referred to by him."   Consideration of your space
and other reasons deter me from adding other proofs than those I
have offered that Creech was one of Burns's best friends, if not
his very best.   Personally, I think, in view of his practical help
to the poor struggling Bard, he was the very best.   Others are
equally entitled to their opinion.   But in proof that I do not stand
alone in my estimate of Creech's helpfulness to and friendship for
Burns, it need only be said that when the idea of memorialising
him in the place where he was born was suggested, all the leading
Burns Clubs in the country subscribed to the movement ;   while
at the service of unveiling, the Masonic Lodge of which both Creech
and Burns were members came from Edinburgh in full force, headed
by their Grand Master, to do honour to Burns's friend and benefactor.
while the head of the Lodge, together with the Provost of Dalkeith
and the descendants of Creech, unveiled the brass in Newbattle Church,
to which most of them had been subscribers.   In a leaflet drawn
up independently for the use of the " Canongate Kilwinning Lodge "
by the Grand Master—specially prepared for his ceremony of unveiling—the ordinarily accepted view of Creech as Burns's friend
and benefactor is taken, and I am quite sure " History " will believe
that Creech would not have had these honours paid him by independent bodies and individuals, had he been the " potato-counting
screw " which your anonymous correspondent would have us to
believe he was.   A great patron of letters and a great Lord-Provost,

his character is well described on the forgotten but splendid monument in Greyfriars' Churchyard, Edinburgh, which the city raised in honour of him at the public expense—a monument which is, alas ! like the others in that historic God's acre, rapidly decaying. Creech was a great literary and social power in his day, and the valuable Raeburn portraits of him, still in the possession of his descendants, Sir Patrick Heron Watson, M.D., Charlotte Square, and Dr Boog-Watson, reveal a fine face. His own magazines and *Fugitive Pieces* show him to have been a man of quick discernment and wide views —not a mere " man with the muck-rake." My friend " History's " story suggests another : When Tom Hood was dining at his friend Jerdan's, a large party being assembled, one of the guests indulged in some wonderful accounts of his shooting, very much after the manner of the " golf lie." " the fisherman's fib " as to the salmon which escaped, the razor which only cost a shilling, and the millionaire who entered the town with only a sixpence in his pocket. Descanting on the number of birds he had killed, the distance at which he had brought them down, and the character of the feathered ones who escaped his deadly fire, he at last raised the irresistible Hood into humour, who thereupon dropped into poetry and said :—

" What he hit is history ;
What he missed is mystery."

When " History " can describe Creech in his relationship to Burns as he does—dwelling only on their temporary disagreement, and forgetting and ignoring all the rest—I think your readers will agree with me that while " what he hit is history " so far as the Burns-Creech quarrel is concerned, still " what he missed is mystery " so far as a proper appreciation of Creech is involved.—I am, &c.

J. C. CARRICK.

Newbattle, 22nd June, 1904.

SIR,—I am quite willing to accept the hint contained in Mr Carrick's last letter that it is no use continuing this correspondence. But if we have not succeeded in convincing each other, we have shown, I hope, that a controversy on a purely historical question can be carried on with perfect courtesy and good-nature.

In exercising my right of replying on the discussion, I put aside as not germane to the question at issue Mr Carrick's references to the function lately held in Newbattle Church in memory of Creech. Nor have I ever attacked what Mr Carrick has written in his book on Creech, from which he makes extracts, as I have not had the pleasure of reading that work. It was the statement in your columns that Creech was one of the best friends Burns ever had that I ventured to challenge, and my friend must permit me to say that the more I. study the history of the subject—and my study is not quite of yesterday—the more amazing the statement appears to me to be.

Mr Carrick implies that I have been unfair to Creech in confining myself to the statements on one side and ignoring the other. I trust not. Mr Creech does not belong to me any more than to Mr Carrick, and I should be ashamed to act unjustly to the memory of the dead. I have honestly tried to draw a fair and true conclusion from all the premises afforded by the facts of the case, neither extenuating nor setting down aught in malice. I do not ignore what Creech did for Burns. I admitted a certain evident admiration that Creech had for the Poet, and held that the remaining interest was easily and naturally accounted for by a publisher's concern for the wares he was selling. I hold yet that the facts in this direction are irresistible to the unbiassed student.

Mr Carrick intends to hit hard, and I most amicably admit his right to do so, when he says that my arguments are reduced to worthlessness, because after Burns grumbled at his publisher two years, he was satisfied at last. As an easy reply to this, I meekly throw myself on facts and dates. It was in February, 1789, that Burns wrote the words which Mr Carrick quotes as the end of the misunderstanding : " I was at Edinburgh lately and settled finally with Mr Creech, and I must own that, at last, he has been amicable and fair to me." It was more than two years after, in October, 1791, that he wrote in the following bitter terms (quoted in full in a former letter) : " Mr Miller's kindness has been just such another as Creech's was. But this for your private ear : 'His meddling vanity, a busy fiend, &c.' I have taken a . . . vengeance of Creech. . . . I owed the gentleman a debt which I am happy to have it in my power to repay." This surely shows that Burns was anything but satisfied, and that his estimate of Mr Creech's friendship was not a particularly high one.

With apologies for intruding so long on your patience and space, and with compliments to my friendly antagonist, I am, &c.

HISTORY.

SIR,—As a lover of all that pertains to Burns, I have read with much interest the several letters which have appeared in the columns of your paper anent Creech and Burns, and while there is a great deal to agree with in what the Rev. J. C. Carrick states in his letters, no unbiassed person can for a moment entertain the idea that Creech was Burns's best friend.

I see Mr Carrick in his last letter twits " History " for calmly passing over all the proofs which he (Mr Carrick) offered of Creech's friendly interest in Burns. I fail to see in any of " History's " letters wherein he does this. He is quite willing to admit, so far as I can see, that Creech did do one or two kindly acts to Burns, but he, like many more, refuses to recognise Creech as " Burns's best friend."

The eulogy of M'Kenzie on Burns did more than any other influence to admit Burns into the literary circles of the time. To say the least of it, was it a friendly act to keep Burns waiting for two years before settling with him ? Creech knew Burns was not a monied man, and it is generally believed that Creech wanted to tire Burns and so snatch a bargain by trying to get the original agreement reduced. Let Burns be what he may have been, not his greatest enemy can accuse him of ingratitude, and had he not had cause he would never have written the lines on Creech which so aptly describes him. I note Mr Carrick lays great stress on the fact that Burns declared that Creech and he had finally come to an honourable settlement. It certainly was honourable in Burns offering two years to accept what he was entitled to, but was it honourable for Creech to keep him waiting two years for it ? Would a " best friend " do this ? Burns did not think so, for, as " History " states, when Creech was about to issue a second edition of Burns's poems he wrote Burns asking for any supplementary poems. Did Burns send them ? No! he remembered the honourable settlement of a few years before !

There is always this passing by or keeping Burns waiting for two years before settling with him which must rob Creech of the honour of ever being considered Burns's " best friend."—I am, &c.

WILL.

TWO ARTISTS OF THE PEOPLE.

A T first thought it may seem far-fetched, if not fantastic, to claim that Robert Burns and Jean Francois Millet are as artists near akin.   But as we look more closely we may come to agree that while the career and the character of the French painter differed much from those of the Scots Poet, yet in the outward circumstances of their lives, in their artistic outlook upon nature and humanity, as well as in the essential message which each as an artist has left us, they have much in common.

Born under very similar conditions, as sons of small tenant farmers ;   subjected in childhood and youth to similar influences ;   growing to manhood through years of toil and self-denial ;   each seeking in the interest of his art his country's capital ;   retiring one to Ellisland and Dumfries, and the other to Barbizon ;   dying both in pecuniary distress and comparative obscurity ;   the fame of each, resting upon much the same popular sentiment and appreciation, has grown through all the passing years.

In temperament, too, the men were in many respects alike ;   though Millet seems to have had little taste for social or convivial pleasures, and either lacked or restrained the ardent, ill-regulated sexual instinct which has repelled many from Burns, and, as he himself deplored, " laid him low and stained his name."   Yet both men, in the home, exemplified the ideal so well expressed by Burns :—

> " To make a happy fireside clime
> For weans and wife,
> That's the true pathos and sublime
> Of Human life."

But to attempt to follow this comparison item by item and trait by trait would soon become uninteresting, if not fantastic.   Rather let us take the life and the artistic career of one of these men, and briefly trace his story and development, trusting that the likeness may, to some extent at least, suggest itself. And, because the incidents of the life and career of Burns are to most of us the more familiar, we will choose the story of Millet.

Few of the thousands of tourists who land each year of normal travel at Cherbourg apprehend how near they are to one of the most beautiful, remote, and interesting districts of France. The city is at the eastern end of a square peninsula that thrusts itself out into the English Channel, north-westerly from the mainland of France. The district is known as La Manche, the very significant French name for the English Channel; and its rolling downs, grey-stone churches, low thatched cottages, its meadows and its orchards, its cattle and sheep, remind one strikingly of Dorset and Devon; and the people are such as those who move in the novels of Eden Phillpotts.

Far out at the north-west corner of this district, ten miles west of Cherbourg, is the headland of La Hogue, looking out across the narrow sea, The Race of Alderney, towards the Channel Islands. The coast is indeed stern and rock-bound. Its granite walls, rising high above the Atlantic and worn by the elements into fantastic shapes, look down upon the spot where the *Kearsage* destroyed the *Alabama* in 1864.

This part of the peninsula comprises the village district of Greville, and out among the cliffs, nestling in a glen almost within stone-throw of the sea, is the tiny hamlet of Gruchy; consisting of eight or ten rough grey-stone houses, strung along one street that runs east and west and is joined by another roadway from the south.

In one of these grey houses farthest to the east was born, a century ago, Jean François Millet, the peasant painter of France. The place to-day is much, indeed one may almost say just, as it was one hundred years ago. The same remote, brooding quiet, save for the surf at the foot of the adjacent rocks. The same rolling pastures. The same copious spring near the fork of the road, where the village women still wash and beat their linen. The same ancient well with its roof of stone ; and the same hard, penurious, peasant life.

It is natural for one familiar with the lives of both men, as he stands beside this stone cottage, to compare this scene with the clay " biggin " on the banks of Doon, near the Irish Sea, in Ayrshire, and Millet's with the career of the peasant-poet of Scotland. Indeed, one biographer of Millet, telling of the associations of his youth, writes · " In their patriarchal simplicity and Puritan virtue these Norman peasants were like the Scottish Presbyterians—and in the natural order of things, out of this life of plain living and high thinking there sprang the great poem of peasant life which was this painter's message to the world."

This might have been written of Burns ; for the circumstances of his early years very closely resemble those of Millet. Both were subject to the same pregnant influence of devout parents and patriarchal home life. Both spent much the same sort of laborious youth amid rural scenes in the remote districts where they were born. Rigid economy, toil and responsibility beyond his years, brought each to an early maturity. In each was developed deep religious faith and strong independence of spirit ; and ultimately, each in his own language forcibly interpreted the dignity of labour, the worth of character, and the value of the individual man. To each was revealed the beauty and the artistic value of the common life of fireside and field, of men and women, of bird and beast and flower. One became a poet and the other a painter of humanity ; each giving expression to new ideals and to modern ideas in striking and original forms.

For twenty years and more Millet lived at Greville and shared the earnest, laborious, and religious life of his home and surroundings. He was fortunate, as it has been suggested Burns was fortunate, in his father, mother and the influences of his home. Education and knowledge were for their own sake greatly esteemed, so that, though books were not easy to come by, Millet, like Burns, acquired a somewhat remarkable mental cultivation, read much and thought deeply. His father, Jean Louis Millet, a tall, slight man, had neither the appearance nor the limitations of the average rustic of his time. He was a man of some refinement both in his appearance and tastes ; with dark eyes, rather long brown hair, and shapely hands. He, too, had a fine voice, was fond of music, and trained the village choir of Greville until it became noted in the neighbourhood and people came from all the vicinity to hear it sing in the low stone Church which his son was to immortalise in one of the last of his paintings, and before which the son's statue now stands. He also modelled in clay, carved wood, and loved and studied, and taught his eldest son to see and note the trees, birds, plants, and scenes of nature about him. His mother, though a hard-working woman in house and field, was one who possessed some education and was noted for her neat and cleanly appearance. Then, too, his grandmother, who made her eldest grandson her special property and took care of him while his parents worked in the field or tended their sheep and cattle, taught him much, as Burns's maternal relative taught him, of the wisdom, sayings, and songs of the countryside.

So Millet grew to manhood amidst scenes and under influences which imparted to him the important truth which he afterwards in a letter thus expressed : " It is essential to use the commonplace in order to express the sublime." And as we read these words, how many of the lines of Burns come to mind ; some as familiar as these :—

> " But mousie, thou art no' thy lane
> In proving foresight may be vain ;
> The best laid schemes o' mice an' men
> Gang aft agley,
> An' lea'e us nought but grief an' pain
> For promised joy ! "

And what more offensively " commonplace " than a louse ! But one seen upon a Sunday bonnet gave us that " sublime " sermon in little :—

> " O wad some Pow'r the giftie gie us
> To see oursels as others see us !
> It wad frae monie a blunder free us
> An' foolish notion
> What airs in dress an' gait wad lea'e us,
> And ev'n devotion ' "

As Millet approached manhood it was his father who appreciated his artistic temperament and capacity; encouraged him to draw, praised his sketches of the men and women and the scenes that attracted the boy's pencil; and finally took him to Cherbourg to see old Mouchel, an artist there. They took with them two of the sketches, and found it difficult to persuade Mouchel that the boy, unaided and untaught, had made them. So this artist kept Millet by him for six months, encouraged him to draw whatever he felt tempted to portray ; and to study the pictures in the small public gallery at Cherbourg.

Then the boy's father died, when, as the oldest son, he had to go home and, as did Burns, in a measure take charge of the family—the grandmother and the mother and the seven brothers and sisters—as well as of the little farm.

But his work at Cherbourg had attracted the attention of some men of influence, and the Mayor wrote him urging him to return to the city and pursue his artistic studies. This his grandmother determined should be accomplished, and so finally it was, and he went into the studio of the principal painter of the town, Langlois, who had studied in Paris and in Italy. He, like Mouchel, recognised Millet's talent at once, and after some months addressed a petition in behalf of young Millet to the town council of Cherbourg, which resulted, after some delays, in an arrangement between the city and the district, by which six hundred francs a year was promised to Millet for his support while he studied his art in Paris.

So, at the age of twenty-two, Millet began the second period of his life. For twelve years he lived, studied and suffered in Paris. At the end of two or three years he was

called home and lived some months there and in Cherbourg, trying, often in the most humble way, to make a
living with his brush. In Cherbourg he now married a
slight, little dressmaker, whose portrait he had painted for
a few francs. With her he returned to his life of privation
in Paris. Only the first instalment of six hundred francs
was paid him by the authorities of Cherbourg. The
second year the sum dwindled to three hundred, and then
ceased altogether ; so that the young artist was thrown
upon his own resources for a living for himself and his
young wife, whose frail constitution gave way until she
died. Millet found Paris and his life there and most of
the artistic development of the time and place thoroughly
distasteful. The Salon and the Beaux-Arts were dominated
by artificial and conventional ideals. Millet, moved,
indeed dominated, by an almost passionate sincerity and
the impulse to seek for essential truth, was filled with
distaste for the classical conventions and theatrical display
of the painters who for the time represented such artistic
taste as found official and public expression in Paris.

On another visit home he had married a young peasant
girl, Catherine Lemaire, and as children came to them fast,
he was compelled to struggle, at times desperately, for the
barest necessaries of life. The work which he was compelled to do, and in doing which he gradually obtained some
renown, was work of necessity rather than of his choice.
He painted much in the nude and did work both in paint
and pastel of a mythological and classical sort such as he
or his friends could sell at some price to the dealers.

Though Millet was essentially a countryfied young
man, shy in disposition, hesitating in speech and awkward
in manner, he had a personality that was in many respects
attractive, and a fine depth of character that had but to
be known to be admired ; so that in the atelier of Delaroche
and among the artists of Paris he made warm friends, and
kept them ; but, in the language of Robert Louis Stevenson, " without capitulation." Among these was the
Spanish painter Dias, who afterwards befriended him

much, and Rousseau, and Jacque, and finally during the latter years of his stay in Paris, Alfred Sensier, his future biographer, his ever faithful and useful friend. By profession a lawyer, Sensier had been appointed to some post in the Museum of the Louvre, which brought him into contact with many of the painters of his day. He was strongly attracted to Millet, visited him much in his studio, loved to watch him at his work, and in many ways made himself liked by and exceedingly useful to the artist, who seems to have possessed even less of worldly wisdom or the money-getting faculty than Burns. Sensier did much to promote Millet among his friends, and finally, when one of his more characteristic pictures was exhibited in the Revolutionary Exhibition in 1848, the picture was purchased, largely through the influence of Sensier, by M. Rollin, the Minister of the Interior. Through Rollin, the same year, Millet obtained a commission from the new Republic for a picture; the subject to be of his own choosing, and the price to be eighteen hundred francs, of which sum 700 francs were paid at once. After several false starts Millet finally began and finished the picture now known as "The Haymakers"; and in April, 1849, he received the other instalment of eleven hundred francs for the canvas.

During the years of his life there the distaste of Millet for Paris had steadily grown, and with it the longing to get once more into the country. This desire was shared by his friend Jacque; so when the eleven hundred francs was paid to him he hurried to Jacque, and though Millet was, as he seems always to have been, considerably in debt, he offered to lend his friend half of his windfall provided he would join him in leaving Paris. Jacque readily accepted this proposal, and with their families they hied them away, first to Fontainebleau and then, after a few days, through the forest to the village of Barbizon—a name which they and their like were destined to make a household word throughout the artistic world.

With Barbizon, the third, final and great period in

the life of Millet began ; and the happiest too in spite of
continued harassment by debt and poverty, and by what
perhaps is best described by the homely phrase " poor
management."

In a little while Millet had rented the curious cottage
in which the next twenty-five years of his life were passed,
in which he died, and which may still be seen in something
of the same condition in which he left it, in the quaint
French hamlet just beyond the great forest of Fontainebleau.   Two rooms eight feet high and twelve feet square
accommodated himself, his wife and growing family ; made
habitable, cheerful and homely by the wise and devoted
wife.   Then came, upon a somewhat lower level, a stable
room with a door and a single window, used by Millet
for the next five or six years as his studio.   Along the
side of this humble dwelling was a rather narrow paved
court, enclosed by a wall, and in this court stood a well
as it is to-day ;   and back of the house was a small orchard,
and beyond was the meadow skirting the forest.   This
scene appeared in many of Millet's subsequent pictures,
and may be seen in " La Becque " ; than which he seldom
painted a better or more characteristic one.

Soon after his removal to Barbizon Millet wrote a
letter to Sensier, a part of which reveals the artist in a
way that the world has learned to recognise as near the
truth about him.   He tells of three pictures he is about
to send his friend for sale, of which he gives the titles as ;
" A Woman Crushing Flax," " A Peasant and his Wife
going to Work in the Fields," and " Gatherers of Wood
in the Forest," and he says :—"

" As you will see by the titles of the pictures there
are neither nude women nor mythological subjects among
them.   1 mean to devote myself to other subjects, not
that I hold that sort of thing to be forbidden, but that I
do not wish to feel myself compelled to paint them.

" But to tell the truth, peasant subjects suit my nature
best ;   for I must confess, at the risk of your taking me
to be a Socialist, that the human side is what touches me

most in art ; and that, could I only do what I like, or at least attempt to do it, I would paint nothing that was not the result of an impression directly received from nature, whether in landscape or in figures. The joyous side never shows itself to me. I know not if it exists, but I have not seen it. The greatest thing I know is the calm, the silence which are so delicious both in the forest and in the cultivated fields. Whether the soil is good for culture or not, you will confess that it always gives you a very dreamy sensation and that the dream is a sad one, although very delicious. You are sitting under a tree enjoying all the comfort and quiet which it is possible to find in this life, when suddenly you see a poor creature loaded with a heavy fagot coming up the narrow path opposite. The unexpected and striking way in which this figure appears before your eyes reminds you instantly of the sad fate of humanity—weariness.

" In cultivated land, or in places where the ground is barren, you see people digging or hoeing and from time to time one raises himself and ' stretches his back,' as they call it, wiping his forehead with the back of his hand, for ' Thou shalt eat bread in the sweat of thy brow.' "

The words are the words of Millet, but the voice certainly resembles the voice of Burns : bringing to mind " Man was made to Mourn " :—

> " When Age and Want, Oh ! ill-matched pair,
> Show man was made to mourn "—

and such poems as " Despondency," " Winter, a Dirge," and even such homely ones as " The Farmer's Address to his Old Mare," " The Cottar's Saturday Night," and others in the same vein. But, while it is true that there was in the artistic temperament of both Millet and Burns a tone, if not sad certainly serious, it is not true of either that " the joyous side never shows itself " to them. Many of Burns's poems and songs are exceeding humorous, some full of fun ; and where can be found a picture more delightfully joyous than Millet's " Springtime," gay with blossoms and sunshine, which hangs beside " The Gleaners " in the Louvre.

Nevertheless, it is obviously true that the appeal made by nature, human-nature, the human side of life closest to nature, was the strongest appeal that could be made to the artistic temperament of both men, the one to which each yielded most readily and with the most memorable artistic results.

And so at Barbizon Millet, the artist, came into his own, and proceeded to exemplify how " essential it is to use the commonplace to express the sublime "—as in The Sower, The Gleaners, The Water Carrier, The Flight of Birds, The Man with the Hoe, The Shepherdess, as she knits in the twilight, The Angelus, and in many other world-famous canvases. And it is significant that these great pictures were, many of them, a growth of years. The first sketch of " The Sower " was made long before he finally left Greville, and repeated with added and ever added power and significance in his portfolio, until it grew to fullness of stature, as the world knows it now. So with " The Gleaners ": first came a sketch of the woman under the green handkerchief (the " marmotte " of the Norman peasant) to the left of the group, leaning down, her worn hand and blunt fingers outstretched to reach the stalk of wheat, and her left arm crossed over her weary back. Then followed from time to time other sketches, first of the second woman in the red marmotte ; and finally the third figure, standing bent and weary but ready to stoop again. Even in the earlier sketches the wide stubble with the growing stacks appear, and gradually there came into the picture the other workers, the loaded waggon and the farmer on his horse over-seeing the work. The whole scene of the completed picture—perhaps Millet's best—can yet be seen at any harvest time at Barbizon ; for the wide plain still stretches away from the trees and walls of the village that close the background of the painting, the wheat is still stacked upon the same spot and the gleaners still follow the harvesters as of old.

With all such scenes of rural life, with the sowing and
the reaping, with the fields and their workers, with the
toil by which a man and the world may live, Millet and
Burns were intimately familiar :—

> " The thresher's weary flingin-tree
> The lee-lang day had tired me "

wrote Burns in " The Vision."

From their own experiences they knew the secrets of
the poor ; the pathos and the poetry of their eternal
struggle. Each apprehended the relationship between
the acts and scenes of the daily life of the lowly men and
women about him and the highest art. Each of them
lived in near companionship with these men and women
and recognised the value, dignity, and integrity of a life
lived worthily amid surroundings however humble. Each,
too, knew something of the life and people of another social
scale, had " dinnered wi' a Lord," and each profoundly,
almost militantly, realised how unessential was social
rank as compared to individual character ; that indeed

> " The rank is but the guinea's stamp,
> The man's the gowd for a' that."

However commonplace these truths may seem now,
we should realise that they were wellnigh revolutionary
an hundred years ago. " At the risk of your taking me
for a Socialist," Millet wrote to Sensier ; and when, the
next year, " The Sower " was exhibited—that strong, tragic,
heroic, typical figure, striding over the plowed and harrowed
soil, flinging abroad the seed of a new harvest on the earth,
the individual man, back of all human life—the profound
sensation it created was political as well as artistic. It
had indeed something of the same social significance as had
" The Cottar's Saturday Night," or " A Man's a Man
for a' that."

It was Gambetta, the most popular statesman of
republican France, an agnostic, who wrote of " The
Angelus " : " That masterpiece, in which two peasants,
bathed in the pale rays of the setting sun, bow their heads,

full of mystical emotion at the clear sound of the bell ringing for evening prayer, compels us to acknowledge the still powerful influence of the religious tradition on the rural population. You feel that the artist is not merely a painter, but that, living ardently amid the passions and the problems of the age, he has his share and plays his part in them. The citizen is one with the artist, and in this grand and noble picture he gives us a great lesson of social and political morality.''

For more than twenty years Millet lived in this quaint out-of-the-way village of Barbizon, which became a Mecca for the world's artistic people, one of the national shrines of France, and gave its name to the artistic renaissance of France. At his death the tardy nation rose to do him honour and to proclaim him one of, if not her greatest modern master. His paintings, pastels, etchings, and drawings are scattered among the great galleries, public and private, of the world ; their value enhanced literally more than a thousandfold since his death ; so that a proof of his early etchings, such as brought ten cents. when printed, now sells for forty and fifty pounds sterling. '' The Angelus,'' for which he received twenty-five hundred francs, sold for five hundred and fifty-three thousand not very long after his death, at one of the most remarkable public sales of pictures that ever took place ; was subsequently purchased by M. Chouchard for some eight hundred thousand francs, and now with his splendid collection rests in the Louvre.

And the Burns Cottage at Ayr is visited annually, in peaceful times, by tens of thousands from all the ends of the earth. And the grave in St. Michael's Churchyard at Dumfries, beside which Wordsworth stood and wrote, ever so long ago :—

> '' Through busiest street, in loneliest glen
> Are felt the flashes of his pen ;
> He rules 'mid winter snows, and when
> Bees fill their hives ;
> Deep in the general heart of men
> His power survives.''

The Kilmarnock edition, in its light blue wrappers, published by subscription at three shillings, selling recently for six thousand dollars! More editions of Burns since his death than of any other book, it is said, save the Bible! More statues of him, in more cities, than of any other man that ever lived! About three hundred " Burns Clubs," scattered through all the English-speaking world, yet federated, just to honour his name and memory! A magazine, ably edited, devoted solely to his cult!

Such wide-spread fame must have its roots deep in congenial soil. Time does not lightly nor mistakenly bestow such guerdon of praise, homage, and affection as she has given Robert Burns and Jean Francois Millet. Great artists both, each in his way unique; and prophets too, interpreters not only of new artistic but of new social ideals. Their pictures and verses are still active, living forces among men; and will continue to be until the day come whose coming they certainly have promoted—

> " That come it may, as come it will for a' that,
>   That man to man, the world o'er,
>   Shall brothers be for a' that !"

Neither of these seers for a moment believed that Nature, whatever her seeming, as Tennyson suggests, is indeed " careless of the single life." Each as artist did much to hearten men, for each in his own way dignified—yea, glorified—the common life of men and women. Each teaches us, with a passion and artistic power which few indeed have equalled, to see and feel and sympathise with the lowly, obscure and poor, the hewer of wood, the sower of seed, the gleaner of the harvest, the cottar by his hearth; to apprehend the worth and the significance of the individual life.

ALBERT DOUGLAS,
Of Washington, D.C.

SHENSTONE AND BURNS.

(No. II.)

A WELL-INFORMED writer in the beginning of last century said : " One of the most elegant literary recreations is that of tracing poetical imitations and similarities, for assuredly similarity is not always imitation."

There is always a great difference between accidental similarity and studied imitation. The attitude of Burns to Shenstone seems to comprise both, though, in cases where the thought is Shenstone's, the expression of the same thought by Burns lifts it into higher poetry, and poetical truths in Shenstone's Elegies have suffered by being couched in expressions that have been described as " mean."

Burns had great respect for Shenstone, the man as well as the author. Both poets lived in a period when the " Pastoral " was in a transitional stage from the Artificial to the Natural, and it is interesting to compare their respective poems " On Pastoral Poetry " and on " Certain Pastorals."

Burns, from his standpoint, says :—

> " Thy rural loves are nature's sel' ;
> Nae bombast spates o' nonsense swell ;
> Nae snap conceits, but that sweet spell
>   O' witchin' love,—
> That charm that can the strongest quell,
>   The sternest move "—

while Shenstone expresses himself as the " man of elegant society and the Warwickshire coterie," when he says :—

> " So rude and tuneless are thy lays,
>   The weary audience vow,
> 'Tis not the Arcadian swain that sings,
>   But 'tis his herds that low."

Yet the foundation of the binding tie of respect and affection is possibly to be found in " Burns in Drama," by James

Hutchison Stirling, wherein this passage, purporting to come from Burns, his brother Gilbert, and Davy Sillar, occurs :—

> *Burns :* "Advantage, man! Do you mind what Shenstone says again ?—' There are numbers in the world who do not want sense to make a figure, so much as an opinion of their own abilities to put them upon recording their observations, and allowing them the same importance which they do to those which appear in print.' "
>
> *Gilbert :* "The sentiment is judicious."
>
> *Burns :* "I should just think it is judicious. Shenstone, man—"
>
> *Gilbert :* "He's a classic, no doubt ; but I do not like his style. He has two ' which's.' "
>
> *Burns :* "I thought of the truth, not the style."*

The love of truth for its own sake was characteristic of both poets, and would form a sentiment of sympathy and reason common to the works of the Oxford cultured Englishman who could not find it " in his nature to be a half friend," and the Scotch peasant who " scorn'd to lie."

A perusal of Shenstone's works shews that Burns's study was by no means confined to the " Divine " Elegies, but had been extended to Shenstone's Life and Prose Works. One must not lose sight of the fact that Shenstone was brought into Burns's life at a very susceptible age, for Burns, though he was continually preaching to his brother to build " Resolve upon Reason," often deviated "a kennin'" from his own advice ; and it is conceivable that he could not regard the foibles of Shenstone in the same light as Campbell, who regretted that Shenstone not only " affected that Arcadianism which gives a certain air of masquerade in his pastoral character " adopted by our earlier poets, but also has " rather incongruously blended together the rural swain with the disciple of virtu."

In comparing the Shenstone and Burns similarities,

---

* Burns practically discarded his English models when his genius came to fruition at Mossgiel.—[ED.].

one is encouraged in the search by Burns's own admission, made in close conjunction with a reference to Shenstone viz., that he adopted models, when he said : " It is an excellent method in a poet—but what I believe every poet does—to place some favourite classic author, in his walks of study and composition, before him as a model."

Burns owed much to this reading and study of the Georgian Poets, and similarities that may be traced to Shenstone may also be found in other poets of the period.

In Henley's notorious Essay on Robert Burns, with its qualified praise and superior criticisms, we are told " He read Pope, Shenstone, Beattie, Goldsmith, Gray, and the rest with so much enthusiasm, that one learned editor has made an interesting little list of pilferings from the works of these distinguished beings." Far be it from us to accuse Burns of pilfering, however petty. Thievings are usually committed surreptitiously, and Burns was careful, and even went out of his way, to acknowledge indebtedness, with a conscientiousness and candour that he inherited from the " ungainly integrity " of his father.

Still, it is difficult to know the exact attitude to adopt when comparing similarities in Burns's and Shenstone's Works ; but in the following quotation from Saintsbury's Introduction to Peacock's *Maid Marian* will be found a passage which sets forth the position one might profitably adopt, as it not only condemns dogmatic assertion, but also disarms captious and pettifogging criticism :—" Nothing comes of nothing ; and though there is no more foolish and useless style of criticism than that which would fain make out that somebody copies somebody else, there is no more sage and more fruitful than that which endeavours to find out what somebody had in his mind, consciously or unconsciously, when he wrote something."

At the outset, before tracing similarities in the works of Shenstone and Burns, it would be educative to enumerate the direct references to Shenstone in Burns's " Works and Letters " (Blackie, 5 vols., 1887).

From Burns's Letters.

1783, January 15th—to John Murdoch (Volume IV., page 20) :—

" My favourite authors are of the sentimental kind, such as Shenstone, particularly his ' Elegies ' ; Thomson's *Man of Feeling*—a book I prize next to the Bible ; *Man of the World* (Sterne), especially his ' Sentimental Journey ' ; Macpherson's *Ossian*, &c. ; these are the glorious models after which I endeavour to form my conduct."

1787, August 2nd—to Dr Moore (Volume I., page 145) :—

" I returned home very considerably improved. My reading was enlarged with the very important addition of Thomson's and Shenstone's Works ; I had seen mankind in a new phasis."

1787, January—to Dr Moore (Volume IV., page 48) :—

" Still, I know very well the novelty of my character has by far the greatest share in the learning and polite notice I have lately had ; and in a language where Pope and Churchill have raised a laugh, and Shenstone and Gray drawn the tear ; where Thomson and Beattie have painted the landscape, and Lyttleton and Collins described the heart, I am not vain enough to hope for distinguished poetic fame."

1788, August 16th—to Mrs Dunlop (Volume IV., page 105) :—

" I am in a fine disposition, my honoured friend, to send you an elegiac epistle ; and want only genius to make it quite Shenstonian ·—

' Why droops my heart with fancied woes forlorn ?
Why sinks my soul beneath each wintry sky ? ' "

—Shenstone's Elegy XX.

1788, September 16th—to Miss Chalmers (Volume IV., page 110) :—

" Shenstone says : ' When one is confined idle within doors by bad weather, the best antidote against ennui is to read the letters of, or write to, one's friends ; in that case then, if the weather continues thus, I may scrawl you half a quire.' "

1787, November 21st—to Miss Chalmers (Volume IV., page 82) :—

" Like those who, Shenstone says, retire because they have made a good speech."

Reference to Shenstone 'from Burns's Poems and Commonplace Book.

1786—From Poems (" The Vision ") :—

" Thou canst not learn, nor I can show,
To paint with Thomson's landscape-glow,
Or wake the bosom-melting throe,
    With Shenstone's art ;
Or pour, with Gray, the moving flow,
    Warm on the heart."

1783—From his Commonplace Book :—

" There are numbers in the world who do not want sense to make a figure, so much as an opinion of their own abilities, to put them upon recording their observations, and allowing them the same importance which they do to those which appear in print."

1783—From his Commonplace Book :—

" Shenstone observes finely that love-verses writ without any real passion are the most nauseous of all conceits."

1784—From his Commonplace Book :—

" I do not see that the turn of mind and pursuits of such an one as the above verses describe—one who spends the hours and thoughts which the vocations of the day can spare with Ossian, Shakespeare, Thomson, Shenstone, Sterne, &c., or as the maggot takes him, a gun, a fiddle, or a song to make, or mend ; and at all times some heartdear bonny lass in view."

Shenstone, in the " Ruin'd Abby," says :—

" I ask not wealth ; but let me hoard with care,
With frugal cunning, with a niggard's art
A few fix'd principles "

and in his Essay on " Man and Manners," writing under " Politics," he writes :—

" Perhaps men of the most different sects and parties very frequently think the same; only vary in their phrase and language. At least, if one examines their first principles, which very often coincide, it were a point of prudence, as well as candor, to consider the rest as nothing more ";

and we find Burns, in a letter to Henry Erskine, of February, 1787, writing :—

" I have a few first principles on religion and politics which, I believe, I would not readily part with."

To examine what those principles were, and how far they were common or similar to Burns and Shenstone, will command attention, which might be even more profitable in estimating the influence of Shenstone on Burns than similarities in the expression and diction. The honest frankness and unenigmatical style of both poets simplify comparison of the ethical standpoints. They formed these principles that both jealously guarded, as guides to the duties to be performed in their excursion through " that Stranger Land and Alien Clime " that Shenstone calls Life, and which expression Burns uses in the opening lines of his " Epistle to Hugh Parker " (see also the Poet's Preface to the 1787 edition) :—

" In this strange land, this uncouth clime."

Possibly one of the most striking principles is the attitude of both poets to money. In common with other great men, money for itself presented no attraction, and both have declared that, while they were not averse to it for the power it conferred on them of exercising generosity in order to relieve distress, yet both expressed the limitations that the want of it imposed. Shenstone says in his famous Seventh Elegy :—

" Yet though averse to gold in heaps amass'd,
   I wish to bless, I languish to bestow ;
And though no friend to Fame's obstreperous blast,
   Still to her dulcet murmurs not a foe.

Too proud with servile tone to deign address ;
   Too mean to think that honours are my due ·
Yet, should some patron yield my stores to bless,
   I sure should deem my boundless thanks were few."

Burns, writing to Miss Chalmers, says :—

" I glory in being a poet, I want to be thought a wise man.
I would fondly be generous, and I wish to be rich."

In Shenstone's Elegy III. we find the same idea expressed by the phrase " to bestow," a phrase that Burns constantly makes use of.　Shenstone says :—

" He little knew the sly, penurious art ;
　　That odious art which Fortune's favourites know
Form'd to bestow, he felt the warmest heart,
　　But envious Fate forbade him to bestow ";

and we find Burns, in the " Brigs of Ayr " :—

" Still, if some Patron's generous care he trace,
Skill'd in the secret, to bestow with grace ;
When Ballantyne befriends his humble name,
And hands the rustic stranger up to fame,
With heartfelt throes his grateful bosom swells,
The godlike bliss, to give, alone excels."

In the " Epistle to Graham of Fintry " we find the same sentiment and the same phrase :—

" But come, ye who the godlike pleasure know—
Heaven's attribute distinguish'd—to bestow."

On the similarities of these views towards money the quotations can be multiplied, but to no further purpose than to confirm that Burns and Shenstone were not by nature fitted to amass wealth ; while both shewed, in their life's practice, an application of the principles, though bestowals were limited to the funds at their disposal

Closely related to their altruistic regard of the use of money is their ideas of duties sacred to the " Social Tie." The two following passages give similarities about Social Duties.　In Elegy IX., wherein Shenstone describes " his disinterestedness to a friend," we find :—

" Scorn'd be the wretch that quits his genial bowl,
　　His loves, his friendships, even his self resigns ;
Perverts the sacred instinct of his soul,
　　And to a ducat's dirty sphere confines.

But come, my Friend ! with taste, with science blest
　　Ere age impair me, and ere gold allure :
Restore thy dear idea to my breast,
　　The rich deposit shall the shrine secure.

Let others toil to gain the sordid ore,
　　The charms of independence let us sing :
Bless'd with thy friendship, can I wish for more ?
　　I'll spurn the boasted wealth of Lydia's king."

Surely one does not draw too much upon the imagination when one concludes that Burns had these lines unconsciously " in his eye " when he wrote to Lapraik :—

" Awa ye selfish, warly race,
Wha think that havins, sense an' grace,
Ev'n love an' friendship should give place
　　To catch the plack !
I dinna like to see your face
　　Nor hear your crack.

But ye whom social pleasure charms,
Whose hearts the tide of kindness warms,
Who hold your being on the terms,
　　' Each aid the others,'
Come to my bowl, come to my arms,
　　My friends, my brothers !'"

The sentiment and language common to both those passages seem to be closely allied, and together they illustrate the general influence of Shenstone on Burns on the common subject of " Social Duties."

It is but a little way from Social Duties to Patriotism, where again we find passages of suggestion in Shenstone. " The Patriot ardour which with life expired " may have suggested the " loud huzzahs "　The two passages are :—

Elegy XI.

" Ah ! let not Britons doubt their social aim,
　　Whose ardent bosoms catch this ancient fire ;
Cold interest melts before the vivid flame,
　　And patriot ardours but with life expire."

This may have suggested the sentiment of the lines from the " Author's Cry and Prayer " :—

" Nae cauld, faint-hearted doubtings tease him ;
　Death comes, wi' fearless eye he sees him ·
　Wi' bluidy han' a welcome gies him ;
　　An' when he fa's,
　His latest draught o' breathin' lea'es him,
　　In faint huzzas."

Shenstone in the above lines boasts the charm of independence, and Burns gave his reasons for being independent in his " Epistle to a Young Friend "—

" Not for to hide it in a hedge,
　Nor for a train-attendant ;
　But for the glorious privilege
　Of being independent."

The meanness that forbade independence also was, in the interests of poets themselves, inveighed against :—

" Ye sons of Wealth ! protect the Muses' train ;
　From winds protect them, and with food supply:
　Ah ! helpless they, to ward the threaten'd pain,
　The meagre famine, and the wintry sky !"

This general invocation of Shenstone is echoed in the more particular one of Burns " To W. Simpson." He complains of the treatment of the poet Ferguson by the Edinburgh Gentry :—

" O Ferguson ! thy glorious parts,
　Ill-suited law's dry, musty arts !
　My curse upon your whunstane hearts,
　　Ye Enbrugh Gentry !
　The tythe o' what ye waste at cartes
　　Wad stow'd his pantry ! "

These particular coincidences in ethical thought and conduct lead one to further search and ascertain what their common opinions were on the larger questions of life. To any thinker there must at times recur the problem of that inevitable dualism that besets Nature, and causes the soundest thinkers to consider that prudence lies *in media via*—or, in other words : "Prudence should be that guide to actions in life," and we find both poets extolling prudence in very similar terms.

A study of these two poets envisaging prudence gives us a further insight to their characters. Burns's opinion on prudence varies according to his moods. On the whole, he was willing to inculcate prudence, as no one who has read " A Bard's Epitaph," which he concludes with—

> " Know prudent, cautious self-control
> Is Wisdom's root "

can gainsay.

At other times he defies prudence, as in his letter to Graham of Fintry :—

> " Let prudence number o'er each sturdy son,
> Who life and wisdom at one race begun,
> Who feel by reason and who give by rule
> (Instinct's a brute, and sentiment a fool !)
> Who make poor *will do* wait upon *I should*—
> We own they're prudent, but who feels they're good ?
> Ye wise ones, hence ! ye hurt the social eye !
> God's image rudely etch'd on base alloy !"

But in the " Epistle to a Young Friend " we find he returns to wisdom's root, when he wishes :—

> " May Prudence, Fortitude, and Truth
> Erect your brow undaunting !"

Shenstone, we find, indulges in the same serious thoughts upon prudence ; but in his Eleventh Elegy he also deviates in his devotion, when he exclaims :—

> " Not all the force of manhood's active might,
> Not all the craft to subtle age assign'd,
> Not Science shall extort that dear delight,
> Which gay Delusion gave the tender mind."

The " wise reflections " return in his Tenth Elegy, where he says :—

> " While guardian Prudence checks my eager hand,
> And, ere the Turf is broken, cries, ' Forbear ' ! "

And, from the point of diction, prudence is often, in both Shenstone and Burns, associated with the expression " to forbear," the same as the " bestowal of riches " is connected with "to bestow." In Shenstone's prose "Essay on Reserve," page 45, we are told—

> "Some reserve is a debt to prudence";

and the quotation from Shenstone—

> "Prudent men lock up their motives; letting familiars have a key to their hearts, as to their garden"

is akin to Burns's maxim :—

> "Aye keep something to yersel' ye scarcely tell to ony."

These acknowledgments to prudence further lead one to examine the philosophy that brought the two poets to confirmatory conclusions in the mode of life. Burns, writing to Mrs Dunlop, says :—

> "A Mathematician without religion is a possible character, an irreligious poet, a monster!"

Before Burns could have come to such a conclusion he must have been influenced from outside, for original genius, however startling the results it may achieve, cannot from itself give utterance to such a remarkable statement. It is not very difficult to shew that Shenstone expressed thoughts that must have influenced Burns; and the claim to that influence being great is that they were first in the field in influencing Burns's mind when it was plastic, and has moulded in a way that first impressions naturally create, especially when they come from a source that is respected and looked up to by one who is conscious of the handicaps of education and social position. In a letter to Gilbert Burns, he says :—

> "We are not shapen out of the common, heavy, methodical clod, the elemental stuff of the plodding, selfish race, the sons of Arithmetic and Prudence; our feelings and hearts are not benumbed and poisoned by the cursed influence of riches, which, whatever blessing they may be in other respects, are no friends to the nobler qualities of the heart: in the name of random sensibility, then, let never the moon change on our silence any more."

In a letter to Richard Brown, he says :—

> " Men of grave, geometrical minds, the sons of ' which was
> to be demonstrated,' may cry up reason as much as they please ;
> but I have always found an honest passion, or native instinct,
> the truest auxiliary in the warfare of this world.   Reason
> almost always comes to me like an unlucky wife to a poor devil
> of a husband, just in sufficient time to add her reproaches to
> his other grievances."

Burns, like Charlotte Bronte, in the " Apostrophe
to Imagination," found reason's gifts little or no better
than " the gnawed bone dogs had forsaken " ; and yet, in
his calmer moments, he is continually telling his brother
to build resolve on reason.   The " pros and cons " of
this philosophy that puzzled Burns could possibly have
been founded on Shenstone's works ;   in fact, the " sense
of geometry and arithmetic " may have been suggested
by the following passage from Shenstone's Works :—

> " Mankind, in general, may be divided into persons of
> understanding and persons of genius ;   much of which will
> admit of many subordinate degrees.   By persons of under-
> standing, I mean persons of sound judgment, formed for mathe-
> matical deductions and clear argumentation.   By persons of
> genius, I would characterise those in whom true and genuine
> fancy predominates ;   and this whether assisted or not by
> cultivation."

It would not do to miss, in the comparison of the two
poets, their opinions of the Legal Profession.   Shenstone's
studied opinion affords food for reflection, which is echoed
in Burns, with the addition of the " righteous anger of the
peasant."

Shenstone had a law-suit which lasted for years, and
his opinion of the tribe in general is stated in these words :—

> " I have known some attornies of reputable families, and
> whose original dispensations seemed to have been open and
> humane.   Yet can I scarce recollect one, in whom the gentle-
> man, the christian, and even the man, was not swallowed up in
> the lawyer.   They are not only the greatest tyrants, but the
> greatest pedants of mankind."

And we find him further expressing his opinion in the following passage :—

> " A Justice and his clerk are now little more than a Blind Man and his Dog. The profound ignorance of the former, together with the *canine rapacity* of the latter, will rarely be found wanting to indicate the comparison. The principal part of the similitude will appear obvious to every one ; I mean that the Justice is as much dependent on his clerk for superior insight and implicit guidance, as the blind fellow on his cur that leads him in a string. Add to this, that the offer of a crust will seduce the conductors of either to drag their masters into a kennel."

Small wonder, then, that Burns, finding his ideas confirmed and coinciding with this, should feel justified in his outburst when he called them the " merciless legal pack— those rapacious hell-hounds that growl in the kennel of justice." Strong language from Burns, but not more damning than Shenstone's on the exponents of " legal thieving." If Shenstone could find no lawyer of his acquaintance whose character he could admire, Burns at least had for his dearest friend a gentleman in word and deed in Gavin Hamilton, the Mauchline lawyer.

Also, in these days of fanatical teetotal reformers, it is interesting to note that Shenstone advocated stimulants to enervate his brain. In his remarks on books and writers in the essay " Man and Manners," he says :—

> " It is often asserted, by pretenders to singular penetration, that the assistance fancy is supposed to draw from wine is merely imaginary and chimerical ; that all which the poets have urged on this head is absolute rant and enthusiasm, and has no foundation in truth or nature. I am inclined to think otherwise. Judgment, I readily allow, derives no benefit from the noblest cordial. But persons of a phlegmatic constitution have those excellencies often suppressed, of which their imagination is truly capable, by reason of lentor, which wine may naturally remove. It raises low spirits to a pitch necessary for the exertion of fancy. It confutes the *non est tanti*, so frequently the maxim with speculative persons. It quickens that ambition, or that social bias, which makes a person wish to shine, or to please. Ask what tradition says of Mr Addison's conversation. But

instances in point of conversation come within every one's observance. Why, then, may it not be allowed to produce the same effects in writing ?"

Whether Burns had this " in his eye " when he wrote,

> " My barmy noddle's workin' prime,
> My fancy's yerket up sublime,"

would be hard to hazard a guess. Both poets, on more occasions than one, coincide in the opinion about the use of alcohol as a stimulus to creative art.

These by no means exhaust the similarities of Shenstone and Burns, but they must suffice for the limits of a magazine article. Possibly a catalogue of similarities in thought and diction may serve as an index to those who would further pursue a delightful exercise. Such a comparative list I shall endeavour to give in a further paper.

A. J. CRAIG.

ROBERT BURNS—ANTIQUARIAN.

IT was in October, 1789, when his most characteristic Scottish poems had been written with the exception of " Tam o' Shanter," and his few and small wanderings over Scotland were limited to his particular Excise area, that Burns wrote his address to Captain Frances Grose, in which he gleefully ridiculed the Trade Antiquarian and " a fouth o' auld nick-nackets." The Bard would have been surprised and decidedly amused if it had then been suggested to him that he had already proved himself a true Antiquarian, and had given irrefutable evidence. It was in 1785, his first year as a freeman, after his father's death, that he became his own master, and it was in that year of exuberant splendour of verse that he wrote " Hallowe'en "—wrote it with the greatest care and concern that none of the manners and traditions of the countryside and of the " principal charms and spells of that night, so big with prophecy to the peasantry in the West of Scotland," should be overlooked or forgotten—and added to it careful notes to explain to all and sundry the peculiar rites and practices of this ancient festival, so that they should be for all time understood.

The Trade Antiquarian comprises—the Minor, who busy themselves in collecting things of the past, material or literary ; then the Major, who apply their minds to learning and recording old days, old ways, and to raising from oblivion the life and work, the skill and art, the manners and customs of the past. Beyond this, there are the very few whose work is national and imperishable. To Burns, as a young and budding poet, jealous of the honour of Carrick and Kyle, and other parts hitherto unsung, his stride towards the preservation of the grand and expressive Auld Scots Tongue was as easy and unpre-

meditated as natural.   And it is to his immortal work in
this direction that his claim to be honoured among
Antiquarians must rest.   Being the most modest of men,
apart from his steadfast knowledge of his own position
and value as the National Bard, he would have smiled
at being compared to John Knox.   But that great man,
two hundred years earlier, had found it necessary to rail
and fulminate against the men of his time who " Knapt
Sudrone "—that is, affected the clipt, quick speech of the
educated Southron, rather than their own broad, vigorous
and dignified Mother tongue.   So it came about that in
Burns's day, when Scotland was reviving after the poverty
of the early eighteenth century and the Jacobite troubles,
and was again giving heed to literature and art, the homely
dialect was in danger of being relegated to the poor and the
countrified, and of losing its place as one of the essences
of national life and character.   The refined and educated
turned more and more to English models of the day, to
the style of Pope and Addison ;   found an admired reflection in the verse of Beattie and Thomson ;   the prose
of Henry Mackenzie and Blair.   To such artificiality and
sententiousness Burns, after a few attempts at imitation,
set himself in opposition with that vigour which so strongly
marked his genius.   His sure sense, naturalness, and
devotion to the soil to which he so peculiarly belonged,
made him unerringly recognise the value of the Scottish
dialect, easily the purest and least contaminated of any
of those which go to make up the English language.   Employed as it was in his verses and songs, it arrested universal
attention, and thenceforth took its place as a true literary
mode.   In this way, by removing it from the idea or reproach of vulgarity, its decay was arrested, its power and
charm made clear, and its permanency secured.

   Although to some extent unconscious, at least as to
the importance of his Antiquarian work, it was a deliberate
aim.   To the boy whose reading began with the *History
of William Wallace*, oddly conjoined with *The Life of
Hannibal*, it was easy and natural that his expanding mind

should rivet itself on his country, its ancient story, and its many beauties. He writes to Mrs Dunlop ·—

" Scottish scenes and Scottish story are the themes I could wish to sing. I have no dearer aim than to have it in my power, unplagued with the routine of business—for which, Heaven knows, I am unfit enough—to make leisurely pilgrimages through Caledonia; to sit on the fields of her battles ; to wander on the romantic banks of her rivers ; and to rest by the stately towers or venerable ruins, once the honoured abodes of her heroes."

He wrote to Doctor Moore that he was—

" to make pilgrimages over some of the classic grounds of Caledonia, Cowden Knowes, Banks of Yarrow, Tweed, &c." ·

and that wish he repeats in his letter to the Earl of Buchan :—

" I wish for nothing more than to make a leisurely pilgrimage through my native country ; to sit and rest on those once hard-contended fields, where Caledonia, rejoicing, saw her bloody lion borne through broken ranks to victory and fame ; and, catching the inspiration, to pour the deathless names in song."

In such few pilgrimages as he was able to carry out he shows, throughout the small notes he took of his Highland and Lowland tours, that he had the true Antiquarian's eye for ancient and beautiful objects, and that he could choicely describe and appraise them almost in a word. Even the prehistoric does not escape him. " Lyon River—Druid's Temple : Three circles of stone, the outermost sunk ; the second has thirteen stones remaining ; the innermost has eight ; two large detached ones, like a gate, to the south-east." " Camelon — the ancient Metropolis of the Picts." " Bochester — the scene of an old encampment (Roman)." Never does he pass Scottish historical remains without mention. " Roxburgh Castle, and the small old religious ruins " ; " Thomas à Rhymer's ruined castle " ; " Linlithgow—tolerably fine castle " ; " Cawdor— where Macbeth murdered King Duncan : saw the bed in which King Duncan was stabbed " ; " Broughty's Castle —a finely situated ruin, jutting into the Tay." For

Ecclesiastical Edifices he has a discerning eye. " Melrose
—that far-famed glorious ruin ; Dryburgh—a fine old
ruined Abbey ; Jedburgh—fine old ruins, a once magnificent cathedral, and strong castle ; Elgin Abbey—a grander
effect at first glance than Melrose, but not near so beautiful ;
stately ruin of Arbroath Abbey ; Dundee's old Steeple."
These are all apposite and discriminating. Dunfermline
Abbey he does not mention, but we know that he went
into a fine fervour as he knelt at the Tomb of the Bruce.
Later, when his limited wanderings were ended, he loved to
pass from the boundary of his farm and sit and meditate
and compose in the quaint, ancient little building known
as the Hermitage at Friars' Carse, where the sculptured
effigy of some old Scottish Knight formed his seat. At
Dumfries, many a time on Sunday, or at eventide, he made
his way to Cluden's silent towers, the beautiful little ruins
of a Nunnery at Lincluden, which is beyond the town, across
the winding Nith. Lower down that well-loved stream—
on the east bank the stately ruins of Caerlaverock Castle ;
on the west the beautiful Church which Devorgilla Baliol
raised to the memory of her husband, the Abbey of the
Sweetheart. In both of these, if you search, you will
find the sign " R.B." boldly engraved on the stones. Thus,
in this wonderful short and busy life, the antiquarian spirit
reveals itself again and again in these ways, as an addition
to his determined effort to preserve in its purity and force
the language of the countryside, the auld Scots tongue,
and to retrieve and preserve the songs and airs which
otherwise might have been lost to the nation.

Looking at the time that has elapsed since Burns's
death, it cannot be wondered at that in his actual writings
there is some part that has in itself passed into the domain
of antiquity. If you wish a picture of old-time farming
you will find it in his poems and his pastoral letters—how
the people lived, were housed and dressed. You shall also
find as well, many notes of customs that have now passed
away, expressed in terms and words no longer in common
use. Thanks to him, these words are decidedly limited

in number.   To-day we do not come across *placks, bodles* and *testers*.   *Tippeny* and *Antiqua* are not our drinks, and barley has taken the place of *bere*.   As mentioned, a large collection of farming terms have passed with the old and poor system of agriculture; and the same applies to the lives and homes of the peasantry, far removed from the poverty, hardships, and meagre fare of his day. That so much has survived and is still in use is one of the finest and most enduring of memorials; and other writers in later days who have eschewed " High English " in favour of the Doric, are best remembered, and have a chance of surviving in the honoured literature of the country.

PHILIP SULLEY.

AT BROW AND AFTER.

And so he came—to Brow by Solway's Firth,
   And eident was his quest.

But love's most earnest wish was unfulfilled,
Day unto day a-numbering out its tale;
For neither shady neuk, a-fragrant with the scent
Of milk-white thorn, so redolent of charm,
Nor healing water from the spring near-by,
Nor rushing wave could bear the spirit up.

   Oh ! could that shady bower but speak,
It, too, might tell the story of the ending of a life
That struggled with the things that tell—
Those eternal things, which the great Father of us all
Has but to few, and that in measure small, revealed
In life's great garden, sometimes rudely kept
By those whose work is but to keep and tend.

   Love's labour lost. . . . He homeward bent his way
Sad thoughts enveloping his soul;
One ray of hope alone enlightening his path—
The ray, that in the radiance of his home
All darkness might dissolve, and in the gleam
Of love for wife and weans, a better day begin.

   Thus he resolved. . . . But all in vain.
The fondly cherished hope did not outspan,
His coming back being like rift in lute,
Or like the tuning up to play the last refrain.

   His work was done. . . . He died—
Died in that madness which ofttimes comes
To those who, after their own order, see things,
And hear and utter sounds yont ordinary ken.

   So thus it was, and so it aye shall be :
The gifted sons of men—the Poet, Prophet, and the Seer—
Go forth. . . . . RESOLVING TO RESOLVE.

                      J. T. G.

Mauchline.

REMOVAL OF THE HIGHLAND MARY MEMORIAL.

IN the last issue of the *Chronicle*, we laid before our readers a full report of the development of the proposal to remove the Monument and remains of Highland Mary from the West Churchyard of Greenock, and also of the discussion which took place at the Annual Meeting of the Federation in connection with the three alternatives offered by Messrs Harland & Wolff to meet the views of the Federation. The alternatives were (1) to remove the remains and the Monument to such a place of sepulture as might be selected by the Executive of the Federation ; (2) to leave the remains interred as at present, and to reverse the existing Monument so as to face the street ; (3) to remove the existing Monument, and to place and maintain a mural tablet in lieu thereof, the remains not being disturbed. After full discussion of these proposals, the finding of the Federation was that " the whole matter be remitted to the Executive along with representatives of the Greenock Burns Club, with full powers to deal with it in the interests of the Federation." Thereafter, acting on instructions, the President and Secretary of the Federation interviewed Mr Kempster, Managing Director in Greenock for Messrs Harland & Wolff, and laid before him the prevailing opinion of the Federation that the remains should not be disturbed, and the Monument interfered with only so far as was necessary to suit the altered circumstances. Mr Kempster received them with the utmost courtesy, and expressed the earnest desire of his firm to meet the wishes of the Federation, even to the extent of bearing the expense of another Monument on any site selected by the Federation, should the alternatives offered be considered out of unison with the sentiment which actuated the opposition to the scheme.

In the meantime the Provisional Order was being rapidly passed through Parliament, and no other course was open to the Federation but to oppose it. The Bill was accordingly blocked by the Hon. A. Shaw, M.P. for the Kilmarnock Division of Ayrshire, who was in communication with the President of the Federation, and the result was that an understanding was come to that Messrs Harland & Wolff would faithfully carry out any of the alternatives chosen by the Federation, and of their own free will supply funds for the erection of a Memorial elsewhere if desired.

In terms of the remit made to them, the Executive then met, and advised the representatives of the Greenock Club that they would visit Greenock and finally determine which of the alternatives should be accepted. After careful examination of the proposed alterations on the Monument if left *in situ*, and the sites offered in the new burying-ground of the West Parish and the Greenock Cemetery, they adjourned to the Burns Club rooms, when it was decided by a majority to accept the site offered by the Corporation in the Greenock Cemetery, it being strongly urged in support of this course that to leave the Monument and grave isolated amid such incongruous, squalid surroundings was a most undesirable solution of the question. Powers were accordingly conferred on the Greenock Burns Club to superintend the removal operations under the direction of Mr M'Whannel, Architect, Glasgow, which work was successfully accomplished by the beginning of November.

To Mr Shaw, the able and popular member for the Kilmarnock Division of Ayrshire, the utmost credit is due for his plucky blocking of the Bill, which only indirectly affected his constituents in the Burns country he represents.

REBURIAL OF THE ASHES.

In chill November weather the ashes of Burns's " Highland Mary " were re-interred in Greenock Cemetery on Saturday, 13th

November, 1920. The ceremony was necessarily attended with all the trappings of woe, but it was not an occasion of mourning. Circumstances provided an opportunity to honour the dust of the Highland girl who inspired some of the most beautiful songs of the Poet, and lovers of Burns, not only in Greenock but throughout the West of Scotland, availed themselves of the opportunity with fitting reverence. Interest in the reburial, however, was not confined to Burns Club members, as was evidenced by the large number of the general public who assembled at the grave-side. Such a gathering as that which came to pay homage to the ashes of a simple peasant girl dead more than 130 years ago could not readily be conceived in any connection other than that of Scotsmen in relation to Burns.

While the company were assembling in Greenock Cemetery there was a brief thunderstorm with vivid flashes of lightning and heavy showers of rain and hail, but the proceedings were carried out during a dry interval. Earlier in the week the remains had been exhumed from their resting place in the Old West Kirk burying-ground, which is required in connection with Messrs Harland & Wolff's shipyard extension, and placed in an oak coffin, which was conveyed to the cemetery house. Here assembled the representatives of the Burns Federation and members of the Greenock and other Burns Clubs. From the house the coffin was borne by relays of prominent Burnsians, others falling in behind, and the procession proceeded at a slow pace up the steep ascent to the site of the new grave in the high part of the cemetery adjoining the James Watt memorial cairn. On the coffin, which bore the simple inscription : "Mary Campbell (Highland Mary), Re-interred 13th November, 1920," were placed three beautiful wreaths. One was from Greenock (the Mother) Burns Club. It was of white heather and laurel, tied with a ribbon of Campbell tartan. The others were from Greenock St. John's Club (of laurel, pink roses, lilies, and ferns) and from Messrs Harland & Wolff (of palm, white roses, and heather).

The scene at the grave was a striking one. Facing the tomb a large canvas shelter had been erected for the accommodation of the members of the Burns Clubs and those specially interested. Around the other three sides of the grave, which had been roped off, were assembled the general public, many being ladies. The monument which was erected in the Old West burying-ground by admirers of the Poet in 1842 was in position. On it is carved the couplet :—

> " O Mary, dear departed shade,
> Where is thy place of blissful rest ?"

In front is the little original headstone bearing the words :—
" This burying-place belongs to Peter M'Pherson, ship carpenter

in Greenock, and his spouse, Mary Campbell, and their children,
1787."

On the arrival of the procession the coffin was placed over the
laurel-lined grave, and the Burns Club members grouped themselves alongside and behind the officiating minister, the Rev. W. J.
Nichol Service, West Kirk, Greenock, who occupied a central position
in the canvas pavilion immediately opposite the burial place. There
followed an impressive service, in which a special choir under Mr
Percy Harmon assisted. It was opened with the singing of verses
13-18 of Psalm 103 to the tune of " Coleshill," and the recitation
of " Sentences and Collect." The coffin was then reverently
lowered into the grave. The pall-bearers were Messrs D. M'Naught,
President of the Burns Federation ; Hugh M'Lean, President of
Greenock Burns Club ; J. B. Morison, Greenock ; Thomas Amos,
Secretary of the Burns Federation ; Dr W. A. Milne, Greenock ;
James A. Morrison, Greenock ; George B. Grieve, Secretary of
Greenock Burns Club ; and Duncan M'Callum, Greenock. Lessons
from the Old and New Testaments were read by Mr D. M'Naught
and Mr Hugh M'Lean, and a prayer :—" O Thou unknown, Almighty
Cause "—written by the Poet " in the prospect of death," was
sung to the tune " Spohr."

The Rev. Mr Service afterwards offered up prayer. In the
course of the petition he said :—" We bless Thee this day, as we
stand by our departed sister's grave, for the love which she called
orth in the heart of our Poet, which inspired his sweetest and his
saddest song, and which drew his soul near to the place of blissful
rest. Help us to cherish the hope that long ago they were re-united
in the fellowship of soul with soul in that place where love is perfect
and immortal ; where there is no more parting or weeping or pain
for ever. O Thou who givest liberally and upbraidest not, we
praise Thee for food and raiment and for all things necessary for the
sustenance of life ; and we thank Thee no less for the sweet voices
that have sounded in this world and made us, in the midst of toil
and trouble, sing in heart along the road of life, giving us kind and
gracious thoughts of our fellows, and drawing us to all that is fair
and beautiful. We praise Thee that their music lingers with us
still when the singers are gone from the sight of our eyes and the
hearing of our ears. Make us, we pray Thee, attentive to them,
that even here we may know the joy and the peace of the heart at
one with Thee."

The service concluded with the singing of part of Paraphrase
66 to the tune " St. Asaph," and with the Benediction. Then the
grave was filled in with earth taken from the grave in the Old West
burying-ground—" dust to dust, ashes to ashes."

The Burns Federation were represented at the service by Messrs D. M'Naught, T. Amos, J. Jeffrey Hunter, Andrew M'Callum, P. Sulley, A. Mackenzie, W. Douglas, H. M'Coll, J. Carmichael, T. Killin, and ex-Provost Wilson, Pollokshaws. Among others present were Sheriff Welsh, Colonel D. F. D. Neill, the Rev. James M'Kechnie, Councillor Hillhouse Carmichael, Messrs Arch. Macphail, Charles L. Brodie, Grierson Macara, A. Foulds, James Campbell, G. Dunlop, W. Morrison, H. D. Scutter, and J. M. Pollock.

HIGHLAND MARY MEMORIAL AT.
FAILFORD.

THE last issue of the *Chronicle* contained an account of the evidence laid before Lord Forteviot by the President of the Federation and Mr J. C. Ewing, Vice-president, in opposition to the proposal contained in the Greenock Provisional Order to remove Highland Mary's remains and Monument, which stood in the way of an extension of the shipbuilding yard of Messrs Harland & Wolff. In pursuance of the policy resolved upon at the last General Meeting of the Federation, Mr Amos, Hon. Secretary, communicated with several Scotch Members of Parliament requesting their support in opposing the Bill. When it reached the House of Commons, the Hon. Alex. Shaw, Member for the Kilmarnock District of Ayrshire, who was in keen sympathy with the views of the Federation, interposed on behalf of his constituents, and blocked the progress of the Bill. Its ultimate passing, however, being a foregone conclusion, he applied himself to secure the best terms he could, and succeeded in obtaining from the promoters an assurance that whichever of the alternatives offered by Messrs Harland & Wolff was accepted by the Federation would be faithfully carried out. When the Bill passed through Parliament, the Executive met with delegates appointed by the Greenock Club on 29th March, 1920, and inspected the practical bearing of each of the alternatives on a satisfactory solution of the question. After debate, it was carried by a majority that the remains and Monument be removed to the site offered by the Greenock Corporation, in the New Cemetery, contiguous to the Monument erected in memory of James Watt. At a subsequent meeting of the Executive, it was agreed to accept Lord Pirrie's generous offer, the site selected being on the banks of the Ayr, near the spot where the parting of Burns and Highland Mary is believed to have taken. place.   Mr James Arthur, of Montgomerie Castle, on being interviewed, very generously granted the site free of any charge, and plans were thereafter prepared by Mr Hay, architect, Kilmarnock, without fee, and the

contract let by the Executive to Mr A. Calderwood, builder, Kilmarnock, the operations to be begun as soon as possible, after approval of the plans by Mr Arthur.

.The accompanying illustration, from a drawing by Mr Hay, conveys a good idea of the Memorial, which will be a prominent object in the landscape.   The unveiling ceremony will take place probably early in 1921, on a date to be fixed by the Executive.

AT MARY'S SHRINE.

Come, Mary, with approving smile,
  From radiant realms divine ;
Light thou this consecrated grove,
  Where rests thy second shrine.

We tell of thee with burning words
  In love's most hallowed page ;
Thy tale of fated love is now
  The nation's heritage.

The spell still haunts Montgomery's hohms,
  And Ayr's song-laden stream ;
And there the mystic music floats,
  Of love's unending dream.

There, in the sanctitude of love,
  When every path was hard,
Love found thee stronger than the fate
  That crushed the hopeless Bard.

He marvelled at thee, but he swayed
  To thine imperious fire,
And, startled into greatness, seized
  And swept his mighty lyre.

Still in these changed, distracted days,
  When olden faiths depart,
Thy love, a constant power, prevails,
  And stays the troubled heart.

Not to thy dust, now doubly dear,
  Our throbbing hearts respond ;
But 'tis thy passionate, fadeless vow
  That holds the world in bond.

'Tis ours to know November glooms,
  And naked woods and plains ;
For thee, in fairer, stainless climes,
  Eternal summer reigns.

This day is dark and fraught with pain,
  Yet, if thou turn thy face,
A ray of immortality
  Will glorify the place.

We stand around a grave, but, lo,
  Thy blinding radiancy !—
The grave, a jewelled casket, lined
  With golden thoughts of thee.

Not now the cypress, not the yew,
  Shall sigh this shrine above ;
But herb o' grace and asphodel
  For memory and for love.

We knew thee near when hitherward
  We bore this dust of thine ;
And thou with Burns again will come
  To bless the holy shrine.

CHAS. L. BRODIE.

Greenock.

MARIA RIDDELL'S LETTERS TO DR JAMES CURRIE, 1796-1805.

PART II.

IN pursuance of the announcement made in the last issue of the *Chronicle* in the preface to this most interesting collection placed at our disposal by its owner, Mr Charles R. Cowie, of Glasgow, we now submit a second instalment—from November, 1797, to December, 1799.

J. C. E.

No. XII.

Christ Church, Hants,
16th November, 1797.

But to be serious. In answer to yours of the 3rd ult., I have no information to afford you relative to such writings of Our Bard's as you have found in Pleyel's selection; his name is prefixed at full length to his own songs there. I can not give you the information you desire as to Johnson's *Miscellany* [*Museum*] neither, just at present, because I am not worth a copy of that publication here; but my Sister has it at Bloxworth, and I will send you all I can afford from thence in the course of a week or ten days. The printed poems you, like a perfidious Doctor (of, I believe, a very perfidious science), still have in your custody, so I cannot refer conveniently, as you request me, to any of them. If I can borrow a copy on my return to Dorsetshire I will do so nevertheless. Have you got among Burns's MS. Letters the copy of one he wrote to old Smellie, dated the 22nd January, 1792? Because it has been thought a very good one, the concluding sentiment, that is to say, is perhaps sufficiently striking to give sanction to the rest of the letter, which is certainly less interesting to the public because relative personally to your humble Servant only. It was an intro-ductory letter he gave me when I first went to Edinburgh to that Naturalist, with whom I was anxious to become acquainted. I could procure you the original letter, if you desired it. Perhaps it was false modesty to suppress it when I gave you his other MSS., but I thought it would appear like wishing to introduce myself to you under the auspices of a too partial narrator if I put it into your hands at that time exactly. Of my own letters you need not be surprised that you have not yet discovered any among the papers, because they were all returned to me at my particular request before I left Scotland. You might see from the tenour of Burns's billets and letters to me that there was no *shining* correspondence between us ; we lived so near, and were so constantly together, that we seldom had recourse for the communication of our thoughts or sentiments to the medium—the cold imperfect medium—of paper. His language might bestow grace to the most trivial subjects, but I did not think my own worth preserving. I regret that the print should be executed by the hand of any artist except the one Roscoe employed for his *Lorenzo*. Have you seen any specimen of this volunteer engraver's performance ? Now, do not let us mar the volumes with an indifferent frontispiece. The price of the sub-scription is considerable, and the print of Burns's head seems an object, I observe, to many of those who are pledged to me as sub-scribers. You have taken an impression of the seal, too, have you not ? It will make a small vignette for the title page. Will you let me know when and where the subscription is open in Edinburgh, and I shall immediately write to Erskine and some of my friends there to patronize it. There are certain Lords of Justiciary there, too, whom I think I have yet some interest with ; these will be of use. You need not be anxious for Bankes's name. I shall set that down without even asking his leave. Among the Peers and Commons I hope to do a good deal. Lewis espouses it warmly, and so will her Grace of Gordon. She wrote me a volume a few days ago, perfectly raving about Roscoe ; his " Vine cover'd hills and gay vallies of France " have deified him with her. She wished extremely to see him while he was in town, and I do not know if he told you how wickedly he gave her, and gave me indeed, the slip about that. However, I have pledged myself, as an encouragement to her activity in our cause, that she shall positively have that gratification when he visits the Capital next. You may tell him this if you like it. I find by a letter I had lately from his son that Dr Moore and you have not corresponded on the arrangements in town yet. It should be set agoing in January, and early in that month. Have you settled how and by whom it is to be conducted there ? Pray let me know if there will be any thing on certain topics, as politics, and so forth, that might render indelicate my requesting persons of any party or persuasion to subscribe. I think if we got the Prince of Wales's name, for instance—I mean by way of ornament, for he will never pay the money. . . .

———

Kingston Hall, 20th.

I now attend to you again, my dear Sir . . . Well ! but of Clarinda's correspondence ! I declare I know not how to act in it, but will be guided willingly by you. You formerly begged me to entrust to you such letters of Clarinda's to myself as related to Burns, as well as those I wrote in return giving her the information she required of the particulars of his death, &c. One or two of these you saw at Liverpool, I believe. Of my own letters, upon my honour, I do not think you can make much use, for half of them are very nonsensical; and Clarinda's contain private anecdotes of his history, his marriage, and so forth, that I can conceive the public will have nothing to do with. Of Burns's letters to her I can only procure a partial selection, as you may suppose, from the fair one herself; but I will write to her to-morrow for all she will give, and if you after this account still wish to have the reading of them, I have nothing to refuse you, and they shall be sent you in any way you will appoint : none occur to me at present except a parcel by the mail, and the thing is whether you think them worth that method of conveyance. Let me know by a line, and your will shall be done immediately. I do not know which of the MSS. you selected, from my *portefeuille*, of Burns's; but I am sure I gave you every elucidation relative to them you asked me, when I was with you. If I neglected any thing material let me know. I pray you forgive me if I have said any thing I ought not to have said, or left unsaid what I ought to have said. I am not able to write six lines without interruption. Just send me your final commands relative to these letters; but if you are not at leisure do not think it necessary to write a letter (it is great virtue in me to admit of this). I will write again when I get Johnson's *Miscellany* [*Museum.*] Believe me, your sincere and obliged

MARIA RIDDELL.

No. XIII.

Bloxworth, 6th December, 1797.

Your letter of the 24th November must have passed one of mine, with what information I could afford you respecting Burns's share in the *Scots Musical Miscellany* [*Museum*], on the road. I have a ready conveyance likely soon to occur for receiving all you have to send me from Liverpool, in the course of this month or very early in the next. One of my female attendants left me on account of bad health last year, is now with her brother at Liverpool, and being quite recovered returns to me as soon as I go to London. She will take great care of the books and papers, and deliver them safely to me. I will let you know before she comes away from Liverpool, or will desire her to call on you for them, if you are not afraid of trusting yourself with the sight of a very uncommonly *bonny Lass*. Hitherto I have been unsuccessful in the enquiry for a volume of the printed poems; when I get one, if I am lucky enough to do so before I go to London, I will certainly set about obeying your commands *de mon mieux ;* if not, will do so as soon as I get my own copy.   I do not comprehend how you came by that contraband copy of Burns's letter to Smellie, unless he (Burns) had retained a copy of it for himself ; *that* you may have procured, but the Original letter young Smellie gave me after his father's death and I have it now in my *scrutore,* unless you deal in magic.   I have not the least acquaintance with Cunningham ;   pray recollect in your next to let me know his address, or rather where the Subscriptions are received—I do not even know Cunningham's Christian name or what he is, I fancy a professional man—because it is impossible for me to desire my friends to subscribe till I can give them some designation where they are to address themselves, &c.   The business would be much better in the booksellers' hands :   Peter Hill's, or Smellie the printer's (a son of the venerable philosopher, and a great protégé of mine ;   I know his worth, and would be responsible for his zeal).   Creech, however, should be avoided like plague or pestilence ;   he is a great rogue as well as an intolerable pedant.   As for Dr Moore, you will never get any thing out of him till I get to town and pull his wig a little ;   I know what a fastidious wretch he is, but I will make him do whatever you like when he is within my reach.   I shall devour Roscoe's Poem with eagerness as soon as it comes out.   I am delighted with your plan about the selection of the Bard's writings.   I will try by speaking to Wilberforce, whenever I see him, if we cannot get Dundas's name, since you wish it ;   but after my contest with the whole clan of Dundas's about Oneil's affair, I dare not attempt an application directly from myself ;   besides, as for the Arch-fiend himself, I never scarcely see him.   I will try, however, an oblique channel, and see what we can do.   Colonel Fullarton I do not know.   You forgot, after all, one of the main purports of my letter—relative to Clarinda.   I now inclose you a letter I received from her two days ago ;   you will read it and let me know in consequence whether you wish for any of these Extracts from Burns's letters, and if any passages concerning *Him*, in mine to her, will be worth your looking over.   Have you heard of these said Memoirs of Burns, by one Heron ?   Clarinda mentions them.   I dare say they are no great things.   If you approve a continuation of this selection from his letters to Clarinda, I conclude you would prefer those delineating his feelings, sentiments, and opinions on every subject, with as little of the love episodes as possible.   The concluding passage in that extract of Clarinda's does great honor to Burns's religion ;   you will be pleased with, and I dare say will find use for, it.   I have, since this was begun, received more papers from Clarinda.   If Syme has not been satisfactory to you on the subject of Burns's *closing scene* I really will, on farther consideration, give my letters to Clarinda into your hands. Now, without sitting down to write me a regular epistle, just scrawl me a line or two by the earliest post, or make one of your young men do so, to let me know if I shall continue to send you any of these extracts, &c., Clarinda forwards to me. The seal I mentioned, and which you propose engraving in the title page, I fancy Gilbert Burns or the Widow will have got in their custody. I gave Burns the stone, and we arranged the *devise* between us, I do firmly believe in despite and violation of all rules of Heraldry : a holly bush with a shepherd's pipe suspended, crest a wood-lark, with the motto from Milton's *Allegro,* "native woodnotes wild"—it is all appropriate enough, and you must not omit to give the Poet's chosen blazon. I shall now busily set about preparing my copies, &c., of my own and Clarinda's letters, with those of Burns's she sends me, *en attendant* your orders for sending them, which I shall look for soon, if at all. If I have time I will digest some of those biographical sketches of mine, since you propose making some use of them, in better form, or at least prune some of the inaccuracies ; they may all go together to Liverpool. I am very angry with you for saying I only "say obliging things to spirit you up to the completion of your task." I must be very insensible to the part you have taken in all this business and to the excellence of those motives that urged you to it, if they certainly did not render you rather more an object of obliging sensations and obliging expressions. . . . Pray lay apart the letters, &c., I send, or may send, you from Clarinda, to return me when done with, as I should not like wholly to resign them. —Addio ! Yours very faithfully,

MARIA RIDDELL.

P.S.—Heron of Heron in Galloway has interested himself much for the publication. Lewis tells me he will do all he can, and be a *ministering spirit* unto me ; and I have been canvassing the *beaux* even here, not totally without success.

No. XIV.

Pluviose, 2de decade [6th February, 1798].

I lost no time on the receipt of your letter, which reached me on Monday evening last, to put your commands in immediate execution. My services you may at all times command as far as they can be useful, and you need never apologise for laying them under contribution. I went to Mr Heron directly—he only said your letter related to Colonel Fullarton rather than to himself, and after a few *shuffling,* evasive speeches and assurances of interest, he dropped the subject; I did not resume it, as I do not think he has acted quite warmly and handsomely, and we can do well enough without him or any of these *tepid* fellows who cannot enter with entire heart and soul into such a business as this. Fullarton has been out of town, which created all this delay. I do not scarcely know him, but he knows me, particularly as a friend of Erskine's. I know the Duchess of Gordon is much occupied, dissipated, and often procrastinates even in her own concerns, so I took courage and wrote to him myself. I have this day received the handsomest and most cordial letter possible from him. I had enclosed him yours, which was worth volumes of what *I* could say; he appears much flattered with your mention of him, and desires me to assure you your insertion of his name in the Proposals required no apology whatever. He promises to befriend us in all points in the prosecution of this business, and has, to conclude, presented me with the enclosed verses, requesting I will transmit them to you, as Syme suggested (for which, by the way, he deserves a rap on the pate) their publication in your volume of Burns. They are by Fullarton's wife, and he seems himself to wish they should appear, so of course appear they must. Now, Fullarton you have at your disposal. As for Heron I would take no more trouble about him: if you want another name you may take Lewis's; or any body's that I know and have influence with I will obtain, if you will fix upon it. Our Duchess has done nothing yet; I sent her a parcel of the printed Proposals to-night, and have announced to her that we *now* expect her to begin her operations. Lewis merits honorable mention in no common degree; nothing can have surpassed his solicitude and activity; he has been the life and spirit of the sub-scription, and his interest is at present in its zenith. My list increases, and I mean to write to Sheridan to-morrow; I have not seen him yet, except at a distance, since I came to town. I am sure you will not complain of the Aristocrates being deficient in my list; I have got few, if any, of the other description. I have had a letter lately from young Smellie; his father's 2nd part of the *Philosophy of Natural History* is published or publishing. The family hope much from it; for their sake, and the memory of the venerable philosopher, as well as for the interests of literature at large, this work should be brilliantly countenanced; pray notice it, and speak of it among your friends. I send you more epistles of Clarinda.

Fullarton has just been with me. I am delighted with him. I have had at least fifty interruptions since I have attempted to finish this to-day; I had begun my letter three days ago. Adieu! *Salut et fraternité*!

Maria Riddell.

No. XV.

' 18 Duke Street, St. James,
10th June, 1798.

There is no getting quite rid of me, you see ; when you do me
the honor to write to me I have your letters to answer ; and now,
your very silence invites me to interrupt it ! I want to know if you
are well and that you have not totally forgotten me. Besides,
here is one-half of the world annoying me with incessant enquiries
when Burns's volume is to appear, and I feel myself in a most mor-
tifying manner disqualified for any satisfactory response. It is
not from " unreasonable impatience " I once more re-iterate them,
but if it does not prove unseasonable interruption to you, you will
oblige me much by a line of information on this head. With regard
to the Subscription, I have had no conversation with Messrs Cadell
and Davies for some time, but I should fancy it went on but heavily
with *them*. My list, the Duchess of Gordon's, Colonel Fullarton's,
Mrs Stratford's, and several other persons, I believe, who have kept
lists, are pretty well *meublés* ; but we do not take the money, as
that was quite impossible, for a variety of reasons unnecessary to
enlarge upon to you at present. I shall be an hundred and fifty
miles out of London at least by the second week in July, therefore
if you have any further commands for me in this part of the world
I give you timely information that you must communicate them
soon, or I shall be removed from the sphere in which I am most
likely to be serviceable to you. . . . We must get Tom Erskine
added to our list of Burns's subscribers, which somehow and very
stupidly I have never managed to do yet ; but I shall probably see
him in a few days and will then demand permission to inscribe him.
What am I to do with my list, &c., now I am leaving town ?' Shall
I send to Mr Davies ? What shall I say to him ? Pray direct me
in every thing at your pleasure ; I am your ministering spirit, and
will obey you in all points. I saw Colonel Fullarton yesterday,
who desired me to tender his obeisance to you likewise. *En passant,*
you have never returned me, or acknowledged even the receipt of,
Clarinda's letters ; I wish, if you have taken your extracts, or in
short done with them, that you would return them to me before I
leave London. Have you not some other papers of mine beside ? . . .
—Adieu ! Health and Fraternity ! MARIA RIDDELL.

No. XVI.

Sunday, 7th July [1798].

Mr dear Doctor, you really and truly are an unreasonable mortal !
On the 20th of June I indeed received a letter from you, desiring

me to send you my list, with Colonel Fullarton's and the Duchess
of Gordon's.   As that seemed the sole purport of your letter I
thought it needless to answer it before I could give you some satisfactory answer to the commands laid upon me.   Colonel Fullarton
is at his Villa; I wrote to him immediately on the receipt of yours,
and I just enclose you his evasive answer.   I shall write again
to-morrow; what can I do more ?   The Duchess of Gordon left
town in a sudden freak a month ago for Scotland.   I had first to
write to her daughter in Huntingdonshire, to enquire her Grace's
address; and then wrote, without losing one day, to herself.   I
wrote the 29th, and as the Duchess is the most fickle of all people,
tho' I directed my letter (as desired) to the *South* of Scotland, it is
ten to one but it has to travel after her as far as Johnny Groat's.
Certain it is that as yet I have had no answer, and hardly expected
one so soon.   You see there has been no negligence on my part,
and I may venture to say that if every one of your ministers and
agents were as punctual as I am, *la besogne en irait mieux*.   I did
not conceive writing to you as little to the purpose as I am doing
now of very essential service ; however, see I do it !   And pray
take it for granted that even when silent I am never indolent or
inactive where I can be of use to you, and am employed.   If your
new plan for the publication of the Works *in toto* answers, it will
be excellent ; but if you can exorcise the *dæmon* of covetousness
out of old Creech—the Age of Miracles is indeed not past !   I will
send my list enclosed to-morrow, if I can get a frank ; if not, the
day after, transcribed in my most legible hand and as unlike that
of this present writing as possible.   I will send it to you, for it is
not considerable enough to assist your " Jew's bargain," I doubt,
till Fullarton's and the Duchess's are added.   So much for business !
. . . I recommend all the MSS. you possess of mine, Clarinda's letters,
&c., to your care till an opportunity occurs to remit them to me. . . .
Here, however, is my list copied, and I have manufactured another
epistle to Fullarton, bidding him, if his list is not in time to catch
me, forward it to you or McCreery at Liverpool.   The Duchess will
know my address, if she chuses to avail herself of it.   Mark that,
owing to Bankes being out of town, I never received your last favor
till yesterday. . . .—Health and fraternity '

MARIA RIDDELL.

No. XVII.

Exmouth, Devon, 15th August, 1798.

My dear Friend !   I sent you a little dispatch just before I
left Town—the 9th, I think, of last month—which I hope reached
you in due course.   I then gave you (with my list) an exact state-

ment of the existing circumstances relative to the negotiation entrusted to me. I told you I had written a second and most peremptory billet to poor Fullarton ; I do not enclose you his epistle in answer on account of postage, but here follows (all and exactly transcribed) what it contains in respect to his mission : " I am shocked and mortified that our list should have been so tardy in its progress, but you may be assured I will not fail to forward it to Dr Currie at Liverpool, and shall continue to solicit additional signatures to the last moment. I was in hopes to have had the honor of saying this in person, &c., &c." Farther on this subject the deponent sayeth not. I gave him your address, and, as I am wandering and you stationary, I think if the Colonel's list ever is completed you will get it before I see or hear any thing of him again myself. I am qualified to afford you just as little *éclaircissement* relative to the Bonny Duchess's exertions. I have had a letter from her since my arrival here, from Monreith, in which she tells me in the most satisfactory manner imaginable, as you will agree, that she left the list very carefully on her table in Piccadilly, and it had slipped her memory to send it to me before she set off for the North. This said list was taken on the *feuilles volantes* of the proposal papers, and her servants have sent me only one of them, with just eight names inscribed upon it. I wrote this dilemma to the Duchess immediately, praying her Grace to write to some of her people in town to search for and recover the remaining sheets, and if that failed, to ransack her recollection for the nominations, &c., of the mass of the subscribers collected by her ; to which I have not yet got the reply, but shall transmit its contents to you as soon as received. In the meantime I would not delay stating to you all I had done in obedience to your desires, and how little stead our coadjutors and coadjutrixes have stood us in hitherto. These are the additional names transmitted to me : Viscount Hinchinbrooke, Bruton Street ; Earl of Fife, Whitehall ; Duke of Athol ; Duchess of Athol ; General Andrew Gordon ; Sir James Pulteney, Bruton Street ; Colonel Ramsay, Guards ; Mrs Morris, N. Audley Street. When the book comes out we will discover the single men's abodes, as they are mostly locomotive. Tell me when my hopes and impatience are likely to be gratified by a perusal of the interesting volume.

I conclude this illegible MS. with Health and fraternity ! and the re-iterated assurance of being faithfully, &c.

MARIA RIDDELL.

No. XVIII.

Richmond, 15th January, 1799.

That your letter of the 20th November has lain so long unanswered, one I wrote to Roscoe a week ago, which he probably mentioned to you, would very sufficiently, I trust, apologize, as well as account, for. I am still confined in " durance vile," but recovering fast and able to enjoy my own society again, and that of my friends ; but in good truth I was very near giving poor Burns an account *viva voce* of the progress of his affairs here below. If Dundas had not fairly overpersuaded me and my fever together, we should perhaps have been riding about the spheres on a comet's tail together at this moment, and I am sometimes half disposed to regret the good society I have so narrowly missed. . ... I wrote again to Fullarton lately for his list ; he is, I find, still in Scotland. I am very sorry he should have lost his great law-suit. If all Burns's subscribers approve as *aveuglément* of all your arrangements as I do, you will find few malcontents. Depend on my discretion as to any communication you may honor me with. I am (pardon and toleration !) all burning with impatience to see the volumes. One of the subscribers has this instant left me (and rendered this letter, by the way, too late for the post) who enquired anxiously after them of me : the Marquiss of Abercorn, he is an enthusiast about Burns. . . This must be a short letter, but let it convey the constant assurance to you of my sincere regard and how faithfully I am your obliged, &c.,

MARIA RIDDELL.

No. XIX.

Kew-road, Richmond, 9th April, 1799.

Many thanks, my dear Doctor, for your long and interesting letter and for your report of Percival's little treatise. ... The Committee for this Monument of our Bard's will not let me be quiet, though I not only declined promoting the subscription in *South Britain*, but conveyed (as well as a letter could do such an office) a very handsome trimming to the said Committee in particular, as well as to the Nation at large, for not feeling more jealous of their own reputation than to admit of, much less solicit, the assistance even of the Sister-country towards the erecting of a monument to a National Poet, in a Church Yard at Dumfries, too ! Do you not conceive Burns's Spirit must feel rather indignant at this ? Mine is, for him. Well ! they have just written again, to request I will fix on the artist who is to be applied to for a plan of the intended monument. I named Flaxman. But who the Committee consists of, besides my correspondent, Mr Sim^n. Mackenzie, I cannot divine, and was so dull as never to ask, indeed. I have perhaps a perverse *pressentiment* that it will be an ill-managed business, and that the artist's genius will not be allowed scope enough, *faute d'argent.* Cannot this people do a handsome thing once in a way ! Do you ever hear from Syme ? I have not for time immemorial, and I foresee (and therefore in a great degree rejoice in the long protraction of the publication) that as soon as Burns's book is completed, your " occupation o'er," and my *petit ministère* at the same time, your pen will become as obstinately silent as his, for your friend Smyth —whom I know you love passing well—says you are a sad Caitiff at epistolary correspondence ; so what may *I* expect ? I did write some songs, or rather I gave Burns some songs I had written (for I never found an obedient Muse at my command in my life) for some of the musical publications he patronized, but none have been published that I know of, at least as yet ; therefore I do not suppose you can have any use for them. If you chuse it I can send you (under a frank) one or two that Burns intended adapting to some Scots airs and giving to Thomson's Collection, but I know you will have no use for them, unless for your own private " crooning." —Believe me to be most faithfully, &c.,

MARIA RIDDELL.

P.S.—. . . When do you mean to return me Clarinda's letters and all the valuable MSS. you contrived to coax me out of ?

No. XX.

Richmond, 12th August, 1799.

Dear Doctor,—Believe me, I have reined in my impatience as long as I possibly could, but enquiries pour in upon me from all quarters which I am unable to satisfy. So favor me with one line, one single line, telling me in what state of forwardness this work of yours is. I hope on many accounts the publication will not be delayed beyond this autumn. I will not say more, as I feel (as a friend of Burns's) too deep a sense of the obligation you have laid us under to think we have a right to press upon your plans any further than suits your own convenience. . . . I desired Whishaw to take charge of those papers you have of mine, from which you have of course extracted all you wanted ere this. I wish I could have a peep at what is already published [? printed], but that cannot be, so I must just take patience. . —Yours truly,

MARIA RIDDELL.

No. XXI.

Richmond, 22nd September, 1799.

You are the most irritable Mortal I know any where ! You know my implicit and blind faith in your infallibility, my patience

and moderation, yet you pretend to " smile inwardly," and rail
outwardly, without considering that the very great eagerness of the
subscribers (I only expressed myself as their organ, and expressly
specified that to you) about this work is the highest compliment
that can be paid to the Editor, while it is yet in embrio at least.
I readily enter into all your vexations, interruptions, and annoy-
ances, but be reconciled, and consoled, and soothed, and calmed,
and modulated, and harmonised—what more shall I say !—in the
expectation of the meed that awaits you.   As to myself, acquit
me of the squeamish delicacy and egotism you allude to ; I have
asked you no selfish questions, and trusted to you to present me in
what form you pleased or leave me out altogether as you judged fit. . . .
All I did was to suppress my own letters, which was all fair, and no
loss to you or the public. . .   With regard to Cadell, &c., I went
yesterday to town purposely to call there, in compliance with
your orders.   The print by Beugo is detestable, not a shadow of
resemblance ; it would disgrace the work completely, and the
old one, indifferent as it is, is far preferable.   Cadell and Davies
agree perfectly with me that if you wish to make the Work complete the Original painting should be sent up to them (the expence
would be trifling, and it might be accomplished in a very short space
of time, if sent for and set about immediately) and the business
put into the hands of a London Artist.   If you object to this, stick
to the old plate ; the new one is worse a thousand times. . .
—Adieu ! Your faithful Disciple,

M. R.

No. XXII.

Kingston Hall Wimborne, Dorset,
28th December, 1799.

My   dear   Doctor,—Make   what   use   you   please   of   me   and
mine.   Those letters to Clarinda are rather fantastical, I believe,
being written under the immediate impression when enthusiasm
about " the archangel . . .," and all that related to him and his
excentricities [sic], was most prevalent in my mind.   I shall not
ask for a review, to correct them, as I would otherwise have done,
since you intend undertaking the office.   It must indeed be base
coin which your improving hand cannot amend so as at least to make
it pass comment.   I have dropped Clarinda's correspondence, which
was quite unnecessary when our aim was once accomplished—in
part at least.   Other circumstances I have since been apprized of,
or rather which have been hinted to me, render me unwilling to have
my correspondence with her noticed further than between Syme,
you, and myself.   So what you let the public participate in must

be as communications to yourself, if you chuse it, to person or persons
unknown, in short certainly not to Her, as her writing that intro-
ductory epistle to me which I believe you have in your custody,
and the romantic spirit that dictated it (which, I confess, I admired
extremely, especially from the frame of mind in which it found me)
not being previously communicated, my intercourse with a woman
so circumstanced might provoke a little good-natured criticism, and
is altogether unfit for the knowledge of the profane. I recollect
(it may seem an affectation, but it is true) not one sentence of the
contents of any of those letters, having retained no duplicates from
the copies I lent you ; but I am sure they contain nothing but facts
and probably some little interesting, but all I did or can recollect,
of that interview, to which I often recur in remembrance with
pleasure and with regret ! Burns said little or nothing about his
Wife to me latterly, but as I believe her conduct, subsequent to their
union by marriage, was exemplary towards him, so it is just to add
that he always spoke of her with a high tribute of respect and esteem.
He did not love her, but he was far from insensible to the indulgence
and patience, " the meekness with which she bore her faculties "
on many occasions very trying to the tempers of most individuals
of our sex. An illegitimate child of his, born after wedlock, who
had lost her mother,* was, I know, adopted by Mrs Burns, and is, I
believe, still an inmate of her house and no distinction shown between that and the rest of their children. This trait He told me
of with much sensibility. Of those " lighter letters and inconsiderate sallies " you allude to he seemed most anxious to procure
the assurance of an entire suppression. He talked to me of many
writings which would perhaps after his decease be usher'd into
light, with considerable apprehension and uneasiness. I have
no verses on the Bard's death but those formerly communicated to
you. I am sorry Roscoe has written another poem on that subject
—not that he has written another, but that the original stanzas
should be suppressed. They had much fire, much excellence. I
liked them extremely myself. . . .—*Vale!*

MARIA R——.

---

* From this, the inference is that Ann Park died shortly after
the birth of her child.

DUMFRIES BURNS CLUB CENTENARY CELEBRATION

THE Burns Club of Dumfries, founded on 18th January, 1820, celebrated its Centenary on Friday, 23rd January last, on the occasion of the Anniversary Dinner in memory of the Poet. These anniversary dinners have been in abeyance during the war, and it was a happy circumstance that their resumption in this year of Peace should have fallen in the year of the Centenary of the Club which inaugurated them, and which has, in that and other useful and signal ways, helped to keep the memory of our National Poet fresh and green in our midst. The Club dinner was eminently worthy of the occasion. Indeed, it will rank as probably the most successful Burns event that has ever taken place in the old burgh.

Mr R. A. GRIERSON, Town Clerk,
President, Dumfries Burns Club.

The company was large and representative, numbering about 160, and including not a few Dumfriesians of note and other distinguished guests. The speaking throughout the evening was on a remarkably high scale of excellence. The note was given by the quite unusually fine oration with which the able and popular President (Mr R. A. Grierson, town clerk) proposed " The Immortal Memory," and it was sustained to the full in such admirable speeches as those of Lord St. Vigeans, Sir Herbert Maxwell, Bart., Sir James Crichton-Browne, Dr MacKenna, Sir J. Lorne Macleod,

Sheriff Morton, Mr Joseph Laing Waugh, and Dr Neilson, each and all of whom, as well as other speakers we may be pardoned for not individualising, were at their best. From first to last there was not a tedious or uninteresting moment, and when, well into " the wee sma' 'oors," the company at length joined in singing " Auld Lang Syne," they did so with the unanimous feeling that the evening spent had been one of rare and unqualified edification and delight. A special tribute of thanks is due to the Hon. Secretary of the Club, Mr John M'Burnie, for his able and valued services.

The President wore the famous Burns Whistle, with which he regulated the proceedings. He explained that it had been very kindly sent for use that night from Craig- darroch, through their friend Mr Irving Edgar. It was very interesting to have it, and it would add a great deal to the fascination of the evening. In addition to her kindness in lending the whistle, Mrs Smith Cuninghame of Craigdarroch had also presented a photograph of the whistle to the Club.

Mr J. W. Whitelaw said :—

I have to tender our sincere thanks to Sir James Crichton- Browne for the able manner in which he has proposed the toast of the Dumfries Burns Club. He has alluded to the formation of the Club 100 years ago, and I would venture in reply to add to what Sir James has so well said a few remarks regarding those three gentlemen who were the original Office-bearers of the Club. They were Mr John Commelin, Mr John Syme, and Mr William Grierson. Mr Commelin was a native of the Stewartry, and was proprietor of King's Grange, in the Parish of Urr.. He was for a time in business as a writer in Kirkcudbright, but afterwards came to Dumfries, and ultimately became agent of the British Linen Bank here. He was a man of excellent literary taste and a good classical scholar. Mr William Grierson was a successful draper in Dumfries, and lived in Irish Street, where his son, the late Dr Grierson, of Thornhill, was born. He seems also to have been interested in agricultural matters, as he was tenant of the farm of Boatford, near Thornhill, and on retiring from business in Dumfries he went to reside at Grovehill, which is quite near Boatford. He was a Justice of the Peace for the County of Dumfries, and seems to have taken a somewhat prominent part in the public life of the town and district. It was Mr John Syme, however, who had most intimate relations with the Poet. He also was connected with the Stewartry, although not, I think, a native of it. His father was a successful Writer to the

Signet, and owned the property of Barncailzie, in the parish of Kirkpatrick - Durham. John Syme at first studied law, but gave that up and joined the Army, and ultimately took up farming at Barncailzie. Subsequently that property had to be sold on account of the failure of the Ayr Bank, in which his father was involved. John Syme then came to Dumfries and took up residence at Ryedale, when he became Distributor of Stamps for the district. His office was on the ground floor of the house near the foot of Bank Street—then known as the Wee Vennel—on the first floor of which Burns occupied] three or four rooms when he came to Dumfries from

Mr J. W. WHITELAW, Solicitor.

Ellisland. A great friendship sprang up between the two men, and Burns was very frequently at Ryedale ; it was with Syme that he made his famous tour through Galloway, and Mr Syme showed many acts of kindness to the Poet during his lifetime, and to his widow and family after his death. Mr Syme seems to have had very considerable literary ability, and there was at one time a question as to whether he should be the editor of the *Work and Life of Burns*, published after the Poet's death for the benefit of his widow and family, and which produced quite a considerable sum. In the end Dr Currie, of Liverpool, who was a Dumfriesshire boy, was chosen as editor, and Mr Syme was at very considerable trouble in collecting material for and in otherwise assisting Dr Currie, who was a personal friend of his own. Those three gentlemen to whom I have referred were the leaders of a coterie of Burns enthusiasts in Dumfries who, before the formation of the Club, used to meet every 25th of January and celebrate the Poet's birthday ; it was that coterie who initiated the movement which resulted in the building of the Mausoleum ; and at the dinner of 25th January, 1819, held in the Globe Inn, they resolved to purchase a punch bowl for use by the subscribers on similar occasions. I mention this fact as it was the nucleus out of which the Club sprang. The bowl was obtained from a well-known manufacturer of the time, Spode of Staffordshire, at a cost of £15, and was exhibited at a business meeting of the subscribers on 18th January, 1820 ; and at that meeting it was resolved to form the subscribers, whose names are given on the bowl, into a society to be called the Burns Club of Dumfries—(applause)—and Mr Commelin was appointed President, Mr Syme Vice-president, and Mr Grierson Secretary and Treasurer of the Society. At the dinner held a week later in the King's Arms Inn, the bowl was " han'selled," and it became a great feature of the annual dinner for many years. It still exists, though in a rather dilapidated condition, and I am glad to see it on the table to-night. Such was the origin of the Dumfries Burns Club, and it is well that we should have in our memories to-night the three gentlemen who acted as sponsers for us at our nativity. In addition to proposing this toast, Sir James has, with his well-known charm of phraseology, made a very valuable and interesting presentation on behalf of Sir James Dewar. This is of such importance that I think it warrants full official recognition, and as our Secretary is also to say a few words in reply, I leave him to deal with the matter. I think, Mr Secretary, I have kept within the time limit you set me, but if you will bear with me a minute longer I would also like to make a presentation to the Club, although on a much lower plane than the one I have just referred to. When Mr Syme's effects were distributed by public roup after his death, my father purchased at the sale a wooden toddy ladle, and the tradition at the time was that this ladle was frequently in use on the occasion of Burns's visits to Ryedale. Therefore it may possibly be a link with the Poet, and it undoubtedly is one with his friend, Mr John Syme, who was one of the authors of our existence. I beg that the Club will become custodiers of it, if they will condescend to accept so humble a gift. (Applause.) Long may the Dumfries Burns Club continue to flourish, to keep green the memory of the Bard, and to preserve that spirit of Scottish nationality of which he was the embodiment, and which, fused to a white heat by the fire of his immortal genius, shines through and illuminates his Works. (Loud applause.)

The Chairman, in calling upon Mr M'Burnie, referred to him as the " heart and marrow of Dumfries Burns Club." Mr M'Burnie said :—

Sir James Crichton-Browne has truly said that the fact of this gift (the snuff box presented to Burns by the Earl of Glencairn) being presented to us cannot remain hidden, and I am certain that our friends of the Press will see that Sir James Dewar's generosity to us is known from John o' Groats to Land's End, aye, and also in those Dominions beyond the seas where our National Poet's name and works are loved, honoured, and revered as warmly and as worthily as they are in the old town of Dumfries. (Applause.) The gift is doubly valuable to us in that it has come to us through one of our oldest surviving Vice-presidents, our illustrious towns-man, Sir James Crichton-Browne. (Applause.) Mr Whitelaw is one of ourselves, and his bringing with him some tangible token of his affection for the Club, of which he is now one of the oldest members, is only what we might expect. (Applause.) The article he has handed over to-night was the property of a gentleman who was not only one of the first mem- bers of our Club, but who was also one of the closest friends of the Poet during these last trying years in Dumfries. It therefore serves to remind us of both Burns and Syme, and so will prove an interesting addition to that collec- tion in the Burns House we are anxious to enrich. (Applause.) I

Mr JOHN M'BURNIE, Sheriff Clerk, Secretary, Dumfries Burns Club.

have now to hand over to the Club, on behalf of Mr James Craik, Dalgrange, Cambuslang, an old son of Dumfries, a bread basket said to have been the property of " Bonnie Jean," and an old banner which was carried in the procession on the occasion of the Dumfries Centenary celebrations in 1859. Mr Craik narrates that the bread basket was given by Jean Armour to an old woman who used to work for her, called Mary Burnie, and was given by the latter to a member of his own family. He states that his father had many times gone messages for " Bonnie Jean," as their houses were not far apart. The history of the banner he does not know quite so well, beyond the fact that it was some time in the Wilson family, one of the members of which, Alex. Wilson, cabman, died recently in Dumfries, and that it was carried in the 1859 procession. Some of you gentlemen may remember Mr Craik, as I myself recollect a brother who carried on business at the Pent House End. He wishes to present these gifts to us in name of his late mother, who resided at the Pent House End for over half a century. (Applause.)

You have before you to-night, I think, the first gift made to our Club, the portrait of Burns, painted by J. Gilfillan, miniature painter, who joined our Club in 1821 and who presented this portrait to the Club, along with a companion portrait of " Bonnie Jean," the following year. These portraits graced the dinner in 1822, and while only one of them is here to-night, it is accompanied by a replica of its companion, the original being now in the National Portrait Gallery in Edinburgh. How it came there is a story too long to tell to-night, but we are satisfied that in the replica before you, which was presented to the Club by Sir John Findlay, Edinburgh, in amicable settlement of a long standing dispute, we have secured a work of art well worthy of hanging in the place from which the original has been removed. (Hear, hear.) I should like to mention only one of those original members whose name is on the old punch bowl in addition to those brought under your notice by Mr Whitelaw, namely, Mr G. W. Boyd, W.S., a brother of the Mrs Maxwell of Gribton of that day. It had been long thought that the last survivor of our original members was the late Mr William Gordon, writer, father of Mr Henry Gordon, Sheriff Clerk, and Mr H. Sharpe Gordon of Glenæ, who both sometime held the office of Secretary of our Club, but I find a minute in Mr Henry Gordon's handwriting stating that at the time of his father's death he had discovered that Mr Boyd was then surviving, and resident at that time in the Isle of Man. I find that Mr Boyd survived until 1887, so that he was a member of this Club for no less than 67 years, and at the time of his death was not only our oldest member, but was also the oldest member of the W.S. Society, of which he had been a member for the long period of 71 years. Mr Whitelaw has mentioned the house in Bank Street, and it may therefore be fitting to read at this stage a communication dealing with this subject sent to me by Dr J. Maxwell Wood, Edinburgh, a former President of the Club, with a request that I should bring it before you in the course of our proceedings to-night. His letter is addressed to the Chairman and members of the Dumfries Burns Club at the Centenary celebrations, 1920, and is as follows :—

" May I, as a life member, be privileged to express the deep pleasure I feel at the very immediate prospect of the Dumfries Burns Club attaining its centenary ? Much water has flowed underneath Devorgilla's bridge since the 18th January, 1820, when the Club came into existence, which, expressed as a century of consistent and useful existence, must give us pause. And now the question arises—at least for those of us not in immediate touch— of how this happy completion of years is to be notched in the post of practical appreciation. For myself, it has been a cherished thought for many years that some day, not alone would the house where the Poet died have its doors thrown wide to the Burns Pilgrim, but also that the house in Bank Street, where the Bard dwelt on retiring from Ellisland, would come to be an additional shrine in Dumfries for his devotees. In a word, is it not possible for the Dumfries Burns Club to acquire possession of the Bank Street House, restore it as far as possible to the semblance of its original condition, and so preserve and throw open to the public an important landmark of the Dumfries period of Burns's life ? A further elaboration of the scheme might be the restoration of Syme's tax office below, which could be utilised as a repository for such things as would appeal to the visitor, much as the ' Old Edinburgh ' bookseller's shop at the base of John Knox's house here. It may be, however, that other plans have been made, or that great difficulties are in the way. Nevertheless, I take this unique opportunity of making the suggestion.''

I hold in my hand the original minute book of the Club, which contains most interesting information, but time forbids us going into it at any length to-night. One is, however, impressed with the care with which the then secretary recorded that '' the company was highly respectable,'' all the more that he concludes his report of several of those early dinners with the note, '' three of the Club glasses were broken at the dinner table.'' (Laughter.) Gentlemen, I think we may feel quite entitled to class ourselves under the description given by that secretary of his company. It is interesting to recall that one of those present at the Club dinner in 1822 was James Hogg, the '' Ettrick Shepherd,'' who was then an honorary member of the Club, and that on that occasion he was one of the singers who entertained the company. At that same dinner there were admitted as honorary members rather a famous group, and it might not be amiss to give their names—Robert, William, and James Glencairn Burns, sons of the Poet ; Sir Walter Scott, Thomas Moore, Thomas Campbell, James Montgomery, Allan Cunningham, George Thomson, General Dirom of Mount Annan, W. R. Keith Douglas, M.P., and Professor Wm. Tennant, Dollar. Before sitting down I might mention two other recent gifts to the Club, those made by Sir J. M. Barrie when he purchased for a hand-some figure the items on exhibition in the Burns House which had belonged to the late Provost James Lennox, and by our good friend and fellow-member, Walter Scott, of New York, who purchased also for a very considerable sum and again restored to our custody the MSS. connected with the Dumfries Centenary celebrations in 1896, and who never forgets to send us a greeting as each Christmas and Anniversary day comes round. These have already been fully brought to your notice, but as this is our first dinner since they were received, I may be pardoned for recalling them to your memory on this historic anniversary. Gentlemen, I ask you to accord your

hearty thanks to the donors of the valuable and interesting gifts
by which the Club has to-night been enriched, and I shall thereafter
endeavour to convey your appreciation to them in suitable form.
(Loud applause.)

[We regret that the pressure on our limited space renders it
impossible to give a full report of the excellent and most interesting
speeches delivered on the occasion, which will be found in the
Dumfries Courier and Herald, 28th January, 1920.]

THE POET'S INSIGHT.

There runs a legend in Dumfries
  Of two men trav'ling Nithsdale side
Who fain would view the tragic place
  Where Coila's minstrel died.

They found the Mill Brae,* now, I ween,
  The best known street in that old town,
And, from a casement, widowed Jean
  Herself was looking down.

They thought her ruddy, care-lined face
  The plainest they had ever seen ;
' Is this,'' said one, with lack of grace,
  '' Our Burns's Bonnie Jean ?''

Jean overheard the idle word,
  And for the moment winced, but tholed,
Nor showed a sign that she had heard—
  So brave and kindly-souled.

She brought them up the narrow stair
  To shrine by foot of Genius trod,
But in the temple small and bare
  They glimpsed nor Pan nor God.

They peeped into the little place—
  The smallest in that tenement—
Where Burns had penned his choicest lays,
  When life was almost spent.

They viewed the treasures of the room,
  But failed, I doubt me, to divine
Either the glory or the gloom
  That made the place a shrine.

Yet still it seemed a wondrous thing
  That here the Muses should engage,
Or that a bird should blythely sing
  In such a narrow cage.

* Afterwards called Burns Street.

Said one—the one who spoke before—
  Not thinking that he turned the dart
He threw unwitting by the door,
  Through Jean's nigh-broken heart :

" I never yet have understood,
  When life went aye from bad to worse,
What moved Burns to poetic mood,
  And write such splendid verse !"

Quick answered Jean : " The thing to me,
  Who knew him best, is no surprise ;
Those who the heavenly vision see
  Are born with poet's eyes.

" The simplest flower within his ken
  The Poet's glowing tribute earns,
We'd see the god in common men
  Had we the eyes of Burns.

" Rab's mind was clear as cloudless sky,
  Love's heart of gold by him was seen,
And to the last his wife was aye
  His bonnie, bonnie Jean !"

The men stood there with heads inclined—
  Jean's frank rebuke left nought to say—
And, with their lesson borne in mind,
  Forthwith they went their way.

JAMES BROWN.

Greenock.

REVIEWS.

"Tam o' Shanter and the Merry Masons." By William Harvey. (F. M. Sparks, Peter Street, Dundee.)

This is a mirth-provoking piece of rollicking rhyme, in which Mr Harvey presents the redoubted Tam as a candidate for the " light " which shines only in the mysterious caves of the Masonic Ceremonial—in fact, its humour cannot be fully enjoyed by the uninitiated, which supplies a good reason for every Mason being in possession of a copy at the modest threepennybit asked for it. How Tam was "made" a mason, with Burns as one of his "makers," the reader must find out for himself by purchasing Mr Harvey's *brochure*. At the crucial point of initiation, we are told, Tam proved himself a formidable rival to his old acquaintance, "Cutty Sark." After all, the *dramatis personœ* are spooks, a race of spiritual beings regarding whose cantrips there is at the present moment a revival of interest among the curious.

Mr A. A. Craig, Secretary of the Burns Club of Atlanta, Ga., has forwarded to us a small book containing 13 pieces, all in praise of Burns, which seem to have been read to the Atlanta Club at successive Anniversary meetings. Every one of these compositions reach a high point of poetic excellence, and the Atlanta Club are to be congratulated on the possession of a poet laureate of such quality as Mr Hubner. The book bears on its title page, " For Love of Burns : Poems by Charles William Hubner," and facing the title is a photograph of a building (an exact reproduction of the Cottage at Alloway) which, we are informed, is " The Burns Club Cottage, Atlanta." As a specimen of Mr Hubner's powers, and the robust commonsense which characterises all the pieces, we quote two stanzas from his " O ! Robert Burns, we miss you not "—

" But all that Death could take of you,
　　Was but your mortal part—
Have we not still your spirit, Burns ?
　　Have we not still your heart ?

This part of you, your dust, he hid
　　Beneath your native sod,
But we will keep the best of you,
　　That came direct from God,"

THE POET'S GENEALOGY.

St. James's, S.W.1,
12th October, 1920.

DEAR SIR,—I enclose, as promised, a Chart of the descendants of Adam Burnes, Notary Public at Montrose, brother of the James and Alexander Burnes who distinguished themselves in India. The bulk of the particulars were sent to me by Adam William Gray Burnes in 1910, and in the same year supplemented by James Henry Napier Anderson Burnes, who was over here in the same year with his wife and daughter. They visited Mrs M'Kay at Londonderry, and generally took stock of the places in the United Kingdom in which they were interested. His death took place some four years later, as you will see from an extract from a New Zealand paper which I enclose. He had not been over here, so he told me, for 32 years. It is pleasing to note that he and his brothers, like others of their race, seem to have attained to positions of responsibility and trust. From the names on the Chart it may also be fairly assumed that individually they show a resolve to perpetuate a strain unmixed with any alien blood !

I hope to hear before the end of the year from Alexander Plunkett Burnes as to any births, marriages, or deaths since 1910. If his eldest brother is dead, the son of the late J. H. N. A. Burnes, viz., Adam-Allan Burnes, is probably the head of the branch—the senior—springing from Provost James Burnes.

In regard to the Broun family, I fear I did not make myself clear. I have the original marriage contract between one Samuel Broun and Agnes Logie. It is dated 23rd October, 1713. It appears to have been thought—from notes made by my grandfather—that these were the grand or great-grand parents of the Poet's mother. If, however, Dr Charles Rogers is accurate [he is often inaccurate in the extreme] this is not the case. It may be a great-grand uncle of the Poet's mother who is one of the contracting parties. Dr Chas. Rogers supports his researches in this particular direction by references to Parochial Registers, so that I am not so inclined to question his accuracy as I am in other directions.

As to The New Psalmody MS., I find that it was published in the Scott Douglas edition, and also in the Gibbie edition (America), 6 vols. ; so that there would not be any point in my copying the original MS.

May I suggest that it would surely be worth while to give a little more publicity to the Annual Burns Chronicle. There would seem to be many in the Colonies who would subscribe. Not a few of the stock, and those nearly and distantly connected, would subscribe, who would not see any object in joining the Federation, but who might, through the Chronicle, easily be led to do so.

I hope the enclosed will be of interest. Some there will be in Montrose still left who remember Adam Burnes, the Notary-Public.—I am, Yours truly,   K. G. BURNS.

John BROUN = Isobe Greg.

Walter BURNES = of Mergie and Bogiorgan. ob. Nov. 1670. Will pd. Brechin.

John BROUN = Janet

John BROUN = ...

William BURNES=Christian Fotheringham. of Bogiorgan. ob. 1715. Sep. Glenbervie.

Robert of Benholm

John, Colonell a.p. (1690) ix. 166.

James BURNES = of Bralinmuir. ob. 23 Jan., 1743, æt. 87. Sep. Genbervie.

Margaret Falconer. ob. 28 Dec, 1749, æt. 90

David

Jean

William BURNES = Elspeth Taylo of Bogiorgan.

Gilbert BROUN=Agnes Rennie.

Robert BURNES = Isabella, dau. of Alxr. Keith o Criggie, Dunottar. b. ante 1690.

1757

Willam BURNES=Ag

. James Armour=Mary Smith.

William BURNES=Helen Thomson, of Bogiorgan, ob. 1779, dau of 1784, æt. 65. Wm. T. of Drumlithie.

Robert BURNES = Margaret Grub, d. at Bervie, circa 1795. 1745

George. Robert BURNES=.....
ob. inf.

4 s. 2 s.

eld. s.

Jean = ROBERT BURN(E)S Poe Descendants at Cheltenham, Eastbourne, and in B. Columbia and Vancouver.

Fanny BURNES=Adam. Descendants

=Anne Greig, dau. of John Greig; ob. Feb., 1796. Sep. Montrose.

James BURNES Notary-Public. b. Montrose. Dec. 1750 ; ob. Ju. 1837. Sep. Montrose.

2nd s.

John BURNES = Margaret Davidson b. 1771 ; d 1826. Author of "Thrummy Cap," and severa p ays.

James BURNES 1745 b. 1717 ; d. July 1761, at Montrose. Town Councillor.

eld. s.

David BURNES=Jean M'Bean. 2nd survg. s.

Thomas=? bapt. 30 July, 1783, Montrose.

Gilbert BURNES=Jean Breckenridge b. 28 Sep., 1760. dau. of James B. His 3rd son, by his wife Thomas Burns, Janet. dau. of D.D., settled at John Aird, Otago and whose 2nd Dunedin, N.Z., husb. was Da. leaving many Sillar, related to descendants. Sir Ja. Shaw, Ld., Mayor of London.

1791.

Isabella = J

Numerous descendants

B Sec. 1.

B.

CHART of the Senior surviving linea MALE (for the most part Descendants o JAMES BURNES, Provost Montrose, in Scotland, together with some collaterals. (*Vide Records*, Lyon Office, Edinburgh; College Arms, London; Dr James Buraes on *Notes on his Name and Family*; Dr Charles Rogers' *Name nd Fam of Robert Burns*; various issues o the *Burns Chronicle*; Burke's *Gentry*, under DAYMAN, 1906 ed *Armor Families* 5th ed.).

Compiled by K. G. BURNS, great-grandson o Gilbert Burns the Poet's brother.

22nd Ap., 1800.

s. James BURNES = Elizabeth, 6th dau. J.P., Provost of of Adam Glegg, Montrose, Chf. Magistrate b. Ap. 1, 1780, of Montrose. d. Montrose; 25th Feb., 1851, d. Brunton Place, æt. 71. Sep. Edinboro, 15th Dairy Cemetery. Feb 1852, æt. 72.

3rd Sep., 1827. | 2 s. 18th Ju., 1838. 2 w.

1 w. Horatia Gordon = Adam BURNES = Isabella Scott, dau. d. 2nd Nov., Notary-Public, of Wm. Scott. 1834 æt. 28. Montrose. b. 19th Feb., 1802; d. 15th Nov., 1872.

28th Mar., 1829. 1 w.

| eld. | s. James BURNES = Sophia, 2nd dau. Knt., LL.D., of Maj.-Gen. Sir F.R.S., J.P., Geo. Holmes, Physician- K.B.C., by his General, Bom- wife, Dame bay Army. b. Sophia Hamilton, Montrose, 12th d. 19th Mar., Feb., 1801; d. 1855, Kensing- at Manchester, ton. 19th Sep, 1862. Sep. Che tenham. 2 w. = Esther Price. d. 27th Aug., 1904, s.p., at Kensington.

6 daughters (4 married).

Young.

Seven sons — all died un- married. Two daughters — both died young.

eld. son. Wellington, N.Z.

Adam BURNES = MaryJane Hatton, b. Montrose, b. Atherstone, 12th Ju., 1832. Warwick; d. Fndr. f (Aus- 29th July, 1884. tralia) Oriental Banking Co. (1st Bank estd. in Colony) Gen. Man. and Insp Nat. Bank, N.Z d. at Sydney N.S.W 9th Ju 1876

son. Alexander Horatio = Mary Jane Harris. BURNES, d. Mar 1910 b. Montrose, 19th Oct., 1834. d. at Hawera, N.Z., 13th July, 1906.

6 sons, 1 dau.

3 | s. Alexander BURNES Sir, Lt.-Col., C.B., F.R.S. b. 16th May, 1805; fell at Cabool, 2nd Nov., 1841. innupt.

Charlotte BURNES. d. at Twicken- ham, 190—, innupt.

4 | s. 20th Oct, 1838. David BURNES = Harlet M.D., R.N., b. Anderson 6th Sep., 1806; d. at Montrose, 2nd Feb., 18 9.

James Anderson BURNES = E Banker at Calcutta. b. 30th Jan., 1845.

14th Dec., 187

16th May, 1866.

1. Anne Eliza Glegg = John Smythe BURNES, M'Kay, of Troy b. Montrose, Hall, London- 15th Sep, 1842, derry; d. 1911. still (1920 living.

2 JAMES BURNES. b. 24th May, 1844 d. 30th

Mary Violet B

Ch L ba fe 2 ir

A.

6 sons, 1 dau.

1. A lam William Gay BURNES; b. We . ign, N.Z., 18th September, 1859. Res at Oamara, N.Z., District Manager Gern ment Life Insurance Department. Md Florence Susette (only daughter of the ate William Tilley), b. at St. Kilda, Mel bourne, W. on 11th na, 1859.

2. Jaes Henry Napier Anderson BURNES; b. Sydney, N.S.W., on 4th My, . Local Mer (Wellington) N.Z. Shipping Co., Married Margaret Jessie Jane, eldest daughter of Hugh M'Neil, of an, N.Z.; b. 9th September, 68, at Me bourne, with issue one son and two daughters. Died at Wellington, N.Z., 19th My, 1914 (Buried Taita 53.
  1. Met Hatton BURNES; b. 18th February, 1892, at Het Church, N.Z.
  2. dam Am BURNES; b. 11th January, 96, at Christ 6th, N.Z.
  3. Ma Eve BURNES; b. 26th May, 1904, at Wellington, N.Z.; died the 29th

3. Alexander Plunkett BURNES: b. "Glenbervie," Me, 8th Mr, 1862. Superintendent , at Life Insurance Department, Mn, N.Z. Md in June 98, M Mary, daughter of J hn Mn; b. Dunedin, N.Z 68, and has issue two sons :—
  1. Alexander J hn BURNES b. 22nd February, 1904.
  2. Robert Hatton BURNES; b. 9th Gr, 108.

4. Ernest Loughnan BURNES; b. "Glenbervie," St. Kilda, Mbourne, 30th August, 63. Assistant-Superintendent Mutua Life and Mr Association, Wellington, N.Z. Md Martha. Mt, daughter of James Reig M'Kerrow b. 5th August, 186 and has issue three sons and one daughter :—
  1. Adam John BURNES; b. Wellington, N.Z., 6th Oer, 09.
  2. William Ernest BNES; b. Wigton, N.Z., 29th Mr, 09.
  3. Jeanie Madeline BURNES; b. 10th February, 1909.
  4. J hn M'Kerrow BURNES; b. 3rd November, 10.

5. George Son BURNES; b. "Glenbervie," St. Kilda, Melbourne, 11th July, 1866. Res at Secretary Australian Ma Po-vident Society, Invercargill, N.Z. Married in April, 99, Anna Mary, daughter of Henry ' Mh, of Invercargill, N.Z., and has issue one daughter:—
  1. Ma Hatton Shea Lalor M'Culloch BURNES b. 6th My, 09, at Ellisland, Invercargill, N.Z.

1. Mary Ethel BURNES ("Mal"); b. "Glenbervie," St. Kilda, 28th May, 1868, residing at Ab, Christ 6th, M. Married 9th Mr, 186, Henry Hamilton LOUGHNAN (2nd son of the late Robert Jnes Loughnan, H.E.I.C.S Bengal Barrister and Solicitor, and has issue two sons and two daughters :
  1. Augustine Real Bede Burnes LOUGHNAN; b. 24th October, 98, at Christ 6th, N.Z.
  2. Anthony ele Barat LOUGHNAN; b. 10th June, 1902, at Christ 6th, N.Z.
  3. Halmai My Violet whan; b. 15th ust, 906, at Christ h, N.Z.
  4. nlies Anthea Hatton Loughnan; b. 3rd Mr, 1908, at Christ ha, N.Z.

6. Doug as Inglis Scott BURNES; b. 2nd April, 18, at the at, Mse Scotland. Living in Vancouver British Co ha, or na in ! 0.

124

EXTRACT FROM AN OBITUARY NOTICE IN THE WELLINGTON NEW
ZEALAND *Evening Post*, 20th May, 1914.

" Mr J. H. N. A. Burnes, Manager of the New Zealand Shipping
Company at Wellington, passed away suddenly at the Wellington
Club yesterday evening.   Shortly before 7 o'clock he was taken
ill, and immediate aid was rendered, but he died half-an-hour later.
Dr Cahill was called in, but could only state that life was extinct.
Mr Burnes had been suffering from heart complaint for a considerable
time, and his death was not unexpected.   The late Mr Burnes was
a son of Mr Adam Burnes, who was a native of Montrose, Scotland.

Mr J. H. N. A. Burnes had been in the service of the N.Z. Shipping
Co. for thirty-six years.   He joined the Wellington Office as a
youth, and was afterwards stationed for several years at Dunedin.
He then became chief clerk in the Company's head office at Christ
Church, and some sixteen years ago·was promoted to the position
of Manager in Wellington.   In his younger days he was a prominent
footballer, and played for the Athletic Club, and represented Wellington Province in the 'seventies.   Some three years ago he took a
trip to England, but after his return he spent some six months in
hospital, and had not since then enjoyed good health.

The late Mr Burnes is survived by a widow and a son and
daughter.

The remains will be interred to-morrow afternoon in the Taita
Cemetery, alongside those of a daughter who died a few years ago.

General regret is expressed in shipping circles at Mr Burnes's
death, and the flags on the various offices and vessels in port were
flown at half-mast to-day as a mark of respect."

CLUB NOTES

[*COMMUNICATED.*]

THE LONDON ROBERT BURNS CLUB.

VERNACULAR CIRCLE NOTES.

The enthusiasm with which the formation of a Vernacular Circle has been welcomed, not only by the members of the London Robert Burns Club, but by many outside, and by the Scottish Press, gives the Committee of the Circle great encouragement to proceed with its work.

The Syllabus prepared by the Committee and incorporated in the programme of the work of the Club for the season 1920-21 includes several items that will give some index of the more public work of the Circle, but this, it must be understood, is only one part of that work.

The Circle has had the good fortune to enlist the sympathy and active service of two men who have done much to foster the use of the Scottish vernacular, Colonel John Buchan, and Dr W. A. Craigie, M.A., LL.D., Professor of English Literature at Oxford University. Professor Craigie has delved deeply into the subject, and his lecture on " The Present State of the Scottish Tongue " will in all probability provide good reasons for the existence of the Circle.

Colonel John Buchan, whose work in vernacular prose and poetry is fine idiomatic Scots, was the first to urge upon us the advisability of making the fostering of the decaying Doric part of the Club's active work. He has been a great friend to the Club, and has willingly given of his valuable time to assist us. A literary treat is in store for members when Colonel Buchan addresses us on the 7th February.

" The Lowland Tongue in Scottish Song," by Mr Garioch Whyte, " The Vernacular Language of Scotland as revealed in Scottish Proverbs," by Mr Spence Leslie, and " Expressive Scottish Words " from many districts (Mr John Anderson leading off with Border words, and Mr M'Farlane with Perthshire words) are all subjects well calculated to bring out the beauty and strength of the Scottish language and its accents.

On the 11th April Mr John Douglas, F.S.A.(Scot.), will compare the Ancient and Modern Vernacular Poets of Scotland, and we shall hear from Mr Douglas wherein poets such as Barbour,

Dunbar, and Douglas differ from Burns, Ramsay, Fergusson, and the men and women who since that great trio lived have kept alive the flame of Scottish poetry.

It is hardly necessary to urge upon members of the Club the desirability of attending regularly to hear papers, lectures, &c., and bringing interested friends with them. The object of the Circle is to make the appeal as wide as possible to Scotsmen and philologists in London ; and the appeal which the Circle is making will fail unless those who love the Auld Scots tongue give this work their active support.

All communications regarding the Vernacular Circle should be sent to Secretary of the Circle, P. N. M'Farlane, Graphic Buildings, Tallis Street, E.C.4. Telephone No., Central 7070.

SOCIAL CIRCLE NOTES.

By the kindness of the President, Mr L. G. Sloan, and Mrs Sloan, you are invited to a Social Evening at 42 Redington Road, Hampstead, N.W.3, on Monday, 8th November, 1920, from 7.30 until 10. This invitation includes your goodwife, or a member of your family. If you would like to bring more than one with you, you are expected to communicate with the Secretary of the Social Committee.

Mr Sloan's message is " come if you can, when you can," but the above-mentioned Secretary makes bold to suggest (for the convenience of Mrs Sloan) that you let him know as soon as you can whether you probably will, and whether in the singular or in the plural.

As the principal object of this gathering is to afford members an opportunity of becoming better acquainted, the evening will be a free and easy one, and you are just to come as you are. There will be some music, so if you can sing a song or play a tune come prepared. If there isn't time for your contribution you will understand that it's only because the trains don't run all night.

Redington Road runs from Frognal to West Heath Road. You can get there by the Hampstead Tube to Hampstead Station or by Metropolitan to Finchley Road Station. If you take a 'bus, alight at Avenue Mansions and proceed up Heath Drive opposite. No. 2 runs *via* Ebury Bridge, Wilton Road, Victoria, Grosvenor Place, Park Lane, Marble Arch, Oxford Street, and Finchley Road, and Nos. 13, 13a, and 13b run *via* Cannon Street, Fleet Street, Charing Cross, Regent Street, Oxford Street, and Finchley Road.

The above information may prove useful later on, so you needn't scrap it just because you can't turn up on 8th November.

The President and Vice-president are anxious to re-develop the Social side of the Club this winter, and to this end the Social

Committee has been formed and is now getting busy. There isn't time for as many Dances and Whist Drives as some of our esteemed Past Presidents would like, and suitable accommodation is not easy to obtain, but the Social Committee, if given sufficient encouragement this winter, will endeavour to supply your needs more amply in 1921-22. Meantime suggestions will be welcomed.

All communications regarding Social Meetings, Dances, or Whist Drives should be sent to the Secretary of the Social Committee, Mr T. J. Wilson, 59 and 60 Old Bailey, E.C.4. (Telephone No.— Central 10160).

GENERAL.—With these notes a list of fixtures for the Winter Session 1920-21 is enclosed, and a notice regarding the Scottish Festival Service on Sunday, 28th November.

HALLOWE'EN DINNER.—There are still some members who have not sent in their application for tickets. In order that proper arrangements may be made for everyone's comfort, please let me know your requirements by return.

IMPORTANT.—The Dinner will be held in the King's Hall, Holborn Restaurant, entrance in Newton Street.

PROGRAMME OF THE VERNACULAR AND SOCIAL CIRCLES, 1920-1921.

1920.

Nov. 8. Social Evening : President's House, at 7.30 p.m.

Nov 22. Vernacular Circle—" The Preservation of the Scottish Vernacular " : Royal Scottish Corporation, Crane Court, Fleet Street, E.C., at 7 p.m.—Mr William Will.

Dec. 6. Cinderella Dance : Wharncliffe Rooms, Hotel Great Central, at 7.30 p.m.

Dec. 13. Vernacular Circle—a. " The Lowland Tongue in Scottish Song "—Mr J. Garioch Whyte ; b. " The Vernacular Language of Scotland, as revealed in Scottish Proverbs " —Mr J. Spence Leslie. Royal Scottish Corporation, at 7 p.m.

1921.

Jan. 10. Vernacular Circle—" The Present State of the Scottish Tongue " : Royal Scottish Corporation, at 7 p.m.— —Prof. W. A. Craigie, M.A., LL.D.

Jan. 25. Birthday Festival : Holborn Restaurant.

Feb. 7. Lecture : Place to be announced later, at 7 p.m.—Col. John Buchan.

Feb. 14. Cinderella Dance : Wharncliffe Rooms, Hotel Great Central, at 7.30 p.m.

Mar. 7. Vernacular Circle—" Expressive Local Words, with Co-relatives in other Districts." Border—Mr John A. Anderson ; Perthshire—Mr P. N. M'Farlane ; Aberdeenshire—Mr W. A. Mutch, M.A. President's House, at 7 p.m.

Mar. 14. Whist Drive : Slater's Restaurant, 192 Oxford Street, W.

April 11. Vernacular Circle—" Old and New Vernacular Poets of Scotland "—Mr John Douglas, F.S.A. (Scot.). Royal Scottish Corporation, at 7 p.m.

April 25. Social Evening : President's House.

Social Circle Secretary : Mr T. J. Wilson, 59 and 60 Old Bailey, E.C.4. (Central 10160).

Vernacular Circle Secretary : Mr P. N. M'Farlane, " Graphic " Buildings, Tallis Street, E.C.4. (Central 7070).

17th ANNUAL SCOTTISH FESTIVAL SERVICE.

The above Service will be held in St. Columba's on Sunday, 28th November, being the Sunday nearest to St. Andrew's Day, at 3.15 p.m. It is a National Celebration, affording an opportunity for the Members of the various Scottish Organisations in London to meet together once a year for common worship.

The sermon will be preached by the gallant French liaison officer, whose eloquence so thrilled last General Assembly—the Rev. Lieut. L. de Saint André, D.S.O., of the French Protestant Church, Tours.

M. de Saint André—whose name itself is a liaison with Scotland and our St. Andrew's Day celebration—was through the whole war as Liasion Officer between the French and British Armies, and as such was present at nearly every big action fought by our troops up to April, 1918.

As in previous years, the Collection will be on behalf of the two great London Scottish Charities, the Royal Scottish Corporation and the Royal Caledonian Schools.

The doors will be open at 2.30, and admission will be by ticket only until 3 o'clock, after which hour no seats will be kept.

Tickets required by members may be obtained from the Secretary of their own organisation, by filling in and sending him the attached form, and an early application for them is requested. No application will be entertained after 12th November.

It is earnestly hoped that members who apply for tickets will make a point of using them, otherwise they leave vacant places in Church, and prevent others who desire to attend the Service from doing so.

Where members belong to more than one organisation, it is particularly requested that application for tickets be made through one only.

A plan of the district near the Church will be printed on the back of the tickets.

P. N. M'FARLANE, *Hon. Secretary.*

SUNDERLAND BURNS CLUB.

REPORT.

In submitting the Annual Report of the work of our Burns Club for the past year we have pleasure in reporting continued progress. We have been able to return to our regular headquarters —the Palatine Hotel—and our meetings have been held as in pre-war days.

The meetings have been most interesting and encouraging, and it is very gratifying to the Officers of the Club that they have been so ably supported. May this friendly fellowship and spirit be cultivated and extended so that we may make our Club life and influence worthy of the " Land of the Mountain and the Flood, Bonnie, Bonnie Scotland."

ANNUAL MEETING.

The Annual Meeting of last year was held in the Palatine Hotel, and a most interesting gathering it proved to be. In compliment to the retiring President, Neil Cameron, the members of the Pipe Band assembled at their practice room in full uniform and marched to the meeting. It was announced that the services of the Band had been placed at the disposal of the Committee having charge of the local Peace Celebration.

ANNIVERSARY CELEBRATION.

The Anniversary Dinner was held on Saturday, 24th January, 1920, when over one hundred members and friends met to celebrate the one hundred and sixty-first anniversary of our Poet's birth.

The President of the Club, Dr A. Stevenson, presided, and was supported by our Hon. Vice-president, Professor Sir Thomas Oliver, Newcastle, together with the past Presidents. The duties of croupier were ably carried out by Vice-president A. R. Calvert. In submitting the toast of the " Immortal Memory," Sir Thomas paid a tribute to the Poet of Mankind, dealing with his songs, his humour and satire in a way which was most enjoyable. It may be interesting to note that Sir Thomas favoured us in a similar capacity in 1899, and on this occasion his fine oration was delivered with as much vigour as of yore. Messrs G. and W. Hynds carried the Haggis round the table preceded by four stalwart pipers, while the " Grace " was given in fine style by Mr MacLennan.

" Chronicle."

For the first time in our history we were unable to secure our usual supply of this important publication for the members of our Club. In the first place I may have been a little later than usual in sending forward our order, and for this I humbly apologise, and in the second place the demand was such that within three days of issue the complete edition was sold out. This is another proof—if such is needed—of the value of this work. Through the courtesy of the Federation Secretary, Mr Thomas Amos, M.A., we were able to procure one copy for our Club Library, thus keeping our set complete and at the same time affording our members an opportunity of perusing it. We are very conscious that the success of this publication is due to the work of the Editor and President of the Federation, D. M'Naught, J.P.

Pipe Band.

The work of the Pipe Band has been continued under the guidance of Pipe-Major Graham. The Band appeared at the Royal Infirmary Fête on Wednesday, 18th June, 1919, and rendered a fine selection of music and dancing. On Saturday, 5th July, 1919, the Band appeared at the Peace Celebration Sports held in the Roker Park Football Ground. The chief event of the year, however, was the Town's Peace Celebration Pageant which was held on Saturday, 19th July, 1919. This proved to be a most imposing spectacle, and being favoured with ideal sunshine, was viewed by huge crowds along the line of route. Our Band led the Scottish section, and a fine impression was made by their smart appearance and splendid piping. They also took part in the celebrations at South Hetton, in addition to appearing at the opening football match at Roker Park, when Aston Villa were the visitors, and at the replayed English Cup Tie, when Burnley were the visitors, and on each occasion the home team were victorious. We are indebted to Mr Donald Gordon for the valuable assistance rendered to the young pipers by teaching them the Highland reels, &c.

In Memoriam.

We have to record the loss of a Past President of the Club during the year by the death of the late Mr W. P. Eastwood, which took place in Edinburgh Royal Infirmary, on 11th September, 1919. He occupied the President's chair in 1912 with much acceptance, was most regular in his attendance at our gatherings, and took a keen interest in all our work. We shall be the poorer by his passing hence. The sympathy of the Club was conveyed to the sorrowing widow.

MEMBERSHIP.

We commenced the session with seventy-one members. During the year we have lost one by death, two have removed from the district, twelve new members have been added. This shows a nett gain of nine and leaves us with eighty active members at the close of the year. We have again been favoured with a fine series of papers, and an interesting feature has been those contributed on " My Native Town." These have proved interesting and inspiring, and we express the hope that they may be continued.

The first St. Andrew's Celebration of the Club was held in the Palatine Hotel, on Wednesday, 26th November, 1919, and took the form of a Social and Musical evening. Dr A. Stevenson presided over a company of one hundred ladies and gentlemen and extended to them a hearty welcome. The Pipe Band gave some excellent selections, while Mr Donald Gordon delighted the company with his excellent Highland dancing. The thanks of the members were duly conveyed to Mr Calvert for his work in the interests of the Club.

SYLLABUS.

1919.

Oct. 8. President's Address—Dr A. Stevenson.
Oct. 22. Musical Evening—Members.
Nov. 12. " Wit and Humour "—Mr H. J. Menzies.
Nov. 26. St. Andrew's Celebration—Ladies' Night.
Dec. 10. " Robert Fergusson "—Mr M. MacLennan.

1920.

Jan. 14. " Sir Walter Scott "—Mr W. M. Donaldson,
Jan. 24. " Immortal Memory "—Sir Thomas Oliver.
Feb. 11. Musical Evening—Members.
Feb. 25. " A Parable "—Mr Stanley Alder.
Mar. 10. " Kilmarnock "—Mr A. W. Semple.
Mar. 24. " Tobermory and the Sound of Mull"—Mr Neil Cameron.
April 14. " Aberdeen, the Silver City "—Mr Geo. MacKay.
May 12. Annual Meeting—Election of Officers.
Sept. 8. Business Meeting.

Our thanks are specially due to Mr Stanley Alder, for his work during the year as accompanist, a work which he has willingly and faithfully carried out to the entire satisfaction of all concerned.

We are indebted to Mr T. E. A. A. Shaw for his gift of two framed pictures of Tam o' Shanter and Souter Johnnie for the Club Room, to the contributors of the excellent papers submitted, to the music provided by singers and musicians, to those who have attended to our creature comforts throughout the year, and may we assure them all we appreciate their efforts. May we all go forward into another year's work resolved to make it better and brighter than any that has gone before it, so that we may make our Club life an influence for good in this town.

M. NEILSON, Hon. Secretary.

ALBANY BURNS CLUB.

The 1919-20 session of this Club was an excellent one, and its monthly meetings were supported by a series of most interesting lectures on topics which appealed to everyone—that by the Rev. Dr Primrose, and another by John Main, M.A., being illustrated by lantern slides.

The Nineteenth Annual Competition in the Songs and Poems of Burns by the senior pupils of Provanside Secondary School was held on 13th December, 1919, and as usual the accommodation in the Gymnasium was somewhat overtaxed to meet the interest taken in this great local event. This competition was instituted by the Albany for the direct purpose of creating interest in our National Bard, and simultaneously continuing a knowledge in the Scottish dialect by teaching it to the young generation, especially as their parents now represent the last of those whose tongues carry the music of the sweet and expressive old vernacular. This ambition of the Albany Club has been warmly fostered by J. Marshall, Esq., M.A., the Headmaster, and his staff of kindred enthusiasts.

Six medals and twelve volumes of literature form the annual prizes in this contest, and these are gifted by members of the Albany, the donors for the last session being Mr John R. Prentice and Past President John A. Headrick.

The Honorary Secretary—Mr Robert Carmichael—with whose industry and successful management the Club has long been familiar, has now joined the directorate, and his successor, Mr D. C. Kennedy, appointed to the office. The new Secretary will thus be able to draw upon the advice and experience of Mr Carmichael.

The President, Dr William Cullen, and his co-directors, are fully alive to the rapidly rising standard of the Burns cult, and to the more extended appeal it commands from an ever-growing and wider circle of people everywhere. All the wide world over, the pioneer Scot in his travels has never failed to announce that it was Burns who unfastened the loops of the heart and let it pulsate freely ; that it was Burns who took the shutters off the mind and let in the clear daylight ; that it was Burns, in fact, who brought man face to face with the world he lived in, and shewed him that it was his own.

1920.

Oct.   6. Opening Remarks—William Cullen, Esq., M.D.

Nov.   3. " The Mediæval Minstrel and his Work "—Geo. Eyre Todd, Esq.

Dec.   1. " A Trip to the Hebrides " (with Lantern Illustrations) —J. Niven Murdoch, Esq.

1921.

Jan.   5. " Burns and the History of his Time "— Rev. Wm. Brownlie, M.A.

Jan.   25. " Immortal Memory " (Annual Dinner, Grand Hotel, at 6.30 p.m.)—William Cullen, Esq., M.D.

Feb.   2. Musical Evening—Members and Friends.

Mar.   2. " Burns and Nature Study " (with Lantern Illustrations) —John Main, Esq., F.G.S., F.E.I.S.

The Club meets on the first Wednesday of each month (from October till March, inclusive), in the Burns House Club, Ltd., 27 India Street, Glasgow, at 7 o'clock p.m.   Members have the privilege of introducing friends.   Subscription for Session, 5s ; Life Member-ship, £2 2s.

D. C. KENNEDY, *Hon. Secretary.*

TAM O' SHANTER BURNS CLUB, GLASGOW.

ANNUAL REPORT FOR 1919-1920.

The Annual Meeting was held on 26th October.

The session opened with the Annual Meeting, which later re-solved itself into a Smoking Concert.   At that meeting the alteration of rules was discussed.

The Annual Dinner took place on 24th January, when Mr Graham Moffat, the celebrated dramatist, proposed the " Immortal Memory," and the speech was well reported in the Press.   A collection was taken at the dinner, amounting to £4, and this was given to the Treasurer on behalf of the Mauchline House Fund.   The question of this Club having a School Competition was discussed at a meeting held on 5th March, and in view of the difficulty of finding a meeting place, the competition was unanimously postponed to next session.   On 30th March a Literary and Musical Evening was held.   Captain Campbell gave an address on " Lord Byron," and an excellent musical programme followed.   On this occasion ladies were present for the first time.

The Annual Outing took place to Loch Lomond on 1st June. A motor boat took the company from Balloch to Ardlui.   Lunch was served at Tarbet, and high tea took place at Ardlui, and the outing was a great success.

The Club was duly represented at the Burns Federation Meeting at London in September, and the kindness shewn by the London Scots will never be forgotten.

The M'Lennan Cup Competition took place in August, and this Club entered three rinks.

The Club agreed to take shares in the newly-constructed Burns House, 27 India Street, and it has been arranged that future meetings shall take place there.

An attractive syllabus has been prepared, and it is hoped that the new session will prove a great success.

The membership stands thus :—Life Members, 58 ; Ordinary Members, 58 ; Honorary Members, 3—total, 119.

BURNS CLUBS ASSOCIATION, GLASGOW.

ANNUAL REPORT FOR 1919-1920.

The Annual Meeting was held in the Burns House, India Street, on 28th October, when a large attendance was presided over by Mr Charles R. Cowie. The Annual Report stated that the Association has now completed its thirteenth year, and had a very successful session.

The various functions of the Association have been carried on successfully, and many lecturers have been sent to Societies and assistance rendered in other forms.

As usual, the Statue in George Square was beautifully decorated, and individual wreaths were sent by the Rosebery, Carlton, Sandyford, and Tam o' Shanter Clubs and by this Association.

The Fourth Anniversary Sermon was preached on 25th January by the Reverend J. H. Dickie, of New Kilpatrick, whose subject was " The Prayers of Burns." The Service was the most successful yet held. There was a crowded congregation—several hundreds of persons being turned away—and the collection on behalf of the Mauchline House amounted to £27 11s.

There are now 44 Clubs affiliated to the Association. Unfortunately a number of Clubs which remained dormant during the war have never been resuscitated, and unless that is done very soon their case seems to be hopeless.

A dinner in honour of Mr Gribbel took place in the Grand Hotel, on 27th July, when the famous Album was presented to him by Mr Duncan M'Naught, as a mark of appreciation of his disinterested conduct in connection with the Glenriddel MSS.

The Annual Outing of the Association took place to Mauchline on 18th September, and proved a very happy event.

The Directors regret to report the removal by death of Mrs Susan Stewart, which sad event took place at Mauchline Station on 6th November, 1919. " Susan," as she was familiarly called by everybody, had from the opening of the Houses faithfully carried out the duties of janitor. She was an excellent old woman, and the news of her death was everywhere received with great regret. Her place has been satisfactorily filled by Mrs Park. Another death that falls to be reported is that of Mrs Brown, one of the beneficiaries. Her house has been filled by another beneficiary.

The Association was represented at the Burns Federation at London on 4th September. The meeting was a conspicuous success, and the kindness of our friends south of the Border will never be forgotten by those privileged to be present.

The most engrossing subject of the year was the search for permanent premises for the Association. In January the dwelling at 27 India Street was purchased, and a Limited Company formed to find the money to pay the purchase price and to alter and furnish the building. The formal opening of the Burns House took place on 22nd October. It now lies with the members to do all in their power to assist the project by every means in their power, so that the Burns House may become as a household word among Burnsians.

THE BURNS HOUSE, GLASGOW.

The Glasgow Association of Burns Clubs and Kindred Societies have for the past year been interested in finding permanent premises. They have hitherto met in the Royal Hotel, Glasgow, and their appreciation of the kindness of the proprietor, Mr Smith, was evidenced by a gift presented to him.

In January last a four-flatted building at 27 India Street, Charing Cross, Glasgow, formerly the home of Colonel Macfarlane, came into the market, and was purchased by Mr J. Jeffrey Hunter solicitor, on behalf of the Association. The house required considerable alteration, and the operations were much impeded by the Glasgow joiners' strike, and also by a strike of electricians. The architects in charge of the job were Messrs John Ballantine, 95 Bath Street, Glasgow, and Ninian M'Whannell, 11 Jane Street, Glasgow, and their arrangements happily resulted in the formal opening of the House on 22nd October. The area flat is occupied by a large billiard room, cloak room, lavatory, &c. The ground floor contains reading room and dining room. The first floor has a lecture hall capable of holding 150 persons. There are also one or two committee rooms. The caretaker, on the upper flat, has a house of three rooms and kitchen.

The contractors for the work have been :—Plumber work—Bailie R. S. Renfrew, 136 North Street, Glasgow ; Mason work—James Bathgate, 482 Pollokshaws Road, Glasgow ; Plaster work—J. Struthers & Son, Pitt Street, Glasgow ; Electric lighting—J. F. Hiddleston, 126 Great Western Road, Glasgow ; Painter work— Neil Toze, 152 North Street, Glasgow.

The House is very handsomely furnished, the bulk of the furniture having been obtained from the Royal Polytechnic Limited, Glasgow.

The Club is owned by a limited company, composed of Burnsians, and the shares have been well taken up. The principal share-holders are—Mr Charles Rennie Cowie, Sir Daniel Macaulay Stevenson, Bailie R. S. Renfrew, Mr Matthew Reid, and Mr Hugh M'Coll.

Already the House has been adopted as a home by a number of the leading Burns Clubs of Glasgow, and already quite a number of large meetings have been held. An appeal has been made, and is being made still, to Burnsians to contribute books, prints, and manuscripts to the library. This appeal has been heartily re-sponded to, and among the donors are Mr Richard Edmiston, jr., Dr Quintin M'Lennan, Mr Hugh M'Coll, Mr Matthew Reid, and Mr J. Jeffrey Hunter. The Burns House is worthy of its name and object. It is meant to be a meeting-place for all good Burnsians in Glasgow, and it is hoped that it will have a long and successful career.

The Office-bearers are as follows :—

Honorary President—C. R. Cowie, 20 Blythswood Square, Glasgow ; *President*—Hugh M'Coll, 278a St. Vincent Street, Glasgow ; *Vice-presidents*—Alex. Mackenzie, 210 Battlefield Road, Glasgow, and Matthew Reid, 82 Dundas Street, Glasgow.

Secretary and Treasurer.—James L. Gillespie, 89 Bath Street, Glasgow.

Committee.—J. Jeffrey Hunter, 89 Bath Street, Glasgow ; Thomas Killin, 2 Stewarton Drive, Cambuslang ; Isaac Chalmers, 104 Crookston Street, Glasgow ; George John M'Callum, 4 Athole Gardens, Newlands, Glasgow ; Hugh Lyon, 35 Cornhill Street, Springburn, Glasgow ; Thomas S. Turnbull, 310 Golfhill Drive, Dennistoun, Glasgow ; James Allan, 2 Broomhill Avenue, Partick, Glasgow ; J. C. Ewing, 167 West Regent Street, Glasgow ; J. M. Brown, 161 Pollok Street, Glasgow ; J. D. Sloan, 151 Queen Street, Glasgow ; R. M. Milholm, 7 Somerville Place, Glasgow ; William Cockburn, N.B. Station, Bowling ; A. G. Andrew, 13 Montgomerie Street, Ardrossan ; John Macfarlane, 6 Gordon Terrace, Shettleston,

Glasgow ; William Gardiner, 83a Broad Street, Camlachie, Glasgow ; T. P. Thomson, 32 Barrington Drive, Glasgow ; Thomas Sutherland, Ashbourne Villa, Minard Road, Partick, Glasgow ; Alexander Duthie, Eversley, Newlands, Glasgow ; John Muir, 13 Kinning Street, Glasgow ; T. C. F. Brotchie, Beechgrove, Bridge-of-Weir ; James Muir, jr., 6 Avon Street, Glasgow.

GLASGOW PRIMROSE BURNS CLUB.

Session, 1919-1920.

Another successful session is credited to the Primrose Burns Club. We commenced the year with 50 active members, and during the session we have added 36 new members. The meetings have been well attended, and speak greatly for the interest and enthusiasm of our members.

Our thanks are due to the President for the excellent paper he gave on the 23rd October, " Notes on Burns's Songs," illustrated with songs and duets by professional artistes : also to Supt. Douglas for his paper on the 18th December, " Burns's Philosophy of Life," which was most interesting and edifying.

The Annual Dinner was held in the Grand Hotel. The President of the Club, Thos S. Turnbull, Esq., occupied the chair, and was supported by James Lucas, Esq., M.A., who submitted the " Immortal Memory," and in doing so paid a high tribute to the genius of Burns.

The Annual Singing and Reciting Competitions from the Works of Burns, by scholars attending Petershill Public School, Springburn, was held in this school on Saturday, 29th March, before an appreciative audience.   There were fourteen prizes in all, contributed by a few members, comprising five handsome medals for the winners, and nine consolation book prizes. The greatest praise is due to Mr Turnbull and his assistants for their work in bringing the competitors to the high state of efficiency in their rendering of the songs and recitations.   The prizes were presented to the winners by Mrs J. Wall, the Club members thereafter being hospitably entertained by the school staff.

Report on Bowling Competition (Jos. Matthews, Convener).— We entered four rinks for the M'Lennan Cup, but owing to the inclemency of the weather the game was anything but pleasant, but with the assistance of the famous " Drooko " we were able to finish the 21 ends.   We were disappointed in not winning the cup, as we feel sure if we had, our popular Vice-president, Matt. Reid, would have filled it with his famous " Blend."   Our highest up rink was

skipped by John Whiteford, better known as the " Provost of Kil-
macolm." With the great enthusiasm which exists among the
bowlers of this Club, they are confident in bringing the cup to the
Primrose Club in the near future.

The Club has arranged to hold their meetings in the Burns
House. Members of kindred Clubs made welcome.

GLASGOW AND DISTRICT BURNS CLUBS' BOWLING ASSOCIATION.

The Association was formed in 1899, to conduct a yearly match
among bowling members of Burns Clubs. The interest was promptly
stimulated by the gift from the late Bailie M'Lennan of a silver
cup. This is a trophy, and on it each year is inscribed the name
of Club and winning rink. Gold badges are presented to the first
and second highest scoring rinks. The " majority year " of the
Association was in 1920, when 130 rinks competed—a record entry.
A rink from Tollcross Club proved the winners, the players being
J. L. Cowan, J. Jack, W. Clarke, and C. S. Mathieson (skip). Second
prize was won by Shettleston Club, the players being A. Perry, A.
Riach, J. Riddell, and W. M'Dowall (skip). The Association has
at various times subscribed to Burns Cult Institutions, and during
the war contributed to local Relief Funds. Particulars of qualifications and entry money can be had from the Secretary.

BUCK'S HEAD BURNS CLUB, ARMADALE.

Annual Report.

A very successful session was carried through under the able
Presidentship of Mr John Mack. The attendance at our meetings
were from 80 to 100. Since the introduction of the lady members
to our Club it has been necessary for us to look for a larger Hall.
Starting at the beginning of the season with 17 male members, we
are pleased to report now a membership of 170 full-paying members,
which is very gratifying.

The Annual Dinner and Anniversary of our Poet was largely
attended—over 120 of our own members and deputations from
four sister Clubs. The musical side of Burns's Works was very
prominent, whilst the readings was a good second. We were
fortunate in having an outstanding good Children's Competition
under the superintendence of the Rev. John Drew, minister of the

parish, and a crowded hall cheered the young ones in song and story of Burns's Works. The performance of the children was most creditable, and the competition will be repeated again in February.

During the season we have subscribed to the Mauchline House £3 3s, and we gave weekly rink prizes to the Bowling Club, and were the means of raising £10 for the Royal Infirmary, Edinburgh. We have started a Choir, and have 18 voices, and the musical director, Mr Samuel Lambie, informs me they will be able for competition singing and concert platform work at an early date. We have also started an Orchestra, which is making very good progress. We have started a Musical Fund for Choir and Orchestra, as it is the desire of the members to give them their music free, and it has only one condition—that is, it must be Scotch music.

During the summer our Outing was to Mauchline, when the travels of Burns was listened to by all the party from a reading by our Vice-president. We only regret, by a mistake that was made for the catering of our dinner and tea at Mauchline, we had not time to visit the beautiful policies of Ballochmyle, which were thrown open to us by the kindness of Sir J. M'Innes Shaw, and we take this opportunity of apologising for not being able to fulfil our promise after his kindness in granting our request to visit his beautiful estate.

The success of the season is due to the energetic work of our worthy President and his committee, and also to Mr Samuel Lambie, Musical Director of the Club, and I take this opportunity of thank ing all who have worked in harmony for the welfare of the Buck's Head Burns Club.

SYLLABUS, 1920-1921.

Dec. 18. " A Nicht wi' Burns "—Vice-president Wm. M'Alpine.
Jan. 22. " Burns's Early Life "—President John Mack.
Feb. 19. Ladies' Night (Musical Evening)—Mr Samuel Lambie.
Mar. 20. Paper—Mr James Mack.

JOHN STEVENSON, *Secretary.*

GOVAN FAIRFIELD BURNS CLUB.

I have pleasure in again wishing you success in the forthcoming publication of the *Chronicle.* You have had a busy year in con- nection with the Federation—the Annual Conference in London, and last Saturday at Greenock included. I have to congratulate you on the successful issue of the " Highland Mary " grave removal, and to remind you that I expressed the hope to you last year that some satisfactory settlement would be reached. About our Club, we have had a successful year, and our membership is full up at present. We had a motor run on 19th June last to Largs, and made a call at the Old West Kirkyard, Greenock.

1920.   SYLLABUS, 1920-1921.

Sept. 1. Harmony.
Oct.   6. " Letters of Robert Burns —Mr J. F. Anderson.
Nov.   3. " Scott "—Mr Jas. Lauder.
Dec.   1. " Wood Notes Wild," with Songs and Illustrations (Ladies' Night)—Mr J. D. Sloan.
1921.
Jan.   5. " Byron "—Mr T. M. Walker, M.A.
Feb.   2. " Scotland's Great Men "—Mr J. J. Hunter.
Mar.   2. Harmony—Members' Night.
Jan. 24. " The Immortal Memory " (Annual Supper)—Mr Jas. Lucas, M.A.

JOHN GORDON, *Hon. Secretary.*

NEWBATTLE AND DISTRICT BURNS CLUB.

1920.   SYLLABUS—SESSION 1920-1921.

Nov. 13. Mr Wm. Kirkwood—Paper.
Dec. 11. Mr John Morris—Paper.
1921.
Jan.   8. Mr Andrew Anderson—Paper.
Jan. 29. Anniversary Meeting (as arranged).
Feb.   5. Councillor Doig—Paper.
Feb. 19. Mr John Carson—Paper.
Mar.   5. Mr John Callender—Paper.
Mar. 19. Mr D. Jameson—Paper.
April 2. Rev. J. N. M'Pherson—Paper.   •

YE CRONIES BURNS CLUB (GOVAN).

SECRETARY'S REPORT. 1919-1920.

A very successful session was carried through under the able Presidentship of Mr Matthew Stirling. The Annual Meeting was held on Saturday, 12th June, when there was a large attendance of members. The reports submitted by the Secretary and Treasurer were of a very gratifying nature, and showed the Club to be in a very flourishing condition. During the session there have been eight ordinary meetings and one special meeting, which were all very well attended by the members.

In the M'Lennan Bowling Competition in August, 1919, the Club entered four rinks, but all failed in winning the coveted trophy. All the players enjoyed the afternoon's outing, and hoped for better luck next year.

On the invitation of the Uddingston Masonic Burns Club, our President, Vice-president, and Secretary visited the above Club in October, 1919, and were very hospitably entertained by the members. In November we held our second Picture Night in the Govan Cross Picture Palace, and were favoured with a deputation from the Hamilton Junior Burns Club, which proved a great success, the balance from same being earmarked for the Club Memoriam Fund.

At the Monthly Meeting in November, Mr J. F. Anderson, President of Glasgow Tam o' Shanter Club, gave us a very interesting address, his subject being entitled " The Philosophy of Robert Burns," which, though to the brief side, was very much enjoyed by the members.

The Anniversary Supper was held in the M'Leod Hall, Pearce Institute, on Saturday, 24th January, 1920, and proved to be a great success, about 300 ladies and gentlemen being present. Mr J. F. Anderson proposed " The Immortal Memory." Greeting cards were exchanged with a large number of Federated Clubs.

On the invitation of the Uddingston Masonic Burns Club, a large number of our members travelled to Uddingston on Saturday the 20th March, 1920, when their new Club-room was formally opened, and we all passed a very pleasant evening.

The Annual Outing this year took place on Saturday, the 29th May, when, along with the members and their lady friends of the Hamilton Junior Burns Club, our members and their lady friends travelled to the High Parks and Cadzow Forest, Hamilton Palace, where an excellent tea was served and everyone spent a fine afternoon, the weather being all that could be desired, and our best thanks are due Mr Wilson and his committee for the perfect arrangements made.

In Memoriam.

It is with sincere regret I have to record during the session the deaths of three of our most esteemed members, and our Club will be much the poorer by their passing, and their presence will be greatly missed at our Club meetings, which they attended very regularly. I refer to Bro. John Orr, who died on the 11th April, 1920, after a very serious illness ; Bro. William Kerr, who was accidently killed while following his employment on Saturday, the 17th April, 1920 ; and Bro. James Roy Kerrigan, who died with startling suddenness on Friday, the 4th June, 1920.   Deputations of the members attended the funerals of the deceased brothers, and floral wreaths were sent on behalf of the members of the Club, also letters of condolence to the relatives of deceased.

Much of the year's success has been due to the untiring energy and enthusiasm of President Stirling and committee, who have always been ready to do all in their power to further the Club's interests, and who were very regular in their attendance at all meetings and committee meetings, which were very numerous.   We are all looking forward to the coming session with confidence, as every member is taking a greater interest in the business, which augurs well for the future of the Club.

JAMES RELLIE, *Secretary.*

HAMILTON JUNIOR BURNS CLUB.

REPORT FOR SESSION, 1919-1920.

I have the pleasure and satisfaction to report another successful year in the activities of the Hamilton Junior Burns Club.   The Annual Meeting was held on the evening of 28th September, when there was practically a full attendance of the members.   Mr David Cross, President, occupied the chair.   The reports submitted by the Secretary and Treasurer showed the brotherhood to be in a good working condition.   To the great regret of the members, the Great Reaper, on 27th March, took from our circle Mr William Ferguson, Past President of the Club.   Mr Ferguson was one of Nature's gentlemen—a large hearted, genial man.   He was widely read in Burns literature, and his addresses from the chair were always models of diction and grace.   He was a source of strength to the Club, and his popular, pawky personality is much missed.   The sympathy of the members was fittingly conveyed to his widow and family in their loss.

During the summer months an interesting series of rambles were again carried through.   The first of these took place to Cadzow Forest on Saturday, 29th May, when a large deputation from Ye Cronies Burns Club, Govan, joined us.   Our Govan friends greatly enjoyed the outing, and were much impressed with the sylvan beauty of the High Parks.   On the invitation of the Govan Burns Club a deputation visited that brotherhood, and had the privilege of being conducted through the Fairfield Shipbuilding Yard.   The visit was one of much interest to the deputation, who were most hospitably entertained during the afternoon.

Messrs D. Cross, J. Brown, and W. Wilson, who were deputed by the members to represent the Club at the Annual Meeting of the

Burns Federation in London on 4th September, gave an interesting report of the proceedings. All spoke of the interest and pleasure which the meeting afforded them, and of the great kindness and hospitality extended to the delegates by the London Robert Burns Club. The London meeting of the Federation will remain memorable to all who had the privilege of taking part in the proceedings.

The Club meetings are held on the first Monday of each month, at 7.30 p.m., at 1 Union Street, Hamilton, when a warm welcome will be accorded to any member of a Federated Club.

W. WILSON, *Secretary*.

BIRMINGHAM BURNS CLUB.

ANNUAL REPORT—SESSION 1918-1919.

The session just closed has been one of great activity. Eight functions were promoted and carried through, and it is pleasing to report that all were of an extremely enjoyable nature.

1918.

Sept. 27. Inaugural Meeting—Grand Hotel.

Oct. 30. Burns Symposium.—Comprising four short papers by members, followed by songs. A collection taken realised £13 for the Lady Mayoress' Fund (Prisoners of War, Warwickshire Regiment). Grand Hotel.

Nov. 22. Lecture : " Sir Walter Scott "—By the President. In aid of War Service Fund. Grand Hotel.

Dec. 20. Ladies' Night. In aid of War Service Fund. Grand Hotel.

1919.

Jan. 24. Burns Anniversary Celebration. Grand Hotel.

Feb. 28. Whist Drive. In aid of Club Funds. Grand Hotel.

April 4. Smoking Concert. White Horse Hotel.

April 11. Lecture : " The Rebirth of the Serbian Nation "—Mrs Robertson, Scottish Women's Hospitals. Queen's Hotel.

During the year 42 ordinary, 3 life, and 12 associate members were elected, but owing to resignations, removals from town, and, I regret to say, the decease of five members, the membership roll now stands at 248 (30 associate members), the highest number in the history of the Club.

Thirteen ordinary members and four associate members were on service with the Colours during the past session.

Our sincere sympathy is extended to the relatives of those members who have passed away, and I am sure you will all read with regret that the Club is the poorer by the decease of Kenneth

Fullarton, Andrew Halley, Patrick J. B. Keiller, Dr M'Call, and Dr Sturrock.

The policy of the Club was again mainly directed to the aiding of War and Local Charities, and the proceeds of several of the functions held have enabled your committee to allocate £50 to the Scottish Women's Hospitals, and to contribute £105 to other Charities.

To those members who worked to attain these objects we tender our sincere thanks.

It is hardly necessary for me to comment on all the meetings seriatim, but the Ladies' Night held on 20th December, 1918, can hardly be passed over without remark. As was confidently expected, this meeting, which took the form of a Whist Drive, was a great success socially, and what is equally important, financially.

The ladies worked with the greatest possible zeal and energy to attain a satisfactory result, and the Club cannot be too lavish in its thanks to them for their able assistance and skilful organisation which enabled them to hand over, as a result of the meeting, the sum of £96 11s 4d for our War Charities Fund.

The cessation of hostilities in the great European conflict having somewhat relieved the feeling of restraint caused by the war, your committee decided to hold the Burns Anniversary Celebration in the orthodox pre-war fashion, and a Burns Dinner was therefore held in the Grand Hotel on 24th January last, at which the Haggis was served with the usual musical honours.

One hundred and sixty-three ladies and gentlemen were present, the largest number a President has ever presided over at any previous Club function of a like nature.

Another function of a very pleasing nature was the meeting held in the Queen's Hotel, on 11th April, when Mrs Robertson, of the Scottish Women's Hospitals, in her lecture entitled, "The Rebirth of the Serbian Nation," gave a very interesting account of the Birmingham Section in the Elsie Inglis Memorial Hospital, Sallanches, France, and told how the money raised by the Flag Day last year was expended in founding this section.

The meeting was an addition to the syllabus, prompted by the desire of the Scottish Women's Hospitals to give some form of recognition of the work done by the Club on their behalf, especially the founding of the City of Birmingham Section mentioned above.

A collection taken at this meeting realised £6 for our War Service Fund.

The committee are indebted to Messrs J. Cumming and C. MacGrath for arranging a Snooker Handicap which realised £15 for our War Service Fund.

Through the courtesy of Mr R. Nelson, brother of the late Dr Nelson, of 78 Hagley Road, Birmingham, a framed steel engraving depicting a meeting between the National Poet, Robert Burns, and Walter Scott (not then Sir Walter), in Sciennes House, Edinburgh, was very kindly presented to the Club and gratefully accepted. The donor has been suitably thanked.

In conclusion, I take this opportunity of thanking all my colleagues in the Club for their kind assistance to me during my year of office.

ANNUAL REPORT—SESSION 1919-1920.

The session just closed has, I am pleased to say, been most successful. Altogether eight functions were held, viz. :—

1919.
Aug. 23. Picnic. Forest Hotel, Knowle and Dorridge.
Oct. 3. Inaugural Meeting. Queen's Hotel.
Oct. 24. Whist Drive. Masonic Rooms, Severn Street (in aid of Club Funds).
Nov. 28. Ladies' Night. Whist Drive, Fletcher's Cafe, Corporation Street.
1920.
Jan. 3. New Year's Party. Grand Hotel.
Jan. 23. Burns Anniversary Celebration. Grand Hotel.
Mar. 5. Social Evening and Sale of Work. Masonic Rooms, Severn Street.
Mar. 26. Smoking Concert. White Horse Hotel.

During the year 48 ordinary, 5 life, and 20 associate members were elected, and 3 ordinary members were transferred to life membership, but owing to resignations and removals from town the membership roll now stands at 287 (43 associate members and 43 life members)—the highest number in the history of the Club.

The policy of the Club was again directed to the aiding of charities, and in this instance donations were confined to local institutions (particulars of the donations made being found in the Hon. Treasurer's report enclosed).

Whilst it is not necessary for me to remark on all the functions held, several cannot be passed over without comment.

The Picnic was a revival of a pre-war custom, and although held late in the summer, was a distinct success. The weather being on its best behaviour, a large number of members and friends were present, and games and sports were indulged in. The proceedings terminated in an impromptu concert in the evening—the talent being mainly supplied by members of the Club.

Burns Anniversary Dinner, 23rd January.—This function was held on a larger scale than any in the history of the Club—167 ladies and gentlemen sat down. Several notable guests were present, and in addition to representatives from kindred societies, we had the pleasure of entertaining the Right Hon. Andrew Fisher, P.C., High Commissioner for Australia; Brig.-Gen. Ludlow, C.B.; Mr H. F. Harvey, Editor of the *Birmingham Daily Mail*; Mr G. A. Smith, President of the Birmingham Rotary Club; and Mr E. Sandford, the Lord Mayor's Secretary.

Out of courtesy to our principal guest, the President surrendered his prerogative by allowing the Right Hon. Andrew Fisher to propose the important toast of the evening, " The Immortal Memory."

Whist Drive, 28th November.—The ladies were again kind enough to organise a special function, and this took the form of a Whist Drive, which realised £11, this sum being earmarked for our Charity Fund.

We are also indebted to the ladies for a special voluntary donation of £21 14s to the funds of the Club. This was raised by means of a series of private Whist Drives held by the ladies and friends throughout the winter months, and we are greatly indebted to them for all their efforts, especially to Mrs Jas. Campbell, as being the prime mover in this direction, and I take this opportunity on behalf of the Club, of thanking the ladies for the great interest and hard work performed in pursuance of the Club's interests.

March 5th. Social Evening and Sale of Work.—Once again our sincere thanks are due to the ladies for their enthusiastic assistance. This function was a distinct success, and resulted in a very substantial sum being added to the Club Funds.

Smoking Concert, 26th March.—It is admitted by all who were present that the talent supplied at this function was the finest of any smoker we ever had. It was very disappointing, however, to the promoters of this function to see such an exceedingly poor attendance of members, and I am desirous of bringing this to your notice as it is no encouragement to those who go to a lot of trouble in arranging these functions to find the support of the Club lacking, and I should be glad if members could see their way wherever possible in future to give their personal support by being present.

It is with regret I have to inform the members that our First President, Mr W. E. Ross, has been for some little time in indifferent health. At present he is away recuperating, and I am sure you will join with me in wishing him a speedy recovery to good health.

LECTURE : " BURNS IN RELATION TO SCOTTISH MUSIC."

Dear Sir or Madam,—The Management Committee is providing an unique programme for Friday, 19th November, at the Queen's

Hotel, at 7 o'clock.   It is in the nature of a lecture entitled :   " Burns
in Relation to Scottish Music."

We have been fortunate in securing Mr Arthur Cranmer to
give the lecture, which will be illustrated with songs by himself
and other artistes.

The Committee believe that this is the first time a serious
attempt has been made in Birmingham to deal with early Scottish
Music up to the period of Burns.

The Management Committee feel that such an important lecture
will be ably supported by the members.   It is an expensive function,
hence the necessity for charging 2s for each ticket.

The accommodation at the Queen's Hotel is limited, and an
early application for tickets from the Secretary or Members of the
Committee is necessary in order to secure a seat.

CHAS. MACGREGOR, *Hon. Secretary.*

SCOTTISH BURNS CLUB

(Instituted 1904),

In which is incorporated " Glasgow Waverley " and " Western "
(1859) and " Ye Saints " (1894) Burns Clubs.

Motto :—" The heart aye's the part aye."

The syllabus for the past season might be termed " A winter
with the Immortals."   Mr J. K. M'Dowall, J.P., led off in September
with " Napoleon " ;   in   November,   Mr George M'Gill handled
"Shakespeare" in a masterly manner ; while, in December, Dr Devon
found a very congenial text in " Knox."   " Burns " was a very
appropriate " Immortal " for January.   Mr John Muir (author
of *Burns and Carlyle*) showed as a Burns student he stands second
to none.   Mr T. A. Fraser concluded in February with " Cromwell,"
concentrating on " the Great Protector " and Scotland.

In addition to the foregoing, musical evenings were held in
October and March, to which ladies were invited.   Mr J. G.
MacKerracher had direction of the programmes on both occasions, and
he introduced the leading musical talent of the city.   Those musical
evenings have become a feature of the Club, the attendance having
to be strictly limited.

" The Immortal Memory " was proposed by Alex. Cargill, Esq.,
J.P., O.B.E., Edinburgh—a well-known authority on our National
Bard.   Again the demand for tickets exceeded the accommodation.

Owing to the cosmopolitan nature of the membership and the

comprehensive name of the Club, it was decided to institute branches to keep in touch with those whom distance deters from attending.

A meeting of members and friends was held in John Knox House, Edinburgh. An Edinburgh Section was formed, and the following Executive elected :—President, Dr James Devon ; Vice-president, Mr John Kelso Kelly ; Treasurer, Mr Joseph Sanders ; Secretary, Mr George M'Gill ; with Messrs A. Drysdale Paterson, Wm. J. Hay, and John Samson to complete the committee. Members of the section are entitled to all the rights and privileges of the Club, including diplomas, &c.

" Glasgow Waverley " and " Western " Burns Clubs, which were instituted in 1859, were incorporated. The property of these pioneer Clubs was handed over, including a solid Georgean silver snuff box in a handsome leather and velvet case, and a wooden snuff mull with a silver plate on lid stating the box is " made of the wood of the bed on which Burns died "—a written guarantee accompanied this. Both lids bear engraved testimony that the boxes were presented to the Glasgow Waverley Burns Club by Dr Francis Hay Thomson and P. P. Alexander, Esq., respectively, while engraving round the silver box states that the Clubs became amalgamated. The keys of the Clubs and a relic of the famous 1859 Centenary were also included—the latter a silver-gilt medal, clasp, and ribbon worn by the Secretary of the Western Burns Club at the Anniversary. On the badge is engraved on the obverse, the Burns crest and motto, and on the reverse, " Western Burns Club," the engraving on the clasp being, " 1859—Secretary."

During the season members of the Club lectured to Burns Clubs and Literary Societies in Glasgow and the West of Scotland with much acceptance, judging from the continued demand this season.

The procedure of the Club at meetings is :—7.30 to 8.30, lecture ; 8.30 to 9, tea ; 9 to 10 p.m., music, song, and entertainment. The average attendance was over 140.

The membership, which is limited to 200 (exclusive of the Edinburgh Section), is full, and waiting applications number about 50.

The first diploma (to which members of three or more years' standing are entitled) takes the form of an artistic lithographic print of scenes from the life of Burns. A handsome gold badge of distinctive design, with name of Club, Burns crest and motto struck on obverse from a specially made die. has now been procured as a second diploma, to which only members of seven or more years' standing are entitled.

The present season has shown no abatement. If the attendances continue to increase, it will be desirable to endeavour to procure larger premises, which will in a sense be unfortunate, as " Reid's Rooms " is a *beau ideal* meeting-place.

Syllabus for Season 1920-1921.

1920.

*Oct.   4. " A Burns Fantasia "—Mr John Muir.

Oct. 25. Musical Evening (Ladies' Night)—Mr J. G. MacKerracher.

Nov. 22. " Dr Johnson and Scotland "—Mr Frank Beaumont, B.A.

Dec. 27. " George Buchanan "—Dr James Devon.

1921.

†Jan. 17. " George Elliot "—Mr W. G. Gray.

Jan. 24. " The Immortal Memory "—The Right Rev. Arch. Ean Campbell, D.D., Lord Bishop of Glasgow and Galloway.

Feb. 28. " Mine Own Romantic Town "—Mr George M'Gill.

Mar. 28. Annual General Meeting, at 6.45 p.m.

           Musical Evening (Ladies' Night), at 7.30 p.m.

    * First Monday in October.   † Third Monday in January.

Edinburgh Section.

Meets on 3rd Friday each month in Observation Tower Rooms, Castle Hill, Lawnmarket.

1920.

Nov. 19. " Burns and Burns Clubs "—Dr James Devon.

Dec. 17. " Shakespeare "—Mr George M'Gill.

1921.

Jan. 21. Musical Evening, Lantern Illustrations (Ladies' Night) —Mr Wm. J. Hay.

Feb. 18. Lecture : Mr John Kelso Kelly.

Mar. 18. Dramatic Recital (Ladies' Night)— Mr A. Drysdale Paterson.

           J. Kevan M'Dowall, *Secretary.*

SHETTLESTON BURNS CLUB.

Secretary's Report, 1918-1919.

" Victory ". Year has proved a record session in the history of the Shettleston Burns Club, our membership and financial position being ahead of any previous year.   At our Anniversary Dinner 84 members and friends were present ; Autumn Social—" Tattie and Herrin'," 53 ; and Spring Social—Ladies' Night, 83.   This was most encouraging to the Office-bearers and Committee who had charge of the arrangements, as it showed keen spirit and enthusiasm amongst our members. The " Immortal Memory " was proposed by J. Seaton Smith, Esq., M.A., a most active member of committee and a thorough Burnsian. His lecture was greatly appreciated and listened to with great attention. At our " Tattie and Herrin' " Supper, ex-President James Lucas, M.A., gave a paper on " Politics in the time of Burns," in his usual earnest and genial manner, which delighted his audience, and gave a further evidence of his great interest in the welfare of our Club. On our Ladies' Night a new feature was introduced ; a lecture on " Bird Life," accompanied with lime-light illustrations, being given by James D. Sloan, Esq., President of Rosebery Burns Club, to whom we were greatly indebted for a most interesting night's entertainment. Mr Sloan was quite at home on the subject of his lecture, and showed a thorough know-ledge of bird life, giving quotations from Burns and other poets, thus adding greatly to the interest of his lecture.

For the M'Lennan Cup Competition six rinks entered. One of our rinks, skipped by Mr James Myles, succeeded in gaining second prize—badges as runner-up, having 30 shots to the good. The Bowling Match—Officials v. Members—played in May last on Mount Vernon Green, was a great success, and all present expressed the opinion that this event should be annual.

During the Session our Club sustained a sad blow in the death of our esteemed Treasurer, Mr Thomas Barrie, one of our oldest members, and for many years a most capable, untiring director of our finances. His genial presence has been greatly missed at our Committee meetings, and future Social Gatherings will be the poorer by the absence of a most earnest and enthusiastic member of our Club. His good work is being continued by the Secretary until next Annual Meeting. As proving the good work done by our late Treasurer, Mr Barrie, the 1918-19 financial statement showed an increase in our funds greatly in excess of any previous year.

Children's Competition—singing and reciting works of Burns—is expected to take place during the coming session. A fund has been inaugurated, showing £2 9s in hand, towards prizes for this event.

I desire to tender my heartfelt thanks to Officials and Members of our Club for the great assistance given me during my year of Secretaryship, and can testify to the good work accomplished by your Committee. There were nine Committee Meetings during the Session, which were well attended by all Members. The Com-mittee are indebted to Messrs Butler and Knight for their kindness in auditing Club's accounts.

ROBERT M. MILHOLM, *Hon. Secretary.*

THORNLIEBANK BURNS CLUB.

In submitting this item for the Club Notes of the *Burns Chronicle*, it is pleasing to report that all the Club functions carried through in pre-war days have during the past year been taken up with much zest by the members, after being in abeyance for 4½ years.

A very successful " Tattie and Herrin' " Supper was held on Hallowe'en, 1919, and the Anniversary Dinner and Hallowe'en Festival of 1920 were things to be remembered by both old and new members. Owing to the difficulty of railway facilities and hotel accommodation it was found impossible to proceed with the Spring Holiday Outing this year, but it is hoped that an Outing of some kind will take place on Spring Holiday of 1921.

The School Children's Competitions, for which the Club is well known to all Federated Clubs, was revived this year, and a most successful contest took place in the Public Hall, Thornliebank, on Friday, 10th December, 1920, a full report of which will be found below.

President T. P. Winter is due to retire this year, and Mr James H. M'Millan, who succeeds him in the office, will be supported by Vice-president John Muir. As the two gentlemen named are enthusiastic Burnsians, a successful *regime* is predicted.

The Club, numerically and financially, is in quite a prosperous state, and the prospects for the next few years appear to be of a rosy nature.

Burns Club School Children's Competition.—The Public Hall was crowded on the evening of Friday, 10th December, 1920, when the final of the School Children's Competition, promoted by the Burns Club, took place. Mr T. P. Winter, who presided, was supported by Mr John Muir. the Rev. R. Harvie Smith, and Mr Robert Hutton, Headmaster of the Public School. Mr Thomas Haddow, Secretary, Mr Hugh Halliday, Treasurer, and the other members of the Committee were untiring in their efforts to make the function a success. Messrs Alex. Pollock, James Andrew, and A. G. Andrew, of the Rosebery Burns Club, were the Judges. While they retired to consider the awards, a concert was given by the Durward Trio ; Mr Sam Love, baritone ; Mr David Low, concertinist ; Mr J. Miller, vocalist ; Miss Dalrymple, reader ; and Mr Alex. Finlay, who is well described as " The Pocket Lauder." The Judges gave their awards as follows :—Seniors—Singing—1. Jean Waterson ; 2. Mary Waterson. Reading—1. Elsie Robinson ; 2. Jean Blair. Juniors—Singing—1. Mary Mewha ; 2. Margaret C. M'Kinlay. Reading—1. Ellen Elder ; 2. Daisy Sinclair. Infants—Singing—1. Isa Strang ; 2. Annie Evans. Reading—1.

Lizzie Sloss ; 2. Rita Cameron. Pianoforte playing—Nan Mathieson. The accompaniments to the competitors were played by Miss M'Kinney, Miss A. Gray, and Mrs M'Kinlay. Mr Harvie Smith presented the prizes, and complimented the Burns Club on the excellent work which they are doing. Acknowledgment was also made of the assistance rendered to the Club by Mr Hutton and his staff in preparing the children for the competition.

THOMAS HADDOW, *Hon. Secretary.*

NOTES AND QUERIES.

TWO BURNS CHAP-BOOKS.

We have received from Mr W. Turner, the able and popular member of the Sunderland Club, two chap-books—one entitled *Poetic Tributes to the Memory of Burns*, received by the Newcastle-on-Tyne Club : Newcastle, G. Angus, 1817 ; the other bears—*An Interesting History of Robert Burns, the Ayrshire Bard* : Glasgow, printed for the Booksellers, No. 60, but has no date. The first-named contains three rhymed epistles to the brethren, two of which are initialled from Newcastle and one from Haddington, under date February, 1816. These compositions are all of superior merit, and they are written in the " raucle tongue " of Burns. The " Interesting History " is an admirable short summary of the Poet's life, expressed in terse and vigorous language. The Poet's salary is given as £35 per annum ; Jean Armour is only once named ; and there is no reference whatever to Highland Mary. In those early days they " didn't know everything down in Judee." Fugitive literature of this kind is valuable for the light it throws upon the popular estimate of Burns in its own period.

EXTRACT FROM " LIFE OF JOHN KEATS."

Less vivid than the above is the invocatory sonnet, apparently showing acquaintance with the geological theory of volcanic upheaval, which Keats was presently moved to address to Ailsa Rock. Coming down into Ballantrae in blustering weather, the friends met a country wedding party on horseback, and Keats tried a song about it in the Burns dialect, for Brown to palm off on Dilke as an original : " but it won't do," he rightly decides. From Maybole he writes to Reynolds with pleased anticipation of the visit to be paid the next day to Burns's Cottage. " One of the pleasantest means of annulling self is approaching such a shrine as the cottage of Burns—we need not think of his misery—that is all gone ; bad luck to it—I shall look upon it all with unmixed pleasure, as I do upon my Stratford-on-Avon day with Bailey."

On the walk from Maybole to Ayr Keats has almost the only phrase which escapes him during the whole tour to indicate a sense of special inspiring power in mountain scenery for a poet : " The approach to it (Ayr) is extremely fine—quite outwent my expectations—richly meadowed, wooded, heathed, and rivuleted—with a grand sea view terminated by the black mountains of the Isle of Arran. As soon as I saw them so nearly I said to myself : " How is it they did not beckon Burns to some grand attempt at an Epic ?" Nearing Kirk Alloway, Keats had been delighted to find the first home of Burns in a landscape so charming. " I endeavoured to drink in the Prospect, that I might spin it out to you, as the Silkworm makes silk from Mulberry leaves—I cannot recollect it." But his anticipations were deceived, the whole scene disenchanted, and thoughts of Burns's misery forced on him in his own despite, by the presence and chatter of the man in charge of the Poet's birthplace :—

The Man at the Cottage was a great Bore with his Anecdotes —I hate the rascal—his life consists in fuzz, fuzzy, fuzziest. He drinks glasses five for the quarter and twelve for the hour—he is a mahogany-faced old Jackass who knew Burns. He ought to have been kicked for having spoken to him. He calls himself " a curious old Bitch "—but he is a flat old dog ; I should like to employ Caliph Vathek to kick him. O the flummery of a birthplace ! Cant ! cant ! cant ! It is enough to give a spirit the guts-ache. Many a true word, they say, is spoken in Jest—this may be because his gab hindered my sublimity : the flat dog made me write a flat sonnet. My dear Reynolds—I cannot write about scenery and visitings. Fancy is indeed less than a present palpable reality, but it is greater than remembrance—you would lift your eyes from Homer only to see close before you the real Isle of Tenedos— you would rather read Homer afterwards than remember yourself. One song of Burns's is of more worth to you than all I could think for a whole year in his native country. His Misery is a dead-weight upon the nimbleness of one's quill—I tried to forget it—to drink Toddy without any care—to write a merry sonnet—it won't do—he talked with Bitches—he drank with blackguards ; he was miserable. We can see horribly clear, in the works of such a man, his whole life. as if we were God's spies. What were his addresses to Jean in the latter part of his life ?   A. J. CRAIG.

Corstorphine.

ELLISLAND FOR SALE.

The farm and estate of Ellisland, so rich in associations with Burns, and a field adjoining Stoke Poges Churchyard, containing a memorial to Thomas Gray, have been on the market during the last week, and have failed to find purchasers.

Some ultra-literary people have been declaring this deplorable, and have read into it a slight to the memory of two justly famed sons of the Muse. I submit that it is nothing of the sort.

Whatever its literary connections, a field or a farm, coming up for sale, is regarded in this practical twentieth century, not as a matter of poetry, but as a matter of agriculture, and lamentations are needless. Ellisland, I do not doubt, will yet be bought, as will the field at Stoke Poges, despite its monument, but on a purely business basis.

And why not ? Need literature come into the question at all ? A poet's worshippers hold every foot of ground sacred that is associated with him, but let the more ardent among them remember that his true memorial is to be found in his works, and that, so long as these still hold the love and admiration of the race, there is no cause to be despondent about set-backs in the sphere of agriculture.

VISITORS TO BURNS'S BIRTHPLACE.

As compared with last year's record figures, a slight decrease in the number of visitors to Burns's Cottage and Monument is shown in the official return for the year ending September 30th. The number who paid for admission to the Poet's birthplace was 64,642, a decrease of 1358, and the number who passed through the turnstiles at the Monument was 71,452, a decrease of 4924. The busiest time at both the Cottage and Monument was the Glasgow Fair week, when there were 10,830 visitors at the Cottage and 11,846 at the Monument.

—*Glasgow Herald*, 5th September, 1920.

CONFESSION OF ANTIQUE SMITH, THE FORGER.

26 George Street,
Edinburgh, 20th November, 1905.

James Cameron, Esq.,
South Street, David Street.

DEAR SIR,—With reference to our recent conversation on the articles which appeared in the *Dispatch* and *Scotsman* newspapers some years ago, relating to Historical MSS., and of which I believe you have made a collection, allow me to state that though a lot of balderdash, there percolates a *soupçon* of truth, but I never really at any time took the trouble of reading or studying them after the first or second issues—I left the result to the Laws of Nature, and did not deem it necessary to answer any of them in public print ; but all the *fac-similes*, as far as I recollect, were in my own workmanship, a fact I did not, and do not, deny. I hope on reading them you will not hold me in any way responsible for the various wonderful theories propounded by some of the writers. They were simply romance, as far as I was concerned.—Yours truly,

A. H. Smith.

Purchased from Macphail, Bookseller, Edinburgh, by me—
30th November, 1917. D. M'Naught.

James Cameron was a bookseller in St. David Street, Edinburgh—a fine specimen of the old school of bibliophiles.—D. M'N.

BURNS RELICS FOR ALLOWAY.

Some interesting additions have just been made to the collection of Burns relics at the Poet's birthplace at Alloway. They consist of articles that were personal to the Poet or to Jean Armour, and have been acquired from a great-granddaughter of the Poet, Mrs Annie V. Burns Scott, whose home is in South Australia. The most important is a manuscript of the poem, "The Lovely Isabella," dated "Edinburgh, 16th March, 1787," and signed by the Poet. It is the only manuscript of the poem known to exist. Its existence was not known to Burns students till 1894, when it was printed in an Australian journal. Other articles included in the collection are one of the Poet's seals, six buttons which belonged to the Poet, a brooch with lock of Mrs Burns's hair, a bracelet with lock of Mrs Burns's hair, silver spoons and sauce ladles which belonged to Mrs Burns, and top of table which belonged to Mrs Burns. The seal is fixed on the end of a silver pen and pencil holder, which, however, is not contemporary with it. The buttons are of brown and white stone, are silver mounted, and of the type used on waistcoats. The brooch, containing a lock of " Bonnie Jean's " hair, is of gold, and is set with seven stones. It bears on its reverse an engraved inscription " From Sarah Burns to her half-sister Annie in memory of their grandmother." The silver spoons, eighteen in number, with two sauce ladles, were a present from James Glencairn Burns to his mother on the occasion of one of his trips home from India.

THE BROWNS OF KIRKOSWALD.

Dear Sir,—Excuse my troubling you on a matter connected with the family on relations of Robert Burns, the Poet.

I have in my possession, amongst other MSS., a " Contract of Marriage " between one Samuel Broun and Agnes Logie, dated

23rd October, 1713.   A note by my grandfather, Gilbert Burns
(youngest son of Gilbert, the Poet's brother), states that these are
the Poet's maternal great-grand parents, but this is qualified by a
query.

Dr Charles Rogers is not a reliable authority, but there seems
to be no doubt that the grandfather of the Poet's mother was John
Broun (Craigentoun), who in December, 1675, married Janet M'Grean,
at Girvan.   This John Broun had a brother Samuel, but I find no
record of any marriage.   The father of this John Broun was named
John (Craigentoun), but I find no record of any brother of his nor
of the name of the woman he married.

Can you tell me if the *Burns Chronicle* is regularly sent to the
British Museum, or other Public Libraries ?   I read the other day
that there were not enough copies to go round to the subscribers.
Would it be possible to get hold of any back numbers ?   I have
from XIV. to XVIII. inclusive only of the series, and should at
least be glad of the complete index of articles and writers' names.

If of interest to readers of the *Chronicle* I will later on send a
very fairly complete chart of the senior branch of the Burns stock.

In a letter of yours to me, dated almost exactly 13 years ago,
you mention Vols. VII. and XIII. which I then wanted, and indeed
still want, but have never been able to procure.   I also want Vols.
II., III., and others of the series which have appeared since 1907.

Could you also tell me if "The New Psalmody" ("O sing a new
song") has ever been printed ?   I have the MS.—Yours faithfully,

K. G. BURNS.

4 Park Place, St. James', S.W.1.

BURNS AND AN AYR TAVERN.

SIR,—I have often wondered how the Robert Burns Tavern
in River Street, Ayr, got its name, or what connection it had with
the Poet.   In the "Brigs of Ayr" he says :—

> "He left his bed and took his wayward rout,
>   And down by Simpson's wheel'd the left about.
>
> .   .   .   .   ,
>
> When, lo ! on either hand the list'ning Bard,
> The clanging sugh of whistling wings is heard ;
> Two dusky forms dart thro' the midnight air,
> Swift as the Gos drives on the wheeling hare ;
> Ane on th' 'Auld Brig' his airy shape uprears,
> The ither flutters o'er the rising piers."

When reading the above lines I thought it might be from this coign of vantage the Poet in fancy listened to the lengthy and interesting dialogue that took place between the two sprites, but on making some enquiries I found my idea was not correct. However, it has been the means of giving some interesting information. It seems that this property at one time belonged to the Poet's mother's family, one of whom had a saddler's shop in it. When the property was first licensed it belonged to two Misses Brown, who would not have it called " Rabbie Burns " Tavern, because his proper name was " Robert," hence the sign. Perhaps he got the inspiration for the " Brigs of Ayr " looking out from his relative's shop door or window. JAS. HYSLOP.

BURNS AND THE LION RAMPANT.

The Schoolhouse,
Buckie, 20th November, 1920.

Mr D. M'Naught, Kilmaurs.

DEAR SIR,—I hope I am still in time in sending you a correction for your next issue of the *Burns Chronicle*, which pressure of duties has prevented me sending sooner.

In his article on " The Heraldry of Burns," the Rev. W. M'Millan repeats an error which occurs in his book on *Scottish Symbols*. He declares that Burns's lines in his " Address to Edinburgh "—

" Wild beats my heart, to trace your steps,
　　Whose ancestors, in days of yore,
　　Thro' hostile ranks and ruin'd gaps
　　Old Scotia's bloody lion bore "—

" refer to Scotland's Kings." The lines do nothing of the sort, as a careful perusal of the whole poem shows. The first two verses of the poem deal with Edinburgh's abstract qualities—wealth, justice, and learning. The third verse is addressed to Edina's sons, and the fourth to Edina's daughters. The fifth stanza refers to the Castle, and the sixth to Holyrood—

" Where Scotia's Kings of other years,
　　Fam'd heroes ! had their royal home :
　　Alas, how chang'd the times to come !
　　Their royal Name low in the dust !
　　Their hapless race wild-wand'ring roam,
　　Tho' rigid law cries out, 'Twas just ! "

And so he leaves the exiled Stuarts. Then follows the seventh verse, of which Mr M'Millan quotes the first half. But the verse clearly refers to the *people of Edinburgh*, and to the fact that Edinburgh's citizens were frequently and naturally first in the field, while provincial Scotland followed. Note the change of person from " their " in verse six to " your " in verse seven—from the dead Kings to his living hearers or readers. And note the second half of the same verse—

> " Ev'n I who sing in rustic lore,
> Haply my sires have left their shed,
> And faced grim danger's loudest roar,
> Bold following where *your fathers* led !"

Whose fathers ? Obviously the fathers of the people of Edinburgh, not " the fathers " of the vacancy that Holyrood now is ! Any reference to royalty is quite impossible. If further proof be needed that Burns is speaking of the Lion as Scotia's, not that of Scotia's Kings, it is found in his letter to the Earl of Buchan, where he expresses his longing to " make a leisurely pilgrimage through my native country ; to sit and muse on those once hard-contended fields, where *Caledonia*, rejoicing, saw *her bloody lion* borne through broken ranks to victory and fame."

Apart from Burns's actual language, it is impossible to think of Robert Burns, the high priest of " A man's a man for a' that," as supporting the narrow-minded modern view of a few heraldic faddists that the emblem of Scotia's ancient people and Kings alike—The Lion Rampant—ought to be regarded as the " personal flag " of the German lairdie whom fate had placed over the Scottish Nation in his day ? Perish the thought !

Mr M'Millan need not be at all surprised that Burns " nowhere mentioned specifically the Scottish National flag, the St. Andrew's saltier of white and blue." Burns is in the same company as Barbour, Blind Harry, Dunbar, Lyndesay, Ramsay, and Hogg, who know of no such banner, national or otherwise, but who reverence and love the Lion, the only national flag dating from, and used by, the Alexanders, Sir Wm. Wallace, and King Robert the Bruce. —Yours sincerely,

CHAS. W. THOMSON,
Author of *Scotland's Work and Worth.*

" THE LAND O' THE LEAL."

The Land o' the Leal—Irrefutably proved to be the Deathbed Valediction of Robert Burns, is the title of a book recently issued by Mr A. Crichton of Albany, Burrelton.

Mr Crichton has been an investigator of the subject on which he writes for more than thirty years, and has borne the gree in many a stiff debate on the disputed authorship in the public prints and elsewhere, and may therefore be trusted to know well what he has written about. His information has been culled from every quarter where a scrap of evidence was likely to be found, and his book, which has been handsomely printed at the office of the *Buchan Observer*, in Peterhead, contains many indisputable proofs of the authorship of the National Bard of Scotland. A special item in the book which ought to appeal to the most prejudiced believers in the Nairne Authorship, is a reproduced photo of the proof letter which is said to have been written by Lady Nairne in her old age. This letter, which has been kept in abeyance for obvious reasons for more than fifty years, is now exposed to public view for the first time, and is clearly seen to be a forgery on the one written by her ladyship. In the letter, as originally written by her, she says distinctly, with reference to the song ("The Land o' the Leal"), "I never wrote it." In the copy now submitted to the public it is clearly seen that the word "never" has been partially erased, and for the want of the word *never* the crown of fame passes from the brow of Robert Burns to that of the Baroness Nairne. It was a villianous deed, for which we may safely say that an untruthful and unscrupulous biographer in the person of Dr Charles Rogers, is ever to be held responsible. More of this gentleman is to be seen in the book.

The book in paper covers is priced at 1s 4d, and may be had handsomely bound in cloth at 2s 6d, post free, from the Author.

[As both sides have the right to be heard, we print the foregoing at the request of Mr Crichton without comment.—ED.].

THE " GEDDES BURNS."

Our reference a few days ago to a distinguished American collector of books and manuscripts reminds a correspondent that Mr Bixby is the possessor of probably the most interesting and certainly the most valuable copy known of the second edition of Burns's *Poems*, published at Edinburgh in 1787. It is the copy that has come to be known as the " Geddes Burns," from the fact that it originally belonged to the Rev. John Geddes, a Roman Catholic priest, in whose praise Burns wrote to Mrs Dunlop, and of whom also " Clarinda " spoke highly in one of her letters to " Sylvander." At the beginning of the volume is inserted the long original letter—unfortunately it is slightly imperfect—that was sent along with the book when the Poet, having had it that he might fill the blanks in the print and add some poetical pieces in his autograph on the blank leaves at beginning and end, returned it to its owner. These additional poems are twelve in number, and fill 27 pages.

This volume—one of the earlier or " skinking " issue, by the way —was reproduced in *fac-simile* by the Bibliophile Society of Boston, Mass., in 1908. The edition was limited to 473 copies, for members of the Society only, so it must always be an uncommon book. The *fac-simile* of the " Geddes Burns " is undoubtedly a wonderful reproduction—portrait, print, and manuscript ; even the armorial bookplate of Bishop Geddes is reproduced inside the front board. The paper throughout is water-marked " Bibliophile Society—Made in Holland," and the volume is bound in calf and enclosed in a slip case. Prefixed is a note telling the history of the volume from the day on which it was forwarded by Burns at Ellisland to Bishop Geddes at Edinburgh till it was purchased by Mr Bixby ; and that note, though it speaks of Alexander instead of John Geddes. reads " more like a romance than a reality."

—*Glasgow Herald.*

THE SYME-CINDER MYTH.

FURTHER CONTEMPORARY EVIDENCE.

At different times the *Burns Chronicle* has sought to rescue the reputation of the National Bard from the evil suggestions of the late Mr Henley and others like-minded ; and it seems to be fairly well established now that, if the Poet was not an abstainer, neither was he a toper during his last unhappy days in Dumfries. I recently came across a little bit of contemporary evidence that further tends to disprove the " burnt-to-a-cinder charge."

In 1898 the late Mr William Lindsay, the well-known book-seller in Aberdeen, published a volume entitled *Some Notes : Personal and Public.* It was the story of his own not unsuccessful career, and dealt with many interests in which he had had a share. Referring to the establishment of the *Commonwealth* newspaper in Glasgow in 1853, he says that Mr Rae, the publisher, paid a visit to Aberdeen sometime before the paper started, and asked him to join the commercial staff. Mr Lindsay did so. His first work was to visit the county of Ayr to see agents and correspondents, and while engaged in these duties he made pilgrimage to " all the parts in the county of note that are immortalised by Burns." These included Mauchline, where he got into conversation with the sexton of the churchyard, " then an old man."

" Our interview with him," writes Mr Lindsay, " added greatly to the value of our visit, for he took us to see every spot to which

Burns had made allusion, and gave us full information on the points connected with each. But we learned, besides, that this man, whose real name was Kirkland, and who belonged to the Border counties, had been unsuccessful in business there, and had gone to Dumfries, where he actually enjoyed the acquaintance of the Poet. When I learned this I was much interested in Bryce, for that's the name he had assumed and was known by in Dumfries and in Mauchline. He volunteered this statement to me :—" Robert Burns was not the intemperate fellow that many people, when he was alive, represented him to be, and do still. Burns was always happy-go-lucky, and never concealed anything about himself, but I always found him to be a warm-hearted, kindly man. For my part, I never believed a hundredth part of the ill that I have heard spoken about Burns by men whom I knew to be fifty times more drunken than ever he was, although they concealed it."

Kirkland, *alias* Bryce, is not new to Burnsiana, but Lindsay's book is probably the first to seek to establish that Bryce was an acquaintance of the Poet. Mr William Wallace, in his revised edition of *Chambers's Burns*, says (vol. I., page 346), when referring to the correspondence which passed between the Bard and David Brice of Glasgow : " A Thomas Brice, from Glasgow, who settled in Mauchline as a weaver and shoemaker about the end of last (*i.e.,* the eighteenth) century, and ultimately became beadle and grave-digger, may have been a son of David Brice. For a time he went by the name of Thomas Kirkland. Latterly, however, he resumed the name of Thomas Brice." I should say that the reference to Bryce in Mr Lindsay's book does not strengthen the view that he was a son of the Poet's intimate friend and correspondent. Lindsay says the man came from the Borders, and as he was apparently proud to recall the fact that he had enjoyed the acquaintance of the Bard in Dumfries, it is unlikely he would have omitted to mention that his father was—as the letters to David Brice undoubtedly indicate—one of Burns's closest personal friends in their Mauchline days.

Mr Lindsay met Bryce in 1853, which was 57 years after the death of Burns. He says that Bryce was " an old man." Even if we allow him to have reached the long age of eighty, he must have been considerably the junior of the Poet. But that is no reason why he should not have known Burns in Dumfries. His evidence is not without value as that of a contemporary, and as Mr Lindsay's volume was strictly limited to private circulation, and is scarce, it seems right that the statement should receive the wider publicity afforded by the *Burns Chronicle.*

WILLIAM HARVEY.

NOTE ON THE WORD "DRIDDLE."

This unusual word occurs only twice in Burns—here and in the Epistle to Major Logan. In both cases the Poet seems to associate the word with the idea of the efforts of an old or feeble fiddler. There seems, however, to be a great deal of uncertainty as to its exact meaning. In a note to the Epistle "driddle" is interpreted "to hobble on a staff" by one authority; by another it is taken to mean "to move slowly, to be constantly in motion but making little progress." According to Reid, it must be applied to "the motion of one who tries to dance, but moves the middle only." The word is sometimes used for "to spill in small quantities," but the more popular interpretation, and the one which is perhaps the most widely accepted, is "to do anything feebly." If this latter meaning be taken as the root idea, it is not difficult to see how Burns has applied it to the feeble music produced by the "pigmy scraper," and how the same word can be used by him to describe the "grey-haired carl" who totters on a "crummock." By taking it in this way we are able to avoid the unwarranted alteration of the text of "The Jolly Beggars," which would be necessary, if we were to read "Wha used *to* trysts and fairs to driddle." The idea of a feeble performance "*at* tryst or fair" is to be preferred, as being more natural and closer to the sense of the verse in which it occurs, to the more laboured notion of the fiddler tottering from one place to another. Is it not legitimate to conclude that the attention of the reader is meant to be fixed rather upon the thinness of the music than upon the physical weakness of the fiddler?

R. FARQUHAR ORR.

Manse of Stanley.

BURNS MSS. AND RELICS FOR SALE.

We have received from Mr K. G. Burns a list of ten original manuscripts, books, relics, and a number of documents connected with the relatives of the Scottish Poet, which are now in the market at a reserve price of £10,000. At least sixteen of the thirty-five detailed were lent by Mrs J. G. Burns, of Knocmaroon, to the Burns Exhibition, held in Glasgow in 1896. No. 1 on the list is the Family Bible (Edinburgh, 1762) of William Burnes, father of the Poet, the "big ha' Bible" of "The Cottar's Saturday Night." In the owner's handwriting at the end of the Old Testament are entered the births of his children : the death of Mrs Burnes is recorded by James Burns, second son of Gilbert Burns, while the Poet himself enters the death of his father. The Bible is said to have been used daily by Mrs Burnes, and on her death passed into the possession of Gilbert and his descendants. As will be recalled, the Family Bible of the Poet himself, sold at auction as Mrs Burns-Hutchinson's in 1904 for £1560, was shortly afterwards acquired at £1700 for the Museum at Alloway. There are also a silver watch, which on the death of William Burnes, was worn by the Poet until he went to Dumfries, when, buying a new one, he gave it to his mother ; a pair of black leather gloves bought by Burns to wear at the funeral of the Earl of Glencairn ; the Poet's riding whip and spurs, used when he was an Exciseman, on his Highland tour, &c., together with a pair of razors, all of which Gilbert Burns received as keepsakes, and a black profile portrait of the Poet, said by his brother Gilbert to be a correct likeness. Of the two copies of the valuable Kilmarnock Edition of the *Poems,* chiefly in the Scottish dialect, both bound in boards, one is a presentation to Lady Elizabeth Cunningham.

ORIGINAL MANUSCRIPTS.

Prominent among the original autographs are those of " The Jolly Beggars," and " Scots Wha Hae." The Huth Manuscript of the first-named realised £490 in 1911, against a cost of £12 in the sixties. The MS. of " Bruce's Address to his Army," differing slightly from the familiar version, was given by Burns to his sister-in-law, Mrs Gilbert Burns. In 1907 the Hamilton autograph of the song was bought at auction for the Burns Museum at £355. In this connection it is worth recalling that about 1870 Henry Stevens purchased an autograph of the " Bannockburn " for £33, thinking that Mr James Lenox, the American of Scottish descent, would be glad to have it at a small profit. Lenox, however, declined to buy, and Henry Stevens kept the autograph for a couple of decades. Now, I believe, it is in the library of Harvard University. There are also MSS. of " The Fête Champetre," sent with a letter to John Ballantine ; the " Stanzas of Psalmody," composed for the general thanksgiving on the King's recovery from mental derangement, held at Kilmarnock, 23rd April, 1789 ; the rough draft of a letter written to the Countess of Glencairn, with innumerable corrections, relates to the patronage of the house of Glencairn, and intimates the Poet's Excise appointment. Probably this is the first form of the long letter written at Ellisland on 23rd December, 1789. The other letters are to Alexander Dalziel, 10th March, 1791 ; to Alexander Cunningham, August, 1791, incomplete ; and two to John Ballantine, the first franked by Mr Miller, and dated 25th October, 1791, the second beginning—" I have been wandering for some time past like Satan in the   " .

The third section includes the original MS. of the " Address to the Sons of Burns," signed by Wordsworth, and sent by an intimate friend of the Lake poet to Gilbert Burns, and various certificates,

agreements, indentures, &c., relating for the most part to William
Burnes and the lands he held at Tarbolton.

—*Glasgow Herald*, 10th December, 1920.

BURNS AND THOMAS BOYD.

On 15th December, Messrs Sotheby will offer for sale as the
property of Miss H. B. Waddell-Boyd, Ravelin House, Portsmouth,
three autograph notes addressed by Burns to Thomas Boyd. All
three relate to the house built for the Poet on the Ellisland Farm,
the first two being inscribed from " Isle," namely, a hut about half
a mile below the farm, near the ivy-covered tower of the Isle, where
he lived till, belatedly, his own home was ready. The first note,
merely dated " Sunday morn," reads :—" I am distressed with
the want of my house in a most provoking manner. It loses me
two hours' work of my servants every day, besides other inconveniences. For G—d's sake let me be but within the shell of it."
On a subsequent " Sunday morn " Burns remained unhoused. " I
arrived from Edin. yesternight, and was a good deal surprised at finding my house still lying like Babylon in the prophecies of Isaiah. . . "
Early in 1789 Burns got into the new house—though it had not been
plastered—and more than two years later, on 16th June, 1791, he
wrote from Ellisland to Thomas Boyd :—" As it is high time that
the account between you and me were settled, if you will take a
bill on Mr Alexr. Crombie's to me for £20 in part . . . Mr Crombie
cannot take it amiss that I endeavour to get myself clear of his
bill in this manner, as you owe him, and I owe you." The bill
dated, Dumfries, 6th April, 1791, goes with the letter. As will be
recalled, Alexander Crombie, Dalswinton, built the farm edifices
at Ellisland, and failed to meet a bill for £20 drawn on him by the
Poet.

Belonging to the late Colonel Henry of Haffield is an autograph
of the two poems beginning " Hear, land o' cakes, and brither Scots,"
and " Thou ling'ring star, with lessening ray ;" while from another
source comes a portable writing desk with a brass plate inscribed
" Dugald Stewart to Robert Burns, Edinburgh, 25th January,
1787."

The Burns Federation.

INSTITUTED 1885.

Hon. President—The Right Hon. The EARL OF ROSEBERY, K.G., K.T.

Hon. Vice-Presidents—WM. WALLACE, LL.D., University Avenue, Glasgow.
Professor LAWSON, D.D., The University, St. Andrews.
Sir ALEX. GIBB, G.B.E., C.B., R.E., Ministry of Transport, 6 Whitehall Gardens, London, S.W.1.

OFFICE-BEARERS.

President—DUNCAN M'NAUGHT, J.P., Benrig, Kilmaurs.

Vice-Presidents—J. JEFFREY HUNTER, 89 Bath Street, Glasgow.
A. M'CALLUM, *News* Office, Pollockshaws.
ALEX. POLLOCK, 52 West Nile Street, Glasgow.
W. H. TURNER, 9 The Oaks, Sunderland.
JOHN CARMICHAEL, 49 Park Road, Glasgow.
P. PATERSON, 23 Bruce Street, Dunfermline.
Ex-Bailie MUNRO, J.P., Howard Park Drive, Kilmarnock.
Ex-Provost M. SMITH, J.P., Glencairn Square, Kilmarnock.
Ex-Provost WILSON, 149 Howard Street, Glasgow.
PHILIP SULLEY, 27 Rutland Square, Edinburgh.
HUGH M'COLL, 278 St. Vincent Street, Glasgow.
DAVID MAIN, Lowther Street, Carlisle.
Col. HENRY S. MURRAY, J.P., Glenmayne, Galashiels.
CHARLES R. COWIE, Blythswood Square, Glasgow.
J. C. EWING, Bailie's Institution, West Regent Street, Glasgow
ALEX. M'KENZIE, 210 Battlefield Road, Langside, Glasgow.
JAMES THOMSON, F.S.A.(Scot.), The Cedars, 21 Fortis Green
East Finchley, London, N.2.
WILLIAM DOUGLAS, 509 Sauchiehall Street, Glasgow.
THOS. KILLIN, 2 Stewarton Drive, Cambuslang.

Hon. Secretary—THOS. AMOS, M.A., 19 Glebe Road, Kilmarnock.

Hon. Treasurer—Major G. A. INNES, M.B.E , 14 London Road, Kilmarnock.

Editor " Burns Chronicle "—D. M'NAUGHT, J.P., Benrig, Kilmaurs.

Auditors—Major D. YUILLE, Burns Avenue, Kilmarnock, and Capt. ADAM MACKAY, The Crescent, Prestwick.

Local Representatives—
London—P. N. M'FARLANE, Tallis House, Tallis Street, London, E.C.
North of England—W. H. TURNER, Sunderland.
Glasgow and District—J. JEFFREY HUNTER, 89 Bath Street, Glasgow

Hon. Secretary of Children's Competitions—ALEX. POLLOCK, 52 West Nile Street, Glasgow (to whom all communications should be addressed).

CONSTITUTION.

1. The Federation shall consist of Hon. Presidents, Hon. Vice-Presidents, Executive Council, and members of each affiliated Club.

2. The Executive Council shall consist of a President, Vice-Presidents, Hon. Secretary, Hon. Treasurer, Editor of the *Burns Chronicle*, and two Auditors—all of whom shall be elected annually, and be eligible for re-election ; also of the President, Vice-President, and Secretary, or any other three members of, and nominated by, each affiliated Club, and other gentlemen of eminence as Burnsians nominated by the Executive Council.

3. All Past Presidents of the Federation shall *ex officio* be members of the Executive Council.

4. The Executive Committee shall consist of the Office-bearers of the Federation, who shall meet quarterly, or when called by the Hon. Secretary, for the transaction of the business of the Federation.

5. Federated Clubs outwith the United Kingdom may be represented by proxy at the meetings of the Federation.

OBJECTS OF THE FEDERATION.

1. To strengthen and consolidate by universal affiliation the bond of fellowship existing amongst the members of Burns Clubs and kindred Societies.

2. To superintend the publication of Works relating to Burns.

3. To acquire a fund for the purchase and preservation of Holograph Manuscripts and other Relics connected with the life of the Poet, and for other purposes of a like nature, as the Executive Council may determine.

4. To repair, renew, and where advisable mark with suitable inscriptions any buildings, tombstones, etc., interesting from their association with Burns.

5. To encourage and arrange School Competitions in order to stimulate the teaching of Scottish History and Literature.

RULES.

1. The Headquarters of the Federation shall be in Kilmarnock, the town in which the Federation was inaugurated and carried to a practical issue, and which contains the only properly organised Burns Library and Museum in the United Kingdom.

2. Properly organised Burns Clubs, St. Andrew's Societies,. and kindred Associations may be admitted to the Federation by application in writing to the Hon. Secretary, enclosing a copy of Constitution, Rules, and list of members, which shall be submitted to the Executive Committee at their first meeting, and the Clubs shall be enrolled if there are not more than two dissentients.

3. The Registration Fee is 21s, on receipt of which the Diploma of the Federation shall be issued, after being numbered and signed by the President and Hon. Secretary.

4. Members of every Burns Club or kindred Association registered by the Federation shall be entitled to receive a pocket Diploma on payment of 1s. These payments are final—not annual.

5. The funds of the Federation shall be vested in the Executive Committee for the purposes before mentioned.

6. A meeting of the Executive Council shall be held annually on the first Saturday of September, at such place as may be agreed upon, when reports on the year's transactions shall be submitted by the Hon. Secretary and Hon. Treasurer, and Office-Bearers elected for the ensuing year.

7. A meeting of the Executive Committee shall take place some time before the Annual Meeting of the Executive Council, to make the necessary arrangements for the same.

8. All nominations for the office of Vice-President must be lodged with the Hon. Secretary two months before the Annual Meeting.

9. Each Federated Club shall subscribe 10s 6d per annum towards the fund for the publication of the *Burns Chronicle*. Clubs failing to pay this subscription for two consecutive years may be struck off the Roll of the Federation. Any surplus profits resulting from the sale of the *Chronicle* shall be added to the general funds.

10. Notice of any amendment or alteration of the Constitution or Rules of the Federation to be considered at the Annual Meeting must be lodged in writing with the Hon. Secretary not later than 30th June.

BENEFITS.

1. Registered Clubs are supplied free with copies of newspapers containing accounts of meetings, demonstrations, etc., organised, conducted, or attended by the Executive Council of the Federation, and of the Annual Meeting of the Kilmarnock Burns Club.

2. Exchange of fraternal greetings on the anniversary of the Poet's natal day.

3. Members of Registered Clubs who have provided themselves with pocket diplomas are entitled to attend meetings of all Clubs on the Roll of the Federation, they being subject to the rules of the Club visited, but having no voice in its management unless admitted a member according to local form.

4. Members are entitled to be supplied, through the Secretaries of their respective Clubs, with copies of all Works published by the Federation at a discount of 25 per cent.

5. A list of Lecturers, Essayists, and Judges for Children's Competitions will be supplied to Clubs on application.

BOOKS PUBLISHED BY THE FEDERATION.

BURNS HOLOGRAPH MANUSCRIPTS in the Kilmarnock Monument Museum, with Notes		1889		1s 6d
BURNS CHRONICLE and CLUB DIRECTORY...		1892		1s 0d
,,	,,	1893		1s 6d
		1894		1s 6d
		1895		1s 6d
		1896		1s 6d
		1897		1s 6d
,,		1898		1s 6d
,,	,,	1899		1s 6d
,,	,, ...	1900		1s 6d
	,, (out of print)	1901		1s 6d
	,,	1902		1s 6d
		1903		1s 6d
		1904		1s 6d
		1905		1s 6d
		1906		1s 6d
		1907 ...		1s 6d
		1908 ...		1s 6d
		1909		1s 6d
		1910		1s 6d
		1911		1s 6d
		1912		1s 6d
		1913		1s 6d
		1914		1s 6d
		1915		1s 6d
		1916		1s 6d
		1917		2s 0d
		1918		2s 0d
		1919		2s 0d
		1920		2s 0d
,,		1921		3s 0d
INDEX	... ...			1s 0d

Copies of the last ten vols. may still be had on application to the Hon. Treasurer.

MINUTES OF THE ANNUAL MEETING

OF THE

BURNS FEDERATION.

ROYAL SCOTTISH CORPORATION HALL,
CRANE COURT, FLEET STREET,
LONDON, 4th September, 1920.

THE Annual Meeting of the Burns Federation was held here to-day. Mr D. M'Naught, J.P., presiding. The following Delegates were present :—

No. 0, Kilmarnock—D. M'Naught, J.P. ; Thomas Amos, M.A. ; Geo. A. Innes, M.B.E. ; ex-Provost M. Smith, J.P. ; J. P. Dickson ; ex-Bailie Munro, J.P. No. 1, London Robert Burns Club—L. G. Sloan, J.P. ; Sir Wm. Noble, P. N. M'Farlane, James Thomson, F.S.A.(Scot.). No. 3, Glasgow Tam o' Shanter—J. Jeffrey Hunter, Alex. M'Kenzie, John Carmichael. No. 9, Glasgow Royalty—Wm. Jamieson, Councillor Jas. Macfarlane, David Gunn. No. 14, Dundee—J. Purves, Jas. Ogilvie, Jas. Neilson. No. 21, Greenock—Hugh M'Lean, Grierson Macara. No. 33,'' Glasgow Haggis—David Macfarlane. No. 36, Glasgow Rosebery—Wm. Craig, Geo. Armour. No. 49, Glasgow Bridgeton—Jas. W. Shaw, J.P. ; David S. Brown, Jas. Craig, Geo. Newton. No. 53, Govan Fairfield—Thomas Fullarton. No. 63, Glasgow Mossgiel—John Hutcheon, Robert Parker, Jas. Robertson. No. 67, Glasgow Carlton—Wm. Gardiner. No. 74, Glasgow Mauchline—Thos. Killin, J. Taylor Gibb, George Smith. No. 85, Dunfermline United —Sir Alexander Gibb, G.B.E., C.B., C.E. ; Wm. Black, P. Donald, Thos. Lessels, P. Paterson. No. 89, Sunderland—T. E. A. A. Shaw, A. W. Semple, M. Neilson. No. 91, Shettleston—Geo. S. Glendinning. No. 113, Vale of Leven Glencairn—William Smith. No. 118, Glasgow Albany—J. Niven Murdoch, Richard Donaldson. No. 121, Hamilton Juniors—David Cross, William Wilson, Jas. Brown. No. 139, Glasgow National—T. M. Hamilton, J. G. Galpine. No. 151, Old Kilpatrick—Wm. C. Cockburn. No. 167, Birmingham—Wright Murray. No. 169, Glasgow B.C.A.—T. Sutherland, Isaac Chalmers. No. 181, Glasgow Primrose—John Hair, T. B. Paton, James Lamb. No. 184, Blairadam Shanter— Thos. C. Anderson. No. 187, Galashiels—Col. H. S. Murray, J.P. No. 189, Clydebank Barns o' Clyde—Lawrence Watt. No. 202, Govan Ye Cronies—Jas. Rellie, J. Hutchison, M. Stirling. No. 207, Cambuslang Wingate—John M'Farlane, John M'Cracken. No. 209, Greenock St. John's—Jas. A. Morrison. No. 212, Portobello —Wm. Baird, J.P., F.S.A.(Scot.). No. 247, Lochgelly Jolly Beggars —Jas. D. Wilson, John Adamson, James Walker. No. 250, Cowdenbeath Tam o' Shanter—George Marshall. No. 251, Glencraig— Thomas Ferguson. No. 275, Ayr—Ex-Provost Hunter, James Wills.

Apologies for absence were intimated from Mr C. R. Cowie, Partick ; Mr Alex. Pollock and Mr Hugh M'Coll, Glasgow ; and Mr Philip Sulley, Edinburgh.

The Minutes of last Annual Meeting and of Committee Meetings held during the year were read and approved.

The Secretary submitted the following Annual Report :—

" To anyone unacquainted with the history of the Burns Federation, our meeting in London to-day may seem out of its proper setting, but that is not so. Wherever Scotsmen may wander they rally round the name of Burns, and in his memory establish Burns Clubs—most characteristic of all the institutions in Scottish social and literary life.

" There are few Scottish towns or villages without a Burns Club, and no one can be surprised that London, the home of so many Scots, has its Burns Clubs, among which the Robert Burns Club, No. 1 on our roll, holds the premier position with a record of more than fifty years' excellent work. At its invitation we gladly visit this mighty city, whose name to the peasant Poet was always associated with wealth, but will henceforth recall to us the kindly fellowship and bounteous hospitality we have experienced during our visit.

" Thirty-five years ago three Scotsmen, Colin Rae Brown of London, and David Mackay and David Sneddon of Kilmarnock, met at the unveiling of the Burns bust in Westminster Abbey. They were perfervid Burnsians, and as they were walking along the Embankment after the ceremony one of-them suggested the formation of a Federation to unify Burns Clubs throughout the world. . From this idea sprang the Burns Federation, which was soon afterwards founded in Kilmarnock, and has increased each year in vigour and usefulness. If an apology is needed for our presence here to-day surely this will suffice.

" I have great pleasure in reporting the continued success of the Federation since our conference in Glasgow a year ago. There are now on our roll 277 Clubs in Scotland, England, Ireland, the United States, Canada, South Africa, and New Zealand. Of these the following seventeen have affiliated during the past year :— Fifeshire Burns Association, Glasgow Masonic, Prestonpans Jolly Beggars, Bingry Jolly Beggars, Newton Jolly Beggars, Prestonpans Mystic, Anderston Cronies, Johnstone Tam o' Shanter, Coquetdale, Trenton (U.S.A.), Stewarton Hodden Grey, Lanark Jolly Beggars, Troon, Ayr, Lumphinnans, Harriman (U.S.A.), and Duluth (U.S.A.). During the year I have issued 315 members' diplomas, which are specially value⟩ as a means of introduction by members who are leaving home.

" Last January No. 29 of the *Burns Chronicle* was published, and there was such an unprecedented run on our Annual that in a few days not a spare copy could be obtained. In the variety and excellence of its articles it maintained the high standard set by its predecessors, and once again we must acknowledge the untiring work of our veteran Editor, who has so successfully conducted the *Chronicle* for twenty-eight years. Each year finds the *Chronicle* more prized by Burnsians, and a complete set of its numbers is regarded by them as a treasure. The two outstanding events in the Burns world during the year have been the recent visit of Mr John Gribbel and the final disposal of the Grave and Monument of Highland Mary in the West Churchyard of Greenock.

" When it was known that the restorer of the Glenriddel MSS. was to visit Scotland, the Federation determined to give him a welcome that would show him how deeply sensible we were of his generosity. At an enthusiastic complimentary dinner in Glasgow, which was attended by 130 delegates, the Scottish Album, containing an illuminated address and thirty-six sketches by famous Scottish artists, was presented to Mr Gribbol. Under the care of the Federation he visited most of the places in the Land of Burns associated with the life of the Poet. He was honoured by a civic reception in Glasgow, Edinburgh, Ayr, Kilmarnock, and Dumfries, and he was also entertained by the National Burns Club, the Burns House, and the Rosebery Burns Club, Glasgow. He has returned to America bearing many gifts from Burnsians who appreciated his disinterested and magnanimous conduct, and best of all, he takes with him the gratitude of a nation that has been profoundly moved by his gift.

" Wherever he went Mr Gribbel left the happiest memories. We found in him a true disciple of our National Bard and an ardent admirer of our country. No Ambassador who has ever come from the United States could have been more earnest in his wish to see a closer and more intimate feeling between Britain and his country. We were grateful for his gift, we were more than grateful for his uplifting presence among us, and we sincerely hope he may long live to have happy memories of his visit to Scotland.

" Four months ago, at a meeting of a Special Committee of the Federation and Delegates from Greenock Burns Club, which was held in Greenock, it was agreed to remove the remains of Highland Mary and the Monument to her memory from the West Parish Churchyard to a suitable resting-place provided by the Town Council in the local cemetery. The majority of the Committee, when they had examined the Churchyard and its surroundings, thought it would be more decent and fitting to remove the remains than to have them isolated in the midst of a great shipyard. A place of reinterment has been fixed in Greenock Cemetery not far from the monument to James Watt, and we hope that the dust of Burns's heroine may henceforth rest in peace. At a recent Executive Committee meeting the Burns Club of Greenock was empowered to carry out the wishes of the Federation, with the professional assistance of Mr Ninian M'Whannell, and so ends this controversy that has lasted for three years.

" Some time ago Lord Pirrie offered the Federation the sum of £300 to erect a monument in memory of Highland Mary. As it was left to us to fix the spot where the monument would be placed, it was agreed, at the suggestion of the President, to erect it at the hamlet of Blackhill, close to the romantic spot where Burns is said to have parted with Highland Mary. Mr James Arthur of Montgomerie has kindly permitted the Federation to erect the monument on his property.

" The country has not yet sufficiently settled down after the Great War to permit the full resuscitation of the Children's Competitions in Scottish song and poetry, which were so successful some years ago, and which were such a marked feature in Burns educational work. We, however, have every reason to hope that we may soon have from Mr Pollock the encouraging reports on this subject which he for many years gave at our annual conferences.

" The excellent work of the Glasgow-Mauchline Society and the Glasgow Burns Clubs' Association in providing Burns Homes for aged poor in Mauchline still goes prosperously forward. There is a rumour that the Mauchline Society propose to add more cottages to those that already cluster round their Memorial Tower close to

Mossgiel.   Of all the monuments that have ever been erected to
the memory of Burns none are nobler or worthier of your support
than these homes.   We heartily wish them success, and commend
them to your consideration.

" The standing of the Federation was never so high as at present.
It is recognised far and wide as the ultimate authority in all matters
pertaining to Burns.   Its Clubs successfully carry on their social,
literary, and philanthropic work, and fill a recognised and necessary
place in our national life ;   while the good they are accomplishing
has killed the old jibe that they exist only for the consumption
of haggis and whisky.

" For many years our Annual Conferences were brightened by
social gatherings, which are being happily renewed this year, after
their abeyance during the war.   We are deeply indebted to the
London Robert Burns Club for its great hospitality, and I have the
greatest pleasure in mentioning the unceasing labours of its indefatigable Secretary, Mr P. N. M'Farlane, to make this visit, at one
time considered ' a dark and perilous adventure,' one of the most
successful in our annals."

In submitting his Annual Financial Statement, the Treasurer
reported that the Federation had a credit balance of £154 8s.   The
income for the year had increased, but the expenditure had been
great.   He suggested that the price of the *Chronicle* should be increased to meet the increased cost of printing.

Mr Jas. Thomson, London, moved, and Mr Wright Murray,
Birmingham, seconded, that the price of the *Chronicle* be 3s to non-
members and 2s 6d to members.   The motion was unanimously
adopted.

In his report on the *Chronicle,* the Chairman stated that Mr
Albert Douglas of Washington, U.S.A., who was present at the
meeting, had, as a labour of love, compiled an Index for the last
29 numbers.   He asked if this Index should be incorporated in the
next volume or published separately.   Mr Douglas offered £25 ;
Col. H. S. Murray, of Galashiels, offered £10 ;   and Sir Alexander
Gibb, G.B.E., C.B., volunteered to make up the balance of the
cost of publishing the Index.

On the motion of Mr Thos. Killin, seconded by Mr T. M. Hamilton, it was agreed to print the Index in a separate volume.

In his report on Highland Mary's grave, the Chairman said that
the decision of the Executive Committee was, on the whole, a very
sensible conclusion.   He informed the meeting that Lord Pirrie
had offered the sum of £300 to erect a Memorial to Highland Mary,
and a site had been chosen at the romantic spot where the parting
took place close to the hamlet of Blackhill, in Ayrshire.   Mr J.
Taylor Gibb asked who would be the custodians of the monument,
and on the suggestion of the Chairman, it was agreed that this
question should be left to the Executive Committee in the meantime.

In the absence of Mr Alex. Pollock, his report on School Children's Competitions was read by the Secretary.

In his report, Mr Pollock stated that he had personally received
reports of competitions in singing and reciting Burns poems and
songs from more than twenty Clubs.   Essay competitions had
been held by two Clubs.

From Press reports and other reliable sources he knew that fifty Clubs had continued, resumed, or initiated this most interesting and valuable work. Bridgeton Club, Glasgow, held competitons in eighteen schools ; Dumfries Club, in five schools ; and the Fifeshire Burns Association in eight schools.

Mr Baird, J.P., Portobello, mentioned that during the past twenty-eight years Portobello Burns Club had distributed £100 in prizes to pupils who entered these competitions in singing and reciting. He agreed with Mr Pollock in leaving these competitions in the hands of the teachers.

On the motion of Mr J. Jeffrey Hunter, seconded by Mr J. Taylor Gibb, Mauchline, it was unanimously agreed to re-elect the Office-bearers.

On behalf of Dunfermline United Burns Club, Sir Alexander Gibb, G.B.E., C.B., invited the Federation to hold the next Annual Meeting in Dunfermline, and Mr Wright Murray, President of Birmingham Burns Club, on behalf of his Club, invited the Federation to meet in Birmingham in 1922. It was agreed to accept both invitations.

On the motion of Mr J. Jeffrey Hunter, seconded by Mr Alexander M'Kenzie, a hearty vote of thanks was given to the Royal Scottish Corporation for the use of their Hall.

A vote of thanks to the Chairman terminated the meeting.

––––––

The Social Gatherings at our London Conference were characterised throughout by the kindly feeling shown to the Delegates by the members of the London Robert Burns Club, who vied with each other in their efforts to promote our pleasure and happiness.

The princely hospitality and genial fellowship of Mr L. G. Sloan, J.P., the President of the local Club, and the untiring kindness of all the members, combined to make our visit one of the most memorable in our annals. Much of the work fell on the able shoulders of the local Secretary, Mr P. N. M'Farlane, who carried out all the details with triumphant success. Nor can we forget the friendly help rendered by our old friend, Mr Jas. Thomson, F.S.A. (Scot.), the former Secretary of the Club. Looking back on the meetings, and noting all the careful planning and willing working of the local Club, one cannot refrain from expressing the lasting gratitude of all the Delegates who attended a meeting which has left so many happy memories.

THE DINNER.

On Friday evening the Delegates were entertained to dinner in the beautiful and historical Vintners' Hall by Mr Sloan, who occupied the chair. Sir William Noble held the position of croupier. After an excellent repast, the Chairman, in a felicitous and appropriate speech, welcomed the Delegates to London. Mr John Douglas, F.S.A.(Scot.), eloquently proposed the toast of the Burns Federation, to which Mr M'Naught replied. Other toasts honoured were " The London Robert Burns Club," proposed by Mr Thomas Amos, and responded to by Messrs P. N. M'Farlane and Wm. Will, and " The

Vintners' Company," proposed by Sir Wm. Noble, and acknowledged by Mr Charles Powell, the Upper Warden. Mr William Anderson, M.P., who was present, also briefly addressed the meeting.

During the evening Miss Bessie Fraser, from Sydney, Australia, Miss Christina Gordon, Mr John Adams, and Mr Neil Kenyon delighted the company with their songs. In addition, some fine recitations were given by Mr Bransby Williams, and an excellent musical programme was contributed by Signor Gandia's Orchestra. On the motion of Major Innes, a hearty vote of thanks was awarded to the Chairman and artistes.

During the evening the Chairman presented to each of his guests a suitably inscribed gold-mounted fountain pen.

AT THE BURNS STATUE.

The Delegates met on Saturday morning at the Savoy Gardens, Thames Embankment, and Mr M'Naught placed a wreath of heather and holly at the base of the Burns Statue. Several photographs of the company were then taken.

THE LUNCHEON.

Immediately after the business meeting, the Delegates and lady friends were generously entertained to luncheon in Anderton's Hotel, Fleet Street, by the members of the Robert Burns Club. Mr L. G. Sloan again acted as Chairman, and after luncheon announced that he had anonymously received the sum of £100 for the funds of the Federation. On the call of Mr M'Naught, a hearty vote of thanks was given to the donor.

Through the kindness of Sir Wm. Noble, each of the company was supplied with a packet of chocolates.

DRIVE TO BUSHEY.

After luncheon the Delegates were taken by motor 'bus to the Royal Caledonian Schools at Bushey. The interesting drive was thoroughly enjoyed by all. On arriving at the Schools, the party was met by the boys' pipe band, and a fine programme of sports and music was submitted. The visitors were entertained to tea in the dining-room of the Institution, and welcomed by Sir William Noble on behalf of the Directors. Major Innes complimented the staff and pupils on their splendid entertainment, and announced that £100 had been given that day to the school, to commemorate the visit of the Federation. At his suggestion, a contribution was taken to help the funds of the school, and under the able direction of Mr Thomas Killin, the sum of £52 was collected and handed to Mr Forsyth, the Treasurer of the Institution. After an excellent concert, in which Miss Bessie Fraser, of Sydney, again took a prominent part, the company joined hands and sang " Auld Lang Syne " before returning to London.

THOMAS AMOS, *Hon. Secretary.*

List of Clubs which have Subscribed to the Publishing Fund.

Aberdeen ...	...£1	1	0
Alexandria ...	0	10	6
Alloway	0	10	6
Anderston Cronies...	0	10	6
Armadale Buck's Head ...	0	10	6
Atlanta, Ga., U.S.A.	1	1	0
Ayr	1	1	0
Baillieston Caledonia	0	10	6
Bannockburn Empire	0	10	6
Bingry Jolly Beggars	0	10	6
Birmingham ...	0	10	6
Blackburn-on-Almond	1	1	0
Blairadam Shanter	0	10	6
Bonnyrigg A man's a' man	0	10	6
Brechin ...	0	10	6
Bristol ...	0	10	6
Broxburn Jolly Beggars ...	0	10	6
Cambuslang Wingate ...	0	10	6
Chattanooga, U.S.A. ...	0	10	6
Clydebank Barns o' Clyde	0	10	6
Colorado Springs Caledonian Society	0	10	6
Coquetdale ...	0	10	6
Cowdenbeath Glencairn ...	0	10	6
Cowdenbeath Tam o' Shanter	0	10	6
Crook, Co. Durham ...	1	1	0
Cumnock Winsome Willie	0	10	6
Cupar	0	10	6
Dalmuir	0	10	6
Derby Scottish Association	0	10	6
Detroit, U.S.A.	0	10	6
Dublin	0	10	6
Duluth U.S.A. Clan Stewart	0	10	6
Dumbarton	0	10	6
Dumfries ...	0	10	6
Dumfries Burns Howff ...	0	10	6
Dundalk and District	1	1	0
Dundee	0	10	6
Dunfermline United	0	10	6
East Calder Jolly Beggars	0	10	6
East Stirlingshire	1	11	6
Edinburgh Ninety	1	1	0
Elgin ...	0	10	6
Fauldhouse...	0	10	6
Fifeshire Association	0	10	6
Garelochhead	0	10	6
Gateshead and District ...	0	10	6
Glasgow Tam o' Shanter ...	0	10	6
Glasgow Primrose	0	10	6
Glasgow Thistle ...	0	10	6
Glasgow Royalty ...	0	10	6
Glasgow Carrick ...	0	10	6

Glasgow Dennistoun Jolly Beggars £0	10	6
Glasgow Mossgiel 0	10	6
Glasgow Carlton 0	10	6
Glasgow Mauchline Society 0	10	6
Glasgow Albany 0	10	6
Glasgow National 1	1	0
Glasgow Kingston 0	10	6
Glasgow Auld Clinkum ... 0	10	6
Glasgow Bridgeton 0	10	6
Glasgow and District 0	10	6
Glasgow Cathcart ... 0	10	6
Glasgow Rosebery... 0	10	6
Glasgow Scottish ... 0	10	6
Glasgow Masonic ... 1	1	0
Glasgow Sandyford 1	1	0
Glasgow and District Bowling Association 0	10	6
Glencairn Vale of Leven ... 0	10	6
Glencraig 0	10	6
Govan Fairfield 0	10	6
Govan Cronies 0	10	6
Gorebridge 1	1	0
Gourock 0	10	6
Gourock Jolly Beggars ... 1	1	0
Greenock 0	10	6
Greenock Cronies 0	10	6
Greenock St. John's 0	10	6
Greenock Victoria 0	10	6
Hamilton 0	10	6
Hamilton Mossgiel 0	10	6
Hamilton Junior ... 0	10	6
Harriman, U.S.A. ... 1	1	0
Hawick 0	10	6
Helensburgh 0	10	6
Hull 0	10	6
Irvine 1	1	0
Johnstone Tam o' Shanter 0	10	6
Kilbowie Jolly Beggars ... 0	10	6
Kilmarnock 0	10	6
Kilmarnock Jolly Beggars 0	10	6
Kinnaird Victoria. 0	10	6
Kirn 0	10	6
Lanark 0	10	6
Lanark Jolly Beggars 0	10	6
Larkhall Cronies . 0	10	6
Liverpool 1	11	6
London Robert Burns Club 0	10	6
Lochore and Rosewell Tam o' Shanter 0	10	6
Lochgelly Thirteen Jolly Beggars 1	1	0

Meikle Earnock Original ...	£0	10	6	Sinclairtown ...	£0 10 6
Mid-Argyll	0	10	6	Stane Mossgiel	0 10 6
Mid-Calder Tam o' Shanter	0	10	6	Stirling ...	0 10 6
Newbattle and District	0	10	6	Stonehouse Jolly Beggars	0 10 6
Newarthill	0	10	6	Sunderland	0 10 6
Newton-on-Ayr ...	0	10	6	Sydney Anniversary Club...	0 10 6
Newton Jolly Beggars	1	1	0	Tarbrax Jolly Beggars	0 10 6
Old Kilpatrick ...	1	1	0	Tollcross	0 10 6
Paisley	0	10	6	Trenton, U.S.A.	1 1 0
Paisley Charleston	0	10	6	Troon	1 1 0
Paisley St. James ...	0	10	6	Uddingston	0 10 6
Paisley St. Mirren	0	10	6	Uddingston Masonic	0 10 6
Partick	0	10	6	Uphall Tam o' Shanter	0 10 6
Partick Western ...	0	10	6	Walker Newcastle ...	1 1 0
Portobello	0	10	6	Vickerstown	0 10 6
Prestonpans Mystic	0	10	6	Wallsend-on-Tyne	0 10 6
Row...	0	10	6	Whitehaven...	0 10 6
Shettleston ...	0	10	6	Whitburn	1 11 6
Shiremoor Blue Bell	0	10	6		

Alphabetical List of Federated Clubs.

No. 40. Aberdeen
84. Abington
23. Adelaide
20. Airdrie
143. Airdrie Gateside
2· Alexandria
6, Alloa
252. Alloway
268. Anderston Cronies
82. Arbroath
174. Ardrossan Castle
257. Armadale Star
258. Armadale Buck's Head
232. Arniston
224. Ashington
238. Atlanta
123. Auchinleck
19. Auckland
275. Ayr
192. Ayrshire Association
157. Ballieston Caledonia
218. Bannockburn Empire
99. Barlinnie
12. Barrow-in-Furness
64. Beith
15. Belfast
265. Bingry Jolly Beggars
167. Birmingham
248. Birtley
30. Blackburn
125. Blackburn-on-Almond
184. Blairadam Shanter
240. Blawarthill
95. Bolton
29. Bolton Juniors
119. Bonhill
142. Bonnybridge
259. Bonnyrigg
76. Brechin
120. Bristol
114. Brodick
106. Broxburn Rosebery
230. Burnbank
185. Burton
228. Calderwaterhead
4. Callander
110. Cambuslang

No. 207. Cambuslang Wingate
87. Campsie
71. Carlisle
102. Carlisle Border
201. Carlisle Newtown
81. Carstairs Junction
171. Chattanooga, U.S.A.
11. Chesterfield
51. Chicago
138. Cleland
166. Cleveland Scottish
Association
93 Clydebank
189. Clydebank Barns o' Clyde
103. Coalburn Rosebery
233. Coalburn Clachan
208. Colorado Springs
270. Coquetdale
79. Corstorphine
127. Cowdenbeath Haggis
128. Cowdenbeath Glencairn
250. Cowdenbeath Tam o'
Shanter
42. Crieff
241. Crook
66. Crossgates
45. Cumnock
86. Cumnock The Winsome
Willie
62. Cupar
179. Dailly
244. Dalmuir
35. Dalry
158. Darlington
122. Darnconner
55. Derby
37. Dollar
278. Duluth, U.S.A
146. Du'. lin
10. Dumbarton
52. Dumfries Mechanics
104. Dumfries Oak
226. Dumfries
112. Dumfries Howff
204 Dundalk
14. Dundee
69. Dunedin

No. 85. Dunfermline United
80. Dunoon Cowal
188. Duns Working Men
134. Duntocher Heron
5. Earlston
229. Eastbourne
108. East Calder
155. East Stirlingshire
22. Edinburgh
111. Edinburgh South
124. Edinburgh Ninety
149. Elgin
217. Eskdale
126. Falkirk
231. Fauldhouse
262. Fifeshire Association
44. Forfar
187. Galashiels
90. Garelochhead
163. Gateshead and District
3. Glasgow Tam o' Shanter
7. ,, Thistle
9. ,, Royalty
24. Bank
27. ,, Springburn
33. ,, Haggis
34. ,, Carrick
36. ,, Rosebery
38. ,, Jolly Beggars
39. ,, St. David's
41. ,, Dennistoun
43. ,, Northern
47. ,, St. Rollox
49. ,, Bridgeton
61. ,, Glencairn
63. ,, Mossgiel
67. ,, Carlton
68. ,, Sandyford
70. ,, St. Rollox
Jolly Beggars
74. Mauchline Soc.
78. ,, Ardgowan
83. ,, Co-operative
88. ,, Caledonian
107. ,, Hutchesontown
109. ,, Caledonia
117. ,, Southern
118. ,, Albany
139. ,, National
145. ,, Central.
153. ,, The Scottish
129. ,, Gorbals
164 ,, Kinning Park
180. ,, Tollcross
81. ,, Primrose

No. 203. Glasgow Dennistoun
Jolly Beggars
206. ,, Daisy
213. ,, Kingston
223. ,, Auld Clinkum
234. ,, Southern Mer-
chants
255. ,, Cathcart
263. ,, Masonic
169. Glasgow and District
282. Glasgow and District B.C.
Bowling Association
251. Glencraig
198. Gorebridge Jolly Beggars
59. Gourock Jolly Beggars
53. Govan Fairfield
202. Govan Cronies
116. Greenloaning
21. Greenock
148. Greenock Cronies
209. Greenock St. John's
152. Hamilton
100. Hamilton Mossgiel
121. Hamilton Junior
136. Hamilton Royal Oak
235. Hamilton Glencairn
210. Hardgate Auld Hoose
277. Harriman, U.S.A.
239. Hawick
225. Helensburgh
222. Hull
137. Ipswich
173. Irvine
96. Jedburgh
154. Johannesburg, S.A.
269. Johnstone Tam o' Shanter
92. Kilbowie
0. Kilmarnock
97. Kilmarnock Bellfield
150. Kilmarnock Jolly
Beggars
178. Kilmarnock Begbie's
186. Kilmarnock Glencairn
245 Kinnaird
115. Kippen
58. Kirkcaldy
75. Kirn
98. Lanark
273. Lanark Jolly Beggars
144. Larbert and Stenhousemuir
170. Larkhall
211. Larkhall Thistle
73. Lenzie
18. Liverpool

No. 247. Lochgelly
246. Lochore
1. London
183. Londonderry
276. Lumphinnans Highland Mary
28. Mauchline Jolly Beggars
175. Meikle Earnock
214. Melrose
249. Mid-Calder Tam o' Shanter
194. Middlebie
242. Montrose
8. Morpeth (dormant)
101. Motherwell
56. Muirkirk Lapraik
65. Musselburgh
199. Newbattle and District
32. Newark
133. Newarthill
156. Newcastle and Tyneside
256. Newton-on-Ayr
266. Newton Jolly Beggars
131. Nottingham
17. Nottingham (dormant)
151. Old Kilpatrick
172. Oregon, U.S.A.
48. Paisley
77. Paisley Gleniffer
161. Paisley Charleston
243. Paisley St. James
205. Paisley St. Mirren
72. Partick
135. Partick Western
227. Penrith
26. Perth
54. Perth St. Johnstone
162. Plymouth and District
140. Pollokshaws
190. Port Glasgow
212. Portobello
221. Prestonpans
264. Prestonpans Jolly Beggars

No. 267. Prestonpans Mystic
177. Prestwick
176. Renfrew
191. Renfrew Moorpark
168. Riccarton
132. Riccarton Kirkstyle
130. Row
105. Rutherglen
193. Rutherglen Jolly Beggars
216. Rutherglen Royal Burgh
31. San Francisco
91. Shettleston
195. Shiremoor
283. Sinclairtown
13. St. Andrews
220. St. Louis, Mo., U.S.A.
182. Stane Mossgiel
271. Stewarton Hodden Grey
50. Stirling
141. Stonehouse
147. Stonehouse Haggis
200. Stonehouse Jolly Beggars
89. Sunderland
16. Sydney
261. Sydney Anniversary
260. Tarbrax
215. Thorniewood
57. Thornliebank
271. Trenton, U.S.A.
274. Troon
219. Uddingston
237. Uddingston Masonic
94. Uphall
113. Vale o' Leven Glencairn
281. Vickerstown
159. Walker-on-Tyne
165. Wallsend-on-Tyne
46. Warwickshire
160. Whitburn
236. Whitehaven
197. Winnipeg
25. Winnipeg St. Andrew's Society
60. Wolverhampton

DIRECTORY

OF

BURNS CLUBS AND SCOTTISH SOCIETIES

ON THE

ROLL OF THE BURNS FEDERATION, 1921.

No 0—KILMARNOCK Burns Club. Instituted 1808. Federated 1885. Place and date of meeting, Art Gallery, 25th January. President, Major James Lang, O.B.E., C.E., Grougar Bank, Kilmarnock ; Vice-president, Sir Alexander Walker, K.B.E., Troon ; Secretary, Major D. Yuille, T.D. Burns Avenue, Kilmarnock. Committee—Ex-Provost M. Smith, O.B.E., J.P. ; D. M'Naught, J.P. ; T. Amos, M.A. ; Major G. A. Innes, M.B.E. ; Bailie Wm. M'Menan B.A. ; John Cuthbertson, M.B.E. ; Jas. Middleton, J.P. ; Ex-Bailie W. Munro, J.P.

No. 1—The LONDON Robert Burns Club. Instituted 1868. Federated 1885. President, L. G. Sloan, J.P., Pen Corner, Kingsway, W.C.2. ; Vice-president, Sir William Noble, Silchester, The Park, Hampstead, N.W. ; Secretary, P. N. M'Farlane, " The Graphic," Tallis Street, E.C.4 ; Treasurer, J. Spence Leslie, Balgownie, Whitehall Road, Harrow. Social Circle—Chairman, L. G. Sloan ; Hon. Secretary, T. J. Wilson, 59-60 Old Bailey, E.C.4. Vernacular Circle—Chairman, William Will, " The Graphic," Tallis Street, E.C.4 ; Hon. Secretary, P. N. M'Farlane.

No. 2—ALEXANDRIA Burns Club. Instituted 1884. Federated 1885. Place and date of meeting, Village School, Alexandria, last Friday each month. President, R. G. Stevenson, Stevenson Place, Alexandria ; Vice-president, Donald M'Dougall, Bridge-End Tavern, Bonhill ; Secretary, Duncan Carswell, Linnbrane Terrace, Alexandria ; Treasurer, James Merrilees, Charleston House, Alexandria. Committee — Dugald Stevenson, John Barton, Wm. M'Gregor, Harry Caldwell, Geo. Wilson.

No. 3 GLASGOW Tam o' Shanter. Instituted 1880. Federated 1885. Place and date of meeting, Burns House Club, 27 India Street, Glasgow, last Tuesday of each month, at 8 p.m. President, T. M. Hamilton, 108 Renfield Street, Glasgow ; Vice-president, John Ballantyne, 95 Bath Street, Glasgow ; Secretary, J. Jeffrey Hunter, Solicitor, 89 Bath Street, Glasgow. Committee—H. J. Altman, Wm. Black, Jas. Fraser, J. H. Hurll, Alex.

Izat, Hugh Lyon, Gerrard Morrison, Alex. M'Kenzie, Dr J. T. M'Lachlan, Thos. Smith, and T. P. Thompson. Special features of Club—Literary evenings and useful movements for the promotion of the Burns cult.

No. 4—CALLANDER Burns Club. Instituted 1877. Federated 1885.

No. 5—ERCILDOUNE Burns Club. Instituted 1885. Federated 26th November, 1885. *Secretary*, A. M. Black, Market Place, Earlston.

No. 6—ALLOA Burns Club. Instituted 1873. Federated 1885.

No. 7—GLASGOW Thistle Burns Club. Instituted 1882. Federated 1885. President, Dr Macdonald, Hawkhead, Crookston ; Vice-president, John Eadie, 5 Miller Street ; *Secretary*, John Vallance, 57 College Street, Glasgow.

No. 8—MORPETH and District Burns Club.

No 9—GLASGOW Royalty Burns Club. Instituted 1882. Federated 1886. President, Councillor James Macfarlane 51 Bath Street, Glasgow ; Vice-president, David Gunn, 4 Finnieston Street, Glasgow ; *Secretary*, George F. Howarth, 188 St. Vincent Street, Glasgow.

No. 10—DUMBARTON Burns Club. Instituted 1859. Federated 1886. Place and date of meeting, Elephant Hotel, 28th January. President, A. Y. Allan, Aitkenbar Farm, Dumbarton ; Vice-president, James Stewart, Dumbuck Crescent, Dumbarton ; *Secretary and Treasurer*, J. M. Menzies, 69 High Street, Dumbarton. Committee —C. MacKinnon, J. M'Clelland, J. M'Pherson, R. M'Murray, J. B. Cameron, H. W. Ballardie, and D. Blackstock. Special feature of Club—Celebration of the Poet's Birthday.

No. 11—CHESTERFIELD Burns Society. Federated 1886.

No. 12—BARROW-IN-FURNESS Burns Club. Federated 1888.

No. 13—ST. ANDREWS Burns Club. Instituted 1869. Federated 1886. Place of meeting, Various. President, Wm. Macbeth Robertson, Esq., Solicitor, Market Street, St. Andrews ; *Secretary*, David Fraser, Lilybank, St. Andrews.

No. 14—DUNDEE Burns Club. Instituted 1860. Federated 5th March, 1886. Place and date of meeting, 36 Nethergate, Dundee, nightly. President, D. G. B. Laing, 7 Hawkhill Place, Dundee ; Vice-president, Wm. F. Mitchell, 302 Strathmartine Road, Dundee ; *Secretary*, James Neilson, 36 Nethergate, Dundee ; Treasurer, D. Brown ; Auditors, P. Davie and Wm. M. Wilkie. Committee — D. Don, R. Watson, and A. Boyack. Special features of Club—Literary and recreation.

No. 15—BELFAST Burns Club. Instituted 1872. Federated 1886.

No. 16—SYDNEY Burns Club, N.S.W. Instituted 1880. Federated 1886. *Secretary,* W. Telfer, School of Art, Pitt Street, Sydney.

No. 17—NOTTINGHAM Scottish Society. Federated 1886.

No. 18—LIVERPOOL Burns Club. Instituted 1866. Federated 1886. Place and date of meeting, Places various, 25th January. President, Dr R. W. MacKenna, M.A., 76 Rodney Street, Liverpool; *Secretary,* Robt. Sinclair, Archer (Major, V.D.), 6 Devonshire Road, Princes Park, Liverpool.

No. 19—AUCKLAND Burns Club. Instituted 1884. Federated 1886.

No. 20—AIRDRIE Burns Club. Instituted 1885. Federated 1886. President, J. Maurice Arthur, Glentore, Airdrie; Vice-president, Geo. E. Swimhoe, Albert House, Airdrie; *Secretary,* G. B. Motherwell, solicitor, 4 East High Street, Airdrie; Treasurer, G. B. Motherwell, solicitor, 4 East High Street, Airdrie; Auditor, C. R. Larkman, Albert Schoolhouse, Airdrie. Committee—Robert Eadie, C. R. Larkman. David Martyn, and Wm. M'Gregor.

No. 21—GREENOCK Burns Club (The Mother Club). Instituted 1802. Federated 1886. Place of meeting, 36 Nicolson Street. President, Hugh M'Lean, Elmhurst, Greenock; Vice-presidents, R. L. Scott, Balclutha, Greenock, and D. M'Callum, 2 Ford Place, Greenock; *Secretary,* George B. Grieve, O.B.E., 25 Robertson Street, Greenock; House Convener, J. B. Morison. Special features of Club —To cherish the name of Robert Burns, and to foster a love for his writings, and, generally, to encourage a taste for Scottish literature.

No. 22—EDINBURGH Burns Club. Instituted 1848. Federated 1886. President, George Williamson, J.P., 178 High Street, Edinburgh; Vice-president, Robert Walker, 6 Royal Terrace, Edinburgh; *Interim Secretary,* Thomas Liddle, S.S.C., 5 Hill Street, Edinburgh.

No. 23—ADELAIDE South Australian Caledonian Society. Instituted 1881. Federated 1886. *Secretary,* H. Tassie, Gray's Arcade, Adelaide, S.A.

No. 24—GLASGOW Bank Burns Club. Instituted 1884. Federated 1886.

No 25—WINNIPEG St. Andrew's Society. Federated 1886. *Secretary,* David Philip, Government Buildings, Winnipeg.

No 26—PERTH Burns Club. Instituted 1873. Federated 1886.

No. 27—SPRINGBURN Burns Club. Instituted 1884. Federated 1886.

No. 28—MAUCHLINE Jolly Beggars Burns Club.

No. 29—BOLTON Juniors Burns Club. Instituted 1881. Federated 1886.

No. 30—BLACKBURN Burns Club. Instituted 1884. Federated 1886. *Secretary*, Robt. Ferguson, 9 Tacketts Street, Blackburn, Lancs.

No. 31—SAN FRANCISO Scottish Thistle Club. Instituted 1882. Federated 1886. *Secretary*, Geo. W. Paterson, 801 Guerero Street, San Francisco, U.S.A.

No 32—NEWARK Burns Club, U.S.A. Federated 1886.

No. 33—GLASGOW Haggis Burns Club. Instituted 1872. Federated 1886. Place and date of meeting, Ferguson and Forrester's, 36 Buchanan Street, last Tuesday from October till March. President, Robert Hamilton, Invershin, Newlands, Glasgow ; *Secretary*, William S. Baird, 121 West George Street, Glasgow.

No. 34—CARRICK Burns Club. Instituted 1859. Federated 1887. Place of meeting, 62 Glassford Street, Glasgow. President, R. A. Wood, Rosevale, Kilmarnock Road, Giffnock, near Glasgow ; Vice-president, T. G. Jamieson, 83 Washington Street, Glasgow ; *Secretary*, David Sutherland, 123 Frederick Street, Glasgow ; Treasurer, Wm. Morrison, 62 Glassford Street, Glasgow.

No. 35—DALRY Burns Club. Instituted 1825. Federated 1887. Place and date of meeting, Turf Inn, Friday, 28th January, 1921. *Secretary*, Patrick Comrie, Waterside, Dalry.

No. 36—ROSEBERY Burns Club. Instituted 1885. Federated 1887. Place and date of meeting, Bath Hotel, 152 Bath Street, first Thursday of month. President, Wm. Craig, Beechcroft, Crow Road, Jordanhill, Glasgow ; Vice-president, T. C. F. Brotchie, Beechgrove, Bridge-of-Weir ; *Joint Secretaries*, James Steel, 10 Cromwell Square, Queen's Park, Glasgow, and George Armour, 19 Kelvinside Gardens ; Treasurer, Ronald Johnstone, 85 Roselea Drive, Dennistoun. Special features of Club—A course of monthly lectures on various literary subjects ; intervisitation of sister Burns Clubs to promote brotherly feeling and give mutual assistance ; encouragement of the young to learn the songs and poetry of Scotland by the institution of school competitions and the giving of prizes. Bluevale School has been the special object upon which the Club has centred its activities. Jointly with the Carlton Club, the Rosebery Club have carried through the publication of Burns Works in Braille type, whereby the blind are able to read Burns for themselves. An edition of the Poet's works in " Moon " type for blind people who are unable to read Braille has also been issued. The Club now admit ladies on an equality with gentlemen to the membership.

No. 37—DOLLAR Burns Club. Instituted 29th December, 1887 Federated 30th December, 1887. *Secretary*, D. Kilpatrick Station Road. Dollar.

No 38—GLASGOW Jolly Beggars Burns Club. Instituted 1877. Federated 1888.

No. 39—GLASGOW St. David's Burns Club. Instituted 1887. Federated 1889.

No. 40—ABERDEEN Burns Club. Instituted 1887. Federated 1889.

No. 41—DENNISTOUN Burns Club. Instituted 1887. Federated 1889.

No. 42—CRIEFF Burns Club. Instituted 1889. Federated 1891.

No. 43—GLASGOW Northern Burns Club. Federated 1891.

No. 44—FORFAR Burns Club. Instituted 1890. Federated 1891.

No. 45—CUMNOCK Burns Club. Instituted 1887. Federated 1891. *Secretary*, John Hume, solicitor, Cumnock.

No. 46—WARWICKSHIRE Burns Club. Instituted 1880. Federated 1891.

No. 47—GLASGOW St. Rollox Burns Club. Instituted 1889. Federated 1891.

No. 48—PAISLEY Burns Club. Instituted 1805. Federated 1891. Time of meeting, First Thursday each month, October to May inclusive. President, Thomas D. Robb, Traquair Potterhill, Paisley ; Vice-president, Robert Marshall, The Cottage, Glen Lane, Paisley ; *Secretary*, Julius F. M'Callum, Mayfield, Sunnyside, Paisley. Special features of Club—Literary and social.

No. 49—BRIDGETON Burns Club. Instituted 1870. Federated 1891. Place of meeting, Albert Hall, Main Street (as arranged). President, James W. Shaw, J.P., Inneraggan, Albert Drive, Rutherglen ; Vice-president, George Brown, Yorville, Maxwell Park, Glasgow, S.S. ; *Secretary*, John G. S. Sproll, 354 Duke Street, Glasgow ; Treasurer, Wm. Reid, 49 West George Street, Glasgow. Directors —David S. Brown, Jas. M. Campbell, J.P., Robt. Miller, Jas. Craig, Dr W. A. Burns, Geo. Newton, Dr T. N. Fletcher, Adam C. Hay, and John M. Watson. Special feature of Club—School competitions—19 schools in district.

No 50—STIRLING Burns Club. Instituted 1887. Federated 1891. Place and date of meeting, Golden Lion Hotel,

25th January, at 7 p.m. President, Councillor William
A. Weir, Forth Crescent, Stirling; Vice-president, Pro-
vost M'Culloch, Clarendon Place, Stirling; *Secretary*,
Alexander Dun, 37 Murray Place, Stirling; Treasurer,
‚ J. P. Crawford. Committee—John Craig, Ridley San-
deman, J. W. Paterson, ex-Bailie Leslie, John Crawford,
W. L. Thomson, David Dick, J. S. Henderson, Robert
Gray, James Duncanson, William Brown, John Ferguson,
Alex. Learmonth, Gilbert Macintosh, Dean of Guild
Buchanan, J. C. Muirhead, J. E. M'Killop, and J. Shirra.

No. 51—CHICAGO Caledonian Society. Fedcrated 1892.

No. 52—DUMFRIES Mechanics Burns Club. Federated 1892.

No. 53—GOVAN Fairfield Burns Club. Instituted 25th January,
1886. Federated 23rd September, 1892. Place and
date of meeting, Eden Villa Restaurant, Govan, 1st
Wednesday, September to March. President, Arch.
B. Allison, 22 Hayburn Crescent, Partick; Vice-president,
John Donald, 883 Govan Road, Govan; *Secretary*,
John Gordon, 13 Hutton Drive, Govan ; Bard, W. MacKay ;
Steward, Geo. Anderson. Committee — G. Wardrope,
A. Phillips, J. Melvin, J. M. Watson, and J. M'Lachlan.
Special features of Club—To increase the knowledge of
the Life and Works of our National Bard, and other
Scottish writers and poets.

No. 54—PERTH St. Johnstone Burns Club. Federated 1892.

No 55—DERBY Scottish Association and Burns Club. Instituted
1890. Federated 1892. Place of meeting, Assembly
Rooms, Market Place, Derby. President, Dr J. A. Watt,
The Walnuts, Littleover, Derby; Vice-president, D. M.
Aird, 42 Vicarage Avenue, Derby; *Secretary*, Chas.
Carmichael, 180 Porter Road, Derby; Treasurer, R. B.
Muir, Derby Road, Belper. Special features of Club—
(1) To unite Scotsmen, and to foster a spirit of friendship,
social and intellectual intercourse among its members;
(2) To perpetuate the memory of the Immortal Bard,
Robert Burns.

    Since the last issue of the *Chronicle*, the name of the
Club has been altered from Derby Burns Club to Derby
Scottish Association and Burns Club. This was done
with a view to widening the scope of the Club, and has
resulted in the membership being doubled. Social
gatherings are held periodically during the winter months,
and also an annual outing in the summer. The children
have been specially catered for, and a Children's Frolic
and Hogmanay Dance will be held on 31st December.
Next year the Club hopes to run a Children's Competition.

No. 56—LAPRAIK (Muirkirk) Burns Club. Instituted 1893.
Federated 1893. President, C. P. Bell, Main Street,
Muirkirk; Vice-president, Peter Mackie, c/o Mrs Fer-
guson, Main Street, Muirkirk; *Secretary*, Hugh Bell,
Roslyn, Wellwood Street, Muirkirk; Treasurer, And.

Pringle, Ironworks Cottages, Muirkirk. Committee—
Thos. Weir, Jno. Taylor, Edgar Anderson, Jas. Hazel,
Wm. Patrick, Wm. Brown, Arch. Fairbairn, Thos. Hazel.
Special features of Club—Annual Celebration and edu-
cational.

No. 57—THORNLIEBANK Burns Club. Instituted 1891. Federated 1893. Place and date of meeting, Village Institute,
Fridays, 8 p.m. President, James H. M'Millan, Woodlands, Shawlands, Glasgow; Vice-president, John Muir,
The Bield, Thornliebank; Secretary, Thomas Haddow,
Hillside Terrace, Thornliebank; Treasurer, Hugh
Halliday, 27 Kennishead Road, Thornliebank. Special
features of Club—School children's competitions, Scotch
concert, annual outing, Hallowe'en festival, Anniversary
dinner, and Club monthly meetings.

No. 58—KIRKCALDY Burns Club. Federated 1892.

No. 59—GOUROCK Jolly Beggars Burns Club. Instituted 1893.
Federated 1893. Place and date of meeting, Club-rooms,
Cove Yard, Gourock, Fridays, at 8 p.m. President,
H. Whyte, The Homestead, Lyle Road, Greenock; Vice-
president, H. Talman, 5 Royal Street, Gourock; Secretary,
W. L. Adam, Torridon Terrace, Gourock.

No. 60—WOLVERHAMPTON Burns Club. Federated 1893.

No. 61—GLASGOW Glencairn Burns Club. Federated 1893.

No. 62—CUPAR Burns Club. Instituted 1892. Federated
1893. President, Col. Sir Alexander Sprot, M.P., Stravithie, Fife; Vice-president, Provost James Stark, Mill-
bank, Cupar; Secretary, David F. Esplin, Dundee Courier
Office, Cupar; Treasurer, Bailie Geo. White; Chairman
of Committee—Geo. Innes.

No. 63—MOSSGIEL Burns Club. Instituted 1893. Federated
1893. Place and date of meeting, Y.M.C.A. Rooms,
Eglinton Toll, 3rd Thursday each winter month. President, Thos. W. M'Nish, 82 Cumberland Street, S.S.;
Vice-president, Wm. Brownlee, 67 Cadder Street, Pollokshields; Secretary, Jos. M'Gregor, 45 Abbotsford Place,
Glasgow; Treasurer, R. Parker. Committee—Wm.
Morrison, J. M. Blair, J. Coulter, J. Saunders, Wm.
M'Neil, R. Johnston, N. M'Luskie, R. Bryden, and Wm.
Morrison, jr. Special features of Club—Annual celebration on 25th January; reunions for the cultivation
of social and intellectual intercourse amongst members;
encouragement of Scottish literature; summer trip ·
and school children's competitions.

No. 64—BEITH Burns Club. Instituted 1892. Federated 12th
December, 1893.

No. 65—MUSSELBURGH Federated Burns Club. Instituted
1886. Federated 3rd January, 1984. Secretary, Herbert Millar, solicitor, High Street, Musselburgh.

No. 66—CROSSGATES Burns Club. Federated 1894

No. 67—CARLTON Burns Club. Instituted 1894. Federated
1894. Place and date of meeting, Kenilworth Hotel,
Glasgow, First Friday each month. President, Wm.
Gardiner, 26 Holyrood Quadrant, Glasgow ; Vice-president,
Wm. Henderson, 912 Sauchiehall Street, Glasgow ; *Secretary,* John C. Brown, 5 Brownlie Gardens, Tollcross,
Glasgow ; Treasurer, Jas. Tudhope, 16 Whitehill Street,
Dennistoun, Glasgow. Directors—D. Cameron, M. M.
Duff, J. Clark, R. Westwater, James Webster, James
D. Sloan, A. Fraser, James F. Gourlay, James M'Blane,
and Past Presidents *ex officio.* Special features of
Club—The perpetuation of the memory of Robert Burns,
and the intellectual and social intercourse of its members
by such means as may from time to time be arranged.

No. 68—SANDYFORD Burns Club. Instituted 1893. Federated
1894. Place of meeting, The Burns House Club, India
Street, Glasgow. Hon. President, J. Gardner, J.P. ;
President, Bailie R. S. Renfrew, 133 North Street, Glasgow ;
Vice-president, Capt. D. C. Davidson, 302 St. Vincent
Street, Glasgow ; *Secretary*, William E. Guest, 47 Kelvinhaugh Street, Glasgow.

No. 69—DUNEDIN Burns Club. Federated 1894.

No 70—GLASGOW St. Rollox Jolly Beggars Burns Club. Federated 1894.

No. 71—CARLISLE Burns Club. Instituted 1889. Federated
1895. *Secretary*, Thomas George Beattie, 200 Warwick
Road, Carlisle.

No. 72—PARTICK Burns Club. Instituted 1885. Federated
1895. President, Charles R. Cowie, Merchant, Woodend
House, Partickhill, Glasgow ; Vice-president, J. Ogilvie
Robertson, solicitor, 111 Balshagray Avenue, Partick ;
Secretary and Treasurer, David Crawford, solicitor, 213
West George Street, Glasgow.

No 73—LENZIE Burns Club. Federated 1896.

No 74—GLASGOW Mauchline Society. Instituted 1888. Federated 1895. Hon. President, Sir Arch. M'Innes Shaw,
Bart., Ballochmyle, Mauchline ; President, J. Leiper
Gemmill, 162 St. Vincent Street, Glasgow ; Vice-president,
John Hyslop, 93 Hope Street, Glasgow ; *Secretary*,
William Campbell, 166 Buchanan Street, Glasgow ;
Treasurer, Thos. Killin, 7 Stewarton Drive, Cambuslang.
Special features of Club—To promote sociability among
natives of Mauchline and friends, and manage the
National Burns Memorial and Cottage Homes, Mauchline.

No. 75—KIRN Burns Club. Instituted 25th January, 1892. Federated 10th February, 1396. Place and date of meeting,
Queen's Hotel, Kirn, 25th January. President, P. F.

More, British Linen Bank, Argyll Street, Dunoon; Vice-president, S. A. Fraser, Silver Ray, Kirn; *Secretary,* John Macnair, house factor, Kirn; Treasurer, Provost Lees. O.B.E., Kirn. Chairman, Recreation Branch, A. Kates; Vice-chairman, A. Balfour; Secretary and Treasurer, J. J. Boyd, Norwood Cottage, Kirn. Special features of Club—Singing and reciting competitions for children; annual excursion; debating and recreation branch; carpet bowling, &c., in Kirn Hall three times every week.

No. 76.—BRECHIN Burns Club. Instituted January, 1894. Federated 7th March, 1896. Place and date of meeting, Masonic Hall, Brechin, 25th January. President, John S. Melrose, Summerbank, Brechin; *Secretary,* F. C. Anderson, 10 St. Mary Street, Brechin. Committee— J. A. Hutcheon, J. S. Lindsay, Robert Anderson, G. W. Mitchell, D. K. Laing, J. F. Lammond, and Alex. Norrie.

No. 77—PAISLEY Tannahill Burns Club. Instituted 1892. Federated 1896.

No 78—GLASGOW Ardgowan Burns Club. Instituted 1893. Federated 1896.

No. 79—CORSTORPHINE Burns Club. Instituted 1887. Federated 1896. *Secretary,* W. M. Wilson, 7 Belgrave Place, Corstorphine.

No. 80—DUNOON Cowall Burns Club. Instituted 1896. Federated 1896.

No. 81—CARSTAIRS Junction Burns Club. Instituted 1896. Federated 1896.

No. 82—ARBROATH Burns Club. Instituted 1888. Federated 1896. President, Dr J. D. Gilruth, Hyde Park House, Arbroath; Vice-president, John R. W. Clark, solicitor, Arbroath; *Secretary,* Ernest F. Cobb, Town Chamberlain, Arbroath; Treasurer. F. W. Moon, solicitor, Arbroath.

No. 83—GLASGOW Co-operative Burns Club. Instituted 1896. Federated 1896.

No. 84—ABINGTON Burns Club. Federated 1896.

No. 85—DUNFERMLINE United Burns Club. Instituted 1812. Federated 12th November, 1896. Date of meeting, 21st January, 1921. Hon. Presidents, The Right Hon. The Earl of Elgin, Broomhall, Dunfermline; Sir Alex. Gibb, K.B.E., C.B., C.E., Gruimard House, Aultbea, Ross-shire; and Sir Richard Mackie, Leith; Hon. Vice-presidents, W. D. Imrie, Wm. Black, P. Donald, Thos. Dow, and R. Taylor; Vice-president, R. Hutchison, Reid Street, Dunfermline; *Secretary,* P. Paterson, Kimmis House, Kimmis Place, Dunfermline. Committee—

John Brown, R. Dunlop, P. Donald, Wm. Black, R.
Taylor, Thos. Lessells, Wm. Crawford, and Adam
Bowman.

No. 86—CUMNOCK Winsome Willie Burns Club. Instituted 1856.
Federated 1896. Place of meeting, Hotel Royal. Presi-
dent, Andrew Hart, Square, Cumnock; Vice-president,
George Young, Glengyron Row, Cumnock; *Secretary*,
Robert Hyslop, Waterside Place, Cumnock. Committee
—Walter M'Crindle, Wm. Hyslop, Thos. Blackwood,
Wm. Jamieson, Robt. Forsyth, Geo. Young, Daniel
Begg, H. M'Crindle. Special feature of Club—Celebrating
the birthday of Robert Burns.

No. 87—CAMPSIE Burns Club. Instituted 1890. Federated
1896.

No. 88—GLASGOW Caledonian Burns Club. Instituted 1896.
Federated 1897.

No. 89—SUNDERLAND Burns Club. Instituted January, 1897.
Federated April, 1897. Place and date of meeting,
Palatine Hotel, 2nd and 4th Wednesdays October to
March; 2nd Wednesday April, May, and September.
President, A. R. Calvert, 11 Side Cliffe Road, Roker,
Sunderland; Vice-president, Tom Fisher, 34 Hunter
Terrace, Sunderland; *Secretary*, M. Neilson, 14 East
Whickham Street, Sunderland; Treasurer, A. W. Semple;
Auditor, E. V. Young; Librarian, G. Mackay; Pianist
S. Alder; Pipe-Major, W. Graham; Trustees, W. H.
Turner and G. Mackay. Committee—Dr A. Stevenson,
W. M. Donaldson, T. E. A. A. Shaw, J. M'Lagan, and D.
Gordon. Special features of Club—Anniversary cele-
bration, reading of papers, pipe band, &c.

No. 90—GARELOCHHEAD Burns Club. Instituted 18th
November, 1895. Federated 25th March, 1897. Place
of meeting, Garelochhead Hotel. President, D. Stark,
Argyle House, Garelochhead; Vice-president, D.
M'Keichan, Mambeg Cottage, Garelochhead; *Secretary*,
John Burnett, I Glencairn Terrace, Garelochhead. Com-
mittee—Messrs D. B. Anderson, P. M'Farlane, Wm.
Grieve, Wm. Espie, J. Gray, J. Miller, J. Martin, and
J. Douglas. Special feature of Club—That we as
Scotchmen should meet and honour Scotland's National
Bard.

No. 91—SHETTLESTON Burns Club. Instituted 1897. Fede-
rated 1897. Place of meeting, Sloan's Arcade Café.
Hon. Presidents, John Cresswell, William Reid, F.E.I.S.,
James Lucas, M.A., F.E.I.S., Robert M. Milholm, James
S. Wilson, and John Ramsey; President, John M'Farlane,
6 Gordon Terrace, Shettleston; Vice-president, John
Brown, J.P., 271 Main Street Shettleston; *Secretary*,
Robert M. Milholm, 7 Somerville Place, off Monteith
Row, Glasgow; Treasurer Edwin S. Thompson, Ardshiel,
Shettleston. Committee—Ambrose Cresswell, George

Farmer, Hugh Fletcher, George Glendinning, William Ross, James Miller, George Stirling, James Cassells, William Smillie, Alexander Riach, and Alfred Perry. Special features of Club—A literary centre as well as social ; lectures on Scottish life and literature by authorities on various subjects and writers. Prizes are provided by the Club for the pupils of the Shettleston and Tollcross schools to foster study of the Works of Burns. Visitors are always welcomed at any of the Club's meetings.

No. 92—KILBOWIE Jolly Beggars Burns Club. Instituted September, 1896. Federated 26th August, 1897. Place of meeting, T. F. Ross's Cross Restaurant. President Alex. M'Donald, 53 Montrose Street, Kilbowie, Clydebank ; Vice-president, David J. Clark, 150 Kilbowie Road, Kilbowie, Clydebank ; *Secretary,* James Chamberlain, 2 Victoria Street, Kilbowie, Clydebank. Committee— Ashcroft, Blair, Crum, Davidson, Deans, Frances, Fleming, Mitchell, Morrison, M'Williams, Philip, Scott, and Walter. Special features of the Club—The cultivation of a better knowledge of the Life and Works of the Bard, and the study of Scottish literature by the reading of papers, &c., original and otherwise, amongst the members.

No. 93—CLYDEBANK Burns Club. Federated 1897.

No. 94—UPHALL Tam o' Shanter Burns Club. Instituted 1885. Federated 12th September, 1897. Place of meeting, Ross's Hall, Uphall. President, James Spence, Beechwood Cottages,Uphall ; Vice-president, Edward Learmond, West Houston, Uphall : *Secretary,* Jas. Purdie, Hawthorn Place, Uphall.

No. 95—BOLTON Burns Club. Instituted 1881. Federated 1897.

No. 96—JEDBURGH Burns Club. Instituted 1869. Federated 13th November, 1897. Place and date of meeting, Spread Eagle Hotel, 25th January, at 8 o'clock. President. ex-Provost John Boyd, J.P., Bongate Cottage, Jedburgh ; Vice-president, Peter Carruthers, Castlegate ; *Secretary and Treasurer,* Joseph Tweddle, Castlegate. Committee —Provost Wm. Oliver, J.P., ex-Bailie A. Walker, Councillor James Veitch, Parish Councillor John Oliver, Messrs Wm. Swanston, John Brown, Wm. Aitken, John Oliver, F. Dyer, and David Heatlie.

No. 97—KILMARNOCK Bellfield Burns Club. Instituted 1895. Federated 1898. Vice-president, Daniel Picken, Glebe Avenue, Kilmarnock.

No. 98—LANARK Burns Club. Instituted 1891. Federated 1898. Place and time of meeting, Market Inn, Monthly, at 7.30 p.m. President, A. S. Boyd, Cordelier Terrace, Lanark ; Vice-president, H. M. Beveridge, Hyndford House, Lanark ; *Secretary,* Thomas Veitch, Dalblair, Wheatland Drive, Lanark. Committee—T. Lithgow,

W. Brown, R. Hamilton, A. Keith, J. Blackhall, and P. MacAuslan. Special features of Club—Papers on the works or influence of Robert Burns are read monthly and discussed and a social evening spent. Last year our Club made special efforts on behalf of local charities, as the result of which the sum of £62 was handed over.

No. 99—BARLINNIE Burns Club. Instituted 1893. Federated 1898. *Secretary*, Alexander Mackay, 10 Officers' Quarters, Barlinnie, Glasgow.

No. 100—HAMILTON Mossgiel Burns Club. Instituted 1892. Federated 4th April, 1898. Place and date of meeting, Masonic Hall, 1st Tuesday of month, at 8 p.m., except June, July, and August. President, James M'Cartney, 99 Quarry Street, Hamilton ; Vice-president, Jas. Drysdale, 3 Glenlee Street, Burnbank, Lanarkshire ; *Secretary*, Wm. Sommerville, 5 Jackson Street, Blantyre ; Treasurer, Wm. Hamilton, Burnfoot, Bent Road, Hamilton.

No. 101—MOTHERWELL Workmen's Burns Club. Federated 1898.

No. 102—CARLISLE Border Burns Club. Instituted 1898. Federated 1898.

No. 103—COALBURN Burns Club. Federated 1898.

No. 104—DUMFRIES Oak Burns Club. Federated 1898.

No. 105—RUTHERGLEN Cronies Burns Club. Instituted 1896. Federated 1898.

No. 106—BROXBURN Rosebery Burns Club. Federated 1898.

No. 107—HUTCHESONTOWN Burns Club. Instituted 1897. Federated 1898. *Secretary*, Robert A. Sinclair, 4 Govanhill Street, Crosshill, Glasgow.

No. 108—EAST CALDER Jolly Beggars Burns Club. Instituted 17th January, 1899. Federated 29th January, 1899. Place of meeting, Grapes Inn, East Calder. President, James Millar, Burn House, Mid-Calder ; Vice-president, James Robertson, East Calder ; *Secretary*, John Watson, 46 Oakbank, Mid-Calder ; Treasurer, John A. Forbes.

No. 109—GLASGOW Caledonia Burns Club. Instituted 1898. Federated 1899.

No. 110—CAMBUSLANG Burns Club. Instituted 1850. Federated 1898.

No. 111—SOUTH EDINBURGH Burns Club. Instituted 1889. Federated 1899.

No. 112—DUMFRIES Burns Howff Club. Instituted 1889. Federated 10th August, 1899. Place and date of meeting, Globe Hotel, monthly. President, William Dinwiddie, 37 Moffat Road, Dumfries ; Past President John Maxwell, English Street, Dumfries ; *Secretary,* Thomas Laidlaw, 3 St. Michael's Terrace, Henry Street, Dumfries ; Treasurer, Thomas Robertson. Committee —J. L. Armstrong, D. Bell, W. Boyd, A. Hamilton, J. W. Blackley, Jas. Smith, A. Shankland, P. M'Murdo, D. Lockerbie, D. Clark, M. Lennox, W.. Robinson, J. B. Wood, .T. Draffan, and W. Carruthers. Special feature of Club—Lectures, &c., during winter months.

No. 113 VALE OF LEVEN Glencairn Burns Club. Instituted 1897. Federated 1899. Place and date of meeting, Albert Hotel, Alexandria, last Saturday of month, at 6.30 p.m. President, Hugh M'Vean, Mossgiel, Dalmonach Road, Bonhill ; Vice-president, Alexander Campbell, 82 Bridge Street, Alexandria ; *Secretary,* Daniel Macmillan, Smollett Street, Alexandria ; Treasurer, Peter Burdon, Viewforth, Balloch. Committee — Daniel M'Innes, John James, James Burdon, Norman M'Crimmon, Thomas Nicol, and William Smith. Special features of Club— Celebration of 25th January ; summer outing ; and occasionally short papers by members.

No. 114—BRODICK Burns Club. Instituted 1899. Federated 1900.

No. 115—KIPPEN and District Burns Club. Instituted 1896. Federated 1900. *Secretary,* Samuel Thomson, Pointend, Kippen.

No. 116—GREENLOANING Burns Club. Instituted 1889. Federated 1900. Place and time of meeting, Greenloaning Inn, at 7.30 p.m. President, S. Watson, Neither Mills, Greenloaning, Braco ; Vice-president, J. Chamers, Bardrill Farm, Blackfora ; *Secretary,* James Bayne, Kinbuck, Dunblane. Committee—R. Taylor, G. Robertson, W. Taylor, A. Graham, and J. M'Naughton.

No. 117—GLASGOW Southern Burns Club. Instituted 1899. Federated 1900.

No. 118—GLASGOW Albany Burns Club. Instituted 1900. Federated 1900. Place and date of meeting, Burns House Club, 27 India Street, Glasgow, 1st Wednesdays, October to March. President, William Cullen, M.D., 3 Queen's Crescent, Glasgow, W. ; Vice-presidents, Richard D. Donaldson, 30 Abbey Drive, Jordanhill, and James Niven Murdoch, 175 Hope Street, Glasgow : *Secretary,* David C. Kennedy, 33 Hope Street, Glasgow ; Treasurer, David Annand, Maxwell Road, East Kilbride. Special features of Club—Monthly lectures by literary gentlemen ; Annual children's competition in Burns songs and readings ; Anniversary dinner.

No 119—BONHILL Burns Club. Instituted 1900. Federated 1900.

No. 120—BRISTOL Burns Club (Incorporated with the Caledonian
Society, 1898). Instituted 1894. Federated 7th
December, 1900. Place of meeting, 24 St. Nicholas Street
(no fixed dates). President, John Turnbull, 1 Baldwin
Street, Bristol; Vice-presidents, A. Cameron, 1 Wine
Street, Bristol, and Angus Turnbull, 26 Florence Park,
Redland, Bristol; *Secretary and Treasurer*, A. K.
Simpson, 24 St. Nicholas Street, Bristol. Special
features of Club—Benevolent and social.

No. 121—HAMILTON Junior Burns Club. Instituted September,
1886. Federated April, 1901. Place and date of meeting, Mrs R. Bell's, Union Street, Hamilton, first Monday
each month. President, David Cross, 127 Quarry Street,
Hamilton; Vice-president, John Cameron, 50 Burnbank Road, Hamilton; *Secretary and Treasurer*, William
Wilson, 5 Haddow Street, Hamilton; Minute Secretary,
J. Hendrie; Stewards, T. Muir and R. Morrison. Committee—J. Brown, G. Fleming, J. Thomson, and R.
Allan. Special features of Club—Reading of essays
on various subjects, concerts, competitions, summer
rambles, and social evenings. (40 members.)

No. 122—DARNCONNER Aird's Moss Burns Club. Instituted
4th November, 1901. Federated 4th November, 1901.
Secretary, William Naismith, Darnconner, *via* Auchinleck.

No. 123—AUCHINLECK Boswell Burns Club. Instituted 25th
January, 1900. Federated 10th December, 1901. Place
of meeting, Market Inn, Auchinleck. President, Peter
Strachan, Dalsalloch, Auchinleck; Vice-president, John
Black, Dalsalloch, Auchinleck; *Secretary*, William Hall,
Dalsalloch, Auchinleck; Steward, David Muir, Dal-
salloch, Auchinleck.

No. 124—EDINBURGH Ninety Burns Club. Instituted 1890.
Federated 1902. Place of meeting, Ferguson & Forrester's,
Princes Street. President, J. Augustus Beddie, 11
Merchiston Crescent, Edinburgh; Vice-president, W.
J. S. Dalling, 199 Bruntsfield Place, Edinburgh; *Secre-
tary*, R. D. Grant M'Laren, 2 Mayfield Road, Edinburgh;
Treasurer, James Bell, 4 Wilfred Terrace, Edinburgh.
Special features of Club—Anniversary dinner, dance,
whist drive, excursion; other social and business meetings.

No. 125—BLACKBURN-ON-ALMOND Rabbie Burns Club.
Instituted 1900. Federated 1902. *Secretary*, Robt.
Carlyle, West-end, Blackburn, Bathgate.

No. 126—FALKIRK Burns Club. Instituted 1866. Federated
1902. Place of meeting, Mathieson's Rooms. Pre-
sident, H. B. Watson, Harlesden, Falkirk; Vice presidents,
T. Callander Wade, Woodcroft, Larbert, and Duncan
Kennedy, 17 Heugh Street, Falkirk; *Secretary and
Treasurer*, R. H. Menzies, Bank Street, Falkirk. Com-
mittee—F. Johnston, R. H. Lochhead, Sheriff Moffatt,
R. S. Aitchison, Rev. Mr Ballard, J. T. Borland, D.

Houston, Andrew Hunter, and J. T. Sinclair. Special features of Club—Annual dinner (24th), and spring and autumn meetings to which ladies are invited.

No. 127—COWDENBEATH Haggis Burns Club. Instituted 1903 Federated 1903.

No. 128—COWDENBEATH Glencairn Burns Club. Instituted 1893. Federated May, 1903. Place and date of meeting, Raith Arms Inn, Cowdenbeath, every alternate Friday from October to April, monthly remainder of year. Hon. President, Wm. Breingan ; Hon. Vice-presidents, Frank Forsyth and David Bowie ; President, Councillor John Sheddon, 28 Woodland Place, Cowdenbeath ; Vice-president, William Archibald, 11 Marshall Street, Cowdenbeath ; Secretary, E. Hunter, 31 Arthur Place, Cowdenbeath ; Treasurer, Thos. Wilson ; Bard, James Murray ; Master of Ceremonies, Jas. M'Kenzie. Committee— John Nisbet, Wm. Foster, Peter Banks, John Banks, and Andrew M'Kechnie. Special features of Club— The mutual improvement of the members ; children's competitions ; essays ; and the annual celebration of the Poet's birthday.

No. 129—GORBALS Burns Club. Instituted 1902. Federated 1903.

No. 130—ROW Burns Club. Instituted 6th February, 1902. Federated 1903. Place and date of meeting, Colquhoun Arms, January, June, and October, at 8 p.m. President Major John M'Farlane, 1 West Clyde Street, Helensburgh ; Vice-president, W. Fraser, F.E.I.S., Clarkfield, 29 Campbell Street, Helensburgh ; Secretary, Robert Sloan, Hollylea, Row, Dumbartonshire ; Treasurer, George Walker, Luggray Lodge, Row. Special features of Club—Social intercourse among its members.

No. 131—NOTTINGHAM Scottish Association. Instituted 1902. Federated 1903. President, John Crawford, J.P. Springfield, Bulwell, Nottingham ; Secretary, John Currie, 24 Arboretum Street, Nottingham.

No. 132—RICCARTON Kirkstyle Burns Club. Instituted 1904. Federated 1904.

No. 133—NEWARTHILL Burns Club. Instituted 26th September, 1903. Federated 28th March, 1904. Place and date of meeting, Mrs H. Watson's, last Saturday every month, at 6.30 p.m. President, John Henshaw, Church Street, Newarthill, Motherwell ; Vice-president, Thomas Law, C.C., Allan Place, Newarthill, Motherwell ; Secretary, Duncan Crawford, 267 High Street, Newarthill, Motherwell. Committee—Thos. Crombie, Thos. Nimmo, and Thos. M'Alpine.

No. 134—DUNTOCHER Heron Burns Club. Instituted 1897. Federated 1904.

196

No. 135—PARTICK Western Burns Club. Instituted 1903. Federated 1904. Place and date of meeting, Windsor Restaurant, Partick, last Friday from October to April. President, William Roy, 47 Byres Road, Partick, Glasgow; Vice-president, James Kyles, 30 Southbrae Drive, Jordanhill, Glasgow; *Secretary*, F. R. Carter, 28 White Street, Partick, Glasgow; Treasurer, Donald Gunn, 592 Dumbarton Road, Partick, Glasgow. Special features of Club—Lectures and harmony and anniversary dinner.

No. 136—HAMILTON Royal Oak Burns Club. Instituted 1898. Federated 1904.

No. 137—IPSWICH Burns Club. Instituted 1902. Federated 1904.

No. 138—CLELAND Burns Club. Instituted 1904. Federated 1904.

No. 139—GLASGOW National Burns Club, Ltd. Instituted 1904. Federated 30th November, 1904. Place and date of meeting, 21 India Street, daily. President, John G. Galpine. 9 Yarrow Gardens, Glasgow; Vice-president, A. Cunningham, 25 Queen Margaret Drive, North Kelvinside, Glasgow; *Secretary*, William Hamilton, National Burns Club, Ltd., 21 India Street, Glasgow. Special feature of Club—Social.

No. 140—POLLOKSHAWS Burns Club. Instituted 1865. Federated 1905. *Secretary*, Jas. Milne, Burgh Halls, Pollokshaws.

No. 141—STONEHOUSE Burns Club. Instituted 1904. Federated 1905.

No. 142—BONNYBRIDGE Burns Club. Instituted 1905. Federated 1905.

No. 143—AIRDRIE Gateside Burns Club. Instituted 1904. Federated 1905.

No. 144—LARBERT and STENHOUSEMUIR Temperance Burns Club. Instituted 1904. Federated 1905.

No 145—GLASGOW Central Burns Club. Instituted 1905. Federated 1905.

No. 146—DUBLIN Burns Club. Instituted 1905. Federated 1905. President, George P. Fleming, Drimnagh House, Inchicore, Co. Dublin; *Secretary*, John Farquhar, 7 Fairview Avenue, Clontarf, Dublin; Treasurer, Alexander Lyon, 111 Botanic Road, Dublin.

No. 147—STONEHOUSE Haggis Burns Club. Federated 1905.

No. 148—GREENOCK Cronies Burns Club. Instituted January, 1899. Federated November, 1905. Place of meeting, Painters' Hall, Charles Street. President, Sandy M'Gavin,

7 Finnart Street, Greenock; Vice-president, William Kelso, 67 Regent Street, Greenock; *Secretary,* James R. Blackley, 20 West Stewart Street, Greenock. Special features of Club—To cherish the name of Robert Burns and foster a love for his writings, and generally to promote good-fellowship.

No. 149—ELGIN Burns Club. Instituted 20th December, 1900. Federated 1905. Hon. President, Sheriff Dunlop, Mar Lodge, Elgin ; President, Thomas North Christie, Blackhills, Lhanbryde,.Morayshire ; Vice-president, Rev. John R. Duncan, Lhanbryde, Morayshire ; *Secretary,* John Foster, Sheriff-Clerk of Morayshire ; Treasurer, John B. Mair, M.V.O., Chief Constable of Morayshire. Committee—Angus Macdonald, H.I.M.S., T. R Mackenzie, Angus Cameron, John Wittot, Alexander Gillan, and D. A. Shiach.

No. 150—KILMARNOCK Jolly Beggars Burns Club. Instituted February 10th, 1905. Federated December, 1905. Place and date of meeting, " Wee Thack," Grange Street, last Monday of every month at 7.30 ; harmony, Saturday evenings at 7.30 ; monthly meeting. President, Wm. Willock, 65 King Street, Kilmarnock ; Vice-president, George M'Donald, Old Irvine Road, Kilmarnock ; *Secretary,* Andrew Niven, 17 Fullarton Street, Kilmarnock ; Treasurer, David Mitchell. Special features of Club— To cherish the name of Robert Burns ; to foster his writings ; to celebrate the anniversary of his birthday ; and to promote friendly and social intercourse amongst the members.

No. 151—OLD KILPATRICK Burns Club. Instituted 20th January, 1906. Federated 20th January, 1906. Place and date of meeting, Barclay U.F. Church Hall, monthly. President, William Cockburn, N.-B. Station House, Bowling ; Vice-president, Robert Newlands, Seyton, Gavinburn Place, Old Kirkpatrick ; *Secretary,* Robert Smith, Maryville, Old Kirkpatrick ; Treasurer, Gavin Irvine, Station House, Old Kirkpatrick. Committee— John Brock, Archie Paul, Alex. Mann, Allan Dawson, William Gallacher, Robert Draper, James Dykes, and James M'Carlie. Special feature of Club—Winter monthly meetings.

No. 152—HAMILTON Burns Club. Instituted 1877. Federated 1906. Place and date of meeting, Commercial Hotel, Hamilton, irregular intervals during year. President, Thomas Arnot, Chaseley, Hamilton ; Vice-president, the Rev. John L. Tulloch, Mansewood, Hamilton ; *Secretary,* Wm. Lang, The British Linen Bank, Hamilton ; Treasurer, W. Martin Kay, Bank of Scotland Chambers, Hamilton. Special feature of Club—Prizes are offered for essays on Scottish literature to pupils in burgh schools.

No. 153—SCOTTISH Burns Club (in which is incorporated " Glasgow Waverley " and " Western " (1859) and " Ye Saints "

(1884) Burns Clubs). Instituted 1904. Federated
1906. Place and date of meeting, Reid's Rooms, 30
Gordon Street, Glasgow, fourth Monday of each month,
at 7.30 p.m. President, ex-Bailie Archibald Campbell,
J.P., Argyll Lodge. Albert Road, Pollokshields; Vice-
presidents, D. S. MacGregor, 185 West Regent Street,
Glasgow, and James G. MacKerracher, 67 Durward Avenue,
Shawlands; Secretary, J. Kevan M'Dowall, 180 Hope
Street, Glasgow (telephone, "Douglas 3755"); Treasurer,
R. W. Reddoch; Financial Secretary, J. D. Bauchop,
LL.D.; Auditors, J. B. Macpherson and D. M. MacIntyre,
M.B.E.; Bard, Thos. Cree. Committee — J. K.
M'Dowall, J.P., J. S. Downie, N. MacWhannell, J.
S. Gregson, Jas. Macfarlane, Sam B. Langlands, and A.
K. Foote. Edinburgh Section.—President, Dr Jas.
Devon; Vice-president, John Kelso Kelly; Secretary,
George M'Gill, 73 Ashley Terrace, North Merchiston,
Edinburgh; Treasurer, Joseph Sanders. Committee
—A. D. Paterson, Wm. J. Hay, and John Samson.
Special features of Club—Burnsiana and literature.
The Club is conducted on temperance principles. Motto
—"The heart ave's the part aye."

No. 154—JOHANNESBURG Burns Club. Instituted 1900.
Federated 1906. Secretary, Richard Rusk, solicitor,
Natal Bank Buildings, Market Square, Johannesburg. .

No. 155—EAST STIRLINGSHIRE Burns Club. Instituted
January, 1905. Federated September, 1906. Place
of meeting, Cross Roads Inn, Bainsford, Falkirk. President, Walter Gibson, 44 Watson Street, Falkirk; Vice-
president, Robert B. Russell, Mungal Place, Bainsford,
Falkirk; Secretary, Alexander Glen, 21 Gordon Terrace,
Carron Road, Falkirk; Treasurer, John Duncan. Committee — Alex. Cruickshanks, George Mallin, and
Wm. Galbraith. Special features of Club—Lectures
(quarterly) and holding of Burns anniversary, and social
intercourse amongst the members.

No. 156—NEWCASTLE and TYNESIDE Burns Club. Instituted
1864. Federated 4th October, 1906. Place and time
of meeting, Central Exchange Hotel, 7 p.m. President,
R. M. Graham; Vice-president, Alex. Sutherland; Secretary, David H. Allan, Tillside, Newlands Road, Newcastle-
on-Tyne; Treasurer, W. Tasker Brown.

No. 157—BAILLIESTON Caledonia Burns Club. Instituted
25th January, 1901. Federated 5th October, 1906.
Place and date of meeting, Free Gardeners' Hall, second
Thursday in each month, 8 p.m. President, John Kerr,
697 Shettleston Road, Glasgow; Vice-president, Geo.
Johnstone; Secretary, John Preston, 21 Church Street,
Baillieston. Committee—W. Lockhart, C. G. Paterson, Alf. Doris, W. Ross, W. Kerr, Jas. Smith, W.
Scott, and Jno. Henry. Special features of Club—To
cherish the name of Robert Burns and to foster a love
for his writings, and generally to encourage a taste for

Scottish history and literature; and to celebrate his memory by an annual social meeting to be held on 25th January, or as near thereto as possible.

No. 158—DARLINGTON Burns Association. Instituted 8th March, 1906. Federated, 18th October, 1906. Place and date of meeting, Temperance Institute, various. President, John Henderson, 7 Southend Avenue, Darlington; Vice-presidents, Jno. M. Galt, The Rand, Cleveland Avenue, Darlington; Jas. Shirlaw, 1 Cliffe Terrace, Woodland Road, Darlington; and J. C. Veitch, Kilbucho, Cleveland Avenue, Darlington; Secretary, R. M. Liddell, 14 Langholm Crescent, Darlington; Treasurer, Geo. Lawson, 5 Holmwood Grove, Harrowgate Hill, Darlington. Committee—Robt. Storar, T. C. Howe, Jas. Anderson, Alexander Luke, T. Henderson. Mus. Bac., Wm. Stevenson (Cleasby Terrace), Wm. Stevenson (Woodlands Road), Alexander Furness, and Jno. M'Gregor. Special features of Club—To promote the study of Burns Works and Scottish literature, history, &c., and the social and intellectual intercourse and enjoyment of the members generally, by such means as may from time to time be agreed upon.

No. 159—WALKER Burns Club. Instituted 1892. Federated 11th November, 1906. Place of meeting, Scrogg Inn, Walker. President, John Keith, 633 Welbeck Road, Walker; Vice-presidents, Dr W. Hutchinson and H. F. Caldwell, Welbeck Road, Walker; Secretary, John Yeats, 114 Middle Street, Walker, Newcastle-on-Tyne; Treasurer, Robert M'Rory, 26 Eastbourne Gardens, Walker. Special features of Club—To promote the cultivation of a better knowledge of the Poet and his Works; to bring together Scotsmen and other admirers of Burns; also promoting Scottish concerts.

No. 160 WHITBURN Burns Club. Instituted November, 1906. Federated 1906. Place and date of meeting, Cross Tavern, on the 2nd Friday of each month. President, Frank M'Gregor, East End, Whitburn, West Lothian; Vice-president, Wm. M'Kenzie, East End, Whitburn, West Lothian; Secretary, Allan Johnston, 184 West Main Street, Whitburn, West Lothian; Treasurer, John Johnston; nine members of Committee. Special features of Club—To further and popularise the Works of Robert Burns; excursion to some historical district annually, destination to be fixed from year to year. In co-operation with the county Clubs for the purpose of restoring the Grave of " Dear Bought Bess," whose remains are interred in the churchyard here.

No. 161 CHARLESTON Burns Club, Paisley. Instituted 25th January, 1905. Federated 20th December, 1906. Place and date of meeting, 17 Stevenson Street, quarterly. President, Peter Shannon, 14 Greenlaw Avenue, Paisley; Vice-presidents, Thos. Peacock, 17 New Stock Street, and Wm. Herd, 25 Stock Street; Secretary, Andrew

Walker, 16 Stevenson Street, Paisley; Auditors, Hugh
Black and Alex. Glasgow. Special features of Club—
The promotion of a friendly feeling among the members
and kindred Clubs; and the celebration of the Poet's
birth.

No. 162—PLYMOUTH and District Caledonian Society. Instituted
8th February, 1898. Federated 8th March, 1907. *Secretary*, P. Robertson, 89 Alcester Street, Devonport.

No. 163—GATESHEAD and District Burns Club. Instituted
1887. Federated 1907. Place and date of meeting,
Royal Hotel, first Thursday of each month, September
to April. President, Donald Morrison, 5 Wensleydale
Terrace, Gateshead - on - Tyne ; Vice - presidents, E.
Bennett, T. Gault, R. Good, T. Hetherington, and J.·
Strachan ; *Secretary*, Wm. Bain, 142 Westminster Street,
Gateshead-on-Tyne ; Assistant Secretary, A. Mansfield,
152 Westbourne Avenue, Gateshead-on-Tyne ; Piper,
Pipe-Major Munro Strachan, Tyneside Scottish, 20 Diamond
Street, Wallsend-on-Tyne ; Treasurer, G. J. Porter,
Durham Road, Gateshead-on-Tyne. Committee—
R. England, J. Guy, A. M'Donald, D. M'Farlane, and
J. Patterson. Special features of Club—To associate
Scotsmen and other admirers of Burns ; to preserve an
interest in Scottish manners, customs, and affairs ; to
cultivate literary pursuits, and more particularly to
advance the study of the Works of Burns and other
Scottish literature.

No. 164—KINNING PARK Burns Club. Instituted 1881. Federated 1907.. *Secretary*, John Downie, 29 Melville Street,
Pollokshields, Glasgow.

No. 165—WALLSEND Burns Club. Instituted 1898. Federated
18th April, 1907. Place of meeting, Assembly Rooms,
Wallsend-on-Tyne. President, D. Walters, 35 North
Road, Wallsend-on-Tyne ; Vice-president, James Heron,
13 Curzon Road, Wallsend-on-Tyne ; *Secretary*, D. E.
Liddle, 72 Northumberland Street, Wallsend-on-Tyne.
Committee—Messrs Stewart, Johnston, M'Kinnon, Glass,
and Murdoch. Special features of Club—To associate
Scotsmen and admirers of Burns ; to cultivate literary
pursuits and love of Scottish song and story by promoting
Scotch concerts ; also to preserve an interest in Scottish
manners and customs.

No. 166—CLEVELAND Scottish Association. Instituted 1907.
Federated 1907. *Secretary*, A. Wallace, 6 Royal Exchange,
Middlesborough.

No. 167—BIRMINGHAM Burns Club. Instituted 1906. Federated 1907. Place and time of meeting, Grand Hotel,
Birmingham, 7 p.m. President, Wright Murray, 130
Oakwood Road, Sparkhill, Birmingham ; Vice-presidents,
John Barr, 6 Springfield Road, King's Heath, Birmingham,
and T. N. Veitch, 33 Victoria Road, Acocks Green, Bir-

mingham ; *Secretary*, Chas. MacGregoi, 46 Tennyson Road,
Small Heath, Birmingham ; Treasurer, R. M'Kenzie, 50
Stirling Road, Edgbaston, Birmingham.   Special features
of Club—To perpetuate the memory of Robert Burns, to
foster a love for his writings, and to promote social and
friendly intercourse between Scotsmen and Scotswomen
in Birmingham and district.

No. 168—RICCARTON Burns Club.   Instituted 7th February,
1877.   Federated, 14th January, 1908.   Place of meeting,
Commercial Inn.   President, Robert Wyllie, Fleming
Street, Riccarton : *Secretary*, Jas. P. Moir, 39 Campbell
Street, Riccarton.   Committee—Geo. Cunningham ("Pate
M'Phun"), Hugh Dale, J. P. Dickson, J. Williamson, and
Wm. Neil.   Special features of Club—Social intercourse
amongst the Burns fraternity ; to spread and become
familiar with the Poet's Works.

No. 169—GLASGOW and DISTRICT Association of Burns Clubs
and Kindred Societies.   Instituted 1907.   Federated
1908.   Place of meeting, Burns House Club, 27 India
Street, Glasgow.   President, C. R. Cowie, 20 Blythswood
Square, Glasgow ; Vice-presidents, Wm Cockburn, N.-B.
Station, Bowling, and Thos. Killin, 2 Stewarton Drive,
Cambuslang : *Secretary*, J. Jeffrey Hunter, solicitor, 89
Bath Street, Glasgow.   Committee — Alex. Pollock,
Hugh M'Coll, Wm. Douglas, Alex. M'Kenzie, J. F. Ander-
son, Geo. Armour, Jas. M. Campbell, Isaac Chalmers,
R. M. Milholm, Wm. Reid, A. C. Riddell, ex-Councillor
Sutherland, Jas. Tudhope, A. R. Young, J. M. Brown,
J. G. Galpine, J. S. Ritchie, T. P. Thompson, Thos. Turn-
bull, J. C. Ewing, Ninian M'Whannell, T. C. F. Brotchie,
J. D. Sloan, and Wm. Gardiner.   Special features of
Club—To further the interests of the Burns cult by promoting closer union between the clubs in the district and
bringing the members of these clubs into more harmonious
relationship, and to take the initiative in instituting and
recommending movements likely to be beneficial to the
cult.

No. 170—LARKHALL Thistle Burns Club.   Instituted November,
1906.   Federated 18th April, 1908.   President, John
Crozier Hislop, 17 Percy Street, Larkhall ; *Secretary*,
William Nicol, Machan, Larkhall.

No. 171—CHATTANOOGA Burns Society, Tenn., U.S.A.   Insti-
tuted 25th January, 1908.   Federated 2nd June, 1908.
Place and date of meeting, Mountain City Club,
Chattanooga, Tenn., 25th January.   President,
James Francis Johnston, 505 Walnut Street, Chat-
tanooga, Tenn. ; Vice-president, Col. Milton B. Ochs,
Times Building, Chattanooga, Tenn. ; *Secretary*, Col. R.
B. Cooke, National Soldiers' Home, Maine, U.S.A. ;
Committee—N. Thayer Montague, Frank Spurlock, Joe
Brown, M.C. and T. R. Preston.   Special features of
Club—Annual dinner, papers, lectures, collection of
library.

No. 172—OREGON Burns Club, Portland, Oregon, U.S.A. Instituted 25th January, 1908. Federated December, 1908. Place of meeting, Chamber of Commerce Building. President, William Bristol, Attorney, Wilcox Building, Portland, Oregon ; Vice-president, Judge George J. Cameron, Chamber of Commerce Building, Portland, Oregon ; Secretary, Alexander T. Smith, 143 Hamilton Avenue, Portland, Oregon. Committee—Dr W. T. Williamson, James Hislop, Alex. G. Brown, Alex. Muirhead. Special features of Club—Meet once a year on January 25th to celebrate the anniversary of the birth of the greatest poet of humanity, the immortal Robert Burns.

No. 173—IRVINE Burns Club. Instituted 1826. Federated 18th November, 1908. Place and date of meeting, King's Arms Hotel, 25th January. President, A. M. Watson, Dyrochburn, Bank Street, Irvine ; Vice-president, Matthew W. Breckenridge, Caldwell, Irvine ; Secretary, R. M. Hogg, Stratford, Irvine ; Treasurer, R. F. Longmuir, Roseville, Irvine.

No. 174—ARDROSSAN Castle Burns Club. Federated 1908. Secretary, Wm. Gibson, Hill Cottage, 90 Glasgow Street, Ardrossan.

No. 175—MEIKLE EARNOCK Original Burns Club. Instituted 16th March, 1906. Federated 21st December, 1908. Place of meeting, John Crowe, Cadzow Vaults, Hamilton. President, James Shepherd, 2 Moore Street, Hamilton ; Vice-president, Alex. Laird, 50 Eddlewood Buildings, Hamilton ; Secretary, John Hepburn, 36 Eddlewood Buildings, Hamilton. Committee—Andrew Hamilton, William Pollock, Robert Lees, and William Ross. Special features of Club—To keep ever green the memory of Scotia's greatest son, and disseminate the principles he strove to inculcate.

No. 176—RENFREW Burns Club. Federated 6th December, 1898. Secretary, Wm. S. Cochran, 20 Renfield Street, Renfrew.

No. 177—PRESTWICK Burns Club. Instituted 1902. Federated 1908.

No. 178—KILMARNOCK Begbie's Burns Club. Instituted 1908. Federated 1909. Place and date of meeting, Angel Hotel, third Wednesday of each month. President, John Stewart, 12 Hill Street, Kilmarnock ; Vice-president Andrew Sinclair, 65 M'Lelland Drive, Kilmarnock ; Secretary, William Lennox, 11 Nursery Avenue, Kilmarnock. Committee—John Brown, A. M'D. Anderson, David Lang, John Douglas, and Wm. Muir. Special features of Club— Reading of papers relative to the Works of Burns and kindred subjects ; celebrating the birthday of the Poet.

No 179—DAILLY Jolly Beggars Burns Club. Instituted 22nd January, 1902. Federated 22nd January, 1902.

No. 180—TOLLCROSS Burns Club. Instituted 1908. Federated 1908. Place and time of meeting, Fullarton Hall, 7.30 p.m. President, John C. Brown, 5 Brownlie Gardens, Tollcross; Vice-president, Robert Irvine, 306 Dennistoun Gardens, Dennistoun; *Secretary*, James L. Cowan, Clydeside Terrace, Tollcross; Treasurer, P. W. Watt, Fielden, Mount Vernon. Special features of Club—To cherish the name of Robert Burns and foster a love for his writings, and generally to encourage a taste for Scottish literature, and to celebrate the memory of our National Bard by an annual social meeting.

No. 181—GLASGOW Primrose Burns Club. Instituted 1901. Federated 11th February, 1909. Place and time of meeting, Burns House Centre, 27 India Street, 7.30 p.m. President, George J. M'Callum, 44 West George Street, Glasgow; Vice-president, Matthew Reid, Benares, Bearsden, Glasgow; *Joint Secretaries*, Geo. R. Hunter, 55 Seamore Street, Glasgow, and R. L. Swann, 104 Hanover Street, Glasgow; Treasurer, John Wall, 263 Hope Street, Glasgow. Special features of Club—The promotion of Burns cult, anniversary dinner, school children's competitions, lectures, and musical evenings.

No. 182—STANE (Shotts) Mossgiel Burns Club. Instituted 3rd February, 1908. Federated 24th February, 1909. Place and date of meeting, Stane Hotel, first Friday of each month, except June, July, and August. President, Jas. Cairns, 121 Torbothie Road, Stane, Shotts; Vice-president, William Rodger, 104 Main Street, Stane, Shotts; *Secretary*, Alexander Walker, 9 Torbothie Road, Stane, Shotts; Treasurer, Jas. White, 1 Stane Place, Stane, Shotts. Special features of Club—Papers and discussion on Poet's Life and Works; school competitions; celebration of anniversaries.

No. 183—LONDONDERRY Burns Club and Caledonian Society. Instituted October, 1905. Federated 15th June, 1909. Place of meeting, Presbyterian Working Men's Institute. President, Alexander MacLean, J.P., Victoria Park, Londonderry; Vice-presidents, Messrs A. Wightman, G. P. Findlay, Jas. MacLehose, T. Wallace, and Geo. Burns; *Secretary*, Wm. Baxter, 12 Harding Street, Londonderry; Treasurer, James H. Wands, Ebrington Gardens, Londonderry; Chairman of Committee, Thos. Wallace, Sunbeam Terrace, Londonderry. Committee — W. Dickie, W. Nichol, J. H. Wands, D. Murray, G. Sidebottom, and A. M'Intosh.

No. 184—BLAIRADAM Shanter Burns Club. Instituted 21st August, 1907. Federated 29th August, 1909. Place of meeting, Blairadam Tavern, Kelty. President, Councillor James Wilkie, Hutton's Buildings, Black Road, Kelty; Vice-presidents, Adam Lees, Adam's Terrace, Kelty, and Arthur Bennett, Stewart's Buildings, Kelty; *Secretary*, Thomas C. Anderson, Blairforge, Blairadam, Kelty, Fife; Treasurer, Wm. Fyfe. Committee—Wm. Clark, Geo.

Cowan, James Mackie, and Geo. Malcolm Special features of Club—Songs, recitations, and readings ; annual school children's competition on the songs and poems of our National Bard.

No. 185—BURTON Burns Club. Instituted 1908. Federated 1909.

No. 186—KILMARNOCK Glencairn Burns Club. Instituted 1909. Federated 1910. *Secretary,* John Thorburn, 12 Fairyhill Road, Kilmarnock.

No. 187—GALASHIELS Burns Club. Instituted 10th December, 1908. Federated 9th December, 1909. Place of meeting—Burgh Buildings. Hon. president, Right Hon. Robert Munro, K.C., M.P. ; President, Councillor George Hope Tait ; Vice-presidents, Provost Dalgleish, H. S. Murray, A. L. Brown ;. *Secretary,* George Grieve ; Treasurer, John Hodge, jun. Committee— W. Addison (chairman of committee), H. M. Tait, David Hislop, W. Young, L. Lennox, Chief Constable Noble, Jas. Walker, Councillor Thos. Brown, Thos. Lamb, ex-Provost Riddle, P. Whyte, Councillor Kemp, Councillor G. T. Sanderson, and ex-Provost Sutherland.

No. 188—DUNS Working Men's Burns Club. Instituted 1902. Federated 1910. *Secretary,* Robt. Cameron, British Linen Bank, Duns.

No. 189—CLYDEBANK Barns o' Clyde Burns Club. Instituted 1896. Federated 9th December, 1909. Place and date of meeting, Boilermakers' Hall, Yoker, 2nd Thursday each month. President, George Latto, 23 Cochno Street, Whitecrook, Clydebank ; Vice-president, James Fowler, 6 Viewfield Terrace, Clydebank ; *Secretary* and *Treasurer,* Alfred Homewood, 35 Taylor Street, Clydebank. Com mittee—G. Gibson, J. Cameron, R. Fowler, J. M'Chlenry, D. Macpherson, J. Doig, A. Raeburn, J. Keane, J. Gibson, R. Carson, W. Middleton, and J. Smith. Special features of Club—To extend the good work of the Poet, and to keep for ever green the memory of the Immortal Bard, Robert Burns, the patriot and prince of song.

No. 190—PORT-GLASGOW Burns Club. Instituted January, 1910. Federated 1910. Place and date of meeting, Oddfellows' Hall, 1st Wednesday each month. President, William R. Niven, Firth View, Port-Glasgow ; Vice-president, John A. Borland, Balfour Place, Port-Glasgow ; *Secretary,* James Hicks, 20 John Wood Street, Port-Glasgow ; Treasurer, William MacDougall, Glenhuntly Terrace, Port-Glasgow. Special features of Club—To foster a love for the works of the National Bard, and to promote good-fellowship amongst the members.

No. 191—MOORPARK Burns Club. Instituted 1908. Federated 1910. *Secretary,* Ebenezer Inglis, Glasdale, Fauldshead Road, Renfrew.

No. 192—AYRSHIRE ASSOCIATION of Federated Burns Clubs. Instituted 1908. Federated 1910. Place and date of meeting, Quarterly, at various places and times in the county. President, Andrew Sinclair, 65 M'Lelland Drive, Kilmarnock; Secretary, William Lennox, 11 Nursery Avenue, Kilmarnock. Committee—Archibald Laird James Moir, Hugh Campbell, Wm. Hall, John M'Gregor, and James Queay. Special features of Club —To further the interests of the Burns cult by promoting closer union between the Clubs in the county, and to render all possible assistance to the work of the Federation.

No. 193—RUTHERGLEN Jolly Beggars Burns Club. Instituted ·1910. Federated 1910.

No. 194—MIDDLEBIE Burns Club. Instituted 1909. Federated 1910. Secretary, Walter A. Mather, Donkins House, Kirtlebridge, Ecclefechan.

No. 195—SHIREMOOR Blue Bell Burns Club. Instituted 1906. Federated 1910. Place and date of meeting, Blue Bell Inn, second Saturday in every month. President, John Wilson, 11 Duke Street, Shiremoor, near Newcastle-on-Tyne; Vice-president, Robert Fyfe, 19 Percy Street, Shiremoor, near Newcastle-on-Tyne; Secretary, Jas. F. Wilson, 11 Duke Street, Shiremoor, near Newcastle-on-Tyne. Committee—Jas. Snedden, A. Messer, T. Young, J. W. Mather, J. Peacock, G. Hancock, and Wm. Brown. Special feature of Club—To foster a love for Burns and his Works.

No. 196—MID-ARGYLL Burns Club. Instituted 11th January, 1909. Federated 27th December, 1910. Place of meeting, Royal Hotel, Ardrishaig. President, Alexander Blue, Kilduskland, Ardrishaig; Vice-president, Robert Finlay, Royal Hotel, Ardrishaig; Secretary, Andrew Y. Roy, Tigh-an-Eas, Ardrishaig. Committee—Captain Jas. M'Bain, R.A.F., J. M. Montgomerie, Archibald Campbell, John M'Alister, A. M. Leckie, and Archibald M'Bain. Special features of Club—Celebration of the Poet's birthday, and to encourage the study of his Works.

No. 197—WINNIPEG Burns Club. Instituted 1905. Federated 1911. Secretary, A. G. Kemp, Box 2886, Winnipeg.

No. 198—GOREBRIDGE Twenty-five Jolly Beggars Burns Club. Federated November 28th, 1913. Place of meeting, Brunton's Inn, Gorebridge. President, Robert Burnside, J.P., Main Street, Gorebridge; Vice-president, Robert Robertson, Store Row, Arniston, Gorebridge; Secretary, John Duncan, 5 Slate Row, Arniston, Gorebridge. Committee—R. Miller, W. Weir, R. Davidson, and R. Hadden.

No. 199—NEWBATTLE and DISTRICT Burns Club. Instituted 1910. Federated March, 1911. Place and date of meeting, Bowling Pavilion, Newtongrange, 1st or 2nd

Saturday of the month, 7 p.m. President, George Humphrey, Saugh Cottages, Newtongrange, Mid-Lothian; Vice-presidents, William Carson, Saugh Cottages, Newtongrange, and James Brown,6 Second Street, Newtongrange ; *Secretary*, John J. Haldane, 7 Sixth Street, Newtongrange, Mid-Lothian. Committee—P. Gray, J. Samuel, J. Gilmour, J. Pryde, J. M'Queen, D. Jamieson, C. Doig, T. Dalgleish, D. Richardson, G. M'Intosh, A. Robertson, and J. Millar. Special features of Club—Encouragement of social intercourse amongst the members and kindred Clubs ; celebration of the Poet's birth ; an annual trip ; meetings for the reading of literary papers relative to the life of Burns and kindred subjects ; promoting entertainments for charitable purposes, &c.

No. 200—STONEHOUSE Jolly Beggars Burns Club. Instituted January, 1911 Federated 21st March, 1911. Place and date of meeting, Buckshead Inn, every alternate Friday. President, Matthew Steel, Camnethan Street, Stonehouse ; Vice-president, David Gavin, Lochart Street, Stonehouse ; *Secretary*, Gavin Hutchison, Boghall Street, Stonehouse ; Treasurer, Robert Anderson, Buckshead Inn, Stonehouse. Special feature of Club—To promote social intercourse amongst the people in the village.

No. 201—CARLISLE Newtown Burns Club. Instituted November, 1910. Federated 27th April, 1911.

No. 202—GOVAN Ye Cronies Burns Club. Instituted 1893. Federated 1911. Place and date of meeting, Red Lamp, Govan, second Saturday each month, at 6 p.m. President, Matthew Stirling, 13 Hutton Drive, Govan ; Vice-president, James Hutchison, 10 Earl Street, Scotstoun · *Secretary*, James Rellie, 18 Elder Street, Govan ; Treasurer, Lachlan M'Laine ; Past Presidents, A. Nicol and E. J. Tait ; Bard, T. M. Walker, M.A. Committee—W. Forbes, T. R. Graham, M. Wardrop, W. Parker, and G. Kinloch. Special features of Club—The Club shall consist of men who honour and revere the memory of Burns ; the membership shall not exceed 100, and each candidate for membership must be a Freemason ; to promote social and friendly intercourse amongst its members.

No. 203—DENNISTOUN Jolly Beggars Burns Club. Instituted 25th January, 1911. Federated 6th June, 1911. Place and date of meeting, Chalmers Street Hall, last Thursday of month, at 8 p.m. President, A. Hainey, 39 Brandon Street, Bellgrove, Glasgow ; Vice-president, Wm. M'Kay, 7 Forrest Street, Mile-end, Glasgow ; *Secretary*, Wm. Fulton, 4 Parkhouse Lane, Dennistoun, Glasgow ; Treasurer, T. Miller, 180 Thomson Street, Dennistoun, Glasgow ; Bard, J. M'Donald ; Piper, A. M'Pherson ; Librarian, W. Forsyth. Past Presidents—W. Hood, G. F. Thomas, W. Williamson, J. M. Broadley, G. Newman Hendry, and J. M'Donald. Committee—A. Napier, J

W. M'Kay, A. Duff, A. Carnan, and R. Combe.
Federation delegates—G. F. Thomas and G. Newman.
Association delegates—A. Hainey, T. Miller, and W.
Fulton. Special features of Club—Celebration of the
birth of Robert Burns; occasional re-union for the
cultivation of social and intellectual intercourse amongst
members and friends; and the encouragement of Scottish
literature.

No. 204—DUNDALK and DISTRICT Burns Club. Instituted
1909. Federated 1911. President, W. Cree, Jocelyn
Street, Dundalk; Vice-president, W. Reid, Park Street,
Dundalk; Secretary, Geo. Williamson, St. Andrew's,
Castle Road, Dundalk.

No. 205—PAISLEY ST. MIRREN Burns Club. Instituted 1910.
Federated 1911. Place of meeting, St. Mirren Bar, 44
Old Sneddon Street. President, John Brown, Rutherglen;
Vice-president, James Jones, Rutherglen Secretary,
Robert Crawford, 44 Old Sneddon Street, Paisley. Special
feature of Club—To maintain and further the interest
of Burns.

No. 206—GLASGOW Daisy Burns Club. Instituted 1911. Federated 1911.

No. 207—CAMBUSLANG Wingate Burns Club. Instituted 1908.
Federated 1912. Place and date of meeting, Masonic
Hall, first Saturday each month. President, Arthur
M'Neil, 14 Longlea, Baillieston; Vice-president, John
Williamson, 431 Hamilton Road, Cambuslang; Secretary,
Robert Forrester, 156 Hamilton Road, Cambuslang;
Assistant Secretary, Robert Tait; Treasurer, John
M'Cracken; Assistant Treasurer, Wm. Stewart; Stewards,
Thos. M'Gilvray and Robt. Harden. Hon. Members
—Wm. M'Lean, Duncan M'Gilvray, A. Young,
Wm. Young, Robt. Tait, John Smith, Dan Smith,
Joseph Laird, and John M'Ginn. Committee—Alex.
Nelson, Dugal Wright, Allan Dunn, Alex. Stevenson,
Robt. M'Allister, Robt. Campbell, and Sam Tait. Special
feature of Club—Furtherance of Scottish song and
sentiment.

No. 208—COLORADO SPRINGS and DISTRICT Caledonian
Society. Instituted 1897. Federated 1912. President,
J. I. M'Clymont, 323 Hagerman Building, Colorado
Springs; Secretary, H. C. Beattie, 524 North Nevada
Avenue, Colorado Springs; Treasurer, Thos. Strachan,
1215 North Weber, Colorado Springs.

No. 209—GREENOCK St. John's Burns Club. Instituted 13th
August, 1909. Federated 17th August, 1911. Place
of meeting, Masonic Temple. President, James A.
Morrison, 39 Brisbane Street, Greenock; Vice-president,
John Broadfoot, 21 Holmscroft Street, Greenock; Secretary, Jacob A. C. Hamilton, 19 Brown Street, Craigieknowes, Greenock; Treasurer Peter Morrison, 66 Welling-

ton Street, Greenock. Special features of Club—To cherish the name of Robert Burns and foster a love for his writings, and generally to promote good-fellowship.

No. 210—HARDGATE Auld Hoose Burns Club. Instituted 28th September, 1912. Federated 30th September, 1912

No. 211—LARKHALL Cronies Burns Club. Instituted May, 1912. Federated 10th October, 1912. Place and date of meeting, Homestead, every Saturday, 7.30 p.m. President, Wm. Kilpatrick, Muir Street, Larkhall ; Vice-president, Chas. Dobbie, 15 Academy Street, Larkhall; Secretary, A. Henderson, 65 London Street, Larkhall. Committee—A. Tannoch, J. Potter, J. Dobbie, G. M'Queen, T. Miller, and R. Morton. Special features of Club—Celebration of the Poet's birthday and to encourage the study of his works ; to promote closer union between other clubs.

No. 212 PORTOBELLO Burns Club. Instituted 25th January, 1892. Federated 1913. President, Bailie James Hastie, J.P., Queen's Bay Hotel, Portobello ; Vice-president, Thomas Bennett, 20 Brighton Place, Portobello ; Secretary, William Baird, J.P., F.S.A.Scot., Clydesdale Bank House, Portobello ; Treasurer, J. Lewis Jenkins, 1 Windsor Place, Portobello. Special features of Club —To commemorate the genius of Robert Burns as the Poet of Humanity, and to create a patriotic love of country through its members to all who seek to advance the brotherhood of man ; to the public schools of the town over twenty book prizes are awarded annually to encourage pupils in the study of Scottish literature, particularly through the works of Burns, Scott, Hogg, &c. ; also the singing of " the Auld Scots Sangs."

No. 213—GLASGOW Kingston Burns Club. Instituted November, 1912. Federated 11th January, 1913. Place and date of meeting, Wheat Sheaf Tea Rooms, 263 Paisley Road, Glasgow, third Thursdays, October to March inclusive. President, Robert Gray, J.P., 83 King Street, Glasgow, S.S. ; Vice-president, John Logan, J.P., 176 Watt Street, Glasgow, S.S. ; Secretary and Treasurer, Hugh A. Begg, 104 Weir Street, Glasgow, S.S. ; Assistant Secretary, Alex. C. Baird, 22 Pollok Street, Glasgow, S.S. Directors—William Robertson, Robert M'Lachlan, John M'Laren, John M. Brown, and John Hannay. Special features of Club—To commemorate the genius of Robert Burns and foster a love for his writings, and to encourage the taste for Scottish literature and music generally ; to celebrate his birthday on the 25th January, or as near thereto as possible. Ladies are now admitted to the Club membership for the first time.

No. 214—MELROSE Burns Club. Federated 22nd February, 1913. President, Dr Henry Speirs, St Dunstan's, Melrose ; Vice-president, Geo. Sanderson, Westhill, Melrose Secretary, Geo. Mackenzie, High Street, Melrose.

No. 215—THORNIEWOOD Burns Club. Instituted 26th February, 1911. Federated 24th February, 1913. *Secretary*, W. Kerr, 54 Thorniewood, Uddingston.

No. 216—RUTHERGLEN Royal Burgh Burns Club. Instituted March, 1913. Federated May, 1913. *Secretary*, James E. Murray, 94 Mill Street, Rutherglen.

No. 217—ESKDALE Burns Club. Federated 29th April, 1913. President, Clement Armstrong, F.S.A.Scot., Eskholm; Vice-president, Thomas Bell, Townfoot; *Secretary*, Wm. Pendreigh, Brewery House, Langholm. Committee— James Barr, Wm. Murray, David Calvert, and Robt. Irving.

No. 218—BANNOCKBURN Empire Burns Club. Instituted 25th January, 1913. Federated 13th June, 1913. Place and time of meeting, Commercial Hotel, Bannockburn, 7 p.m. President, William R. Lennie, Newlands, Bannockburn; Vice-president, Thomas Rattray, West Murrayfield, Bannockburn; *Secretary*, William Wark, Helenslea, Bannockburn; Treasurer, James Kirkwood, Cauldhame, Bannockburn. Committee — J. Fulton, W. Neill, C. Palmer, W. Stitt, P. Wilson, J. Forsyth, and M'Gilchrist. Special features of Club—Monthly meetings during the year (our meetings consist of recitations and songs, and tend to create good-fellowship amongst our members); and to render all possible assistance to the work of the Federation.

No 219—UDDINGSTON Burns Club. Instituted 1st April, 1913. Federated 21st June, 1913. Place of meeting, Magdala Hall, Uddingston. President, Thos. Hamilton, Alpine Terrace, Uddingston; Vice-president, James Ross, Greenrig Street, Uddingston; *Secretary*, Henry Rowan, 50 Hamilton Place, Uddingston; Treasurer, John Hunter, c/o Thos. Latta, Uddingston.

No. 220   ST. LOUIS Burns Club, Mo., U.S.A. Instituted 1904. Federated 1913. Date of meeting, 25th January. President, W. K. Bixby, Century Buildings, St. Louis, Mo.; Vice-president, David R. Francis, St. Louis, Mo.; *Secretary*, Walter B. Stevens, Jefferson Memorial, St. Louis, Mo.; Treasurer, Hanford Crawford, 722 Chestnut Street, St. Louis, Mo. Special features of Club—Annual meetings; issuing printed reports from time to time.

No. 221—PRESTONPANS Burns Club. Instituted 25th January. 1913. Federated 16th August, 1913. *Secretary*, T. W. Watson, Moat House, Prestonpans.

No. 222—HULL Burns Club. Instituted 1863. Federated 1913. Place and date of meeting, Albion Hall, Baker Street, Hull, last Friday of month, 7.45 p.m. President, Councillor Dr G. W. Lilley, J.P., 22 Williamson Street; Past President, Alderman W. Hakes, F.R.G.S., 61 Louis Street, Hull; *Joint Secretaries*, Robert A. Speirs, 24

Marlborough Avenue, Hull, and Albert Hockney, 51
Clumber Street, Hull; Treasurer, J. R. Robinson, 20
Spring Street, Hull. Special features of Club—Social
and literary. Membership, 300.

No. 223—GLASGOW Auld Clinkum Burns Club. Instituted
3rd April, 1913. Federated, 6th October, 1913. Place
of meeting, Masonic Hall. Overnewton. President, J.
Wilson, 17 Albany Terrace, Shettleston; Vice-president,
James Muir, 13 Kinning Street; Secretary, James Robertson, 21 James Orr Street, Glasgow; Treasurer, D. Moir,
16 Blackie Street, Overnewton. Delegates, J. Wilson,
42 Dover Street, and D. M'Farlane, 4 Tower Street,
Kinning Park. Special features of Club—Annual
trip; celebration of the Poet's birthday; literary and
musical evenings; short papers by members, and otherwise to encourage interest and teaching of Scotland's
National Bard.

No. 224—ASHINGTON Burns Club. Instituted 1891. Federated
1913. Place of meeting, Portland Hotel. President,
Dr F. Beaton; Vice-president, Dr J. M'Lean; Secretary,
D. Robertson, 20 Sixth Row, Ashington; Treasurer,
S. W. Strong. Special feature of Club—Celebration of
Burns anniversary.

No. 225—HELENSBURGH Burns Club. Instituted 2nd February,
1911. Federated 14th November, 1913. Place and
date of meeting, Masonic Hall—choir and ordinary meetings on Tuesdays. President, John Brown, Cairndhu
Lodge, Helensburgh; Vice-presidents, John Somerville,
Woodland Place, Helensburgh, and Silas Maclean, 52
John Street, Helensburgh; Secretary, Robert Thorburn,
Albion Cottage, Helensburgh. Special features of
Club—Hallowe'en and anniversary festivals, with lectures
and debating nights between. Ladies now admitted
to membership. In place of the male voice choir (which
has been a notable feature of the Club since its institution),
a choir of mixed voices has been formed, which promises
well. Membership, 150.

No 226—DUMFRIES Burns Club. Instituted 18th January,
1820. Federated 1913. Place and date of meeting,
Annual Meeting, Sheriff Court-house, Dumfries, first
week in November. President, Lieut.-Col. P. Murray
Kerr, V.D., 30 Castle Street, Dumfries; Vice-president,
R. A. Grierson, Town Clerk, Dumfries; Secretary, John
M'Burnie, Sheriff Court-house, Dumfries. Committee—
David H. Hastie; W. A. Hiddleston, Dr Joseph Hunter,
A. C. Penman, Robert Adamson, and Peter Biggam.
Special features of Club are—(a) To maintain the Burns
Mausoleum in good repair, and provide for its proper
supervision; (b) To discharge the obligations laid upon
the Club by the testamentary disposition of Colonel William
Nichol Burns with respect to Burns's House and the
Mausoleum; (c) To celebrate in suitable manner the
anniversary of the Poet's birth, and to honour his memory

in such other ways as may be from time to time determined ; (d) To foster a knowledge of the life and works of Burns by means of an annual competition amongst local school children, prizes being awarded to the successful competitors.

No. 227—PENRITH Burns Club. Instituted 27th January, 1911. Federated 1913. Place of meeting, Station Hotel. President, D. S. M'Ghie, Kirkby Thore, near Penrith ; Vice-president, Thomas Heskett, Plumpton Hall, Plumpton, Penrith ; Secretary, J. S. M'Grogan, 94 Lowther Street, Penrith, Cumberland ; Treasurer, R. Gardiner, 8 Brunswick Square, Penrith. Special feature of Club—Honour to memory of Burns.

No. 228—CALDERWATERHEAD Burns Club. Federated 23rd May, 1914. President, James Taylor, Shotts ; Vice-president, Jno. Gilfillan, Calderhead Farm, Shotts ; Secretary, Wm. R. Moir, Mossbank, Hall Road, Shotts.

No. 229—EASTBOURNE and DISTRICT Scottish Association. Federated 23rd May, 1914. President, Sir John Nisbet Maitland, 69 Silverdale Road, Eastbourne ; Vice-president, Alex. Campbell, 14 Blackwater Road, Eastbourne ; Secretary, R. Prentice, 110 Terminus Road, Eastbourne.

No. 230—BURNBANK Burns Club. Instituted November, 1913. Federated 23rd May, 1914. Secretary, William Jamieson, 140 Glasgow Road, Burnbank, Hamilton.

No. 231—FAULDHOUSE and EAST BENHAR Burns Club. Instituted 1907. Federated 28th May, 1914. Place and date of meeting, Caledonian Hotel, Fauldhouse, last Saturday of every month, 6 p.m. President, John Salmond, Co-operative Buildings, West End, Fauldhouse ; Vice-president, Thomas Forsyth, Caledonian Hotel, Fauldhouse ; Secretary, John Kinniburgh, Co-operative Buildings, West End, Fauldhouse ; Treasurer, Robert Clark, Portland Terrace, Fauldhouse. Special features of Club — To cherish the name of Burns and foster a love of his writings, and generally promote good-fellowship ; and to visit Burns Clubs and receive visitations from other Clubs.

No. 232—ARNISTON Tam o' Shanter Burns Club. Federated 23rd May, 1914. Secretary, George Russell, 1 Victoria Street, Arniston, Gorebridge.

No. 233—The CLACHAN Burns Club. Instituted February, 1914. Federated 23rd May, 1914. Secretary, Donald M'Leod, Ivy Cottage, Braehead, Coalburn.

No. 234—GLASGOW Southern Merchants' Burns Club. Instituted 1914. Federated 1914. President, Bailie Campbell, Govan Road, Glasgow ; Vice-president, W. L. Hutchison, 1 and 3 Cathcart Road, Glasgow ; Secretary, A. J. Ruglen, 36 Dundas Street, Glasgow (City).

No. 235—HAMILTON Glencairn Burns Club.   Instituted 1894.
Federated 8th August, 1914.

No. 236—WHITEHAVEN Burns Club.   Instituted 24th January,
1914.   Federated August, 1914.   Place and date of
meeting, Masonic Hall, Duke Street, Whitehaven, January,
March, and November.   President, Dr Dickson, Queen
Street, Whitehaven ; Vice-president, Robert T. Bell,
Woodend Gardens, Whitehaven ; *Secretary*, John David-
son, 9 Edge Hill Terrace, Whitehaven.   Committee—
A. Anderson, T. C. Bell, J. R. Clark, John Forbes,
J. M. Gibson, Wm. Glenn, A. Kilpatrick, A. Lockhart,
W. H. Miers, Dr Muir, J. Murray, Alderman Palmer,
John Sewell, P. Turner, and J. Young.   Special features
of Club—To foster a knowledge of the life and works of
Robert Burns, and to perpetuate his memory by an
annual festival on the 25th January.

No. 237—UDDINGSTON Masonic Burns Club.   Instituted July,
1914.   Federated 8th August, 1914.   Place of meeting,
Rowan Tree Inn Hall, Uddingston.   President, Jas.
Donald, Bothwell Castle, Bothwell ; Vice-president,
Thos. Cameron, Gas Work Cottage, Uddingston ; *Secretary*, D. N. Miller, 601 Shettleston Road, Glasgow ; Treasurer, Thos. Barr, 4 Croftbank Place, Uddingston.   Committee—Wm. Beattie, Chas. M'Williams, Donald M'Leod
Paton.

No. 238—ATLANTA, Ga., Burns Club, U.S.A.   Instituted 1896.
Federated 1914.   Place and date of meeting, The Burns
Cottage, Atlanta, Ga., first Wednesday of each month.
President, H. H. Cabaniss, 136½ Marietta Street, Atlanta,
Ga., U.S.A. ; Vice-president, R. M. M'Whirter, 1 Terry
Street, Atlanta, Ga. ; *Secretary*, H. C. Reid, 44 Fairbanks
Street, Atlanta, Ga. ; Treasurer, E. F. King ; Superin-
tendent, Robert Murray ; Chaplain, R. K. Smith. . Direc-
tors—Jas. Carlisle, T. S. Scoggins, Jas. Duffy, Alex.
Strachan, and Thos. Scott.

No. 239—HAWICK Burns Club.   Instituted 1878.   Federated
8th August, 1914.   Place and time of meeting, Club
Rooms, 12 Teviot Crescent, 10 a.m. to 10 p.m.   President,
John Hume, 5 Wellington Road, Hawick ; Vice-president,
Wm. Fairholm, 12 Dickson Street, Hawick ; *Secretary*,
Alex. Pringle, 24 Garfield Street, Hawick.   Committee
— Peter Walker, Thomas Laidlaw, George Brooks,
Robert Butler, Peter Johnstone, and George Armstrong.
Special features of Club—To honour the name and per-
petuate the memory of Robert Burns, and to afford its
members the means of social intercourse, mutual help-
fulness, intellectual improvement, and rational recreation.

No. 240—BLAWARTHILL Burns Club.   Federated 6th December,
1914.   President, Wm. Blair ; Vice-president, J. Paterson ; *Secretary*, T. G. King, 917 Yoker Road, Yoker ;
Treasurer, D. J. Lindsay.

No. 241—CROOK Burns Club. Instituted 1906. Federated 4th January, 1915. President, J. Tillotson, School-house, Crook ; Vice-president, S. Wraith, Railway Avenue, Crook ; Secretary, A. B. Rutherford, Church Street, Crook, Co. Durham ; Treasurer, C. Wand, St. Mary's Avenue, Crook.

No. 242 MONTROSE Burns Club. Instituted 1908. Federated 1915. President, John Yorston, M.A., Rector, Montrose Academy ; Vice-p-esident, Rev. Professor D. Russell Scott ; Secretary, Alex. Miller, 6 Wellington Gardens Montrose ; Treasurer, Alex. Low ; Past President, ex-Provost Thomson.

No. 243 PAISLEY St. James Burns Club. Instituted 1912. Federated 23rd December, 1915. Place of meeting, 4 St. James Street, Paisley. President, Wm. Alexander, 28 Glen Street, Paisley ; Vice-president, John Aitken, 1 Maxwell Street, Paisley ; Secretary, John M'Kechnie, 2 Douglas Terrace, Paisley ; Treasurer, James Fleming 33 Glen Street, Paisley. Special features of Club —The encouragement of social intercourse amongst the members and kindred Clubs ; the celebration of the Poet's birth ; meeting for the reading of literary papers relative to the life and works of Burns, and kindred subjects.

No. 244 DALMUIR Burns Club. Instituted 1914. Federated 1916. Place of meeting, Trades Restaurant. Hon. President, Bailie Jno. Young, The Crescent, Dalmuir ; President, John Will, 9 French Street, Dalmuir ; Vice-president, Robert Ferguson, Learig Place, Dalmuir ; Secretary, Alex. Dillon, 21 Trafalgar Street, Dalmuir Literary Secretary and Bard, Jno. Rae (" Invis ") ; Auditors, Wm. Boyle and D. M'Nair. Committee— R. Ferguson, A. M'Gregor, J. Chalmers, J. Holmes, and Wm. Gordon. Special features of Club — The perpetuation of the memory of the Immortal Bard and the cultivation of Scottish poetry and literature.

No 245—KINNAIRD Victoria Burns Club. Instituted 9th October, 1910. Federated 3rd January, 1917. Place and date of meeting, Victoria Inn, 2nd Saturday each month, at 6 p.m. President, James Turnbull, Bothy Row, Carronshore, by Carron ; Vice-president, Alexander Reid, North Main Street, East End, Stenhousemuir ; Secretary, George Jenkins, 12 Kinnaird, by Falkirk. Committee — George Cowan, George Easton, Samuel Marshall, William Russell, and George Smith. Special features of Club—To meet in a social capacity to uphold the name of Burns and his works ; annual picnic to places of interest connected with the Poet ; and to celebrate the anniversary of the Poet's birth.

No. 246- LOCHORE and ROSEWELL Shanter Burns Club. Instituted 29th September, 1916. Federated 15th January, 1917. Place and date of meeting, Rosewell

Bar, first Tuesday each month. President, William
Morton, Waverley Street, Lochore, by Glencraig, Fife;
Vice-president, John Mackie, sen., Waverley Street,
Lochore, by Glencraig, Fife; *Secretary*, Alex. Ross, 149
Waverley Street, Lochore, by Glencraig, Fife. Com-
mittee—A. Arnott, T. Wilson, T. Nailon, John Mackie,
jun., and Geo. Young. Special feature of Club—The
encouragement of sound intercourse among admirers of the
Poet by means of literary and social meetings.

No 247—LOCHGELLY Thirteen Jolly Beggars Burns Club. Instituted 12th March, 1916. Federated 1st September, 1917.
Place and date of meeting, Victoria Bar, monthly meetings. President, William Whisker, Opera House Buildings, Main Street, Lochgelly; Vice-president, George
Arrol, 16 South Street, Lochgelly; *Secretary*, William
M'Kechnie, 64 Melville Street, Lochgelly; Treasurer,
D. Thomson; Croupier, J. Kippen; Bard, R. Mackie;
Horn Bearer and Sentinel, J. Walker. Special features
of Club—(1) To celebrate in suitable manner the anniversary of the Poet's birth, and to honour his memory
in such other ways as may be determined; (2) To foster
a knowledge of the works of Burns by means of school
competitions in songs and recitations, for which prizes
are awarded; (3) Social intercourse with kindred Clubs.

No. 248—BIRTLEY Burns Club. Instituted 10th December, 1915.
Federated 18th October, 1917. Place and date of meeting,
Railway Hotel, Birtley, alternate Thursdays, 7.30 p.m.
President, T. Fenwick, Harras Bank, Birtley, Co. Durham;
Vice-president, John Young, Durham Road, Birtley,
Co. Durham; *Secretary*, James Mann, Wellington House,
Station Road, Birtley, Co. Durham; Assistant Secretary,
J. W. Stirling; Treasurer, Dr J. Johnston, Brookside,
Birtley, Co. Durham; Organist, R. H. Richardson. Com-
mittee—R. Wade, R. G. Wilson, A. Stewart, R. H. Robson,
T. Foster, G. Jackson. Special features of Club—To
celebrate in a suitable manner the Poet's birth, and to
honour his memory in such other way as may from time
to time be determined; social well-being of the members;
to institute competitions in local schools in Scottish songs
and literature.

No. 249—MID-CALDER Tam o' Shanter Burns Club. Instituted
25th November, 1916. Federated 1917. Place of
meeting, Market Inn, Mid-Calder. President, John
Gordon, 74 Oakbank, Mid-Calder; Vice-president, Thos.
Dalziel, Oakbank, Mid-Calder; *Secretary*, D. M'Kerracher,
North Gate, Livingston, Mid-Calder. Committee—
Peter Cross, Samuel M'Manus, William Dudgeon, John
Liffay, James Denholm, and James Samson.

No. 250—COWDENBEATH Tam o' Shanter Burns Club. Instituted 19th October, 1917. Federated 28th November,
1917. Place and date of meeting, Monthly (Saturdays),
5.30 p.m. President, Walter M. Miller, Moss-side Road,
Cowdenbeath; Vice-president, Robt. M'Gregor, 85 Main

Street, Lumphinnans ; *Secretary,* Jno. Black, 25 Natal
Place, Cowdenbeath ; Treasurer, Thos. Waugh. Committee—W. Jack (Bard), A. Bradford (Croupier), and
W.ʹ Wilson. Special features of Club—The study of
Scottish literature ; delivery of lectures, &c., on subjects
pertaining to Scottish life and character ; and to assist
the intellectual, moral, and social improvement of the
members.

No 251—GLENCRAIG Burns Club. Instituted 9th February,
1918. Federated 7th December, 1918. Place and
date of meeting, Hunter's Bar, 3rd Saturday of month.
President, Robert Glencross, Lofty View, Glencraig ;
Vice-president, John Scott, 35 North Glencraig ; *Secretary,* Thos. Ferguson, 125 South Glencraig. Special
features of Club—To uphold the cult of our Bard ; to
instil the love of his poetical works by having yearly
competitions among the children ; to hold literary and
harmony meetings monthly during season.

No 252—ALLOWAY Burns Club. Instituted 1908. Federated
1918. Place and date of meeting, Alloway, 25th January,
1921. President, Rev. J. M. Hamilton, B.D., The
Manse, Alloway, Ayr ; Vice-president, James Turnbull,
The Schoolhouse, Alloway, Ayr ; *Secretary and Treasurer,*
Andrew J. Gray, 29 Northpark Avenue, Ayr. Council—
J. R. Dickson, A. Cunningham, T. Auld, Jas. M'Cutcheon,
C. Auld, and W. Monaghan. Special features of Club
—School children's competition ; annual concert, featuring
Scottish items.

No. 253—GALSTON Jolly Beggars Burns Club. Instituted 1916.
Federated 1918. Place and time of meeting, Burns
Tavern, Galston, 7 p.m. President, Alex. Frew ; Vice-
president, Jas. M'Caw ; *Secretary,* Thos. Morton, 37
Brewland Street, Galston. Committee—John Paterson,
Jas. Haggarty, and Robt. Howatt.

No. 254—GREENOCK Victoria Burns Club. Instituted 2nd
October, 1914. Federated 1918. Place and date of
meeting, Victoria Bowl House, monthly. President,
Dr W. A. Milne, Hillend House, East Crawford Street,
Greenock ; Vice-president, D. M'G. Clark, 2 Octavia
Street, Port-Glasgow ; *Secretary,* Matthew W. Linn,
19 Belville Street, Greenock ; Treasurer, J. Armstrong,
36 Grant Street, Greenock. Special features of Club
—(a) Monthly meetings (social) ; (b) draughts, dominoes,
darts, cards (monthly competitions); (c) to celebrate in
suitable manner the anniversary of the Poet's birth, and
to honour his memory in such other ways as may be
from time to time determined.

No. 255—CATHCART Burns Club. Instituted January 22nd,
1916. Federated January, 1919. Place and date of
meeting, Unionist Rooms, Cathcart, last Thursday each
month. President, Robert Laurie, 1132 Cathcart Road,
Mount Florida ; Vice-president, James Kerr, 17 Marl-

borough Road, Cathcart ; *Secretary,* David B. Wilson,
9 Craig Road, Cathcart. Special features of Club—
To foster an intimate knowledge of the Poet's works
and general Scottish folk-lore ; giving prizes in local
schools in competitions, &c. At the meetings papers
are read followed by discussion.

No. 256—NEWTON-ON-AYR Burns Club. Instituted 1904.
Federated 1919. Place and date of meeting, Robert
Burns Tavern, Ayr, every Tuesday, at 7.30 p.m. Hon.
President, Sir George Younger, Bart., M.P. ; President,
John S. Jackson, 23 Bellesley Hill Avenue, Ayr ; Vice-
president, H. M. Giles, Monkswell, Prestwick : *Secretary,*
and (*pro tem.*) *Treasurer,* James Dobbie, 1 Falkland Park,
Ayr ; Auditors, D. Mullen and James Templeton.
Committee—W. M'Dowall, Thos. M'Creadie, R. Morris,
D. Mullen, and Thos. Reid.

No. 257—ARMADALE Star Burns Club. Instituted 2nd February,
1918. Federated 17th May, 1919. Place of meeting,
Star Inn, Armadale. President, Thomas Milne, Star
Inn, Armadale ; Vice-president, James M'Hattie, Heather-
field, Armadale ; *Secretary,* Robert Cunningham, East
Main Street, Armadale ; Treasurer, Alexander Samuels,
East Main Street, Armadale.

No. 258—ARMADALE Buck's Head Burns Club. Instituted
12th October, 1918. Federated 17th May, 1919. Place
of meeting, Federation Hall, Armadale. President,
John Mack, Polkemmet Cottage, Armadale, West Lothian ;
Vice-president, Wm. M'Alpine, Unity Terrace, Armadale, West Lothian ; *Secretary,* John Stevenson, New
Street, Station Road, Armadale, West Lothian. Committee—John Rodgers, Wm. Ferguson, Wm. Brown,
Tom Gibson, and Meikle M'Lay. Special features
of Club—To consider and discuss subjects, questions,
and reading of papers directly concerning Burns's life
and works ; to promote the efficiency, knowledge, and
attainments of the members on the works and life of Rabbie
Burns ; anniversary dinner celebration ; visitation to
places of interest and kindred Clubs ; holding of Hallowe'en
special night ; annual public schools competition ; visitors
cordially invited.

No. 259—BONNYRIGG A Man's a Man for a' That Burns Club.
Instituted 17th May, 1919. Federated 20th May, 1919.
Place and date of meeting, Calderwood Arms, monthly.
President, Andrew Ross, 13 Arniston Place, Bonnyrigg ;
Vice-president, James Harper, 44 Camp View, Bonny-
rigg ; *Secretary* (*pro tem.*), George Weatherstone, 8 Camp
View, Bonnyrigg ; Treasurer, J. Anderson. Committee
—A. Hill, J. Purvies, W. Temple, J. Brown, J. Brand,
J. Crozier, and G. Knox. Special features of Club—
Social and literary.

No. 260—TARBRAX Jolly Beggars Burns Club. Instituted
21st January, 1916. Federated 17th May, 1919. Place

and date of meeting, Institute, 28th January, 1921, at 8 p.m. President, David Black, Moorview, Tarbrax, Cobbinshaw ; Vice-presidents, Jas. Roberts, Fineview, Tarbrax ; W. Forsyth, M.A., Schoolhouse, Tarbrax ; Dr J. M. Johnstone, Leven, Fifeshire ; *Secretary*, Hugh M'Glone, 239 Tarbrax, Cobbinshaw ; Chairman of Committee, Robert Crichton. Committee — John Graham, David Smith, Thos. Reid, Thos. Kerr, Geo. Watson, and Chas. M'Connachie. Special features of Club—Educating the young by means of concerts and competitions on the works of Burns ; annual festival.

No. 261—SYDNEY Anniversary Burns Club, N.S.W. Instituted 25th January, 1895. Federated 1919. Place and date of meeting, Protestant Hall, Sydney, last Saturday in the month. President, David R. Rogers, J.P., A.C.I.S., Bannockburn, Marlowe Street, Campsie, Sydney ; Vice-presidents, W. H. Johnston, Balgownie, Robey Street, Mascot, Sydney, and A. MacRae, Loch Kithorn ; *Secretary*, James Buchan, Logie Brae, York Street, Forest Lodge, Sydney, N.S.W. ; Assistant Secretary, James Campbell ; Treasurer, John Campbell ; Past President, James Kelman ; Trustees, John Irvine and H. J. Ranger ; Choir Conductor, Hector Fleming ; Musical Director (acting), William H. Johnston ; Masters of Ceremonies, James G. Baillie and Eric Hill ; Inner Guardian, F. MacCabe ; Country Representative, John MacKinlay. Committee—J. R. Ca pbell, W. Campbell, W. Auld, Jas. Duncan, John Duncan. W. H. Hill, E. Martin, A. S. Peters, W. Taylor, James Toddie, M.M., James Tunnie, and C. Watt.

No. 262—FIFESHIRE Burns Association. Instituted 17th May, 1919. Federated 6th September, 1919. Place of meeting, Associated Club Rooms. President, Jas. Wilkie, J.P., Hutton's Buildings, Black Road, Kelty ; Vice-presidents, Walter Millar (Cowdenbeath), and Peter Paterson (Dunfermline) ; *Secretary*, George Marshall, 38 Natal Place, Cowdenbeath. Committee—R. Glencross (Glencraig), E. Hunter (Cowdenbeath), R. Dunlop (Dunfermline), J. Black (Cowdenbeath), Geo. Pratt (Lumphinnans), T. Anderson (Kelty), W. Whisker (Lochgelly), and Geo. Clark (Lochore). Special features of Association —To further the interests of the Burns cult by promoting closer union between Clubs and kindred Societies, and bringing them into more harmonious relationship.

No. 263 GLASGOW Masonic Burns Club. Instituted 31st January, 1919. Federated 6th September, 1919. Place and date of meeting, Burns House Club, 27 India Street, Glasgow, last Fridays. President, Hugh M'Quat, 1 Hazelwood Drive, Ibrox ; Vice-president, J. S. Jamieson, Glenwood, Newlands ; *Secretary*, H. Stuart Girvan, B.L., 252 West George Street, Glasgow ; Treasurer, A. D. Campbell, 116 Trongate, Glasgow. .

No. 264—PRESTONPANS Jolly Beggars Burns Club. Instituted 28th June, 1919. Federated 20th September, 1919. Place of meeting, Mr Mather's Railway Tavern, Prestonpans. President, William Edmond, Harlaw Hill, Prestonpans; Vice-president, David Bruce, 90 Montgomery Street, Edinburgh; *Secretary*, William Watt, 59 High Street, Prestonpans; Treasurer, Wm. Cunningham; Bard, Andrew M'Leod; Croupiers, George and William Doigg. Special features of Club—Scottish literature; study and rehearsal of Burns's works · educating the young into the works of Burns.

No. 265—BINGRY Jolly Beggars Burns Club. Instituted 25th October, 1919. Federated March, 1920. Place and date of meeting, Gothenburg, Lochore, 3rd Saturday each month. President, James Gold, 166 Waverley Cottages, Lochore, Fife; Vice-president, John Pratt, Flockhouse, Lochore, Fife; *Secretary*, Wm. C. Clark, 169 Waverley Cottages, Lochore, Fife; Treasurer, Andrew Stewart. Committee — P. Moffat, William Crawford, R. Crawford, and R. Agnew. Special features of Club—To promote the works of our National Bard and keep his name ever green, and celebrate the annual festival.

No. 266—NEWTON Jolly Beggars Burns Club. Instituted 15th September, 1919. Federated 15th March, 1920. Place and date of meeting, Newton Brae, last Saturday in month, at 4 p.m. Hon. President, Geo. Paterson, Darnley Place, 435 Rutherglen Road, Glasgow; President, James Buchanan, 15 Pitt Street, Newton, Hallside, Glasgow; *Secretary*, Wm. M'Intosh, 12 Clyde Street, Newton, Hallside, Glasgow; Treasurer, John Russell. Committee— Wm. Duncan, Jas. Currie, Tom Whyte, Don. Griffiths. Special features of Club—To consider and discuss subjects, questions, and reading papers on the life and works of Burns; visitation to places of interest and kindred Clubs; anniversary dinner celebration; holding of Hallowe'en special night; annual schools competition on essays on the life and works of Burns.

No. 267—PRESTONPANS Mystic Burns Club. Instituted May, 1919. Federated October, 1919. Place and date of meeting, Black Bull Inn, Prestonpans, 1st and 3rd Saturdays of month, June to September, at 6 p.m. President, Charles Rowan, 10 Front Street, Cuthill, Prestonpans; Vice-presidents, James Hunter, Beach Cottage, and Wm. Hewitt, Morrisonhaven, Prestonpans; *Secretary*, Daniel M'Clure, 11 Mitchell Street, Musselburgh; Hon. Members —Geo. Don, Prestonpans; Wm. Murray, Haddington; Geo. Walker, Musselburgh. Committee — John Black, Wm. Ford, Geo. Cunningham, Neil Livingstone, Angus Boyd, Wm, Barr, and R. Tweedie. Special features of Club—To foster the works of Burns; and hold open competition in the various schools in the community annually.

No 268—ANDERSTON Cronies Burns Club. Instituted January, 1905. Federated 1919. Place and date of meeting, 109 Argyle Street, Saturdays, January, May, September, and November. President, Quintin Henderson, 614 Cathcart Road, Glasgow ; Vice-president, Thos. M'Guire, 1019 Sauchiehall Street, Glasgow ; Secretary, Frank M'Ewan, 4 North Street, Glasgow. Committee—Andrew Nixon, Robert M'Neil, Robert Cowan, and Geo. Lockhart. Special features of Club — Social and educational intercourse ; study of Burns's songs, life, and characteristics.

No 269—JOHNSTONE Tam o' Shanter Burns Club. Instituted 6th December, 1912. Federated January, 1919. Place of meeting, Masonic Hall, Johnstone. President, F. W· C. Aitken, Bank House, Collier Street, Johnstone ; Vice-president, Thos. Gillespie, Ashcot, Kilbarchan Road, Johnstone ; Secretary, Andrew Walker, 5 Armour Street, Johnstone.

No. 270—COQUETDALE Burns Club. Instituted 22nd January, 1898. Federated 6th March, 1920. Place and date of meeting, Jubilee Hall, Rothbury, as necessary. President, Richard Charlton, Snitter, Rothbury, Northumberland ; Vice-president, David Dippie Dixon, Cragside, Rothbury ; Corresponding Secretary, George Rae Patterson, Burleigh House, Rothbury ; Minutes Secretary, John Walker, The Station, Rothbury ; Treasurer, J. Percival, Bridge Street, Rothbury ; Bard, Thomas Walker, Glasgow. Special features of Club—Winter lectures ; and summer excursions per char-a-banc to the Burns country.

No. 271 -TRENTON Burns Club, U.S.A. Instituted 19th February, 1919. Federated 30th March, 1920. Place and date of meeting, 33 West State Street, 2nd Saturday evening of each month. President, Robert Ness, 1275 Hamilton Avenue, Trenton, New Jersey, U.S.A. ; Vice-president, James Barrowman, 908 Jefferson Street, Bristol, Pa., U.S.A. ; Secretary, Andrew Carmichael, 48½ Wall Street, Trenton, New Jersey, U.S.A. ; Inside Guard, John Young. Committee — James Ballantine, J. Black, and D. Graham. Special features of Club— It is our avowed purpose to foster, encourage, and cultivate a love for the songs of Scotland, and chiefly to perpetuate the memory and works of Robert Burns, commemorate his birth, and enjoy that boundless wealth of song with which he has endowed our nature and his native land, and which flows through the world in dignified and manly sentiments, enlightening and enobling all humanity.

No. 272 STEWARTON Hodden Grey Burns Club. Instituted January 30th, 1920. Federated 27th March, 1920. Place and date of meeting, Institute Hall, by arrangement. President, Harry Gordon, 26 Lainshaw Street, Stewarton ;

Vice-president, John Gillies, Dean Street, Stewarton ; *Secretary*, Thos. J. Boyd, Bellevue, Graham Terrace, Stewarton ; Treasurer, Matt. Muir, Quarryhouse, Stewarton. Special features of Club—Lectures, debates, &c., pertaining to the National Bard and Scottish life and character.

No. 273 LANARK Jolly Beggars Burns Club. Instituted 23rd December, 1919. Federated 27th March, 1920. Place and date of meeting, Club Room, 32 Bannatyne Street, 7.30 p.m. President, William Foster, Ladyacre Road, Lanark ; Vice-president, Andrew Watson, 26 Dovecot Lane, Lanark ; *Secretary*, James Kay, 34 Bonnet Road, Lanark ; Treasurer, John Glaister. Committee — D. Muir, W. Gracie, R. Gray, and J. Mitchell. Special features of Club—To foster the spirit of Burns's manly independence as depicted in his poem, " A man's a man for a' that " ; annual supper to celebrate the birthday of the Poet ; annual trip to places of interest.

No. 274—TROON Burns Club. Instituted 28th January, 1920. Federated 30th March, 1920. Place and date of meeting, Troon, monthly. President, Provost Muir, St. Monnena, Troon ; Vice-president, Councillor Young, Elmbank, Bentick Drive, Troon ; *Secretary*, James C. Brown, 21 Templehill, Troon. Committee—Robt. Cochrane, Wm. White, Bailie Johnston, John Laing, Wm. Kellie, F. Beaumont, D. M'Nab, and James Nicol.

No 275—AYR Burns Club. Federated, 12th June, 1920. Place of meeting, Council Chambers, Ayr. President, Geo. Willock, J.P. ; Vice-presidents, ex-Provost James Hunter, J.P., Hugh M'Quiston, and J. R. Gordon ; *Secretary*, James Wills, 27 High Street, Ayr ; Treasurer, J. L. Wilson, 15 High Street, Ayr. Special features of Club—School competitions ; lectures.

No 276—LUMPHINNANS Highland Mary Burns Club. Federated 12th June, 1920. Hon. President, William Campbell ; Hon. Vice-president, Alexander Robertson ; President, George Anderson ; Vice-president, John Doherty ; *Secretary*, Alexander Easson, 47 Sligo Street, Lumphinnans, Fife ; Treasurer, James Binnie.

No. 277—HARRIMAN Burns Club, Pa., U.S.A. Federated 12th June, 1920. President, Angus M. Cameron, 1208 Pond Street, Harriman, Pa., U.S.A. ; Vice-president, Wm. Tait, 233 West Circle, Harriman, Pa., U.S.A. ; *Secretary*, Wm. M'Nee, 266 Madison Street, Harriman, Pa., U.S.A.

No. 278—DULUTH Clan Stewart, No. 50 (Order of Scottish Clans), Burns Club, U.S.A. Federated 29th August, 1920. *Secretary*, A. G. M'Knight, Attorney-at-Law, 319 Providence Building, Duluth, Minnesota, U.S.A.

No. 279—BROXBURN Jolly Beggars Burns Club. Date and time of meeting, Fridays, 7 p.m. President, Wm. M'Queen, 13 Shrine Place, Broxburn ; Vice-president, J. Black, Violet Cottage, Port Buchan, Broxburn ; *Secretary*, J. Cruickshanks, P.O. Buildings, Broxburn ; Treasurer, T. Goodall, 119 Pumpherston, Mid-Calder. Special feature of Club—To try and keep good the good work of Rabbie Burns.

No. 280—DETROIT Burns Club, U.S.A. Instituted 25th January, 1912. Federated 13th November, 1920. Place and date of meeting, Tuller Hotel, 2nd Friday of each month. President, Edward Goodwillie, 47 Casgrain Avenue, Detroit, Michigan ; 1st Vice-president, John Smith, 70 Kaier Avenue, Detroit; 2nd Vice-president, John Cameron, 646 Wabash Avenue, Detroit ; *Secretary*, W. S. Allen, Service Dept., Burrough's Adding Machine Co. Special features of Club—Erection of Burns statue ; annual Burns banquet ; literary and social evenings.

No. 281—VICKERSTOWN Burns Club. Instituted September, 1919. Federated 14th November, 1920. Place and date of meeting, George Hotel, Walney, Barrow-in-Furness, quarterly. Hon President, Sir James M'Kechnie, K.B.E., The Abbey House, Furness Abbey, Lancs ; Acting Hon. President, James C. Ferguson, 9 Promenade, Walney, Barrow-in-Furness ; Vice-presidents—William Pollock, O.B.E., John Donald, O.B.E., Alex. Smith, M.B.E., James Haddow, William M'Lung, D. M'Farlane, William Simpson, and Arthur Taylor ; *Secretary*, James D. Cowley, 82 King Alfred Street, Walney, Barrow-in-Furness ; Treasurer, Adam M'Gregor, 44 Powerful Street. Special features of Club—To revere the memory of our National Bard, and foster an interest in his incomparable literary works ; to develop a friendly spirit between Scotsmen resident in Barrow by affording them occasional opportunities of meeting together in a social capacity.

No. 282 GLASGOW and DISTRICT Burns Clubs Bowling Association. Instituted 1899. Federated 1920. Place of meeting, Bank Restaurant, 41 Queen Street, Glasgow. President, David Davidson, 85 Armadale Street, Dennistoun ; Vice-president, J. M. Blair, 162 Hospital Street, Glasgow. *Secretary*, Robt. Parker, 5 Barrland Street, Pollokshields, Glasgow. Committee—John Hutcheon, A. B. Allison, H. A. Begg, N. M'Kelvie, A. Izat, and R. M. Milholm. Special features of Club— To hold a competition every year for the M'Lennan Cup (presented by the late Bailie M'Lennan), providing badges for first and second highest-up rinks. The Association has repeatedly donated portion of its funds to institutions connected with the Burns cult, and during the war subscribed to various funds.

No. 283—SINCLAIRTOWN Burns Club. Instituted 26th March, 1920. Federated 13th November, 1920. Place and

date of meeting, Sinclairtown Station Hotel, monthly.
Hon. President, Councillor James Roberts ; Hon. Vice-
president, William Smith ; President, Councillor Thomas
Laing, 100 St. Clair Street, Kirkcaldy ; Vice-president,
William Crombie, 148 St. Clair Street, Kirkcaldy ; *Secretary,* Robert Keddie, 2 M'Kenzie Street, Kirkcaldy ;
Treasurer, D. Harley. Committee—R. Blyth, B. Brown,
J. Brown, J Innes, J. Beattie. and W. Kidd. Special
features of Club—To foster the study of the works
of Burns, and to promote social and intellectual intercourse
amongst the members by lectures and discussions.

ROBERT DINWIDDIE, Printer, &c., High Street, Dumfries.

BURNS CHRONICLE
&
CLUB DIRECTORY

INSTITUTED
SEPTEMBER 1891.

Edited by
D. McNAUGHT, J.P., LL.D
KILMAURS.

WOOD NOTES WILD

BETTER A WEE BUSH THAN NAE BIELD

No. XXXI.
JANUARY, 1922.

PRICE
THREE Shillings.

PUBLISHED BY THE
BURNS FEDERATION,

PRINTED BY
ROBERT DINWIDDIE,

CONTENTS.

Page.

Annotations of Scottish Songs by Burns—*Davidson Cook, F.S.A.Scot.* 1

Burns as an Employer—*Rev. Wm. M'Millan, M.A., F.S.A.Scot.* 22

Robert Tannahill (1774-1810)—*Wm. M'Ilwraith* 27

The Skinner Bi-Centenary 42

Burns Clubs and Burns's Songs—*J. Jeffrey Hunter* 55

Glenriddell—*Dr J. Maxwell Wood* 64

Shenstone and Burns (III.)—*A. J. Craig* 68

Highland Mary's Re-interment 77

The End of an Old Song—*Arch. MacPhail* 78

The Story of the Kilmarnock Burns Temple Hoax— *John Aitken* 82

Burns and the Beggars—*N. Farquhar Orr, B.A., B.D.* 87

Unveiling of Robert Burns Statue at Detroit—*R. K. Young* 92

Honorably Discharged—*Capt. Douglas* 94

Burns and the Kingdom of Fife—*Rev. Wm. M'Millan. M.A., F.S.A.Scot.* 95

The Murison Collection : Sir A. Gibb Honoured 104

Reviews 108

Notes and Queries 112

Club Notes 119, 203

Federation Office-bearers, &c. 143

Annual Conference of the Federation 147

Club Directory 160

PREFACE.

To avoid disappointment, we again impress upon the Secretaries of Clubs the necessity of ordering their copies of the *Chronicle* as early as possible, so as to secure delivery shortly after the date of publication. Though the supply has been increased, it is still scarcely equal to the demand : and most of the back issues have been sold out.

We have again to thank our correspondents and contributors for their kindly assistance in compiling the present volume, and trust its contents will be found interesting by our readers.

D. M'NAUGHT.

BENRIG, KILMAURS
January 1st, 1922.

ANNOTATIONS OF SCOTTISH SONGS BY BURNS:

An Essential Supplement to Cromek and Dick,

In which, on the authority of an important Burns Manuscript now in the Edinburgh University Library, many Notes hitherto deemed " Spurious " and " Garbled," are restored to textual currency as authentic emanations of the Poet's song-lore.

WHEN R. H. Cromek, in his *Reliques of Robert Burns*, 1808, included the writings of the Bard as a song annotator, he prefaced them thus :—

" The chief part of the following *Remarks* on Scottish Songs and Ballads exist in the handwriting of Robert Burns, in an interleaved copy, in four volumes octavo, of *Johnson's Scots Musical Museum*. They were written by the Poet for Captain Riddel of Glenriddel, whose auto. graph the volumes bear. These valuable volumes were left by Mrs Riddel to her niece, Miss Eliza Bayley, of Man. chester, by whose kindness the Editor is enabled to give to the public transcripts of this amusing and miscellaneous collection."

For years, editor after editor, in edition after edition, copied the " Strictures on Scottish Songs," as printed by Cromek ; for the whereabouts of the Interleaved Volume being unknown to them, they had perforce to lean upon the *Reliques*. A second edition of that work appeared in 1809, and the following year Cromek published, in two volumes, his *Select Scotish Songs*. This is how he begins his preface :—" The following *Remarks* from the pen of Burns appeared in the publication of the *Reliques*." That statement is a bit wide of the truth. The " Remarks " in many cases do not follow the order of their first publication, thus making comparison awkward, but persistent collation shews that though Stenhouse and other authorities

ROBERT RIDDELL OF GLENRIDDELL,

From a Frontispiece Drawing in one of his Manuscript Volumes now in the Library of the Society of Antiquaries, London, to whose courtesy we are indebted for this, probably the first published, portrait of the friend of the Poet.

cite the *Reliques* of 1808 in quoting a comment by Burns on " The boatie rows," that note, and twenty-one others printed in the 1810 volumes, did *not* appear in the *Reliques ;*

and of those which did make their debut in that work, two are omitted in *Select Scotish Songs*.

At long last J. C. Dick, the scholarly editor of that invaluable volume, *The Songs of Robert Burns*, 1903, got access to the veritable Interleaved Copy of *The Scots Musical Museum*—a book so enriched by Burns that when it passed through Sotheby's it fetched £610. It is now in the collection of Dr John Gribbel, of Philadelphia, to whose splendid generosity Scotland owes its possession of two other treasure-books which link the names of Burns and Glenriddell for ever with his own.

The results of Mr Dick's careful scrutiny of the Interleaves appeared in a volume—of which only 255 copies were printed—published posthumously in 1908, exactly a hundred years after *The Reliques of Robert Burns*. Dick's book (another splendid contribution to real Burns literature) is entitled *Notes on Scottish Song by Robert Burns*, &c. In it he dissects Cromek's *Reliques* version of Burns's "Strictures," and sets forth (1) the Notes found in the actual handwriting of Burns ; (2) Notes written by Riddell and interspersed among those in the Poet's holograph, all of which (Riddell's) had for a century been accounted the legitimate prose offspring of Burns ; (3) Notes which could not be verified, as the Interleaves, where presumably Cromek found them, have been abstracted from the volume. It would be a great find if they could be located, especially that leaf with the note on Highland Mary. Dick, in further introducing his volume, says : "The last part (4) consists of a series of Spurious Notes, also printed by Cromek in the *Reliques*. These are not in the (Glenriddell) volumes, and never were there." Referring to Cromek's 1810 additions, he says : "All the additions were written either by himself or by his friend in deception Allan Cunningham."

Mr Dick branded fifteen Notes as "Spurious," and others, he says in his Appendix, "Cromek has garbled."

By a lucky chance a friend sent me three cuttings from the *Kilmarnock Standard* (v.d. May, 1921) of an article written by Mr David Cuthbertson, Sub-Librarian of Edinburgh University, the subject being " Manuscripts of Robert Burns : The property of Edinburgh University." It was an interesting article all through, but the parts which made me open my eyes wide were certain quotations of Song Annotations by Burns, taken from " a separate manuscript written on Excise paper, and consisting of twelve folio pages," entirely in the handwriting of the Poet.

To my amazement, I found that the passages cited were, word for word, the same as some of the Notes classified as " spurious " by Mr Dick. This appeared very significant, and seemed to indicate that while, as Cromek says—and there is great virtue in his phraseology—" the chief part " of the Notes printed in his *Reliques of Robert Burns* were, as stated, from the Interleaved copy of the *Scots Musical Museum*, he had also drawn upon at least one other *unstated* source—this very Burns Manuscript of twelve folio pages, which is one of the Laing MSS. now treasured in the Library of Edinburgh University.

The correctness of this deduction was amply confirmed by a verbatim transcript of this most important and illuminative manuscript, obligingly and with helpful courtesy furnished by Mr Frank C. Nicholson, M.A., Chief Librarian of the University, whose great kindness and generous permission to make the fullest use thereof for the information of students of Burns literature has made this article possible. For purposes of reference the Editor was strongly of opinion that the manuscript should be printed in full in the *Annual Burns Chronicle*, and I had no hesitation in placing it at his disposal.

TRANSCRIPT OF A BURNS MANUSCRIPT OF 12 FOLIO PAGES IN EDINBURGH UNIVERSITY LIBRARY.

(p. 1) : *Waukin o' the Fauld.*—There are two stanzas still sung to this tune, which I take to be the original song when Ramsay composed his beautiful song of that name in the " Gentle Shepherd." It begins :—

O will ye speak at our town,
As ye come frae the fauld.   &c.

I regret that, as in many of our old songs, the delicacy of this old fragment is not equal to its wit and humor.

Maggie Lauder.

Mill, Mill, O.—The original, or at least a song evidently prior to Ramsay's, is still extant.   It begins :

As I cam down yon waterside,
And by yon shillin-hill, O,
There I spied a bonie, bonie lass,
And a lass that I lo'ed right weel, O.

Chorus

The mill, mill, O, and the kill, kill, O,
And the coggin o' Peggy's wheel, O,
The sack and the sieve, and a' she did leave,
And danc'd the Miller's reel, O.

The remaining two stanzas, though pretty enough, partake rather too much of the rude simplicity of the " olden time " to be admitted here.

(p. 2) :   *Bob o' Dumblane.*—Ramsay, as usual, has modernised this song.   The original, which I learned on the spot, from my Hostess in the principal Inn there :—

Lassie, lend me your braw hemp heckle,
And I'll lend you my thripplin-kame ;
My heckle is broken, it canna be gotten,
And we'll gae dance the bob o' Dumblane.

Twa gaed to the wood, to the wood, to the wood,
Twa gaed to the wood—three came hame :
An' it be na weel bobbit, weel bobbit, weel bobbit,
An' it be na weel bobbit, we'll bob it again.

1 insert this song to introduce the following anecdote which I have heard well authenticated.   In the evening of the day of the

battle of Dumblane (Sheriffmoor), after the action was over, a Scots officer in Argyle's army observed to His Grace that he was afraid the rebels would give out to the world that *they* had gotten the victory. " Weel, weel," returned His Grace, alluding to the foregoing ballad ; " if they think it be na weel bobbit, we'll bob it again."

————

O'er the Muir amang the Heather.—

> O, vow ! an' I had her,
> O'er the muir, amang the heather,
> A' her friends should na get her
> Till I made her lo'e me better.

————

The Moudiewort.

————

(p. 3) : *Kirk wad let me be.*—Tradition in the Western parts of Scotland tells this old song, of which there are still three stanzas extant, once saved a Covenanting Clergyman out of a scrape. It was a little prior to the Revolution, a period when being a Scots Covenanter was' being a Felon, one of their clergy who was at that very time hunted by the merciless soldiery, fell in, by accident, with a party of the military. The soldiers were not exactly acquainted with the person of the Rev. gentleman of whom they were in search ; but from some suspicious circumstances they fancied that they had got one of that cloth and opprobious persuasion among them in the person of this stranger. " Mass John," to extricate himself, assumed such a freedom of manners (very unlike the gloomy strictness of his sect), and among other convivial exhibitions, sung (and, some traditions say, composed on the spur of the occasion) " Kirk wad let me be," with such effect, that the soldiers swore he was a d——d honest fellow, and that it was impossible *he* could belong to these hellish conventicles, and so gave him his liberty.

The first stanza of this song, a little altered, is a favourite kind of dramatic interlude at country weddings in the south-west parts of the kingdom. A young fellow is dressed up like an old beggar ; a peruke, commonly of carded tow, to represent hoary locks ; an old bonnet ; a ragged plaid, or surtout, bound with a straw-rope for a girdle ; a pair of old shoes, with straw-ropes twisted round his ancles, as is done by shepherds in snowy weather (p. 4) ; his face disguised as like wretched old age as they can. In this plight he

is brought into the wedding house, frequently to the astonishment
of strangers who are not in the secret, and begins to sing :

> O, I am a silly auld man,
> My name it is auld Glenae.* &c.

He is asked to drink, and by and by to dance, which, after
some uncouth excuses, he is prevailed on to do, the fiddler playing the
tune, which here is commonly called " Auld Glenae "; in short,
he is all the time so plied with liquor that he is understood to be
intoxicated, and with all the ridiculous gesticulations of an old drunken
beggar, he dances and stagg(ers) untill he falls on the floor, yet
still in all his ri(ot), nay in his rolling and tumbling on the floor,
with some or other drunken motion of his body, he beats time to
the music, till at last he is supposed to be carried out dead-drunk.

--- --- ---

(p. 5)   *Wat ye what my Minnie did ?*

> Wat ye what my minnie did,
> My minnie did, my minnie did,
> An' wat ye what my minnie did,
> My minnie did to me, jo ?
>
> She put me in a dark room
> A dark room, a dark room,
> She put me in a dark room,
> A styme I could na see, jo.
>
> And there came in a lang man,
> A meikle man, a strang man,
> And there came in a lang man,
> He might hae worried me ! jo.   &c.

--- --- ---

If ever I marry, I'll marry a wright.—(See this tune in Oswald).

> If ever I marry, I'll marry a wright,
> He'll set up my bed, and he'll set it up right.   &c.

---

* Glenae, on the small river Ae, in Annandale ; the seat and
designation of an ancient branch, and the present representative
of the gallant, but unfortunate, Dalziels of Carnwath.

Lass, an' I come near ye.—(See this tune in Aird's "Selec.
tion of Airs and Marches.")

> Lass, an' I come near ye,
> Lass, an' I come near ye,
> I'll gar a' your ribbands reel
> Lass, an' I come near ye !

———

Little wats thou o' thy daddie, hiney. — (Sometimes called
Elsie Marley.)—

> O little wats thou o' thy daddie, hiney,
> An' little wats thou o' thy daddie, hiney ;
> For lairds and lords hae kiss'd thy minnie,
> An' little wats thou o' thy daddie, hiney.

———

(p 6) : *The King o' France he rade a race.* — (Oswald &
Macgibbon's Collections, now altered into a modern reel called
The lass o' Loncarty)—

> The King o' France he rade a race
> Out o'er the hills o' Syria,
> His eldest (*sic*) has followed him,
> Upon a gude grey marie, O ;
> They were sae high, they were sae skeigh,
> Naebody durst come near them, O ;
> But there cam a Fiddler out o' Fife
> That dang them tapsalteerie, O.

———

Rob shoor in hairst. — (See this tune in Oswald's and other
Collections.)—

> O Robin shoor in hairst,
> I shoor wi' him ;
> Fient a heuk had I,
> Yet I stack by him. *&c*

———

Jockie's gray breeks.—Though this has certainly every evidence
of being a Scotish air, yet there is a well-known tune and song in
the North of Ireland, call'd " The weaver and his shuttle, O," which
though sung much quicker, is, every note, the very tune.

Corn rigs are bonie.—All that ever I could meet of old words to this air were the following, which seems to have been an old chorus :—

> O corn-rigs and rye-rigs,
> O corn-rigs are bonie,
> And where'er ye meet a bonie lass,
> Preen up her cockernony.

———

The Posie.—It appears evident to me that Oswald composed his " Roslin Castle " on the modulation of this air.   In the second part of Oswald's, in the three first (p. 7) bars, he has either hit on a wonderful similarity to, or else he has entirely borrowed the three first bars of the older air ;   and the close of both tunes is almost exactly the same.   The old verses to which it was sung, when I took down the notes from a country girl's voice, had no great merit. The following is a specimen :

> There was a pretty May, and a-milkin' she went,
> Wi' her red, rosy cheeks and her coal-black hair :
> And she has met a young man a-comin' o'er the bent ;
> With a double and adieu to thee fair May.

> O whare are ye goin', my ain pretty May,
> Wi' thy red, rosy cheeks and thy coal-black hair ;
> Unto the yowes a-milkin', kind Sir, she says
> With a double and adieu to thee fair May.

> What if I gang alang wi' thee, my ain pretty May,
> Wi' thy red, rosy cheeks and thy coal-black hair ;
> Wad I be ought the warre o' that, kind Sir, she says,
> With a double and adieu to thee fair May.   *&c.*

———

Saw ye nae my Peggy. — The original words, for they can scarcely be called verses, seem to be as follows, a song familiar from the cradle to every Scotish ear :—

> Saw ye my Maggie,
> Saw ye my Maggie,
> Saw ye my Maggie,
>   Linkin' o'er the lea ?

> High kilted was she,
> High kilted was she,
> High kilted was she,
>   Her (coa)ts aboon her knee.

(p. 8) :   What mark has your Maggie,
      What mark has your Maggie,
      What mark has your Maggie,
      That ane may ken her be ? (*by*). &c.

Though it by no means follows that the silliest verses to an air must, for that reason, be the original song, yet I take this ballad, of which I have quoted part, to be the old verses.

The two songs in Ramsay, one of them evidently his own, are never to be met with in the fireside circle of our peasantry ; while, what I take to be the old song is in every shepherd's mouth. Ramsay, I suppose, had thought the old verses unworthy of a place in his Collection.

Fy, gar rub her o'er wi' strae.—It is self-evident that the first four lines are part of a song much ancienter than Ramsay's beautiful verses which are annexed to them. To this day, among people who know nothing of Ramsay's verse, the following is the song, and all the song that ever I heard :—

    Gin ye meet a bonie lassie,
     Gie her a kiss and let her gae ;
    But gin ye meet a dirty hizzie,
     Fye, gae rub her o'er wi' strae.

    Fye, gae rub her, rub her, rub her,
     Fye, gae rub her o'er wi' strae ;
    An' gin ye meet a dirty hizzie,
     Fye, gae rub her o'er wi' strae.

(p. 9) : *The Lass o' Liviston.*—The old song, in three eight-line stanzas, is well known, and has merit as to wit and humour ; but is rather unfit for insertion. It begins :—

    The bonie lass o' Liviston,
     Her name ye ken, her name ye ken,
    And she has written in her contract,
     To lie her lane, to lie her lane. &c.

The lass o' Patie's Mill. — In the *Statistical Account of Scotland* this song has been claimed by a Clergyman in Shire as belonging to a place in Ayrshire and his parish, and by the Clergyman of Galston as belonging to that country. The following is the fact : Allan Ramsay was residing with the then Earl of Loudon at Loudon

Castle for some little time ; and one day Mr Ramsay, accompanying
his Lordship in a forenoon's walk or ride, at a place still known by
the name of Patie's Mill, on the banks of the Irvine, they saw a
pretty girl " Tedding o' the hay, Bareheaded on the green." My
Lord observed to Allan that she would be a charming subject for
a song. Ramsay took the hint ; and loitering behind, on their
return home, he set about the composition ; and at dinner produced
the first copy of The lass o' Patie's Mill.

This anecdote I had of my much-esteemed friend Sir William
Cunningham of Robertland, who had it of the late John, Earl of
Loudon.

(p. 10) : *Highland Laddie.* — As this was a favourite theme
with our later Scotish muses, there are several airs and songs of
that name. That which I take to be the oldest is to be found in
the *Musical Museum*, beginning " I hae been at Crookie-den."
One reason for my thinking so is, that Oswald has it in his collection
by the name of " The auld Highland laddie." It is also known
by the name of " Jinglan Johnie," which is a well-known song of
four or five stanzas, and seems to be an earlier song than Jacobite
times. As a proof of this, it is little known to the peasantry by
the name of " Highland Laddie "; while every body knows " Jinglan
Johnie." The song begins :—

> Jinglan John, the meikle man,
> He met wi' a lass was blythe and bonie.

Another " Highland Laddie " is also in the *Museum*, vol. V.,
which I take to be Ramsay's original, as he has borrowed the chorus :
" O, my bonie Highland lad," &c. It consists of three stanzas,
besides the chorus ; and has humour in its composition. It begins :—

> As I cam' o'er Cairney-Mount,
> And down amang the blooming heather. *&c.*

This air and the common " Highland Laddie " seem only to
be different sets.

Another " Highland Laddie," also in the *Museum*, vol. V., is
the tune of several Jacobite fragments. One of these old songs
to it, only exists, as far as I know, in these four lines ·—

> Whare hae ye been a' day,
> Bonie laddie, Highland laddie ?
> Down the back o' Bell's brae,
> Courtin' Maggie, courtin' Maggie.

Another of this name is Dr Arne's beautiful air, called " The
new Highland Laddie."

(p. 11): *Clout the Caldron.*—A tradition is mentioned in *The Bee*, that the second Bishop Chisholm, of Dunblane, used to say, that if he were going to be hanged, nothing would soothe his mind so much by the way as to hear " Clout the Cauldron " played.

I have met with another tradition, that the old song to this tune—

> " Hae ye ony pots or pans,
> Or onie broken chanlers ?"—

was composed on one of the Kenmure family, in the Cavalier times ; and alluded to an amour he had, while under hiding, in the disguise of an itinerant tinker.   The air is also known by the name of

> " The Blacksmith and his Apron,"

which, from the rhythm, seems to have been a line of some old song to the tune.

Auld Lang Syne. — Ramsay here, as usual with him, has taken the idea of the song, and the first line, from the old fragment, which may be seen in the *Museum*, vol. V.

Dainty Davie.—This song, tradition says, and the composition itself confirms it, was composed on the Rev. David Williamson's begetting the daughter of Lady Cherrytrees with child, while a party of dragoons were searching her house to apprehend him for being an adherent to the Solemn League and Covenant.   The pious woman had put a lady's night-cap on him, and had laid him a-bed with her own daughter, and passed him to the soldiery as a lady, her daughter's bed-fellow.   A mutilated stanza or two are to be found in Herd's Collection, but the song consists of five or six stanzas, and has merit in its way.   The first stanza is :—

> Being pursued by the dragoons,
> Within my bed he was laid down ;
> And weel I wat he was worth his room
> For he was my daintie Davie.

Ramsay's song, " Luckie Nansie," though he calls it an old song with additions, seems to be all his own, except the chorus :—

> I was ay telling you,
> Luckie Nansie, luckie Nansie,
> Auld springs wad ding the new,
> But ye wad never trow me—

which I should conjecture to be part of a song prior to the affair of Williamson.

(p. 12): *Tweedside.* —I have seen a song calling itself the original " Tweedside," and said to have been composed by a Lord Yester. It consisted of two stanzas, of which I still recollect the first :—

> When Maggy and I was acquaint,
> I carried ma noddle fu' hie ;
> Nae lintwhite on a' the green plain,
> Nor gowspink sae happy as me
> But I saw her sae fair, and 1 lo'ed ·
> I woo'd, but I came nae great speed ;
> So now I maun wander abroad,
> And lay my banes far frae the Tweed

ELUCIDATIONS

Note.—When J. C. Dick's work is cited it should be understood that, unless otherwise stated, the reference is to his *Notes on Scottish Song by Robert Burns*, 1908.

MS. Item 1 : *" Waukin o' the Fauld."*—This note is in Cromek's *Reliques*, 1808, 232. Dick prints it (p. 77) as a Spurious Note. According to the manuscript, the word *" whence "* of the printed version should be *" when."*

Item 2 : *" Maggie Lauder."*—Only the title is written on the manuscript. There is no notice of " Maggie Lauder " in the *Reliques*, but in *Select Scotish Songs*, 1810, I., 93, Cromek has a note thereon which, be it marked, follows immediately after the one on " The Waukin o' the Faulds." It reads · " This old song, so pregnant with Scottish naivieté and energy, is much relished by all ranks, notwithstanding its broad wit and palpable allusions.— Its language is a precious model of imitation : sly, sprightly, and forcibly expressive.— Maggie's tongue wags out the nicknames of Rob the Piper with all the careless lightsomeness of unrestrained gaiety."

Item 3 : *" Mill, Mill, O."*—This is in the *Reliques*, p. 244, with chorus and verse in reverse order, and the last sentence printed in smaller type as a footnote. Cromek must have forgotten that the words so treated were in the manuscript, for in reprinting them in his *Select Scotish Songs* (vol. I., 133) he appropriates the footnote by adding " Ed." No doubt that explains why Mr Dick, in classing the item with his " Spurious Notes " (p. 77), omitted the sentence entirely. There is one slight verbal discrepancy in the printed versions. For " It *begins*—" in the manuscript, Cromek printed " It *runs thus :—*"

Item 4 : " *Bob o' Dumblane.*"—This interesting anecdote, reminiscent of the Poet's Highland Tour, with its glimpse of his work as a gleaner of traditional song, will be welcomed back to the canon of his authentic writings. It was printed in the *Reliques*, p. 305, and numbered among Dick's " Spurious Notes " (p. 80). The manuscript and printed renderings agree, with the slight exception that the " *is* " printed immediately before the poetry is evidently an interpolation.

Item 5 : " *O'er the Muir amang the Heather.*"—Here the manuscript yields an interesting little discovery. Burns wrote in the interleaved *Museum* a spicy note (*Reliques*, p. 296) on the song of this title, in which he ascribed it to an erring daughter of Killie called Jean Glover. Dick's comment (p. 109) is · " Except for what Burns has said on this beautiful song, absolutely nothing else is known, except that the tune, with the title, is in Bremner's *Reels*, 1760, at the time when Jean Glover, the assumed writer of the song, was only two years of age. Therefore, a song of some sort existed in 1760, of which there is now no trace. I have long thought that Burns himself did much more than edit this fine song."

The verse in the manuscript is quite different from any in the song as published in the fourth volume of the *Scots Musical Museum* (1792), and in all likelihood we have here an otherwise unrecorded fragment of the old song, as sung by the strolling singer. Thanks to Mr Frank Kidson, of Leeds, I am able to supplement Mr Dick's information about the tune. It is in Thompson's *Country Dances for* 1758 as " In the moor among the heather," probably published in the autumn of 1757, and exactly the same set is in the *Universal Magazine* for March, 1758.

Item 6 : " *The Moudiewort.*"—The title only is noted on the manuscript. It is the tune for " O, for ane-and-twenty, Tam," which, though not dealt with in the *Reliques*, is printed in *Select Scotish Songs*, 1810, II., 171, prefixed with the remark : " This song is mine."

Item 7 : " *Kirk wad let me be.*"—This very long and rather interesting note (*Reliques*, 252), branded as spurious by Mr Dick (p. 78), was printed by Cromek with the words appended to the footnote : " This is the *Author's* note." Mr Dick had abundant grounds for scepticism, and no one could blame him for applying his literary branding-iron, but with all his faults as an editor, and they were many, the Edinburgh University Manuscript proved that Cromek was right, and that note and footnote are alike *genuine Burns.*

Item 8 : " *Wat ye what my Minnie did ?*"—Cromek seems to have made no use of these lines, which do not appear in either of his works.

Item 9 : " *If ever I marry, I'll marry a wright.*"— Another fragment of song not used bv Cromek when he handled the manuscript.

Item 10 : " *Lass. and I come near ye.*"—Cromek like-wise ignored this little Note and snatch of song, probably because he printed, as if it were by Burns, one of Riddell's notes relating to " Wha is that at my bower-door ?" and the same tune, inferentially signing Burns's name to it by the unauthorised addition of the formula, " The words are mine " (see *Reliques*, 301). The air mentioned is, as Burns says, in Aird's work. It is in the first book, which Mr Dick dates 1782, but which Mr Frank Kidson, an even greater authority on Antiquarian Music, says he has good proof was earlier—about 1775-6.

Item 11 : " *Little wats thou o' thy Daddie, hiney* "—
This is another scrap of song not noted by Cromek. The
tune, " Elsie Marley," is in Bremner's *Reels*, 1759, and
in later Collections, including Gow's *Fourth Repository*.

Item 12 : " *The King o' France he rade a race* "—This
hitherto unpublished Note has a special interest, because
it unexpectedly furnishes us with a verse of the old song
which Burns used as a model for " Amang the trees where
humming bees," published in Cromek's *Reliques*, 1808, p.
453, to the tune, " The King of France he rade a race."
In his last two lines—

> He fir'd a fiddler in the North
> That dang them tapsalteerie, O,

it will be seen how closely Burns followed the original, and
taking the verse as a whole, how little he was indebted to it.

Item 13 : " *Rob shoor in hairst.*"—Ignored by Cromek.

Item 14 : " *Jockie's gray breeks.*"—Printed in the
Reliques, p. 205, with the word " certain " of the manuscript altered to " certain*ly*." Dick includes it among
the " Spurious Notes " (p. 75), but there cannot now be
any doubt of its authenticity, even though the original is
not in the interleaved *Museum*.

Item 15 : " *Corn rigs are bonie.*"—The note given by
Cromek (*Reliques*, p. 231), though slightly varied in sequence
of words, is manifestly copied from the Edinburgh University Manuscript. A somewhat similar note in the
interleaved *Museum* (Dick, p. 22) reads : " There must
have been an old song under this title ; the chorus of it is
all that remains "—

> O corn-rigs and rye-rigs,
> O corn-rigs are bonie,
> And where'er ye meet a bonie lass,
> Preen up her cockernony.

Mr Dick seems, in this instance, to have overlooked the
discrepancy between the *Reliques* version and the Burns
holograph in the interleaved *Museum*.

Item 16 : " *The Posie.*"—This is the undoubted original of the note in Cromek's *Reliques* (p. 214) which Dick—failing to find in the interleaved copy of the *Scots Musical Museum*, and quite evidently unsuspicious of any other authentic manuscript source—printed in his volume (p. 76) among the " Spurious Notes."

Item 17 : " *Saw ye nae my Peggy ?*"—In Dick's Appendix (p. 83), he says : " Cromek has a long note in his *Reliques* which is not in the manuscript." Nevertheless it is no " invention " of Cromek, who, with two annotations of the song in Burns's handwriting in front of him—as we now for the first time know—in this case printed what he found in the Glenriddell volume, and eked it out with the longer note from the Excise Paper Manuscript of twelve folio pages.

Item 18 : " *Fy, gar rub her o'er wi' strae.*"—Dick says (p. 84) " Cromek reconstructed and made additions to this note " In a sense that is very true. The note as printed in the *Reliques* (p. 202), is the whole of that in the Excise Paper MS., with the interleaved *Museum* note—minus the first sentence—sandwiched into it. It is peculiar editing, but it is all genuine Burns lore.

Item 19 : " *The lass o' Liviston.*"—Dick's observation is : " Here again Cromek has garbled the note. The part of the old song which he quotes incorrectly is . . . in the *Merry Muses*. What Cromek did do was to give preference to his alternative manuscript, his indebtedness to which—with a laxity too common in his time—he did not even trouble to mention. He followed it faithfully however (*Reliques*, 204), and the verse also, though not agreeing with the rendering in the *Merry Muses*, is as Burns penned it in the manuscript under review.

Item 20 · " *The lass o' Patie's Mill.*"—This note is very similar, but not quite identical with the one in the Interleaved Glenriddell Volume, which Cromek printed in his *Reliques*, p. 205.

Item 30 · "*Highland Laddie.*"—Referring to this note, as given in the *Reliques* (p. 207), Mr Dick, in his special summing up of the " Spurious Notes " (p. 123), remarks : " ' Highland Laddie ' is a long composite invention, superseding the short note which Burns wrote." We know now that it was no " invention," but a genuine Burns commentary which Cromek selected from his Manuscript No. 2, giving it place rather than the note in the interleaved *Museum,* from which, however, he borrowed almost verbatim the sentence in parenthesis—-" it is an excellent but somewhat . licentious song "—which is not in the Edinburgh University Manuscript. Continuing, Dick stresses another objection to the authenticity of this note thuswise : " Here Cromek refers to the " fifth " volume of the *Museum,* which did not exist. It was not published until six months after the death of Burns, and therefore could not have been noticed by him, particularly as the last notes in the interleaved *Museum* were penned about three or four years before the volume was published, and before any arrangement was made for sketching its contents." Nevertheless, this other manuscript, which was probably written towards the close of the Poet's life, shows that he did mention the *fifth* volume of the *Scots Musical Museum.* He must have done a lot of work upon it, apart from his own contributions, in the way of determining its contents, and probably correcting proofs, and, expecting its early publication, speaks of it here as already in being. By the way, when was volume V. published ? Dick gives December, 1796, but John Glen—unfortunately without indicating his reasons—dates it March, 1797.

Item 31 : "*Clout the Caldron.*"—This comes first in the "Spurious Notes," as given by Mr Dick (p. 74). The manuscript is exactly as printed in Cromek's *Reliques of Robert Burns,* p. 199.

Item 32 : "*Auld Lang Syne.*"—Once more in this manuscript we find Burns referring to the fifth volume of the *Museum.* Dick says (p. 123) Cromek " omits what Burns wrote." What Burns wrote in the interleaved copy

The original & by much the best set of the
words of this song is as follows
Should auld acquaintance be forgot
And never brought to mind?
Should auld acquaintance be forg
And days o' lang syne?
    Chorus
And for auld lang syne, my jo,
    For auld lang syne,
We'll tak a cup o' kindness yet,
O For auld lang syne.
And surely ye'll be your pint-stowp.
And surely I'll be mine!
And we'll tak a cup o' kindness yet
O For auld lang syne. —
    And for &c
We twa hae run about the braes,
And pou'd the gowans fine;
But we've wander'd mony a weary foot
Sin auld lang syne.
    And for &c.
We twa hae paidl'd i' the burn,
Frae mornin sun till dine;
But seas between us braid hae roar'd
Sin auld lang syne. —
    And for &c.
And there's a hand, my trusty fiere!
And gie's a hand o' thine!
And we'll tak a right gude-willy waught,
O For auld lang syne. And &

FIRST PUBLISHED FACSIMILE,

From the Interleaved Copy of *The Scots Musical Museum* (by kind permission
of the owner of the original, Dr John Gribbel, of Philadelphia).

of the *Scots Musical Museum* was a copy of " Auld Lang Syne," headed, ' The original and by much the best set of the words of this song is as follows :" A *facsimile* of that page—one of the most interesting in the whole of that unique and remarkable volume—was kindly given to me by Mr Gribbel, and is herewith illustrated, being, I believe, the first portion of the famous interleaved copy of the *Scots Musical Museum* published in *facsimile*

Item 33 : " *Dainty Davie*."—Mr Dick (p. 123), speaking of Cromek's note in the *Reliques* (p. 304), says : " . . . that on ' Dainty Davie ' is a suppression of the note in the manuscript, to interpolate and repeat in detail the old chesnut about the Rev. David Williamson and the daughter of the Laird of Cherrytrees." The fact is that Cromek used both manuscripts. He took the anecdote from the one we now distinguish as the Excise Paper, or Edinburgh University Manuscript, and then, far from *suppressing* the short note in the interleaved *Museum*, neatly dovetailed " a kennin " more than half of it—reading : " and were their delicacy equal to their wit and humour they would merit a place in any collection "—into the other. He also took the word " original " from the *Museum* holograph, and inserted it before " song " in his printing of its less famous fellow, as well as cutting out the words " and has merit in its way " as in our MS., the expansion of the sentence having rendered them superfluous.

The earliest printed account of the " Dainty Davie " story, I have found, is in the first edition of *The Scotch Presbyterian Eloquence*, 1692, p. 5, a work which has also what is probably the first use in literature of the vernacular phrase, " For ald lang syne." Mr Dick cites the second edition of 1694, p. 64, for that distinction (64 is probably a printer's error, for it should be 68) ; but it is on page 101 of the first edition, and also on page 80 of an earlier second edition dated 1693.

Item 34 : " *Tweedside*."—J. C. Dick (p. 87) says : " The verses quoted in Cromek's *Reliques* are not in the manuscript " Here again Cromek has simply utilised both manuscripts, making the one note follow the other, and the portion on page 214 of the *Reliques*, beginning " I have seen a song," is from his supplementary manuscript—the one now in the Library of Edinburgh University.

After this wholesale restoration, there remain of the Notes labelled " Spurious " by Mr Dick three very short ones—" Polwart on the Green," " The Shepherd's Complaint," " We ran and they ran "—and a longer one entitled " The bonie lass made the bed to me," which are not to be found in either of the Burns Manuscripts known to be used by Cromek. These are naturally open to suspicion, and till further evidence transpires may be regarded as doubtful ; but in view of the readjustment of opinion rendered necessary by this latest discovery, I would, even while remembering R. H. Cromek's editoral idiosyncrasies, hesitate to brand them as " spurious." Cromek may have had access to still another unsuspected Burns Manuscript, and even the additional Notes of the *Select Scotish Songs*, while still more open to doubt, may prove in the end to be the work of Robert Burns.

Incidentally, the increase of confidence in the Cromek-Burns text goes a long way towards establishing the authenticity of that important note on " Highland Mary," of which I believe some of us have had suspicions since Mr Dick's disclosure of Cromek's shortcomings as an editor, and his revelation of the fact that the interleaf, which should, according to the *Reliques*, contain nearly all that Burns wrote about Highland Mary, is, with others, missing from the book. By whatever hand it was abstracted, it is to be hoped that the " Highland Mary " leaf and its fellows will some day be discovered, and eventually restored to the volume annotated by Burns for his friend Robert Riddell of Glenriddell.

DAVIDSON COOK, F.S.A. (Scot.).

BURNS AS EMPLOYER.

IT is very often forgotten by admirers of our National
Bard that he belonged to that class which, in those
latter days, is sometimes regarded in anything but a
favourable light—the class composed of employers of labour.
While he is everywhere hailed as the poet of democracy,
as the champion of the working-man, the fact that he was
an employer, and not an employee, during a large part
of his working life, is too often neglected. Indeed, we
can hardly speak of Burns as having ever been an employee
in the usual sense of the word, for in his early life he worked
with his father, with whom he never regarded himself as
a servant ; while as an exciseman he was the servant,
not of a " capitalist," but of the Nation. Burns, both
on his father's and his mother's side, was sprung from
farmers who were themselves employers, and in his
autobiographical poem he makes it his boast : " My father
was a farmer upon the Carrick Border." When the future
Poet was only seven years old his father took the farm of
Mount Oliphant, and though it is generally asserted that
there were no hired helpers employed, Murdoch, Burns's
teacher, referring to this period, says : " William Burnes
had the art of gaining the esteem and goodwill of those
who were labourers under him."

In 1777 the Burnes family removed to Lochlea, and
of the Poet's experiences as a farmer here we have an
interesting glimpse in a letter written to his cousin, James
Burnes, just about six years after they had entered the
farm :—" Farming is at a pretty low ebb with us. . . . We
are much at a loss for want of proper methods in our improvements. Necessity compels us to leave our old
schemes, and few of us have opportunities of being well
informed in new ones."

Later in the year in which this letter was written
(1783) Robert and Gilbert Burns became farmers of Mossgiel,
which was sublet to them by Gavin Hamilton, and now
became employers on their own account. While Gilbert
took chief charge of the farm, Robert was by no means
indifferent to the success of the venture. We know from
his own words that he tried hard to become a successful
farmer. "I read farming books," he says, "I calculated
crops, I attended markets." The methods of farming
differed considerably in those days from the methods
employed to-day. For one thing, there were few labour-
saving devices in the latter part of the eighteenth century.
Considerable portions of the country (as at Ellisland)
were still unenclosed, and were cultivated on the "run-rig"
system. Such conditions meant that larger numbers of
farm servants had to be employed. Thus we find that
at Mossgiel, a farm of only 118 acres, there were three male
servants (one of whom indeed—Wee Davock—was only
a boy), in addition to the members of the family—eight
in number.

In the "Inventory" the Bard tells us that two of
the servants were "a gaudsman ane, a thresher t'other."
Neither gaudsman nor thresher now appear in lists of farm
servants. The former's duty was to drive, or rather
"goad," the "owsen" or horses in the plough, which was
a great lumbering affair in those days. Grey Graham,
in his book *Social Life in Scotland in the Eighteenth Century*,
remarks that the gaudsman was required to exercise his
skill in whistling in order to stimulate his charges—a
practice Burns refers to in one of his poems. At Lochlea
a married ploughman named Hutchison was employed
by William Burnes. His health broke down, and he
died of a low fever. His family of two boys and two
girls were thrown on the world. Two of them—Janet and
David—the wee Davock of the poems—remained with
the family at Mossgiel, getting practically all their education
at the hands of the Poet. Janet remained with Mrs Burns
for many years.

In 1786 Robert made over his interest in the farm to his brother Gilbert, in trust for his " dear bought Bess," and not until two years later did he again enter the ranks of the employers of labour, when he took the farm of Ellisland.   Here his duties were more varied than at Mossgiel, for when he went south the steading had not been built, and in addition to the duties of farmer he had to add those of " Superintendent of Works," as Allan Cunningham informs us.   After the steading was completed and Mrs Burns duly installed, the Bard settled down to a farmer's life, but even as early as January, 1789, he knew that he had little reason to be satisfied with his venture.   At Ellisland his household included a domestic servant, as well as two women and two men engaged as outworkers. His idea was to make the place a dairy farm, where " Bonnie Jean," who had received instruction from her mother-in-law, might preside over the mysteries of butter-making. He was no mere gentleman farmer.   While looking after others he was always ready to lend a hand at the farm-work.   He did much of the sowing himself, and was altogether a model of laborious industry.   In the words of one who investigated this period of his life closely, " The first year of his sojourn in the new house at Ellisland passed happily away. . . .   We see him during this period as a faithful husband, as a good master, as the honoured head of a decent household."

Among those who served the Poet here were three of his cousins—two sons (William and John) and a daughter (Fanny, afterwards Mrs Armour)—of " poor uncle Robert," who, with the Bard's father, had left his home in Kincardineshire to seek his fortune in the South.   John Burns lived to 1844, and to the end spoke of his cousin as having been a good master, " though somewhat restless and absent-minded."   Another of the Ellisland servants—William Clark—has left on record his impressions of Burns as an employer.   He states that his master was quite as good a manager as the generality of farmers.   He was a kind and indulgent master, spoke familiarly to his servants,

both in the house and out of it, though he did not take his
food with them as was the custom in most farm-houses.
If there was extra work to be done the men usually got a
dram, but, adds Clark, " I have been with masters who were
more flush in that way with their servants." When the
young man left, Burns not only gave him a certificate of
character, but also a " fairing."

Another sidelight on the Poet's character as an
employer is seen in his transactions with two " orra "
workers. The one was a drainer, and in a letter to the
factor with regard to his work and pay, Burns says : " I
have stated the wage at 20d the rood, as in fact, even at
that, they have not the wages they ought to have had, and
I cannot for the life of me see a poor devil a loser at my
hand."

In another account relating to dike building, a document still preserved shows that he gave the worker ten
shillings more than was due. Allan Cunningham, whose
testimony, however, is not above suspicion, says of the
farming operations at Ellisland : " Burns's skill in hus-
bandry was but moderate. . . He employed more servants
than the number of acres demanded, and spread for them a
richer board than common."

Burns, as can be easily understood, did not grudge his
servants their share of the merry-makings of those days.
His well-known poem, " Hallowe'en," shows how much
he himself enjoyed these periodical celebrations, while
his description of the roup of his crops in 1791 indicates
that he was no laggard where the provision of refreshments
was concerned. A letter from his friend Robert Ainslie
to " Clarinda " gives an interesting account of a " kirn "
(harvest home) at Ellisland. When the evening passed,
with the fun going fast and furious, Ainslie appears to have
enjoyed himself thoroughly, though he did not think " the
menage and company worthy of the Poet."

All things considered then, Burns seems to have been
an employer of the best kind, taking a sympathetic and
intelligent interest in his employees and doing his best for

them. As the head of the household, he catechised them in the good old-fashioned way. Apparently, too, he superintended the education of the younger servants. But it may be questioned whether he was paid back in kind. At Ellisland, at any rate, there appears to be evidence that slackness on the part of the servants, and indifference to their master's interests, had partly to do with the failure there.

WM. M'MILLAN.

ROBERT TANNAHILL.

(1774-1810.)

PERHAPS no Scots poet since Burns is entitled to
rank higher in the ranks of the lyrical muse than
Robert Tannahill, the weaver poet of Paisley.

He was born fifteen years after Burns, and he lived
twenty-two years after the death of the National Bard.
That he was inspired and stimulated by the genius of the
greater poet there is no question. This view is not only
supported by the personal admiration he manifested for
Burns, but also by the testimony of numerous contemporary poets. Let us take one of the many for example.
John Mitchell, the shoemaker poet of Paisley, whose education was superior to that of Tannahill, is not unworthy
of a place among the minor poets of Scotland. This is
what he says :—

> " His master, Burns, with giant stride,
>   Had reached the dizzy steep,
> Where genius' sons, in modest pride
>   Unfading laurels reap.
>
> And Tannahill, with eager eye,
>   The stately pile survey'd,.
> And fondly hop'd at least to lie
>   Beneath his cheering shade.
>
> .   .   .   .   .
>
> His ' Bonnie Wood o' Craigilea,'
> His ' Jessie o' Dunblane,'
> Will match with any melody
>   Auld Scotland calls her ain.

At the time of Tannahill there was so large a coterie
of poets in Paisley and its vicinity that one may say of it,
as the Americans say of Boston, that it was not so much
a place as a state of mind.

It is difficult to determine whether the artistic and
poetic temperaments were induced by the atmosphere,

the scenery of the locality, or the delightful fabric designs which were thrown off from the weavers' shuttles of Paisley, but the fact remains that it has a history of which any town may well be proud. It has long been a popular belief that a zealous devotion to trade and manufacture fosters the commercial spirit which is prejudicial to the cultivation of refined sentiment and literary tastes, but it is one of those generalities that must be taken *cum grano salis*. Although trade and manufacture have been the chief enterprises of the industrial capital of Renfrewshire for generations, Paisley is a notable exception. The working classes have long been distinguished by a keen desire for the acquisition of knowledge and intellectual pursuits.

The inhabitants, generally speaking, are well informed, and keep a critical eye on all religious, social and political questions. Any political candidate who appears at the hustings must expect a severe heckling on the contents of his political programme. The prevailing sentiment from time immemorial appears to have been an ardent desire for the diffusion of education, consequently Paisley has been the birthplace of many men of distinction. Among these may be mentioned the celebrated Dr Witherspoon, and Alexander Wilson, the Ornithologist, who has already been noticed in the *Burns Chronicle*. The former did some of his best work while minister of Paisley, and the first published poem of Robert Tannahill was written on the emigration of Wilson to America. In the last stanza but one he pays him this fine tribute :—

> " Since now he's gane, and Burns deid,
>   Ah ! wha will tune the Scottish reed ?
> Her thistle, dowie, hings its heid,
>   Her harp's unstrung,
> While mountain, river, loch, an' mead
>   Remain unsung."

It was the literary reputation of Paisley which induced the late Lord Houghton to visit the burgh town some years ago, and, as the story goes, he was desirous of cele.

brating his visit by providing a banquet for the poets and *literati* of the town. To his great surprise, some three hundred responded to the invitation.

This, then, was the environment of our poet, Robert Tannahill, who was born at Paisley in June, 1774. In his infancy he was a weak and delicate child, and his young life was only preserved by the tender care of a devoted mother. As a boy he was shy, and bashful to an inordinate degree. This disposition clung to him throughout his manhood, and it was only by a supreme effort he could fortify himself against a constitutional melancholy which preyed upon his feeble body and sensitive mind—a struggle finally reaching the breaking-point before he reached the 37th year of his age.

It must not be inferred from this that he was void of a sense of humour, for he could be bright and humorous in the society of his boon companions and frequently in his writings, but there lurked behind it all the gloomy atmosphere of melancholy and despondency. In mental character and disposition, Tannahill was a Grimaldi in miniature, who, when behind the footlights, could keep thousands of his admirers in roars of laughter. Yet, when off the stage, he was so weighed down with sadness and despondency that he was driven to seek medical advice. After careful diagnosis, the physician, by whom he was not recognised, said he was suffering from aggravated mental depression and must seek cheerful society and amusement, finally urging him to pay a visit to Grimaldi's entertainments, when the distressed patient sorrowfully exclaimed : " Ah ! I am Grimaldi !"

James Tannahill, the poet's father, was above the rank and file in education and intelligence, and so was the poet's mother. His father built the cottage he dwelt in, and in which all the children were brought up. The domestic felicity which prevailed in the family circle was of a high order, and answered all the conditions of those pictured in Burns's " Cottar's Saturday Night."

The father of the family was elected one of the nine

Directors of the Hospital in New Sneddon Street, and was re-elected annually for five successive years. He frequently was returned at the head of those chosen outside the Town Council, from which it may be inferred that the poet's parents belonged to the lower middle classes in social status, and they had an ardent desire to give all their children the best education they could afford. During his school days Robert did not distinguish himself from other boys of average ability, and no one dreamt that there lay in the boy latent talents capable of great development. After he left school, however, he was assiduous in his efforts to improve himself in the art of speaking and writing correctly, and, judging from his poetical productions and letters, he succeeded in no small degree. As a letter writer, however, in comparison with Burns, Cowper, Gray, Shelley, Keats and Matthew Arnold, he does not rank high Judging from the score or so that have been published, all that can be said is, that they are concise and businesslike. He never indulges in philosophical flights ; rather the impression conveyed is that he kept a strict watch on his pen for fear it would run away with him, and unconsciously let him slip into the " grand style."

Thus it is scarcely possible to make his letters a medium through which his innermost character and personality might be revealed. From his extensive knowledge of literature, it is obvious that he must have been an omnivorous reader, both in poetry and prose, being particularly well read in both the Scots and English poets. Like Burns, the lyrics of Shenstone specially appealed to him, and we gather from " The Choice " that his ambition was to imitate Thomson and the Shropshire poet.

In 1786, when Tannahill was twelve years of age, he became an apprentice to the weaving trade with his father for a period of five years, which was the custom at the time whether they learned with their parents or strangers. Obviously it was the rigid apprenticeship system then in vogue which resulted in the fabrics of Paisley attaining their high reputation in so many parts of the world. Having served five years with his father, his apprenticeship was terminated in 1791, the same year in which Burns's "Tam o' Shanter" was published in Captain Grose's *Antiquities of Scotland.* The poem evoked much interest among the natives of Paisley, as the heroine of the tale was dressed in "her cutty sark o' Paisley harn."

Among the admirers of Burns, few of the natives of Paisley were more appreciative than Tannahill, and he was one of the founders of the Paisley Burns Club, acting for long as its secretary.

The first Anniversary of Burns was celebrated at Paisley on 29th January, 1805, the exact date of the Poet's birthday being not definitely known among the founders of the Club, though the Poet had given it himself in the song, "There was a Lad," where he writes :—

> " Our monarch's hindmost year but ane
> Was five-and-twenty days begun,
> 'Twas then a blast o' Jan'war' win'
> Blew hansel in on Robin."

Tannahill, in the exordium with which he prefaced the minutes of the Club, places Burns among the great immortals of all time, from which we give the following enthusiastic excerpt :—

"Shall we, then, suffer such characters to pass unnoticed ? No ! Ye illustrious benefactors of the world, we shall cherish, we shall celebrate your memories ; your virtues are already engraven on our hearts, and the tears of honest gratitude shall bedew your tombs ; posterity will imitate and applaud the deed, and your proud names shall roll through an eternity of years."

In addition to this tribute, Tannahill contributed several pieces in honour of the dead Poet on the occasion of the anniversary celebrations, and, indeed, was looked upon as the Poet Laureate of the Club. The best of these is, perhaps, "The Dirge," which shows a wonderful descriptive power and facility of expression. The concluding verse may be quoted by way of example :—

" All dismal let the nicht descend,
Let whirling storms the forest rend,
Let furious tempests sweep the sky,
And dreary howling caverns cry :
He's gone, he's gone, he's frae us torn,
The ae best poet e'er was born."

Up till his death, the life of Tannahill was a singularly uneventful one, except for a little love romance which to the outside world may seem but trivial, for there is a diversity of opinion as to what extent it affected his subsequent career. Indeed, the question would probably never have been raised had it not been for his melancholy end. In any case, the old adage fitly applies to Tannahill's case, that " a faint heart never won a fair lady." He was exceedingly shy and reserved in the company of women. Indeed, this characteristic manifested itself on every occasion he was thrown into the society of those whom he thought above. him in social position. In this respect he was the antithesis of Burns, who " could crack his thoom and tell his tale afore them a'."

Considering his three years' engagement to Jenny Tennant, he was too precipitate in breaking it off. Although her heart was sound at the core, his shyness seemed to make her feel that he was " like a star that dwelt apart." At any rate, no one can accuse him of being indifferent in the matter, for the pang of disappointment was acute and deep, as we ascertain from the allusion he makes to the incident in the following lines from " The Farewell ":—

" But when I knew thy plighted lips
Once to a rival's prest,
Love-smothered independence rose,
And spurned thee from my breast.

The fairest flower in Nature's field
Conceals the rankling thorn ;
So thou, sweet flower, as false as fair
This once kind heart has torn."

The idea suggested here is, that it was rather in-
judicious for one who was not quite sure of his own position
with his lady fair to have given his consent for her to
go to the dance, even with his own friend. No sooner
was the consent given than jealousy began to assert itself,
and when the rival impressed a kiss on the lips of the fair
enchantress at their parting, her jealous Robert, who was
concealed near-by, had all his worst suspicions confirmed.
It would have been more considerate on the poet's part
to have first ascertained whether it was not an impulsive
act on the part of his rival for which his Jenny should
not have been held responsible without being heard.
The estrangement which followed produced much un-
happiness and misery to himself, and it was also a severe
blow to Jenny Tennant. This is an incident in the poet's
life which must be regarded in a spirit of charity, for
philosophical circumspection is hardly to be expected
from a man who has been so severely wounded by Cupid's
dart, even though he tread the exalted path of the Muses.

In 1799, about a year after Jenny Tennant was wed
to another, Tannahill left Paisley for Bolton, in Lancashire,
where he remained for two years, during which period the
voice of the Muse was silent. This, it is said, was on
account of slighted love, but we must not overlook the fact
that the weaving trade of Paisley was in a very depressed
condition at the time. and the cause of his migration to
Bolton was probably due to reasons of a more material
kind. It was not till a few years before he passed away
that Tannahill's poetical abilities became fully recognised ;
he was under the shadow of the Ayrshire Bard, who had
laid the whole country under contribution to his genius,
not to mention his other famous contemporaries—Walter
Scott, Christopher North, and the Ettrick Shepherd. With
the exception of the last-named, the weaver poet does not
appear to have awakened much interest amongst them.

In March, 1810, the Ettrick Shepherd paid Tannahill a flying visit when returning from a tour in the
Highlands on his way to Glasgow. The two poets

spent the evening together at the Sun Tavern, Paisley, and we gather from a letter from Tannahill to James King—a military friend and a poet also—that Hogg and he had a good deal of conversation about the poets of the day. It would have been exceedingly interesting if that conversation between two individuals so different in character and disposition had been recorded in detail. On the one hand, there was the robust Hogg, the cherry optimist, who could meet his own threatened ruin with a jest and a smile ; on the other, the weak and sensitive Tannahill, who could only see despair and blackest night in the slightest reverse of the wheel of fortune.

Considering the nature and temperament of our poet, it is surprising to find he was so enamoured of the drama and the stage. In his love and appreciation of the theatre he was as enthusiastic as Allan Ramsay, who severely shocked the rigidly righteous of the Edinburgh of his day by building a theatre in the city. When a company of comedians visited Paisley, Tannahill seldom failed to attend the theatre, and he formed a friendly attachment with Richard Pollock and William Livingston—both men of culture and education, who had earned a high reputation in their profession.

The Interlude in "The Soldier's Return" was originally suggested by Pollock, who, unfortunately, died before the Poet had well commenced it. James Moss, an Edinburgh comedian, was another of his theatrical friends with whom he was on terms of more than a mere nodding acquaintance. "The Soldier's Return" was the poet's first and last attempt at dramatic composition, and his was but another case, among many, in which the author had failed to correctly estimate his own limitations. One does not need to read far into the piece before discovering that the model he constantly kept before him during its composition was Allan Ramsay's "Gentle Shepherd." Throughout the piece Tannahill failed to attain the natural simplicity and spontaneous sequence of Ramsay's rural scenes, and the rustic habits which he portrayed so faithfully to the life.

This, as we take it, is the pith and kernel of the pastoral drama. In "The Soldier's Return" the Interlude is by far the best of the piece, showing, as it does, Tannahill's lyrical gift in a marked degree. "The Soldier's Return" was not included in the first collected edition of his works, and, when subsequently published, it was severely criticised. Even the six beautiful songs which constitute the Interlude did not save the drama from sweeping condemnation by the critics. This reception greatly disappointed the author, and haunted him to the end of his days. His dream of dramatic fame which had raised his hopes and aspirations so high proved but the baseless fabric of a vision, and to his sensitive mind was gall and bitterness, which all but impelled him to hang his harp on the willow tree.

A more robust mind would have realised that he was not the first or only author who had failed to form a correct estimate of his own limitations. Granting all this, he was deserving of more merciful treatment at the hands of his critics, on account of his other and more excellent work. As the saying goes, disappointment usually runs in double harness, and the Poet was destined to see another illusion dispelled when he published his collected Irish Airs. Desirous of having them included in George Thomsons's *Musical Collection*, to which Burns had ready access, he sent them to Thomson at Edinburgh, who rejected them on the ground that he did not consider them up to the high standard of his musical publication. He bore this disappointment more heroically, for he continued his search for Irish airs, and he published fourteen in all, and many of the verses convey the Hibernian spirit in greater or less degree. The impression conveyed by the majority of his critics was that Tannahill had not the necessary genius to handle effectively the subject of Irish songs.

In the light of more recent times, however, this is not the only effective critical charge which may be advanced. After a comparison with Thomas Crofton Croker's collection of the *Popular Songs of Ireland*, we are of opinion that it could scarcely be lack of talent or breadth of knowledge which accounted for Tannahill's defects in the treatment of the subject. Indeed, it was rather on account of Tannahill's superior talent in versification, and his inability to descend to so commonplace a poetical level. The popular *Songs of Ireland* are so local and baldly realistic that they are best suited for the swaggering blade twirling his shillelah on the streets of Donnybrook Fair—

" Who goes to a tent, and spends half-a-crown,
He meets with a friend, and for love knocks him down
With his sprig of shillelah, and shamrock so green.

At evening retiring, as homeward he goes,
His heart soft with whisky, his head soft with blows
From a sprig of shillelah, and shamrock so green."

In fact, these songs are quite unworthy of the careful editing bestowed upon them by Croker. True, they may serve some purpose as human documents, but what a sordid picture of unpoetical commonplaces and the squalid depravity of human nature do they present. It would have been no great loss to the world had they been left to slumber in oblivion. In the poems and songs of Burns and Tannahill we have abundance of local colour, native scenery, and social customs introduced, but they seldom, if ever, lack that poetic touch that appeals to the whole world. In the popular *Songs of Ireland* the would-be rhymsters appear to keep their befuddled gaze too intently turned upon the rest of creation, and reserve their clearer vision for the mere glorification of their abandoned and rollicking ways. Judging from the characters of the heroes and heroines introduced, self-restraint always seems to be a burden too grievous to be borne, and their gyrations are akin to those of the uncultured barbarian. They know that they are naked and yet they are not ashamed, and, for lack of the broader outlook, it has been for generations " the winter of their discontent." There are a few exceptions, but they are very few.

The one specially deserving of notice is Callanan's " Gougaune Bazra," which in an inferior posthumous collec-

tion of his poems is entitled the " Recluse of Inchidony."
Even in that excellent song, however, the author could
not lay down his pen without discharging a poisoned
arrow at the cold-blooded Saxon.

Despite all that has been said in justification of Tannahill's Irish Collection, his reputation would not have suffered
had he left the subject to be dealt with by other hands.
It is as a lyrical poet on his own native heath, and in his
own homely environment, that Tannahill must be judged.
And we are not wide of the mark when we say that his
achievements in this particular sphere have not been
adequately recognised by a near posterity.

If " The Soldier's Return " has failed to fulfil the
higher canons of dramatic art, it has added to, rather
than diminished, his reputation as a lyrical poet, and it is
entitled to notice by virtue of the Interlude, which comprises such excellent lyrics as those beginning—" Lang-
syne, beside the Woodland burn," " We'll meet
beside the dusky glen on yon burn side," " Blyth was
the time when he fee'd wi' my faither "—all of which
are in keeping with the rustic setting of the pastoral
drama, whatever other defects they may possess. Had
his friend, Archibald Pollock, not passed away so suddenly, " The Soldier's Return " would probably have
been ultimately placed upon the stage and the ambition
of the author to that extent satisfied. There are reasons
for believing however that, even as a song-writer, Tannahill's
reputation suffered from the circumstances attending his
tragic end, which prevented his work from being judged
on its merits. For a man to put an end to himself was
then regarded as an unpardonable sin, precluding all hope
beyond the grave for the unfortunate victim. Aberration
of mind was not considered any palliation or excuse for
such an act, though, from a psychological point of view,
it is a direct negation of the normal state of the mental
functions—a fact not sufficiently recognised even at the
present day.

Having thus briefly endeavoured to rescue the reputation of Tannahill from the early bias which clouded his work and his memory, we proceed to notice one or two of his most famous songs. Among these there is the " Bonnie Wood o' Craigielea," which is far from being the least important of his lyrics. It has achieved a popularity greater than his very best, and has often been sung while the others have been neglected.

His description of Nature is realistic rather than romantic, and the introduction of the cushat, or wood-pigeon, is neither original nor incongruous, though unfamilar perhaps to southern ears. Burns introduced it, and several poets before him ; but making every allowance for poetical licence, it may be made a point of dispute whether Tannahill's simile is not the more appropriate of the two, and closer to Nature :—

> " Far ben thy dark plantin's shade,
> The cushat croodles am'rously."

Burns's reference is as follows :—

> " While through the braes the cushat croods
> With waefu' cry."

To Tannahill's lyrical gift may be added a fertile imagination, which is as necessary to the poet as it is to the novelist, and even the historian. In his songs he introduced many imaginary fair ones, and associated them with scenes and localities which he had never seen or visited. For instance, the locus of the " Lass o' Arranteenie " was unknown to him, yet there is nothing incongruous in the description of the scenery with which she is associated.

Again, there is " Jessie, the Flower o' Dunblane," one of his finest songs, which has had a popularity quite in keeping with its merits. Several of his commentators have endeavoured to associate it with Jenny Tennant, his lost love, but it may fairly be assumed that Jessie was quite an imaginary personage. Were there no other evidence to rest upon, its sentiment is quite inconsistent with the tone and spirit of "The Farewell" quoted above.

The song, "Gloomy Winter's noo awa'," was written for R. A. Smith, who adapted the words to the melody, and on its publication it immediately became a general favourite. In May, 1874, it was included in the programme of the Crathie Choir a few days before the celebration of the Tannahill Centenary, when that choir sang at Balmoral Castle in presence of Queen Victoria in honour of Her Majesty's birthday. "The Braes o' Balquhidder" was also a popular favourite in the Highlands, especially among the fair sex ; and D. T. Holmes, in his *Literary Tour in the Highlands and Islands of Scotland*, found that the people of Ross-shire placed Tannahill on a level with Shakespeare. This recalls the incident of the Scotsman who paid a visit to the Metropolis while John Home's tragedy of "Douglas" was staged in one of the London theatres. The country-man of the author was so carried away on witnessing the play that when the applause began to subside he was heard to exclaim at the top of his voice, "Whar's yer Wullie Shakespeare noo ?"

"Loudoun's Bonnie Woods and Braes" is also deserving of special mention. It was written in honour of the Marquis of Hastings on the occasion of his going abroad on military service soon after his marriage to the Countess of Loudoun. He was appointed Commander-in-Chief of the Forces in Scotland in view of the threatened invasion of Great Britain by Napoleon Bonaparte, then Consul of the French Republic. The Poet's native Paisley was among the first places which raised two regiments of volunteers. This song was one of the author's first favourites, though critical opinion scarcely endorses that view.

The once popular song, "O are ye sleeping, Maggie," first appeared in the *Glasgow Nightingale* in 1806, and if not the best, it was one of the most spontaneous effusions of the poet's muse, being composed while plying his rod and line in the river. The heroine of this song was not an imaginary fair one, as was the case in others of his songs, but Margaret Pollock, the author's own cousin on the mother's side.   If he was ever actually in love with her he evidently did not earnestly urge his suit, for she died with her maiden name unchanged.   "The Braes o' Gleniffer" also first appeared in the *Glasgow Nightingale* in 1806, and was set to music by John Ross, of Aberdeen. It was regarded by the inner circle of his literary associates as the best of all his poetical productions, and really the descriptive power and imagery throughout will rank among the finest flowers of Scottish poetry.

The songs here referred to are but a few samples of the author's productions, but they are among the choicest of his lyrics.   In addition to his songs of love and senti ment, he could sing on other keys with no faltering voice. He has written several amusing Bacchanalian songs, amongst which mav be mentioned the "Five Frien's," which is perhaps the most famous and amusing, and "The Coggie." The former was originally intended for private circulation only, and to enhance the humour the author represents himself as being "As blin' as an owl," which was not the case in reality, and must be put down as a poetical ex- aggeration, for he lived an exceptionally temperate life, and despised excess in others.   The following lines from his rhymed Epistle to his friend Alexander Borland, will best express his true sentiments on the subject :—

> Retired, disgusted, from the tavern roar,
> Where strong-lung'd ignorance does highest soar,
> Where silly ridicule is passed for wit,
> And shallow laughter takes her gaping fit ;
> Where selfish sophistry out-brother's sense,
> And lords it high at modesty's expense."

Again. there are in this connection the author's two Bacchanalian poems. "Scotch Drink" and the "Baccha- nalians," which may be mentioned in passing.

His Bacchanalian songs, as well as many other of his songs and poems, manifest a strong sense of humour, which makes it all the more puzzling to understand why. this sense did not save him from the tragic end which threw his native Paisley into a state of sadness and gloom. When the rising tide of the poet's reputation commenced to flow beyond the confines of his own literary circle, and when his love songs had begun to fascinate the blythe milkmaid and the artless young lassie at her spinning-wheel, the sad intelligence of his melancholy end arrested the flowing tide. On the 16th of May, 1810, Tannahill walked to Glasgow to see his friend Alexander Borland, with whom he had a long conversation, in the course of which his friend became alarmed by his incoherent and rambling speech. Observing it was vastly different from the clear and well-ordered speech of the Tannahill of other days, he resolved to accompany him to Paisley. When opposite Crookston Castle, almost at the spot where the Poet and the Ettrick Shepherd parted only a few weeks previously, he made an effort to break away from his friend. By this strange action Borland deemed it prudent not to leave him till he saw him safe in his mother's dwelling, with whom he had lived since he returned from Bolton. He was put to bed and left under his mother's care, who, unfortunately, dozed off to sleep on her vigil. About three o'clock in the morning she discovered that he had stolen from his bed and could not be found. An alarm was quickly raised, and a search made. At length his coat and watch were found on the bank of Caudren Burn, and his lifeless body, discovered near-by, was carried to his mother's house by five o'clock on Thursday morning, 17th May, 1810.

Thus terminated the career of one whose intellectual faculties should have been at their highest and best. From his high poetic gifts and past achievements, the world had reason to expect much more in the future, and this expectation would no doubt have been realised had it not been that a mind diseased thrust him into the merciless grip of relentless Fate.

WM. M'ILWRAITH.

THE SKINNER BI-CENTENARY.

ON the evening of Monday, 3rd October, 1921, under
the auspices of the Vernacular Circle of the London
Burns Club, a large and distinguished company met in
the Holborn Restaurant to do honour to the memory of
John Skinner.

Canon Wilkinson, Peterhead, who proposed the toast
of the evening, said that in Scotland that night many
grateful tributes were being paid to the memory of John
Skinner. At his own beloved village of Longside, half
a mile from the famous house of Linshart, his successor
in office was at that moment extolling the genius and
limning the personality of his great predecessor. But
none of those rejoicings had the significance of that
gathering in the heart of London ; for their commemoration was proof, if proof were needed, not only that
Skinner's place in literature was acknowledged far beyond
the boundaries of his own land, but that his message was
of that indomitable stuff which, like Betty Buchan's wincey
petticoat, would stand " soakin', and scourin', and wring-
in', and rubbin', and then be as gweed as on the day it
was made !"

No Miltonic Spirit.

Skinner was no Miltonic spirit who sounded his trumpet among the stars. He kept to the ingle-neuk and the
King's highway, where there were weel-kent faces and
friendly hearts ; and there with unerring insight he read
and interpreted and declared the character of his own
people and the conscience of his father's house. The
modern poet, with his feet in Piccadilly and his mind
sweeping the sands of Sahara for a new and startling simile,
might be pardoned if he failed to perceive the essential
greatness of a genius so beset with limitations that it
preferred to find its inspiration, not at the ends of the earth,

but at home.   For Skinner was undoubtedly a provincial. He was provincially born, provincially reared, provincially trained.   The high road to England was possibly too crowded for his liking ; but at any rate his honest brogues never ventured upon it, and only faint adumbrations of the great world-movements of his age penetrated the obscurity of his homely surroundings.   Indeed, practically the whole of his long life was passed in one Scottish county, and by far the greater part of it in one secluded corner of the shire.   " I'm a faur-traivelled man," boasted the Kirkintilloch shoemaker, " I've been twice tae Mullguy, and ance at Arran, and I've veesited the wife's mother at Auchtermuchty ;   and, eh, sirs, what an awfu' warld we leeve in !"   Skinner, being only a village parson and not a cosmopolitan shoemaker, did not attempt to envisage the universe from the reeking lums of Linshart ;   and therefore, thanks to the littleness of his environment, he saw less of the grandeur of the world, with its turmoil and its wickedness, and more of its simplicity, its tranquility, and its grace.   That was why in his writings there is no vast campus on which the forces of good and evil are arrayed in eternal rivalry, and no great peaks on which the devil strives for the mastery of man's soul.

Scottish Dialect Poetry.

This, indeed, was the strength, or weakness, just as they cared to regard it, of the great body of Scottish dialect poetry.   Their country was peculiarly rich in vernacular verse.   Every village had its laureate, every considerable township its little nest of singing-birds.   The output was tremendous and persistent, and inevitably there was much that did not rise or get beyond the boundaries of the parish.. Pegasus in the paddock had grace, sprightliness, and no small beauty ;   but his limitations were manifest even to himself, and they welcomed the splendid moment when he broke bounds and pranced bravely on the mountain side, where the winds of heaven played around him and the vision of the world was unrolled.   They knew, of course, that not all true poetry had this universal note, but they knew also that there could be no great poetry without it ; and that was one chief reason why, though Skinner was a fairly prolific writer and gave us many winsome thoughts alluringly expressed, it is simple truth to say that his fame rests almost exclusively on the " Ewie " and " Tullochgorum." The most fruitful themes of Scottish lyrical poetry had been threefold—bonnie bruilzies, bonnie sichts, and bonnie Jeans—in other words, the adventure of war : the wantonness and witchery of Nature ; and the love of a man for a maid : from Barbour to Burns and from Burns to Charles Murray they had enriched our literature and quickened the springs of our national life. But none of these themes inspired the pen of the poet-priest of Linshart. The " pomp and circumstance of glorious war " touched no responsive chord in his nature and set no thought aflame ; he never saw " the budding rose above the rose full blown," or if he did he let it bud unlyred ; and though the tender passion was real to him, real and beautiful, he chose not to sing of it, and turned to other loves that are no less inseparable from the human heart, and as precious to the understanding of every age. What Burns saw in the " wee, modest, crimson-tipped flower," Skinner saw in " our ewie wi' the crookit horn "—helplessness, innocence, simplicity ruthlessly done to death ; and he sang of it so wistfully, with such homely grace and couthy humour, that the pools of pity which lie deep among the bents of the Scottish character were stirred instantly by the compassion of his appeal. " Tullochgorum," on the other hand, is a song of sunny-hearted fellowship ; it lifts brotherhood out of the atmosphere of the coldly ethical, and reveals it as a neighbourly thing, full of the joy of life, of genial, understanding tolerance and of the charity that suffereth long and is kind. Thus, notwithstanding the limitations to which he had referred, John Skinner sounded two notes that had an eternal meaning and a universal range ; and the obscure village parson, the casual clinker of rhymes, became one of the most notable figures of his generation, a poet whose niche in the temple of remembrance and whose place in the hearts of his ain folk were assured till a' the seas gang dry.

The Theologian Turns Poet.

If disembodied spirits had chins to rub and minds that were capable of analysing their emotions, John Skinner's fingers must be busy and his thoughts in a " sair trauchle " as in the Land of Shades he pondered the ploy that a humorous but long-headed fate had played upon him. For if he ever hoped to win fame and the gratitude of posterity it was certainly not as the manufacturer and retailer of what he himself, in his " Epistle to a Young Bookseller," has called " a decent stock of poetrie." It was a relaxation " now and then to spin a line," but only a relaxation. Such modest expectations as he cherished pointed in an altogether different direction. The son of an accomplished parochial dominie who gave him an admirable grounding in the Latin tongue, he entered Marischal College, Aberdeen, at the age of thirteen, graduated four years later, and began at Kemnay a schoolmastering career which ended abruptly at Monymusk. There two things happened that not only influenced his immediate future but shaped his whole life—he " dropped into poetry " and embraced the tenets of Scottish Episcopacy. He (Canon Wilkinson) would not presume on their good nature by discussing at any length John Skinner's position in Scotland as a theologian and ecclesiastic ; but they would permit him to say this —that while his theology was now as dead as the dodo, it was during his lifetime a factor of first-rate importance in the religious and intellectual life of Aberdeenshire, while in the Church of his adoption his influence as an ecclesiastical statesman lingered unto this day. Honesty, sincerity, and utter fearlessness were not simply engraven on his character—they were woven into the woof and fibre of his personality ; and until they had grasped this primary fact, the man John Skinner must elude them. Destined for the ministry of the Scottish Establishment

he forsook for conscience' sake a life of dignity and comfort
to identify himself with a Church which had not even a
bare subsistence to offer to the majority of its clergy, a
Church, moreover, which since the abortive Jacobite rising
of 1715 had been under the continuous ban of the Government.   His sufferings would have broken the spirit and
soured the mind of a lesser man ; but John Skinner was
—Tullochgorum.   He had the capacity, as an old Peterhead worthy once said, of " adapting himsel' to the
suitabeelity o' the consequences "; and though he was
never the man to take dunts and forget to return them,
his philosophy of life was too broadly human, too genially
tolerant, to let the canker of bitterness eat into his soul.
At Longside he took to farming to eke out the scanty
emoluments of his office ; but the experiment was a ghastly
failure, and in the end he was glad to—-

> " Sell corn and cattle off ; pay every man ;
> Get rid of debts and duns as fast's I can ;
> Give up the farm and all its wants, and then,
> Betake me to the book and pen."

It was about this period that his two great songs were
written ; and, like nearly every line that came from his
pen, they were dashed off and put into circulation without
any thought of futurity.   Skinner indeed, as a poet, never
took himself seriously.   He wrote chiefly for friendship's
sake or to gratify the girls at Linshart—those lassies of
his who teased him for words to fit old tunes, and being a
good father, with an eye in his head and knowledge of
marriageable daughters' ways, he did his best on occasion
to provide them with material for the entertainment of
the village swains.   This explained the inequality of his
published writings ; and the speaker felt bound to say
that in his humble judgment those amiable persons who
in the past had been at pains to retrieve the *disjecta membra*
of his fugitive poems and publish them under his name,
had done his reputation a signal disservice.   Give me,
continued Canon Wilkinson, " Tullochgorum," " The Ewie
wi' the Crookit Horn," " John of Badenyon," and " The

Old Man's Song," and who will may have the rest, with the possible exception of two verses of "Lizzie Liberty." Among his non-lyrical pieces I give the place of honour to "The Monymusk Christmas Ba'ing," not because it is finished poetry, but for two very different reasons—first, because it is a wonderfully vivid description of village customs, village philosophy, and village character in the early years of the eighteenth century; and second, because it preserves inviolate those ancient forms of speech which were once the pride and are now rapidly becoming a mere reminiscence of the Scottish people :—

> " Has ne'er in a' this countra been
>   Sic shoudering and sic fa'ing,
> As happened but few ouks sinsyne,
>   Here at the Christmas ba'ing.
> At evening syne the fallows keen
>   Drank till the neist day's da'ing,
> Sae snell that some tint baith their een
>   And couldna pay their la'ing
>   Till the neist day."

What Scottish poet except Charles Murray could write to-day of " bumbees bizzing frae a bike," or describe so inimitably what happened when—

> " Francy Winsy steppit in,
>   A sauchin slivery slype,
> Ran forrat wi' a furious din,
>   And drew a swinging swype.
> But Tammy Norrie thought nae sin
>   To o'er him wi' a snype,
> Levell'd his nose flat wi' his chin,
>   And gart his swall'd een sype
>   Sawt tears that day "

The poem was a descriptive masterpiece in the pure vernacular, and reminded them of what they had lost, not only in forms of speech that were racy of the soil and steeped in the memories of an interesting historic past, but in the characteristics of life and thought which once they incarnated, are now only dimly and bemusedly expressed. They had lost more than they could ever hope fully to recover ; but at least, by the intelligent and loving study of such vernacular literature as had survived the undiscerning passion for " gentility," and the Anglicising influences in politics, letters, religion, and education that were steadily converting the sons of the sturdy North into base imitations of the West-end Edinburghian Scots —by such study, faithfully directed and zealously pursued, they might at least save for their children and their children's children something of the glamour, the romance, the beauty, the soft witcheries and the vivid directness of the ancient speech of an ancient people, the mither-tongue of the brave folk, the dear folk, the kind folk o' aul' lang syne.

In that goodly company the venerable and venerated figure of John Skinner took an honoured place. They saluted his memory—the memory of a great Scot, a true poet, and a man whose name was still a synonym in the North for honour and integrity, for loyalty to kith and kin, and for brave, buoyant, large-hearted humanity.

The other toasts included " Skinner's County," proposed by Colonel Sir James Cantlie, K.B.E., and responded to by Sir Edward Troup, K.C.B., K.C.V.O. ; and " The Vernacular Circle," proposed by Sir William Noble, and replied to by Mr John Douglas, F.S.A.(Scot.). The artistes were Mr Tom Kinniburgh, Miss Christine Gordon, Miss Muriel Macgregor, and Miss Maud Cooper.

COMMEMORATION AT LONGSIDE.

Longside, for the greater part of his lifetime the home of John Skinner, was fittingly chosen as the headquarters of the Tullochgorum Club, with his successor in office, the Rev. Canon Mackay, as the first President, Dr Wood as Vice-president, and Mr George Martin Gray as Secretary and Treasurer. Monday, 3rd October, 1921, was the two hundredth anniversary of the poet's birth ; and the inaugural dinner of the Club was held in S. John's Hall. There was a large attendance of members.

The President occupied the chair, and after the toast of "The King," proposed "The Memory of John Skinner." He said that Lord Rosebery in his *Miscellanies*, published the other day, speaks of the tropical tangle of centenaries that has grown up in recent years, but Lord Rosebery would be the last man to admit that any excuse was needed for the commemoration of the poet-parson of Linshart. Two hundred years ago on this date, John Skinner first saw the light of day among the hills of Birse. It has been said that every great man is the son of his mother, but Skinner's case was a notable exception. "A Mother! Ah! The venerable name which my young lips were never taught to frame" are the words in which he refers to the loss which he sustained when only two years of age. He therefore owed little or nothing to maternal guidance beyond the moulding process of his pre-natal training, but he was born to one great privilege, that of having as his father one of the class of old parochial schoolmasters of Scotland—a class that more than any other has made Scotland and Scotsmen what they are. His mother's death served to make him all the more the object of paternal care and affection, and as the bud of early life began to open and expand, his father was not slow to observe the latent spark of genius that was kindling within, and which was destined to burn so brightly in the coming man. Entering Marischal College as a bursar at the early age of thirteen, he passed with distinction through all the stages of the Arts curriculum graduated with honours when seventeen, and then, without a shilling in his pocket, went out into the world to make his living. Eighteen months of school-mastering at Kemnay and Monymusk, a year's tutoring in the far-off Shetlands, then back to his native shire to study theology with a view to entering the Ministry of the Church,. his ordination by Bishop Dunbar at Peterhead in 1742, and then a few months later his institution to the pastoral charge of the congregation of Longside, where in a position of genteel poverty he ministered for the long period of sixty-five years—

> " A man to all the country dear,
> And passing rich with forty pounds a year."

Such, in brief, are the leading landmarks in the life history of the man to the outstanding gifts and graces of which posterity will always do homage.

An Impressive Personality.

When we regard Skinner in his character as a man, there rises up before us a personality massive and impressive in its rich blend of indomitable courage, loyalty to conscience, indifference to worldly rewards and advantages, buoyant optimism and cheerfulness, and a fascinating genius for friendship. It required no small courage on the part of the young schoolmaster at Monymusk to give up the prospect of entering the pulpit and adorning the ministry of a rich Established Church, and to throw in his lot with a disestablished, impoverished, and persecuted religious body. " With his eyes open," as Bishop Mitchell remarks, " Skinner gave up the career as a parish minister to which his schoolmastering was meant to lead. and embraced a life of genteel poverty in which his great talents never received adequate scope or recognition." Not less, though of a different complexion, was the courage—which some people would regard as a tempting of Providence, but in his case the outcome of a buoyant optimism and trust—which led him while yet a stripling without a home or means of sustenance, to enter the bonds of matrimony, and then, leaving his young wife in the care of her father, returning to Aberdeenshire to settle down with a firlot of meal for his food and a barrowful of peats for fuel to prepare himself for the ministry.

When, after the Battle of Culloden, the storm of persecution burst upon his Church, and when (although he himself was no Jacobite) his house was pillaged and his chapel burnt, Skinner went calmly on, and even his six months' imprisonment in the jail of Aberdeen failed to crush his noble spirit or impair the vigour of his activities. It was this buoyant spirit animating him no less in adversity than in prosperity that endowed him with his great genius for friendship. Strong Churchman that he was, and ever ready to enter into a polemical duel, he never cherished any feeling of intolerance towards those who differed from him. One of the most pleasing pictures in his life of social intercourse is presented to us in the friendship which sprang up between himself and John Brown, the parish minister of Longside, a friendship which, with the exception of a temporary estrangement consequent on Skinner's suspicion of Mr Brown having been in league with the Lady of Kinmundry, at whose instigation soldiers were brought to Longside to burn down his chapel, continued till death. So close was their intimacy that they could afford to chaff each other even on their differences in religious practices without giving or taking offence.

Of Skinner as a parson and ecclesiastic, this is not the time or the place to say much, if anything. My sole object in briefly alluding to him in this capacity, is to show how he fulfilled the wishes of his father after he accepted the principles of Episcopacy. His defection from the Presbyterian Church was naturally a great disappointment to his father, who intended him for the Establishment Church, but instead of remonstrating with him, the worthy dominie expressed the fervent wish that his son might be sincere in his new profession, and do credit to the principles which he had adopted. How abundantly this wish was realised is well known to all, and to none more fully than to Skinner's own fellow-churchmen of the past and present generations.

As a scholar and writer, Skinner occupied a position of eminence in the literary world of his day. His ecclesiastical history, theological works, and his contributions to the *Encyclopædia Britannica* and to other contemporary writings of his time, all bear the stamp of ripe scholarship. But it is not as a historian or theologist or a controversialist that the name of Skinner is recalled with reverence to-day. It is as the " brother bard," and " the loon who did it " of Burns that he lives in the hearts of his countrymen. His love of poetry and his turn for poetical compositions were conspicuous at an early age. He was only seventeen years of age when he wrote " The Monymusk Christmas Ba'ing " —a poem full of graphic power and " Homeric vigour." This poem is perhaps the best example of the pure vernacular that the eighteenth century has produced. Its language is so archaically Scotch that few a hundred years ago, and fewer still to-day, could read it intelligently without the aid of a glossary. How many people are there to-day who could say right off what is meant by a " skypel skate," a " yap gilpy," or a " sauchin slype "? Notwithstanding that the " Ba'ing " was written in imitation of a poem by King James, it has considerable originality and great wealth of expression. What more delightful pen-picture of a football match as played in those days could we have than in the words :—

> " Like bumbees bizzing frae a bike
> Whan hirds their riggins tirr ;
> They yowff'd the ba' frae dyke to dyke
> Wi' unco speed and virr."

When the late Professor Geddes gave his estimation of Skinner as " a far-off second " to Burns, he was no doubt thinking of quantity more than of quality, forgetful of the fact that poetic composition was regarded by him only as an amusement, and further, that, being a clergyman, he could not use the same unrestrained freedom as Burns, either in the choice of his themes or in his treatment of them. Whatever may be thought of a number of songs which he tossed off at a moment's notice, there are two which stand out unchallenged in the estimation of all song lovers as being almost on a level with the best of Burns, namely, " Tullochgorum " and " The Ewie wi' the Crookit Horn," both of which called forth unstinted praise from Burns himself, who regarded the former as the " best Scotch song ever Scotland saw," and when on reading the latter, exclaimed, " Oh, an' I had the loon that did it." In praise of these two songs I cannot do better than quote the words of my friend, Canon Wilkinson, whose unrivalled knowledge of Skinner and his times, and his ardent admiration of his genius, enabled him to speak with an authority and with a sense of appreciation which few can exercise. "There are," he says, "few things in Scottish literature to match the joyous humanity, the buoyant ringing tolerance, and the lilt of couthly, canty fellowship in the one, and the pathos, the tenderness, the heart-wrung grief, and the over-flowing compassion of the other." The spirit of these songs will ever keep his name fresh and green, and produce a rich harvest of affection and admiration in the hearts of generations to come.

The toast was drunk in silence. Dr Wood proposed "Skinner's Church," which was replied to by the Bishop. "His Ain Folk" was spoken to by Captain A. M'D. Younie, and a letter was read from the Very Rev. John Skinner Wilson, D.D., formerly Dean of Edinburgh, from which we extract the following :—

"Aros, Strathtay, Perthshire.

"I understand that your Committee proposes to include among their toasts one to John Skinner of Linshart's 'ain folk.' They are a numerous body, composed, I hope, of men and women of whom he would not be ashamed.

"In 1807, when the old man was spending his closing days on earth with his second son and Bishop of Aberdeen, he had one of his great-grandchildren in his arms when he quoted from the Psalm (with a slight extension of the original) 'Yea, thou shalt see thy children's grandchildren, and peace upon Israel.' I have cherished the idea that the child in his arms may have been my mother, then a year old. It may, on the other hand, have been one of the children of John Skinner of Forfar, the Fourth John Skinner in his well-known list, whose humility he fanned by predicting (but not veraciously) 'the fourth shall be a fool.'

"Anyhow, the old man's memory is held in highest honour among his 'ain folk,' who have sprung from two of his grandsons, John Skinner of Forfar, Dean of Dunkeld, and William Skinner, who was Bishop of Aberdeen from 1816 to 1857. My mother was the only child of the latter.

" If I have drawn from her breast the spirit of Tullochgorum to a very limited degree, it has shown itself in me, not in poetic genius, nor in theological learning, nor in brilliance in conversation, nor in ready wit—in all of which he excelled—but solely in life-long devotion to that branch of the Church of Christ in Scotland of which he in his generation was the most distinguished of its clergy for wise and statemanlike vision. I have spent close on fifty years among these self-same pastoral duties in which he found his delight ; but my lines have fallen in pleasant places and in more prosperous days. May it be long before there is no descendant of his to carry on in the service of his Church. I have done my best to pass on the tradition.

" But besides the Skinner's and the Wilson's sprung from the stock of " Tullochgorum," and still at home, there are many others—Cummings in New York, Skinners in Canada and India, whose hearts will rejoice to learn that the old man's memory is being honoured in Longside on the bi-centenary of his birth.

" In the name of them all I beg to tender respectful thanks to the members of the ' Tullochgorum' Club for all they are doing to keep that memory green.—I am, yours faithfully, " J. S. WILSON, D.D."

" Tullochgorum " was sung by Mr J. S. Smith, and " The Ewie wi' the Crookit Horn " was recited by Mr G. M. Gray.

The following greeting was sent by the Secretary to the Vernacular Circle of the London Burns Club :—

" Dear brither Scots in Lunnon toon,
    Fa meet this nicht wi' pride to soun'
The praises o' oor Buchan loon,
      In speech and sang galorum ;
We greet ye a' richt cheerilie,
Richt cheerilie, richt cheerilie
      And pledge wi' a' decorum
Richt cheerilie, richt cheerilie,
The toast which aye baith you and we
Will honour till the day we dee
      The toast of Tullochgorum."

BURNS CLUBS AND BURNS'S SONGS

I WAS rather surprised lately to read in an article in the *Glasgow Herald*, entitled "A Scots Revival," that the London Robert Burns Club had just inaugurated a new departure in trying to create an interest amongst children in the Songs of Scotland. I am sure our good friends in London know, and acknowledge, that this is a work dear to the Burns Federation, which for many years has not only "done things," but has regularly presented an annual report on what had been accomplished.

Scotland is the greatest song-writing country in the world, and Burns is the greatest song-writer. When I use the word song I am speaking of the spontaneous and natural lyrics which no artiste need be ashamed of. The lilts of the Hebrides and the similar folk-songs of all lands are often charming, but tend to monotony and gloom, and I am of opinion that the worthy people who, during the past few years, have been striving hard to get us to admire these often fantastic fragments would be doing a better service to Scotland if they were content to "push" Burns, Lady Nairne, Scott, Hogg, Tannahill, and others at their best. For (as I shall try to show presently) of the 300 songs or thereby that Burns wrote, about one-half are never heard of in public, and others but seldom, though they *ought* to be sung into popularity.

The Burns cult had for a time a struggle for existence. It is true that Greenock founded a Burns Club in 1802, and that other towns soon followed the example, though only with qualified success. But when we review the dead years that followed Waterloo, the political excitements of the 'twenties and 'thirties, the hunger and misery of the 'forties and 'fifties, we are not surprised that song-singing was not much in vogue in Scotland. The publication of Carlyle's *Essay on Burns* in 1835 gave a new interest to Burns, and prepared the way for the triumphant celebrations of the Poet's Centenary in 1859.

But even after that there were set-backs. Following on the American Civil War came a mass of Transatlantic trash called "Christy Minstrelism," &c.—songs certainly, but of a kind not to be desired. These covered our country like a flood. The easy, tricky tunes, and the sickly sentimentality of the words, for the time thrust the grand but more difficult Scots songs to one side. It was one of these freaks of popular folly over which one can only groan in later years. Read such rubbish as " Annie Lisle," " The Prairie Flower," " In the hazel dell my Nelly's sleeping," and " Let me kiss him for his mother." In most of them the death of a sweet little cherub girl was absolutely essential; but in the nigger songs it was usually a grand old black man who went to Heaven, as in " Poor Old Jeff," " Poor Old Joe," and the rest of them. This minstrelsy was one of the worst " imports " ever obtained from America, followed in due course by Moody and Sankeyism (which, for a time, swept away our best hymns), freak religions, absurd social movements, and lastly, Prohibition.

In addition to the American invasion, Scots songs have had to compete in more recent years with equally sickly stuff from England, such as the " works " of Claribel, Weatherley, *et hoc genus omne*. It was one of those periods when " Scotch " was considered vulgar in Snobdom, and ignorant Scottish " mammas " taught their children to ape the worst forms of Cockneyese. Last of all, Burnsians had to contend with the latest thing (it was discovered in London) in " Scotch " Comedy ; but surely the persons who apply the time-honoured word " comedy " to the antics of music hall artistes don't know what they are talking about.

In face of all difficulties, I claim that Burns Clubs have kept the flag of Scottish song flying. I wish to say something about their work, especially in the direction of music. I have been going out and in among them for over thirty years in all four countries of the United Kingdom, and in my capacity as Secretary of the Glasgow

and District Burns Club Association and a Vice-president
of the Burns Federation, I am every day in touch with
Clubs over a great part of Scotland.

In Scotland, by the way, Burns's sovereignty is not
so strong geographically as one could wish. He is almost
unknown in the Highlands ; few Highlanders have ever
had much appreciation of Sassenach poetry. In the
Lowland North Burns has been heard of, but he is
hardly known beyond Aberdeen except amongst educated
people. His " Kingdom " really begins in the Kingdom
of Fife, and drawing a line from there to Dumbartonshire,
all South (including the Cowal district of Argyll) may be
described as Burns Country.' In the Border counties,
however, the Bard has strong " competitors " in Scott and
Hogg, and Burns Clubs are few.

The old taunt of " Haggis and Whisky " thrown at
Burns Clubs was in days gone by frequently justified, but
for years past it has been a pointless and baseless jeer.
The number of Clubs which have merely an annual dinner,
or supper, is steadily diminishing. A large number of
Scottish Clubs (also many Clubs in England, notably
London) are doing splendid work of varied quality, essay-
ing tasks at once patriotic, philanthropic, antiquarian,
literary, and artistic. And I am not sorry to see from the
numerous syllabuses published in the *Burns Chronicle,*
that Burnsians are everywhere alive to the propriety of
extending their literary horizon. They include not only
most Scots authors, but English and foreign ones as well.
Among the subjects discussed last session are John Galt,
Shakespearian Tragedy, Miss Ferrier's Novels, The Kail-
yarders. J. M. Barrie, Lord Byron, John Keats, Beranger,
and Heine. And in addition we have numerous papers
on social, political (non-party), and even religious subjects,
e.g., The Covenanters, The Scots Sabbath, &c.

I have sometimes thought that instead of calling our
institutions *Burns* Clubs, it would make a wider appeal if
we named them Caledonian or Scottish National Societies.
We have now Walter Scott Clubs, and R. L. Stevenson

Clubs, and it might be well if we tried to rope in all literary Scots into one common circle.

In addition to the lectures and papers, the talent now in evidence in Burns circles shews a vast improvement on what we found twenty years ago. Elocution is (unfortunately or otherwise) suffering from slump ; " Dunga Gin " and " Shannahan's Ould Shebeen " were for long bellowed at us with maddening monotony. But happily they are now laid on the shelf. There are, perhaps, not many good Scots pieces suitable for recitation at a festive gathering. " Tam o' Shanter " and " The Cottar " are too long for such a sederunt, but some of Burns's shorter poems, such as " Holy Willie's Prayer " and the " Address to the Deil " are sure to please if capably rendered. But save us from such mispronunciations as—

> " And scarcely had he Maggie *railed*,
> When out the hellish legion *sailed* ;

or,

> " But, let me whisper i' your lug,
> Ye're *Albion's* nae temptation,"

and others equally reprehensible.

With regard to the *Songs* my experience is that the City Clubs are not so faithful to the Poet as Country ones. There are some Clubs where, even now, Burns is seldom sung, and, when he is, we have the hackneyed (if anything of Burns can be called so) " Lea Rig " and " Willie brew'd." But worse than this, it is disappointing to find such doggerel songs as " The Cottage where Burns was Born " and " The Star o' Rabbie Burns " sung with amazing frequency. Burns Clubs should make it a point of honour to taboo such productions, as well as the bastard " Scots " songs—some of which have attained great popularity—*e.g.*, " Within a Mile o' Edinburgh toon," and others of like nature. There is, of course, a better type of Scots song which is of varying degrees of excellence in words and melody, *e.g.*, " Bonie Marv Hay," " Gloomy Winter," " Annie Laurie," " Mary of Argyle," &c., &c.

Twenty years ago I presided at a " Smoker " of a

large and prosperous Club. For an hour we had a spate
of the comic stuff of Harry Lauder, W. F. Frame Harry
Linn, and the music halls, and then the master of ceremonies handed me a slip legended " The Lea Rig." " Good
Heavens !" I said, " You must have made a mistake."
" Not at all ; it's a Burns song." " Exactly," I replied.
" That's my point ; a *Burns* song. Are you sure we can
stand it ?" The gentleman bestowed a withering look
on me, but later he made the *amende honorable* by sending
on more stuff from Mauchline and Dumfries. That kind
of thing is not so much in evidence now at Club meetings.

One respect in which many Burnsians are culpably
negligent is the loose way of rendering the master's words.
Take " Auld lang syne," for instance. In certain circles
nine times out of ten we get this fatuous rendering (second
couplet of first verse) : " Should auld acquaintance be
forgot, *For* the days of auld lang syne." The last line
of the chorus again is very frequently rendered " *For* the
days, &c." In the fourth verse " fiere " is nearly always
given as " frien." Then some obliging idiot often volunteers a new verse beginning " And you'll gang hame to your
ain hoose, and I'll gang hame to mine." Good Burnsians
must frown upon such innovations.

The " Lea Rig " is frequently mutilated. " *Altho'*
the nicht was eer," " And I was eer," &c. I have even
heard that line in " My Nannie's awa' "—" And listen the
lambkins that bleat o'er the braes "—rendered ridiculous by
the substitution of "lamb-skins" for little Mary's favourites ;
and once I heard a raucous voice shouting " Scots wi' wha
and Wallace bluid " as the first line of the immortal ode,
followed by an emendation on " *servile* chains," which
changed them into " silver " manacles.

But the worst outrage is on " Of a' the airts." The
mistakes begin with the first word " O," instead of " Of ";
and then verses that Burns never wrote are tagged on.
the most favoured containing that excruciating couplet :—

" And bring the lassie back to me
That's aye sae neat and clean."

No doubt some of the music books are to blame for the mistakes. I recently went over a music book published by an excellent firm, and Burns's songs were given with many irritating mistakes, *e.g.*, in " Oh, wert thou in the cauld blast," instead of " Thy bield " it read " Thy shield should be." The moral is—for the words consult the best editions, such as Dr Wallace's or Henley and Henderson's.

Burns's songs deal with patriotism, politics, social life, and love—especially the last. The love-songs are unique. They deal with the subject in all its phases. Sometimes the swain is the victim and sometimes the lass, and the sad ones have, as Sir Wm. Robertson Nicoll says, " an almost unendurable pathos "—*e.g.*

> " My fause lover staw my rose,
> And left the thorn wi' me."
>
> .   .   .   .
>
> " The wan moon is setting behind the white wave,
> And time is setting fast wi' me, oh."
>
> .   .   .   .
>
> " I hae parted wi' my love
> Never to meet again, my dear,
> Never to meet again.

And we have the joy of love, the majesty of it, the comfort of it, and also the fun of it. What better funny things, from the woman's point of view, can we have than " Last May a braw wooer "; or, from the man's point of view, than " Husband, husband, cease your strife "?

Judging from my experience of Burns Clubs, public concerts, and private parties, I should say that the most popular of all Burns's songs are " Auld lang syne," " Rantin', rovin' Robin," " Scots wha hae," " A man's a man," and " Willie brew'd." None of these concerns love. Of the love songs, those oftenest heard are the " Lea Rig " (easily the first, and not a bad choice), and " Of a' the airts." The other beautiful song in praise of Jean Armour (" Parnassus Hill ") is rarely heard. Next come two songs in honour of Clarinda (" Ae fond Kiss " and " My

Nannie's awa' "). The songs in memory of Mary Campbell are only rarely heard, and only one of the " Chloris "
songs is really popular.

The next hot favourites are " Bonnie Wee Thing,"
" Ye Banks and Braes " (but not the beautiful original
version which was Tennyson's favourite Burns song),
" Mary Morrison," " Oh, wert thou in the cauld blast,"
" Green grow the rashes," " Ay Waukin'," " O Whistle
and I'll come," " Last May a braw wooer," and " Corn
Rigs." These are all of the first class. Two of the Poet's
second-class songs, " The Lass o' Ballochmyle " and " Flow
gently, sweet Afton," are sung as often as any of the above,
and the same may be said of " Comin' thro' the Rye "—
an old song touched up, but still little better than doggerel.
However, as Henley truly remarks, it's the *motif*, or idea,
that counts most in a song. Given, he suggests, a hint,
a refrain, an idea, " and the song writes itself " Well,
very often it does, but it may not always turn out a gem
of Poesy.

A *secondary division* of good songs (and some are of
the finest) *rarely* sung, include " John Anderson," " My
love she's but," " Whistle o'er the lave o't," " Wandering
Willie," " Open the door," " I gaed a waefu' gate," the
two " Swan " songs, *e.g.*, " Here's a health " and " Fairest
maid on Devon banks," " A Hieland Lad," " The Farewell," " Somebody," " My Nannie, O," " Turn again,"
" Birks of Aberfeldy." " My heart's in the Highlands,"
" O luve will venture in," " She's a winsome wee thing,"
" O poortith cauld," " Come, let me take thee," " Wilt
thou be my dearie ?" " O wha is she ?" " Lay thy loof
in mine," " Here's a health to them that's awa," " Does
Haughty Gaul ?" and " This is no my ain lassie."

And I may give a *third division* of songs, which I have
never heard sung except amongst a few Burns enthusiasts,
some of them, again, of the very finest quality—*e.g.*, " Montgomery's Peggy," " Young Peggy," " Cessnock Banks,"
" The gloomy night," " Macpherson's farewell," " Stay,
my charmer," " Thickest night, surround," " The Plough-

man," " How long and weary," " Blythe was she," " Beware
o' bonnie Ann," " O May, thy morn," " The Braes o'
Ballochmyle," " There'll never be peace," " Thou hast me
forsaken," " Lord Gregory," " Gat ye me," " I'll ay ca'
in," " Logan Water," and " Phyllis the fair."

I am not forgetting that a number of Burns's finest
songs are set to difficult and exacting music—frequently
to old fiddle tunes. That is in some respects a misfortune.
Our modern composers would do a service if they could
give to some of the songs easier, but still characteristically
Scots settings, for, after all, it is the melody which catches
the public ear.

Mr Alexander Pollock, Glasgow, who looks after
School Competitions for the Burns Federation, and who is
always glad to assist Clubs in connection with these, has
an excellent lecture (illustrated) entitled, " The Lesser-
known Songs of Burns." If a few more enthusiasts
would follow his example, and press the claims of many
of these neglected gems, they would engage in a useful
and patriotic work.

The Music Hall is supposed to be a place mainly for
fun. It is believed to be good for worried business men
who, at the close of an anxious day, are not able to stomach
Shakespearian Tragedy, or even to have sufficient mental
equipment for an old English Comedy or one of the modern
masterpieces of Pinero, Masefield, or Galsworthy. If that
is so, what is wrong with Burns's humour ? Sir Harry
Lauder is a member of the London Robert Burns Club,
which has recently credited him with services to Scottish
song. I am sorry I have never heard of those services.
What Burns or other good Scottish song does the footlights
knight ever sing ? Surely it is not claimed that his
characteristic repertoire is Scottish song ? " Last May a
braw wooer " and " Whistle and I'll come tae ye," are
worth a wilderness of " Roamin' in the gloamin' " and
" I love a lassie."

I fear that many good Burnsians neglect the humorous
side of Burns, and love him exclusively on his tender and

pathetic side. This is a great mistake. Just let them take this list of rollicking ditties, and see what can be made of them : " O whistle, and I'll come tae ye," " Whistle o'er the lave o't," " Willie Wastle," " Duncan Gray," " I'm ower young to marry," " Duncan Davison," " Anna," " Findlay," " To daunton me," " Tibbie, I hae seen," "My love she's but a lassie," "There's a youth," " A Waukrife minnie," " Willie brew'd," " Rantin', rovin' Robin," " Naebody," " The weary pund," " The Deil's awa' wi' the Exciseman," " Here's to thy health, my bonnie lass," " Meg o' the Mill," &c.

In the old Scottish music hall Burns was by no means neglected. Davie Brown, Johnie Muir (both of Glasgow), and others, rendered real Scottish songs, I believe, quite adequately and with acceptance. But the modern variety theatre, with its amazing mixture of cross-talk comedians, ventriloquists, performing fleas, jugglers and wrestlers, seems to have little use for the melodies of old. Why then should not the Burns cult organise a travelling Scottish Choir on the lines of the famous old Glasgow Select Choir ? There will always be an audience for such if the thing be well done.

Finally, brethren, I would beg most seriously to say to the leaders of Burns Clubs everywhere (1) Support the Burns Federation in all its works and in no stinted, half-hearted way ; (2) Raise the standard of your Club and extend its literary and musical operations ; (3) Enlist the sympathies of your schoolmaster and his staff, and set agoing a School Competition—you will find the children eager to assist, and I have *never* found the slightest difficulty in collecting a few pounds for prize money ; (4) Insist on a high percentage of Burns's best at your concerts (whilst not forgetting the other Immortals of Caledonia), and frown fiercely and finally on the modern rubbish masquerading as " Scotch " comic song.

J. JEFFREY HUNTER.

man." " How long and weary," " Blythe was she," o' bonnie Ann." O May, thy morn," "The D Ballochmyle." " Lere'll never be peace." " Tho: 1 forsaken, " Lord Gregory," " Gat ye me." " I'll in." " Logan Watr," and " Phyllis the fair."

I am not foretting that a number of Burns': songs are set to difficult and exacting music—freq to old fiddle tunes That is in some respects a misfc Our modern comosers would do a service if they give to some of the songs easier. but still characteri Scots settings, for after all, it is the melody which the public ear.

Mr Alexandr Pollock. Glasgow. who look School Competitios for the Burns Federation, and always glad to asist Clubs in connection with th an excellent lectre (illustrated) entitled. "The 1 known Songs o Burns." If a few more enth: would follow his example, and press the claims of of these neglectd gems, they would engage in & and patriotic wok.

The Music lall is supposed to be a place ma: fun. It is believed to be good for worried busine: who, at the close f an anxious day, are not able to stc Shakespearian Tagedy, or even to have sufficient 1 equipment for a old English Comedy or one of the r: masterpieces of inero, Masefield, or Galsworthy. is so, what is vong with Burns's humour ? Sir Lauder is a meiber of the London Robert Burr which has recenty credited him with services to S song. I am sory I have never heard of those : What Burns or cher good Scottish song does the fc: knight ever sin ? Surely it is not claimed the characteristic reertoire is Scottish song ? "Last braw wooer " ad " Whistle and I'll come tae y worth a wilderess of " Roamin' in the gloamin' " I love a lassie'

I fear that many good Burnsians neglect the hu: side of Burns, ad love him exclusively on his ten:

pathetic side. ... ...
take this list of ... ...
made of them: "... ... ...
"Whistle o'er the lave o't," ... ...
Gray," "I'm owre young to ... ...
"Anna," "Findlay," "... ... ...
seen," "My love she's but a lass ..."
"A Waukrife minnie," "... ...
Robin," "Macherly," "... ...
awa' wi' the Exciseman," "... ...
lass," "Meg o' the Mill," &c.

In the old Scottish music itself Burns was ...
neglected. Dowie Dowus, Johnnie Faa, ...
and others, rendered and themselves ...
adequately and with ... ...
theatre, with its ... ...
ventriloquists, ...
seems to have little ... for the ...
then should not the Burns club ...
Choir on the lines of Sir ...
There will always be an audience for ...
well done.

Finally, brethren, I would ... ...
to the leaders of Burns Clubs ...
Burns Federation in all its works ...
hearted way: ... Burns the ...
extend its literary and musical ...
sympathies of your schoolmaster ...
aging a School Competition ... ...
eager to assist, and I have never ...
in collecting a few pounds for ...
on a high percentage of Burns ...
not forgetting the other ...
frown frankly and ...
quarreling as "...

man," "How long and weary," "Blythe was she," "Beware o' bonnie Ann," "O May, thy morn," "The Braes o' Ballochmyle," "There'll never be peace," "Thou hast me forsaken," "Lord Gregory," "Gat ye me," "I'll ay ca' in," "Logan Water," and "Phyllis the fair."

I am not forgetting that a number of Burns's finest songs are set to difficult and exacting music—frequently to old fiddle tunes. That is in some respects a misfortune. Our modern composers would do a service if they could give to some of the songs easier, but still characteristically Scots settings, for, after all, it is the melody which catches the public ear.

Mr Alexander Pollock, Glasgow, who looks after School Competitions for the Burns Federation, and who is always glad to assist Clubs in connection with these, has an excellent lecture (illustrated) entitled, "The Lesser-known Songs of Burns." If a few more enthusiasts would follow his example, and press the claims of many of these neglected gems, they would engage in a useful and patriotic work.

The Music Hall is supposed to be a place mainly for fun. It is believed to be good for worried business men who, at the close of an anxious day, are not able to stomach Shakespearian Tragedy, or even to have sufficient mental equipment for an old English Comedy or one of the modern masterpieces of Pinero, Masefield, or Galsworthy. If that is so, what is wrong with Burns's humour? Sir Harry Lauder is a member of the London Robert Burns Club, which has recently credited him with services to Scottish song. I am sorry I have never heard of those services. What Burns or other good Scottish song does the footlights knight ever sing? Surely it is not claimed that his characteristic repertoire is Scottish song? "Last May a braw wooer" and "Whistle and I'll come tae ye," are worth a wilderness of "Roamin' in the gloamin'" and "I love a lassie."

I fear that many good Burnsians neglect the humorous side of Burns, and love him exclusively on his tender and pathetic side.   This is a great mistake.   Just let them take this list of rollicking ditties, and see what can be made of them : " O whistle, and I'll come tae ye," " Whistle o'er the lave o't," " Willie Wastle," " Duncan Gray," " I'm ower young to marry," " Duncan Davison," " Anna," " Findlay," " To daunton me," "Tibbie, I hae seen," "My love she's but a lassie," "There's a youth," " A Waukrife minnie," " Willie brew'd," " Rantin', rovin' Robin," " Naebody," " The weary pund," " The Deil's awa' wi' the Exciseman," " Here's to thy health, my bonnie lass," " Meg o' the Mill," &c.

In the old Scottish music hall Burns was by no means neglected.   Davie Brown, Johnie Muir (both of Glasgow), and others, rendered real Scottish songs, I believe, quite adequately and with acceptance.   But the modern variety theatre, with its amazing mixture of cross-talk comedians, ventriloquists, performing fleas, jugglers and wrestlers, seems to have little use for the melodies of old.   Why then should not the Burns cult organise a travelling Scottish Choir on the lines of the famous old Glasgow Select Choir ? There will always be an audience for such if the thing be well done.

Finally, brethren, I would beg most seriously to say to the leaders of Burns Clubs everywhere (1) Support the Burns Federation in all its works and in no stinted, half-hearted way ;   (2) Raise the standard of your Club and extend its literary and musical operations ;   (3) Enlist the sympathies of your schoolmaster and his staff, and set agoing a School Competition—you will find the children eager to assist, and I have *never* found the slightest difficulty in collecting a few pounds for prize money ;   (4) Insist on a high percentage of Burns's best at your concerts (whilst not forgetting the other Immortals of Caledonia), and frown fiercely and finally on the modern rubbish mas-querading as " Scotch " comic song.

J. JEFFREY HUNTER.

GLENRIDDELL.

" Unchanged, thence pass'd Deloraine,
To ancient Riddell's fair domain."
—*The Lay of the Last Minstrel.*

THE antiquity and importance of the family of Riddell is written large in Scottish family records, and shews a descent from Gervase de Ridel, a Norman Baron, who accompanied David I. from England (*circa* 1225), and who, from the King's hand, received the appointment of Sheriff of Roxburghshire, together with grants of land in the neighbourhood.

To Walter, son of Gervase, passed the possession of his father's lands in Roxburghshire, and from these lands was formed the Barony of Glenriddell, from which the Dumfriesshire Glenriddell was long afterwards to take its name.

Down the long years many family events of importance occurred, of which, perhaps, the most outstanding was the creation by Charles I., in 1628, of John Riddell of Riddell a Baronet.

Sir John was succeeded in the title by his son Walter, whose second son, William, became an advocate at the Scottish Bar, and who later inherited Glenriddell.

In his turn, William Riddell was succeeded by his son Walter, whose marriage, in 1694, with Catherine, daughter of Sir Robert Laurie of Maxwelton, brought the family connection into touch with Dumfriesshire and the Ellisland district, a bond which was strengthened by the purchase of a property in the Dumfriesshire parish of Glencairn.

This property, a possession of the Cunningham family, which had come into the market, was the Barony of Snade, originally known as Gilmoreston. For purposes of sale, it was divided into two lots, one-half going to John Laurie of Maxwelton, father of Sir Robert. The other portion, and that which contained the old baronial residence, was purchased by Walter Riddell; and following upon a family custom, it was renamed Glenriddell, after the original family seat.

To Walter and Catherine Riddell, in this quiet country home, were born two sons and two daughters, the elder son, Robert, in course of time succeeding to the estate, and somewhere about the year 1731 an alliance was formed with another family, well-known in the annals of Burns story, by his marriage with Jean, daughter of Alexander Fergusson of Craigdarroch.

From this marriage a large family followed (three sons and seven daughters, it is said); but several of these young people seem to have died. Certainly the sons did not survive, for upon one of the daughters, Annie, descended the succession; and she it was, who. by her marriage into yet another branch of the Riddell family, became the mother of Robert and Walter Riddell, the friends and contemporaries of Burns.

On the father's side the family descent is quite as interesting to follow out.

In the neighbouring Parish of Tynron there had lived and laboured a man of strong personality, Simon Riddell, the parish minister, descended from the Riddells of Roxburghshire. A Master of Arts, he was licensed by the Presbytery of Jedburgh in 1699, and received a call to Tynron the following year.

The troubles of the " 'Fifteen " proved the manner of man he was. Briefly told, the memory of the persecution at the hands of the Stuarts in the South of Scotland was too recent and vivid to lead to any support to the scheme for their restoration. No sooner, indeed, were the seeds of rebellion sown than, under Alexander Fergusson of Craigdarroch, a band of loyal and influential gentlemen of the district gathered themselves together to oppose it heart and soul, among whom was the sturdy and zealous minister, and, at the head of a body of his parishioners, he marched to Stirling to aid in the defence of his Majesty and the religious faith he had been trained to teach.

In less strenuous times, Simon Riddell had married a Miss Riddell of Newhouse (also of Roxburghshire), and to them there was born an only son, Walter, of the same fearless temperament as his father, who was destined to play a considerable part in the later rebellion of the " 'Forty-five.''

As heir to his father, Walter inherited the property of Newhouse, in Roxburghshire, and is styled " Walter Riddell, of Newhouse.'' Following his marriage with Annie Riddell, the heiress of Glenriddell, he acquired, by right of his wife, not only Glenriddell, but the adjacent properties of Carse (Friars') and Lincluden, in the neighbouring Parish of Irongray.

Glance for a moment now at the connection of Walter Riddell with the Jacobite affair of the " 'Forty-five,'' and here it may be said that when the rebellion broke out Riddell appears to have been in trade in the neighbouring town of Dumfries, as he is referred to in the historical account of the occupation of that town by Prince Charlie, as one of the merchant councillors.

The retreat from Derby had taken place. At Longtown the rebels crossed the Esk, where they divided into two portions, one proceeding north ; the other, the main body, marching upon Dumfries, which was entered without opposition.

The situation may be briefly summed up by the quotation of an extract from a letter from James Fergusson, jun., of Craigdarroch, Commissioner to the Duke of Queensberry (28th December, 1746) :—" At Dumfries they behaved very rudely, stript everybody almost of their shoes, obliged the town to grant them £1000 and a considerable quantity of shoes, and carried away Provost Crosbie and Mr Walter Riddell, merchants, as hostages for £1000 more.''

Ex-Provost Crosbie of Holm (afterwards known as Goldielea, and later, Woodley Park), with Walter Riddell of Glenriddell, were taken on to Glasgow. The balance of the £2000, however, soon followed, and they were then enabled to return home, not much the worse for their adventure.

To Walter and Annie Riddell, in this Dumfriesshire
home of Glenriddell several children were born, two of
these destined to play a part, as we shall more fully see,
in the life-story of Burns. Robert, the eldest, afterwards
to become the antiquary, was born 3rd October, 1755 ;
while Walter, afterwards of Woodley Park, was born 4th
March, 1764. Allusion may also be made to a sister
(Elinor or Sophy), who died unmarried in 1797, for doubtless this was the Miss——, to whom Burns, after the death
of Robert Riddell, wrote the touching letter from Dumfries
(May or June, 1794), requesting the return of what is now
the first volume of the Glenriddell MSS. This letter is
regularly associated with the name of Miss Woodley, but
the two sisters of Marie Riddell had been married long
before—Frances in 1784, and Harriet in 1788.

Mention must also be made of a third brother, Alexander
John, who died at Hampton Court, 24th June, 1804, without
issue, and who was styled " Esquire of Glenriddell."

Walter Riddell, the father, survived to a good old
age, dying in the year 1788. He was naturally succeeded
by Robert, his oldest son, who, preferring Friars' Carse,
in which he had resided since his marriage in 1784, disposed
of the property of Glenriddell in 1792.

A fragment of this old home of the Riddells may
still be seen. Passing from the picturesque little station
of Dunscore, on the Dumfries and Moniaive Railway, the
high road is left, and the Cairn crossed by the footbridge
a mile away. The site will be found close to the farmhouse
of Snade, almost encircled by a group of yew trees ; and
on the northern aspect a double row may be distinguished,
indicating the original approach to the house.

Purchased by the Society for the Propagation of
Christian Knowledge in Edinburgh, the property now
belongs to the Governors of the Trust for Education in
the Highlands and Islands of Scotland.

Dr J. MAXWELL WOOD.

SHENSTONE AND BURNS

I N a letter to Mrs Dunlop, of 7th February, 1791,
Burns says :—

> " Any new idea on the business is not to be expected. It
> is well if we can place an old idea in a new light."

Such an expression of opinion on the limitations of
originality and invention is interesting, as it shews how
the Poet would have regarded an idea, and what literary
use he would make of it, and, as a guide, it ought to be kept
in mind when considering the effects of ideas and the use
Burns put them to.

The Poet may possibly have been aware that, as a
matter of scientific fact, there is not such a thing possible
as Invention in the vulgar understanding of the word.
All inventions are but a recombination of what has already
been, and any attempt to seek to invest Burns with a halo
of metaphysical glory is doing the intensely human Burns
an injustice, and detracting from the social man, whose
fondest and constant wish through life was to see " all
tears wiped away from all eyes." Burns's life is not like
Shakespeare's, " unguessed at." It has been " weel
ryped " open, and after all his imperfections have been
exposed he still lives in the hearts' core of humanity.

At any rate, Burns's admission that he can only place
an old idea in a new light, takes the sting out of any charge
of pilfering that critics of the Henley order have insistently
drawn attention to.

Shenstone, in his first Essay on " Man and Manners,"
remarks :—

> " It is with real concern that I observe many persons of
> true poetical genius endeavouring to quench their *native fire*,
> that they may exhibit *learning* without a single *spark of it.*"

It is not far-fetched to say that Burns must have had this in his mind when he wrote the lines :—

> " Gie me ae spark o' Nature's fire
> That's a' the learnin' I desire."

This is only one of the many instances where the sense of a passage by Shenstone is transmuted into the pithier expression of Burns, and sometimes with added beauty, as in the case of the somewhat " mean " lines from Shenstone's Elegy XII. :—

> " The star of Venus ushers in the day,
> When other stars their friendly beams resign."

This becomes in Burns's poetry :—

> " Thou ling'ring star, with less'ning ray
> That lov'st to greet the early morn,
> Again thou usher'st in the day."

If the object of true literature is to interpret feeling and convey emotion, the above two passages illustrate degrees of emotion that characterise utterances by Shenstone and Burns.

Another striking similarity may be found when comparing the lines in Shenstone's Elegy I. with Burns, page 1, Elegy X.—

> " At noon the poor mechanic wanders home,
> Collects the square, the level, and the line "—

with the picture of—

> " The toil-worn cottar from his labour goes,
> Collects his spades, his mattocks, and his hoes."

Logie Robertson, in his *Furth of Scotland*, draws attention to Elegy VII., and particularly to the passage :—

> " Stranger, amidst this pealing rain,
> Benighted, lonesome, whither wouldst thou stray ?
> Does Wealth or Power thy weary step constrain ?"

with the passage in " Man was made to mourn " :—

> " Young stranger, whither wand'rest thou ?
> Dost thirst of wealth thy step constrain."

Also in " Man was made to mourn," the phrase "Manhood's active might " is to be found in Shenstone's Eleventh Elegy.

This Seventh Elegy was commented upon by Isaac D'Israeli :—

> " This fanciful subject was not chosen capriciously, but sprang from an incident. Once, on his way to Cheltenham, Shenstone missed his road, and wandered till late at night among the Cotswold Hills ; on this occasion he appears to have made a moral reflection, which we find in his *Essays* :—
>
> ' How melancholy is it to travel late upon any ambitious project on a winter's night, and observe the light of cottages, where all the unambitious people are warm and happy, or at rest in their beds.' "

This fanciful idea or moral reflection must have been very " dear " to Burns's heart, and Dugald Stewart's remarks upon Burns add interest to the reflection :—

> " The variety of his engagements while in Edinburgh, prevented me from seeing him so often as I could have wished. In the course of the spring he called on me once or twice, at my request early in the morning, and walked with me to the Braid Hills, in the neighbourhood of the town, when he charmed me still more by his private conversation than he had ever done in company. He was passionately fond of the beauties of Nature ; and I recollect once he told me, when I was admiring a distant prospect in one of our morning walks, that the sight of so many smoking cottages gave a pleasure to his mind, which none could understand who had not witnessed, like himself, the happiness and worth which they contained."

In fact, the whole *motif* of the Seventh Elegy finds an echo in the execution of the " Cottar's Saturday Night."

Again, this elegy is in the Poet's mind when he writes to Mrs Dunlop on the 15th January, 1787. Burns, then in the zenith of his popularity in Edinburgh, and fearful of the fate that the future had in store for him, introduces a reflection to remarks by a line from this same elegy. The quotation is :—

> " ' And when proud Fortune's ebbing tide recedes,' you will bear me witness that, when my bubble of fame was at the highest,

I stood unintoxicated with the inebriating cup in my hand, looking forward with rueful resolve to the hastening time when the blow of Calumny should dash it to the ground, with all the eagerness of vengeful triumph."

The next verse in the Seventh Elegy is :—

> " Too proud with servile tone to deign address
> Too mean to think that honours are my due ;
> Yet should some patron yield my store to bless,
> I sure should deem my boundless thanks were few."

A similar coupling of pride and servility is to be found in Burns's letter to the Earl of Eglinton, in January, 1787 :—

> " Selfish ingratitude I hope I am incapable of ; and mercenary servility, I trust, I shall ever have so much honest pride as to detest."

And about the same time he writes to Mrs Dunlop :—

> " For my part, Madam, I trust I have too much pride for servility, and too little prudence for selfishness."

The sentiment of the line—

> " Check not my speed where social joys invite,"

requires no comparison in the often-expressed sentiments of Burns.

Taken over all, the Seventh Elegy must have made a considerable impression on the memory of the Scottish Poet.

The whole of the Eleventh Elegy, in which Shenstone complains " How soon the pleasing novelty of life is over," must have been the direct inspiration for a letter from Burns to Richard Brown, of 24th February, 1788. In both elegy and letter life is compared to a " Faery scene," and the line—

> " O Youth, enchanting stage, profusely blest,"

is quoted as from the elegy. The letter also says that " almost all that deserves the name of enjoyment or pleasure is only a charming delusion ; and in comes repining age, in all the gravity of hoary wisdom, and wretchedly chases away the bewitching phantom." This is a paraphrase of the lines in the Elegy :—

> " But now 'tis o'er, the dear delusion's o'er,
> Not Science shall extort that dear delight
> Which gay Delusion gave the tender mind."

The tenderness and affectionate disposition of Shenstone would naturally appeal to Burns, and the quotation from Burns's letter to Peter Hill, on 2nd March, 1790 :—

> " Even the knaves who have injured me, I would oblige them ; though, to tell the truth, it would be more out of vengeance, to show them that I was independent of and above them, not out of the overflowing of my benevolence,"

is an adaptation of the peculiar kind of revenge that Shenstone indicates in paragraph 51 of his " Man and Manners " :—

> " The only kind of revenge which a man of sense need take upon a scoundrel, is, by a series of worthy behaviour, to force him to admire and esteem his name, and yet irritate his animosity by declining a reconciliation. As Sir John Falstaff might say, ' Turning even quarrels to commodity.' "

Burns, writing to Mrs Dunlop on 16th August, 1788, says :—

> " I could indulge these reflections till my humour could ferment into the most acid chagrin that would corrode the very thread of life,"

an idea of chemical action that he very likely got from the following observation of Shenstone, p. 116 :—

> " A poet that fails in writing, becomes fast a morose critic. The weak and insipid white-wine makes at length excellent vinegar."

A direct similarity occurs, when Burns in writing to Gavin Hamilton, April, 1788, says :—

> " The language of refusal is to me the most difficult thing on earth."

This expression, it is obvious, he must have got from Shenstone's—

" Not Hebrew, Arabic, Syriac, Coptic, not even the Chinese language, seems half so difficult to me as the *language of refusal*."

Whether Burns was conversant with Dodsley's description of Shenstone's *ferme ornée* " The Leasowes " is not very evident, but when we find that one of Shenstone's inscriptions, " at the bottom of a large root on the side of a slope," contains—

" The trout bedropp'd with crimson stains,"

one is inclined, though the same idea occurs in other Georgian poets, to conclude that Burns might have taken his description from Shenstone, for in " Tam Samson's Elegy " we find the words :—

" Trouts bedropp'd wi' crimson hail."

The word " bedropp'd " is common to both.

Burns may have perused Shenstone's letters, but a perusal of them does not suggest any ideas that Burns may have benefited from that are not used also in his observations upon " Man and Manners."

l Similarities, of course, may be found in the letters, but these are not frequent enough to repay research, and may be neglected.

One authority has it that Burns was largely influenced by Shenstone's " Schoolmistress " as regards the rhyme and theme and rhythm. Such coincidences or similarities as we find common to both are not very numerous, and to say that Burns took the Spenserian stanza from Shenstone is open to doubt, when we consider that Mrs Dunlop tells Burns that he taught her to know Spenser : and in Thomson's works, which Burns acquired simultaneously with Shenstone's at Kirkoswald, there is the " Castle of Indolence " in true Spenserian stanza. Yet there is undoubtedly more than a hazy idea and a sough between the " Cottar's Saturday Night " and the " Schoolmistress." The expression "modest worth" applied to the School Dame, is also applied to Coila in the "Vision, and "russet weed" is used by Burns in contradistinction to "silk" in the lines "Written in Friars' Carse Hermitage," to indicate modest position in the world. Still one can only bring oneself to the opinion that, whatever influence Shenstone's "Schoolmistress" had on Burns, such influence is not so marked as other similarities cited.

Claims have been made as to the greater influence of Shenstone's "Schoolmistress" or Fergusson's "Farmer's Ingle" on the "Cottar's Saturday Night." These contentions exhibit in different aspects two kinds of influence of different classes of poets on Burns's literary work. When a solution is sought of the question—where did Burns get his ideas to clothe in a new light?—we must recognise the influence of Shenstone as of a different kind from that he derived from Ramsay and Fergusson. The relationship of Burns and Fergusson is almost, one might say, personal. Burns and Fergusson belonged to the same era and the same stage. Fergusson died only thirteen years before Burns came to Edinburgh. Burns addresses Fergusson in homely and affectionate terms as "My elder brother in misfortune, by far my elder brother in the Muses." Such a familiar term of affinity would be absurd, indeed untrue, if applied to Shenstone.

Burns knew Shenstone as a popular poet and a cultured man, with all the advantages of an Oxford education. He also recognised in Shenstone's life and works the social man of tender and sincere feeling, combined with a simplicity and a love of truth. Burns's envisaging of Shenstone was not that of a man he could be familiar with yet could love and respect in the abstract. He did not find in Shenstone models for the plots of "Tam o' Shanter" or the "Cottar's Saturday Night." He rather looked to Shenstone's essay on "Man and Manners" for moral and philosophical reflections. In these respects the influences were different—on the one hand, the homely influences of his Scottish poetical forebears, and on the other, the educative influences of such poets as Shenstone, Crabbe, and Goldsmith, and others of the early Georgian era shed their influences or conveyed ideas.

In Elegy VII. we have :—

> " 'Tis no Italian song nor senseless ditty cheers
> the vernal tree,"

and in Elegy IX. :—

> " Nor boast the produce of Peruvian mines,
> Nor with Italian sounds deceive the day."

Compare those two references to Italian music with the line in the " Cottar's Saturday Night "—

> " Compared with these, Italian trills are tame,"

and, without enquiries whether Shenstone and Burns interested themselves in the contemporaneous discussion on the merits of the French and Italian Schools, it is evident that they both preferred the tunes of their native country to any foreign innovation. In this predilection they were joined by Fergusson in his Elegy on " Scots Music," where " the sounds fresh from Italy " are called " a bastard breed."

Allusions to Peruvian mines are to be found in Burns. In the " Vision " he says :—

> " And trust me not Potosi's mine."

It would be hypercritical to discount this allusion because Potosi happened to be in Bolivia and not Peru.

Other allusions to Potosi will be found in the apostrophe to " Frugality," in a letter to Peter Hill, of 2nd April, 1789.

It is curious to note that Shenstone, in one of his best-known poems, " Nancy of the Vale," describes " Her leg so taper, straight and fair," while Burns's Coila in the " Vision," is described as " Sae taper, tight and clean," so that one is inclined to think that the lilt of the one description infected the other.

In Shenstone's " Man and Manners " there occurs, in contiguity, two lines :—

" When thou are from me every place is desert."

" Surely Paradise is round me."

These lines from Otway's " Tragedy of the Unhappy Marriage " might be got by Burns from Otway's poem direct, but there is also the possibility of the two lines in Shenstone's essay suggesting the line :—

" That desert were a Paradise if thou wert there."

If one felt inclined to give further points of similarity, many more quotations could be found. To show the influence of Shenstone on Burns enough has possibly been said.

These three articles have been a labour of love and a source of information to the writer. He is surprised to find that a certain critic, and a well-known student of Burns, objected strongly to them because they might detract from Burns's reputation.

The writer, speaking for himself, has not found his admiration for the Poet or the man diminished in the slightest as the result of a research which has proved delightful as a literary exercise. Rather the contrary, and he would no more think of accusing Burns of pilfering than he would of accusing Shakespeare of stealing the play of " Hamlet " from " *The Historia Danica of Saxo Grammaticus.*"

A. J. CRAIG.

HIGHLAND MARY'S RE-INTERMENT

(13th November, 1920).

LEAVING THE MORTUARY.

ON THE WAY TO THE NEW GRAVE.

THE END OF AN OLD SONG.

" An honest man was Duncan Dow ; his native place was Glendaruel,
A wee bit hallan in the west, some miles ayont the hills o' Cowal ;
But whaur he's frae it mak's nae odds, be it Mull or Skye or be it
Cary,
Some auchty years hae slipped awa' since he dug the grave o'
Highland Mary.
Then, if e'er ye gang tae Greenock toon, an'd hae a half-an-hoor
tae tarry,
Gang wast intae the auld kirkyard and see the grave o' Highland
Mary "

THOSE simple lines, popular in the early 'seventies
of last century, no longer apply. The song is out
of date, and a revised version called for. The Old West
Kirkyard no longer contains the resting-place of Highland
Mary.

On the forenoon of Monday, 8th November, 1920,
the grave dug by honest Duncan Dow away back in the
eighteenth century was again opened, this time not to be.
filled in again. That which had formed its contents was,
with reverent care, transferred to Greenock Cemetery,
for interment in a new place of sepulture prepared for its
reception.

The work of transference was carried out under the
personal direction of Mr Robert Sheridan, Superintendent
of Cemetery and Parks, his staff including Messrs Hugh
Campbell, Robert Chalmers, William Elliot, Robert Alcorn,
and Patrick Boyle. There were also present :—Ex-Bailie
William Hillhouse Carmichael, Convener of Cemetery and
Parks Committee ; and Mr James Christie, Chief Constable,
Greenock Corporation ; Mr Ninian M'Whannel, F.R.I.,
B.A., Burns Federation ; Messrs Duncan M'Callum, Junior
Vice-President ; Arch. MacPhail, Director ; Thomas
Graham, Musical Director ;- George B. Grieve, O.B.E.,
Honorary Secretary, Greenock Burns Club ; and Mr Charles

G. Macara—fourteen persons all told. The surface of the ground had been removed as the first of the Burns contingent arrived, and already several small bones found.

The excavation took two hours, four men relieving each other in turns. Four large boxes were provided for the earth, and a small box to hold any bones or remains. The proceedings were carried through decently and in order. The grave was only four feet deep, stopping at the gravel and clay. Three skulls were unearthed, as well as a number of thigh and smaller bones, and part of a jaw bone with four teeth in a good state of preservation, also some human remains which were black and quite hard. One got a better idea of the number of interments from the considerable quantity of wood unearthed.

At the foot of the grave the bottom of an infant's coffin was found. This to appearance had been interred at a later period, the wood being quite sound. The unusual experience was suggestive of the well-known scene in " Hamlet," as the grave-diggers from time to time paused in their discovery of now an arm or thigh bone, again a jawbone, and anon a skull.

Standing by the opened grave, glancing backwards over the dim past, there may be discerned the shadowy forms of pilgrims from many lands, near and far, directing their steps to this spot ; generation following generation, led by Burns's guiding star to the place hallowed by his genius. Here until recently stood the memorial stone erected by loving hearts to mark, for ever as they fondly imagined, the shrine of Highland Mary. But changes great have taken place in Greenock town since then, and no more shall the pilgrims come hither to muse on the Poet's inspired words :—

> " O Mary ! dear departed shade !
> Where is thy place of blissful rest ?
> See'st thou thy lover lowly laid ?
> Hear'st thou the groans that rend his breast ?"

The place that knew them shall know them no more.

To what uses this spot of earth may be put we know not, but "Forward though we canna see, we guess and fear." It may be an entrance through which in times of prosperity shall pass thousands of eager, bustling workers to the great industrial hive within to ply their various crafts, or to which, when "times are bad," may come bands of unhappy pilgrims, weary and dejected because no man hireth them, begging "a brother of the earth to give them leave to toil," exemplifying Burns's conception of Life's saddest sight, a man seeking for work. At this place where once might be carved in stone Burns's undying lines, "To Mary in Heaven," perchance may be erected a dismal study in black and white paint, "To workmen in search of employment." What a fall was there, my countrymen!

The men stooping over their spades, the solitary aspect, and the church spire showing distant in the grey haze, impart a touch of Millet's "Angelus" to the scene. The hour of noon is at hand, and, in imagination, the bell in the old tower may almost be heard, faint and low, calling from worldly thoughts to meditation in paths of pleasantness and peace, and to blissful forgetfulness of life's toil and strife.

But only for a moment. The spell is quickly broken, and the dreamers rudely recalled to reality by a loud blast from a giant trombone close by. It is the sound of the dinner horn proclaiming a brief respite to the builders of ships. Its nearness also acts as a rough reminder to grave-digger and looker-on alike, that they are almost trespassers on territory dedicated and devoted to the service of a strange new order. They are but a few paces from the borderland of a mysterious region in which an army of alchemists is at work, transmuting coal and iron and lives into gold, directed, controlled, and dominated by an all-conquering force designated *The Spirit of Modern Commercialism*. To this spirit the words "love" and "friendship" are meaningless sounds. It impatiently sweeps sentiment aside. It scoffs and laughs alike at the Psalms of David and the songs of Burns. It is the destroying angel at whose blighting approach the living and the dead, the Church and the tombs, must go west but to whose high priests and blind votaries, as to heretics outwith its pale, the kirkyard must ultimately and inevitably have the last word :—

> " Let them troll in pleasure or toilfully spin,
> I gather them in—I gather them in."

The work of disinterment goes steadily and silently on, and soon is at an end. The men lay their spades aside ; their work is done. Those Burnsians who have waited get ready to leave. With their leave-taking the long, hitherto unbroken, line of devotees is broken at last. They are the last of the pilgrims to this place, so long tended with jealous, loving care.

The shrine is gone !

Soon shall the fragrant birch and hawthorn hoar give place to towering cranes and derricks, and ere long the steam whistle shriek where once the birds sang love on every spray.

Never again may the singer as of old lilt the lines :—

> " Gang wast intae the auld kirkyard
> And see the grave o' Highland Mary."

The end of an old song.

ARCH. MacPHAIL,

Greenock Burns Club.

THE STORY OF THE KILMARNOCK BURNS
TEMPLE HOAX.

[As all feeling in connection with this incident, save amusement, has evaporated, the following account can wound the susceptibilities of none of the actors in it.—(ED.)

THE *History of Kilmarnock* (1911) makes no distinct reference to the Burns Temple except to say that the chief hoaxer resigned his seat in the Town Council, was re-elected the following year, and raised to the position of Dean of Guild—surely an appropriate honour. A résumé of the events leading up to this will give the lovers of the ludicrous a fuller understanding of our amusing narrative. On Saturday, 29th August, 1903, Mr Andrew Carnegie of Skibo Castle arrived in Kilmarnock in answer to the combined invitation of our Civic and Educational Authorities. He received the Freedom of the Burgh, laid the memorial stone of the Loanhead School, and was afterwards entertained to dinner. All went well till a delicate hint from the chairman informed Mr Carnegie that he would now have an opportunity to part with a modicum of his £60,000,000. "You have spoiled my day," was the unexpected answer of the millionaire, and the subsequent proceedings interested him no more. The reply affected some of our humorists to such an extent that they resolved to have revenge, and thus originated the Burns Temple Hoax. Viewed from this standpoint the sequence of events which followed was natural and logical, and may be briefly summarised. The concocting of the plot, the composing of the epistle, and its reproduction on paper that gave a semblance of authority by employing a typewriter in one of the public offices, were alike simple and easily accomplished. The reception and acceptance of the epistle as genuine, by the Council, public, and

Press, was enthusiastic. The subsequent elucidation of the mystery, together with the confession of the perpetrator, were inevitable; but who shall say that a temple more glorious than that outlined may not one day adorn the ancient town of St. Marnock, thereby proving that truth is stranger than fiction. As for the gentleman who shouldered the responsibility, and to whom consequently the honour is due, one may venture to amend the well-known couplet, and say :—

> " The *jesting* that men do lives after them.
> The rest is oft interred with their bones."

One memorable night eighteen years ago, the Amalgamated Civic Galoots held a special meeting to decide the momentous question whether Burns should have a temple or a pyramid.

Now I shall not give the names of the humorous conspirators, nor will I reveal the spot at which their meetings took place; suffice it to say, that if the whole of us get our deserts we'll all be there soon enough.

That night in Kilmarnock there was concocted a sensation that caused the whole inhabitants of the civilised world to realise that they possessed risible faculties, with the exception of one millionaire whose name will be forgotten while that of the chief humorist will live in the Pantheon of burlesque. This Burns Temple proved no evanescent pleasantry, but a perennial jest that has never been surpassed even in the House of Commons, whose members are paid to provide us with entertainment. The laughter was so great everywhere that it was forgot, for the time being, that the Gulf Stream would be frozen in a million years and mangold-wurzel extinct. Thanks to a learned member of the Galoots, who spoke with contempt of Michael Angelo and Sir Christopher Wren, it was known that the ancients always erected temples to their great men and women, who had in their time contributed to the party funds, and who in the course of time were created deities. The brilliant idea of building one to Burns that would ensure him divine honours was proposed, seconded, and carried *nemine contradicentur* amid manifestations of sorely over-strained diaphragms.

Temples were built and adorned with all possible splendour, as can be read by those so inclined of the one erected by King Solomon, who employed 30,000 men for seven years in its construction. His anti-porcine subjects disliked the great monarch's levies in men and money as much as their offspring do Noah for calling one of his sons Ham, without specification of its constituent elements. *Tempus fugit*, and now, it is said, there is not a stone, precious or otherwise, left to tell the tale. But the Burns Temple was a half-million job, and Solomon had not the advantage of Portland cement and the 8-hours' day. As yet, there is no such building to attract hordes of pilgrims to Kilmarnock, but any respectable citizen suffering in the vicinity of the Cross, the morning after the night before, will be glad to show the stranger within our gates the hypothetical site at Braehead.

Theodore Hook and his friends were the world's practical jokers, *par excellence*, till succeeded by our Amalgamated Galoots, who surpassed their predecessors' greatest efforts. This is how they did it. On the memorable night of February, 1904, the Town Clerk read the following communication to a full meeting of the Town Council :—

"THE PUBLIC LIBRARY, GEORGE IV. BRIDGE,
EDINBURGH, 9th February, 1904.

THE PROVOST OF KILMARNOCK,

DEAR SIR,—I have just received word by this mail that Mr Carnegie, who was deeply impressed with the progressive tendencies of Kilmarnock during his recent visit, has had under consideration a project of more closely identifying the town with the name of our National Bard. He recognises Kilmarnock as the Mecca of Burns lore, where the peerless poems were first published to the world, and where all literature associated with his honourable name has been carefully compiled and widely disseminated. Mr Carnegie has therefore decided to erect at his own cost, within the town of Kilmarnock, a temple to the memory of our national pride, provided the Town Council will grant a free site. It is his intention to make the memorial a most elaborate one, the building to be constructed of granite, white marble, or some superior material, and to be of magnificent design, while the interior will contain statues of Burns contemporaries, and the principal characters of his creation, and under the dome a chaste figure of the immortal genius will stand. Artistic panels will embellish the walls, illustrative of scenes depicted in his poems, and the whole building will be lavishly treated at a cost not exceeding £500,000. While Mr Carnegie will retain in his own hands the plans and details of construction, he wishes the management of the temple to be vested in a committee of trustees, consisting of the Provost, Magistrates, and three of the people's representatives in the Town Council ; the president, vice-president, secretary, and other three members of the Kilmarnock Burns Club ; and the Editor of the *Burns Chronicle*. In selecting a site, Mr Carnegie has confidence in the judgment of the Kilmarnock Town Council, but when in Kilmarnock he was impressed with a commanding position at the entrance of your Park, opposite to Tam Samson's house ; imposing flights of steps could be led up to the structure and made add to the effect.

Mr Carnegie will be glad to learn if the Kilmarnock Town Council are prepared to entertain the conditions of this gift, so that he can make the necessary arrangements for immediately proceeding therewith.—Yours faithfully,

HEW MORRISON (per J. C.)."

The perusal of the above document, needless to say, was received with acclamation, and Mr Carnegie was accorded an enthusiastic vote of thanks, amid cheers that might have been heard at Skibo Castle. At the same time there were men present, and one of them a Magistrate, who knew that the letter just read was bogus. Then was the psychological moment for an honest confession, which would have received hilarious absolution, but the chief hoaxer remained silent, the far-reaching effects of the joke depriving him of his usual presence of mind as he slowly —too slowly—realised them. The next morning Kilmarnock wakened up and found itself famous ; though people with no sense of humour said, infamous. Dr Hew Morrison, Mr Carnegie's confidential agent, wrote to the Chief Magistrate—

" DEAR PROVOST,—I offer my sympathy in this wretched and silly hoax, which, I learned last night at 11.30, has been perpetrated upon you ; a hoax which I think not only silly, but an insult to the people of the town over which you worthily preside. I at once repudiated the letter, and characterised it as an impudent and cruel hoax. I am very much distressed that such a trick should have been so far successful."

The makers of artificial thunder, who might have given the real temple a short paragraph. now treated the spurious one to columns, and there was quite a renaissance of burlesque. The local and district papers were filled with letters breathing sanguinary reprisals on the hoaxer, and hinting at the suppression of the Habeas Corpus Act. The chief local worshippers of the National Bard were all suspected of the forgery, whether they loved him for the first Kilmarnock edition, which had so increased in value, or from the gastronomical motives kindly suggested by Mr Henley.

The mystery, for a time, remained unsolved, but at length the lawyers met and, by the system of Sherlock Holmes, traced the culprits to their lair. A typewritten letter like the one that deceived the Town Council naturally suggested a typewriter, and on examining the various machines in town the identical one was found. The chief conspirator, emulating Coriolanus, now came manfully forward and said—" Alone I did it ! " This was the truth, but not all the truth, and the plea was accepted with a solatium of £50, and expressions of regret. The local papers called the hoax " an audacious and unscrupulous outrage," but it may be said for the Amalgamated Galoots—

> " They sat in folly side by side,
> And caused much idle chaff,
> But their excuse is good enough,
> They caused the world to laugh."

JOHN AITKEN
Author of *Humours of Ayrshire*

BURNS AND THE BEGGARS.

IT is part of a poet's reward that he is able, by the force of his genius, to confer a kind of immortality on many things that might else be lost in oblivion. The light of his imagination first illuminates, then fixes in a permanent focus, features in the life of his time in a fashion that can never be forgotten. Thus he lays posterity under an obligation from which it can never be free and for which it should be eternally grateful. The poetry of Burns passes this high test of genius triumphantly; for one of the proofs of the enduring merit of his power over the minds of men clearly lies in the faithful remembrance with which we cherish to-day the portrait of the Cottar with his simple faith, or the lovely landscape of the Doon ; nor can we forget, because he has enshrined them in immortal verse, the worth and independence of Scottish character, the value and reality of Scottish religion, and the life and manners of Scottish peasantry in the eighteenth century. To him, along with one other, falls the honour of having unfolded, so that he who runs might read, the secret greatness of those qualities which have created an historic race in Northern latitudes.

We find a further illustration of this fact in the happy and characteristic fashion in which Burns has deftly caught and preserved for us some of the most picturesque features of what was already in his day a dying race—we mean that race which acknowledged no King, which claimed no country for its own, which regarded no law save that of hunger, which bowed before no authority save that of misfortune, and which claimed no fellowship save that of a common want. In bygone days the beggars of Scotland had been a hardy and a numerous people, healthily free from many of the vices which disgraced and degraded their successors. But in Burns's time, as his Cantata " The Jolly Beggars " reveals, they had fallen upon evil fortune and dwindled until only the last, and worst, and most parasitic type remained.

In the chance which led the Poet to Poosie Nancy's on that winter night when the wild blast of Boreas had driven to their humble shelter for an evening's merriment the "randie gangrel bodies" of the road, we must recognise the good hand of Fortune.   It gave him the opportunity, which he was quick to seize, of recording for the future, where otherwise lay complete forgetfulness, some of the best elements in this fast-disappearing race, who

> "Ranged a' from Tweed to Spey,
> An' lived like lords and ladies gay."

Herded together by the "bitter skyte" of hailstones and the bite of "infant frosts," he found a mixed assembly. Here was the Sons of Mars with the "auld red rags"— signs of his former glory—still hanging unwillingly upon him ; beside him the Merry Andrew that "tumbles for sport," and is a fool by profession ; the "raucle carlin wha kent fu' weel to cleek the sterling," but who could yet sing with infinite pathos the ballad of the "waefu' woodie"; the "pigmy scraper, wi' his fiddle, wha used at trysts and fairs to driddle," but who lacks the courage to face a "sturdy caird" armed with his rusty rapier.   Truly a "mountebank squad !"   They had little in common save rags, roguery, and unsavouriness, yet they provided Burns with an inspiration for his Muse.

Is it too much to assert that he saw in this company the last remnant of what was once an honourable race ? The time had been when the "Wight o' Homer's craft" had lived without reproach or shame.   Once the wandering minstrel, even when "infirm and old," had needed not to beg "his bread from door to door."   For him the gate stood always open in welcome, and lords or commons wearied not in listening to his lay.   Then "a gentle trade indeed" it was "to carry the gaberlunzie on."   Com- passion was lavished upon the blind Sons of Tobit and Timaeus ; nor did authority look sternly upon poor Tom o' Bedlam who enlivened the countryside with his mad song.

The cripple or paralytic was carried from farm to farm with the same care and regularity as the stage conveyed its travellers from one post to another. All these found crust and clothing and kindness wherever they chanced to wander. The Lords of Little Egypt lived in something that resembled a regal state, while cairds and tinklers, fiddlers and gaberlunzies, minstrels and mountebanks, rejoiced in an easy tolerance. No one counted it a disgrace when a Scottish King assumed the " blue-gown badge and claithing." The " aumos dish "—a wooden vessel carried for broken meats and oatmeal—the " mealy bags and knapsack a' in order," the horn or fiddle or staff, even the " orra duds " were a passport to the pity and the pockets of a generation which had not forgotten to be charitable. But now—

> " Old times were changed, old manners gone ;
> The bigots of the iron time
> Had called his harmless art a crime,"

and with the minstrel every wanderer passed beneath the frown and ban of Society. The better and more honest types soon vanished and, as Burns wrote in " A Winter Night," the sons of affliction became brothers " in distress." One feature, however, remained which was worth preserving. The vigilant eye of the Poet perceived it as he watched the carouse of the beggarly rant that filled the kitchen. Prowling tinklers they might be, thievish cairds, mis-shapen fiddlers, rough, daft, or wretched, but the freemasonry of the road had handed down to them from their forebears a traditional gift of song. With this they were able and wont to defy " Daddy Care " with such success that they could bid him " Whistle o'er the lave o't." The last vestiges of an ancient minstrelsy lingered in their recollection. Of each one it might be said—

> " He had nae wish but to be glad,
> Nor want but when he thirsted,
> He hated nought but to be sad,
> And thus the Muse suggested
> His sang that night "

Perhaps none but a genuine poet could have detected the
native gift which lay hidden beneath such an unpromising
exterior, or discovered that the "Jolly Beggars" drew
their melody from so reputable a spring. His own fate
had taught him to honour

> " The bard of no regard
> Wi' gentle folks and a' that,"

just as his unstilted and unstinted genius enabled him
to recognise a fellow-poet in the one who could say—

> " I never drank the Muse's stank (pool),
> Castalia's burn, and a' that ·
> But there it streams, and richly reams,
> My Helicon I ca' that."

The true test of the singer's power lay in the fascination
which, like the Pied Piper of Hamelin, he exercised over
" the glowran byke (staring swarm) " that, following, he
drew " frae town to town."

So then Burns adds another debt to the many which
we owe him. He has fixed for ever this one last glimpse
of a fading and fugitive company. Would any other
have brought to the task such large-heartedness, such quick
sympathy ? Was there not in Burns something that drew
him into instinctive fellowship with the flotsam and jetsam
of Society ? Scattered through his poems we have lines
which seem to bear this out. Thus, in the Epistle to
Davie, he says " the best o' chiels are whiles in want,"
showing that he knew too well the pinching poverty which
lightened the never heavy wallet of the beggar. In the
same poem he numbers himself among those " wha drudge
and drive thro' wet and dry," fathoming yet another
experience of the vagrant. And had he not also the
Wanderlust in his own veins ? For in the Second Epistle
he exclaims—

> " Of a' the thoughtless sons of men.
> Commen' me to the bardie clan,
> Nae thought, nae view, nae scheme of livin',
> Nae cares to gi'e us joy or grievin'—
> But just the pouchie put the nieve in
> An' while aught's there."

That he had thought of such a life and found much to recommend its liberty, we gather from the Second Epistle to Lapraik, in which occurs this prayer—

> " O Thou wha gi'es us each guid gift,
> Gi'e me o' wit an' sense a lift,
> Then turn me, if Thou please, adrift
> Through Scotland wide."

No one could better appreciate the life which reduces its wants to a minimum, or the power of Nature to console its child for what the world and Fortune denied, than Robert Burns. Light in pocket, light of heart, he was himself the Prince of Beggars ; he had all the insignia of the royal minstrel clan, and with them found fellowship. Whatever happiness he had, came to him as he sought the woods and hills, and only when he freed himself from convention or restraint could he find the inspiration which bade him say

> " I'll be merry and free,
> I'll be sad for naebody,
> If naebody care for me,
> I'll care for naebody."

It is in the genuine spirit of healthy vagabondage that he pledges the toast—

> " Here's to budgets, bags, and wallets !
> Here's to all the wandering train !"

N. FARQUHAR ORR, B.A., B.D.

UNVEILING OF ROBERT BURNS STATUE AT DETROIT.

ON 23rd July, 1921, Royal Tanist Colonel Walter Scott unveiled a statue of Robert Burns in the city of Detriot amid scenes of enthusiasm never to be forgotten by any of that vast gathering of American Scots. This is an event of which the Order of Scottish Clans may well feel inordinately proud. It seems fitting that a tribute of respect be paid Past Royal Deputy Edward Goodwillie, who originated the plan and worked indefatigably to carry it to a successful issue. That statue standing in beautiful Cass Park is a monument not only to our National Bard, but a monument to Scottish perseverance and steadfast fidelity to a Herculean task. Brother Goodwillie laid the foundation of his work by compiling a book on the Burns Statues that is world-wide in its scope. In spite of all difficulties, he started out with splendid courage to present the city of Detroit with one of the finest statues of the " Poet of Humanity" that has ever been erected, and his heart must have swelled with the pride of achievement, as he turned the statue out to Mayor Couzens as a gift to the city of Detroit.

In 1912 Goodwillie organised the Burns Club, and has been its president continuously. At the same time Mrs Goodwillie ably seconded her husband's efforts by forming the Jean Armour Club, which under her presidency has laboured all these years wholeheartedly for the success of the great work. Inspiring and cheery when the hours were darkest, only the indominable courage of the Scot could have carried the work through the dark days of 1914. When the war-clouds swept over us and the storm broke over the world, Detroit was a border city, and when the

call to arms sounded, the Scots crossed to Canada and cast
in their lot with the Motherland. The sons and daughters
of Scotia gave themselves and all they had to the cause.
and the statue had to take second place. But when the
storm-clouds had been swept away, their work was resumed
and carried to a successful finish. We, as Clansmen, feel
proud that, in spite of the tremendous handicap, Scottish
grit made possible what Mayor Couzens said was the greatest
day Detroit had ever seen. It is peculiar that the very
busy men, the men of big affairs, are always the men who
have time to do something for their fellow-men. Brother
Goodwillie is chief chemist of the greatest chemical company
in this country, and devotion to his work has placed him
where every minute of his time is full of problems that
call for his best thought; and time devoted to this labour
of love must of necessity have been taken from his leisure
hours and the lamp must have burned many hours in his
study as he wrought out his plans to honour Burns and
Scotland. Fortunately for him and his work, Mrs Goodwillie was just as full of enthusiasm. She inspired every
Scotswoman with whom she came in contact.

Belonging to a family of sculptors, the Royal Deputy
was peculiarly qualified to pass judgment on the Burns
Statues already erected, and give to Detroit what is probably the finest in the world. Early in his campaign
he succeeded in enlisting the interest of the Royal Tanist,
and if there is a busier man in America or a more loyal
Scot nobody has ever found him, yet he found time to
give his loyal support to Brother Goodwillie's work, and it
must have been a proud moment for him when he saw
the wheels of industry stopped and the streets filled with
a happy multitude doing honour to the land he loves and
her matchless Burns. The photographer fortunately
caught him with that eager happy smile as he read a tele-
gram of regret from the Vice-President of this great land,
who deemed it a high honour to have been invited to honour
Robert Burns. That the Order of Scottish Clans has

men in its membership of the calbre of Walter Scott and
Edward Goodwillie is an indication of its worth, and should
be an inspiration to every member to devote himself with
unswerving loyalty to his Clan and the Order.

R. K. YOUNG.

HONORABLY DISCHARGED

May 16th, 1921.

Thanks be to God, who gave me in my day
Youth, strength, and nerve sufficient for the hour.
Out of the Army ;   none can take away
The memory of duty done, and power
Used in good faith to serve my country's need.
Thanks be to God, who gave me in my time
To watch the bombing-squadrons eastward speed—
The flame and thunder of that night sublime
Before we broke the Hun at Saint Mihiel
Were worth ten years of life.   And now to know
Of faced and conquered fear—bullet and shell,
Gas, darkness of the night and savage foe ;
    Wounded and lame, discharged to take my chance
    Against whole men, thank God I fought in France !

CAPTAIN DOUGLAS.

Washington. U.S.A.

BURNS AND THE KINGDOM OF FIFE.

IN his *History of Scotland*, published in 1582, George Buchanan states that "all the country between the Forth and the Tay grows narrow like a wedge eastwards even to the sea, and it is called Fife, a district provided within its own bounds with all things necessary for the use of life." It will be observed that, as defined by this ancient historian, Fife includes more territory than is contained in the present county. The greater part of Clackmannan and Kinross is included "in the country between the Forth and the Tay." In the early days of Scottish history the Earls of Fife were among the greatest in the land, and the antiquity of the title is proved by the fact that the first chief or "Maormor" of Fife was no other than that Macduff who was the enemy of Macbeth, whom he defeated in 1056. Fife was one of the seven provinces into which all Scotland was divided previous to the 13th century, and this accounts for the name "Kingdom" which is still applied to it. In this connection, it is of interest to note that the arms of the ancient Earls were almost identical with those of the Kings of Scotland, being "a red lion rampant on a golden field."

Burns would catch his first glimpse of the "Kingdom' when he entered Edinburgh, 28th November, 1787. From that day until he left the Capital some months later, Fife must have been more or less always before his eyes, yet one is rather surprised to find that neither in letter nor in poem is there a single reference to the Firth of Forth or to the country lying to the north of it. We have the testimony of Nasmyth that Burns much enjoyed the prospect from the top of Arthur's Seat. The two often had a walk there while the first "Nasmyth" was being painted, but so far not a line has been discovered in which he wrote of the charms of the land and seascape. One might have expected that the islands of the Forth, "the emeralds chased in gold " of Sir Walter Scott, might have roused his muse, more especially as Fergusson, whom Burns regarded as his master, had already celebrated the most prominent in lines of beauty. Scott Douglas conjectures that Burns must have paid a visit to the " Fifian coast through the medium of the pleasure smacks that plied betwixt Leith and Pettycur." Such trips seem to have been the " correct thing " for visitors to Edinburgh in the latter end of the 18th century, but, as I have already said, we have no evidence that Burns followed the fashion.

It was not until after his second visit to Edinburgh that we find any reference to Fife in the works of Burns. In the diary he kept when on his Highland tour we find the following under date 25th August, 1787 : " Pleasant distant view of Dunfermline, and the rest of the fertile coast of Fife as we go down to that dirty, ugly place, Borrowstouness." Burns, it will be noticed, mentions the fertility of Fife, a fertility which was at that time proverbial. Pennant, who visited the county just fifteen years earlier, writes thus : " The peninsula of Fife, a county so populous that, excepting the environs of Loudon, scarce one in South Britain can vie with it, fertile in soil, abundant in cattle, happy in collieries, in iron, stone, lime, and freestone, blest in manufactures, the property remarkably well divided, none insultingly powerful to distress and often depopulate a county—the most of the fortunes of a useful mediocrity."

It was not long till the Bard was on the borders of the " Kingdom." The entry in his diary for 27th August reads : " Go to Harvieston, Mrs Hamilton and family, Mrs Chalmers, Mrs Shields. Go to see Cauldron Linn and Rumbling Brig and the Deil's Mill. Return in the evening to Stirling." Harvieston lies in the valley of the Devon in Clackmannanshire, and the Mrs Hamilton whom the Poet met there was the stepmother of his friend and landlord, Gavin Hamilton, of Mauchline. The short notice in the dairy is supplemented somewhat by a letter written to Gavin Hamilton from Stirling. There is little in the letter about the scenery, though there is a good deal about the persons he had met, and he sums up his experiences in the words, " One of the most pleasant days I ever had in my life." On his return from this tour Burns passed through the " Kingdom." He left Perth on Saturday, September 15, and passing by Endermay, where he dined, he came that evening to Kinross, where he spent the night. Next morning he left there and travelled to North Queensferry, where he crossed the Forth. The extract from his diary runs : " Pass through a cold, barren country to Queensferry—dine—cross the ferry, and on to Edinburgh." The extract shows us that the Poet had realised the truth of King James' words regarding this part of Scotland, " Fife is a beggar's mantle with a fringe of gold." Doubtless the Bard would follow the old highwav still known as the Great North Road. It was then in a very different condition to what it is now, for, writing just a few years after the Poet's visit, Dr Thomson, of Markinch (a nephew of the Poet of " The Seasons ") declares that the wretched conditions of the road was among the chief obstacles to improvement in the county. The road runs from North Queensferry through the ancient burgh of Inverkeithing (a burgh in the days of Alexander I., 1107-1124), and heads in a north-easterly direction. It does not touch the burgh of Dunfermline, though for some distance it forms the eastern boundary of the parish, evidence of its ancient origin.

So far then, our National Poet does not appear to have been greatly impressed by our county, and though in the letters written from Edinburgh after his return there are references to many of the places he visited, there do not appear to be any regarding the places immediately north of the Firth, although it is possible we have one in the lines—

" Not Gowrie's rich valley, nor Forth's sunny shores,
To me hae the charms of yon wild mossy moors."

It was no great time, however, till the Poet was across the Forth again. In Dr Currie's " Life " there is an account

given of a visit paid by Burns to Harvieston and Ochter-
tyre in company with Dr Adair, the son of a physician
in Ayr. Dr Adair (who was related to Mrs Dunlop) places
this visit in August, 1787, but a somewhat later date must
be assigned to it. Most probably it took place in the
following October. This proved a rather eventful journey
for the Doctor, for at Harvieston he was introduced by
Burns to Miss Charlotte Hamilton, whom he married in
1789. Miss Hamilton was a half-sister of Gavin Hamilton,
and it was in her honour that the Bard wrote the lines—

"" How pleasant the banks of the clear winding Devon,
    With green spreading bushes and flow'rs blooming fair !·
But the bonniest flow'r on the banks of the Devon
Was once a sweet bud on the braes of the Ayr.''

It is interesting to note that in the last days of his life the
Bard's thoughts turned to the few days spent on Devon's
banks, and the last poem he ever wrote was one in praise
of Miss Hamilton, then Mrs Adair—

" Fairest maid on Devon Banks."

While at Harvieston the two visitors were storm-stayed,
but apparently the great floods did not keep them indoors,
for Dr Adair records excursions to Castle Campbell at Dollar,
the Cauldron Linn, and Rumbling Brig. He expresses
some surprise that none of these scenes should have called
forth the exertions of Burns's muse. " I doubt," he adds,
" if he had much taste for the picturesque." It was while
on this tour that the famous visit was paid to Mrs Bruce,
of Clackmannan, who claimed—not that she was sprung
from the family of the hero King of Scotland—but that
the latter was sprung from her family. She possessed what
were alleged to be the helmet and two-handed sword which
belonged to King Robert, and with the latter she conferred
the order of knighthood on the Poet, doubtless pleasing
him greatly with the remark that she had a better right
to confer that title than " some people." The old lady
was the last of her particular line (which, it may be mentioned, was descended from a Sir Robert Bruce whom David

II., in a charter, designated "his beloved and faithful cousin "). When she died it was found that she had bequeathed the sword and helmet to the then Earl of Elgin—also a Bruce—and they are still preserved at the family seat at Broomhall, Dunfermline.

Ere they returned to Edinburgh the two travellers, Burns and Adair, visited the city of Malcolm and Margaret. They travelled *via* Kinross, where it has been conjectured

" Dumferline Abbey, in Fifeshire."

Burns wanted to see once again the island fortress which had been the prison of Queen Mary.

" At Dunfermline," says Dr Adair, " we visited the ruined Abbey and the Abbey Church, now consecrated to Presbyterian worship. Here I mounted the cutty stool, or stool of repentance, assuming the character of a penitent for fornication, while Burns from the pulpit addressed to me a ludicrous reproof and exhortation, parodied from that which had been delivered to himself in Ayrshire, where he had, as he assured me, been one of seven (the Mauchline Session Records say five) who had mounted the seat of

shame together.   In the churchyard two broad flag-stones
mark the grave of Robert Bruce, for whose memory Burns
had more than common veneration.   He knelt and kissed
the stone with sacred fervour, and heartily (*suus ut mos
erat*) execrated the worse than Gothic neglect of the first
of Scottish heroes.   The portion of the Abbey Church
then in use was that now known as the Old Abbey.   It
was originally the Parish Church of Dunfermline, and
continued to be so until the opening of the new church in
1821.   The new portion covers the site of the former Abbey
Church, for it has to be remembered that in pre-Reformation
times there were two churches here, though both were under
the one roof.   The Parish Church formed the nave, and
the Conventual or Abbey Church formed the choir of the
building.   After the Reformation there was no need for
the Abbey Church, as the monks had all gone; and as the
lands which provided the funds for its upkeep were seized
by neighbouring landlords, it soon fell into ruins, though
had there been a Carnegie one hundred years ago it might
have been restored.   The last portions of the Abbey
Church (with the exception of St. Margaret's Shrine, which
is still in existence) were removed in 1818 to make room
for the present church.   The pulpit from which Burns
addressed his friend has disappeared, though I have heard
that it was still to the fore comparatively recently.   The
seats, &c., in the older building were disposed of by auction
in 1822.   The Royal Gallery, which was in the church
when Burns visited it, is still preserved in the new portion.
The remains of King Robert were re-interred with considerable ceremony during the rebuilding of the edifice,
and the grave is now marked with a handsome brass of
mediæval style bearing the figure and arms of the Bruce.
Above the grave stands the arched pulpit, one of the finest
in Scotland.   Burns returned to Edinburgh on 20th
October, travelling by the road which is associated with
memories of Queen Margaret, to Queensferry.

In Burns's Common-place Book there are two references to the " Kingdom."   The first is given thus in Currie:

"*Ah, Chloris!* Sir Robert Halket, of Pitferran, the author. *Note.*—He married her, the heiress of Pitferran." Apparently the reference is to a song, but so far I have not been able to trace it, and though there are several references to Sir Peter in local histories, *The Scottish Nation*, &c., no mention is made of his being a poet. Another of the family, Lady Elizabeth Halket, who married Sir Henry Wardlaw, of Pitreavie, in 1696, is the reputed authoress

" Dunfermling Fratery "

of the ballad, " Hardy Knute." Pitferran is an estate lying to the south-west of Dunfermline, and the Sir Peter who married the heiress was Sir Peter Wedderburn, who took as his wife Janet Halket, sister of Elizabeth mentioned above. In consequence of this marriage he and his descendants were obliged to take the name and arms of Halket. Another Halket, who was not, however, of the same family, was the author of the popular song, " Logie o' Buchan," and the Jacobite ballad, " Wherry Whigs awa man."

The other reference is given thus : " Fife and a' the

land about it.—R. Fergusson." This probably refers to some poem of Robert Fergusson's, but in my copy of that poet's works, edited by Robert Aiken, there is no poem of that name, though, as has been already said, there are several references to the "Kingdom" in his works. It is possible, of course, that some other Fergusson is meant. There was a family of Fergussons, of Raith, Fifeshire, who were of some note in Burns's day. Perhaps the note may refer to one of these.

In Johnson's *Museum* (1792) there appears a song, "The Carls o' Dysart," which owes its present form to the National Bard, though its basis was an old Fifeshire boat-song :—

> "Up wi' the carls o' Dysart,
>   And the lads o' Buckhaven,
>   And the kimmers o' Largo,
>   And the lasses o' Leven."

In Cromek's *Reliques* (1808) there is given an epitaph on one William Michie, "Schoolmaster of Cleish Parish, Fifeshire," which runs as follows :—

> "Here lie Willie Michie's banes ;
>   O Satan ! when ye tak' him,
>   Gie him the schulin' o' your weans,
>   For clever deils he'll mak' them."

According to Allan Cunningham, Michie was introduced to Burns in Edinburgh. Scott Douglas states that no further information has been vouchsafed to us regarding this clever dominie, but in Wallace's edition of *Chambers's Life* we are told that Michie, whose name is given as Ebenezer, was introduced by Nicol to Burns while they were taking an evening stroll together in Edinburgh. Michie was "dominie" first at Kettle, in the centre of Fife, and afterwards at Cleish. The latter place, it may be mentioned, is not in Fifeshire but in Kinross-shire. There is some reason to believe, however, that this epitaph is not genuine Burns.

A number of the friends of the Bard had a connection with the "Kingdom." William Creech, who published the first Edinburgh editions of his poems, was the grandson of a farmer in the county. Peter Hill, bookseller, who was on very intimate terms with the Poet, and who supplied him with many of his books, was a Fifeshire man. He was the son of James Hill, collector of shore dues at Dysart, by his wife, Margaret Russell, who was a native of Dunfermline. Peter was himself a Fifer, having been born at Dysart in 1754.

George Thomson, who was on very intimate terms with Burns, and to whose book on the melodies of Scotland the Poet contributed so much, was a native of Limekilns, near Dunfermline. His father, Mr Robert Thomson (as he is styled in the Register of Baptisms), was schoolmaster there for a few years, and it was there that George his eldest son, was born in 1757.

When Burns resided in Dumfries he sometimes attended the Secession Church there (now Loreburn U.F. Church). The minister in his day was the Rev. William Inglis, who was a native of the Fifeshire village of Freuchie.

WM. M'MILLAN.

Dunfermline.

THE MURISON COLLECTION.

SIR ALEXANDER GIBB, the donor of the Murison Collection of Burns's Works to the Carnegie Library, Dunfermline, was honoured at dinner in the Burns House, Glasgow, on 9th December last, by the Burns Federation, and from the hands of the president, Duncan M'Naught, LL.D., who presided over a large and enthusiastic meeting, received an illuminated address enclosed in a case of Levant morocco, bearing in gilt the arms designed by the Poet himself. The address is executed in black, red, and gold. Among those present were Dr M'Naught, Sir Alexander Gibb, Mr Thomas Amos, secretary of the Federation; Major G. A. Innes, treasurer : Mr J. Jeffrey Hunter, senior vice-president ; Mr Thomas Killin, Glasgow Mauchline Society ; Sir Robert Wilson, Mr Hugh M'Coll, president, Old Glasgow Club ; Provost Norval, Dunfermline ; Mr Andrew Shearer, Town Clerk, Dunfermline ; Mr P. Paterson, Mr J. C. Ewing, and Mr T. C. F. Brotchie.

After the usual royal and patriotic toasts the Chairman, in presenting Sir Alexander Gibb with the address, said they would remember that 18 months ago he had the honour to present an illuminated address and commemorative album to Colonel John Gribbel, of Philadelphia. Two valuable manuscripts of Robert Burns were carried off to America, and they considered they were lost to the Scottish nation, but they were agreeably surprised when they were returned by Mr Gribbel, into whose possession they had come. Acting on that good example they had Sir Alexander Gibb coming forward in the same way. It might be said his gift was a local gift, but just as Mr Gribbel's was a national gift united with a locality, so Sir Alexander Gibb's was a local gift which was associated with the whole nation, for the manuscripts were placed in the Carnegie Library, open to all students of Burns. They would all have noticed, in Mondays *Glasgow Herald* the sad news of the death of Mr Murison, and they regretted deeply the passing of a very old friend. Continuing, Dr M'Naught con-

SIR ALEXANDER GIBB.

gratulated Sir Alexander Gibb on his enterprise and generosity. Whenever he received the report of this collection and its value, he at once purchased it. If the collection had not been purchased at that time it would assuredly have gone to the salerooms and been dispersed, never again to be brought together. Speaking of the personal qualities of Sir Alexander, he said the highest compliment he could pay him was to tell him he was a thorough Burns man, imbued with the Burns spirit, the man of independent mind, and '' the manly heart with love o'erflowing.'' The *deus ex machina* all through had been Mr Peter Paterson, who had manv good qualities, but he (the president) admired most his perseverance and tenacity of purpose.

Mr Amos then read the terms of the Address, which were as follow :—

'' To Sir Alexander Gibb, G.B.E., C.B., Hon. President Burns Federation.

'' Sir,—The Burns Federation, representing 300 Burns clubs throughout the world, hereby desire to convey to you their high appreciation of your generosity in presenting to Dunfermline the valuable collections of Burns books and relics known as the Murison Collection.

'' They also desire to acknowledge the wisdom you have displayed in the housing of your valuable gift in the Burns Room of the Carnegie Public Library, where every facility will be provided for the convenience of all admirers and students of the works of our National Bard, thereby rendering your gift a national one, entitling you to the gratitude of all your fellow-countrymen.

'' We ask you to accept this address as an inadequate expression of the feelings which inspired it, accompanied by the fervent hope that your honoured and useful life may long be spared to your country.—D. M'Naught, hon. president ; Thomas Amos, hon. secretary ; Geo. A. Innes, hon. treasurer.''

The president handed the address to Sir Alexander Gibb and invited the company to pledge the long life, continued health, and prosperity of their guest.

Sir Alexander Gibb, in reply, said he felt overwhelmed that such an honour should have been done him by the Federation on account of so light an act on his part, but he could assure them he appreciated it from the bottom of his heart, and there was nothing he had in his possession which he prized more than that beautiful address. It would go down as an heirloom. He had only one other heirloom—a silver tray presented to his great-grandfather, John Gibb, who built the old Glasgow Bridge. (Applause.) Continuing, Sir Alexander said that anything to do with Burns lay very close to his heart. The Burns spirit was one of the finest spirits in the whole world. He was exceedingly proud to be there, and to add another to the many links he had with Glasgow. He worked in Glasgow 28 years ago, and he had carried away with him a great love of the city and its people. There was a feeling of homeliness and kindness that one did not meet with elsewhere.

Provost Norval, proposing " The Burns Federation," to which Mr J. Jeffrey Hunter replied, said that they had now completed the equipment of the Burns Room in the Carnegie Library, and he thought Sir Alexander would agree that a most adequate setting had been given to the magnificent jewel he had presented to them. It had already proved a great attraction to Burns lovers, not only through-out our own country, but all over the world, and Dunfermline was exceedingly proud of it.

REVIEWS.

"THE TRUTH ABOUT BURNS." By Duncan M'Naught, LL.D. [Review by James A. Morris, A.R.S.A., F.R.B.A., Alloway Burns Club.]

Dr M'Naught's book, *The Truth About Burns*, has been worth waiting for, and in its opening sentence he states its purpose : " This volume is the outcome of many urgent representations from all quarters that the time had arrived for a new Life of Burns in the light of the countervailing evidence which has accumulated during the last quarter of a century." That is the intention and spirit of the book : to discount error and establish truth, and in doing so to " nothing extenuate, nor set down aught in malice."

He shows how Currie, Burns's first biographer, was perhaps among the least fitted of all men to write about Burns, much less to attempt to portray Burns. Depending upon second-hand information lamentably inaccurate and imperfectly understood, Dr Currie yet set himself to the task. Pathetically incompetent and inept, seeking largely his own glorification, he essayed that which was beyond him, as beyond most men : the delineation of the incomprehensible, the portraiture of the soul from the skeleton of death. Yet this travesty of the truth, this web of fiction and pedantry spun by Currie with no doubt excellent intent, has, until recent years, been accepted almost universally as authoritative, and it has been largely built upon by successive biographers as an established record of fact. It was high time, therefore, that a more modest book should be written, recording the actual data as disclosed by recent research, and so clear away the unkind myths and cobwebs initially spun by Currie. Lockhart and Chambers did good work patiently and with care, and Scott Douglas recorded and tabulated diligently ; but even these, while noting errors and discrepancies, laboured under the difficulty of a middle period, in which the truth was only partially known. Dr Wallace's *Life* was the first of real authority, but even it is in part judicially inconclusive and temperamentally over-cautious regarding certain of the more pronounced episodes. All interested in Burns must needs be grateful to him for his scholarly volumes, while the publication of his " Robert Burns and Mrs Dunlop " letters did much to increase the general knowledge of the man. Henley's *Life* may be largely discounted, for while full of brilliant and incisive invective, not so much against Burns as against the cult of Burns, and salted with bitterness against all cant and pretence, it is yet a sincere effort to understand Burns through Henley spectacles. Himself a poet and an able writer upon Art, Henley had neither the patience nor the aptitude of the student, and in his Burns he took much at first hand and without real examination. Stevenson, again—and whatever his master hand touched he turned into wonderful melody—in his writings upon Burns and Burnsiana, imaged them as he thought they were, or ought to be ; for that exquisite romancer made all he wrote about live, as lived the creations of his own vivid brain. Carlyle, outstandingly and of all writers, perhaps best understood Burns, and he had, moreover, the most penetrating and enduring insight into the inherent greatness and immortality of the man.

Dr M'Naught has not written a new Life, yet for clearness of narrative and faithful delineation of the most salient events of the Poet's career, hiding nothing and exaggerating nothing, it is as notable in its directness and cogency as in its convincing fairness and impartiality ; while in its quiet conviction of knowledge, and of not a little unquestionable authority, it has a potency peculiarly its own. It must ever be difficult, if not beyond the humanly possible, to write of a man who was minting untold gold for posterity yet himself living amidst much of the dross and hardship of life, ever with his head in Olympus and his feet almost continuously treading the laborious matter-of-fact struggle for existence, ·vainly trying to extort a bare pittance from unproductive soil. With a heart above it all, soaring into realms unpeopled and unseen by his fellows, it beat warmly toward the sons and daughters of men, as to all living, yearning, striving things. To try to explain or excuse Burns is alike fatuous and futile, for how can the lesser explain the greater, or how measure, as Lord Rosebery has happily phrased it, " the miracle called Burns ? "

> " A fire of fierce and laughing light,
> That clove the shuddering heart of night,
> Leapt earthward, and the thunder's might,
> That pants and yearns,
> Made fitful music round its flight
> And earth saw Burns."

So sang another great lyric poet, one who read the heart with a fire and heat touching that of Burns but without his faith.

The Truth About Burns tells also of the times in which Burns lived, and those who have touched minds with it ; though those who themselves saw or heard of it at first hand know that Burns, in this also, as in all else, was better than his time. In shredding fact from fancy and fiction, Dr M'Naught follows closely the life of Burns from Alloway to Dumfries, touching mainly on the fundamental facts of his life and the sequence of his poetry, dwelling much upon those things where spleen or ignorance or controversy has most rested ; recording the essential and leaving the immaterial aside. The book impresses by its transparent sincerity and con-- vinces by its candour ; besides, it is the work of a devoted student, of one who through nearly all his life, and certainly for thirty years of it, as Editor of the *Burns Chronicle,* has given careful and un- wearied attention to the records of the Poet as they have successively been made manifest. Few possess Dr M'Naught's knowledge and authority, and these qualities have given to the book a quiet dignity that is not its least manifest charm. Summarised, the book stands to-day as the last word upon the Poet, and those who may follow would seem to have but little of new material left to them after Dr M'Naught's careful gleaning

[I note that the volume has been most favourably reviewed in the following journals :—*The Spectator,* the *British Weekly,* The Literary Supplement of the *London Times,* the *Westminster Gazette,* the *Newspaper World,* the *Warrington Examiner,* the *Elgin Courant,* the Glasgow *Evening Times,* the Glasgow *Evening Citizen,* the Glasgow *Evening News,* the Glasgow *Bailie,* the *Scotsman,* the *Glasgow Herald,* the *Kilmarnock Standard,* the *Kilmarnock Herald, Perthshire Advertiser,* &c., &c.]

" ROBERT BURNS AS A FREEMASON." By William Harvey, J.P.
(T. M. Sparkes, Dundee.)

We have received a forward copy of this elegant little volume, which deals with the masonic side of Burns in brief yet compre- hensive terms which leave nothing to be said which the enquiring reader desires to know. Mr Harvey, who, by the way, is the author of a *Complete Manual of Freemasonry,* tells us in his preface that he has endeavoured to collect the scattered references to Freemasonry that are found in the record of the Poet's life, and to weave them into a connected narrative. In this he has been most successful ; he keeps closely to his subject, avoiding the temptation of irrelevant padding ; and he has been at the most laudable pains to secure accuracy in matters of fact. The text is illustrated with a number of excellent photogravures which give added interest to the narrative, and a handy index completes the work, which Mr Harvey dedicates to the " Brethren of the Mystic Tie " at home and abroad. The Burnsian student and general reader will also find much to interest them in this study of one phase of Burns's character, and we cordially recommend it as the best short treatise on the subject which has come under our notice.

" The Scottish Lion as a National Possession." By Charles
W. Thomson, M.A., B.A., F.E.I.S., Buckie. (Robt.
Gibson & Sons (Glasgow) Ltd.)

This book is published, Mr Thomson informs us, with the
approval of the Scottish Patriotic Association, Glasgow, the inspiring motive being a condemnatory and convincing reply to the
Police Circular of March 17th, 1907, prohibiting the private use
and exhibition of the Scottish Lion rampant without special permission of the mandarins who keep a myopic official eye on the gew-
gaw trivialities which they imagine to be part of the " divinity which
doth hedge a king." Mr Thomson, in some 50 pages of informative
historical references, clearly shows how shallow and untrue is the
contention that the people are debarred from using the Lion Flag
where and when they choose, unless by the high permission of the
nearest policeman. Among his authorities he cites Burns, who
refers very seldom to the national emblems, but always in a way,
Mr Thomson contends, that puts beyond doubt that he deemed the
Red Lion a national and not a royal possession. As a contribution
to heraldry alone, Mr Thomson's book is well worth possessing.

" Under the Red Lamp—Songs of Yarrow, &c." By G. W. T.
M'Gown, M.A., F.E.I.S. (Selkirk : James Lewis.)

We have had previous knowledge of Mr M'Gown's abilities
in his handy and concise *Primer of Burns*, for which we had a highly
commending word to say at the date of its publication. The
present is a volume of verse, mostly in the vernacular, and redolent
of the glamour of Yarrow, which has inspired so many Border
singers and prose writers. All the pieces do great honour to the
head and heart which conceived them, while his fifteen sonnets
at the end of the volume prove him no mean versifier in the English
tongue. Its late arrival precluded any notice of its merits in our
last issue.

NOTES AND QUERIES.

A FRAGMENT BY ROBERT BURNS.

We (*Dumfries Courier*) have before us a copy of the poetical works of Mr William Collins, published in London, in 1765. On one of the fly-leaves of the book there is written in pencil, but perfectly legible,

To Jean Lorimer, a small but sincere mark of friendship, from
ROBT. BURNS.

in the peculiar upright and rounded hand of the poet. Under this is written in ink, in a very good hand,

JANE LORIMER, 1794.

Jean Lorimer was the " Chloris " of Burns, and many of his songs were addressed to her—the first, according to Mr Chambers, in September, 1794. She was a remarkably beautiful young woman, then residing with her father at Kemishall, near Dumfries. Her romantic but truly melancholy story is well known.

On the first fly-leaf of the book mentioned there are a few lines in the Poet's handwriting, and, like the inscription already mentioned, in pencil. We have deciphered them, with the exception of one line, after some difficulty, and append them, not for their intrinsic merit, but because anything that Burns wrote is regarded with interest, and because they tend to show the same feeling though not the same power which produced the glorious song of " Scots wha hae." As far as we know they have never been published.

His royal visage seamed with many a scar
That Caledonian reared his martial form ;
Who led the tyrant-quelling war,
When Bannockburn's ensanguined flood,
Swelled with mingling hostile blood,
Saw Edward's myriads struck with deep dismay,
And Scotia's troop of brothers win their way,
   .   .   .   .   tyrant's band ;
Oh heavenly joy to free our native land,
While high their mighty chief poured on the doubling storm.

[The above is a clipping from the *Kilmarnock Post* of April 14th, 1860. The " Fragment " seems to be part of the projected drama of Bruce's exploits, but it is so elliptical or imperfectly copied that one is inclined to question its authenticity. Can any of our readers give any information regarding this volume of poems perused by the editor of the *Dumfries Courier* about the date mentioned ?—ED.].

FUSION OF THE LONDON BURNS CLUBS.

The Annual Meetings of our Club and the London Burns Club (Scots) were held in separate rooms at Anderton's Hotel, Fleet Street, E.C., on Thursday, May 26th.

The following Resolution was passed by each Club separately, by large majorities, and subsequently at a combined meeting presided over by Mr Will :—That the report and recommendations of the Committee with regard to fusion be adopted, and that the London. Robert Burns Club (No. 1) and the London Burns Club (Scots) be united under the name and title of " The Burns Club of London (No. 1)," incorporating The London Robert Burns Club (No. 1) and The London Burns Club (Scots), and it was afterwards agreed that the rules framed by the Special Committees of the two Clubs be adopted *in toto*, and that the following office-bearers be appointed for the ensuing twelve months :—President, Sir William Noble ; Vice-President, P. N. M'Farlane ; Hon. Secretary, John A. Brown, 38 Vaughan Gardens, Cranbrook Road, Ilford ; Hon. Assistant Secretary, S. J. Fraser ; Hon. Treasurer, J. Spencer Leslie ; Committee (24), to be appointed, 12 from the London Robert Burns Club and 12 from the London Burns Club, and our Members were elected as follows :—Messrs John Anderson, A. T. Bromfield, J. M. Bulloch, W. B. Buyers, T. S. Cockburn, John Douglas, A. P. Florence, H. M'Michael, Geo. Pocock, T. E. Price, W. Williamson, and T. J. Wilson.

The above named gentlemen immediately assumed office, and the business of the Burns Club of London was commenced.

P. N. M'FARLANE.

THE BOHN AUTOGRAPHS.

The late Mr Henry G. Bohn, a famous publisher in Victorian days, collected a number of interesting manuscripts and autograph letters, which are to be sold in November in Messrs Knight, Frank & Rutley's Rooms. There are four Burns documents of importance, including the letter to James Smith, of Mauchline, as to the Poet's intended voyage to the West Indies, also the lines written in Glenriddel Hermitage beginning, " Thou whom chance may hither lead," and a holograph of 48 lines entitled, " Nature's Law," a humorous appreciation of being blessed with twins. The fourth manuscript of 16 lines is " Nithsdale's Welcome to Terreagles."

THE BURNS—BISHOP FAMILY.

The following genealogical table of the descendants of "Dear Bought Bess" has been kind
warded by Mr Alex. Frugh, Glenshellach, Lochgelly, for publication in the *Chronicle*
Burnsiana item worthy of preservation.

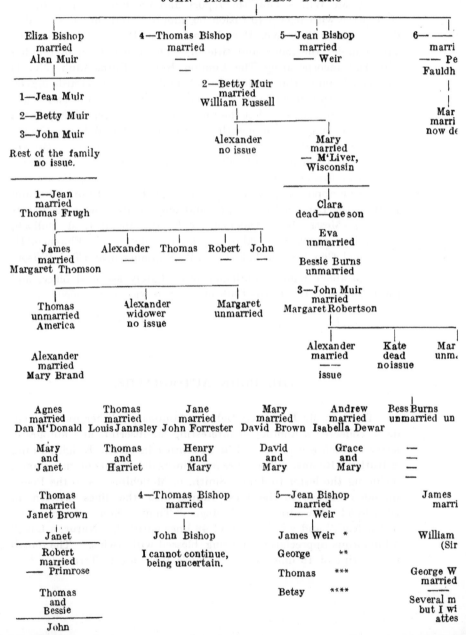

ROBERT BURNS———LIZZIE PATON, of Largieside

BESS BURNS
"The sonsie, smirking, dear bought Bess."
Married JOHN BISHOP, Overseer at Polkemmet
viz.—
JOHN BISHOP——BESS BURNS

Eliza Bishop married Alan Muir	4—Thomas Bishop married — —	5—Jean Bishop married — Weir	6— — marri — Pe Fauldh
1—Jean Muir	2—Betty Muir married William Russell		
2—Betty Muir			Mar marri
3—John Muir	Alexander no issue	Mary married — M'Liver, Wisconsin	now de
Rest of the family no issue.			
1—Jean married Thomas Frugh		Clara dead—one son	
James married Margaret Thomson	Alexander — Thomas — Robert — John —	Eva unmarried Bessie Burns unmarried	
Thomas unmarried America	Alexander widower no issue	Margaret unmarried	3—John Muir married Margaret Robertson
Alexander married Mary Brand		Alexander married — — issue	Kate dead no issue	Mar unm.

Agnes married Dan M'Donald	Thomas married Louis Jannsley	Jane married John Forrester	Mary married David Brown	Andrew married Isabella Dewar	Bess Burns unmarried un
Mary and Janet	Thomas and Harriet	Henry and Mary	David and Mary	Grace and Mary	— — —
Thomas married Janet Brown	4—Thomas Bishop married —	5—Jean Bishop married — Weir			James marri
Janet	John Bishop	James Weir *			William (Sir
Robert married — Primrose	I cannot continue, being uncertain.	George **			
		Thomas ***			George W married
Thomas and Bessie		Betsy ****			Several m but I wi attes
John					

HERALDRY OF BURNS.

To the article in No. XXIX., 1920 *Chronicle*, there falls to be added the interesting information that Burns had at least one Manual of Heraldry on his shelves.   A book bearing the somewhat lengthy title, *A Summary View of Heraldry in Reference to the Usages of Chivalry and the General Economy of the Feudal System, with an Appendix respecting such Distinctions of Rank as have place in the British Constitution*, was published in Edinburgh in 1795.   The author was Thomas Brydson, F.A.S., Edinburgh.   This volume was published by subscription, and the list of subscribers is printed at the beginning.   The list includes the name of "Mr Robert Burns," together with those of his friends, Mr William Nicol, Patrick Heron of Heron, M.P., Major Logan, Dr Blair, and others.

W. M'MILLAN.

JESSE COLLINS ON BURNS.

In the autobiography of the Rt. Hon. Jesse Collins, of "three acres and a cow" fame, the following passage occurs :—" Among the books of poetry I was a close reader of Robert Burns—a master of song describing the joys, sorrows, and feelings of those who labour for their daily bread.   His ' Address to the Unco Guid' is one of the greatest incentives to human charity that was ever written."

W. M'MILLAN.

A BURNS MANUSCRIPT.

1 Cambridge Villas, The Promenade,
Cheltenham, Gloucestershire, June 2, 1921.

DEAR SIR,—Quite recently I have come across the enclosed page of *The Illustrated London News* for November 17, 1855, which contains an interesting letter from a correspondent concerning a MS. of " Tam o' Shanter."   I thought you might like to make use of it in the next volume of *The Burns Chronicle*.   I expect you know where this particular MS. is located at the present time.   I wonder if it is at Alloway.

No doubt you are aware that there is a Miss Burns still living in Cheltenham, though old and infirm.

In the churchyard at Charlton Kings, a village about 2½ miles from Cheltenham, but connected by electric tram, I copied the following inscription from a gravestone :

" Sacred to the memory of Sarah Burns Hutchinson, widow of Berkley Hutchinson, M.D., and daughter of Lt.-Col. James Glencairn Burns, died 12th July, 1909, aged 87 years. Also of Margaret Constance Burns Hutchinson, her daughter. Died 8th December 1919, aged 57 years.

A PRAYER.

When soon or late they reach that coast,
O'er life's rough ocean driv'n,
May they rejoice, no wand'rer lost
A family in Heaven.   BURNS."

MANUSCRIPT OF BURNS.—Will you have the goodness to inform me, under your head " Memorabilia," whether an original MS. of Burns's celebrated poem, " Tam o' Shanter," of which I became the purchaser about thirty years ago, is of much value in the market for relics ?   The copy alluded to was evidently one of the very first penned by the Poet, containing as it does several interlineatory corrections previous to publication, or to even circulation in the MS. state among his most intimate friends.   The manuscript in question, I was told, was given by Burns to a friend of his in Dumfriesshire, just after its having been composed, and long before having been printed.   It is written on quarto-size post paper, and worn through on the outer leaf where folded for the pocket—no doubt to show to friends ; and there are some memoranda written on the outside blank leaf in allusion to Melrose Abbey as being mentioned in Grose's *Antiquities of Scotland*. I had this relic preserved in morocco half binding, and titled on the back " *Burns's Tam o' Shanter : Original MS.*," with the intention of presenting it to Lord Byron, having just then (about 1824-5) read his eulogium on the Scottish Bard ; but the death of the noble Poet interfered with my design. *Apropos* of Burns : I may here observe that about thirty years ago, while passing through the small town of Lockerby, a young minister of the Scotch Kirk, named Duff, told me he was in possession of a considerable number of Burns's original manuscript pieces, chiefly verses, never published, which his father, then a small tradesman in that place, received at various times from Burns, who used not unfrequently in his poverty to share the humble bed of his friend Duff.   It often happened during these times that Burns—under the powerful influence of his native " mountain dew," while sitting round the small three-legged table of the humble public-house— would repeat or pen down the extemporaneous flashes of his wit (" which used to keep the table in a roar ") or let fall his withering sarcasm upon some hapless wight who had attracted the lightning of his muse's ire.   Copies of these effusions he would frequently, at the time, present to Mr Duff, sen.   I endeavoured to advise Mr D., jun., to publish these pieces, along with any other unpublished effusions of the poet that could be found, with the interlineations or corrections of the manuscripts faithfully given ; but I never heard that my suggestion was ever acted upon, nor what became of the relics then in Mr Duff's possession.—J. J.

> Believe me, dear sir, yours faithfully,
> WILLIAM WALE.

AN UNPUBLISHED BURNS LETTER.

[Dr Maxwell Wood has obligingly forwarded us the following interesting communications.—ED.]

Portland, Maine, July 27, 1921.

Dr J. Maxwell Wood,
3 Comely Bank, Edinburgh, Scotland.

MY DEAR SIR,—Enclosed please find the letter of Burns for which you asked.   It has been a pleasure to copy it, as it is always a privilege to be connected, even in so simple a capacity, with the words of a true poet.

Our autograph collection, from which this letter was copied, was a bequest to the Maine Historical Society, made by John S. H. Fogg, M.D., who was born in Eliot, Maine, May 21, 1826, and died in South Boston, Mass., October 16, 1893.   For the last twenty years of his life Dr Fogg was completely paralyzed in his feet and legs, so that he could neither stand nor walk.   To keep his mind from his sufferings, he devoted himself to his autograph collection, and his faithful wife was his assistant.   Together they gathered, prepared, and mounted what is said to be the third best collection in the United States—the very best in point of mounting.

When this collection came to our society it was appraised at $25,000, which is ridiculously low.   Colonel James Manning, of Albany, himself a noted collector, told me that the two volumes containing the signatures of the   Signers of the   Declaration of Independence were worth at least that ; and we have fifty-seven volumes besides.

Trusting that these few particulars may be what you wish, I am

> Yours very truly,
> EVELYN L. GILMORE, Librarian.

N.B.—The erasures and insertions of the letter are those which Burns made in the original.

[Burns Letter referred to.]

SIR,

It would be [a†] reason sufficiently just, if I were to tell you that I have not sent you my Poetic Epistle to Fintry, because I actually could not find time to transcribe it; but a better reason is, I am out of conceit with it myself, & transcribing a thing of my own I do not like is a drudgery I know not how to bear.—I dare say if you have [not†] met with Captn. Matthew Henderson about Edinr., you must have heard of him.—He was an intimate acquaintance of mine; & of all Mankind I ever knew, he was one of the first [I ever met with‡] for a nice sense of honor, a generous contempt of the adventitious distinctions of Men, and sterling tho sometimes *outré* Wit.—The inclosed Elegy has pleased me beyond any of my late poetic efforts.—Perhaps 'tis " the memory of joys that are past," and a friend who is no more, that biasses my criticism.—It is likewise, ever since I read your Aiken on the poetical use of Natural History, a favorite study of mine, the characters of the Vegetable & the manners of the Animal kingdoms.—I regret much that I cannot have an opportunity of waiting on you to have your strictures on this Poem—How I have succeeded on the whole —if there is any incongruity in the imagery—or whether I have not omitted some apt rural paintings altogether.—I will [not†] pretend to say whether it is owing to my prejudice in favor of a gentleman to whom I am so much indebted, or to your critical abilities; but in the way of my trade, as a Poet, I will subscribe more implicitly to *your* strictures than to any individual on earth.—

I have written Captn. Grose, & inclosed him a billet to you.— If he comes to your neighbourhood you will probably see him.— I shall have leisure soon to write off for you several of my pieces.—

I have the honor to be,

    Sir,

        Your obliged humble ser[vt]*

              ROBT. BURNS.

Ellisland,
30th July, 1790.

    Professor Stewart,
        Catrine.

(From the Fogg Collection of Autograph Documents and Letters in the library of the Maine Historical Society, Portland, Me.)

† Insertions.
‡ Erasures.
* Letters in brackets beneath paper strip pasted on for hinge. Cannot be seen through paper.

CLUB NOTES.

[COMMUNICATED.]

BURNS CLUB OF LONDON.

REPORT OF THE VERNACULAR CIRCLE COMMITTEE.

It was inevitable that for the first session the work of the Vernacular Circle should be explanatory, that is, that while many conflicting opinions had to be reconciled, it was necessary for us to carry out a first-session programme that would provide entertainment and instruction, and at the same time help us to form some idea of the volume of support that we might expect, in London and at home, for more extended educational work. Although this Circle was formed as an appendage of the London Robert Burns Club, not one of us would have been satisfied had ordinary club work —the reading of papers and delivery of lectures to our members —been the beginning and end of the Circle's activities. Had there been nothing else before us, the Circle in a few years would have gone the way of all such things. Our real work lies outside London.

The end of our first session's programme will form but the jumping-off ground for the educational work which has now to be undertaken. We are certain that here in London those of the Lowland Scottish people who know of our work sympathise with it, and are ready to support it. We know also that we can show the Scottish education authorities a great volume of opinion in favour of the more extended use in schools than hitherto of the Vernacular Language of Lowland Scotland.

DR CRAIGIE AND COL. JOHN BUCHAN'S LECTURES.

It can be no reflection upon those of us who have contributed to the session's programme to say that the outstanding contributions were those of Dr W. A. Craigie, Professor of Anglo-Saxon at Oxford University, and Colonel John Buchan, novelist and historian. Dr Craigie gave the work of the Circle a direction that it needed. His knowledge of the renaissance of other languages similarly placed to our own gave great heartening, and the lecture attracted considerable attention in Scotland. Colonel John Buchan's lecture also was of great value to the Circle. No man living would have put the subject more eloquently, more lucidly, or more pawkily ; and while it had not the particular reference to the work of the Circle that Dr Craigie's lecture had, it was of great value to the patriotic Scots whom we are anxious to interest in our work. Colonel Buchan warned us that if the decay of our language continued, Scots people would be identified by their accent rather than by their language.

WORLD-WIDE APPEAL TO SCOTS.

Now that the work of the session is over, we have already turned to the future. First we are appealing for the co-operation as corresponding Associations of Burns Clubs and other Scottish organisations throughout Scotland, England, America, Canada, Australia, New Zealand, South Africa, India ; indeed, wherever Scotsmen gather.

Professor Craigie proposes visiting India and the United States next winter, and he is prepared to address Scotsmen on the work of our Circle and what we are doing to arrest the decay of the Scottish language, and how they can help. We are communicating with Scottish organisations in those towns which he will visit, asking them to arrange for lectures by the Professor.

OUR OBJECTS.

It is undesirable at this stage, even if it were possible, to lay down a hard and fast programme ; but generally our work may be indicated as the encouragement by every means possible of the use of the Vernacular Language, oral and written. Naturally, the first attention will have to be paid to the children, who are fast losing their grip of the Lowland tongue. We have evidence of the sympathy of many schoolmasters, and we will support them by the presentation of prizes for singing and reciting of pieces of classical Scots, and for the composition of prose and verse, leaving to them and the education authorities the fixing of conditions that will secure the greatest possible educational advantages.

The presentation of prizes in Primary, Secondary, and Continuation Schools and Universities is bound to have a great influence on the future of the language.

SCHOOL PRIZES.

Until we are able to raise a Scottish Language Fund, which will have to be undertaken sooner or later, it is suggested that individual members of the Circle, and through them non-members, should give prizes annually to their mither-schools for singing and reciting, or composition in verse or prose, or all of these things

PRIZES IN UNIVERSITIES.

As was suggested when this Circle was founded, an important matter to be considered is the presentation of annual prizes in Scottish Universities for the best poem for the year in the Lowland Vernacular. This was suggested for more than one reason. As we are aiming at killing the false pride that is choking the use of the Scottish Vernacular, we know of nothing better calculated to assist us than the approval of the authorities of a Scottish University. Aberdeen University has already accepted Sir William Noble's prize, and when the Senati of St. Andrews, Edinburgh, and Glasgow Universities accept prizes for the best poem or prose piece in the Vernacular a great step forward will have been taken.

OUTSIDE SCHOOLS : SINGING CONTESTS.

It will be the aim of the Circle to form four great centres—Edinburgh, Glasgow, Dundee, and Aberdeen—and invite entries at these four centres, and award four prizes (probably medals) for soprano, contralto, tenor, and bass at each centre.

COMPOSITION IN POETRY OR PROSE.

Under the auspices of the Circle, with a committee of Scottish literary men and women that would command national confidence, there should be two annual prizes, one for a poem or play and one for a prose piece. These two competitions would be open to the world, and would be advertised through the corresponding or affiliated members and the Scottish newspapers. The recitation or reading of the successful poem, play, or prose piece will be arranged for a Hallowe'en meeting or concert.

ABERDEEN'S EXAMPLE.

The Circle's prize scheme has had a splendid start, As has been said, Aberdeen University has accepted Sir William Noble's prize of ten guineas per annum for the best poem in any dialect of braid Scots. It is open to all matriculated students, and to graduates in any faculty, provided not more than seven years have elapsed since the date of their first matriculation.

Into the matter of Sir William Noble's prizes to Primary and Secondary Schools in Aberdeen, the Aberdeen Education Authority have entered enthusiastically. A Secondary Schools Noble Prize Committee has been appointed, with Professor Gilroy as convener, and the prizes for recitations have been divided into two classes —for Secondary and Primary Schools. The prizes in the Secondary Schools will this year be given to scholars in the High School and in the Grammar School, and the winner of the first prize will have an opportunity of giving the piece at the School Prize Distribution. In addition to the mere recitation, each candidate will be examined as to his or her knowledge of the subject matter prescribed.

THE DECAY OF THE LANGUAGE.

For the Primary School Prizes thirty-three schools are interested, and the competitions will be begun this year. The subjects will be prose or poetry in the Scots Vernacular or one of Burns's poems.

The Burns Club of London offer no excuse for the formation of their Vernacular Circle. There are those who profess that there is no decay in the spoken language of Scotland, but evidence continues to come to us from all parts of Scotland as to the need for a combined effort to promote the use of the language.

THE ACTIVITY OF WRITERS IN SCOTS.

Notwithstanding these signs of deterioration the outlook is bright. At present in many parts of Scotland, young and old men and women are writing verse and prose in the Vernacular, amateur playwrights are writing local plays or playlets in the Doric, and generally there is great activity in these departments of literature. The work of the Circle, by encouraging in every way the development of the Vernacular, can help the efforts of those authors, and it will be surprising if there do not emerge from our activities some great figure or figures that will revivify the Auld Scots tongue, and assist us in forming a great defensive wall around the language of our beloved land.

———

Since the above report was framed, the Circle has the gratifying announcement to make that Mr L. G. Sloan, the past President of the Club, has most generously gifted the sum of £500 for the establishment of prizes at the University of his native city of Edinburgh and at the University of St. Andrews, for the encouragement of the use and study of the Vernacular Language of Lowland Scotland.

These prizes will give a further great impetus to the movement which has been so successfully inaugurated.

JOHN DOUGLAS,
Chairman, Vernacular Circle.
WM. WILL,
Hon. Secy. Vernacular Circle,
" The Graphic," Tallis St., E.C.

———

COMPLIMENTARY DINNER TO SIR ALEXANDER GIBB, G.B.E., C.B.

Sir Alexander Gibb, who recently purchased the Murison Collection of Burnsiana and has presented it to Scotland, is one of our Life Members, and the Council at their last meeting on the 8th inst., unanimously agreed to entertain Sir Alexander and Lady Gibb to dinner.

The Dinner was held at the Victoria Hall, Hotel Cecil, Strand, W.C., on Friday, 8th July, at 6.30, and was attended by a large and appreciative number of members and friends.

LONDON ROBERT BURNS CLUB.

President's Report, 1920-1921.

In presenting my report for a year of great activity, I am able to say that the Club is in a most healthy condition, and that its work is so greatly appreciated that although death and other causes have robbed us of nine members, 54 life and ordinary members have joined, thus leaving an addition to the membership of 45.

Thanks to a consistent policy that has necessitated active, unostentatious work, and continuous effort to keep the Burns movement strongly humanitarian and literary, the London Robert Burns Club retains its position as one of the most important in the Federation. Its work for the Burns movement is known throughout the world, as is evidenced by the fact that services of many kinds are required of our members from all over the habitable globe. Our work is known in Southern and Tropical Africa, India, in America, and in Australia and New Zealand. As an example of the work that our members are sometimes called upon to perform, I may mention the fact that only a few weeks ago four of our number acted as a committee to supervise the preparation of a Burns statue—the replica of the Ayr statue by Lawson—which a Burns Club in the United States of America have ordered for erection in the States.

Our Birthday Festivals are recognised as the most important literary gatherings in the Burns movement, and so anxious are we to retain this position that already preparations have been made for the 1922 celebration. Professor Grierson, professor of Rhetoric and English Literature at Edinburgh University, one of the greatest living literary critics, has consented to propose " The Immortal Memory," and applications have already been received for tickets.

Contributions to Charities, &c.

This Club has never made it a practice to hold any considerable sums of money. All surpluses from subscriptions and concerts have been disbursed for charitable and other objects, so that our exchequer at the end of the year never shows a big surplus, if any This year the Club and its members have raised considerable sums for various deserving objects, among them being ·—

Scots Corporation ...	...	...	...	...	...	... £205
Caledonian Schools ...	...	...	...,	...	...	... 155
Burns Federation ...	...	...	...	...	...	. 100
Scottish National War Memorial ...	...	...	...	...	130

These amounts have been contributed without ostentation, and without any appeal outside our own members.

THE FEDERATION MEETINGS.

The outstanding event of the year's work was the visit of the Burns Federation to London. This visit was to have been made in September, 1914. All arrangements were then made for the meetings, but the outbreak of war necessitated their abandonment. To London, last September, 95 gentleman came as delegates from the various federated Burns Clubs, and the series of meetings which were arranged for them kept their time well occupied with work and entertainment.

To inaugurate the proceedings, on Friday evening, 3rd September, the delegates accepted my invitation to dine with the members of the Council of the London Robert Burns Club at Vintners' Hall, and a most enjoyable evening was spent. The speeches were homely and hearty, and the music was good. The fine old hall of the Vintners' Company, which was kindly placed at our disposal through the good offices of Mr Powell, the senior warden, was an object of great interest to the delegates.

On the following (Saturday) morning, the delegates met members of the London Robert Burns Club at the Burns Statue on the Embankment, and Mr Duncan M'Naught, as president of the Federation, placed a wreath at the base of the statue.

The company immediately proceeded to the Scots Corporation Hall, Crane Court, Fleet Street, where the annual meeting of Federation delegates was held. Our club was represented by myself, Sir William Noble, vice-president, and Mr M'Farlane, hon. secretary. In the course of the meeting a cheque for £100 was handed to the treasurer for Federation purposes by an anonymous donor.

On the conclusion of the business the company lunched at Anderton's Hotel. After luncheon it was announced that in connection with the visit to the Caledonian Schools at Bushey, a member who wished to remain anonymous had presented a cheque for £100 to the schools.

The visit to the schools—the journey was made in motor busses —was one of the most enjoyable parts of the programme arranged for the entertainment of the delegates. The happy boys and girls in their neat uniforms, marched past to the music of the bagpipes; they swam, danced, ran races, and generally showed themselves a healthy, happy, and athletic band of children. The delegates were so greatly impressed with the excellence of the institution that during a high tea, provided by Mr Peter D. Graham, secretary, a collection of £55 was made. After tea, a concert was held in the hall, at which the children provided part of the programme. Here I would like to say how grateful we were to Mrs Price (Miss Bessie

Fraser), of Australia, for her kind services in singing at our various functions.

The delegates during their London visit enjoyed themselves heartily, as will be seen by the report in the *Burns Chronicle*, 1920-21, and many of them sent expressions of their grateful thanks to Mr M'Farlane, our hon. secretary.

The Birthday Festival.

The Club's 52nd Celebration of the Poet's Birthday will be remembered as one of the most successful and certainly the best-attended in the history of the Club.   451 members, friends, and club guests, sat down to dinner in the King's Hall, Holborn Restaurant, and an attractive programme of speeches and music was carried through.

After a word of welcome by the President, Miss Annie S. Swan proposed " The Press," to which Sir Andrew Caird replied.   Mr Edmund Gosse, in his address in proposing " The Immortal Memory," paid his tribute to the work of Burns as a Scottish song preserver and restorer.   In his speech on Burns Lovers Abroad, Sir Harry Lauder told of the heart-hunger of the Scot abroad for his native land and for the songs and poems of Robert Burns.

The Vernacular Circle.

A movement which has already attracted a deal of attention, and which is bound to have a great influence on the future of the language of Lowland Scotland, although inaugurated during the year 1919-20, concluded its first session during the year just ending. Begun with the blessing of many of the professors of Scottish Universities and of Oxford and Cambridge, the Vernacular Circle has secured the support of many schoolmasters, literary men, and other patriotic Scots who love their mither-tongue, and who lament the fact that it is dying on the tongues of the people.   The Circle hope by their efforts to do a good deal to arrest the decay that is all too apparent.   The Vernacular Circle Committee have prepared a full report of their work for the session and their programme for the future, and this relieves me of the necessity of referring further to the matter.

Domestic Matters.

As the members are aware, our Club has a particularly strong domestic side.   As the annual reports of the Past Presidents will disclose, we take special interest in the life and work of our members outside the actual Club work.   In keeping with this tradition, I wish on my own and my wife's behalf, to thank the members for their kindness on the occasion of our daughter's wedding to Mr Donald Mackay, by sending us congratulations, and presenting to our daughter a beautiful wedding gift. For your kind thoughts and gift we are all grateful to you.

We congratulate Dunfermline and our brethren there on receiving, at the hands of one of our members, Sir Alexander Gibb, G.B.E., C.B., the great Burns Collection known as the Murison Collection, one of the finest collections of Burnsiana in the world. Sir Alexander Gibb, the honorary president of the Dunfermline Club, most generously purchased the collection and handed it over to Dunfermline. While congratulating Dunfermline, we wish to thank Sir Alexander Gibb for his great public spirit. Sir Alexander's action has most probably prevented the collection from being purchased for America, where so many valuable Burns books and collections have gone.

During the year we have lost the services as honorary treasurer, but fortunately not the membership or support, of our old friend and past president, Mr Wilkinson-Pimbury, who has rendered great service to us, and who for these services the members conferred on him life-membership and a beautifully bound copy of the Poet's works. Happily, Mr Wilkinson-Pimbury has been succeeded as hon. treasurer by an able accountant in Mr J. Spence Leslie.

We have recently congratulated Dr J. M. Bulloch, one of our members, on having had conferred upon him the degree of LL.D. by his Alma Mater, Aberdeen. Dr Bulloch has done much literary work for Scotland, and his hosts of friends inside and outside this Club are proud of the honour conferred upon him. Dr Bulloch has just undergone a serious operation, and we all wish him a speedy and complete recovery.

Among what may be considered as domestic events, I wish to refer to the recovery from his period of illness of our worthy hon. secretary, who has given such great service to the Club. Mr M'Farlane, at the Federation Meetings, at the Hollowe'en Dinner, at our great Birthday Festival, and at our Committee meetings, has been the life and soul of our Club, as he has been since he took up office. His illness cannot altogether be separated from the work that he has done for the Club ; and often when he might have claimed exemption on account of illness, he has stuck to his work with the cheerfulness and joviality that make association with him so pleasant.

Among minor matters to be recorded are the facts that the Club assisted with the visit of the Orpheus Choir ; and with the petition for securing a Civil List Pension for Mr Scott Skinner, the eminent Scottish composer and violinist.

During the year we have lost several of our brethren by death. Among these are :—Mr Peter Bonthron, a life member, a gentleman whose interest in the Poet's works was most intelligent, and who attended our gatherings consistently. Mr Robert C. Annand, who was elected to membership only in December, one of the leading manufacturers of printing machinery of the present time; Mr G. Simpson, an old and valued member of the Club; Mr A. D. Ferguson, Mr J. Campbell Walker, and Mr D. Scully, whose presence we shall greatly miss from our gatherings.

FUSION OF BURNS CLUBS IN LONDON.

The most important matter that our Club has had to consider during the past twelve months is the proposal to unite the two Burns Clubs in London. In 1917, I may recall, this Club made an effort to effect a union, but the time apparently was not ripe and the negotiations failed. In March last, as the result of informal conversations, the London Burns Club (Scots), made overtures to our committee. These were heartily welcomed by us, and the result may be—we hope it will be—that to-night the two clubs, having similar ideals, will be united under the title, " The Burns Club of London." With a united body of Burns lovers in London the good work on which we have all been engaged will go forward with increased zest.

IN CONCLUSION—THANKS.

In conclusion I would like to thank the Officials and Council for the enthusiastic support they have given me during the past year. I have already referred to the extraordinary hard work of Mr M'Farlane, and while emphasising his good work, I do not overlook the work of the members of the different committees who have given excellent service to the Club; and in particular I wish to refer to the support given to me by our Vice-President, Sir William Noble.

We have had a year of great interest, and I feel sure of great good to the Burns cult. We have reached an important point in the history of our Club; and should the fusion of the two Clubs actually follow the negotiations, much more can be done for the literary and charitable sides of our work. We shall go forward in the expectation of doing great things together.

My last words are words of gratitude to you all for the support you have given me in the chair.

L. G. SLOAN, *President.*

ROSEBERY BURNS CLUB.

The past session's work, it is pleasing to note, has been markedly progressive. All the meetings have been largely attended, and it is evident from the number of ladies present that it was a wise move on the part of the Club to admit them as members.

Probably one of the most interesting meetings held was on 17th August, 1920' when Mrs Gribbel was duly elected our first Honorary Lady Member. A splendid evening's entertainment resulted, and will long remain a pleasant memory in the minds of all present.

The Syllabus was quite up to, if not better than, its predecessors, and to judge from the titles of the lectures, we had quite a " Poetic Session," addresses being delivered on " Tannahill, Cowper, and Burns," as well as on " The Poetry of Business."

All the social functions were well partonised, and a large and appreciative gathering heard Prin. Chas. S. Dougall, M.A., of Dollar Academy, give the oration on the 25th January.

The Ladies' Night consisted of a Whist Drive on 23rd December, and a high tea on 31st March. At the latter function an Auction Sale was held whereby the Infirmaries benefited to the extent of over £30.

The School Competition at Bluevale Public School proved an unqualified success, and while the members of the Rosebery provided the incentive, we cannot allow the occasion to pass without recording our appreciation of Mr Lucas, the Headmaster of the School, and his well qualified staff, who took such pains with the children. As a result of the competition and the whole-hearted enthusiasm of the children, it is pleasing to record that a goodly sum was donated to the Bellahouston Hospital.

As all Burnsians know, the Rosebery, in co-operation with the Carlton Burns Club, had taken in hand the publication of Burns Works in Braille and Moon type, so that those of our brethren who had not their sight might be able to appreciate and enjoy our Bard's literary masterpieces. This grand work is now completed, and at the parting of the ways of the joint committee a balance of nearly £62 was donated to the Scottish Institution for the Blind, whose headquarters are in Edinburgh.

From the foregoing it will be seen that the Club is in a flourishing condition, and we anticipate continuing our forward march in the session now started. So far, everything augurs well for this hope being realised. JOHN M. ALEXANDER, *Hon. Secy.*

TAM O' SHANTER BURNS CLUB, GLASGOW.

ANNUAL REPORT FOR 1920-1921.

The Annual Report was submitted at the meeting on 25th October.

The Club has met three times during the session, the Committee seven times, and the Sub-committee four times.

The Session opened with the Annual Meeting, which later resolved itself into a Smoking Concert. At that meeting the alteration of rules was discussed.

The Annual Dinner took place on 25th January in the Trades House Restaurant, when Professor Rait proposed the " Immortal Memory " in a scholarly and masterly manner, and was enthusiastically applauded.

It has been arranged to have a School Competition in Govanhill School early next year, under the auspices of Mr Edward Patience.

Owing to the difficulties connected with the railway strike, there was no outing this year.

On 29th March a Literary and Musical Evening was held. President Hamilton gave an address on " Charles Dickens," and an excellent musical programme followed. Ladies were present at the function for the first time, and the experiment was considered successful and will be repeated.

The Club was duly represented at the Burns Federation Meeting at Dunfermline in September by Messrs Hamilton and Ballantyne. The M'Lennan Cup Competition took place in August, and the Club entered three rinks. The membership stands thus :—Life Members, 70 ; Ordinary Members, 52 ; Honorary Members, 6—total, 128. an increase of 9.

It was remitted to a Committee to consider the erection of a Memorial Tablet to Douglas Graham, the " original " of Tam o' Shanter. Mr J. D. Sloan, ex-President of the Rosebery Club, and the Rev. James Muir, Parish Minister of Kirkoswald, are both interested in the subject.

The Annual Meeting was held on 25th October, when the Annual Report revealed a very satisfactory state of affairs. Arrangements were made for the Annual Dinner, when Mr Fred. A. M'Quisten, M.P., would give the " Immortal Memory." Arrangements were made for a School Competition in the Annette Street School. Mr J. Blair Smith, of the *Record and Mail*, addressed the meeting on the subject of the action of Licensing Authorities in restricting the hours of licensed houses.

A syllabus for the session was fixed as follows :—

Oct. 25 " Scots Songs and School Competitions "—Mr J. Jeffrey Hunter.

Nov. 29. " Men Worth Knowing "—Ex-Bailie Shaw Maxwell, J.P.

Feb. 28. " Burns and the Poets "—Mr Jas. D. Sloan.

Mar. 28. " Some Modern Scots Poets of the Vernacular "—Mr Ninian M'Whannel.

April 25. Smoking Concert and Whist Drive.

June 1. Annual Outing.   J. J. H.

GLASGOW AND DISTRICT BURNS CLUBS ASSOCIATION.

ANNUAL REPORT, 1920-21.

The annual report was submitted at the meeting on 27th October.

The Association has now completed its 14th year.

All the meetings of the year were largely attended, and the various functions have been carried on successfully. Many lecturers have been sent to Societies and assistance rendered in other forms.

As usual the statue in George Square was beautifully decorated, and individual wreaths were sent by the Rosebery, Sandyford, and Tam o' Shanter Clubs, and by this Association.

The 5th Anniversary Sermon was preached on 23rd January by the Rev. Dugald Clark, of the Parish Church, Springburn, whose subject was " The Religious Teaching of Burns." The service was one of the most successful yet held, and there was a crowded congregation. The collection on behalf of the Mauchline House amounted to £14 6s 3d.

The Westland Club, Whiteinch ; the Shawlands Club, and Southern Merchants' Club have been admitted to membership, making the total membership 47.

On 13th November the re-interment of Highland Mary took place at Greenock, and was an impressive and memorable ceremony. The hospitality of the Greenock Burnsians will not be forgotten by those present.

A legacy of £50 was given to the Association from the estate of the late W. P. Lowrie, and this was handed over to the Burns House, Mauchline. Application has also been made for a legacy of similar amount bequeathed by a Helensburgh lady to the Haggis Club.

The Association was represented at the Burns Federation at Dunfermline on 4th September by Messrs Sutherland, Chalmers, and Cockburn. The meeting was a great success.

The Annual Outing of the Association took place to Mauchline on Saturday, 1st October, and proved a very happy event. The Highland Mary Memorial at Failford was visited, the beneficiaries were seen, and the members and friends dined in Poosie Nancy's.

The Museum at Mauchline has received several gifts, and has, during the past summer, been visited by a large number of people from all parts of the world.

At the Annual Meeting Mr Cowie presented to the Association :

(1) A pair of razors which belonged to Robert Burns.

(2) A silver watch which was the property of Burns's father, and was worn by Burns till he went to Dumfries, when he got a new one. ˙ The watch afterwards came into the possession of Gilbert Burns, and descended to his relations. Mr Cowie purchased all these at Sotheby's in July last. Mr Ewing gave an interesting description of the gifts, and stated they were absolutely genuine.

The Burns House Club promoted by the Association has had an extraordinary success, and is now the rendezvous of the principal Burns Clubs of the City and District.

At the Annual Meeting on 27th October Mr Cowie reported on the proposed Memorial to the Earl of Glencairn at Falmouth Church, and it was agreed to support same. It was agreed to re-thatch the Burns House at Mauchline, and to continue the allowances to the beneficiaries.

It was reported that an effort was being made to establish a Federation of the Edinburgh Burns Clubs, and it was agreed to give this project every possible assistance.

It was also agreed to support the proposed dinner to Sir Alexander Gibb on 9th December.

Letters were read from Mr Philip Sulley in connection with Entertainment Tax on Burns Dinner Tickets. These were reckoned very satisfactory, and it was agreed that Mr Sulley be heartily thanked for his gratuitous services.

It was unanimously agreed to heartily congratulate Dr M'Naught on receiving the degree of LL.D. from Glasgow University, and for the successful publication of his book, *The Truth About Burns*. J. J. H.

SCOTTISH BURNS CLUB.

(Instituted 1904),

In which are incorporated " Glasgow Waverley " and " Western " (1859) and " Ye Saints " (1884) Burns Clubs.

(Edinburgh Section formed 1919).

Motto :—" The heart aye's the part aye."

Success continues to follow the Club.

The syllabus was again a special feature. Mr John Muir (editor of the first *Burns Chronicle*) opened the session on 4th October, 1920, with " A Burns Fantasia." On November 22nd

Mr Frank Beaumont gave a delightful lecture on "Dr Johnson and Scotland." On 27th December Dr James Devon made a welcome re-appearance and gave one of his characteristic addresses, his subject being "George Buchanan." On 17th January Mr Walter Gray made his *debut* as a lecturer to the Club, treating "George Elliot" in a most interesting manner. February 28th saw Mr George M'Gill back to the scene of his former triumphs, his subject being "Mine Own Romantic Town."

Musical evenings were held on 25th October, 1920, and 28th March, 1921, to which ladies were invited. Mr J. G. MacKerracher as usual undertook the direction of the programme, and fully sustained his high reputation in submitting entertainments for which the Club has become famous.

The "Anniversary" was held on Monday, 24th January, when "The Immortal Memory" was proposed by the late The Right Rev. Archibald Ean Campbell, D.D., Lord Bishop of Glasgow and Galloway, who was in his best vein. The demise of this eminent divine shortly afterwards was a great shock to the community at large, and his loss to the Burns world is a blank which will not be easily filled. In addition to his many great gifts, he was a master of Burnsiana.

The Edinburgh Section is proving a great success. A splendid syllabus was successfully carried through. The Club meet on the third Friday of each month from October to March inclusive in The Outlook Tower—Scotland Room, Castle Hill, Edinburgh. The parent Club was represented at several of the meetings, and this season a lecturer will officially represent "headquarters."

The Scottish Burns Club seems to be getting a reputation for lecturers. It is well within the mark to say that Club members would deliver over two dozen lectures during the season to Burns Clubs and other societies.

The Club meetings begin at 7.30 p.m., opening with the lecture, which generally lasts until 8.30 p.m. Tea is served from then until 9 p.m., when a musical evening follows for an hour.

The membership is limited to 200, exclusive of life and honorary members and the Edinburgh Section. The list of waiting applicants is somewhere in the region of 50.

Owing to the increased attendance, the Club had reluctantly to leave their old quarters in Reid's Rooms in 30 Gordon Street —which can only comfortably accommodate slightly over 100. They have now gone to the "Ca'doro," 132 Renfield Street, and it is safe to say that no club is better housed in the city. It is hoped that the increased accommodation will allow the limit on the membership to be raised.

The Club diplomas are very unique. The first diploma is a lithographed print of Burns views, while the second diploma is a handsome gold badge bearing the Burns crest and motto. Three years entitle members to the first diploma, and seven years to the second diploma.

The present season is promising well, and the following syllabus provides interesting and instructive evenings.

1921.   SYLLABUS—1921-22.

*Oct.   3. " Burnsian Memories "—Mr John Muir.
Oct.   24. Musical Evening (Ladies' Night)—Mr J. G. MacKerracher.
Nov. 28. " James Boswell "—Dr J. T. T. Brown.
†Dec. 19. " Some Auld Scots Folk "—Dr James Devon.
1922.
†Jan. 16. " Ossian "—Mr Angus M'Intyre.
Jan.   23. " The Immortal Memory "—Sir William Martin.
Feb.   27. " British Literature "—Mr R. W. Brown.
Mar.   27. Annual General Meeting at 6.45 p.m.
            Musical Evening (Ladies' Night) at 7.30 p.m.—Mr J. G. MacKerracher.

* First Monday in October.   † Third Monday of month.

EDINBURGH SECTION.
1921.   SYLLABUS—1921-22.
Oct. 21. " Scotland in the Time of Burns "—Mr Martin Anderson.
Nov. 18. Scots Concert (Ladies' Night)—Arranged by Mr A. Drysdale Paterson.   (Meeting place to be arranged later.)
Dec. 16. " Burns Library : Some Edinburgh Items "—Mr John Muir, Scottish Burns Club, Glasgow.
1922.
Jan. 20. " Humour of Bench and Bar "—Mr J. Samson.
Feb. 17. Lantern Lecture on " Burns in Edinburgh " (Ladies' Night)—Mr W. J. Hay.
Mar. 17. "Northern Forebears of Robert Burns"—Mr Chas, Irvine, S.S.C.

J. KEVAN M'DOWALL, Hon. Sec. and Treasurer.

GLASGOW PRIMROSE BURNS CLUB.

SESSION 1920-1921.

We have pleasure in submitting the Annual Report of our last year's work. An average attendance of over 90 was maintained. Two ladies' evenings were held during the session, and a large turnout gave evidence of the popularity of such gatherings. The Annual Dinner took place in the Grand Hotel. Dr Steel, Rector of Allan Glen School proposed the " Immortal Memory."

A collection was taken at the dinner amounting to 5 guineas, which was handed to the Treasurer of the Mauchline House Fund.

The Annual School Competition was held in the Petershill Public School, Springburn. The President, Mr George M'Callum, occupied the chair. The excellence of the solo singing, and intelligent rendering of recitations, were features thoroughly enjoyed by the enthusiastic audience of parents, members, and friends. The principal prize-winners (silver medal lists) were :—Singing —Mary Leithhead, David Stewart, and James Leithhead ; Recitations—Mary Begg and James Duff. There were 19 prizes in all, contributed by our members. The prizes were gracefully handed to the winners by Mrs John Duncan, the club members thereafter being hospitably entertained bv the School Staff.

In the M'Lennan Bowling Competition we entered four rinks, *all being up*, but failed to win the coveted trophy.

Members of kindred clubs made welcome.

1921.   SYLLABUS.
Oct.   14. Opening Meeting—Musical Evening.
Nov.   18. Musical Evening—Ladies' Night.
Dec.   16. Musical Evening (" Our Trip to London ")—Tom Paton.
   1922.
Jan.   25. (Annual Dinner, Grand Hotel).   "The Immortal Memory"
             —Rev. Alex Moffatt, B.D.
Feb.   17. Ladies' Night and Whist Drive.
Mar.   17. Musical Evening.

All the above meetings to start 7.30 prompt.

                                                    J. W.

THE COQUETDALE BURNS CLUB.

1921, the second year of resuscitation of the above Club, has been somewhat less active than the previous year for various reasons, one being that the re-formation after the long war years was naturally most enthusiastic, and men travelled long miles over the hills to the Burns Dinner of 1919, held at Rothbury. Also money was plentiful. But the past year has been an anxious time amongst the hill farmers.

We had a most successful Burns Club Dinner in January,

1921. Mr Thomas Walker, the indefatigable · Burns enthusiast and authority, travelled all the way from Govan to propose the toast of the " Immortal Memory," which he honoured splendidly and with supreme literary skill. The Club is greatly indebted to Mr Walker for the real helpful interest he has taken in our ongoings.

On March 29, 1921, Mr Walker was again with us at the Jubilee Hall, Rothbury, and delivered a most illuminating lecture on " Robert Burns, the Poet and Man." Our veteran Vice-President, the far-famed archæologist, historian of the border country, and *littérateur*—Mr David Dippie Dixon, F.S.A., of Cragside—occupied the chair. The Burns Club Glee Party and others contributed Scottish music to illustrate the lecture. A large audience followed the course of the lecture with interest, and at the close the Rev. Ashby Mays moved a hearty vote of thanks to lecturer and singers, which was responded to by Mr Thomas Walker. Altogether it was a most delightful evening, to be remembered long by those privileged to attend.

1921 may be recorded as a fairly successful year, but not so good as we hope the coming years will be for the spread of the Burns cult in Coquetdale. We are sorry to have to report that owing to increasing years our worthy President, Mr R. Charlton of Sistler, feels compelled to retire this year from all office. He, with the famous John Carruthers, that sturdy border man of Barrow, well known round the Cheviots, are a fast-dwindling type of Burns lovers we can ill spare.

GEORGE RAE PATTERSON, *Secretary.*

ALBANY BURNS CLUB.

1921. SYLLABUS.

Oct. 5 Opening Meeting—William Cullen, Esq., M.D.
Nov. 2. " Clyde Steamers, Skippers, Trippers, and Scenery " (with Lantern Studies)—James Brown, Esq.
Dec. 7. " Braid Scots "—Geo. Eyre Todd, Esq.
Dec. 17. Children's Concert and Competition—Provanside Public School, at 3.30 p m.
Jan. 11. " Cottar's Saturday Night "—John Wilson Bain, Esq.
Jan. 25. " Immortal Memory " (Anniversary Dinner, Grand Hotel, at 6.30 p.m.).
Feb. 1. Music and Tea—Ladies' Night.
Mar. 1. " Millais and Burns "—John M'Ghie, Esq.

HELENSBURGH BURNS CLUB.

1921.   SYLLABUS FOR SESSION 1921-1922.

Oct.   7. Annual General Meeting.
Oct.   31. Hallowe'en.
Nov.   21. Essay : " Oliver Goldsmith "—Mr Findlay M'Kichan.
Dec.   5. Hat Night.
1922.
Jan.   16. Essay : " Tannahill "—Mr Matthew Allan, with Musical
            Illustrations by Choir and Soloists.
Jan.   25. Anniversary Celebration.
Feb.   — Concert in Victoria Hall (date not yet decided).

BUCK'S HEAD BURNS CLUB, ARMADALE.

REPORT FOR SESSION 1920-1921.

I have the pleasure and satisfaction to report another successful year of the Buck's Head Burns Club under the able Presidentship of Mr John Mack. The Annual Meeting of the Club was held on the 18th of September, 1920, with a large turnout of the members. The reports of Secretary and Treasurer were submitted, and showed the Club to be in a very flourishing condition. Our Hallowe'en Nicht of tatties and herrin', with a social and dance following, was a great success. A free New-Year's Day treat to the members' children brought a fairly good turnout of future Burnsites. The New-Year's Night social and dance was one of our most successful events, there being 110 couples present. The Annual Dinner in honour of our National Bard was held on 28th January, 1921, and proved to be a great success, there being 250 ladies and gentlemen present, while deputations from three sister clubs were present, viz., Newarthill, Whitburn, and Mid-Calder. Mr William M'Alpine proposed the " Immortal Memory," and Mrs J. Peden, a lady member of the committee, replied to " The Lassies." We have held meetings throughout the county to get an association of the county clubs formed, and in the near future we see hopes of our work getting rewarded. Owing to the coal strike some of our most enterprising features had unfortunately to be abandoned, our school children's competition did not come off, and our annual outing, which had been fixed to take place on the first Saturday of June, 1921, to Dumfries, had also to be cancelled for the same reason. Seven of our lady members have now got their membership cards, and others are desirous of having theirs. We are greatly indebted to the lady members of our Club for a special voluntary donation of £8 14s to the funds of the Club. This was raised by a series of presents brought to the Club and sold by auction, and I take this opportunity of thanking the ladies on behalf of the Club for the great interest and hard work performed in .pursuance of the Club's interests. The success of the session is due to the energetic work of our worthy President and his committee, and also to Mr Samuel Lambie, Musical Director of the Club, and I take this opportunity of thanking all who have worked in harmony for the welfare of the Buck's Head Burns Club.

SYLLABUS—1921-1922.

Dec. 17. " Burns and the Common People "—Vice-President Mr Wm. M'Alpine.

Jan. 16. Paper—Mr John Strang.

Jan. 29. Anniversary Dinner—As arranged.

Feb. 20. Musical Evening (Ladies' Night)—Mr Samuel Lambie.

Mar. 19. Paper—Mr John Mack.

JOHN STEVENSON, *Hon. Secretary.*

———————

YE CRONIES BURNS CLUB (GOVAN).

SECRETARY'S REPORT, 1920-1921

I am very pleased to report that the session just closed has been a very successful one. The Annual Meeting was held on Saturday, the 12th June, 1920, when there was a large attendance of members. The reports submitted by the Secretary and Treasurer were of a very gratifying nature, and showed the Club to be in a very flourishing condition. During the session there have been ten ordinary monthly meetings and two special lectures, which were all very well attended by the members. In the M'Lennan Bowling Competition in August, 1920, the Club entered five rinks, but all failed in winning the coveted trophy, although all the players enjoyed the afternoon's outing and hoped for better luck next year. The Annual Outing took place on Saturday, 28th August, 1920, to Hamilton Palace and Mausoleum, when there was a large turnout of members and their lady friends, dinner and tea being provided inside the policies. A large programme of sports was carried through, and handsome prizes awarded to the winners of the various events. Our best thanks are due Mr Wilson, Secretary of the Hamilton Junior Burns Club, and his committee, for the perfect arrangements made for our comfort.' The President, Vice-President, and Secretary attended the Annual Meeting of the Burns Federation in London on September 4th, 1920, and reported the great interest and pleasure the meeting afforded them and the princely hospitality extended to the delegates by the members of the London Robert Burns Club. On Saturday, the 23rd October, 1920, Mr Amos, the genial Secretary of the Burns Federation, gave us a lecture in Men's Clubroom, Pearce Institute, Govan, when there was a very large audience, Mr Amos's subject being "Dunbar, the Pre-Reformation Burns," which he handled in a masterly manner, everyone present being delighted with the lecture; and Mr Parker, Musical Director, submitted an excellent programme of music. At November Monthly Meeting Mr L. M'Laine, Treasurer, gave the members a very interesting address on Burns Clubs, pointing out where the activities of clubs could be greatly increased and show to the public that our admiration for the Poet was sincere. At the December Monthly Meeting Mr Parker addressed the members on "Burns's Works," several members assisting Mr Parker in illustrating his address. The Anniversary Supper was held in M'Leod Hall, Pearce Institute, on Saturday, 22nd January, 1921, and proved a great success. Mr T. M. Walker, M.A., proposed "The Immortal Memory," and in doing so paid a high tribute to the genius of Burns. Greeting cards were exchanged with a large number of federated clubs. At the February Monthly Meeting Mr C. B. Moodie addressed the members, his subject being "The Life and Songs of Baroness Nairne." Mr Moodie had a thorough grasp of his subject, and pointed out had Lady Nairne wrote no more than the three songs, "The Rowan Tree," "The Auld Hoose," and "Caller Herrin'," she was entitled to a high place in the lyric minstrelsy of Scotland. On Tuesday, 22nd March, 1921, Dr J. H. Steel, M.A., D. Litt., Headmaster, Allan Glen's School, Glasgow, gave us a lecture in Men's Clubroom, Pearce Institute, before a very large and attentive audience, his subject being "Tam o' Shanter," which he handled in a brilliant manner for over an hour, which proved the Doctor to be one of our foremost lecturers and able to hold any audience by his fine oratory. Mr Parker again submitted an excellent programme of music. The Annual Meeting was held on the 11th June, 1921, when all the reports submitted were of a satisfactory nature, and showed the Club to be still progressing. In the M'Lennan Bowling Competition, the Club entered five rinks, and the one skipped by Mr D. Fisher were successful in winning the cup and badges, being 36 shots up. The President, Vice-President, Secretary, and Past President (Mr Stirling) attended the Annual Meeting of the Burns Federation in Dunfermline on Saturday, 3rd September, 1921, and reported the great pleasure they had at being at the conference and the great hospitality shown to them by the Dunfermline Club, Sir Alexander Gibb, and Lord Elgin, who did all in their power to make the delegates feel at home.

The Dunfermline meeting will long be remembered by those who had the privilege of taking part in the proceedings.

In Memoriam.

It is with sincere regret I have to record during this session the deaths of five of our most esteemed members, and our Club will be much the poorer by their passing, and their presence will be greatly missed at our Club meetings. I refer to Bro. Robert Coutts, a past Secretary of the Club, who died on 17th August, 1920, after a long and serious illness ; Bro. John Brown, the genial manager of our Clubroom, who died on the 13th September, 1920, after a serious operation ; Bro. Robert M'Kissock, who died on 29th September, 1920, from the effects of gas poisoning received while serving his King and Country ; Bro. Nathan M'Kelvie, a past Vice-President of the Club, who died very suddenly on the 5th March, 1921 ; and Bro. Lauchlan M'Laine, Treasurer of the Club, who died with tragic suddenness on September 9th, 1921. Deputations of the members attended the funerals of the deceased Brothers, and floral wreaths were sent on behalf of the members of the Club, also letters of condolence to the relatives of deceased.

Much of the year's success has been due to the untiring energy and enthusiasm of Past President Stirling and Committee, who have always been ready to do all in their power to further the Club's interests, and who were very regular in their attendance at all meetings and committee meetings, which were very numerous. Our new President, Mr J. Hutchison, seems assured of a very prosperous session, as all our members are taking a very active part in the work of the Club, which augurs well for its future success.

James Rellie, Secretary.

SINCLAIRTOWN BURNS CLUB (KIRKCALDY).

Following the Annual Dinner in January last, the Sinclairtown Club has pursued a career of social and edifying activity, and at the present moment is inundated by applications from many prospective members. Early in March the first President of the Club, Councillor Tom Laing, gave up both his office and membership, but in October he was prevailed upon to take his place in a group showing the original office-bearers of the resuscitated Club, which group we have pleasure in reproducing. Next to the Annual Dinner the most successful of the Club's functions is the Annual Drive, which took place in June, and in which the ladies participated. Callander was the venue, with a considerable halt at Stirling, and the drive was voted a complete success, notwithstanding an unavoidable mishap in the latter part of the day caused by a transport difficulty. Delegates from the Club attended the conference of Burns Federations in Dunfermline, and reported to general meeting their impressions of the proceedings, their conviction being that this conference is an undoubted stimulus to lovers of the Poet and his works. At the annual meeting in October office-bearers for the ensuing year were elected as follows :—Hon. President, Mr James Roberts, Sinclairtown Hotel (the Club's headquarters); Hon.

Vice-President, Mr Henry W. Hogarth; President, Mr William Crombie; Vice-President, Mr Robert Keddie; Treasurer, Mr D. Harley; Secretary, Mr Thomas Hunter, Dryburgh House, 181 St. Clair Street; Members of committee—Messrs John Innes, David Brown, Alexander Justice, William Kidd, Robert Blyth, James Brown, and William Mackie. It has now been arranged to hold general meetings of the Club in November, January, and March. A very healthy tone pervades the Club all through, and every effort is being made to provide the members with those social opportunities which do their part to hasten the day of which the Bard wrote so hopefully—

> " When man to man the world o'er
> Shall brithers be   "

THOMAS HUNTER, *Secretary.*

WHITBURN BURNS CLUB.

The Annual Meeting of Whitburn Burns Club was held in the Cross Tavern. Mr Frank M'Gregor, President, presided. The Secretary, Mr A. Johnston, gave an outline of the work done during the session just closed, also an outline of the Burns Federation meeting held at Dunfermline on September 3rd. The balance sheet was gone over and approved of. The income showed that, including brought forward from session 1920 £1 17s 6d, and the members' fees, &c., during session 1920-21 forthcoming £3 8s 9d, the funds realised £5 6s 3d. From this fell to be deducted expenditure of £3 15s 5d, leaving net credit balance of £1 11s 10d. The following appointments for session 1921-22 were made :—President, Mr Frank M'Gregor ; Vice-President, Mr Wm. M'Kenzie ; Treasurer, Mr John Johnston ; Secretary, Mr Allan Johnston ; Delegate to S.B.C.A. Council Meetings, Mr Wm. Clark ; Members of Committee—Messrs John Greig, Wm. Gray, David Reid, John Easton, James Brown, James Donald, John Brown (No. 1), John Ferguson, Alex. M'Laren (sen.), A. M'Laren (jun)., and Andrew Clark. Agreed that meetings during session be held thus—Business meeting, first Friday of each month ; socials on third Saturday of each month. Agreed to ask any member willing to give a paper, or a musical evening, to hand his name to the Secretary. Arranged to hold two essay competitions in November, and singing and reciting competitions in March. Membership fee was fixed at 2s 6d.

THE CATHCART BURNS CLUB.

ANNUAL REPORT.

The session of 1920-21 has been a most enjoyable and prosperous one, both for the Club and for the members individually. The syllabus was very attractive, and the Monthly Meetings were very well attended. The Annual Supper in the Couper Institute was a great success, about 60 gentlemen sitting down to a first-class purvey. " The Immortal Memory " was proposed by Mr Wm. Douglas. The Club entered a rink for the M'Lennan Bowling Trophy, but met better men. The Club also had an evening's bowling tournament on the Cathcart Bowling Club's green, and another on Weir's Recreation Grounds, Cathcart, when two very enjoyable evenings were spent. The Secretary attended and represented the Club at the dinner given to Mr Gribbel in the Grand Hotel, Glasgow. The committee are making arrangements to have competitions in the local schools on Scottish History, but the details are not yet settled. From the number of new names handed to the Secretary it looks as if 1921-22 were going to eclipse its predecessors.

1921.   SYLLABUS.

Sep. 29. " Behind the German Lines "—Capt. the Rev. G. C Smith, M.C., M.A.

Oct. 27. " A Trip to Canada with the British Bowlers "—Mr W. Scott.

Nov. 24. " Egypt "—Mr Graham.

Dec. 29. " Some Characteristics of Scottish Song " — Mr W. Douglas.

1922.

Jan. 25. Annual Supper in Couper Institute, at 7.30 p.m.

Feb. 23. " Scott "—Mr W. Glen.

Mar. 30. Selected—Mr J Hyslop.

Apr. 27. Business Meeting.

THE ABERDEEN BURNS CLUB.

1921.   SYLLABUS—1921-1922.

Aug. 13. Annual Picnic at Hazlehead.

Oct. 4. Open Social Evening—Address by Dr J. F. Tocher, County Analyst.

Nov. 9. " Natural History in Burns "—Professor J. Arthur Thomson.

Dec. 5. Entertainment in Y.M.C.A. Hall.

1922.

Jan. 3. Illustrated Lecture on Mountaineering—Mr William Garden, Advocate.

Jan. 25. Annual Celebration and Supper.

Feb. 6. Lecture—Dr W. J. Profeit, Lecturer on Agriculture.

Mar. 6. Open Social Evening—Address by Mr George Duncan, Advocate.

Apr. 3. Annual General Meeting.

All meetings are held in the Imperial Hotel, except otherwise notified, and commence at 7.30 p.m prompt.

The Burns Federation.

INSTITUTED 1885.

Hon. Presidents-The Right Hon. The EARL OF ROSEBERY, K.G., K.T.
Sir ALEX. GIBB, G.B.E., C.B., Grunard, by Aultbea, Ross-shire.

Hon. Vice-Presidents — Col. JOHN GRIBBEL, M.A., LL.D., St.
Austell's, Wyncote, Philadelphia.
WM. WILL, *Graphic*, Tallis Street, London, E.C.4.

OFFICE-BEARERS.

President—DUNCAN M'NAUGHT, J.P., LL.D., Benrig, Kilmaurs.

Vice-Presidents—J. JEFFREY HUNTER, 89 Bath Street, Glasgow.
A. M'CALLUM, *News* Office, Pollockshaws.
ALEX. POLLOCK, 52 West Nile Street, Glasgow.
W. H. TURNER, 9 The Oaks, Sunderland.
JOHN CARMICHAEL, 49 Park Road, Glasgow.
P. PATERSON, 23 Bruce Street, Dunfermline.
Ex-Bailie MUNRO, J.P., Howard Park Drive, Kilmarnock.
Ex-Provost M. SMITH, J.P., Glencairn Square, Kilmarnock.
Sir ROBERT WILSON, 149 Howard Street, Glasgow.
PHILIP SULLEY, 27 Rutland Square, Edinburgh.
HUGH M'COLL, 278 St. Vincent Street, Glasgow.
Col. HENRY S. MURRAY, J.P., Glenmayne, Galashiels.
CHARLES R. COWIE, 20 Blythswood Square, Glasgow.
J. C. EWING, Bailie's Institution, West Regent Street, Glasgow.
ALEX. M'KENZIE, 210 Battlefield Road, Langside, Glasgow.
JAMES THOMSON, F S.A.(Scot.), The Cedars, 21 Fortis Green,
East Finchley, London, N.2.
THOS. KILLIN, J.P., 2 Stewarton Drive, Cambuslang.
HUGH M'LEAN, Elmhurst, Greenock.
ALBERT DOUGLAS, LL.D., Washington, U.S.A.
WM. BAIRD, J.P., F.S.A.(Scot.), 11 Pitt Street, Portobello.
L. G. SLOAN, J.P., Pen Corner, Kingsway, London, W.C.2.
J. TAYLOR GIBB, M.A., Mauchline.

Hon Secretary—THOS. AMOS, M.A., 19 Glebe Road, Kilmarnock.

Hon. Treasurer—Major G. A. INNES, M.B.E., 14 London Road,
Kilmarnock.

Editor " Burns Chronicle "—Dr D. M'NAUGHT, J.P., Benrig, Kilmaurs.

Auditors—Major D. YUILLE, Burns Avenue, Kilmarnock, and Capt. ADAM MACKAY, The Crescent, Prestwick.

Local Representatives—
London—P. N. M'FARLANE, Tallis House, Tallis Street, London. E.C.
North of England—W. H. TURNER, Sunderland.
Glasgow and District—J. JEFFREY HUNTER, 89 Bath Street Glasgow.

Hon Secretary of Children's Competitions—ALEX. POLLOCK, 52 West Nile Street, Glasgow (to whom all communications should be addressed).

CONSTITUTION.

1. The Federation shall consist of Hon. Presidents, Hon. Vice-Presidents, Executive Council, and members of each affiliated Club

2. The Executive Council shall consist of a President, Vice-Presidents, Hon. Secretary, Hon. Treasurer, Editor of the *Burns Chronicle*, and two Auditors—all of whom shall be elected annually, and be eligible for re-election ; also of the President, Vice-President, and Secretary, or any other three members of, and nominated by, each affiliated Club, and other gentlemen of eminence as Burnsians nominated by the Executive Council.

3. All Past Presidents of the Federation shall *ex officio* be members of the Executive Council.

4. The Executive Committee shall consist of the Office-bearers of the Federation, who shall meet quarterly, or when called by the Hon. Secretary, for the transaction of the business of the Federation.

5. Federated Clubs outwith the United Kingdom may be represented by proxy at the meetings of the Federation.

OBJECTS OF THE FEDERATION.

1. To strengthen and consolidate by universal affiliation the bond of fellowship existing amongst the members of Burns Clubs and kindred Societies.

2. To superintend the publication of Works relating to Burns.

3. To acquire a fund for the purchase and preservation of Holograph Manuscripts and other Relics connected with the life of the Poet, and for other purposes of a like nature, as the Executive Council may determine.

4. To repair, renew, and where advisable mark with suitable inscriptions any buildings, tombstones, etc., interesting from their association with Burns.

5. To encourage and arrange School Competitions in order to stimulate the teaching of Scottish History and Literature.

RULES.

1. The Headquarters of the Federation shall be in Kilmarnock, the town in which the Federation was inaugurated and carried to a

practical issue, and which contains the only properly organised Burns Library and Museum in the United Kingdom.

2. Properly organised Burns Clubs, St. Andrew's Societies, and kindred Associations may be admitted to the Federation by application in writing to the Hon. Secretary, enclosing a copy of Constitution, Rules, and list of members, which shall be submitted to the Executive Committee at their first meeting, and the Clubs shall be enrolled if there are not more than two dissentients.'

3. The Registration Fee is 42s, on receipt of which the Diploma of the Federation shall be issued, after being numbered and signed by the President and Hon. Secretary.

4. Members of every Burns Club or kindred Association registered by the Federation shall be entitled to receive a pocket Diploma on payment of 1s. These payments are final—not annual.

5. The funds of the Federation shall be vested in the Executive Committee for the purposes before mentioned.

6. A meeting of the Executive Council shall be held annually on the first Saturday of September, at such place as may be agreed upon, when reports on the year's transactions shall be submitted by the Hon. Secretary and Hon. Treasurer, and Office-Bearers elected for the ensuing year.

7. A meeting of the Executive Committee shall take place some time before the Annual Meeting of the Executive Council, to make the necessary arrangements for the same

8. All nominations for the office of Vice-President must be lodged with the Hon. Secretary two. months before the Annual Meeting.

9. Each Federated Club shall pay a minimum subscription of one guinea annually. Clubs failing to pay this subscription for two consecutive years may be struck off the Roll of the Federation. Any surplus profits resulting from the sale of the *Chronicle* shall be added to the general funds.

10. Notice of any amendment or alteration of the Constitution or Rules of the Federation to be considered at the Annual Meeting must be lodged in writing with the Hon. Secretary not later than 30th June.

BENEFITS.

1. Registered Clubs are supplied free with copies of newspapers containing accounts of meetings, demonstrations, etc , organised, conducted, or attended by the Executive Council of the Federation, and of the Annual Meeting of the Kilmarnock Burns Club.

2. Exchange of fraternal greetings on the anniversary of the Poet's natal day.

3. Members of Registered Clubs who have provided themselves with pocket diplomas are entitled to attend meetings of all Clubs on the Roll of the Federation, they being subject to the rules of the Club visited, but having no voice in its management unless admitted a member according to local form.

4. Members are entitled to be supplied, through the Secretaries of their respective Clubs, with copies of all Works published by the Federation at a discount of 25 per cent.

5. A list of Lecturers. Essayists, and Judges for Children's Competitions will be supplied to Clubs on application.

BOOKS PUBLISHED BY THE FEDERATION.

BURNS HOLOGRAPH MANUSCRIPTS in the Kilmarnock Monument Museum, with Notes	1889	1s 6d
BURNS CHRONICLE and CLUB DIRECTORY...	1892	Is 0d
,,	1893	1s 6d
	1894	Is 6d
	1895	1s 6d
	1896	Is 6d
	1897	1s 6d
	1898	Is 6d
	1899	1s 6d
,,	1900	1s 6d
,, (out of print)	1901	1s 6d
,,	1902	1s 6d
	1903	1s 6d
	1904	Is 6d
	1905	1s 6d
	1906	Is 6d
	1907	1s 6d
	1908	1s 6d
	1909	1s 6d
	1910	1s 6d
	1911	1s 6d
	1912	Is 6d
	1913	1s 6d
	1914	1s 6d
	1915	1s 6d
	1916	1s 6d
	1917	2s 0d
	1918	2s 0d
	1919	2s 0d
	1920	2s 0d
	1921	3s 0d
,,	1922	3s 0d
INDEX		1s 0d

Copies of the last eleven vols. may still be had on application to the Hon. Treasurer.

MINUTES OF THE ANNUAL CONFERENCE

BURNS FEDERATION.

BURGH COURT ROOM, DUNFERMLINE
3rd September, 1921.

THE Annual Conference of the Burns Federation was held here to-day at 11 a.m. Dr D. M'Naught, President of the Federation, occupied the chair. The following delegates were present :—

Executive Committee—J. Jeffrey Hunter, A. M'Callum, A. Pollock, W. H. Turner, J. Carmichael, P. Paterson, W. Munro, Sir Robt. Wilson, P. Sulley, H. M'Coll, J. C. Ewing, Alex. M'Kenzie, J. Thomson, W. Douglas, T. Killin, P. N. M'Farlane, G. A. Innes, and T. Amos.

No. 0, Kilmarnock—J. Ford, J. P. Dickson. No. 1, London —Sir W. Noble, J. A. Brown, T. W. B. Ramsay. No. 9, Glasgow Royalty—Councillor Jas. M'Farlane, D. Gunn, Wm. Jamieson. No. 14, Dundee—D. Brown, J. Neilson, M. Gibson. No. 21, Greenock—D. M'Callum, W. Nicoll, G. B. Grieve, H. M'Lean. No. 22, Edinburgh—R. Duncan. No. 36, Glasgow Rosebery— W. Craig, A. G. Andrew, J. M. Alexander. No. 40, Aberdeen —A. W. Mackie, L. M. Gordon. No. 49, Bridgeton—G. Brown, Dr W. A. Burn, J. G. Sproll. No. 50, Stirling—R. Sandeman. No. 53, Govan Fairfield—J. Donald, J. M'Lachlan, T. Fullarton. No. 63, Glasgow Mossgiel—J. M. Blain. No. 67, Glasgow Carlton —Jas. Robertson. No. 68, Glasgow Sandyford—Lieut.-Col. J. G. Robertson, Bailie Renfrew, A. Duthie. No. 74, Glasgow Mauch. line Society—J. T. Gibb. No. 76, Brechin—R. Anderson, J. S. Melrose, F. C. Anderson. No. 81, Glasgow Primrose—J. Hair, W. G. Robertson, T. B. Paton, T. Sutherland. No. 85, Dunferm. line United—Thos. Lessells. No. 86, Cumnock Winsome Willie —Jas. Neil. No. 89, Sunderland—Thos. Fisher. No. 91, Shettleston—G. S. Glendinning, A. M'Kay, J. M'Farlan. No. 92, Kilbirnie Jolly Beggars—A. Davidson, Robt. Patrick, W. Patrick. No. 97, Kilmarnock Bellfield—Wm. Flannagan. No. 113, Vale of Leven Glencairn—J. James, J. L. Ritchie, P. Burdon. No. 118, Glasgow Albany—R. Carmichael, Dr W. Cullen, J. Niven Murdoch. No. 121, Hamilton Junior—R. Brown, D. Cross, W. Wilson. No. 128, Cowdenbeath Glencairn—W. Foster, J. Nisbet, E. Hunter. No. 133, Newarthill—C. Johnstone. No. 135, Partick Western—Albert V. Smith. No. 139, Glasgow National—J. M. Ritchie, J. G. Galpine, G. Black. No. 151, Old Kilpatrick— R. Smith, T. M. Walker. No. 155, East Stirlingshire—A. Glen, W. Galbraith, W. Gibson. No. 156, Newcastle and Tyneside— R. M. Graham, J. Gibb. No. 157, Baillieston—J. Kerr. No. 160, Whitburn—Allan Johnston. No. 165, Wallsend—D. Carruthers. No. 167, Birmingham—A. Barclay, R. Kerr. No. 169, Glasgow

B.C.A.—W. C. Cockburn, Isaac Chalmers. No. 175, Meikle Earnock Original—Jas. Shepherd, Alex. Laird. No. 182, Stane Mossgiel—Alex. Walker, Geo. Meikle. No. 184, Blairadam Shanter —A. Bennet, W. Fyfe, A Richardson. No. 186, Kilmarnock Glencairn—John Ferguson. No. 189, Clydebank Barns o' Clyde —A. Homewood. No. 192, Ayrshire B.C.A.—W. Lennox. No. 198, Gorebridge Jolly Beggars—J. Learmonth, J. Dunlop, J. Deans. No. 199, Newbattle and District— J. F. Haldane, J. Gilmour. No. 202, Ye Cronies (Govan)—W. Parker, J. Rellie, J. Hutchison. No. 207, Cambuslang Wingate—W. Stewart, J. Campbell, A. M'Neil. No. 209, Greenock St. John's — J. A. Morrison, J. A. C. Hamilton, P. Morrison. No. 211, Larkhall Cronies—W. Kilpatrick, R. Ramage, C. Dobbie. No. 212, Portobello—W. Baird, Bailie Hastie, T. Bennett. No. 218, Bannockburn Empire—J. Forsyth, W. R. Lennie. No. 223, Glasgow Auld Clinkum—J. Wilson. No. 231, Fauldhouse and East Benhar— W. Salmond, J. Salmond, W. Thompson. No. 237, Uddingston Masonic—G. Anderson, D. N. Miller. No. 243, Paisley St. James —J. M'Kechnie, W. Alexander, J. P. Stewart. No. 244, Dalmuir —C. F. Kean, A. M'Gregor. No. 245, Kinnaird Victoria—R. Easton, T. Aitken, S. Marshall. No. 246, Rosewell Shanter— A. Rankin, W. Morton, A. Arnott. No. 247, Lochgelly Jolly Beggars—J. Adamson, J. D. Wilson, W. M'Kechnie, J. Walker. No. 250, Cowdenbeath Tam o' Shanter—J. Black, T. Waugh, J. M'Queen. No. 251, Glencraig — J. Dodds, R. Glencross, A. Garrie. No. 258, Armadale Buck's Head—J. Mack, J. Stevenson. No. 262, Fifeshire B.C.A.—W. M. Millar, G. Marshall. No. 263, Glasgow Masonic—C. W. Crofts, J. Veitch, F. S. Russell. No. 264, Prestonpans Jolly Beggars—R. Tripney, R. White. No. 265, Bingry Jolly Beggars—J. Gold, W. C. Clark, A. Stewart. No. 274, Troon—H. Thomson. No. 275, Ayr—J. M'Kay, J. Wills, J. L. Wilson. No. 276, Lumphinnans Highland Mary—R. Bulloch, G. Pratt. No. 282, Glasgow B.C.A. Bowlers—R B. Allison, R. Parker. No. 283, Sinclairtown—W. Crombie, T. Thorrat, J. G. Brown. No. 288, Beith Caledonia—A. P. Craig, J. Fulton. No. 289, Coatbridge Bricklayers—A. Young, J. Hill. No. 290, Blantyre Masonic—G. Gourlay, A. Airns, A. M. Gourlay. No. 291, Kilmarnock Highland Mary—H. Strachan, W. Blacklock. No. 292, Grahamston — J. Lapsley, J. Finnie. No. 294, Hill of Beith— W. Lees, J. Barclay.

Apologies for absence were intimated from Col. H. S. Murray, Galashiels ; ex-Provost Smith, Kilmarnock ; and Chas. R. Cowie, Glasgow.

Minutes of previous Conference were read and approved.

SECRETARY'S REPORT.

Mr Amos submitted his annual report, which was in the following terms :—

" Twelve years have passed since the Burns Federation last met in this hall, and at the invitation of the Dunfermline United Burns Club we gladly renew our acquaintance with ' the Auld Grey Town,' and its memories of poets and kings.

" Our first duty to-day is to congratulate Dr M'Naught on his recent honour. The University of Glasgow by conferring the degree of LL.D. on our president has justly crowned a lifetime's

work for the Burns cult.   Since he became editor of the *Chronicle*
thirty years ago our annual has been enriched each year with
articles from his pen, and the extent and scope of his work can
easily be gauged by reference to the recently published Index.
His book, *The Truth About Burns*, which will soon be published
in Glasgow, has at his request been dedicated to the Federation.
and we can best show our appreciation of this honour by our careful
reading of this volume—the garnered wisdom of a life-long study
of Burns.

"During the year death has removed several well-known
Burnsians.   I have only to mention the names of Dr Wallace,
Professor Lawson, Joseph Martin, David M'Farlane, Robert Dunlop, and Andrew Sinclair to show how difficult it will be to refill their
vacant places.   We were proud to have Dr Wallace as our president, and at his retiral from office we appointed him an honorary
vice-president.   His scholarly work as a Burns editor is known
and appreciated by all Burnsians, and his untiring efforts, both
for the establishment of a Chair of Scottish Literature and the
restoration of the Auld Brig of Ayr, will always be gratefully
remembered by the Federation.   Professor Lawson, another of our
hon. vice-presidents, for many years adorned the Chair of English
Literature at St. Andrews University.   He was greatly interested in the Federation, and not long before his death, edited, along
with his wife, an excellent anthology of Scottish verse.   Dunfermline and Kilmarnock are poorer through the passing of Robert
Dunlop and Andrew Sinclair.   Both were men of strong personality,
steeped in Burns lore, and intimately acquainted with the homes
and haunts of the Poet.   They were also both men of high attainments in natural science, and their greatest joy was either to lead
a geological excursion or a Burnsian ramble.   Joseph Martin, one
of our senior vice-presidents, was for many years one of our most
faithful workers.   In the movement for the foundation of a Chair
of Scottish Literature he acted as joint secretary, and he was for
long one of the outstanding Burnsians in Glasgow.   His genial
presence and wise counsel are greatly missed by a wide circle of
friends.   To the bereaved relations of all we respectfully tender
our sincerest sympathy.

"I am pleased to report that the Federation is still growing
in numbers and usefulness.   At present there are 295 Clubs on
our roll.   During the past year the following sixteen Clubs have
been affiliated :—Broxburn Jolly Beggars, Detroit (U.S.A.), Vickerstown, Glasgow Burns Clubs Bowling Association (Sinclairtown),
Jean Armour (Cowdenbeath), Shawlands, Queen Anne (Glasgow),
Caledonia (Beith), Coatbridge Bricklayers, Blantyre and District
Masonic, Highland Mary (Kilmarnock), North Eastern (Philadelphia), Grahamston, Poosie Nancy (Newcraighall), and Hill of
Beath.   It is interesting to note that through the efforts of Detroit
Burns Club a statue to Burns was erected six weeks ago in that
city.   We send the Club our congratulations.

"In the month of January No. 30 of the *Burns Chronicle* was
published, and the whole issue was quickly sold out.   In its literary
matter the number was abreast of its predecessors, and its hearty
welcome by the Press must have been some recompense to our veteran editor, whom we again thank most sincerely for his arduous
and honorary labours.   Owing to the illness of Mr Albert Douglas,
of Philadelphia, U.S.A., the Index to the first thirty copies of the

Chronicle was not published until June.   Through the generosity of Mr Douglas, Col. H. S. Murray, and Sir Alexander Gibb the Index was supplied to members at a nominal cost, and should prove invaluable as a book of reference to all who have a set of the *Chronicle.*

" On Saturday, 13th November, 1920, according to the wish of the Executive Committee, the dust of Highland Mary was removed from the West Kirk burying ground and re-interred in Greenock Cemetery.   Notwithstanding the inclement weather a great gathering witnessed the ceremony, which was conducted under the direction of the Greenock Burns Clubs and attended by many members of the Executive Committee.   At the grave a dignified and impressive service was held by the Rev. W. J. Nichol Service, of the West Kirk, Greenock, who was assisted by a special male voice choir under Mr Percy Harmon.   Mr Hugh M'Lean, President of Greenock Burns Club, and the Committee who worked with him, deserve the thanks of the Federation for the admirable manner in which the details of the ceremony were conceived and carried out.

" As you may remember, Messrs Harland & Wolff offered £300 to the Federation for the purpose of erecting a memorial to Highland Mary.   At our meeting in London it was announced that a site for the memorial had been fixed at Blackhill, Ayrshire, near the spot where Burns and Highland Mary are said to have parted. In the month of May a Masonic demonstration was organised by the Rev. J. C. Higgins, of Tarbolton, and the foundation stone of this memorial was laid with full Masonic honours by Mr James Arthur, of Montgomerie, upon whose ground the memorial stands. It was the intention of the Federation to formally inaugurate the memorial in September, but Mr Arthur wishes an unclimbable iron railing erected for the protection of the memorial and also an iron fence from the public road to the memorial.   The distance of the memorial from the public road is about 52 yards, and it is esti- mated, that it will cost at least £150 to fence this path and erect the railing.   In view of the amount of money required the Presi- dent thought that no further action was possible until the whole matter was brought before the Executive Council at this meeting.

" We congratulate the Burns Club of London on its recently published report of the Vernacular Circle Committee, which has aroused great interest in Scotland.   The Circle is trying to encourage by every means possible the use of the vernacular language, oral and written, and for that purpose is offering prizes in schools and universities.   Aberdeen University has accepted a prize of ten guineas per annum for the best poem in any dialect of braid Scots. This prize, as well as prizes for recitations open to the schools of Aberdeen, has been generously awarded by Sir William Noble, President of the Club, whom we are pleased to have present with us. Mr L. G. Sloan, whose hospitality at our memorable London meeting will never be forgotten, has also generously gifted the sum of £500 to the Universities of St. Andrews and Edinburgh for the estab- lishment of prizes in Scottish vernacular literature.   We in Scot- land can thoroughly sympathise with this endeavour by our countrymen in London, as for years a great many of our Scottish Burns Clubs have been quietly doing work of a similar nature. Mr Pollock's report on school children's competitions will give Scotsmen at home who are unaware of what we have done some idea of the effort that is being made by Burns Clubs in Scotland to arrest the decay of our dialect.

" The Burns Homes for the aged in Mauchline are still being successfully conducted by the Glasgow Mauchline Society and the Glasgow B.C.A. We heartily wish them success.

" I cannot close without recording our grateful appreciation of the enthusiastic welcome we have had from the Burns Club of this ancient royal city. Their President, Sir Alexander Gibb, has overwhelmed us with his more than generous hospitality. Their Secretary, Mr Paterson, not content with the success of our last meeting here, has worked without ceasing for several months to make this meeting an unqualified success, and his work has not been in vain. We most sincerely thank him and all those who worked for our pleasure along with him."

The Treasurer submitted his Annual Statement, which showed a credit balance of £231 13s 6d.

Dr M'Naught reviewed the work done during the past year in connection with the Highland Mary Memorial. The ground proprietor, Mr James Arthur, had stipulated as a condition for his gift of the site, that a fence should be erected round the monument, and that the road to the monument should also be fenced. As the site originally fixed had been changed, a much greater length of railing was necessary, and it was estimated that £150 would be required to cover the expenses. Mr Philip Sulley moved, and Mr T. Killin seconded the motion, that the Federation proceed with the railing of the monument and pathway. This was agreed to, and the matter was remitted to the Executive Committee with powers to raise the money required.

Mr Alex. Pollock reported that since last Conference, three additional Clubs had initiated competitions for children in Scottish song and poetry. He also offered his help and guidance to any Club beginning this important work.

The Secretary reported that several Burns Clubs had complained that the Entertainment Tax had been levied on their meetings. Mr Philip Sulley suggested that the complaint should be brought before the Inland Revenue Commissioners and their expert advisers.

In the absence of Mr Chas. R. Cowie, Mr J. C. Ewing moved that a monument be erected in the Parish Church of Falmouth in memory of Burns's patron, the Earl of Glencairn, who died there in 1791. Mr Alex. M'Kenzie seconded the motion. After a division, it was agreed to remit to the Executive Committee with power to add to their numbers.

Mr J. Jeffrey Hunter brought forward the following motion :—
" To appoint a Special Committee with powers (a) to appeal to Scottish Educational Authorities, and to individual schoolmasters in likely districts, to establish School Competitions in Scottish Literature and History, (b) to make a general appeal for financial assistance for such competitions, and for bursaries, &c." Mr Wm. Baird, Portobello, seconded the motion. Mr Hunter read an in-

teresting letter from Professor Rait, Glasgow University, who commended the motion. After a division, it was agreed to entrust the subject to the following Special Committee :—The three officials, the two senior vice-presidents, and Messrs Pollock, M'Coll, Galpine, Cowie, and Ewing, with power to add to their numbers. Mr Thos. Killin, J.P., proposed that part of the funds of the Federation be invested in the Burns House Club, Ltd., 27 India Street, Glasgow. Mr Alex. M'Kenzie seconded the motion. Major Innes, seconded by Mr Jas. Thomson, London, moved the rejection of the motion, and this became the finding of the meeting after a vote had been taken. Ex-Councillor T. Sutherland, Glasgow, moved, and Mr H. M'Coll seconded, the following motion :—" That a Rule be inserted in the Constitution that the office of President can only be held by the same individual for two consecutive years." Owing to the opposition aroused by the motion Mr Sutherland agreed to withdraw it.

Mr Jeffrey Hunter moved, and Mr P. N. M'Farlane, London, seconded : — " That in the future the affiliation fee be doubled, and the minimum annual subscription be one guinea." The motion was unanimously adopted.

Owing to his advancing years, and the amount of work involved in his offices, Dr M'Naught intimated that he wished to retire from the presidentship. Mr W. H. Turner, Sunderland ; Mr M'Farlane, London ; and Mr Jeffrey Hunter having expressed their deep appreciation of the President's work and worth, and also their desire to find some means to lighten his work, Dr M'Naught agreed to remain in office for another year. It was left to the Executive Council to devise some means of relieving Dr M'Naught in the performance of his duties as President and Editor of the *Burns Chronicle.*

The following new office-bearers were appointed :—Hon. President, Sir Alex. Gibb, G.B.E., C.B. ; Hon. Vice-Presidents—Col. John Gribbel, M.A., LL.D., Philadelphia, and Wm. Will, *Graphic* Office, London ; Vice-Presidents—Albert Douglas, LL.D., Washington, U.S.A ; Wm. Baird, J.P., F.S.A. (Scot.), Portobello ; Hugh M'Lean, Greenock ; L. G. Sloan, J.P., London ; and J. Taylor Gibb, M.A., Mauchline.

On the motion of Sir Wm. Noble, seconded by Mr Alex. Pollock, the sum of £50 was granted to the Hon. Secretary as an honorarium.

Sir Wm. Noble read a letter from Col. H. B. Hans Hamilton making an appeal on behalf of Robert Burns Hutchison, a great-grandson of Burns, who was in distress in Vancouver. On the motion of the President it was agreed to remit the matter to the Executive Committee, who would act along with the Burns Club of London.

On behalf of the Burns Club of Birmingham, Mr A. Barclay assured the Federation that a very hearty welcome would await them in that city at next year's conference.

The question of recognising in some suitable manner the generosity of Sir Alex. Gibb in presenting the Murison Burns

Collection to Dunfermline was left in the hands of the Executive Committee.

The Secretary submitted a letter from Dundalk Burns Club, asking assistance to erect a monument to Edward Bruce, brother of King Robert Bruce, who was killed near Dundalk. Owing to the many schemes the Federation has at present on hand, it was considered impossible to accede to the request.

On the motion of Mr P. N. M'Farlane, London, the Federation conveyed its warmest congratulations to Dr M'Naught on receiving the degree of LL.D. from Glasgow University.

A vote of thanks to the Chairman terminated the meeting.

DINNER TO THE DELEGATES.

Through the generosity of Sir Alexander Gibb, President of the Dunfermline Burns Club, the Delegates were entertained to dinner in the Masonic Hall on Friday evening. Sir Alexander occupied the chair, and was supported by the Right Hon. The Earl of Elgin, Sir William Noble, Admiral Sir John F. E. Green, Sir William Robertson, Lord-Lieutenant of Fife ; Sir John Ross, Provost Norval, Mr Andrew Shearer, Town Clerk ; Mr Howard D. Van Sant, U.S. Consul ; and the President, Secretary, and Treasurer of the Federation.

After the loyal and patriotic toasts had been honoured, the Chairman proposed the toast of the Burns Federation, to which Dr M'Naught eloquently replied. The toast of " The Lasses " was felicitously proposed by Sir John Ross, and the Earl of Elgin on their behalf made a clever and humorous reply. The President, on rising to reply to the toast of his health, received a great ovation.

During the evening a most enjoyable musical programme was sustained by the members of the local Club, and Mr T. Don recited a spirited " Address to the Federation." A toast to the Chairman by Dr M'Naught, which was received with great enthusiasm, concluded a thoroughly successful function.

CIVIC RECEPTION.

Before the Business Meeting on Saturday, the Federation was accorded a Civic Reception in the Burgh Municipal Buildings. On behalf of the Corporation, Provost Norval offered the Delegates a hearty welcome to Dunfermline. Mr Jeffrey Hunter returned thanks on behalf of the Delegates.

PRESENTATION OF THE MURISON BURNS COLLECTION.

Immediately after the Business Meeting the Delegates proceeded to the Carnegie Library, where the Murison Burns Collection was formally handed over to the city by Sir Alexander Gibb.

Provost Norval, who presided, detailed the arrangements that had been made by the Town Council for the suitable housing of the Collection. Sir Alexander Gibb, in handing over his gift, hoped that the Collection would be a real asset to Dunfermline. Provost Norval thanked Sir Alexander for the very handsome addition to the attractions of Dunfermline.

Councillor P. Paterson, Secretary of Dunfermline Burns Club, called on Mr Robert Taylor, the oldest member of the Club, who presented to Lady Gibb a 'gold key, with which she opened the newly-dedicated Burns Room. Lady Gibb, in a graceful speech, hoped the Collection would grow in size and interest, and that the citizens of Dunfermline and visitors to the town would, through it, obtain a greater knowledge of the priceless legacy which had been bequeathed to them by Robert Burns.

VISIT TO BROOMHALL.

The Delegates afterwards proceeded by char-a-banc to Broomhall, where they were entertained to lunch by the Earl and Countess of Elgin. After lunch, which was served in a large marquee erected on the lawn, they were conducted through Broomhall, and had an opportunity of inspecting the many interesting historical relics and portraits of the Bruce family. The sword and helmet of King Robert Bruce attracted much attention. The Earl heartily welcomed the Delegates to his home, and on their behalf Mr Amos thanked the Earl and Countess for their charming hospitality.

VISIT TO PITTENCRIEFF GLEN.

After a hurried visit to H.M. Dockyard and Rosyth, the Delegates returned to Dunfermline and were entertained to tea in Pittencrieff Park by the Carnegie Trust. Excellent music was discoursed by military and pipe bands. On the call of Sir Robert Wilson, a hearty vote of thanks was passed to the Carnegie Trust, on whose behalf Sir John Ross, the veteran Secretary, replied. Major Innes moved a similar compliment to Councillor P. Paterson, whom he warmly praised for the admirable way in which all the arrangements had been carried out in connection with the visit of the Federation to Dunfermline.

THOMAS AMOS, *Hon. Secretary.*

List of Clubs which have Subscribed to the Publishing Fund

Aberdeen (arrears)	...£0	10	6	Glasgow Tam o' Shanter ...£1	1	0
Aberdeen	... 1	1	0	Glasgow Thistle ... 1	1	0
Alexandria	0	10	6	Glasgow Royalty ... 1	1	0
Alloway	... 1	1	0	Glasgow Carrick ... 1	1	0
Armadale Star ...	... 1	1	0	Glasgow Rosebery... 1	1	0
Armadale Buck's Head	... 1	1	0	Glasgow Bridgeton 0	10	6
Ashington	... 0	10	6	Glasgow Bridgeton 1	1	0
Atlanta, Ga., U.S.A.	1	1	0	Glasgow Masonic ... 1	1	0
Auchinleck	0	10	6	Glasgow Mossgiel ... 1	1	0
Auchinleck	1	1	0	Glasgow Carlton ... 1	1	0
Bannockburn Empire	1	1	0	Glasgow Sandyford ... 1	1	0
Blairadam Shanter	1	1	0	Glasgow Mauchline Society 1	1	0
Bonnyrigg	1	1	0	Glasgow Southern 0	10	6
Blantyre	0	10	6	Glasgow Albany ... 1	1	0
Blantyre District ...	1	1	0	Glasgow National ... 2	2	0
Bristol	... 1	1	0	Glasgow Scottish ... 1	1	0
Cambuslang Wingate	... 1	1	0	Glasgow Kinning Park 1	1	0
Clydebank Barns o' Clyde	1	1	0	Glasgow Primrose 1	1	0
Coquetdale	1	1	0	Glasgow Auld Clinkum ... 1	1	0
Cowdenbeath Tam o'				Glasgow Cathcart ... 1	1	0
Shanter	1	1	0	Glasgow and District 1	1	0
Cowdenbeath Hill of Beath	1	1	0	Glasgow and District B.C.		
Cowdenbeath Hill of Beath	0	10	6	Bowling Association ... 1	1	0
Coatbridge Bricklayers	0	10	6	Glasgow Shawlands ... 1	1	0
Coatbridge Bricklayers	1	1	0	Glasgow Anderston Cronies 1	1	0
Cupar	... 0	10	6	Glasgow Queen Anne ... 1	1	0
Dalmuir	... 1	1	0	Glasgow Burns House Club 1	1	0
Darlington	0	10	6	Glencraig 1	1	0
Derby	1	1	0	Gourock Jolly Beggars ... 1	1	0
Detroit, Mich., U.S.A.	1	1	0	Govan Fairfield . 1	1	0
Dollar ...	0	10	6	Govan Cronies . 1	1	0
Dollar ...	1	1	0	Greenock Cronies . 1	1	0
Duluth, U.S.A.	1	1	0	Greenock St. John's 1	1	0
Dumbarton	0	10	6	Greenock Victoria 1	1	0
Dumbarton	1	1	0	Hamilton 1	1	0
Dumfries ...	1	1	0	Hamilton Mossgiel 1	1	0
Dumfries Howff	1	1	0	Hamilton Junior 1	1	0
Dundalk	... 1	1	0	Hawick 1	1	0
Dundee ...	1	1	0	Helensburgh 1	1	0
Dunfermline United	1	1	0	Irvine 1	1	0
East Calder	1	1	0	Jedburgh 1	1	0
East Stirlingshire	1	1	0	Johnstone Tam o' Shanter 1	1	0
Edinburgh Ninety.	1	1	0	Kilmarnock 0	10	6
Elgin	1	1	0	Kilmarnock 1	1	0
Falkirk	1	1	0	Kinnaird Victoria 1	1	0
Falkirk Grahamston	1	1	0	Kirn 1	1	0
Fauldhouse... .	1	1	0	Kilbowie Jolly Beggars ... 1	1	0
Fifeshire Association	1	1	0	Lanark 1	1	0
Galston	... 1	1	0	Lanark Jolly Beggars 1	1	0
Galston (arrears) ...	... 1	1	0	Larkhall Cronies ... 1	1	0
Garelochhead ...	1	1	0	Liverpool 0	10	6
Gateshead and District	1	1	0	Liverpool 0	10	6

London	...£1	1	0	Row... ...	...£1	1	0
London	... 0	10	6	Shettleston	1	1	0
Mid-Argyll ...	1	1	0	Shiremoor ...	1	1	0
Montrose	1	1	0	St. Andrew's	0	10	6
Newbattle and District ...	1	1	0	St. Andrew's ...	1	1	0
Newcraighall Poosie Nancy	1	1	0	St. Louis, Mo., U.S.A.	0	10	6
Newton-on-Ayr	1	1	0	Stane Mossgiel	1	1	0
Newton Jolly Beggars	1	1	0	Stirling ...	1	1	0
Nottingham (arrears)	1	11	6	Sunderland	1	1	0
Nottingham	1	1	0	Tarbrax ...	1	1	0
Oregon, U.S.A.	1	1	0	Thornliebank	0	10	6
Oregon, U.S.A.	0	10	6	Uddingston Masonic	1	1	0
Paisley ...	1	1	0	Uphall Tam o' Shanter	1	1	0
Paisley Charleston	1	1	0	Vale o' Leven	1	1	0
Paisley St. James ...	1	1	0	Vickerston	... 1	1	0
Paisley St. Mirren	1	1	0	Walker-on-Tyne ...	1	1	0
Partick	... 1	1	0	Wallsend-on-Tyne	1	1	0
Partick Western ...	... 1	1	0	Whitburn ...	1	1	0
Portobello	1	1	0	Whitehaven	1	1	0
Prestonpans Jolly Beggars	1	1	0				

Alphabetical List of Federated Clubs.

No. 40. Aberdeen
   84. Abington
   23. Adelaide
   20. Airdrie
 143. Airdrie Gateside
   2. Alexandria
   6. Alloa
 252. Alloway
 268. Anderston Cronies
  82. Arbroath
 174. Ardrossan Castle
 257. Armadale Star
 258. Armadale Buck's Head
 232. Arniston
 224. Ashington
 238. Atlanta
 123. Auchinleck
  19. Auckland
 275. Ayr
 192. Ayrshire Association
 157. Baillieston Caledonia
 218. Bannockburn Empire
  99. Barlinnie
  12. Barrow-in-Furness
  64. Beith
 288. Beith Caledonia
  15. Belfast
 265. Bingry Jolly Beggars
 167. Birmingham
 248. Birtley
  30. Blackburn
 125. Blackburn-on-Almond
 184. Blairadam Shanter
 290. Blantyre and District
 240. Blawarthill
  95. Bolton
  29. Bolton Juniors
 119. Bonhill
 142. Bonnybridge
 259. Bonnyrigg
  76. Brechin
 120. Bristol
 114. Brodick
 106. Broxburn Rosebery
 230. Burnbank
 185. Burton
 228. Calderwaterhead
  4. Callander
 110. Cambuslang

No. 207. Cambuslang Wingate
  87. Campsie
  71. Carlisle
 102. Carlisle Border
 201. Carlisle Newtown
  81. Carstairs Junction
 171. Chattanooga, U.S.A.
  11. Chesterfield
  51. Chicago
 138. Cleland
 166. Cleveland Scottish
     Association
  93. Clydebank
 189. Clydebank Barns o' Clyde
 103. Coalburn Rosebery
 233. Coalburn Clachan
 289. Coatbridge Bricklayers
 208. Colorado Springs
 270. Coquetdale
  79. Corstorphine
 127. Cowdenbeath Haggis
 128. Cowdenbeath Glencairn
 250. Cowdenbeath Tam o'
     Shanter
 285. Cowdenbeath Jean
     Armour
  42. Crieff
 241. Crook
  66. Crossgates
  45. Cumnock
  86. Cumnock The Winsome
     Willie
  62. Cupar
 179. Dailly
 244. Dalmuir
  35. Dalry
 158. Darlington
 122. Darnconner
  55. Derby
  37. Dollar
 278. Duluth, U.S.A.
 146. Dublin
  10. Dumbarton
  52. Dumfries Mechanics
 104. Dumfries Oak
 226. Dumfries
 112. Dumfries Howff
 204. Dundalk
  14. Dundee

No. 69. Dunedin
85. Dunfermline United
80. Dunoon Cowal
188. Duns Working Men
134. Duntocher Heron
5. Earlston
229. Eastbourne
108. East Calder
155. East Stirlingshire
22. Edinburgh
111. Edinburgh South
124. Edinburgh Ninety
149. Elgin
217. Eskdale
126. Falkirk
231. Fauldhouse
262. Fifeshire Association
44. Forfar
187. Galashiels
90. Garelochhead
163. Gateshead and District
3. Glasgow Tam o' Shanter
7. ,, Thistle
9. ,, Royalty
24. ,, Bank
27. ,, Springburn
33. ,, Hággis
34. ,, Carrick
36. ,, Rosebery
38. ,, Jolly Beggars
39. ,, St. David's
41. ,, Dennistoun
43. ,, Northern
47. ,, St. Rollox
49. ,, Bridgeton
61. ,, Glencairn
63. ,, Mossgiel
67. ,, Carlton
68. ,, Sandyford
70. ,, St. Rollox
Jolly Beggars
74. ,, Mauchline Soc.
78. ,, Ardgowan
83. ,, Co-operative
88. ,, Caledonian
107. ,, Hutcheson-
town
109. ,, Caledonia
117. ,, Southern
118. ,, Albany
139. ,, National
145. ,, Central
153. ,, The Scottish
129. ,, Gorbals
164. ,, Kinning Park
180. ,, Tollcross
81. ,, Primrose

No. 203. Glasgow Dennistoun
Jolly Beggars
206. ,, Daisy
213. ,, Kingston
223. ,, Auld Clinkum
234. ,, Southern Mer-
chants
255. ,, Cathcart
263. ,, Masónic
286. , Shawlands
287. Queen Anne
295. ,, Burns House,
Ltd.
169. Glasgow and District
282. Glasgow and District
B.C. Bowling Asso-
ciation
251. Glencraig
198. Gorebridge Jolly Beggars
59. Gourock Jolly Beggars
53. Govan Fairfield
202. Govan Cronies
292. Grahamston
116. Greenloaning
21. Greenock
148. Greenock Cronies
209. Greenock St. John's
152. Hamilton
100. Hamilton Mossgiel
121. Hamilton Junior
136. Hamilton Royal Oak
235. Hamilton Glencairn
210. Hardgate Auld Hoose
277. Harriman, U.S.A.
239. Hawick
225. Helensburgh
294. Hill of Beath
222. Hull
137. Ipswich
173. Irvine
96. Jedburgh
154. Johannesburg, S.A.
269. Johnstone Tam o'
Shanter
92. Kilbowie
0. Kilmarnock
97. Kilmarnock Bellfield
150. Kilmarnock Jolly
Beggars
178. Kilmarnock Begbie's
291. Kilmarnock Highland
Mary
186. Kilmarnock Glencairn
245. Kinnaird
115. Kippen
58. Kirkcaldy
75. Kirn

No. 98. Lanark
273. Lanark Jolly Beggars
144. Larbert and Stenhousemuir
170. Larkhall Thistle
211. Larkhall Cronies
73. Lenzie
18. Liverpool
247. Lochgelly
246. Lochore
1. London
183. Londonderry
276. Lumphinnans Highland
Mary
28 Mauchline Jolly Beggars
175. Meikle Earnock
214. Melrose
249 Mid-Calder Tam o'
Shanter
194. Middlebie
242. Montrose
8. Morpeth (dormant)
101. Motherwell
56. Muirkirk Lapraik
65. Musselburgh
199. Newbattle and District
32. Newark
133. Newarthill
156. Newcastle and Tyneside
293. Newcraighall Poosie
Nancy
256. Newton-on-Ayr
266. Newton Jolly Beggars
131. Nottingham
17. Nottingham (dormant)
151. Old Kilpatrick
172. Oregon, U.S.A.
48. Paisley
77. Paisley Gleniffer
161. Paisley Charleston
243. Paisley St. James
205. Paisley St. Mirren
72. Partick
135. Partick Western
227. Penrith
26. Perth
54. Perth St. Johnstone
284. Philadelphia North
Eastern
162. Plymouth and District
140. Pollokshaws

No. 190. Port Glasgow
212. Portobello
221. Prestonpans
264. Prestonpans Jolly
Beggars
267. Prestonpans Mystic
177. Prestwick
176. Renfrew
191. Renfrew Moorpark
168. Riccarton
132. Riccarton Kirkstyle
130. Row
105. Rutherglen
193. Rutherglen Jolly
Beggars
216. Rutherglen Royal Burgh
31. San Francisco
91. Shettleston
195. Shiremoor
283. Sinclairtown
13. St. Andrews
220. St. Louis, Mo., U.S.A.
182. Stane Mossgiel
271. Stewarton Hodden Grey
50. Stirling
141. Stonehouse
147. Stonehouse Haggis
200. Stonehouse Jolly
Beggars
89. Sunderland
16. Sydney
261. Sydney Anniversary
260. Tarbrax
215. Thorniewood
57. Thornliebank
271. Trenton, U.S.A.
274. Troon
219. Uddingston
237. Uddingston Masonic
94. Uphall
113. Vale o' Leven Glenca'rn
281. Vickerstown
159. Walker-on-Tyne.
165. Wallsend-on-Tyne
46. Warwickshire
160. Whitburn
236. Whitehaven
197. Winnipeg
25. Winnipeg St. Andrew's
Society
60. Wolverhampton

DIRECTORY

OF

BURNS CLUBS AND SCOTTISH SOCIETIES

ON THE

ROLL OF THE BURNS FEDERATION, 1921.

No. 0—KILMARNOCK Burns Club.   Instituted 1808.   Federated
1885.   Place and date of meeting, Art Gallery, 25th
January.   President, Sir Alexander Walker, K.B.E.,
Troon ;   Vice-president, John Dickson, *Standard* Office,
Kilmarnock ;   *Secretary,* ✓ David Yuille, Burns Avenue,
Kilmarnock.   Committee—Ex-Provost M. Smith, O.B.E.,
J.P. ;   D. M'Naught, LL.D., J.P. ;   T. Amos, M.A. ;   Major
G. A. Innes, M.B.E. ;   Jas. Middleton, J.P. ;   ex-Bailie
W. Munro, J.P. ;   John Cuthbertson, M.B.E. ;   Major
Jas. Lang, C.E., O.B.E.

No. 1—THE BURNS CLUB OF LONDON.   Instituted 1868.
Federated 1885.   President, Sir Wm. Noble, Silchester,
The Park, Hampstead, N.W. ;   Vice-president, P. N.
M'Farlane, " The Graphic," Tallis House, E.C. 4 ;   *Secre-
tary,* J. A. Brown,✓ C.E.. M.C.I., M.S.I., 38 Vaughan
Gardens, Cranbrook Road, Ilford, Essex ;   Hon. Trea-
surer, J. Spence Leslie,ᵛ Balgownie, Whitehall Road,
Harrow.   Vernacular Circle—Chairman, John Douglas,
F.S.A.(Scot.) :   Hon. Secretary,✓ William Will, " The
Graphic," Tallis Street, E.C. 4.

No. 2—ALEXANDRIA Burns Club.   Instituted 1884.   Fede-
rated 1885.   Place of meeting, Village School.   Presi-
dent, R. G. Stevenson, Stevenson Place, Alexandria ;
Vice-president, Donald M'Dougall, Bridge-End Tavern,
Bonhill ;   *Secretary,* ᵛ Duncan Carswell, 120 Linnbrane
Terrace, Alexandria ;   Treasurer, James Merrilees,
Charleston House, Alexandria.   Committee—Dugald
Stevenson, John Burton, William M'Gregor, Harry
Caldwell, George Wilson.

No. 3—GLASGOW Tam o' Shanter.   Instituted 1880.   Federated
1885.   Place and date of meeting, Burns House Club,
27 India Street, Glasgow, last Tuesday of each month,
at 8 p.m.   President, ✓ John Ballantine, architect, 95
Bath Street, Glasgow ;   Vice-president, ex-Councillor
Hugh Lyon, 17 Oswald Street, Glasgow ;   *Secretary,* J.
Jeffrey Hunter,ʳsolicitor, 89 Bath Street, Glasgow.   Committee—J. F. Anderson, Arch. Campbell, Matthew Comrie,
D. Conway, W. Munro Denholm, James Fraser, T. M.

Hamilton, J. H. Hurll, Alex. Izat, Gerrard Morrison, James Murray, Alex. Mackenzie, Wm. Renfrew, T. P. Thomson, Peter Webster. Special features of Club —Literary evening and useful movements for the promotion of the Burns cult.

No. 4—CALLANDER Burns Club. Instituted 1877. Federated 1885.

No. 5—ERCILDOUNE Burns Club. Instituted 1885. Federated 26th November, 1885. *Secretary*, A. M. Black, Market Place, Earlston.

No. 6—ALLOA Burns Club. Instituted 1873. Federated 1885.

No. 7—GLASGOW Thistle Burns Club. Instituted 1882. Federated 1885. President, J. Eadie, 7 Miller Street, Glasgow ; Vice-president, G. Thomson, Pollokshaws Road ; *Secretary*, J. Vallance, 57 College Street, Glasgow; Treasurer (*pro tem*), J. Eadie, 7 Miller Street, Glasgow.

No. 8—MORPETH and District Burns Club.

No 9—GLASGOW Royalty Burns Club. Instituted 1882. Federated 1886. Place and date of meeting, Grand Hotel, Charing Cross, last Thursday of October. President, Councillor James Macfarlane, 51 Bath Street, Glasgow ; Vice-president, David Gunn, 4 Finnieston Street, Glasgow ; *Secretary*, George F. Howarth, 188 St. Vincent Street, Glasgow.

No. 10—DUMBARTON Burns Club. Instituted 1859. Federated 1886. Place and date of meeting, Elephant Hotel 25th January, 1922. President, James Stewart, Dumbuck Crescent, Dumbarton ; Vice-president, Provost J. G. Buchanan, Dumbarton ; *Secretary*, J. M. Menzies, 69 High Street, Dumbarton. Committee—Charles M'Kinnon, John M'Clelland, John M'Pherson, J. B. Cameron, Robert M'Murray, H. W. Ballardie, D. Blackstock, and A. Y. Allan. Special feature of Club —Celebration of the Poet's birthday

No. 11—CHESTERFIELD Burns Society. Federated 1886.

No. 12—BARROW-IN-FURNESS Burns Club. Federated 1888.

No. 13—ST. ANDREW'S Burns Club. Instituted 1869. Federated 1886. Place of meeting, Various. President, Wm. Macbeth Robertson, solicitor, Market Street, St. Andrews ; *Secretary*, David Fraser, Lilybank, St. Andrews.

No. 14—DUNDEE Burns Club. Instituted 1860. Federated 5th March, 1886. Place and time of meeting, 36 Nethergate, Dundee, nightly. President, ex-Bailie Wm. F. Mitchell, Dalmeny, 302 Strathmartine Road, Downfield, Dundee ; Vice-president, H. Pettie, Ingleside, 26 Lammerton Terrace, Maryfield, Dundee ; *Secretary*, J. Neilson,

36 Nethergate, Dundee; Treasurer, D. J. Brown; Auditors, J. Gorrie and J. M'Kelvie; Librarian, J. Brown. Committee—Messrs J. A. Purves, P. G. Speed, and J. Ogilvie. Special featues of Club—Literary and recreation.

No. 15—BELFAST Burns Club. Instituted 1872. Federated 1886.

No. 16—SYDNEY Burns Club, N.S.W. Instituted 1880. Federated 1886. *Secretary*, W. Telfer, School of Art, Pitt Street, Sydney.

No. 17—NOTTINGHAM Scottish Society. Federated 1886.

No. 18—LIVERPOOL Burns Club. Instituted 1866. Federated 1886. Place and date of meeting, Places various, 25th January. President, Dr R. W. MacKenna, M.A., 76 Rodney Street, Liverpool; *Secretary*, Robt. Sinclair Archer (Major, V.D.), 6 Devonshire Road, Princes Park, Liverpool. Special features of Club—Annual dinner; also prizes offered to pupils of Liverpool Caledonian Schools for Burns's (or Scottish) poetry.

No. 19—AUCKLAND Burns Club. Instituted 1884. Federated 1886.

No. 20—AIRDRIE Burns Club. Instituted 1885. Federated 1886. President, J. Maurice Arthur, Glentore, Airdrie Vice-president, Geo. E. Swimhoe, Albert House, Airdrie, *Secretary*, G. B. Motherwell, solicitor, 4 East High Street, Airdrie; Treasurer, G. B. Motherwell, solicitor, 4 East Street, Airdrie; Auditor, C. R. Larkman, Albert Schoolhouse, Airdrie; Committee—Robert Eadie, C. R. Larkman, David Martyn, and Wm. M'Gregor.

No. 21 GREENOCK Burns Club (The Mother Club). Instituted 1802. Federated 1886. Place of meeting, Club-Rooms, 36 Nicholson Street. President, ex-Bailie D. M'Callum, 21 Cathcart Street, Greenock; Vice-presidents, Chas. L. Brodie, 9 Margaret Street, and Wm. Nicoll, 29 Finnart Street; *Secretary*, George B. Grieve, O.B.E., 35 Robertson Street, Greenock; House Convener, J. B. Morison. Special features of Club—To cherish the name of Robert Burns and to foster a love for his writings, and, generally, to encourage a taste for Scottish literature.

No. 22—EDINBURGH Burns Club. Instituted 1848. Federated 1886. President, George Williamson, J.P., 178 High Street, Edinburgh; Vice-president, Robert Walker, 6 Royal Terrace, Edinburgh; *Interim Secretary*, Thomas Liddle, S.S.C., 5 Hill Street, Edinburgh.

No. 23—ADELAIDE South Australian Caledonian Society. Instituted 1881. Federated 1886. *Secretary*, H. Tassie, Gray's Arcade, Adelaide, S.A.

No. 24—GLASGOW Bank Burns Club. Instituted 1884. Federated 1886..

No. 25—WINNIPEG St. Andrew's Society. Federated 1886. *Secretary*, David Philip, Government Buildings, Winnipeg.

No. 26—PERTH Burns Club. Instituted 1873. Federated 1886.

No. 27—SPRINGBURN Burns Club. Instituted 1884. Federated 1886.

No. 28—MAUCHLINE Jolly Beggars Burns Club.

No. 29—BOLTON Juniors Burns Club. Instituted 1881. Federated 1886.

No. 30—BLACKBURN Burns Club. Instituted 1884. Federated 1886. *Secretary*, Robt. Ferguson, 9 Tacketts Street, Blackburn, Lancs.

No. 31—SAN FRANCISCO Scottish Thistle Club. Instituted 1882. Federated 1886. *Secretary*, Geo. W. Paterson, 801 Guerero Street, San Francisco, U.S.A.

No. 32—NEWARK Burns Club U.S.A. Federated 1886.

No. 33—GLASGOW Haggis Burns Club. Instituted 1872. Federated 1886. Place and date of meeting, Ferguson and Forrester's, 36 Buchanan Street, last Tuesday from October till March. President, Robert Hamilton, Invershin, Newlands, Glasgow : *Secretary*, William S. Baird, 121 West George Street, Glasgow.

No. 34—CARRICK Burns Club. Instituted 1859. Federated 1887. Date of meeting, last Friday of each month. President, R. A. Wood, Rosevale, Kilmarnock Road Giffnock, near Glasgow ; Vice-president, H. D. M'Neill, 264 Darnley Street, Glasgow ; *Secretary*, David Sutherland, 123 Frederick Street, Glasgow.

No. 35—DALRY Burns Club. Instituted 1825. Federated 1887. Place and date of meeting, Turf Inn, Friday, 25th January, 1922. *Secretary*, Patrick Comrie, Waterside, Dalry.

No. 36—ROSEBERY Burns Club. Instituted 1885. Federated 1887. Place and date of meeting, Bath Hotel, Bath Street, Glasgow, second Thursday each month, at 7.45 p.m. President, Wm. Craig, Beechcroft, Crow Road, Jordanhill, Glasgow ; Vice-president, T. C. F. Brotchie, F.S.A.(Scot.), Camphill House, Glasgow ; *Secretary*, Jno. M. Alexander, 223 Cumbernauld Road, Dennistoun, Glasgow ; Treasurer, Ronald Johnstone, 85 Roslea Drive, Dennistoun, Glasgow. Special features of Club —A course of monthly lectures on various literary subjects ; inter-visitation of sister Burns Clubs ; school competitions, &c.

No 37—DOLLAR Burns Club. Instituted 29th December, 1887. Federated 30th December, 1887. Place and date of meeting, Masonic Hall, Dollar, 25th November, 1922. President, W. D. Congalton, M.A., Burnbrae, Dollar ; *Secretary*, J. M. C. Wilson, B.Sc.,✓Institution Place, Dollar. Special features of Club—To keep the Poet's works before the members, and to arrange suitable competitions amongst the school children.

No. 38—GLASGOW Jolly Beggars Burns Club. Instituted 1877. Federated 1888.

No. 39—GLASGOW St. David's Burns Club. Instituted 1887. Federated 1889.

No. 40—ABERDEEN Burns Club. Instituted 1887. Federated 1889. Place and date of meeting, Imperial Hotel, Aberdeen, first Monday of each month, at 7.30 p.m. President, Chas. S. France, 13 Cairnfield Place, Aberdeen ; Vice-president, L. W. Gordon, 8 Academy Street, Aberdeen ; *Secretary*, Alex. W. Mackie, 5 Station Road, Woodside, Aberdeen. Special features of Club—The membership has trebled itself in three years. Outing every summer. Obtaining new members by having syllabus prepared about end of August, and showing it to friends before the session commences in October. Celebration and supper on 25th January.

No. 41—DENNISTOUN Burns Club. Instituted 1887. Federated 1889.

No. 42—CRIEFF Burns Club. Instituted 1889. Federated 1891.

No. 43—GLASGOW Northern Burns Club. Federated 1891

No. 44—FORFAR Burns Club. Instituted 1890. Federated 1891.

No. 45—CUMNOCK Burns Club. Instituted 1887. Federated 1891. *Secretary*, John Hume, ✓solicitor, Cumnock.

No. 46—WARWICKSHIRE Burns Club. Instituted 1880. Federated 1891.

No. 47—GLASGOW St. Rollox Burns Club. Instituted 1889. Federated 1891.

No. 48—PAISLEY Burns Club. Instituted 1805. Federated 1891. Time of meeting, First Thursday each month, October to April inclusive. President, Robert Marshall, The Cottage, Glen Lorne, Paisley ; Vice-president, James Paton, Shirbrooke, Johnstone ; *Secretary*, Julius F. M'Callum,✓Mayfield, Sunnyside, Paisley. Special features of Club—Literary and social.

No. 49—BRIDGETON Burns Club. Instituted 1870. Federated 30th November, 1891. Place of meeting, Albert Hall, 46 Main Street. President, George Brown, Yorville, Maxwell Park, Glasgow; vice-president, Dr W. A. Burns, Belmont, Rodger Drive, Rutherglen; *Secretary*, John G. S. Sproll,✓354 Duke Street, Glasgow; Treasurer, David S. Brown, 79 Canning Street, Glasgow. Directors—James W. Shaw, J.P., Adam C. Hay, James Craig, Dr T. M. Fletcher, Robert Miller, W. Reid, John M. Watson, John M'Donald, Dr David M'Kail, Robert Cowper. Examiners—Peter White, J.P., and George Newton.

No. 50—STIRLING Burns Club. Instituted 1887. Federated 1891. Place and date of meeting, Station Hotel, 25th January, at 7 p.m. President, Councillor William A. Weir, Forth Crescent, Stirling; Vice-president, Provost M'Culloch, Clarendon Place, Stirling; *Secretary*, Alexander Dun,✓37 Murray Place, Stirling: Treasurer, J. P. Crawford. Committee—John Craig, Ridley Sandeman, J. W. Paterson, ex-Bailie Leslie, John Crawford, W. L. Thomson, David Dick, J. S. Henderson, Robert Gray, James Duncanson, William Brown, John Ferguson, Alex. Learmonth, Dean of Guild Buchanan, J. C. Muirhead, J. E. M'Killop, and J. Shirra.

No. 51 CHICAGO Caledonian Society. Federated 1892.

No. 52—DUMFRIES Mechanics' Burns Club. Federated 1892.

No. 53—GOVAN Fairfield Burns Club. Instituted 1886. Federated 1892. Place of meeting, Eden Villa Restaurant, Carmichael Street. President, John Donald, 883 Govan Road, Govan; Vice-president, George Wardrope, Merryflatts Cottages, Govan; *Secretary*, John Gordon,✓13 Hutton Drive, Govan: Treasurer, Alex. George. Committee—A. Phillips, J. Melvin, J. Watson, J. MacLachlan, and J. M'Cartney. Special features of Club—To promote interest in the Life and Works of the National Bard, and to have intercourse with other Burns Clubs.

No. 54—PERTH St. Johnstone Burns Club. Federated 1892.

No. 55—DERBY Scottish Association and Burns Club. Instituted 1890. Federated 1892. Place of meeting, Assembly Rooms, Market Place, Derby; President, D. M'Call Aird, 42 Vicarage Avenue, Derby; vice-presidents, J. Dobson, Conservative Club; and Dr A. K. MacLachlan, 38 Charnwood Street, Derby; *Secretary*, A. Dunlop Ferguson,✓100 Friar Gate, Derby; Treasurer, D. Dow, Lindley House, Porter Road, Derby. Special features of Club—To unite Scotsmen and to foster a spirit of friendship; social and intellectual intercourse among the members: and to perpetuate the memory of the Immortal Bard, Robert Burns.

No. 56—LAPRAIK (Muirkirk) Burns Club. Instituted 1893. Federated 1893. President, C. P. Bell, Main Street, Muirkirk; Vice-president, Peter Mackie, c/o Mrs Ferguson, Main Street, Muirkirk; *Secretary*, Hugh Bell,

Roslyn, Wellwood Street, Muirkirk ; Treasurer, And. Pringle, Ironworks Cottages, Muirkirk. Committee— Thos. Weir, Jno. Taylor, Edgar Anderson, Jas. Hazel, Wm. Patrick, Wm. Brown, Arch. Fairbairn, Thos. Hazel. Special features of Club—Annual Celebration and educational.

No. 57—THORNLIEBANK Burns Club. Instituted 1891. Federated 1893. Place and date of meeting, Village Institute, Fridays, at 8 p.m. President, James H. M'Millan, Woodlands, Shawlands, Glasgow, S. ; Vice-president, Thomas R. Murray, Unitas, Thornliebank ; Secretary, Thomas Haddow, ✓ Hillside Terrace, Thornliebank : Treasurer, Hugh Halliday, 27 Kennishead Road, Thornliebank. Special features of Club—School children's competitions, Scotch concert, annual outing, Hallowe'en festival, Anniversary dinner, and Club monthly meetings.

No. 58—KIRKCALDY Burns Club. Federated 1892.

No. 59—GOUROCK Jolly Beggars Burns Club. Instituted 1893. Federated 1893. Place of meeting, Gamble Institute. Hon. President, Harry White ; President, Hugh Talman, 17 Royal Street, Gourock ; Vice-president, Peter M. Weir, Parklea, Adam Street, Gourock ; Secretary, W. L. Adam, ✓ Oakdene, Manor Crescent, Gourock ; Hon. Treasurer, Joseph Wilson, Avonmore, John Street, Gourock. Auditors, W. Callender and W. M'Kerrol. Committee —M. E. Campbell, E. Hepburn, Jas. King, John M'Cracken, Neil M'Kechnie, A. Olding, and H. W. Philip. Special features of Club—To foster the love of our National Bard ; to promote competitions among the school children ; and to have lectures and essays on Burns, &c.

No. 60—WOLVERHAMPTON Burns Club. Federated 1893.

No. 61—GLASGOW Glencairn Burns Club. Federated 1893.

No. 62—CUPAR Burns Club. Instituted 1892. Federated 1893. Place and date of meeting, Royal Hotel, 25th January, 1922. President, Col. Sir Alex. Sprot, C.M.G., M.P., Stravithie, by St. Andrews ; Vice-presidents, Provost Stark, Cupar ; and R. Osborne Payne, W.S., Cupar ; Secretary, Robert G. Brown, 27 Crossgate, Cupar.

No. 63—MOSSGIEL Burns Club. Instituted 1893. Federated 1893. Place and date of meeting, Y.M.C.A. Rooms Eglinton Toll, Third Thursday each winter month. President, Wm. Brownlie, 67 Cadder Street, Pollokshields ; Vice-president, Robt. Bryden, Torthorwald, Muirend, Cathcart ; Secretary, Jas. M'Gregor, 45 Abbotsford Place, Glasgow ; Treasurer, Wm. Morrison, jun. Committee —Thos. M'Nish, Wm. Morrison, J. M. Blair, J. Coulter, J. Saunders, Wm. M'Neil, R. Johnstone, N. M'Luskie, Councillor J. L. Johnston, J.P., and M. Waddel. Special features of Club—Annual celebration in January ; reunions for social and intellectual intercourse ; encouragement of Scottish literature; summer trip; and school children's competitions.

No. 64 BEITH Burns Club. Instituted 1892. Federated 12th December, 1893.

No 65—MUSSELBURGH Federated Burns Club. Instituted 1886. Federated 3rd January, 1894. *Secretary*, Herbert Millar, solicitor, High Street, Musselburgh.

No. 66—CROSSGATES Burns Club. Federated 1894.

No. 67—CARLTON Burns Club. Instituted 1894. Federated 1894. Place of meeting, Kenilworth Hotel, Glasgow. President, Wm. Henderson, 912 Sauchiehall Street, Glasgow; Vice-president, Duncan Cameron, 10 Blackie Street Glasgow; *Secretary*, John Clark, 665 Cathcart Road, Crosshill, Glasgow; Treasurer, James Tudhope, 16 Whitehill Street, Dennistoun, Glasgow. Directors—M. M. Duff, Thos. Drysdale, J. F. Gourlay, J. R. M'Blane, Jas. Webster, J. D. Sloan, Alex. Clark, J. C. Brown, Mungo Wallace, and Past Presidents *ex officio*. Special features of Club—To perpetuate the name of Burns; musical evenings; annual outing; dinner; bowling games.

No. 68—SANDYFORD Burns Club. Instituted 1893. Federated 1894. Place of meeting, The Burns House Club, India Street, Glasgow. Hon. President, Bailie Robert S. Renfrew, 133 North Street, Glasgow; President, George Calder, 1117 Argyle Street, Glasgow; Vice-president, James G. Robertson, 350 St. Vincent Street, Glasgow; *Secretary*, William E. Guest, 47 Kelvinhaugh Street, Glasgow. Special features of Club—To cherish the name of Robert Burns; to promote the cultivation of a better knowledge of the Poet and his Works; and to encourage social intercourse amongst the members.

No. 69—DUNEDIN Burns Club. Federated 1894.

No. 70—GLASGOW St. Rollox Jolly Beggars Burns Club. Federated 1894.

No. 71—CARLISLE Burns Club. Instituted 1889. Federated 1895. *Secretary*, Thomas George Beattie, 200 Warwick Road, Carlisle.

No 72—PARTICK Burns Club. Instituted 1885. Federated 1895. President, J. Ogilvie Robertson, 111 Balshagray Avenue, Partick, Glasgow; Vice-president David Robinson, 1 Park Drive, North Partick; *Secretary*, David Crawford, 213 West George Street, Glasgow.

No. 73—LENZIE Burns Club. Federated 1896.

No. 74—GLASGOW Mauchline Society. Instituted 1888. Federated 1895. Hon. President, Sir. Arch M'Innes Shaw, Bart., Ballochmyle, Mauchline; President, J. Leiper

Gemmill, 162 St. Vincent Street, Glasgow ; Vice-president, John Hyslop, 93 Hope Street, Glasgow ; *Secretary*, William Campbell, ⌄166 Buchanan Street, Glasgow : Treasurer, Thos. Killin, 7 Stewarton Drive, Cambuslang. Special features of Club—To promote sociability among natives of Mauchline and friends, and manage the National Burns Memorial and Cottage Homes, Mauchline.

No. 75—KIRN Burns Club. Instituted 25th January, 1892. Federated 10th February, 1896. Place and date of meeting, Queen's Hotel, Kirn, 25th January. President, Samuel A. Fraser, Silver Ray, Kirn ; Vice-president, William Johnston, Meridine, Hunter's Quay ; *Secretary*, John Macnair, Netherton, Kirn ; Treasurer, ex-Provost Lees, O.B.E., Ferny Crag, Kirn : Secretary of Recreation Branch, J. J. Boyd, Norwood Cottage, Kirn. Special feature of Club—Debating and recreation branch meets every Monday in Kirn Parish Hall.

No. 76—BRECHIN Burns Club. Instituted January, 1894. Federated 7th March, 1896. Place and date of meeting, Masonic Hall, Brechin, 25th January. President, John S. Melrose, J.P., Summerbank, Brechin ; Vice-president, Alexander Philip, J.P., LL.B., The Mary Acre, Brechin ; *Secretary*, F. C. Anderson, 10 St. Mary Street, Brechin. Committee—Messrs Robert Anderson, J. F. Lammond, D. K. Laing, W. S. Leslie, J. W. Bisset, George Cumming, and James Duncan.

No. 77—PAISLEY Tannahill Burns Club. Instituted 1892. Federated 1896.

No. 78.—GLASGOW Ardgowan Burns Club. Instituted 1893. Federated 1896.

No. 79—CORSTORPHINE Burns Club. Instituted 1887. Federated 1896. *Secretary*, W. M. Wilson, 7 Belgrave Place, Corstorphine.

No. 80—DUNOON Cowall Burns Club. Instituted 1896 Federated 1896.

No. 81—CARSTAIRS Junction Burns Club. Instituted 1896. Federated 1896.

No. 82—ARBROATH Burns Club. Instituted 1888. Federated 1896. President, Dr J. D. Gilruth, Hyde Park House, Arbroath ; Vice-president, John R. W. Clark, solicitor, Arbroath : *Secretary*, Ernest F. Cobb, Town Chamberlain, Arbroath ; Treasurer, F. W. Moon, solicitor, Arbroath.

No 83—GLASGOW Co-operative Burns Club. Instituted 1896. Federated 1896.

No. 84—ABINGTON Burns Club. Federated 1896.

No 85—DUNFERMLINE United Burns Club. Instituted 1812. Federated 12th November, 1896. Place and date of meeting, D.C.I. Rooms, 25th January, 1922. Hon Presidents, The Right Hon. The Earl of Elgin, Broomhall · Sir Richard Mackie, Leith ; Hon. Vice-presidents, W. D. Imrie, Wm. Black, P. Donald, Thos. Dow, R. Taylor, and R. Hutchison; President, Sir Alex. Gibb, G.B.E., C.B., Gruinard, by Aultbea, Ross-shire ; Vice-president, Provost Norval, Dunfermline · Secretary, P. Paterson, Kinnis House, Kinnis Place, Dunfermline. Committee—Wm. Black Charlestown, J. Donald, R. Taylor, Thos. Lessells, R. Hutchison, J. Brown, Wm. Crawford, John Bissett, Robt. Muir (Dunfermline), and Adam Bowman (Rosyth).

No. 86—CUMNOCK Winsome Willie. Instituted 1856. Federated 1896. Place of meeting, Hotel Royal, Cumnock. President, Andrew Hart, Square ; Vice-president, James Neil, Lugar Street ; Secretary, Robert Hyslop, Waterside Place, Cumnock. Committee—Wm. Hyslop, Walter M'Crindle, Wm. Jamieson, and Robt. Forsyth. Special features of Club—To celebrate Burns's birth and a special meeting at Hallowe'en.

No. 87—CAMPSIE Burns Club. Instituted 1890. Federated 1896.

No. 88—GLASGOW Caledonian Burns Club. Instituted 1896. Federated 1897.

No 89—SUNDERLAND Burns Club. Instituted January, 1897. Federated April, 1897. Place and date of meeting, Palatine Hotel, 2nd and 4th Mondays October to March ; 2nd Monday April, May, and September. President, Tom Fisher, 34 Hunter Terrace, Sunderland ; Vice-president, H. J. Menzies, Linden House, East Boldon, Newcastle-on-Tyne ; Secretary, M. Neilson, 14 East Whickham Street, Sunderland ; Treasurer, A. W. Semple ; Auditor, E. V. Young ; Librarian, G. Mackay ; Trustees, W. H. Turner and G. Mackay. Committee—A. R. Calvert, T. E. A. A. Shaw, W. M. Donaldson, J. M'Lagan, and D. Gordon. Special features of Club — Burns anniversary gathering ; St. Andrew's celebration ; reading of papers, &c. Visitors always welcome.

No. 90—GARELOCHHEAD Burns Club. Instituted November 18th, 1895. Federated March 27th, 1897. Place and time of meeting, Garelochhead Hotel, 7 o'clock p.m. President, David Stark, Argyle House, Garelochhead ; Vice-president, Duncan M'Keichan, Mambeg Cottage, Garelochhead ; Secretary, John Burnett, 1 Glencairn Terrace, Garelochhead. Committee—William Grieve, J. Gray, Wm. Espie, P. M'Farlane, J. Millar, J. Douglas, S. Dane, and Major D. B. Anderson. Special feature of Club—That we as Scotchmen should meet to honour Scotland's National Bard.

No. 91—SHETTLESTON Burns Club. Instituted 1897. Federated 1897. Place of meeting, Royal Restaurant, Glasgow.

Hon. Presidents, John Cresswell, William Reid, F.E.I.S., James Lucas, M.A., F.E.I.S. ; Robert M. Milholm, James S. Wilson, John Ramsey, and John M'Farlane ; President, John Brown, J.P., 88 Westmuir Street, Parkhead, Glasgow ; Vice-president, William Ross, 20 Mansion house Drive, Shettleston ; *Secretary*, William Brown, 88 Westmuir Street, Parkhead, Glasgow ; Treasurer, E. S. Thompson, Ardshill, Hillhead Avenue, Shettleston. Committee—Ambrose Cresswell, George Farmer, Geo. G. Glendinning, Councillor James Miller, George Stirling, James Cassells, William Smillie, Alexander Riach, Alfred Perry, Isaiah Hardstaff, and Thomas Morrison. Special features of Club—A literary centre as well as social ; lectures on Scottish life and literature by authorities on various subjects and writers. Prizes are provided by the Club for the pupils of the Shettleston and Tollcross schools to foster study of the Works of Burns. Visitors are always welcome at any of the Club meetings.

No. 92—KILBOWIE Jolly Beggars Burns Club. Instituted September, 1896. Federated 26th August, 1897. Place of meeting, T. F. Ross's Cross Restaurant. President, Alex. M'Donald, 53 Montrose Street, Clydebank ; Vice-president, David J. Clark, 150 Kilbowie Road, Clydebank ; *Secretary*, James Chamberlain, 2 Victoria Street, Clydebank ; Treasurer, Jas. Walker. Committee— Messrs Crum, Davidson, Deans, Francis, Morrison, M'Williams, R. Patrick, W. Patrick, Phillips, Walters, and Watson. Special features of Club—The cultivation of a better knowledge of the Life and Works of the Bard, and the study of Scottish literature by the reading of papers, &c., original and otherwise, amongst the members.

No. 93—CLYDEBANK Burns Club. Federated 1897.

No. 94—UPHALL Tam o' Shanter Burns Club. Instituted September, 1885. Federated 12th September, 1897. Place and date of meeting, Uphall Hotel, First Friday of month, 7 p.m. President, James Spence, Beechwood Cottages, Uphall Station ; Vice-president, James Wilson, Beechwood Cottages, Uphall Station ; *Secretary*, James Purdie, Hawthorn Place, Uphall. Special feature of Club— To further the memory of the National Bard.

No. 95—BOLTON Burns Club. Instituted 1881 Federated 1897.

No. 96—JEDBURGH Burns Club. Instituted 1869. Federated 13th November, 1897. Place and date of meeting, Royal Hotel, Jedburgh, 25th January, 1922. President, John S. Boyd, J.P., The Cottage, Bongate, Jedburgh ; Vice-president, Peter Carruthers, 33 Castlegate, Jedburgh ; *Secretary and Treasurer*, Alex. Walker, The Dispensary, Jedburgh.

No. 97—KILMARNOCK Bellfield Burns Club. Instituted 1895. Federated 1898. Vice-president, Daniel Picken, Glebe Avenue, Kilmarnock.

No. 98—LANARK Burns Club. Instituted 1891. Federated 1898. Place and time of meeting, Market Inn, 7.30 p.m. President, A. S. Boyd, Cordelier Terrace, Lanark ; Vice-president, H. M. Beveridge, Town Buildings, St. Leonard Street, Lanark : Secretary, Thomas Veitch, Dalblair, Wheatland Drive, Lanark. Committee—W. Brown, T. Lithgow, R. Hamilton, J. Howe, A. Keith, J. B. M'Auslan, and J. Blackhall. Special features of Club —The holding of social meetings during the winter months, when papers on the Works of Burns are read and discussed. To help all local deserving institutions. During the last three years our Club has handed over the sum of £96 to local charities.

No. 99—BARLINNIE Burns Club. Instituted 1893. Federated 1898. Secretary, Alexander Mackay, 10 Officers' Quarters, Barlinnie, Glasgow.

No. 100—HAMILTON Mossgiel Burns Club. Instituted 1892. Federated 4th April, 1898. Place and date of meeting, Commercial Hotel, First Tuesday in month excepting June, July, and August. President, James M'Cartney, 99 Quarry Street, Hamilton ; Vice-president, H. C. Evans, 11 Guthrie Street, Hamilton ; Secretary, Wm. Sommerville, 5 Jackson Street, Blantyre ; Treasurer, Wm. Hamilton, Burnfoot, Bent Road, Hamilton.

No. 101—MOTHERWELL Workmen's Burns Club. Federated 1898.

No. 102—CARLISLE Border Burns Club. Instituted 1898. Federated 1898.

No. 103—COALBURN Burns Club. Federated 1898.

No. 104—DUMFRIES Oak Burns Club. Federated 1898.

No. 105—RUTHERGLEN Cronies Burns Club. Instituted 1896. Federated 1898.

No. 106—BROXBURN Rosebery Burns Club. Federated 1898.

No. 107—HUTCHESONTOWN Burns Club. Instituted 1897. Federated 1898. Secretary, Robert A. Sinclair, 4 Govanhill Street, Crosshill, Glasgow.

No. 108—EAST CALDER and DISTRICT Jolly Beggars Burns Club. Instituted 25th January, 1897. Federated 17th January, 1899. Place of meeting, Grapes Inn, East Calder. President, James Millar, Burn House, East Calder ; Vice-president, James Robertson, East Calder ; Secretary, John Watson, 46 Oakbank, Mid-Calder : Treasurer, John Forbes, 18 Oakbank, Mid-Calder.

No. 109 GLASGOW Caledonia Burns Club. Instituted 1898. Federated 1899.

No 110—CAMBUSLANG Burns Club. Instituted 1850. Federated 1898.

No. 111—SOUTH EDINBURGH Burns Club. Instituted 1889. Federated 1899.

No. 112—DUMFRIES Burns Howff Club. Instituted 1889. Federated 10th August, 1899. Place and date of meeting, Globe Hotel, monthly. President, Alexander Hutchison, Nith Place, Dumfries ; Past President, William Dinwiddie, 37 Moffat Road, Dumfries ; Secretary, Thomas Laidlaw. 3 St. Michael's Terrace, Dumfries ; Treasurer, Thomas Robertson, Dumfries. Committee—J. W. Howat, W. E. Boyd, J. Maxwell, T. Waugh, James Smith, P. M'Murdo, D. Lockerbie, D. Clark, W. Robinson, J. B. Wood, W. Carruthers, G. Hastings, W. Fraser, T. M'Connell, and M. M'Cubbin. Special features of Club—Lectures, &c., during winter months.

No. 113—VALE OF LEVEN Glencairn Burns Club. Instituted 1897. Federated 1899. Place and date of meeting, Albert Hotel, Alexandria, last Saturday of month, at 6.30 p.m. Hon. President, Hugh M'Vean, Mossgiel, Dalmarnock Road, Bonhill ; President, John L. Ritchie, 1 Park Street, Renton, Dumbartonshire ; Vice-president, Daniel Macmillan, Smollett Street, Alexandria ; Secretary, John James, c/o Mrs T. Young, 7 John Street, Renton, Dumbartonshire ; Treasurer, Peter Burden, Viewfield, Balloch. Committee—James Burdon, Daniel M'Innes, Norman M'Crimmon, Thomas Nicol, and William Smith. Special features of Club—Celebration of 25th January ; summer outing ; and occasionally short papers by the members.

No. 114—BRODICK Burns Club. Instituted 1899. Federated 1900.

No. 115—KIPPEN and District Burns Club. Instituted 1896. Federated 1900. Secretary, Samuel Thomson, Pointend, Kippen.

No. 116—GREENLOANING Burns Club. Instituted 1889. Federated 1900. Place and time of meeting, Greenloaning Inn, at 7.30 p.m. President, S. Watson, Neither Mills, Greenloaning, Braco ; Vice-president, J. Chalmers, Bardrill Farm, Blackford ; Secretary, James Bayne, Kinbuck, Dunblane. Committee—R. Taylor, G. Robertson, W. Taylor, A. Graham, and J. M'Naughton.

No. 117 GLASGOW Southern Burns Club. Instituted 1899. Federated 1900.

No. 118—GLASGOW Albany Burns Club. Instituted 1900. Federated 1900. Place and date of meeting, 27 India Street, Glasgow, W., First Wednesdays, October to March. President, William Cullen, M.D., 3 Queen's Crescent, Glasgow, W. ; Vice-presidents, R. D. Donaldson, 50 Abbey

Drive, Jordanhill, and Jas. N. Murdoch, 175 Hope Street, Glasgow ; *Secretary*, D. C. Kennedy, 33 Hope Street, Glasgow ; Treasurer, D. Annand ; Librarian, Wm. Dall. Special features of Club—Lectures by prominent gentlemen ; children's singing and reciting competitions : music and harmony ; anniversary dinner, 25th January, 1922.

No. 119—BONHILL Burns Club. Instituted 1900. Federated 1900.

No. 120—BRISTOL Caledonian Society. Caledonian Society established 1820 : The Burns Club established 1894. Amalgamated 1898. Federated 10th December, 1900. Place and date of meeting, 24 St. Nicholas Street, Bristol, no fixed dates. Chairman, John Turnbull, 1 Baldwin Street, Bristol ; Vice-presidents, A. C. Turnbull, 26 Florence Park, Bristol, and R. W. French, 39 Shadwell Road, Bristol ; *Secretary*, A. K. Simpson, 24 St. Nicholas Street, Bristol. Special features of Club— Social and benevolent.

No. 121 HAMILTON Junior Burns Club. Instituted September, 1886. Federated 1901. Place and date of meeting, Mrs R. Bell's, Union Street, Hamilton, first Monday each month. President, Robert Brown, Coursington Forge, Motherwell ; Vice-president, John Cameron, 50 Burnbank Road, Hamilton ; *Secretary and Treasurer*, William Wilson, 5 Haddow Street, Hamilton ; Minute Secretary, W. M'Laren ; Stewards, R. Morrison, S. Naismith, and James M'Neil. Committee — James Brown, D. Cross, G. Fleming, Jas. Thomson, and R. Allan. Special features of Club—Reading of essays on various subjects, concerts, competitions, summer outings, and social evenings (40 members).

No. 122—DARNCONNER Aird's Moss Burns Club. Instituted 4th November, 1901. Federated 4th November, 1901. *Secretary*, William Naismith, Darnconner, *via* Auchinleck.

No. 123—AUCHINLECK Boswell Burns Club. Instituted 25th January, 1900. Federated 10th December, 1901. Place of meeting, Market Inn, Auchinleck. President, James Muir, Dalblair Cottage, Mauchline Road, Auchinleck ; Vice-president, Alex. Dalziel, Common Farm, Auchinleck ; *Secretary*, William Hall, 181 Dalsalloch, Auchinleck ; Treasurer, John Black, 189 Dalsalloch, Auchinleck. Special features of Club—Hallowe'en supper (with Burns's songs and recitations) ; monthly meeting, last Saturday of every month, to instruct and be instructed in Burns's works. On 25th January to celebrate the Poet's birth.

No. 124—EDINBURGH Ninety Burns Club. Instituted 1890. Federated 1902. Place of meeting, Ferguson & Forrester's, Princes Street. President, W. J. S. Dalling, 199 Bruntsfield Place, Edinburgh ; Vice-president, James Bell,

4 Wilfrid Terrace, Edinburgh ; *Secretary*, R. D. Grant ✓ M'Laren, 2 Mayfield Road, Edinburgh ; Treasurer, W. M. M'Burnie, 21 Plewlands Terrace, Edinburgh. Special features of Club—Anniversary dinner, dance, " at home," excursion, social evenings (with short addresses and songs), and business meetings.

No. 125—BLACKBURN-ON-ALMOND Rabbie Burns Club. Instituted 1900. Federated 1902. *Secretary*, Robt. Carlyle,✓ West-end, Blackburn, Bathgate.

No. 126—FALKIRK Burns Club. Instituted 1866. Federated 1902. Place of meeting, Mathieson's Rooms, High Street. President, H. B. Watson, Harlesdene, Major's Loan, Falkirk ; Vice-presidents, T. Callander Wade, M.B.E., Woodcroft, Larbert, and Duncan Kennedy, W.S., M.B.E., Heugh Street, Falkirk ; *Secretary*, R. H. Menzies,✓Bank Street, Falkirk. Committee—Fred Johnston, J.P., James M. Wilson, Rev. J. M. Ballard, Andrew Hunter, J. T. Borland, J. T. Sinclair, D. Houston, R. J. Aitchison, M.B.E., and Dan. Robertson.

No. 127—COWDENBEATH Haggis Burns Club. Instituted 1903. Federated 1903.

No. 128—COWDENBEATH Glencairn Burns Club. Instituted 1893. Federated 1903. Place and date of meeting, Raith Arms Inn, every alternate Friday from October to April, monthly remainder of year. Hon. President, W. Breingan ; Hon. Vice-presidents, F. Forsyth and D. Bowie ; President, Thos. Harower, 49 Arthur Street, Cowdenbeath ; Vice-president, John Nisbet, 61 Thistle Street, Cowdenbeath ; *Secretary*, E. Hunter,✓31 Arthur Place, Cowdenbeath ; Treasurer, Peter Banks ; Bard, Jas. Murray ; Master of Ceremonies, Jas. M'Kenzie. Committee—J. Wilson, William Foster, George Russell, A. Taylor, A. M'Kechnie, and G. Howie. Special features of Club—Anniversary dinner and social intercourse.

No. 129—GORBALS Burns Club. Instituted 1902. Federated 1903.

No. 130—ROW Burns Club. Instituted 1902. Federated 1903. *Secretary*, Robert Sloan, Hollylea, Row, Dumbartonshire.

No. 131—NOTTINGHAM Scottish Association. Instituted October, 1902. Federated November, 1903. Place of meeting, Mikado Cafe, Long Row, Nottingham. President, John Crawford, J.P., Springfield, Bulwell, Nottingham ; Vice president, Charles T. Craig, 2 Orston Road, West Bridgford, Nottingham ; *Secretary and Treasurer*, John Currie, 24 Arboretum Street, Nottingham. Special features of Club—Social intercourse among members ; celebration of Burns birthday and other national festivals.

No. 132—RICCARTON Kirkstyle Burns Club. Instituted 1904. Federated 1904.

No. 133—NEWARTHILL Burns Club Instituted 20th September, 1903. Federated 28th March, 1904. Place and date of meeting, Mrs H. Watson's, last Saturday of month, 6.30 p.m. President, John Henshaw, Church Street, Newarthill, Motherwell ; Vice-president, Thomas Law, C.C., Allan Place, Newarthill, Motherwell ; Secretary, Duncan Crawford,✓267 High Street, Newarthill, Motherwell. Committee—Thos. Crombie, Thos. Nimmo, and Thos. Macalpine.

No. 134—DUNTOCHER Heron Burns Club. Instituted 1897. Federated 1904.

No. 135—PARTICK Western Burns Club. Instituted 1903. Federated 1904. · Place of meeting, Windsor Restaurant, Partick. President, Alexander MacLellan, 20 Balshagry Avenue, Whiteinch, Glasgow ; Vice-president, Thomas Sutherland, Ashbourne Villa, Minard Road, Partickhill, Glasgow ; Secretary, F. R. Carter,✓28 White Street, Partick, Glasgow. Special features of Club—Lectures and harmony and anniversary dinner.

No. 136 HAMILTON Royal Oak Burns Club. Instituted 1898. Federated 1904.

No. 137—IPSWICH Burns Club. Instituted 1902. Federated 1904.

No. 138—CLELAND Burns Club. Instituted 1904. Federated 1904.

No. 139—GLASGOW National Burns Club, Ltd. Instituted 1904. Federated 1905. Place and date of meeting, 21 India Street, Glasgow, daily. President, John G. Galpine, 9 Yarrow Gardens, Glasgow ; Vice-president, William Emslie, 48 West Princes Street, Glasgow ; Secretary, Wm. Hamilton,✓21 India Street, Glasgow. Special feature of Club—Social.

No. 140 POLLOKSHAWS Burns Club. Instituted 1865. Federated 1905. Secretary, Jas. Milne, Burgh Halls, Pollokshaws.

No. 141—STONEHOUSE Burns Club. Instituted 1904. Federated 1905.

No. 142—BONNYBRIDGE Burns Club. Instituted 1905. Federated 1905.

No. 143—AIRDRIE Gateside Burns Club. Instituted 1904. Federated 1905.

No. 144—LARBERT and STENHOUSEMUIR Temperance Burns Club. Instituted 1904. Federated 1905.

No. 145—GLASGOW Central Burns Club. Instituted 1905. Federated 1905.

No. 146—DUBLIN Burns Club. Instituted 1905. Federated 1905. President, George P. Fleming, Drimnagh House, Inchicore, Co. Dublin ; Secretary, John Farquhar, 7 Fairview Avenue, Clontarf, Dublin ; Treasurer, Alexander Lyon, 111 Botanic Road, Dublin.

No. 147—STONEHOUSE Haggis Burns Club. Federated 1905.

No. 148—GREENOCK Cronies Burns Club. Instituted 1899. Federated 1905. Place and date of meeting, Painters' Hall, Charles Street, monthly. President, William Kelso, 67 Regent Street, Greenock ; Vice-president, John Dewar, 37 Dempster Street, Greenock : Secretary, James R. Blackley, 20 West Stewart Street, Greenock. Committee—D. Hamilton, Alex. Moffat, and Joseph Innes. Special features of Club—To cherish the name of Robert Burns and foster a love for his writings, and to promote good-fellowship.

No. 149—ELGIN Burns Club. Revived 20th December, 1900. Federated 1905. Date of meeting, annual business meeting in December, annual dinner in January. Hon. President, Sheriff Dunlop, Mar Lodge, Elgin : President Thomas North Christie of Blackhills, Morayshire ; Vice-presidents, Rev. J. R. Duncan, Lhanbryde, Morayshire, and R. B. Gordon, P.-F., Elgin ; Hon. Secretary, John Foster, Sheriff-Clerk of Morayshire ; Hon. Treasurer, J. B. Mair, M.V.O., Chief Constable of Morayshire. Committee—John Wittet, Col. Johnston, T. R. Mackenzie, D. A. Shiach, Alex. Gillan, and Angus Cameron.

No. 150—KILMARNOCK Jolly Beggars Burns Club. Instituted February 10th, 1905. Federated December, 1905. Place and date of meeting, "Wee Thack," Grange Street, last Monday of every month at 7.30 ; harmony, Saturday evenings at 7.30 ; monthly meeting. President, Wm. Willock, 65 King Street, Kilmarnock ; Vice-president, George M'Donald, Old Irvine Road, Kilmarnock ; Secretary, Andrew Niven, 17 Fullarton Street, Kilmarnock ; Treasurer, David Mitchell. Special features of Club— To cherish the name of Robert Burns ; to foster his writings ; to celebrate the anniversary of his birthday ; and to promote friendly and social intercourse amongst the members.

No. 151—OLD KILPATRICK Burns Club. Instituted 20th January, 1906. Federated 20th January, 1906. Place and date of meeting, Barclay U.F. Church Hall, monthly. President, William Cockburn, N.-B. Station House, Bowling ; Vice-president, Robert Newlands, Seyton, Gavinburn Place, Old Kilpatrick ; Secretary, Robert Smith, Maryville, Old Kilpatrick : Treasurer, Gavin Irvine, Station House, Old Kilpatrick. Committee— John Brock, Archie Paul, Alex. Mann, Allan Dawson, William Gallacher, Robert Draper, James Dykes, and James M'Carlie. Special feature of Club—Winter monthly meetings.

No. 152—HAMILTON Burns Club. Instituted 1877. Federated 1906. Place and date of meeting, Commercial Hotel, Hamilton, at irregular intervals during year. President, Thomas Arnot, Chaseley, Hamilton ; Vice-president, Rev. John L. Tulloch, Mansewood, Hamilton ; Secretary, Wm. Lang, The British Linen Bank, Hamilton ; Treasurer, W. Martin Kay, Bank of Scotland Chambers, Hamilton. Special feature of Club—Prizes are offered for essays on Scottish literature to pupils attending burgh schools.

No. 153—SCOTTISH Burns Club (in which are incorporated " Glasgow Waverley " and " Western " (1859) and " Ye Saints " (1884) Burns Clubs. Edinburgh Section formed 1919). Instituted 1904. Federated 1906. Place of meeting, " Ca'doro," 132 Renfield Street, Glasgow. President, D. S. Macgregor, 185 West Regent Street, Glasgow ; Vice-presidents, J. G. MacKerracher, 67 Durward Avenue, Shawlands, and A. K. Foote, Larkfield, Newlands Road, Newlands ; Secretary and Treasurer. J. Kevan M'Dowall, 180 Hope Street, Glasgow (telephone, " Douglas 3755 ") ; Auditors, Jas. B. Macpherson and D. M. M'Intyre, M.B.E., F.C.I.S. ; Bard, Thos. Cree. Committee—J. K. M'Dowall, J.P. ; J. S. Downie, M.A. ; N. MacWhannell, F.B.I.B.A., I.A. ; J. S. Gregson, Jas. Macfarlane, Sam. B. Langlands, R. W. Reddoch, J. Spears, and ex-Bailie Arch. Campbell, J.P. ; with President, Vice-presidents, and Secretary and Treasurer ex officio. Edinburgh Section.—President, Dr James Devon ; Vice-president, J. Kelso Kelly ; Secretary, J. M. Beaton, 2 Lily Terrace, North Merchiston Committee—A. Drysdale Paterson, Wm. J. Hay, John Samson, George M'Gill, and office-bearers ex officio. Special features of Club—Burnsiana and literature. The Club is conducted on temperance principles. Motto—" The heart aye's the part aye."

No. 154—JOHANNESBURG Burns Club. Instituted 1900. Federated 1906. Secretary, Richard Rusk, solicitor, Natal Bank Buildings, Market Square, Johannesburg.

No. 155—EAST STIRLINGSHIRE Burns Club. Instituted January, 1905. Federated September, 1906. Place and date of meeting, Cross Roads Inn, Bainsford, Falkirk, quarterly. President, Walter Gibson, 14 Watson Street, Grahamston, Falkirk ; Vice-president, Robert A. Russell, 2 Mungal Place, Bainsford, Falkirk ; Secretary, Alexander Glen, 21 Gordon Terrace, Carron Road, Falkirk ; Treasurer, John Duncan. Committee—William Galbraith, Wm. Philip, and George Milroy. Special features of Club—To foster and maintain a thorough knowledge of the Works of Burns ; to celebrate the anniversary of his birth in supper, song, and sentiment ; and to propagate and encourage a kind, social, and brotherly feeling one towards another.

No. 156—NEWCASTLE and TYNESIDE Burns Club. Instituted 1864. Federated 4th October, 1906. Place and

12

time of meeting, Central Exchange Hotel, 7 p.m. President, R. M Graham ; Vice-president, Alex. Sutherland · Secretary, David H. Allan, Tillside, Newlands Road, Newcastle-on-Tyne ; Treasurer, W. Tasker Brown.

No. 157 BAILLIESTON Caledonian Burns Club. Instituted January, 1901. Federated October, 1906. Place and date of meeting, Free Gardeners' Hall, Baillieston, second Friday in each month. President, John Kerr, 697 Shettleston Road, Shettleston ; Vice-president, Geo. Johnstone, 24 Longlea, Baillieston ; Secretary, Charles Paterson, 55 Muirside Road, Baillieston ; Treasurer and Delegate, Donald Macfarlane. Committee — John Preston, William Ross, William Kerr, James Smith, John Hendry, Alex. Johnstone, Arch. Page, John Scobbie, and John Wilson. Special features of Club—To cherish the name of Robert Burns and foster a love for his writings, and generally to encourage a taste for Scottish history and literature ; also to celebrate the memory of our National Bard by an annual s cial meeting to be held on 25th January, or as near thereto as possible.

No. 158—DARLINGTON Burns Association. Instituted March, 1906. Federated October, 1906. Place and date of meeting, Temperance Institute, various. President, Jno. Henderson, 7 Southend Avenue, Darlington ; Vice-presidents, J. M. Galt, Jas. Shirlaw, and J. C. Veitch ; Secretary, R. M. Liddell, 14 Langholm Crescent, Darlington ; Treasurer, Geo. Lawson, 5 Holmwood Grove, Harrogate Hill, Darlington. Committee—Robt. Storar, T. C. Howe, Jas. Anderson, Alexander Luke, T. Henderson Mus. Bac., Wm. Stevenson (Cleasby Terrace), Wm. Stevenson (Woodlands Road), Alexander Furness, and Councillor R. Nichol. Special features of Club—To promote the study of Burns's works and Scottish literature, history, &c., and the social and intellectual intercourse and enjoyment of the members generally, by such means as may from time to time be agreed upon.

No. 159—WALKER Burns Club. Instituted 1892. Federated 11th November, 1906. Place of meeting, Scrogg Inn, Walker. President, John Keith, 633 Welbeck Road, Walker ; Vice-presidents, Dr W. Hutchison, H. F. Caldwell, Welbeck Road, Walker, and T. Smith, 84 Mitchell Street, Walker ; Secretary, John Yeats, 168 Middle Street, Walker, Newcastle-on-Tyne ; Treasurer, Robert M'Rory, 26 Eastbourne Gardens, Walker. Special features of Club—To promote the cultivation of a better knowledge of the Poet and his works ; to bring together Scotsmen and other admirers of Burns ; also promoting Scottish concerts.

No. 160—WHITBURN Burns Club. Instituted 1906. Federated 1906. Place and date of meeting, Cross Tavern, Whitburn, first Friday and third Saturday each month. President, Frank M'Gregor, East Main Street, Whitburn ; Vice-president, Wm. M'Kenzie, East Main Street, Whitburn ; *Secretary*, Allan Johnston, 184 West Main Street, Whitburn, West Lothian ; Delegate to S.C.B.C.A., Wm. Clark ; Stewards, John Brown and Alex. M'Laren, sen. Special features of Club—Competitions among the young, viz. : Essay writing, singing and reciting, &c. We have just brought off an essay writing competition confined to Whitburn School. Other items are socials, papers from members on Scottish history and literature, and summer excursion to some historical district or town.

No. 161—CHARLESTON Burns Club, Paisley. Instituted 25th January, 1905. Federated 20th December, 1906. Place and date of meeting, 17 Stevenson Street, quarterly. President, Wm. Herd, 25 Stock Street ; Vice-president, Andrew Walker, 16 Stevenson Street ; *Secretary*, A. R. Rowand, 7 South Park Drive, Paisley ; Auditors, Hugh Black and Andrew Shannon. Special features of Club —The propagation of the knowledge of the writings of Burns in the district : the promotion of a friendly feeling among the members and kindred Clubs : and the celebration of the Poet's birth.

No 162 PLYMOUTH and District Caledonian Society. Instituted 8th February, 1898. Federated 8th March, 1907. *Secretary*, P. Robertson, 89 Alcester Street, Devonport.

No. 163—GATESHEAD and District Burns Club. Instituted 1887. Federated 1907. Place and date of meeting, Royal Hotel, Prince Consort Road, Gateshead-on-Tyne, first Wednesday of each month, September to April. President, John Drape, Shannon House, Low Fell : Vice-presidents, Thomas Gault, 187 Windsor Avenue, Gateshead-on-Tyne, W. Bain, E. Bennett, R. Good, T. Hetherington, and D. Morrison ; *Secretary*, A. Mansfield, 152 Westbourne Avenue, Gateshead-on-Tyne ; Treasurer, G. J. Porter, 6 Trevelyan Terrace, Durham Road, Gateshead-on-Tyne ; Piper, Pipe-Major Munro Strachan, Tyneside Scottish, 20 Diamond Street, Wallsend-on-Tyne. Committee—D. Buchan, D. Dick, R. England, J. Guy, J. D. Jardine, T. Lumsden, A. M'Donald, J. S. Mason, G. Paterson, and T. Watson. Special features of Club—To associate Scotsmen and other admirers of Burns ; to preserve an interest in Scottish manners, customs, and affairs ; to cultivate literary pursuits, and more particularly to advance the study of the Works of Burns and other Scottish literature.

No. 164 KINNING PARK Burns Club. Instituted 1881 ; re-instituted 1921. Federated 1907. Place and date of meeting, Wheatsheaf Rooms, once monthly. President, Thomas Deans, 159 Stanley Street, Glasgow, S.S. ; Vice-president, J. W. Forsyth, 12 Fleurs Avenue, Dumbreck, Glasgow ; *Secretary*, John Henderson, 48 Pollok Street, Glasgow, S.W. : Auditors, Robert Bain and Malcolm Chisholm. Committee—James Mason, James Hay, James Douglas, Thomas Porter, David Lorimer, John Simpson, and James Adam. Special features of Club

—Annual celebration of the birthday of Robert Burns ; occasional meetings for the cultivation of social and intellectual intercourse ; the encouragement of Scottish literature amongst members and friends.

No. 165 WALLSEND Burns Club. Instituted 1898. Federated 18th April, 1907 Place and date of meeting, Jolly Sailors' Hotel, Wallsend-on-Tyne, third Wednesday every month. President, James Heron, 13 Curzon Road, Wallsend-on-Tyne ; Vice-president, Peter Smith, 30 Myrtle Grove, Wallsend-on-Tyne ; Secretary, D. E. Liddle, 72 Northumberland Street, Wallsend-on-Tyne ; Treasurer, T. M'Ewan. Committee—Messrs Carruthers, Walters, M'Kinnon, Rae, and Lough. Special features of Club—To associate Scotsmen and admirers of Burns ; to cultivate literary pursuits and love of Scottish song and story by promoting Scotch concerts ; also to preserve an interest in Scottish manners and customs.

No. 166—CLEVELAND Scottish Association. Instituted 1907. Federated 1907. Secretary, A. Wallace, 6 Royal Exchange, Middlesborough.

No 167—Birmingham Burns Club. Instituted 1906. Federated 1907. Place of meeting, Grand Hotel. President, T. N. Veitch, 33 Victoria Road, Acocks Green, Birmingham ; Vice-presidents, John Barr, 6 Springfield Road, King's Heath, Birmingham, and C. Macgrath, 82 Oakfield Road, Balsall Heath, Birmingham ; Secretary, Wright Murray, 130 Oakwood Road, Sparkhill, Birmingham ; Treasurer, Robt. M'Kenzie, 50 Stirling Road, Edgbaston, Birmingham.

No. 168—RICCARTON Burns Club. Instituted 7th February, 1877. Federated 14th January, 1908. Place of meeting, Commercial Inn. President, Robert Wyllie, Fleming Street, Riccarton ; Secretary, Jas. P. Moir, 39 Campbell Street, Riccarton. Committee—Geo. Cunningham (" Pate M'Phun "), Hugh Dale, J. P. Dickson, J. Williamson, and Wm. Neil. Special features of Club —Social intercourse amongst the Burns fraternity ; to spread and become familiar with the Poet's works.

No. 169—GLASGOW and DISTRICT Association of Burns Clubs and Kindred Societies. Instituted 1907. Federated 1908. Place of meeting, Burns Club House, 27 India Street, Glasgow. President, Wm. Cockburn, North British Railway Station, Bowling ; Vice-presidents, Thomas Killin, J.P., 2 Stewarton Drive, Cambuslang, and J. C. Ewing, 167 West Regent Street, Glasgow : Secretary, J. Jeffrey Hunter, solicitor, 89 Bath Street, Glasgow. Committee—J. M. Alexander, J. F. Anderson, J. M. Brown, T. C. F. Brotchie (Art Gallery), James M. Campbell, Isaac Chalmers, Thos. Deans, Wm. Gardiner, J. G. Galpine, R. M. Milholm, John Macfarlane, Ninian M'Whannell, Hugh Paton, Wm. Reid, A. C. Riddall, J. S. Ritchie, J. D. Sloan, T. P. Thomson, and Thomas

S. Turnbull. Special features of Club—To further the interest of the Burns cult by promoting closer union between the clubs in the district and bringing the members of these clubs into more harmonious relationship, and to take the initiative in instituting and recommending movements likely to be beneficial to the Burns cult.

No 170—LARKHALL Thistle Burns Club. Instituted November, 1906. Federated 18th April, 1908. President, John Crozier Hislop, 17 Percy Street, Larkhall ; *Secretary,* William Nicol, Machan, Larkhall.

No 171—CHATTANOOGA Burns Society, Tenn., U.S.A. Instituted 25th January, 1908 Federated 2nd June, 1908. Place and date of meeting, Mountain City Club, Chattanooga, Tenn., 25th January. President, James Francis Johnston, 505 Walnut Street, Chattanooga, Tenn. ; Vice-president, Col. Milton B. Ochs, *Times* Building, Chattanooga, Tenn. ; *Secretary,* Col. R. B. Cooke, National Soldiers' Home, Maine, U.S.A. ; Committee—N. Thayer Montague, Frank Spurlock, Joe Brown, M.C., and T. R. Preston. Special features of Club—Annual dinner, papers, lectures, collection of library.

No. 172—OREGON Burns Club, Portland, Oregon, U.S.A. Instituted 25th January, 1908. Federated December, 1908. Place of meeting, Chamber of Commerce Building. President, William Bristol, Attorney, Wilcox Buildings, Portland, Oregon ; Vice-president, Judge George J. Cameron Chamber of Commerce Building, Portland, Oregon ; *Secretary,* Alexander T. Smith, 143 Hamilton Avenue, Portland, Oregon. Committee—Dr W. T. Williamson, James Hislop, Alex. G. Brown, Alex. Muirhead. Special features of Club—Meet once a year on January 25th to celebrate the anniversary of the birth of the greatest poet of humanity, the immortal Robert Burns.

No. 173—IRVINE Burns Club. Instituted 1826. Federated 18th November, 1908. Place of meeting, King's Arms Hotel. President, Matthew Breckenridge, Caldwell, Irvine ; Vice-president, Provost Muir, Roselea, Irvine ; *Secretary,* R. M. Hogg, B.A., Stratford, Irvine ; Treasurer, R. F. Longmuir, Roseville, Irvine.

No. 174 ARDROSSAN Castle Burns Club. Federated 1908. *Secretary,* Wm. Gibson, Hill Cottage, 90 Glasgow Street, Ardrossan.

No. 175—MEIKLE EARNOCK Original Burns Club. Instituted 16th March, 1906. Federated 21st December 1908. Place of meeting, John Crowe, Cadzow Vaults, Hamilton. President, James Shepherd, 2 Moore Street, Hamilton ; Vice-president, Alex. Laird, 50 Eddlewood Buildings, Hamilton ; *Secretary,* John Hepburn, 36 Eddlewood Buildings, Hamilton. Committee—Andrew Hamilton, William Pollock, Robert Lees, and William Ross. Special features of Club—To keep ever green the memory of Scotia's greatest son, and disseminate the principles he strove to inculcate.

No. 176 RENFREW Burns Club. Federated 6th December, 1898. *Secretary*, Wm. S. Cochran, 20 Renfield Street, Renfrew.

No. 177—PRESTWICK Burns Club. Instituted 1902. Federated 1908.

No 178—KILMARNOCK Begbie's Burns Club. Instituted 1908. Federated 1909. Place and date of meeting, Angel Hotel, third Wednesday of each month. President, John Stewart, 12 Hill Street, Kilmarnock ; Vice-president, Andrew Sinclair, 65 M'Lelland Drive, Kilmarnock ; *Secretary*, William Lennox, 11 Nursery Avenue, Kilmarnock. Committee—John Brown, A. M'D. Anderson, David Lang, John Douglas, and Wm. Muir. Special features of Club— Reading of papers relative to the works of Burns and kindred subjects ; celebrating the birthday of the Poet.

No. 179—DAILLY Jolly Beggars Burns Club. Instituted 22nd January, 1902. Federated 22nd January, 1902.

No. 180—TOLLCROSS Burns Club. Instituted 1908. Federated 1909. Place and date of meeting, Fullarton Hall, first Friday of each month, 7.30. President, Robert Irvine, 306 Dennistoun Gardens, Dennistoun ; Vice-president, James Hodgins, 18 Trainard Avenue, Tollcross ; *Secretary*, James L. Cowan, Clydeside Terrace, Tollcross : Treasurer, P. W. Watt. Directors—John Kerr, sen., A. Meikle, W. Clarke. D. Waddell, D. Campbell, J. Paterson. Special features of Club—To cherish the name of Robert Burns and foster a love for his writings, and generally to encourage a taste for Scottish literature, and to celebrate the memory of our National Bard by an annual dinner or social meeting.

No. 181 GLASGOW Primrose Burns Club. Instituted 1901. Federated 11th February, 1909. Place and date of meeting, Burns House, 27 India Street, 7.30. President, Alex. Webster, 7 Willowbank Crescent, Glasgow ; Vice-president, John Duncan, 14 Willowbank Crescent, Glasgow ; *Secretary*, George R. Hunter, 55 Seamore Street, Glasgow ; Treasurer, John Wall, 263 Hope Street, Glasgow. Special features of the Club—The promotion of Burns cult, anniversary dinner, school children's competitions, lectures, and musical evenings.

No. 182—STANE (Shotts) Mossgiel Burns Club. Instituted 3rd February, 1908. Federated 24th February, 1909. Place and date of meeting, Stane Hotel, first Friday of each month, except June, July, and August. President, Jas. Morris, Greenview, Shotts ; Vice-president, William Rodger, 104 Main Street, Stane, Shotts ; *Secretary*, Alexander Walker, 9 Torbothie Road, Stane, Shotts ;

Treasurer, Jas. White, 1 Stane Place, Stane, Shotts. Special features of Club—Papers and discussion on Poet's life and works ; school competitions ; celebration of anniversaries.

No. 183—LONDONDERRY Burns Club and Caledonian Society. Instituted 1905. Federated 1909. Place of meeting, Presbyterian Working Men's Institute, The Diamond, Londonderry. President, Thos. Wallace, Elderslie, Sunbeam Terrace, Londonderry ; Vice-presidents, Jas. F. Wands, G. P. Findlay, Jas. MacLehose, Wm. Dickie, Geo. Burns, D. Murray, W. Nichol, Wm. Mason, W. G. S. Ballantyne, and Alexander Wightman ; Lady Vice-presidents, Mrs Wallace, Mrs Dickie, and Mrs Wands ; Secretary, Wm. Baxter,ᵛ 12 Harding Street, Londonderry. Special features of Club—To cherish the memory of Burns and to study his works, also to cultivate a closer social union amongst all classes of Scotsmen.

No. 184—BLAIRADAM Shanter Burns Club. Instituted 21st August, 1907. Federated 29th August. 1909. Place and date of meeting, Blairadam Tavern, Kelty, alternate Saturdays. President, Councillor James Wilkie, Hutton's Buildings, Black Road, Kelty ; Vice-presidents, Adam Lees, Adam's Terrace, Kelty, and Arthur Bennett, Stewart's Buildings, Main Street, Kelty ; Secretary, Thos. C. Anderson, Blairforge, Blairadam, Kelty ; Treasurer, Wm. Fyfe. Committee—Wm. Clark, Alex. Richardson, James Lees, Alex. Penman, and Peter Bett. Special features of Club— Songs, recitations, and readings annual school children's competitions on the songs and poems of our National Bard.

No. 185—BURTON Burns Club. Instituted 1908. Federated 1909.

No. 186—KILMARNOCK Glencairn Burns Club. Instituted 1909. Federated 1910. Secretary, John Thorburn, ⱴ 12 Fairyhill Road, Kilmarnock.

No. 187—GALASHIELS Burns Club. Instituted 10th December, 1908. Federated 9th December, 1909. Place of meeting, Burgh Buildings. Hon. President, Right Hon. Robert Munro, K.C., M.P. ; President, Councillor George Hope Tait ; Vice-presidents, Provost Dalgleish, H. S. Murray, A. L. Brown ; Secretary, George Grieve : Treasurer, John Hodge, jun. Committee—W Addison (chairman of committee), H. M. Tait, David Hislop, W. Young, L. Lennox, Chief Constable Noble, Jas. Walker, Councillor Thos. Brown, Thos. Lamb, ex-Provost Riddle, P. Whyte, Councillor Kemp, Councillor G. T. Sanderson, and ex-Provost Sutherland.

No. 188—DUNS Working Men's Burns Club. Instituted 1902. Federated 1910. Secretary, Robt. Cameron, ⱴ British Linen Bank, Duns.

No. 189—CLYDEBANK Barns o' Clyde Burns Club. Instituted 1896. Federated December, 1909. Place and date of meeting, Hutcheon's Restaurant, first Thursday each month. President, Geo. Latto, slater, Canal Street, Clydebank ; Vice-president, Jas. Fowler, 6 Viewfield Terrace, Clydebank ; *Secretary*, A. Homewood ' 35 Taylor Street, Clydebank. Committee—G. Gibson, J. Cameron, J. M'Chleary, R. Fowler, A. R. Raeburn, D. Macpherson, J. Kean, W. Middleton, J. Gibson, R. Carson, J. Smith, D. Sutherland, J. Dunsmore. Special features of Club —To extend the good work of the Poet, and to keep for ever green the memory of the Immortal Bard, Robert Burns, the patriot and prince of song.

No. 190—PORT-GLASGOW Burns Club. Instituted 13th January, 1910. Federated 5th April, 1910. Place and date of meeting, Oddfellows' Hall, second Wednesday April to September. President, J. A. Borland, Balfour Place ; Vice-president, C. Young, Plantation Cottage, Clune Brae ; *Secretary*, Wm. R. Niven, 53 Firth View ; Treasurer, Wm. M'Dougall ; Stewards, J. Louden, D. Simpson, G. H. Anderson, and M. Phill ps ; Chief Auditors, T. Wyllie, and A. Morrison. Committee—G. Bannerman, J. Cameron, and M. Phillips.

No. 191 MOORPARK Burns Club. Instituted 1908. Federated 1910. *Secretary*, Ebenezer Inglis, Glasdale, Fauldshead Road, Renfrew.

No. 192—AYRSHIRE ASSOCIATION of Federated Burns Clubs. Instituted 1908. Federated 1910. Place and date of meeting, Quarterly, at various places and times in the county. *Secretary*, William Lennox, 11 Nursery Avenue, Kilmarnock. Committee—Arch. Laird, Jas. Moir, H. Campbell, Wm. Hall, and John M'Gregor. Special features of the Club—To further the interests of the Burns cult by promoting closer union between the Clubs in the county, and to render all possible assistance to the work of the Federation.

No. 193 RUTHERGLEN Jolly Beggars Burns Club. Instituted 1910. Federated 1910.

No. 194—MIDDLEBIE Burns Club. Instituted 1909. Federated 1910. *Secretary*, Walter A. Mather, Donkins House, Kirtlebridge, Ecclefechan.

No. 195—SHIREMOOR Blue Bell Burns Club. Instituted 1906. Federated November, 1910. Place and date of meeting, Blue Bell Hotel, second Saturday in every month. President, John Wilson, 11 Duke Street, Shiremoor, Northumberland : Vice-president, Robert Fyfe, 19 Percy Street, Shiremoor, Northumberland ; *Secretary*, Jas. Fyfe Wilson, 11 Duke Street, Shiremoor, Northumberland. Committee—J. Peacock, J. Sneddon, A. Messer, J. W. Mather, T. Young, and W. S. Brown. Special feature of Club—To foster a love for the Poet and his Works.

No. 196 MID-ARGYLL Burns Club. Instituted 11th January, 1909. Federated 27th December, 1910. Place of meeting, Royal Hotel, Ardrishaig. President, Alexander Blue, Kilduskland, Ardrishaig ; Vice-president, Robert Finlay, Royal Hotel, Ardrishaig ; Secretary, Andrew Y. Roy, 'Tigh-an-Eas, Ardrishaig. Committee—J. M. Montgomerie, John M'Arthur, Archibald Campbell, and Archibald M'Bain. Special features of Club—Celebration of the Poet's birthday, and . to encourage the study of his works.

No. 197 WINNIPEG Burns Club. Instituted 1905. Federated 1911. Secretary, A. G. Kemp,' Box 2886, Winnipeg.

No. 198—GOREBRIDGE Twenty-five Jolly Beggars Burns Club. Federated 28th November, 1913. Place of meeting, Brunton's Inn, Gorebridge. President, Robert Burnside, J.P., Main Street, Gorebridge ; Vice-president, Robert Robertson, Store Row, Arniston, Gorebridge : Secretary, John Duncan,'5 Slate Row, Arniston, Gorebridge. Committee—R. Miller, W. Weir, R. Davidson, and R. Hadden.

No. 199—NEWBATTLE and DISTRICT Burns Club. Instituted 1910. Federated March, 1911. Place and time of meeting, Bowling Pavilion and Band Hall, 7 p.m. President, William Carson, Saugh, Newtongrange, Mid-Lothian· Vice-presidents, James Brown, 6 Second Street, Newtongrange, and Andrew Anderson, Newtongrange ; Secretary, John J. Haldane,' 7 Sixth Street, Newtongrange, Mid-Lothian. Committee—P. Gray, J. Samuel, J. Gilmour, D. Jamieson, Councillor Doig, D. Richardson, G. M'Intosh, A. Robertson, T. Gardner, J. Vickers, R. M'Laren, and W. Thomson. Special features of Club—Encouragement of social intercourse amongst the members and kindred Clubs ; celebration of the Poet's birth ; an annual trip ; meetings for the reading of literary papers relative to the life of Burns and kindred subjects ; promoting entertainments for charitable purposes, &c.

No. 200 STONEHOUSE Jolly Beggars Burns Club. Instituted January, 1911. Federated 21st March, 1911. Place and date of meeting, Buckshead Inn, every alternate Friday. President, Matthew Steel, Camnethan Street, Stonehouse ; Vice-president, David Gavin, Lochart Street, Stonehouse ; Secretary, Gavin Hutchison,' Boghall Street, Stonehouse ; Treasurer, Robert Anderson, Buckshead Inn, Stonehouse. Special feature of Club—To promote social intercourse amongst the people in the village.

No 201 CARLISLE Newtown Burns Club. Instituted November, 1910. Federated 27th April, 1911.

No. 202—GOVAN Ye Cronies Burns Club. Instituted 1893. Federated 1911. Place and date of meeting, Red Lamp, Govan, second Saturday each month, at 6 p.m. President, Jas Hutchison, 10 Earl Street, Scotstoun ; Vice-president, William Parker, 11 Moss Road, Govan ; Secretary, James Rellie, 18 Elder Street, Govan : Treasurer, Alex. Munro ; Bard. T. M. Walker, M.A. ; Past Presidents, A. Nicol, E. J. Tait, and M. Stirling. Committee— W. Forbes, G. Kinloch, J. Curtis, A. P. Gowans, and W. Watson. Special features of Club—The Club shall consist of men who honour and revere the memory of Burns ; the membership shall not exceed 100, and each candidate for membership must be a Freemason ; to promote social and friendly intercourse amongst its members.

No 203—DENNISTOUN Jolly Beggars Burns Club. Instituted 25th January, 1911. Federated 6th June, 1911. Place and date of meeting, Chalmers Street Hall, last Thurdsay of month, at 8 p.m. President, Thomas Miller, 180 Thomson Street, Dennistoun, Glasgow ; Vice-president, J. Hendry, 189 Bellfield Street, Dennistoun, Glasgow ; Secretary, Wm. Fulton, 4 Parkhouse Lane, Dennistoun, Glasgow ; Bard, J. M'Donald ; Piper, A. M'Pherson ; Librarian, W. Forsyth. Past Presidents—W. Hood, G. F. Thomas, W. Williamson, J. M. Broadby, G. Newman, J. M'Donald, and A. Hainey. Committee—J. Hendry, A. Duff, A. Carnan, A. Napier, W. Forsyth, and J. Lennox. Federation delegates—G. F. Thomas and T. Miller. Association delegates—W. Fulton, A. Hainey, and J. Hendry. Special features of Club—Celebration of the birth of Robert Burns ; occasional re-union for the cultivation of social and intellectual intercourse amongst members and friends ; and the encouragement of Scottish literature.

No. 204—DUNDALK and DISTRICT Burns Club. Instituted 1909. Federated 1911. President, W. Cree, Jocelyn Street, Dundalk ; Vice-president, W. Reid, Park Street, Dundalk ; Secretary, Geo. Williamson, St. Andrew's, Castle Road, Dundalk.

No. 205—PAISLEY St. Mirren Burns Club. Instituted 1910. Federated 1911. Place of meeting, St. Mirren Bar, 44 Old Sneddon Street. President, John Brown, Rutherglen ; Vice-president, Aaron Jones, Main Street, Neilston ; Secretary, Robert Crawford, 44 Old Sneddon Street, Paisley. Special feature of Club—To maintain and further the interest in the Life of Burns.

No 206 GLASGOW Daisy Burns Club. Instituted 1911. Federated 1911.

No. 207—CAMBUSLANG Wingate Burns Club. Instituted 1908. Federated 1912. Place and date of meeting, Free Gardeners' Hall, first Saturday every month. President, Arthur M'Neil, 14 Longlea, Baillieston ; Vice-president, John Williamson, 431 Hamilton Road, Cambuslang.

Secretary, John Cowie Smith, 14 Church Street, Cambus-
lang ; Assistant Secretary, Robert Tait ; Treasurer,
Wm. Stewart ; Stewards, Jno. M'Farlane and Robt.
Campbell. Hon. Members—Wm. Young, A. H. Young,
Daniel Smith, sen., Robt. Tait, Wm. M'Lean, Duncan
M'Gilvray, John C. Smith, and John M'Cracken. Com-
mittee—Dugal Wright, Allan Dunn, Alex. Stevenson,
John Anderson, Alex. H. Young, Robt. Harden, Donald
Robertson, and Robt. Forrester, jun. Special feature
of Club—Furtherance of Scottish song and sentiment.

No. 208—COLORADO SPRINGS and DISTRICT Caledonian
Society. Instituted 1897. Federated 1912. President,
J. I. M'Clymont, 323 Hagerman Building, Colorado
Springs ; *Secretary*, H. C. Beattie, 524 North Nevada
Avenue, Colorado Springs ; Treasurer, Thos. Strachan,
1215 North Weber, Colorado Springs.

No. 209 GREENOCK St. John's Burns Club. Instituted 13th
August, 1909. Federated 17th August, 1911. Place
of meeting, Masonic Temple. President, James A. Morri-
son, 39 Brisbane Street, Greenock ; Vice-president, John
Broadfoot, 21 Holmscroft Street, Greenock ; *Secretary*,
Jacob A. C. Hamilton, 19 Brown Street, Craigieknowes,
Greenock ; Treasurer, Peter Morrison, 66 Wellington
Street, Greenock. Special features of Club—To cherish
the name of Robert Burns and foster a love for his
writings, and generally to promote good-fellowship.

No. 210—HARDGATE Auld Hoose Burns Club. Instituted 28th
September, 1912. Federated 30th September, 1912.

No 211—LARKHALL Cronies Burns Club. Instituted May,
1912. Federated 10th October, 1912. Place and
date of meeting, The Volunteer Bar, every Saturday
evening. President, William Kilpatrick, c/o Anderson,
41 Marshall Street, Larkhall ; Vice-president, Charles
Dobbie, 15 Academy Street, Larkhall ; *Secretary*, John
M'Leod, 52 Muir Street, Larkhall ; Treasurer, Robert
Ramage. Committee—John Potter, Robert Morton,
George M'Queen, Alexander Currie, and William Anderson. Special features of Club—Celebration of the
Poet's birthday and to encourage the study of his works ·
to promote closer union between other clubs.

No. 212 PORTOBELLO Burns Club. Instituted 25th January,
1892. Federated 1913. President, Bailie James Hastie,
J.P., Queen's Bay Hotel, Portobello ; Vice-president,
Thomas Bennett, 20 Brighton Place ; *Secretary*, William
Baird, J.P., F.S.A.Scot., 11 Pitt Street, Portobello ;
Treasurer, J. Lewis Jenkins, 1 Windsor Place, Portobello.
Special features of Club—To encourage a study of Scottish
literature, and particularly to interest the members
in all that pertains to the life of Burns and his works.
Frequent social meetings are held during the winter months,
when papers bearing upon these are read and concerts
of Scottish music given. These meetings have been of

late eminently successful. Twenty-one prizes (in books) were awarded to the children of the two public schools of Portobello this year, and are highly valued by teachers and children alike. The membership has gone steadily up, and is now over 140.

No. 213—GLASGOW Kingston Burns Club. Instituted 1912. Federated 11th January, 1913. Place and date of meeting, Kingston Hall, Paisley Road, third Thursday of month. President, Robert Gray, J.P., 83 King Street, Glasgow, S S. ; Vice-president, John Logan, J.P., 176 Watt Street, Glasgow, S.S. ; Secretary, Alex. Baird, 22 Pollok Street, Glasgow, S.S. : Treasurer, Hugh A. Begg, 104 Weir Street, Glasgow, S.S. Special features of Club —To commemorate the genius of Robert Burns and foster a love for his writings, and to encourage the taste for Scottish literature and music generally.

No. 214—MELROSE Burns Club. Federated 22nd February, 1913. President, Dr Henry Speirs, St. Dunstan's, Melrose ; Vice-president, Geo. Sanderson, Westhill, Melrose ; Secretary, Geo. Mackenzie, High Street, Melrose.

No. 215—THORNIEWOOD Burns Club. Instituted 26th February, 1911. Federated 24th February, 1913. Secretary, W. Kerr, 54 Thorniewood, Uddingston.

No. 216—RUTHERGLEN Royal Burgh Burns Club. Instituted March, 1913. Federated May, 1913. Secretary, James E. Murray, 94 Mill Street, Rutherglen.

No. 217—ESKDALE Burns Club. Federated 29th April, 1913. President, Clement Armstrong, F.S A.Scot., Eskholm ; Vice-president, Thomas Bell, Townfoot : Secretary, Wm. Pendreigh, Brewery House, Langholm. Committee— James Barr, Wm. Murray, David Calvert, and Robt. Irving.

No 218 BANNOCKBURN Empire Burns Club. Instituted 25th January, 1913. Federated 13th June, 1913. Place and time of meeting, Commercial Hotel, Bannockburn, 7 p.m. President, Thomas Rattray, West Murrayfield, Bannockburn ; Vice-president, William Still, Wallace Street, Bannockburn ; Secretary, William Wark, Helenslea, Bannockburn ; Treasurer, James Kirkwood, Cauldhame, Bannockburn. Committee — John Fulton, William Neill, Edward Wright, Wm. Lennie, Jno. Love, And. M'Gilchrist, C. Palmer, and James Forsyth. Special features of Club—Monthly meetings during the year (our meetings consist of recitations and songs, and tend to create good-fellowship amongst our members) ; and to render all possible assistance to the work of the Federation.

No. 219—UDDINGSTON Burns Club. Instituted 1st April. 1913. Federated 21st June, 1913. Place of meeting, Magdala Hall, Uddingston. President, Thos. Hamilton,

Alpine Terrace, Uddingston ; Vice-president, James
Ross, Greenrig Street, Uddingston ; *Secretary,* Henry
Rowan,✓50 Hamilton Place, Uddingston ; Treasurer,
John Hunter, c/o Thos. Latta, Uddingston.

No. 220 ST. LOUIS Burns Club, Mo., U.S.A. Instituted 1904.
Federated 1913. Date of meeting, 25th January. Presi-
dent, W. K. Bixby, Century Buildings, St. Louis, Mo. ;
Vice-president, David R. Francis, St. Louis, Mo ; *Secre-
tary,* Walter B. Stevens, Jefferson Memorial, St. Louis,
Mo. ; Treasurer, Hanford Crawford, 722 Chestnut Street
St. Louis, Mo Special features of Club—Annual meet-
ings ; issuing printed reports from time to time.

No. 221—PRESTONPANS Burns Club. Instituted 25th January,
1913. Federated 16th August, 1913. *Secretary,* T.
W. Watson,✓ Moat House, Prestonpans.

No. 222—HULL Burns Club. Instituted 1863. Federated 1913.
Place and time of meeting, Albion Hall, Baker Street,
7.45 p.m. President, Councillor Dr G. W. Lilley, J.P.,
22 Williamson Street, Hull ; *Joint Secretaries,* Robt.
A. Speirs, 24 Marlborough Avenue, Hull, and Albert
Hockney, 51 Clumber Street, Hull. Special features
of Club—Social and literary.

No. 223 GLASGOW Auld Clinkum Burns Club. Instituted
3rd April, 1913. Federated 6th October, 1913. Place
and date of meeting, Burns Club House, 27 India Street,
first Saturday each month. President, James Wilson,
17 Albany Terrace, Shettleston ; Vice-president, James
Muir, 6 Avon Street, Glasgow ; *Secretary,* James Robertson,✓21 James Orr Street, Glasgow ; Treasurer, William
Harris, 972 Argyle Street, Glasgow. Delegates, Charles
M'Kenna and C. M. Kelly. Special features of Club
—Cultivating a friendly feeling amongst the members ;
helping in a practical way in assisting widows and children
of deceased members ; annual trip ; celebration of
Poet's birthday ; lectures on other great literary men ;
musical entertainments to encourage interest in the
works and teaching of Scotia's National Bard.

No. 224 ASHINGTON Burns Club. Instituted 1891. Federated 1913. Place and date of meeting, Portland Hotel,
monthly. President, Dr F. Beaton, Lintonville, Ashington ; Vice-presidents, Dr M'Lean, F. Beattie, County
Councillor J. J. Hall, and Councillor S. Strong ; *Secretary,*
J. A. Robertson, 2 Eighth Row, Ashington ; Treasurer, R.
Hamilton ; Chairman, T. Boutland. Special features
of Club—Monthly meetings and celebration of Burns
anniversary.

No. 225—HELENSBURGH Burns Club. Instituted 2nd February,
1911. Federated 14th November, 1913. Place and
time of meeting, Masonic Hall, 8 p.m. President, John
Brown, Cairndhu Lodge, Helensburgh ; Vice-presidents,
John Somerville, Woodlands Place, and Silas Maclean,

John Street ; *Secretary,* Robert Thorburn, Albion Cottage, Helensburgh. Special features of Club—Special observance of Hallowe'en and anniversary festivals. Only Burnsiana allowed on 25th January. Lecture and debating nights between festivals. Successful public concert held in February, 1921 (may be repeated in 1922). A choir of mixed voices (conducted by the President) lends variety and charm to the social gatherings, illustrates essays on song-writers, and has been of considerable use by giving concerts in the villages around in aid of various charitable objects. Membership of Club, 170.

No. 226—DUMFRIES Burns Club. Instituted 18th January, 1820. Federated 1913. Place and date of meeting, Annual meeting, Sheriff Court-house, Dumfries, first week in November. President, Joseph Hunter, M.B., Ch.B., 31 Castle Street, Dumfries ; Vice-president. Lieut.-Col. P. Murray Kerr, V.D., 30 Castle Street, Dumfries ; *Secretary,* John M'Burnie, Sheriff Court-house, Dumfries. Committee—A. C. Penman, Robert Adamson, Peter Biggam, William J. Stark, T. S. Hunter, and John White. Special features of Club are—(a) To maintain the Burns Mausoleum in good repair, and provide for its proper supervision ; (b) To discharge the obligations laid upon the Club by the testamentary disposition of Colonel William Nichol Burns with respect to Burns's House and the Mausoleum ; (c) To celebrate in suitable manner the anniversary of the Poet's birth, and to honour his memory in such other ways as may be from time to time determined : (d) To foster a knowledge of the life and works of Burns by means of an annual competition amongst local school children, prizes being awarded to the successful competitors.

No. 227 PENRITH Burns Club. Instituted 27th January, 1911. Federated 1913. *Secretary,* J. S. M'Grogan, 94 Lowther Street, Penrith, Cumberland.

No. 228—CALDERWATERHEAD Burns Club. Federated 23rd May, 1914. *Secretary,* Wm. R. Moir, Mossbank, Hall Road, Shotts.

No. 229—EASTBOURNE and DISTRICT Scottish Association. Federated 23rd May, 1914. *Secretary,* R Prentice 110 Terminus Road, Eastbourne.

No. 230—BURNBANK Burns Club. Instituted November, 1913. Federated 23rd May, 1914. *Secretary,* William Jamieson, 140 Glasgow Road, Burnbank, Hamilton.

No. 231—FAULDHOUSE and EAST BENHAR Burns Club. Instituted 1907. Federated 28th May, 1914. Place and date of meeting, Caledonian Hotel, Fauldhouse, last Saturday of every month, at 6 p.m. President, John Salmond, Co-operative Buildings, West End, Fauldhouse ; Vice-president, Robert Mutter, Co-operative

Buildings, West End, Fauldhouse ; *Secretary*, William Salmond, Hawthorn Place, Quarry Road, Fauldhouse ; Treasurer, William Forsyth, Hawthorn Place, Quarry Road, Fauldhouse. Special features of Club—To cherish the name of Burns and foster a love for his writings, and generally promote good-fellowship ; to visit Burns Clubs and receive visitations from other Clubs ; to foster a knowledge of the life and works of Burns by means of an annual competition amongst local school children, prizes being awarded to the successful competitors.

No. 232—ARNISTON Tam o' Shanter Burns Club. Federated 23rd May, 1914. *Secretary*, George Russell, 1 Victoria Street, Arniston, Gorebridge.

No 233—The CLACHAN Burns Club. Instituted February, 1914. Federated 23rd May, 1914. *Secretary*, Donald M'Leod, Ivy Cottage, Braehead, Coalburn.

No. 234—GLASGOW Southern Merchants' Burns Club. Instituted 1914. Federated 1914. Place and date of meeting, Kennilworth Hotel, monthly as per syllabus. Hon. Presidents, Provost Paxton, M. Montgomery, and ex-Bailie A. Campbell ; President, ex-Councillor M'Neil, Heath Park, Belmont Drive, Giffnock ; Vice-president, Councillor Martin, 62 Nithsdale Road, Strathbungo ; *Secretary*, D. Macgregor, 5 Barrland Street, Pollokshields, E. Special features of Club—Monthly lectures to promote interest in Burns's works ; annual dinner, &c.

No. 235—HAMILTON Glencairn Burns Club. Instituted 1894. Federated 8th August. 1914.

No 236—WHITEHAVEN Burns Club. Instituted 24th January, 1914. Federated August, 1914. Place and date of meeting, Masonic Hall, Whitehaven, January, March, and November. President, Robert T. Bell, Woodend Gardens, Whitehaven ; Vice-president, John Davidson, 9 Edge Hill Terrace, Whitehaven ; *Secretary*, John Davidson, 9 Edge Hill Terrace, Whitehaven ; Bard, Wm. Glenn, The Schoolhouse, Hensingham. Committee —A. Anderson, T. C. Bell, Dr Dickson, J. Forbes, J. M. Gibson, W. Glenn, D. Jamieson, A. Kilpatrick, A. Lockhart, Dr Manson, Dr Muir, J. Murray, G. Palmer, J. Sewell, P. Turner, and J. Young. Special features of Club — To foster a knowledge of the life and works of Robert Burns, and to perpetuate his memory by an annual festival on 25th January.

No. 237 UDDINGSTON Masonic Burns Club. Instituted 2nd May, 1914. Federated 8th August, 1914. Place and date of meeting, Rowan Tree Hall, Old Mill Road, Uddingston, third Saturday in month, except June, July, and August, 6 p m. President, Thos. Cameron, 59 Bothwell Road, Bothwell ; Vice president, Thos. Barr, 4 Croftbank Place, Uddingston ; Secretary, David N. Miller, 601 Shettleston Road, Glasgow ; Treasurer,

G. Anderson ; Past President, J. Donald ; Stewards, Bros. Cuthbertson and R. Black. Committee—Messrs Beattie, M'Williams, Wright, and R. M'Donald. Special features of Club—Each candidate for membership must be a Freemason ; to promote social and friendly intercourse amongst its members by visiting other Burns Clubs and receiving visitations from other Clubs ; receive and give assistance when required from kindred Clubs ; holding of Hallowe'en a special night ; annual anniversary dinner ; annual outing to places of interest connected with the Poet. Membership limited to 40.

No. 238—ATLANTA, Ga., Burns Club, U.S.A. Instituted 25th January, 1896 ; Incorporated June 3rd, 1907. Federated 1914. Place and date of meeting, Burns Cottage, Atlanta, Ga., first Wednesday of each month. President, H. H. Cabaniss, 671 Piedmont Avenue, Atlanta, Ga. ; First Vice-president, R. M. M'Whirter, 1 Terry Street, Atlanta, Ga. ; Second Vice-president, A. S. Taylor ; Secretary, H. C. Reid, 44 Fairbanks Street, Atlanta, Ga. ; Treasurer, E. F. King ; Superintendent, Robert Murray ; Chaplain, Rev. R. K. Smith. Directors— Thos. Scott, Fred Turner, David Buchan, Jas. Carlisle, and Kenneth M'Kenzie.

No. 239 HAWICK Burns Club. Instituted 1878. Federated 8th August, 1914. Place of meeting, Club Rooms, 12 Teviot Crescent. President, Henry Mitchell, 10 Bright Street, Hawick ; Vice-president, Izaac Edmondson, 12 Gladstone Street, Hawick ; Secretary, Adam Millar, 5 Teviot Crescent, Hawick ; Treasurer, P. Walker, 4 Green Terrace, Hawick. Committee—Messrs Scott, Butler, R. Butler, D. Russell, and Stewart. Special features of Club—To honour the name of Robert Burns ; to celebrate the anniversary of his birth and otherwise endeavour to perpetuate his memory ; to afford the members the means of social intercourse, mutual helpfulness, intellectual improvement, and social recreation.

No. 240—BLAWARTHILL Burns Club. Federated 6th December, 1914. Secretary, T. G. King, 917 Yoker Road, Yoker.

No. 241—CROOK Burns Club. Instituted 1906. Federated 4th January, 1915. Secretary, A. B. Rutherford, Church Street, Crook, Co. Durham.

No. 242—MONTROSE Burns Club. Instituted 24th February, 1908. Federated 1915. Place and date of meeting, Town Buildings ; Council, as required ; annual meeting, December ; festival, 25th January. President, William Jolly, J.P., Caxton House, Gendera Road, Montrose ; Vice-president, James Christieson, J.P., F.S.A.(Scot.), Library House, Montrose ; Secretary, Alex. Miller, 6 Wellington Gardens, Montrose ; Treasurer, Alex. Low, 9 Melville Gardens. Special feature of Club—Annual competition for children in rendering Scottish songs.

No. 243—PAISLEY St. James Burns Club. Instituted 1912. Federated 1915. Place of meeting, 4 St. James Street, Paisley. President, Wm. Alexander, 28 Glen Street, Paisley ; Vice-president, John Aitken, 1 Maxwell Street, Paisley ; Secretary, John M'Kechnie, 2 Douglas Terrace, Paisley. Special features of Club—The encouragement of social intercourse amongst the members and kindred Clubs ; the celebration of the Poet's birthday ; meetings for the reading of literary papers relative to the life and works of Burns, and kindred subjects.

No. 244—DALMUIR Burns Club. Instituted 1914. Federated 1916. Place of meeting, Trades Restaurant. Hon. President, Bailie Jno. Young, The Crescent, Dalmuir ; President, John Will, 9 French Street, Dalmuir ; Vice-president, Robert Ferguson, Learig Place, Dalmuir ; Secretary, Alex. Dillon, 21 Trafalgar Street, Dalmuir ; literary Secretary and Bard, Jno. Rae, Invis ; Auditors, Wm. Boyle and D. M'Nair. Committee—R. Ferguson, Wm Gordon, R. Raitt, R. Woodburn, Jno. Holmes, Wm. Boyle, J. Forsyth, C. F. Kean, and J. B. M'Intyre. Special features of Club—The perpetuation of the memory of the Immortal Bard, and the cultivation of Scottish poetry and literature.

No. 245 KINNAIRD Victoria Burns Club. Instituted 9th October, 1910. Federated 3rd January, 1917. Place of meeting, Victoria Inn, Carronshore. President, James Turnbull, Bothy Row, Carronshore, by Carron ; Vice-president, George Jenkins, Kinnaird, by Falkirk ; Secretary, George Jenkins, 12 Kinnaird, by Falkirk. Committee—George Easton, James Kemp, George Cowan, Thomas Aitken, and Robert Wilson. Special features of Club—To meet in a social capacity to create an interest in the works of Burns among the members ; annual picnic to places of interest connected with the Poet ; annual celebration of the Poet's birthday.

No. 246—LOCHORE and ROSEWELL Shanter Burns Club. Instituted 16th October, 1920. Federated 11th January, 1921. Place and date of meeting, Rosewell Bar, Lochore, fortnightly. Hon. President, George B. Garry ; President, William Morton, Waverley Cottages, Lochore ; Vice-president, Edward M'Quillan, Waverley Street, Lochore ; Secretary, Thomas Nailen, 106 Waverley Street, Lochore ; Treasurer, Archibald Rankine. Special features of Club—Draughts and dominoes ; to further a knowledge of the works of Burns.

No. 247 LOCHGELLY Thirteen Jolly Beggars Burns Club. Instituted 12th March, 1916. Federated 1st September, 1917. Place and date of meeting, Victoria Bar, monthly. Hon. Presidents, Provost Walker, J. D. Wilson, Dr Stephen, and Alex. Hugh ; President, G. Arrol, 36 South Street, Lochgelly ; Vice-president, Arch. Lowe, Melville Street, Lochgelly ; Secretary, William M'Kechnie, 64 Melville Street, Lochgelly ; Treasurer, C. Wright ;

Croupier, C. Wright ; Bard, R. Mackie ; Horn-bearer,
H. Hannah.   Special features of Club—The encouragement of social intercourse amongst the members and
kindred Clubs ; the celebration of the Poet's birth, and
to honour his memory in such other way as may from time
to time be determined ; annual excursion to places of
historical interest.

No. 248   BIRTLEY Burns Club.   Instituted 10th December, 1915.
Federated 18th October, 1917.   *Secretary*, James Mann,
Wellington House, Station Road, Birtley, Co. Durham.

No. 249—MID-CALDER Tam o' Shanter Burns Club.   Instituted
25th November, 1916.   Federated 1917.   *Secretary*,
D. M'Kerracher, North Gate, Livingston, Mid-Calder.

No. 250—COWDENBEATH Tam o' Shanter Burns Club.   Instituted 19th October, 1917.   Federated 28th November,
1917.   Place and date of meeting, Commercial Hotel,
monthly, at 5.30.   President, Walter M. Miller, Moss-
side Road, Cowdenbeath : Vice-president, John Duff,
10 Sligo Street, Lumphinnans ;   *Secretary*, John Black,
333 West Broad Street, Cowdenbeath ; Treasurer, Jno.
Bain ; Croupier, Adam Bradford ; Bard, T. Burns ;
Director of Ceremonies, W. Spence.   Special features of
Club—The study of Scottish literature ;   delivery of
lectures, &c., pertaining to Scottish life and character ;
school children's competitions ;   and   to   assist   the
intellectual, moral, and social improvement of the
members.

No. 251—GLENCRAIG Burns Club.   Instituted 1916. Federated
23rd November, 1918.   Place and time of meeting,
The Houf, Hunter's Bar, third Saturday of month at
6 p.m.   President, Alex. Garry, baker, Cowdenbeath ;
Vice-president, John Scott, 35 North Glencraig ; *Secretary*,
Robert Glencross, Lofty View, Glencraig, Fife ; Treasurer,
Robert Ferrans, Largo Cottages, Glencraig.   Special
features of Club — To advance the Burns cult ;   the
preservation of the Doric ; social harmonies ; discussions
on Burns literature ; and the holding of children's competitions.

No. 252—ALLOWAY Burns Club.   Instituted 1908.   Federated
1918.   Place of meeting, Alloway.   President, Rev
J. M. Hamilton, B.D., The Manse, Alloway, Ayr ; Vice-
president, James Turnbull, F.E.I.S., The Schoolhouse,
Alloway, Ayr : *Hon Secretary and Treasurer*, Andrew
J. Gray, 29 Northpark Avenue, Ayr.   Council—J. R.
Dickson, A. Cunningham, T. Auld, Jas. M'Cutcheon,
C. Auld, and W. Monaghan.   Special features of Club
—School children's competition ; annual concert featuring
Scottish items.

No. 253—GALSTON Jolly Beggars Burns Club.   Instituted
1916.   Federated 1918.   *Secretary*, Thos. Morton, 37
Brewland Street, Galston.

No 254—GREENOCK Victoria Burns Club. Instituted 2nd October, 1914. Federated 1918. Place and date of meeting, Co-operative Hall, monthly. President, D. M'G. Clark, 2 Octavia Street, Port-Glasgow ; Vice-president, Jas. Cameron, 5 Highholm Street, Port-Glasgow : Secretary, Matthew W. Linn, 19 Belville Street, Greenock ; Treasurer, J. Armstrong 36 Grant Street, Greenock. Special features of Club—To cherish the name of Robert Burns and to foster a love for his writings, and generally to encourage a taste for Scottish literature and history, and to celebrate the memory of our National Bard by an annual supper held on January 25th, or as near thereto as possible.

No. 255—CATHCART Burns Club. Instituted January, 1916. Federated 1918. Place and date of meeting, Couper Institute, Cathcart, last Thursday of month. President, John Kerr, 27 Dixon Road, Govanhill, Glasgow ; Vice-president, James Ewing, 271 Kilmarnock Road, Shawlands, Glasgow ; Secretary, David B. Wilson, 9 Craig Road, Cathcart ; Treasurer, R. Bannatyne. Special features of Club—The study of Burns and Scots literature ; papers ; discussions ; and good-fellowship.

No. 256—NEWTON-ON-AYR Burns Club. Instituted August, 1904. Federated 1919. Place and date of meeting Robert Burns Tavern, every Tuesday. President John S. Jackson, 23 Bellesley Hill Avenue, Ayr ; Vice-president, H. M. Giles, Monkswell, New Prestwick, Ayr ; Secretary, James Dobbie, 1 Falkland Park, Ayr ; Treasurer, Wm. Beattie, 49 Content Street, Ayr.

No. 257 ARMADALE Star Burns Club. Instituted 2nd February, 1918. Federated 17th May, 1919. Place and date of meeting, Star Inn, Armadale, first Saturday of each month, 6 p.m. President, Thomas Milne, Star Inn, Armadale ; Vice-president, James M'Hattie, Heatherfield, Armadale ; Secretary, Robert Cunningham, 6 M'Donald's Square, Armadale. Committee—R. Currie, J. Swan, J. Brown, G. Menzies, J. Martin, and J. Scott. Special features of Club—Social and literary monthly meetings (federated Burnsians specially welcomed) ; anniversary supper ; and summer outings.

No. 258—ARMADALE Buck's Head Burns Club. Instituted 12th October, 1918. Federated 17th May, 1919. Place of meeting, Masonic Hall, Armadale. President, John Mack, Polkemmet Cottage, Armadale, West Lothian ; Vice-president, William M'Alpine, Unity Terrace, Armadale, West Lothian ; Secretary, John Stevenson, New Street, Station Road, Armadale, West Lothian ; Treasurer, Joseph Wilson, Mayfield Place, Armadale. Committee—Tom Gibson, Meikle M'Lay, John Campbell, and Wm. Brown. Special features of Club—To consider and discuss subjects, questions, and reading of papers directly concerning Burns and his works ; to promote the efficiency, knowledge, and attainments of the members on the works and life of Rabbie Burns ; visitations to places of interest and kindred Clubs ; anniversary dinner celebration ; holding of Hallowe'en special night ; annual school children's competition ; visitors cordially invited.

No 259—BONNYRIGG A Man's a Man for a' That Burns Club. Instituted 29th March, 1919. Federated 3rd May, 1919. Place and date of meeting, Calderwood Arms, monthly. President, Andrew Ross, 13 Arniston Place, Bonnyrigg : Vice-president, James Harper, 44 Camp View, Bonnyrigg ; Secretary, Andrew Hill, jun., 21 Camp View, Bonnyrigg : Treasurer, J. Anderson. Committee—J. Crozier, A. Hill, J. Purves, W. Temple, J. Brown, J. Brand, and G. Knox.

No 260—TARBRAX Jolly Beggars Burns Club Instituted 21st January, 1916. Federated 19th May, 1919 Presi‐ dent, David Black, Moorview, Tarbrax, Cobbinshaw ; Vice-presidents, J. K. Roberts, Wm. Forsyth, M.A., Dr G. M'Lean, Tarbrax, Cobbinshaw ; and Dr J. M. John‐ stone, Leven, Fife ; Secretary, Hugh M'Glone, 239 Tarbrax, Cobbinshaw ; Committee—R. Crichton (chair‐ man), John Graham, Thos. Reid, David Smith, Arch. Barrie, Chas. M'Connachie, and Geo. Watson. Special features of Club—Annual supper ; to encourage the study of Burns in the young by holding concerts and com‐ petitions confined to his works (we have good entries on these lines).

No. 261—SYDNEY Anniversary Burns Club, N.S.W. Insti‐ tuted 25th January, 1895. Federated 1919. Secretary, James Buchan, Logie Brae, York Street, Forest Lodge, Sydney, N.S.W.

No 262—FIFESHIRE Burns Association. Instituted 17th May, 1919. Federated 6th September, 1919. Place of meeting, Associated Club Rooms. President, Walter M. Millar, Moss-side Road, Cowdenbeath ; Vice-presidents, Peter Paterson, Kinnis House, Kinnis Park, Dunferm‐ line, and Robt. Glencross, Lofty View, Glencraig ; Secre‐ tary and Treasurer, Geo. Marshall, 38 Natal Place, Cowden‐ beath ; Bardess, Miss M. Moir, Rumdewan, Kingskettle. Committee—J. Black (Tam o' Shanter, Cowdenbeath), Thos. Anderson (Shanter, Blairadam), Wm. M'Kechnie (Thirteen Jolly Beggars, Lochgelly), John Nisbet (Glen‐ cairn, Cowdenbeath), Robt. Balloch (Highland Mary, Lumphinnans), Ed. M'Quillan (Rosewell Shanter, Lochore), Jas. Gold (Bingry Jolly Beggars, Lochore), and Jno. Dodds (Glencraig). Special features of Club—To further the interests of the Burns cult by promoting closer union between Clubs and kindred Societies and bringing them into more harmonious relationship ; also to promote and carry through school children's competitions in the county, and organise excursions to places of interest in the summer.

No. 263—GLASGOW Masonic Burns Club. Instituted 31st January, 1919. Federated 6th September, 1919. Place and date of meeting, Burns Club House, Glasgow, last Fridays, monthly. President, Charles Crofts, 219 Main Street, Cambuslang : Vice-president, John Waddell, 189 St. Vincent Street, Glasgow ; Secretary, H. Stuart Girvan, 252 West George Street, Glasgow : Treasurer, Arch. D. Campbell, 116 Trongate, Glasgow.

No. 264—PRESTONPANS Jolly Beggars Burns Club. Instituted 28th June, 1919. Federated 20th September, 1919. Secretary, William Watt, 59 High Street, Prestonpans.

No. 265—BINGRY Jolly Beggars Burns Club. Instituted 25th October, 1919. Federated March, 1920. Secretary, Wm. C. Clark, 169 Waverley Cottages, Lochore, Fife.

No. 266—NEWTON Jolly Beggars Burns Club. Instituted January, 1920. Federated 6th March, 1920. Place and date of meeting, Newton Brae, last Saturday in month, at 4 p.m. President, James Buchanan, 15 Pitt Street, Newton ; Vice-president, Arch. Barr, 1 Dunlop Street, Newton ; Secretary, Wm. M'Intosh, 12 Clyde Street, Newton, Hallside, Glasgow. Committee—John Russell, Donald Griffiths, Thomas Whyte, Campbell Gilmour, and William Duncan. Special features of Club—To consider and discuss subjects, questions, and reading papers on the life and works of Burns ; visitation to places of interest and kindred Clubs ; anniversary dinner celebration ; holding of Hallowe'en special night ; annual schools competition in essays on the life and works of Burns.

No. 267 PRESTONPANS Mystic Burns Club. Instituted 12th April, 1919. Federated 24th December, 1919. Place of meeting, Black Bull Inn, Prestonpans.. President, Charles Rowan, 10 Front Street, Prestonpans ; Vice-presidents, Wm. Hewitt and Geo. Cunningham : Secretary, William Ford, 15 Front Street, Prestonpans ; Treasurer, And. Brown. Special features of Club—To foster and encourage a love of Burns's poems and songs in the community ; social intercourse among members of kindred Clubs ; encouragement of the young to learn the songs and poems of Burns by school competitions and prizes ; and to commemorate the Poet's birthday.

No. 268 ANDERSTON Cronies Burns Club. Instituted January, 1905. Federated 1919. Place and date of meeting. 109 Argyle Street, by arrangement. President, Quintin Henderson, 614 Cathcart Road, Glasgow ; Vice-president, Tho. M'Guire, 7 Ardgowan Terrace, Sauchiehall Street, Glasgow ; Secretary, Frank M'Ewan, 4 North Street, Anderston, Glasgow : Auditors, A. Barnetson and W. Boyd. Committee—R Cowan, A. Nixon, G. Lockhart, and R. M'Neil. Special features of Club—Social and educational converse ; study of Burns's songs, life, and characteristics.

No. 269 JOHNSTONE Tam o' Shanter Burns Club. Instituted 6th December, 1912. Federated 6th March, 1920. Place of meeting, Masonic Hall, Johnstone. President, Thomas Gillespie, Ascot, Kilbarchan Road, Johnstone ; Vice-president, Alexander Hutton, Dunconnell, Thomson Avenue, Johnstone ; Secretary, Andrew Walker, 5 Armour Street, Johnstone. Special features of Club—To revere the memory of our National Bard, foster and encourage a love of his works, and promote school competitions.

No. 270—COQUETDALE Burns Club. Instituted 1919. Federated 6th March, 1920. Place and date of meeting, Jubilee Hall, as arranged, 7.30 p.m. President, Dr J. A. Smail, Stewart House, Rothbury ; Vice-president, Geo. Rae Patterson, Burleigh House, Rothbury ; Secretary, John Walker, 6 Whitton Terrace, Rothbury ; Assistant Secretary, A. Munro ; Treasurer, Isaac Percival. Special features of Club—Lectures, concerts, and annual outing.

No 271—TRENTON Burns Club, U.S.A. Instituted 19th February, 1919. Federated 30th March, 1920. Secretary, Andrew Carmichael, 48½ Wall Street, Trenton, New Jersey, U.S.A.

No. 272—STEWARTON Hodden Grey Burns Club. Instituted January 30th, 1920. Federated 27th March. 1920. Secretary, Thos. J. Boyd, Bellevue, Graham Terrace, Stewarton.

No. 273—LANARK Jolly Beggars Burns Club. Instituted 23rd December, 1919. Federated 27th March, 1920. Place and time of meeting, The Albion, 7 p.m. President, William Foster, Ladyacre Road, Lanark ; Vice-president, William Gracie, Burgh Cottages, St. Leonard's Street, Lanark ; Secretary, Jas. Kay, 34 Bonnet Road, Lanark. Committee—John Mitchell, David Muir, John Glaister, Robt. Gray, and Robt. Flemington. Special features of Club—To foster the spirit of Burns's manly independence as depicted in his poem, " A man's a man for a' that " ; annual supper to celebrate the birthday of the Poet ; annual trip to places of interest.

No. 274—TROON Burns Club. Instituted 28th January, 1920. Federated 30th March, 1920. Secretary, James C. Brown, 21 Templehill, Troon.

No. 275—AYR Burns Club. Federated 12th June, 1920. President, James Wills, 27 High Street, Ayr ; Secretary, James M. Kay, 100 High Street, Ayr ; Treasurer, John L. Wilson, 15 High Street, Ayr. Special features of Club—School competitions ; lectures.

No 276—LUMPHINNANS Highland Mary Burns Club. Federated 12th June, 1920. Secretary, Alexander Easson, 47 Sligo Street, Lumphinnans, Fife.

No. 277—HARRIMAN Burns Club, Pa., U.S.A. Federated 12th June, 1920. *Secretary,* Wm. M'Nee,'266 Madison Street, Harriman, Pa., U.S.A.

No. 278—DULUTH Clan Stewart, No. 50 (Order of Scottish Clans), Burns Club, U.S.A. Federated 29th August, 1920. *Secretary,* A. G. M'Knight,' Attorney-at-Law, 319 Providence Building, Duluth, Minnesota, U.S.A.

No. 279—BROXBURN Jolly Beggars Burns Club. Instituted 21st May, 1920. Federated November, 1920. Place of meeting, Strathbrock Hotel. President, Wm. M'Queen, Shrine Place, Broxburn ; Vice-president, Jno. Black, Port Buchan, Broxburn ; *Secretary,* Jno. W. Cruickshank, 64 Greendykes Road, Broxburn ; Treasurer, Thos. Inglis, Falconer's Buildings, Broxburn.

No. 280 DETROIT Burns Club, U.S.A. Instituted January 25th, 1912. Federated 15th November, 1920. Place and date of meeting, Hotel Tuller, second Friday of each month. President, Edward Goodwillie, 795 Casgrain Avenue, Detroit, Mich., U.S.A. First Vice-president, John Smith, 9491 Kaier Avenue ; Second Vice-president, John Cameron, 3632 Wabash Avenue. *Recording Secretary,* W. S. Allan, 1149 West Ferry Avenue, Detroit, Mich., U.S.A. ; Financial Secretary, W A. V. Edward, 2455 Canton Avenue ; Treasurer. Thos. G. White, 1130 Seward Avenue. Trustees—J. C. Robertson, 344 Glendale Avenue ; Wm. Ross, 2635 West Forest Avenue ; and John F. M'Kinlay, 933 Hazelwood Avenue. Special features of Club—The Club was organised for the purpose of erecting a statue to Robert Burns. This was accomplished on July 23rd, 1921. New constitution and byelaws are now in preparation to incorporate the Club for the study of the works of Robert Burns, and to erect a statue to Sir Walter Scott as a companion to the Burns statue.

No. 281—VICKERSTOWN Burns Club. Instituted September, 1919. Federated 14th November, 1920. Place and date of meeting, George Hotel, Walney, Barrow-in-Furness, quarterly. President, Sir James M'Kechnie, K.B.E., The Abbey House, Furness Abbey, Lancs. ; Vice-president, James C. Ferguson, 9 Promenade, Walney, Barrow-in-Furness ; *Secretary,* James D Cowley, 82 King Alfred Street, Walney, Barrow-in-Furness ; Treasurer, Adam M'Gregor ; Chairman, Alexander Craig. Special features of Club—To revere the memory of our National Bard and foster an interest in his incomparable literary works ; to develop a friendly spirit between Scotsmen resident in Barrow by affording them occasional opportunities of meeting together in a social capacity.

No. 282—GLASGOW and DISTRICT Burns Clubs Bowling Association. Instituted 1899. Federated 1920. Place of meeting, Bank Restaurant, 21 Queen Street. President, J. M. Blair, 162 Hospital Street, Glasgow ; Vice-president, A. B. Allison, 24 Hayburn Crescent, Partick ; *Secretary*, Robt. Parker, 5 Barrland Street, Pollokshields, Glasgow. Committee—R. M. Milholm, A. Izaat, D. Fisher, D. Gunn, D. Mackin, W. Craig, and D. Davidson. Special features of Club—To hold a bowling competition every year for the M'Lennan Cup, providing badges for the first and second highest-up rinks. The Association has very frequently donated portions of its funds to institutions and objects connected with the Burns cult. The competition is held usually on the first Tuesday in August. One hundred and fifty rinks entered in 1920, Ye Cronies, Govan (Dan Fisher, skip), being the winners.

No. 283—SINCLAIRSTOWN Burns Club. Instituted 1920 (reconstituted). Federated 13th November, 1920. Place of meeting, Sinclairstown Hotel. President, Wm. Crombie, 148 St. Clair Street, Kirkcaldy ; Vice-president, Robt. Keddie, 2 Mackenzie Street, Kirkcaldy ; *Secretary*, Thomas Hunter, Dryburgh House, 181 St. Clair Street, Kirkcaldy ; Treasurer, David Chalmers, Kidd Street. Special features of Club—To study the works of Burns and promote social and intellectual intercourse among members by lectures and discussions.

No 284—PHILADELPHIA North-Eastern Burns Club, U.S.A. Federated 1921. President, Wm. Dallas, 4526 Mulberry Street; Vice-president, Daniel Thompson, 2543 East Dakota Street ; *Secretary*, Robt. M'Lean, 2863 North Howard Street, Philadelphia, Pa., U.S.A. ; Treasurer, Wm. Millar, 3037 North 4th Street. Committee—John Burgess, H. J. Nelson, S. Hawthorne, J. M. Gray.

No. 285 COWDENBEATH Jean Armour Burns Club. Federated 1921.

No. 286—GLASGOW Shawlands Burns Club. Instituted 9th January, 1920. Federated 4th June, 1921. Place and date of meeting, 1097 Pollokshaws Road, monthly. President, Robert Mair, M.B.E., Moraig, Peveril Avenue, Shawlands ; Vice-president, Arch. Lindsay, 65 Stevenson Drive, Langside ; *Secretary*, Harry R. Dinsmore, F.F.S., 59 Durward Avenue, Shawlands, Glasgow ; Treasurer, James Thom. Committee—The President, Vice-president, Treasurer, Secretary, and J. Wallace, George Woodburn, and J. G. M'Farlane. Special features of Club—To encourage a study of Scottish literature, particularly the works of Burns. " When man shall clasp, frae strivings torn, the hand o' brither, brither-born."

No. 287 GLASGOW Queen Anne Burns Club. Instituted November, 1919. Federated 9th June, 1921. Place and date of meeting, Queen Anne Restaurant, second Friday each month. President, J. F. M'Nicol, 141 Clarkston Road, Langside ; Vice-president, Edward M'Gregor, butcher, West Scotland Street, Kinning Park, Glasgow ; *Secretary*, Robert Gourlay, jun., 1155 Pollokshaws Road, Shawlands, Glasgow. Committee—H. Rimmer, C. N. Exley, J. Denniston, J. G. Lees, A. Rankin, W. Haddon, and J. Sinclair.

No. 288 BEITH Caledonia Burns Club. Instituted 10th November, 1911. Federated 3rd June, 1921. Place and date of meeting, Caledonian Inn, Beith, monthly. President, John S. Snodgrass, Eglinton Street, Beith ; Vice-president, Duncan M'Kechnie, King's Road, Beith ; Secretary, William White, 6 Church Road, Beith. Committee —A. P. Craig, J. Danks, W. Breckenridge, S. Irving, J. Kennedy, R. Dalzell, W. Seggie. Special feature of Club—Literary meetings.

No. 289—COATBRIDGE Bricklayers Burns Club. Instituted 17th November, 1920. Federated 4th June, 1921. Place and date of meeting, Y.M.C.A., Bank Street, third Wednesday of month. Hon. President, Provost Lavelle ; Hon. Vice-presidents, Dr Murray and R. B. Crombie ; President, Archibald Young, 16 Corswall Street, Coatbridge ; Vice-president, John Lang, 34 Wallace Street, Coatbridge ; Secretary, Archibald M. Raeside, 30 Corswall Street, Coatbridge ; Treasurer, Wm. Donald ; Librarian, Peter Gentles ; Musical Director, David Angus. Committee—J. Stocks, W. Dick, W. Nicol, T. Neilson, P. M'Gregor, J. Hill, and J. Curran. Special features of Club—Monthly lectures.

No. 290—BLANTYRE and DISTRICT Masonic Burns Club. Instituted October, 1919. Federated June, 1921. Place and date of meeting, Masonic Hall, Blantyre, fourth Saturday of each month, 6.30 p.m. President, Alexander Gourlay, 24 Carscallen Row, Quarter ; Vice-president, Zecheriah Nimmo, 265 Glasgow Road, Blantyre ; Secretary, Abraham Airns, 1 Clark Street, Blantyre.; Treasurer, Wm. Murray, jun. Committee—A. Reid, Wm. M'Mann, S. Courtney, J. Fulton, J. Hammell, J. M'Garvie, G. Rainey, W. Findlay, and R. Tinto. Special features of Club—The furtherance of Scottish song, poetry, and story, with special attention to the works of Robert Burns ; also school competitions.

No. 291—KILMARNOCK Highland Mary Burns Club. Instituted November, 1920. Federated 4th June, 1921. Place and date of meeting, Khadikoi, first Friday each month, 7 p.m. President, Wm. Lambie, 36 Bonnyton Road, Kilmarnock ; Vice-president, David M'Ewen, Hayside, Crosshouse, Kilmarnock ; Secretary, John Ballantyne, 44 Bonnyton Road, Kilmarnock ; Treasurer, Arch. M'Pherson. Committee—J. Train, P. Welsh, R. Brown, A. Hamilton, J. Milligan, H. Strachan, J. M'Fadzean, and W. Blacklock. Special features of Club—Study of the life and works of Robert Burns ; papers and readings on kindred subjects ; benevolence towards distressed members.

No. 292 GRAHAMSTON Burns Club. Instituted 9th November, 1920. Federated 6th August, 1920. Place and

date of meeting, Empire Bar, Graham's Road, Falkirk,
7.30 p.m. Hon. President, R. C. Liddell, Empire Bar
Grahamston ; President, John Lapsley, 1 Canal Street,
Grahamston, Falkirk ; Vice-president, Andrew Buch-
anan, 17 James Street, Grahamston, Falkirk ; *Secretary*,
James Finnie, 18 Boyd Street, Grahamston, Falkirk ;
Treasurer, Wm. Watmore, David's Loan, Bainsford,
Falkirk. Special feature of Club—To foster and develop
the works of Burns.

No. 293—NEWCRAIGHALL Poosie Nancy Burns Club. Instituted 19th February, 1921. Federated 6th August, 1921.
Place and time of meeting, Sheephead Inn, Duddingston,
6 p.m. Hon. President, Col. David Whitelaw ; Hon.
Vice-president, Wm. Muir ; President, Robert Porteous,
23 Main Avenue, Newcraighall ; Vice-president, William
Watson, 48 Main Avenue, Newcraighall ; *Secretary*,
Matthew Love, 49 Whitehill Street, Newcraighall. Special
features of Club—The study of the works of Burns ; to
foster and encourage a love of his poems and songs in the
community ; social intercourse amongst members of
kindred Clubs ; encouragement of the young to learn
the songs and poems of Burns by school competitions
and prizes ; to commemorate the Poet's birthday.

No. 294—HILL OF BEATH Burns Club. Federated 23rd August,
1921. Place of meeting, Hill of Beath Tavern. President, John Turcan, 1 Hall Row, Hill of Beath ; Vice-
president, John Burt, Hill of Beath Tavern, Hill of Beath ;
Secretary, James Barclay, 1 Reading Room Row, Hill
of Beath.

The following "Club Note" was received too late for classification.

SUNDERLAND BURNS CLUB.

REPORT.

In submitting the Twenty-fourth Annual Report of the Sunderland Burns Club, it is a pleasure to be able to say that the progress during the year has been most encouraging. The meetings have been well attended, while the special functions arranged during the year have been highly successful.

ANNUAL MEETING.

The Annual Meeting is always a most interesting gathering, as it affords the members an opportunity of discussing the affairs of the Club in a way not afforded at any other meeting. The Report of our Treasurer, Mr A. W. Semple, is always looked forward to with more than a passing interest, as they are always presented in such a pleasing manner.

ANNIVERSARY GATHERING

The Twenty-fifth Dinner of the Club and the One Hundred and Sixty-second Anniversary of our Poet's birth was held in the Palatine Hotel on Tuesday, January 25th, 1921. The President, Mr A. R. Calvert, occupied the chair, and was supported by a company of one hundred and thirty-nine gentlemen. An excellent repast was put on the festive board by Mr J. W. Hugil and his staff, which included the time-honoured "Haggis," which was duly ushered in with all the honours, preceded by the pipers.

The Club was honoured by having as guest of the evening Joseph Jardine, Esq., the Provost of the ancient burgh of Annan. In submitting the principal toast of the "Immortal Memory," the Provost paid an eloquent tribute to our beloved Bard.

The gathering will rank as one of the best we ever had, and we are indebted to those who contributed to its success, particularly to our President for entertaining the worthy Provost during his stay in Sunderland.

" Chronicle."

After our experience of the previous year, it was quite fitting that we should have on this occasion a great demand for this most useful publication. Each issue seems to improve with the years, and it reflects the utmost credit on the indomitable energy and labour of Dr M'Naught in collecting and compiling such valuable information. May we hope that he may be spared for many years to supervise this important part of the Federation work.

Picnic.

After a lapse of many years the Summer Picnic of the Club was held on Wednesday, June 30th, 1920, to Wynyard Park, the beautiful seat of Lord Londonderry, who had kindly granted permission for the visit. The party, which numbered ninety ladies and gentlemen, left the headquarters at 1 p.m. in three fine motor coaches. The weather was beautifully fine, and the drive was much enjoyed. On arrival at the Park a visit was paid to the mansion house and gardens, after which tea was served on the lawn. A programme of sports was carried through, the prizes being provided by the Committee, while several dances were indulged in at the close of the proceedings. The full Pipe Band was present as guests of the Club, and added much to the success of the outing. The prizes were gracefully handed over to the winners by the President's daughter, Miss Calvert, who was accorded a hearty vote of thanks. The return journey was commenced about 8 o'clock, and Sunderland was safely reached shortly before ten, all having spent a most enjoyable afternoon.

In Memoriam.

We have to record the loss of two members during the year. It is seldom indeed the members receive such a shock as they did by the sudden death of Piper William Clark, which took place on December 12th, 1920. By his death the Club has lost one of its most faithful members, while the Band has lost its most devoted member. Of a genial and kindly disposition, he was always ready and willing to do whatever lay in his power to further the interests of the Club. At the funeral, which took place on December 16th, a fitting tribute was paid to his memory. His late Battalion Band, the 2nd Tyneside Scottish, from Newcastle, along with a firing party, were present, while the members of our own Pipe Band acted as pall-bearers. A large number of the Club members were present to pay their last tribute of respect. In the gathering dusk of a

December afternoon, the Pipers playing the " Lament " and his comrades firing the volleys over the grave, there was laid to rest one who was beloved by all who knew him.

The death of Mr John Saxon took place on May 5th, 1921. Though a severe illness left him very much aged in appearance, his spirit was young, and he enjoyed our meetings and was always a most regular attender. The sympathy of the Club was conveyed in suitable form to his sorrowing relatives.

SYLLABUS.

1920.

Oct. 13. Presidents' Address.
Oct. 27. " The Jolly Beggars "—Mr R. C. Lyness.
Nov. 10. " Greenock "—Mr T. Fisher.
Nov. 30. St. Andrew's Celebration—Ladies' Night.
Dec. 15. " Kilwinning "—Dr A. Stevenson.

1921.

Jan. 12. " Girvan "—Mr W. H. Turner.
Jan. 25. " Immortal Memory "—Mr J. Jardine, Provost of Annan.
Feb. 29. " Parish of Glencairn "—Mr W. M. Donaldson.
Feb. 24. Visit of Newcastle Burns Club.
Mar. 9. " Vale of Atholl "—Mr D. Gordon.
Mar. 23. " Lochmaben "—Dr J. Wells.
Apr. 13. " Islay "—Mr A. Short.
May 11. Annual Meeting—Election of Officers.
Sept. 12. Business Meeting.

MEMBERSHIP.

We commenced the year with eighty members, we have lost two by death, while lapses and removals account for four. Eleven new members have been added, leaving us with eighty-five active members, a nett gain of five on the year.

The Complimentary Dinner arranged by the Burns Federation to Mr John Gribbel, of Philadelphia, U.S.A., was held in the Charing Cross Hotel, Glasgow, on Tuesday, July 27th, 1920, and this Club was represented by Messrs W. H. Turner and A. W. Semple. The gathering was a fitting tribute to Mr Gribbel for his generosity in purchasing and restoring to Scotland the Glenriddel Manuscripts.

The St. Andrew's Celebration was held in the Burnville Cafe, Fawcett Street, on Tuesday, November 30th, 1920, and was attended by upwards of one hundred and fifty ladies and gentlemen. The President of the Club, Mr A. R. Calvert, occupied the chair. The first part of the programme consisted of an excellent concert sustained by Misses Auld, Joseph, and Darce ; Messrs Wight, Fisher, Thompson, Hall, and Fidler ; the Pipe Band : and Highland dances by Mr Gordon. Supper was served in good style, after which a dance followed. A word of praise is due to Mr Neil Cameron and Mr D. Gordon, who acted as M C.'s and did much towards the success of the gathering

We cannot close this report without expressing our gratitude to our President, Mr A. R. Calvert. He has guided the affairs of the Club with a very marked degree of success, while his painstaking and efficient attention to the details has earned the gratitude and esteem of the members.

M. NEILSON, *Hon. Secretary.*

ROBERT DINWIDDIE, Printer, &c., High Street, Dumfries.

Lightning Source UK Ltd.
Milton Keynes UK
UKOW06f1908220617

303924UK00013B/456/P